The Dorling Kindersley

ILLUSTRATED FAMILY ENCYCLOPEDIA

VOLUME 1 · A-I

Aboriginal Australians to *India, History of*

A DORLING KINDERSLEY BOOK

DK

LONDON, NEW YORK, MUNICH,
MELBOURNE AND DELHI

Senior Editor Jayne Parsons   **Senior Art Editor** Gillian Shaw

Project Editors
Marian Broderick, Gill Cooling,
Maggie Crowley, Hazel Egerton,
Cynthia O'Neill, Veronica Pennycook,
Louise Pritchard, Steve Setford, Jackie Wilson

Project Art Editors
Jane Felstead, Martyn Foote,
Neville Graham, Jamie Hanson,
Christopher Howson, Jill Plank, Floyd Sayers,
Jane Tetzlaff, Ann Thompson

Editors
Rachel Beaugié, Nic Kynaston, Sarah Levete,
Karen O'Brien, Linda Sonntag

Art Editors
Tina Borg, Diane Clouting,
Tory Gordon-Harris

DTP Designers
Andrew O'Brien, Cordelia Springer

Managing Editor Ann Kramer   **Managing Art Editor** Peter Bailey

Senior DTP Designer Mathew Birch

Picture Research Jo Walton, Kate Duncan, Liz Moore

DK Picture Library Ola Rudowska, Melanie Simmonds

Country pages by PAGE*One*: Bob Gordon, Helen Parker,
Thomas Keenes, Sarah Watson, Chris Clark

Cartographers Peter Winfield, James Anderson

Research Robert Graham, Angela Koo

Editorial Assistants Sarah-Louise Reed, Nichola Roberts

Production Louise Barratt, Charlotte Traill

First published in Great Britain in 1997.
This edition published in Great Britain in 2002
by Dorling Kindersley Limited,
80 Strand, London WC2R 0RL

Copyright © 1997, © 2002 Dorling Kindersley Limited, London
A Pearson company

A CIP catalogue record for this book is available from the British Library

ISBN 0 7513 3929 6

Colour reproduction by Colourscan, Singapore
Printed and bound in China by Toppan Printing Co. (Shenzhen) Ltd.

See our complete catalogue at www.dk.com

ILLUSTRATED
FAMILY
ENCYCLOPEDIA

Indonesian bank note
see MONEY

Colt Peacemaker
see WEAPONS

Straw boater *see* SAILING AND
OTHER WATER SPORTS

Shipping signal
see FLAGS

1970s platform shoes
see CLOTHES AND FASHION

Postage stamps
see STAMPS AND
POSTAL SERVICES

Yu'pik family, Alaska
see ARCTIC OCEAN

King and Queen
see CHESS

Picture book
see CHILDREN'S
LITERATURE

Tenor horn
see MUSICAL
INSTRUMENTS

Gecko *see* LIZARDS

Honey fungus
see MUSHROOMS

Monarch butterfly
see EVOLUTION

Clown fish *see*
ECOLOGY

Hoverfly
see INSECTS

Paradise riflebird egg
see EGGS

Kiwanos
see FRUITS AND SEEDS

Duckling
see DUCKS, GEESE, AND SWANS

Bloodhound *see* DOGS

SLR camera
see CAMERAS

Personal stereo
see RADIO

Ethane molecule
see ATOMS AND MOLECULES

Hubble space telescope
see SPACE
EXPLORATION

Light bulb
see INVENTIONS

Jaguar XK120
see CARS AND TRUCKS

Mobile phone
see TELEPHONES

DNA double helix
see GENETICS

Chemical reactions
see CHEMISTRY

Dagger
see
WEAPONS

Amulet
see EGYPT, ANCIENT

Board Game
see VIKINGS

Throwing dice
see ROMAN EMPIRE

Thumbscrew
see WITCHES AND WITCHCRAFT

Portable sextant *see* EXPLORATION

Flint arrowhead
see STONE AGE

Clasp *see* CHINA, HISTORY OF

Ceremonial dress
see NORTH AMERICA,
HISTORY OF

Ancient coins
see SUMERIANS

Sabaton *see* ARMS AND ARMOUR

CONTRIBUTORS AND CONSULTANTS

Simon Adams BSc MSc
Historian and writer

Norman Barrett MA
Sports writer and consultant

Dr Martin R. Bates BSc, PhD
Institute of Archaeology
University of London

David Burnie BSc
Science and natural history writer

Jack Challoner BSc, ARCS, PGCE
Science writer, formerly with the Education
Unit, Science Museum, London

Julie Childs BSc
Zoologist and natural history writer,
former Head of Public Affairs, Zoological
Society of London

Neil Clark BSc
Paleontologist, Hunterian Museum and
University of Glasgow

Paul Collins MA
Institute of Archaeology
University College, London

Dr Gordon Daniels
Reader in History,
University of Sheffield

Veronica Doubleday
Lecturer, Historical and Critical Studies,
University of Brighton

John Farndon
Writer and consultant

Roger Few BA
Author on natural history and the
environment

Theresa Greenaway BSc, ARCS
Botanist and natural history writer

Frances Halpin BSc
Science consultant and teacher at
Royal Russell School

Dr Austen Ivereigh D Phil
Lecturer in Latin American History
University of Leeds

Robin Kerrod FRAS
Science writer and consultant

Bruce P. Lenman
Professor of Modern History
University of St Andrews

Nicky Levell
Curator Collections History,
The Horniman Museum

John E. Llewellyn-Jones BSc
Zoologist and botanist; writer and lecturer

Miranda MacQuitty BSc, PhD
Zoologist and natural history writer

Kevin McRae
Writer and consultant

Haydn Middleton MA
Historian and author

Mark O'Shea BSc, FRGS
Curator of Reptiles, West Midland Safari
Park; tropical herpetologist and zoologist;
natural history author

Chris Oxlade BSc
Writer and consultant, specializing in
science and technology

Douglas Palmer BSc, PhD
Writer, lecturer, and Open University tutor
specializing in palaeobiology

Steve Parker BSc
Zoologist, science writer and scientific
fellow of the Zoological Society

Tom Parsons MA
Art historian and writer

James Pickford BA
Writer and
electronic editor FT Mastering

Richard Platt BA
Writer and consultant

Matthew Robertson
Senior invertebrate keeper, Bristol Zoo

Theodore Rowland-Entwistle BA, FRGS
Writer and consultant

Noel Simon
Member emeritus of the Species Survival
Commission of IUCN; original compiler
mammalia volume, Red Data Book

Carole Stott BA, FRAS
Astronomy and space writer;
formerly Head of the Old Royal
Observatory, Greenwich, London

Jonathan Stroud BA
Writer and consultant: literature

Barbara Taylor BSc
Environmental scientist and
natural history writer

Louise Tythacott
Writer and consultant Southeast Asia

Richard Walker BSc PhD
Human biology and natural history writer

Marcus Weeks B Mus
Composer and writer

Philip Wilkinson MA
Historian and writer

Elizabeth Wyse BA
Writer and consultant

Dorling Kindersley Cartography
in conjunction with leading cartographic
consultants, embassies, and consulates

LIST OF MAIN ENTRIES

See index for further topics

Jupiter, the largest planet,
comparative to the Sun

Sun *see* Sun and solar system

COMPARATIVE PLANET SIZES

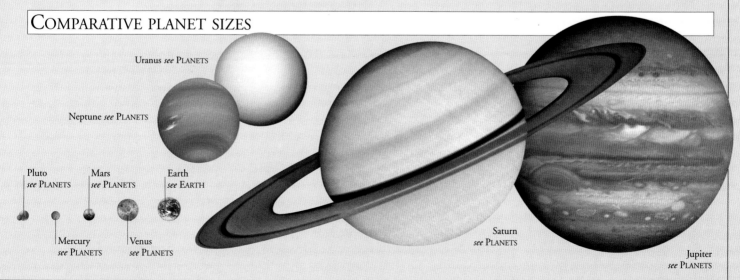

Uranus *see* PLANETS

Neptune *see* PLANETS

Pluto
see PLANETS

Mars
see PLANETS

Earth
see EARTH

Mercury
see PLANETS

Venus
see PLANETS

Saturn
see PLANETS

Jupiter
see PLANETS

HOW TO USE THIS ENCYCLOPEDIA

THE FOLLOWING PAGES WILL HELP YOU get the most out of your copy of the *Dorling Kindersley Illustrated Family Encyclopedia*. The encyclopedia consists of three volumes. Volumes 1–2 contain nearly 700 main entries organized alphabetically, from Aboriginal Australians through to Zoos. To find the entry you want, simply turn to the correct letter of the alphabet.

If you cannot find the topic you want, then turn to Volume 3. This volume includes an index and gazetteer for the whole encyclopedia, which will direct you straight to the page you need. In addition, Volume 3 contains hundreds of reference charts, fact boxes, lists, and tables to supplement the information provided on the main entry pages.

MEASUREMENTS AND ABBREVIATIONS

Most measurements are supplied in both metric and imperial units. Some of the most common abbreviations used in the encyclopedia are shown below in **bold** type.

°C = degrees Celsius
°F = degrees Fahrenheit
K = degrees kelvin
mm = millimetre; **cm** = centimetre
m = metre; **km** = kilometre
in = inch; **ft** = foot; **yd** = yard
g = gram; **kg** = kilogram
oz = ounce; **lb** = pound
ml = millilitre; **l** = litre
pt = pint; **gal** = gallon
sq km (km²) = square kilometre
sq ft (ft²) = square foot
kmh = kilometres per hour
mph = miles per hour
mya = million years ago
BC = before Christ
AD = anno Domini (refers to any date after the birth of Christ)
c. = circa (about)
b. = born; **d.** = died; **r.** = reigned

THE PAGE LAYOUT

The pages in this encyclopedia have been carefully planned to make each subject as accessible as possible. Main entries are broken down into a hierarchy of information – from a general introduction to more specific individual topics.

Alphabet locators
Letter flashes help you find your way quickly around the encyclopedia.

Sub-entries
Sub-entries provide important additional information and expand on points made in the introduction.

This sub-entry explains how rainbows are caused by raindrops in the air.

Diagrams
Clear diagrams help explain complex processes and scientific concepts.

The diagram here shows how a raindrop splits sunlight into its constituent colours.

Introduction
Clear introductions are the starting point for each entry. The introduction defines and provides an overview of each subject.

In the main entry on COLOUR, the introduction explains that colours are different forms of light, and that sunlight contains light of many different colours.

COLLEGES see SCHOOLS AND COLLEGES • COLOMBIA see SOUTH AMERICA.

COLOUR

A WORLD WITHOUT COLOUR would be dull and uninspiring. Colour is a form of light. Light is made up of electromagnetic waves of varying lengths. The human eye detects these different wavelengths and sees them as different colours. White light – like that from the Sun – is a mixture of all the different wavelengths. Objects look coloured because they give out or reflect only certain wavelengths of light.

White light spectrum
Passing white light through a transparent triangular block called a prism separates out the different wavelengths of light. The prism refracts (bends) each wavelength by a different amount, forming a band of colours called a white light spectrum, or a visible spectrum. The seven main colours are red, orange, yellow, green, blue, indigo, and violet. Red has the longest wavelength and violet the shortest. Here, a convex lens combines the colours back into white light.

Rainbow
If it rains on a sunny day, you may well see a rainbow if you stand with your back to the Sun. A rainbow is a curved white light spectrum that forms when light is reflected and refracted by raindrops in the sky.

A rainbow at dawn

How a rainbow forms
When white sunlight passes through a raindrop, the raindrop acts like a tiny prism. The raindrop refracts the light and splits it up into its separate colours. The colours fan out and emerge as a spectrum. A rainbow is made up of spectra from millions of raindrops.

Sunlight
Spectrum
Colours refract again.
Light refracts.
Colours reflect off back surface.

Colour and temperature
Objects at room temperature emit (give out) electromagnetic waves, but these waves are too long for human eyes to see. Heating an object, such as this steel bar, gives the waves it emits more energy and makes them shorter. The waves eventually become short enough to be seen, and the bar begins to glow. As the bar's temperature rises, it glows with different colours.

Steel bar at 630°C (1,170°F)
Steel bar at 1,530°C (2,790°F)

Spectroscope
An instrument called a spectroscope is used to analyze the light given out by hot substances. Inside the spectroscope, a prism or diffraction grating (a glass slide scored with fine lines) splits light from a glowing substance into its component wavelengths.

Light source
Diffraction grating

Emission spectrum
Each chemical element gives out a unique range of light wavelengths when heated. Seen through a spectroscope, these wavelengths appear as a set of bright lines on a dark background. This is the element's emission spectrum. A compound's emission spectrum is a combination of spectra from the elements that make up the compound.

Emission spectrum of a sodium flame
Sodium flame

Cone cells
At the back of the eye there are special cells called cones that enable humans to see colours. There are three types of cone, called red, green, and blue cones. Each type of cone is sensitive to a different range of light wavelengths. White light stimulates all three types of cone.

Cone cells

Sensitivity of red cones
Sensitivity of green cones
Sensitivity of blue cones
Visible spectrum

Sensitivity of cone cells in the human eye

Glowing white
Glowing red
Visible spectrum

Red hot and white hot
As the steel bar gets hotter, it emits more and more of the visible spectrum. At about 630°C (1,170°F), it is "red hot" and emits light from the red end of the spectrum. At about 1,530°C (2,790°F), the "white hot" bar emits the entire white light spectrum.

Hot stars
The colour of a star gives a clue to its age. To the naked eye, most stars look white, but their true colours can be seen using a telescope. Young stars are hot and glow with white light. Older stars are relatively cool and glow red or orange.

A cluster of young stars

Joseph von Fraunhofer
The German physicist Joseph von Fraunhofer (1787–1826) became interested in the nature of light while training as a mirror maker and lens polisher. His training enabled him to make spectroscopes of great precision. From 1814–17, he used them to make the first scientific study of the Sun's emission spectrum.

Munsell colour system
Describing colours exactly using words alone is not easy. To avoid confusion, manufacturing industries use standard colour-identification systems. The Munsell system is used to specify colours for dyes and pigments. It defines a colour by its value (brightness), its chroma (strength), and its hue (position in the spectrum).

Colour matching systems
Graphic designers use swatches of colour cards to match the colours in their work with those available from printers. The designer supplies the printer with the reference number of the colour, so the printer knows exactly what is wanted.

Each colour has a reference number.

226

Strong chest muscles pull down the wings.

Penguin rises through the water to break through the surface.

act as rudders.

Huddling reduces heat loss.

emperor penguins carry chicks around on their feet.

KING PENGUIN

SCIENTIFIC NAME	*Aptenodytes patagonica*
ORDER	Sphenisciformes
FAMILY	Spheniscidae
DISTRIBUTION	Islands and ocean north of Antarctica
HABITAT	Coasts and open sea
DIET	Fish and squid
SIZE	Length, including tail 95 cm (37.5 in)
LIFESPAN	About 20 years

Labels help to identify images.

Natural history data boxes
On the natural history pages, data boxes summarize essential information about a key animal featured in the entry. The box contains information about the animal's size, diet, habitat, lifespan, distribution, and scientific name.

This data box gives you key facts about the King Penguin.

Biography boxes
Most main entry pages have biography boxes that tell you about key people who have contributed to our knowledge of the subject. The encyclopedia also has single-page entries on the life and work of more than 50 major historical figures.

This biography box describes the work of the physicist Joseph von Fraunhofer.

Headings
The topic headings enable you to see at-a-glance which subjects are covered within the main entry.

The heading Colour matching systems refers to the way designers use reference numbers to match the colours on their work to the colours of printers' inks.

INDEX

Volume 3 contains an index and a gazetteer. The index, which comes first, lists all the topics mentioned in the encyclopedia and the pages on which they can be found. The gazetteer follows on, with references to help you find all the features included on the maps.

• page numbers in **bold** type (eg Knights and heraldry **495-6**) show that the subject is a main A–Z entry in Volumes 1–2.
• page numbers in plain type (eg armour 69) send you to sub-entries, text references, and the reference section.
• grid references (eg Cremona Italy 475 C3) are letter-number combinations that locate features on maps.

Knights and heraldry 495-6
armour 69
feudalism 329
Crusades 247, 883
Knights of Malta 70
Knights of St John 247
Knossos, Crete 557
Knowledge, epistemology 651

Craiova Romania 727 C7
Cremona Italy 475 C3
Cres Island Croatia 105 B4
Crete Island Greece 403 E11
Crete, Sea of Mediterranean Sea 403 E10
Crimea Peninsula Ukraine 727 I7
Croatia Country SE Europe 105
Crotone Italy 475 G8

Running head

There is an A–Z running head at the top of most pages to help you find important topics that are not main entries within the encyclopedia.

This two-page entry discusses the main types of primate.

The running head on PRINTING tells you that although there is no main entry on primates, you can find the topic on MONKEYS AND OTHER PRIMATES.

Illustrations

Each main entry is heavily illustrated with models, photographs, and artworks, adding a vibrant layer of visual information to the page.

This annotation tells you how different colours can be produced by mixing red, green, and blue light.

Annotation

The illustrations are comprehensively annotated to draw attention to details of particular interest and to explain complex points.

Pigments

A pigment is a chemical that absorbs only certain colours from white light. This process is called colour subtraction. Yellow, magenta, and cyan are primary pigments. Each absorbs one of the primary colours of light and reflects the other two. For example, a yellow pigment absorbs blue light but reflects green and red, which mix to give yellow. An equal mix of all three pigments absorbs all the colours from white light, giving black.

Coloured lights

Different amounts of red, green, and blue light can be mixed to form light of any other colour. This process is called colour addition. Unlike paints, red, green, and blue are the primary colours of light. Equal amounts of any two primary colours give a secondary colour (yellow, cyan, or magenta). When all three primaries are mixed in equal amounts, white light is produced.

Colour television
The principle of adding coloured lights is used in colour television. The screen is covered with tiny strips that glow with red, green, or blue light. They are so small that, at a normal viewing distance, the human eye mixes the light coming from them. By adjusting the intensities of these three colours, the sensation of any other colour can be produced.

Image is formed by tiny glowing strips.

Colour printing
To print a full-colour image, three single-colour images are printed on top of each other – one in cyan, one in magenta, and one in yellow. Each picture is made up of tiny coloured dots. The dots overlap and absorb the right wavelengths of light to give all the other colours required. A black image is then added to make the picture sharper.

Mixing paints
Paints are pigments mixed with water or oil. Any colour except white can be made by mixing the three primary pigments. Mixing paints has the effect of evenly mixing the pigments, and absorbing more of the white light spectrum.

Painting with dots
"Pointillism" is a style of painting in which an artist uses thousands of tiny coloured dots to build up a picture. When viewed close up, the colours of the individual dots are clearly visible. Like the coloured strips on a television screen, the dots are too small to be seen from close by. When viewed from a distance, the dots seem to merge, giving areas a single colour.

Scattering and interference

Two processes, called scattering and interference, can remove colours from the spectrum. Interference occurs when light from two sources meets and combines. In scattering, some parts of the spectrum are briefly absorbed by particles of matter and then radiated out again in all directions.

Blue sky
Sunlight includes all the colours of the spectrum. The sky appears blue during the day because air molecules in the atmosphere scatter light from the blue end of the spectrum in all directions.

Soap bubble
When white light strikes a soap bubble, it reflects off both the inner and outer surfaces of the bubble. The reflected light rays interfere, making some colours cancel each other out but others appear bright.

Interference creates a pattern of bright colours and dark bands.

Using interference
Stress is a force that can stretch or bend objects. Engineers shine light through plastic models of their designs to test their ability to withstand stress. The plastic molecules make the light rays split up and interfere. The interference patterns show the points of greatest stress.

High stress

Thomas Young
The English doctor and physicist Thomas Young (1773–1829) carried out many experiments to prove that light travels as waves. He realized that colours are light waves of different lengths, and that interference colours occur where light waves meet and combine. Young also investigated colour vision. In 1801, he proposed that the human eye contains three types of colour sensor (now called cone cells), sensitive to blue, red, and green light.

Reflecting colours

Objects have colour only when light falls upon them, because colours do not exist in total darkness. An object that appears one colour in white light may look different when illuminated by coloured light. The yellow pot in this sequence of pictures appears yellow only in white light.

White light
The yellow pot reflects the red and green parts of the white light spectrum, but absorbs the blue part.

Red light
The yellow pot reflects red light, and therefore appears red when illuminated by red light.

Green light
When illuminated by green light, the yellow pigment reflects the green light and so appears green.

Blue light
When only blue light is available, the yellow pot absorbs the blue light, making it look black.

FIND OUT MORE | DYES AND PAINTS | EYES AND SEEING | LIGHT | PHOTOGRAPHY | PRINTING | TELEVISION

227

Find out more

The Find Out More lines at the end of each entry direct you to other relevant main entries in the encyclopedia. Using the Find Out More lines can help you understand an entry in its wider context.

On COLOUR, the Find Out More line directs you to the entry on PRINTING, where there is a detailed explanation of the colour printing process and how printing presses work.

PRINTING

Before the 15th century, books were copied out and illustrated by hand. The development, in the 1450s, of a printing press capable of using movable type led to an information revolution. Large numbers of books and leaflets could be reproduced mechanically, quickly and cheaply, allowing learning to spread rapidly. Today we are surrounded by printed material, from magazines, packaging, and posters to the prints made by artists.

The PRINTING timeline stretches from the printing of the first books in ancient China to the computerization of modern printing.

Timelines

An entry may include a timeline that gives the dates of key events in the history or development of the subject.

PRINTING'S Find Out More line sends you to CHINA, HISTORY OF, which lists ancient Chinese inventions, including printing.

COLLECTION PAGES

There are more than 70 pages of photographic collections, which follow main entries and provide a visual guide to the subject. They are organized under clear headings.

The entry on the history of China is followed by a collection page showing Chinese jewellery and ornaments.

CONTINENT AND COUNTRY PAGES

The encyclopedia contains entries on all the world's continents and countries, each containing a detailed map. Continent entries focus on the physical geography of the region; country entries provide information about the society and economy of the country. Below is the single-page entry on the Netherlands

The country's flag appears by its name.

Locator map

A small map in the top left-hand corner of the page shows you where the region lies within a continent or in relation to the rest of the world.

Map of Netherlands' position in Europe.

The introduction defines the region and provides an overview to the entry.

Compass points north

Scale bar

Scale bar and compass

Each map has a scale bar that shows how distances on the map relate to actual miles and kilometers. The compass shows you which direction on the map is north (N).

Grid reference

The numbers and letters around the map help you find all the places listed in the index.

The index gives Amsterdam's grid reference as C4, so you can find it on the map by locating the third square along (C) and the fourth square down (4).

Population density

A population density diagram shows how many people there are to every square mile or square kilometer.

The Netherlands is a very densely populated country

KEY TO MAP

International border	Lake	●	Capital city
Disputed border	Seasonal lake	◉	Major town
Road	River	●	Minor town
Railroad	Canal	▲	Spot height (feet)
International airport	Waterfall	▼	Spot depth (feet)

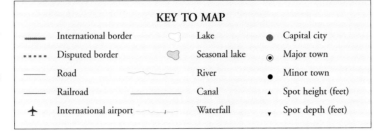

NETBALL see BALL GAMES

NETHERLANDS

ALSO CALLED HOLLAND, the Netherlands straddles the deltas of five major rivers in northwest Europe. The Dutch people say they created their own country because they have reclaimed about one-third of the land from sea or marshland by enclosing the area with earth barriers, or dikes, and draining the water from it. Despite being one of the most densely populated countries in the world, the Netherlands enjoys high living standards. Amsterdam is the official capital, although the government is based at The Hague.

NETHERLANDS FACTS

CAPITAL CITY Amsterdam
(seat of government The Hague)
AREA 37,330 sq km (14,413 sq miles)
POPULATION 15,800,000
MAIN LANGUAGE Dutch
MAJOR RELIGION Christian
CURRENCY Euro
LIFE EXPECTANCY 78 years
PEOPLE PER DOCTOR 385
GOVERNMENT Multi-party democracy
ADULT LITERACY 99%

Physical features

The Netherlands is mainly flat, with 27 per cent of the land below sea level, and protected from the sea by natural sand dunes along the coast, and by artificial dikes. Wide sandy plains cover most of the rest of the country, falling into a few, low hills in the eastern and southern parts of the country.

Canals
The Netherlands is a land of canals, which drain the land and serve as waterways for the movement of people and freight. Amsterdam alone has more than 100 canals.

Windmills
For centuries the Dutch landscape was dotted with 10,000 windmills, which powered pumps to drain water from the land. Electric pumps now do this work in the battle to keep the sea back.

37°C (99°F) / -25°C (-13°F)
16°C (62°F) / 2°C (36°F)
580 mm (23 in)

Climate
The Netherlands has mild, rainy winters and cool summers. In winter northerly gales lash the coast, damaging dikes and threatening floods. Frosts sometimes freeze canals.

Land use
Almost one-third of the land has been reclaimed from the sea. These areas are known as polders and are extremely fertile. The country has large natural gas reserves in the north, and there is some offshore oil drilling in the North Sea.

Forest 3.5% / Farmland 84.5% / Built-up 12%

Farming and industry
The Dutch economy is one of the most successful in Europe. Most imports and exports travel through Rotterdam, the world's biggest port. In addition to high-tech sectors such as electronics, telecommunications, and chemicals, the Netherlands has a successful agricultural industry. Productivity is high, and products such as vegetables, cheese, meat, and cut flowers are significant export earners.

Amsterdam

The Dutch capital is built on 70 islands, linked by about 500 bridges, which span its many canals. The best way to get around is by bicycle, and around 750,000 people cycle to school or work each day. Today, Amsterdam is a busy centre for tourism and diamond trading.

One of Amsterdam's many canals

People
The Dutch see their society as the most tolerant in Europe, with relaxed laws on sexuality, drugs, and euthanasia. The country has a long history of welcoming immigrants, often from former Dutch colonies. Most of these people are now assimilated as Dutch citizens. However, members of the small Turkish community, which makes up just one per cent of the population, do not enjoy full citizenship.

Street scene, Amsterdam

466 per sq km (1,206 per sq mile) / 89% Urban / 11% Rural

Dutch tulips

FIND OUT MORE | DAMS | EMPIRES | EUROPE | EUROPE, HISTORY OF | EUROPEAN UNION | FARMING | NETHERLANDS, HISTORY OF | PORTS AND WATERWAYS

601

Country file

On each country page there is a fact box containing key details about the country, such as its population, capital city, area, currency, political system, and main language and religion. Other categories of information include:

Literacy – the percentage of people over 15 years old who can read and write.
People per doctor – a rough guide to the availability of medical facilities.
Life expectancy – how long an average person can expect to live.

Climate

A climate diagram gives details of rainfall levels and temperatures in the country, region, or continent.

Average summer temperature
Average winter temperature
Average rainfall

Single country's average in capital city

Average summer temperature
Average winter temperature
Average rainfall

Regional average is the average of all capital cities on map

Concise explanation of the country's main physical characteristics.

Land use

The land-use diagram tells you how much of the the country's total land area is taken up by, for example, woodland, agriculture, and urban developments such as villages, towns, and cities.

Most of the land in the Netherlands is used for farming.

Urban/rural split

A small diagram shows the percentage of people living in urban (built-up) areas and rural (country) areas.

The majority of people in the Netherlands live in urban areas.

REFERENCE PAGES

Volume 3 of the Encyclopedia contains an illustrated reference section with essential facts, figures, and statistical data, divided into the five main strands described here.

International world

This strand contains a double-page map showing all the countries of the world, and data on the world's population, economy, and resources.

History

The history strand features a timeline of key historical events, stretching from 40,000 BC to the present day, together with the dates of major wars, revolutions, battles, and great leaders.

Living world

The centrepiece of this strand is a detailed guide to the classification of living things, supported by lists of species in danger, and many other facts about the natural world.

People, arts, and media

This strand is crammed full of information about television, theatre, music, art, philosophy, architecture, literature, dance, and much

Science

A double-page spread on the periodic table is supported by key data on the weather, mathematics, the Earth and the Universe, and measurement conversion tables.

ABORIGINAL AUSTRALIANS

THE ABORIGINALS settled the Australian continent more than 40,000 years ago. They lived in total isolation from the rest of the world, existing by hunting and gathering. In the 18th century, the Europeans arrived, forcing the Aboriginals off their territories. Today, many feel isolated from white society, but still try to preserve their tribal identity.

Some early peoples crossed by means of a land bridge.

Settlers stayed near the coast and rivers where more food was available.

Aboriginal history

Aboriginals first reached Australia during the last Ice Age. Sea levels were low, and they were able to cross from southeast Asia over land bridges and small stretches of water. When the ice melted and sea levels rose again, the continent was completely cut off. Initially, the settlers clung to the coasts and rivers, but gradually moved across the continent. By the time Europeans arrived, there were about 500 different tribal groups living in Australia.

Ways of life

Traditionally, Aboriginals lived by hunting and gathering. They were nomadic, roaming over large stretches of territory, setting up temporary camps near watering places, and moving on when food supplies were exhausted. They traded with other tribes, exchanging goods such as spears.

Hunting and gathering

Aboriginals lived by hunting animals such as kangaroos, and supplemented their diet with wild plants, nuts, and berries. The hunters used spears with stone blades and wooden boomerangs, a type of missile that flies back to the thrower. Some tribes developed an elaborate sign language, so that they could send silent messages to each other when they were stalking game.

Aboriginal hunters used silent signals to avoid disturbing the game. The sign for kangaroo starts with a closed hand and moves to an open shape.

Corroborees

Aboriginal peoples have handed down stories, songs, and traditions from generation to generation. This culture is kept alive at corroborees, ceremonial dances where tribes gather together to retell the tales of Australia's past through songs, music, and dance.

Dreamtime

The Aboriginals believe that Dreamtime is a period when Ancestral Beings shaped the land, creating all species and human beings. These beings are thought to live on eternally in spirit form. Human beings are believed to be a part of nature, closely associated with all other living things. Images of spirits of Dreamtime, such as Lightning Man, cover sacred cliffs and caves in tribal areas.

Lightning Man, also known as Namarrgon

Lightning Man was believed to have created thunder and lightning.

Barrkinj – wife of Lightning Man

Aboriginals today

European colonists arrived in Australia in 1788, and displaced Aboriginal tribes from their territory. Today, there are about 250,000 Aboriginals in Australia, many of whom live in urban areas. Although there is still discrimination, Aboriginals are beginning to benefit from government aid, and to assert their civil rights.

Land rights

When the Europeans arrived in Australia they claimed that the land was *Terra nullius*, that it belonged to no one, and that they were entitled to occupy it. More recently, the Aboriginals have campaigned to regain their lost territory and sacred sites. In 1993, the Australian government reversed its *Terra nullius* policy.

Education

During early contact with the Europeans, Aboriginal languages were lost or fell into disuse. In 1972, the government established a bilingual education programme. Many children are now taught in their tribal languages before learning English. Books, radio, and television broadcasts are all available in many Aboriginal languages.

Uluru (Ayers Rock)

Aboriginals believe that the Ancestral Beings created the Australian landscape, and established customs and traditions still followed today. They have left evidence of their presence in the many sacred places, such as Uluru in central Australia. This is revered as a sacred place by the local Aranda people. Once called Ayers Rock by the Australian government, the rock regained its Aboriginal name in 1988.

FIND OUT MORE ART, HISTORY OF | AUSTRALASIA AND OCEANIA | AUSTRALIA | AUSTRALIA, HISTORY OF | COOK, JAMES | MYTHS AND LEGENDS | RELIGIONS | SOCIETIES, HUMAN

ACIDS AND ALKALIS

LEMON JUICE AND VINEGAR taste sour because they contain weak acids. An acid is a substance that dissolves in water to form positively charged particles called hydrogen ions (H^+). The opposite of an acid is an alkali, which dissolves in water to form negatively charged ions of hydrogen and oxygen, called hydroxide ions (OH^-). Alkalis are "anti-acids" because they cancel out acidity. Toothpaste, for example, contains an alkali to cancel out acidity in the mouth that would otherwise damage teeth.

Hydrochloric acid

There is a tremendous fizzing as hydrogen gas is given off.

Zinc replaces the hydrogen in the acid to form zinc chloride.

Zinc nuggets

pH scale

The concentration of hydrogen ions in a solution is known as its pH. Scientists use the pH scale to measure acidity and alkalinity. On the pH scale, a solution with a pH lower than 7 is acidic, and a solution with a pH greater than 7 is alkaline. Water is neutral, with a pH of 7. A solution's pH can be tested with universal indicator solution or paper, which changes colour in acids and alkalis.

Universal indicator pH colour chart

Universal indicator paper

1 Strong acids
Digestive juices: pH 1
Lemon juice: pH 3
Acid rain: pH 5
7 Neutral
Human blood: pH 7.4
Oven cleaner: pH 13
14 Strong alkalis

Hydrochloric acid (pH 1)

Vinegar (pH 4)

Liquid soap (pH 8–9)

Household cleaner (pH 10)

Strong acids

The more hydrogen ions an acid forms in water, the stronger it is, and the lower its pH. Strong acids, such as sulphuric acid and nitric acid, are very dangerous and must be handled carefully.

Sulphuric acid

Carbon

Sugar

Sulphuric acid
Concentrated sulphuric acid will dehydrate (remove water from) any substance with which it comes into contact. For example, the acid dehydrates sugar, a carbohydrate, to leave a mass of smouldering black carbon.

Cork

Nitric acid

Nitrogen dioxide gas and smoke are given off as acid reacts with cork.

Nitric acid
Organic matter, such as paper, cork, rubber, fabric, and skin, is rapidly decomposed by nitric acid. The acid is so corrosive because it oxidizes (supplies oxygen to) any material with which it comes into contact.

Svante Arrhenius

Swedish scientist Svante Arrhenius (1859–1927) won acclaim for his research into how compounds form ions in solution. This work led him to realize that it is hydrogen ions that give acids their special properties.

Acids and metals

Even the weakest acids cannot be stored in metal containers because acids are corrosive to most metals. When an acid reacts with a metal, hydrogen gas is given off and the metal dissolves in the acid to form a compound called a salt. The reaction is very violent with metals such as potassium and sodium, and quite vigorous with metals such as magnesium and zinc.

Salts
When the hydrogen in an acid is replaced by a metal during a chemical reaction, a neutral compound called a salt is formed. For example, when copper reacts with nitric acid, the copper takes the place of the hydrogen to make the salt copper nitrate. Like other metals, copper forms a variety of salts when mixed with different acids. Most salts are crystals, and many are coloured. Some salts, such as sodium chloride (common salt), occur naturally.

Copper nitrate

Nitric acid

Sulphuric acid

Copper sulphate

Hydrochloric acid

Copper turnings

Copper chloride

Acid industry

Acids are widely used in industry because they react so readily with other materials. For example, sulphuric acid is used in the production of dyes and pigments, artificial fibres, plastics, soaps, and explosives. The acid is made by sulphur and oxygen reacting together.

Sulphuric acid chemical plant

Acid rain
Burning fossil fuels to produce energy for use at home and in industry releases polluting gases into the air. The gases dissolve in water in the clouds to form nitric acid and sulphuric acid. This water falls as acid rain, which erodes stone buildings and statues, kills trees and aquatic life, and reduces the soil's fertility.

Bases and alkalis

The acidity of vinegar (ethanoic acid) can be neutralized, or cancelled out, by adding chalk (calcium carbonate). Any substance that neutralizes acidity, such as chalk, is called a base. An alkali is a base that dissolves in water. An alkali's strength is measured by the number of hydroxide ions it forms in water. Strong alkalis, such as sodium hydroxide, are just as corrosive as strong acids.

Chalk and vinegar react together and release carbon dioxide gas.

The product of the reaction is a salt called calcium ethanoate.

The mixture spills out of the flask.

Testing the mixture with universal indicator solution proves that it is now neutral – the acidity has been cancelled out.

Soaps and detergents

Alkalis are good at dissolving oil and grease, so they are widely used in the manufacture of soaps and detergents. Most dirt is bound to skin, clothes, or eating utensils by grease. The grease makes it difficult to remove the dirt with water alone, because water and grease do not mix. A soap or detergent, such as washing-up liquid, breaks the grease up into tiny drops and allows the water to wash away the dirt.

Once the washing-up liquid has broken down the grease, the water can wet the plate and dissolve the rest of the dirt.

Oil slicks

Accidents with oil tankers at sea can create huge oil slicks (spillages) on the water's surface. Strong detergents called dispersants may be used to break up the oil. Wildlife experts use weaker detergents, such as washing-up liquid, to clean the feathers of oil-coated seabirds. If the birds' feathers – which usually keep them warm and dry – become clogged with oil, the birds may lose their buoyancy and drown, or die of exposure to the cold.

Batteries

Acids, alkalis, and salts are electrolytes, meaning that they conduct electricity when in solution. Batteries consist of an electrolyte – usually in the form of a moist paste or liquid – between two rods or plates called electrodes. The most common battery is the dry cell, which uses the salt ammonium chloride as an electrolyte. Long-life batteries contain alkaline electrolytes, such as potassium hydroxide; car batteries have electrolytes of sulphuric acid.

Car battery

Long-life battery

Dry cell

Alkali industry

The main raw material in the alkali industry is brine (salt water). Sodium hydroxide, which is used to make soaps and paper, is produced from brine by electrolysis (passing electricity through it). Brine will also absorb carbon dioxide to make sodium carbonate, which is used in textile treatment, photography, and glass making.

Electrolysis of brine to make sodium hydroxide

Neutralizing acids

An alkali and an acid react together to give a neutral salt. In addition, hydroxide ions (OH⁻) in the alkali combine with the acid's hydrogen ions (H⁺) to produce water (H_2O). In daily life, problems of unwanted acidity are solved by adding an alkali of the appropriate strength.

Soil acidity

The pH of soil varies from area to area. Few crops grow well in highly acidic soil, because the acid dissolves vital minerals that the plants need for healthy growth and allows them to be washed away. Farmers treat acidic soil by spreading lime (calcium oxide) over their fields. This is a cheaply produced alkali made from limestone. It neutralizes the acid in the soil, making it more fertile.

Farmer liming acidic soil

Curing indigestion

The human stomach uses hydrochloric acid to break down food. Some foods cause your stomach to produce so much acid that it gives you discomfort. Stomach powders or indigestion tablets can cure this. They contain weak alkalis that neutralize the acidity, but do not harm your stomach, or react too vigorously with the acid.

Stomach powder fizzes as it reacts with lemon juice (citric acid).

Bee and wasp stings

A bee sting is painful because it is acidic. Treating the sting with a weak alkali, such as soap or bicarbonate of soda, relieves the pain by neutralizing the acid. In contrast, a wasp sting is alkaline, so it can be neutralized by a weak acid, such as vinegar or lemon juice.

Wasp

Bee

Fritz Haber

In 1908, the German chemist Fritz Haber (1868–1934) developed a process for making the alkali ammonia, which is used to make fertilizers and explosives. The Haber process involves reacting nitrogen from the air with hydrogen at high pressure and temperature. Haber later devised a way of making nitric acid by heating ammonia in air.

Timeline

c.600 BC The Phoenicians use alkaline wood ash to make soap.

11th century AD Arab chemists make sulphuric, nitric, and hydrochloric acids.

1780s World's first sulphuric acid factory opens in France.

1865 Ernest Solvay, a Belgian chemist, develops the first commercially successful process for making the alkali, sodium carbonate, on a large scale.

Sodium carbonate

1887 Svante Arrhenius proposes that it is hydrogen ions that give acids their special properties.

1908 Fritz Haber invents a process for making ammonia.

1909 The Danish chemist Søren Sørensen (1868–1939) devises the pH scale.

FIND OUT MORE   ATOMS AND MOLECULES   BEES AND WASPS   CHEMISTRY   DIGESTION   ELECTRICITY   MIXTURES AND COMPOUNDS   POLLUTION   ROCKETS   SOIL

ADVERTISING AND MARKETING

WHEN A COMPANY WISHES TO SELL or improve the sales of its products or services, it may decide to advertise. Newspapers and magazines carry advertisements, as do billboards, television, and radio. Marketing is the wider process of creating a product or service, advertising it, and selling it. Advertising and marketing are vast industries that affect all our lives.

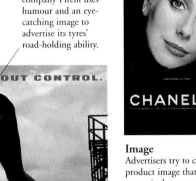

Copy line gives us product information. Here, the tyre-making company Pirelli uses humour and an eye-catching image to advertise its tyres' road-holding ability.

How advertising works

Advertisements use humour and strong images to get our attention. Short, memorable catchphrases called slogans become associated with the product. An advertising campaign often combines posters and television advertisements so that repetition ensures people remember the product.

Well-known athlete

The striking image of an athlete in high heels grabs our attention.

POWER IS NOTHING WITHOUT CONTROL.

Product name

Image
Advertisers try to create a product image that will appeal to particular customers. An advertisement for perfume, for example, may project an image of beauty and sophistication. Well-known personalities may be shown endorsing a product to strengthen its image.

Marketing

A company's marketing strategy includes market research, product development, publicity, advertising, and point of sale displays. The marketing department researches the products people want, and works with other departments to make sure that products meet the customer's needs and expectations.

Public relations
Many companies use public relations, or PR, to improve their standing with the people who buy their products. The two main branches of PR are research and communication. Research tries to find out what people think about the company and its products. Companies communicate with people through press coverage, advertising, and sponsorship.

Pepsi-Cola painted Concorde blue to gain publicity.

Market research
The purpose of market research is to find out what sort of people are likely to buy a product, and what will make them buy one product rather than another. Researchers get this information from interviews, questionnaires, and government statistics.

Point of sale
Shops use posters and display units to encourage people to buy products. Point of sale displays try to catch the customer's eye where he or she can buy the product immediately. Shop window displays aim to draw customers into a shop.

Advertising agencies

Companies use advertising agencies to advise them on their advertising strategy. Advertising agencies conduct market research, plan which forms of media the client's advertisements should appear in, and finally prepare the client's advertisements.

The film is combined with a sound track, and then edited.

Storyboards
The first stage of producing a television advertisement is to present a storyboard of ideas to the client, showing how the final advertisement will look. A storyboard looks rather like a comic strip, with a series of pictures showing how the action will run. If the client approves the storyboard, production can go ahead.

Production
The advertising agency hires a production team to film the advertisement. This will include a producer, who supervises the rehearsal schedule, and a director, who directs the action when the commercial is being filmed. Once the film has been shot, a sound track is added. The sound track may be a voice-over repeating the product name and a catchy tune called a jingle.

Advertisement
Once the advertisement has been completed, it is shown to the client. If the client approves the film, it is taken to the television stations to be aired. Television advertising is by far the most expensive form of advertising, but it is the most effective since it reaches people in their own homes.

FIND OUT MORE DESIGN • FILMS AND FILM-MAKING • MONEY • SHOPS • TELEVISION • TRADE AND INDUSTRY

AFRICA

THE SECOND LARGEST CONTINENT after Asia, Africa is dominated in the north by the vast Sahara Desert and in the east by the Great Rift Valley. A belt of rainforest lies along the Equator, and grasslands provide grazing for herds of wild animals. Africa is home to many different peoples, each with their own distinctive languages and customs. Islam and Christianity are widespread, but many Africans adhere to their own traditional beliefs.

Physical features

Most of Africa is a high plateau covered with deserts, lush rainforests, and dry grasslands. It is crossed by rivers, which bring water to dry regions and provide communications. Although they lie on the Equator, the high peaks in the east are snow-capped all year. Africa has several volcanoes.

Sahara

The world's largest desert, the Sahara, covers much of northwestern Africa. It has an area of 9,065,000 sq km (3,263,400 sq miles) and is rapidly expanding as land at its edges is overgrazed. With less than 100 mm (4 in) of rainfall every year and daytime temperatures of up to 50°C (122°F), only a few specially adapted plants and animals survive here.

River Nile

The Nile is the world's longest river. From its source in Lake Victoria, it flows 6,695 km (4,160 miles) north through Uganda, Sudan, and Egypt to the Mediterranean Sea. Africa's third longest river, the Niger, flows 4,180 km (2,597 miles) in a big loop through western Africa, ending in Nigeria in a delta bigger than that of the Nile.

River Nile at Aswan in Egypt

Mountains rise from the Great Rift Valley.

Great Rift Valley

The mountains of Ethiopia are divided by the Great Rift Valley that stretches 6,000 km (3,750 miles) north from Mozambique, through east Africa and the Red Sea, into Syria. The valley is formed by massive cracks in the Earth's crust. It is up to 90 km (55 miles) wide, and in millions of years will eventually divide the African continent.

Simen Mountains, Ethiopia

Okavango Delta

Many rivers end in deltas at the sea, but the Okavango River in southern Africa has a delta that forms a swamp in the Kalahari Desert. The Okavango rises in Angola and flows 974 km (605 miles) to Botswana, where its delta and swamps cover more than 22,000 sq km (8,500 sq miles).

Cross-section through Africa

Africa rises sharply from the Atlantic Ocean up to about 1,000 m (3,280 ft) before dropping down into the marshes of the Zaire Basin. The Ruwenzori Mountains and Great Rift Valley lie to the east, and the plateau falls gently to the Indian Ocean.

São Tomé

Atlantic Ocean

Lush, wet Zaire Basin

Mt. Stanley 5,110 m (16,765 ft)

Ruwenzori Mountains

Lake Victoria

Great Rift Valley

Mt. Kilimanjaro 5895 m (19,341 ft)

Indian Ocean

A — Approximately 4,100 km (2,550 miles) from A to B — B

AFRICA FACTS

AREA	30,335,000 sq km (11,712,434 sq miles)
POPULATION	783,800,000
NUMBER OF COUNTRIES	53
BIGGEST COUNTRY	Sudan
SMALLEST COUNTRY	Seychelles
HIGHEST POINT	Kilimanjaro (Tanzania) 5,895 m (19,341 ft)
LONGEST RIVER	Nile (Uganda/Sudan/Egypt) 6,695 km (4,160 miles)
BIGGEST LAKE	Lake Victoria (East Africa) 68,880 sq km (26,590 sq miles)

Map labels

Mediterranean Sea, Atlas Mts., TUNISIA, Gulf of Sirte, Nile Delta, Suez Canal, Qattara Depression, ASIA, Red Sea, Madeira (Portugal), Toubkal 4165m, MOROCCO, Canary Is. (Spain), ALGERIA, LIBYA, EGYPT, Libyan Desert, WESTERN SAHARA (Occupied by Morocco), Tropic of Cancer, Ahaggar 2918m, Tibesti 3145m, Nubian Desert, MAURITANIA, MALI, NIGER, CHAD, SUDAN, ERITREA, Senegal, Niger, L. Chad, Blue Nile, White Nile, DJIBOUTI, Gulf of Aden, SENEGAL, GAMBIA, GUINEA-BISSAU, BURKINA, 4620m, Ethiopian Highlands, Assal 156m, GUINEA, SIERRA LEONE, IVORY COAST, GHANA, TOGO, BENIN, NIGERIA, Benue, CAMEROON, CENTRAL AFRICAN REPUBLIC, Ubangi, Sudd, Shebeli, ETHIOPIA, Elemi Triangle, LIBERIA, ATLANTIC OCEAN, Niger Delta, EQUATORIAL GUINEA, SAO TOME & PRINCIPE, GABON, Congo, Congo Basin, Mt Stanley 5110m, UGANDA, L. Victoria, KENYA, Kirinyaga 5200m, Equator, ANGOLA (Cabinda), DEM. REP. CONGO (ZAIRE), RWANDA, BURUNDI, Kilimanjaro 5895m, Pemba, Zanzibar, L. Tanganyika 1482m, TANZANIA, SEYCHELLES, Kasai, L. Nyasa, COMOROS, Mayotte (France), ANGOLA, MALAWI, ZAMBIA, Zambezi, MOZAMBIQUE, Mozambique Channel, MADAGASCAR 2658m, Victoria Falls 108m, ZIMBABWE, L. Kariba, NAMIBIA, Okavango Delta, BOTSWANA, Namib Desert, Kalahari Desert, SWAZILAND, INDIAN OCEAN, Orange, LESOTHO 3482m, Drakensberg, SOUTH AFRICA, Tropic of Capricorn, Cape of Good Hope

0 km 1000 / 0 miles 1000

Climatic zones

Although most of Africa is warm or hot all year round, the climate varies greatly because of the wide range of landscapes. Parts of the north coast have hot, dry summers and cooler, moist winters. Desert regions have cold nights, scorching hot days, and almost no rain at all. On the Equator the climate is hot and humid, with high rainfall. Mountain regions have warm summers and cool winters.

Scrubland *Desert* *Grassland* *Tropical rainforest* *Wetland* *Mountain*

Fantastically shaped dunes are formed by strong desert winds.

Scrubland

Much of the northern coast of Africa has a warm Mediterranean climate. Coastal cliffs and hills are covered in sparse, low-growing, often fragrant plants and shrubs that are able to thrive in the poor, stony soils. Many of the plants have thorns and small, leathery leaves to prevent them from drying out in the fierce heat of the sun and frequent sea breezes.

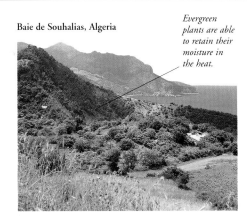

Baie de Souhalias, Algeria

Evergreen plants are able to retain their moisture in the heat.

Deserts

About 40 per cent of Africa is desert. The Erg of Bilma in Niger is part of the vast Sahara. In Arabic, *erg* means a sandy expanse. The sand is blown by the wind into ripples and into huge dunes, some of which may be nearly 200 m (650 ft) high. Two other main desert areas are the Kalahari and the Namib, both in southern Africa.

Occasional stunted trees offer animals some protection from the harsh sun.

Many streams and rivers cross the rainforest.

Savannah

About 40 per cent of Africa is covered with savannah, which is the name given to grassland with scattered trees and shrubs. This type of land forms a wide loop around the Zaire (Congo) Basin. Vast herds of grazing animals, such as antelopes and zebras, move around the savannah seeking fresh grass to eat.

Masai Mara, Kenya

Low shrubs cover some of the mountains' lower slopes and foothills.

Tropical rainforest

Dense, tropical rainforest covers less than 20 per cent of Africa. The most extensive areas lie close to the Equator in West Africa and in Central Africa's Zaire (Congo) Basin. Thousands of species of tree flourish in the hot, humid climate, which produces rain all year round. However, large-scale felling of trees for timber hardwoods, such as teak and mahogany, threatens to destroy this environment.

Mahogany leaf

Oil

Mountain

Africa's highest ranges include the Drakensberg, in southeast Africa, which runs for about 1,130 km (70 miles) through South Africa and Lesotho and forms part of the rim of the great South African Plateau. The highest point is Thabana Ntlenyana at 3,482 m (11,424 ft). Even higher mountain ranges are the Atlas range in Morocco, and the Ruwenzori on the border between Uganda and Congo (Zaire).

People

One in eight of the world's people lives in Africa, mostly along the north and west coasts, and in the fertile river valleys. Although traditionally people live in small villages, a growing number are moving to towns and cities to look for work. Birth rates in many countries are high and families are large. About half the population is under 15 years old.

Ghanaian girls   Tanzanian girl   Egyptian boy

Resources

Africa has many resources, but they are unevenly distributed. Libya and Nigeria are leading oil producers, southern Africa is rich in gold and diamonds, and Zambia is a leading copper producer. Tropical forests yield valuable timber but are being felled at an alarming rate. Africa is a leading producer of cocoa beans, cassava, bananas, coffee, and tea.

Cocoa beans and pod

Diamond

 FIND OUT MORE   AFRICA, HISTORY OF   AFRICAN WILDLIFE   CLIMATES   CONTINENTS   DESERTS   FORESTS   GRASSLAND WILDLIFE   MOUNTAINS AND VALLEYS   OIL   RAINFOREST WILDLIFE

AFRICA, HISTORY OF

CIVILIZATION IN AFRICA BEGAN TO appear more than 5,000 years ago with the rise of ancient Egypt. From about 2,500 years ago in sub-Saharan Africa, many other different kingdoms also developed. The Sahara acted as a barrier to keep this area separate from the rest of the world until the arrival of Arab traders in the 8th century. From the 15th century, the arrival of Europeans, the subsequent slave trade, and European imperialism had a profound effect on the continent. Since the 1950s, all African nations have reclaimed independence, although modern Africa continues to struggle with its post-colonial legacy and environmental problems.

Ancient empires

North Africa was in a good position to trade with western Asia. This caused rich empires to develop, including Meroë (modern Sudan, c.600 BC–AD 350), and Aksum (a trading state in northern Ethiopia, c.100 BC–AD 1000). Ghana (in West Africa, c.500–1300) developed for similar reasons.

Meroë
From the city of Meroë, the Kushites controlled trade in the Red Sea and the Nile River from 600 BC. They exported luxury goods, such as ostrich feathers and leopard skins, and built fine temples and flat-topped pyramids over the graves of their dead.

Ruined temple, Meroë

Ghana
Ghana (located on the borders of modern Mali and Mauritania), one of Africa's most important empires, controlled the trans-Saharan trade in gold. Ghana's kings wore gold jewellery, and gold-embroidered clothes and turbans. Surviving gold artefacts show the incredible wealth of this kingdom.

Heads of gold, often of royalty, played an important part in rituals.

Carving was made of wood and coated with gold.

Head weighs 1.5 kg (3 lbs).

Figures were attached to royal thrones.

Bird ornament

Rings were often decorated with flowers.

Finger rings

Stela, Aksum

Aksum
From c.300, Egyptian scholars introduced Christianity to Aksum, which then became famous as a holy city. During this period, Aksum took over the empire based at Meroë. Aksum's people built tall, stone stelae (monuments) to mark the tombs of dead kings.

Early inhabitants

Humans have inhabited Africa for 4 million years. The Sahara was once a fertile land rich in plants and animals. But thousands of years ago, it dried up, and people moved south to the savannah to farm there.

Rock paintings
Rock and bone pictures often depicted everyday events, such as dancing, hunting animals, and fishing. Painters used animal fat coloured with vegetable dyes.

Vegetable dye

Animals

Painted bone

Nok culture
The earliest evidence of Iron Age settlement is called the Nok culture (500 BC–AD 200), which existed in what is now central Nigeria. Nok people lived in farming communities. They made iron weapons and tools for farming, and also produced fine terracotta sculptures.

Terracotta head, Nok culture

Spread of religions

From the 8th century, trade, conquests, and colonialism spread religions such as Islam in Africa. In North Africa, Islam completely replaced traditional religions, which often included the worship of ancestors.

Festival mask

Ancestor worship
In many parts of Africa, communities had sacred shrines where they placed offerings for the spirits of their dead ancestors. Today, during certain annual festivals, members of the community wear special masks, sing, dance, and tell stories in honour of their ancestors.

Islam
By c.800, Middle Eastern Arabs had taken Islam to North Africa. From the 11th century, trade helped spread Islam across the Sahara into West Africa and up the River Nile into Sudan.

Ait Benhaddou, Morocco

Slave trade
By the 1470s, the Portuguese were trading copper, brass, gold, and slaves with Benin in West Africa. In the 1480s, the Portuguese arrived in the islands of Principe and São Tomé in the Gulf of Guinea, just off the west African coast. They established sugar plantations, and forced African captives (mainly kidnapped in Senegal and Gambia) to work as slaves on the plantations. This was the beginning of European domination in Africa.

Plaque showing Portuguese soldier, 1500s

A

Colonialism

During the 1800s, Europeans colonized areas in Africa, introducing Christianity, and taking economic control. They used African workers to grow or mine precious raw materials, but sent the materials to be manufactured in Europe and America – where profits stayed. During this period, slavery was at its height as Europeans kidnapped Africans to work in the Americas.

African Diaspora

The slave trade scattered more than 20 million Africans throughout the Americas and Europe, undermining African culture in the process. Over the centuries, the dispersed descendents of these slaves became known as the African Diaspora.

African carving of a European

Christianity

Europe sent missionaries to Africa to set up schools and churches, and to convert Africans to Christianity. They also tried to abolish African traditional religions, often punishing those who still practised them.

Traditional witch doctors

Voodoo voice disguiser

Voodoo

In 19th-century Caribbean colonies, traditional ancestor worship combined with Christianity to produce a religion called voodoo.

Scramble for Africa

In 1884, European leaders decided that their countries could claim African territories as colonies when occupied by Europeans. This started a scramble to the interior in search of new lands. By 1902, all of Africa was colonized, except Liberia and Ethiopia.

Carving of Queen Victoria

Morocco
Tunisia
Egypt
Algeria
Libya
Liberia
Nigeria
British Somaliland
Sierra Leone
Ethiopia
British East Africa (Kenya)
French
British
German
Portuguese
Belgium
Spanish
Italian
Anglo-Egyptian
Angola

World Wars I and II

Although both world wars were European, thousands of Africans lost their lives as colonial rulers forced them to join the army. One cause of World War I was German resentment against other European countries during colonization. In World War II, North Africa became a battleground, as German and Italian forces invaded British- and French-ruled territories.

Troops at El Alamein, Egypt

World War I

When World War I broke out in 1914, the Ottoman Empire controlled North Africa. The Egyptians colluded with the British to overthrow Turkish rule, and they were helped from 1916 to 1918 by the eccentric soldier and author Thomas Edward Lawrence (1888–1935), who became famous as Lawrence of Arabia. After the war, Egypt became a British protectorate but signed a treaty for independence in 1922.

El Alamein

In 1941, Italian and German forces invaded North African territories held by the British. The British recruited soldiers from their colonies of Nigeria, Ghana, and Sierra Leone to join the fight on their behalf. In 1942, the British defeated the Germans at the historic battle of El Alamein. This battle was a turning point in the war.

Herero and Nama tribes fight German colonialists, Namibia, 1904

African resistance

Africans strenuously resisted colonialism. The Ethiopians fought to stay independent and won (1896); Zimbabwe and Sudan rebelled against the British (1896 and 1920); tribes in Angola tried to overthrow the Portuguese (1902); in Namibia and Tanzania, thousands were killed in uprisings against the Germans (1904–1908); and in Nigeria, tribes revolted against French rule (1920s).

Operation Torch

In 1942, American and British soldiers landed in Morocco and Algeria in an invasion called Operation Torch. Joined by the French, the Allies attacked the German and Italian armies, forcing them into Tunisia. After a bloody battle, Germany's Afrika Korps surrendered. The war on African soil was over by May 1943.

African Front

TE Lawrence

Haile Selassie

Emperor Haile Selassie of Ethiopia (r.1930–74) led his troops against the Italian invasion of 1935. The Italians forced the emperor into exile in 1936, but he returned in 1941. Haile Selassie instituted reforms, suppressed slavery, and worked with the Organization of African Unity. In 1974, the army overthrew the emperor, installing military rule. He died in exile in 1975 aged 84.

A

Independence

After World War II, many Africans wanted to end colonial rule, and govern their own countries. Colonial powers such as France, Portugal, and Britain fought to prevent this, and there were bloody wars of independence in Algeria, Mozambique, Angola, and Zimbabwe. By the late 1960s most African countries had gained independence, but political and economic problems remained.

Returning refugees, Angola

Ghanaian Independence Day stamps

Gold Coast
One of the first colonies to become independent was the former British colony of the Gold Coast. After World War II, anti-colonial feeling had intensified, and, in 1957, the state of Ghana (which was named after a powerful West African medieval empire) became independent. A leading nationalist, Kwame Nkrumah (1909–72) became the new country's first prime minister. In 1960, Nkrumah declared Ghana a republic and himself president for life. He became increasingly dictatorial, while drawing ever further away from the west. In 1966, a police-military coup overthrew Nkrumah.

OAU member states now number 50.

OAU summit, Tunisia

Organization of African Unity
In 1963, the heads of 30 independent African states met to form the OAU (Organization of African Unity). Its aim was to promote political and economic co-operation between the states, and help colonies achieve independence.

Angola War
In 1961, Angola's people rose in revolt against the Portuguese colonial government. The Portuguese army crushed the rebels, who fled into exile in Zaire. While in exile, the rebels formed liberation movements, and waged guerrilla warfare in Angola. In 1974, the liberation forces staged a military uprising, and overthrew the Portuguese, who finally granted independence in 1975. After independence, a bitter civil war erupted between two political groups, both of whom wanted to govern Angola. One side was backed by South African troops, the other by Russian troops. The Angolan factions agreed to a ceasefire in 1994.

Electronics technician

Game park, Kenya

Apartheid
By the 1980s, only South Africa was still trying to retain white-minority power. The white government had passed the Apartheid (separateness) Policy in 1948, which classified people according to race. Under apartheid, those classified as Black, Coloured, or Asian had few rights. Apartheid was abolished in 1994.

A taxi stand for whites, South Africa, 1967

Modern Africa

Mineral-rich Africa has a thriving mining industry. More recently, new African electronics plants are specializing in the assembly of imported electronic components.

Tourism
A century ago, East African governments established game reserves and parks to protect wildlife from hunters. Today, tourists pay to stay in the parks and go on safari to see the wild animals. Kenya now makes more money from tourism than from any other source.

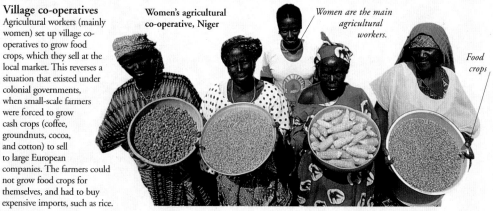

Village co-operatives
Agricultural workers (mainly women) set up village co-operatives to grow food crops, which they sell at the local market. This reverses a situation that existed under colonial governments, when small-scale farmers were forced to grow cash crops (coffee, groundnuts, cocoa, and cotton) to sell to large European companies. The farmers could not grow food crops for themselves, and had to buy expensive imports, such as rice.

Women's agricultural co-operative, Niger

Women are the main agricultural workers.

Food crops

Deforestation, Somalia

Environmental devastation
In semi-arid areas of Africa, such as Somalia, land is gradually turning into desert. Since the 1950s, there has been a fall in the average annual rainfall, and much of the land has become very dry. The people have often over-used the land for cash crops, and cut down the trees for firewood.

Ken Saro-Wiwa
Ken Saro-Wiwa (1941–1995), a human rights campaigner, was hanged along with eight others by Nigeria's military government. His "crime" was to speak out against the pollution of tribal lands by government-backed international oil companies.

Timeline

African carving

2500 BC Climatic changes in the Sahara region force people to move southward.

c.600 BC Kushite people of Sudan expand and base their capital at Meroë.

c.AD 320–25 King Ezama of Aksum becomes Christian.

500–1300 The kingdom of Ghana controls trans-Saharan trade.

641 Arabs conquer Egypt, and convert it to Islam.

600s The empire based at Aksum begins to decline.

1497 Portuguese explorers land on east coast, after sailing around Africa.

1900 Most of the Sahara region comes under French colonial rule.

1940 Italian forces invade North Africa; Germans follow one year later.

1945 League of Arab States is founded; it includes eight African nations.

1973–75 Horn of Africa suffers a severe drought.

1994–95 In Rwanda 800,000 Hutus are massacred by Tutsis; millions flee the country.

FIND OUT MORE   BENIN EMPIRE   GREAT ZIMBABWE   MALI EMPIRE   MANDELA, NELSON   RELIGIONS   SLAVERY   SONGHAI EMPIRE   SOUTH AFRICA, HISTORY OF

AFRICA, CENTRAL

THE EQUATOR RUNS THROUGH Central Africa, affecting not only climate but also ways of life. There are ten countries. All were European colonies with a history of a cruel slave trade. Although these countries were all independent by the end of the 1960s, they have experienced mixed fortunes. Cameroon is stable, while Democratic Republic Congo (Zaire) and the Central African Republic, have suffered dictatorships. Most Central Africans live by farming.

Physical features

The landscape varies according to its distance from the Equator. Much of the region is rolling hills and valleys, with craggy mountains in the north and east. The arid Sahara desert and Sahel cover the extreme north. Farther south, is the vast equatorial basin of the River Congo, surrounded by some unspoilt tropical rainforest.

Dry woodland
Tropical rainforests give way to woodland, where the climate is much drier. Acacia and baobab trees grow in this region. The baobabs have very thick trunks that can hold water to feed themselves. Some baobabs on Cameroon's central plateau live for 1,000 years.

Tibesti
The dramatic cliffs of the volcanic Tibesti Mountains dominate the border between Chad and Libya, in the Sahara Desert. At 3,415 m (11,204 ft) above sea-level, Emi Koussi is the highest peak.

River Congo
One of the longest rivers in the world, the Congo, formerly the Zaire, flows in a great curve for 4,666 km (2,900 miles), crossing the Equator twice. It drains an area of about 3,630,000 sq km (1,400,000 sq miles).

Equatorial rainforest
The hot, humid basin of the River Congo is Africa's largest remaining region of tropical rainforest. Competing for light, a wide variety of trees grow tall, forming a protective canopy that teems with plant and animal life.

Regional climate
The north of the region, the Sahara and Sahel area, is a broad band of dry, dusty land that is starved of rain. By contrast, in the steamy equatorial forests more than 38 mm (1.5 in) of rain falls every day in places. The south experiences the monsoon season between May and October.

29°C (84°F)   27°C (81°F)
1,434 mm (56 in)

Ethnic diversity

There are hundreds of different peoples in Central Africa, each with their own customs and languages. Large groups include the Kongo and Luba, and there are several pygmy groups including the Twa, BaKa, and Mbuti, who live in clearings deep in the rainforests. A growing number of people are moving to towns to escape war, drought, or famine, and because larger centres offer more jobs and food.

Village chief, Brazzaville, Congo

Chad

The land-locked republic of Chad is one of the world's poorest countries. Nearly half of the land is desert or lies in the Sahel, where rainfall is erratic. More than half of the people work on farmland near the Chari river in the south, but lack of food is still a problem. Chad has some valuable mineral deposits, but they are unexploited.

Muslim nomads
More than 100,000 nomadic Muslims live in the desert and northern Sahel regions of Chad. They include the Kanimbo people, who are related to the Arabs and Berbers of North Africa. Every day, Kanimbo women must walk long distances in the heat to fetch water for their families.

Camels
One of the only ways to cross the vast Sahara Desert is by camel. Camels are used as pack animals to transport forest products and minerals from Lake Chad, as well as for farming, pumping water, and carrying people. Herders value their milk, meat, and hides.

Dried gourds used as bowls for making butter.

Fulani
Throughout Africa a nomadic group called the Fulani herd cattle and roam wherever there is grazing land. They drink the cows' milk and use it to make butter and cheese. Bottle-shaped gourds, a type of fruit, are dried and decorated for use as water carriers and bowls.

CHAD FACTS

CAPITAL CITY	N'Djamena
AREA	1,259,200 sq km (486,177 sq miles)
POPULATION	7,700,000
MAIN LANGUAGES	French, Arabic, Sara
MAJOR RELIGIONS	Muslim, Christian, traditional beliefs
CURRENCY	CFA franc

A

Cameroon

On Africa's west coast, Cameroon was once a colony divided between the French and the British. The two parts gained independence and became a united country in 1961. Despite initial troubles, Cameroon now has one of the most successful economies in Africa, exporting oil, bauxite, and a range of natural products, including cocoa, coffee, and rubber. The country has a diverse culture with more than 230 ethnic groups.

Timber
Like many other African countries, Cameroon sells hardwood logs, including mahogany, ebony, and teak from its rainforests to earn foreign currency. Although the trade represents one tenth of the country's total exports, it poses a serious threat to the future of the forests.

CAMEROON FACTS

CAPITAL CITY	Yaoundé
AREA	465,400 sq km (179,691 sq miles)
POPULATION	15,100,000
MAIN LANGUAGES	French, English, Fang, Duala, Fulani
MAJOR RELIGIONS	Traditional beliefs, Christian, Muslim
CURRENCY	CFA franc

Dried gourds amplify sounds made by strings.

Football
One of Cameroon's leading amateur sports, football is widely enjoyed and people play it whenever they have time. Games draw large crowds of spectators. Cameroon's national football team was acclaimed as one of the best in Africa, after displaying its skills in the 1990 World Cup.

Music
Makossa is a popular style of African folk music that originated in Cameroon. It is played on traditional instruments, including this one, known as a *mvet*. It is made using a wooden stick, horsehair strings, and hollowed-out gourds. *Mvet* players are specially trained and highly regarded in the community.

Several strings are stretched along the stick and plucked to make a range of sounds.

Central African Republic

Lying in the very heart of Africa, the Central African Republic, or CAR, has a complicated history. Drought and 13 years of repressive government have made the CAR one of the poorest nations in the world. Only two per cent of the people live in the semi-arid north, and the majority are clustered in villages in the southern rainforests.

Bantu woman

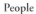

Cotton
Coffee and cotton together form about 13 per cent of the country's exports. Grown on large plantations, all parts of the cotton plant are used. The fibre, known as a boll, is spun into yarn to make fabric. The seed's oil forms the base of many foods, whilst the plant's stalks and leaves are ploughed back into the soil to fertilize it.

CENTRAL AFRICAN REPUBLIC FACTS

CAPITAL CITY	Bangui
AREA	622,980 sq km (240,530 sq miles)
POPULATION	3,600,000
MAIN LANGUAGES	French, Sango, Zande, Banda, Sara, Arabic
MAJOR RELIGIONS	Traditional beliefs, Christian, Muslim
CURRENCY	CFA franc

After drying in the sun, cotton bolls are sorted by hand.

Millet

People
Seven major Bantu language groups and many smaller ones make up the population of the CAR. Several thousand hunter-gatherers live in the rainforests in harmony with nature. They survive by eating forest fruits and build their homes from banana leaves.

Food
The people of the CAR grow nearly all their own food by subsistence farming. Root crops, such as cassava, yams, and vegetables, are cultivated alongside grains including millet, maize, and sorghum. Fish from the CAR's rivers, including the Chari and Ubangi, is a vital source of protein.

Cassava

Congo

The Republic of Congo was a French territory until 1960. It is a hot, humid land, and its densely forested north has few inhabitants. Nearly half the country's people are members of the Kongo group; the rest include Batéké, M'Bochi, and Sangha. The mineral and timber industries have made Congo wealthy, but many people are still subsistence farmers, growing barely enough food to survive.

Coffee beans

Crops
About 50 per cent of the work-force are farmers who grow cassava, maize, rice, peanuts, and fruit to feed their families. Much food is imported. The steady export of coffee and cocoa beans has saved Congo from economic problems.

Animal skin is stretched across the drum.

Each cocoa pod contains about 30 beans, for use in chocolate and cosmetics.

Cocoa pods

Drum
An essential part of African life, drums are used for signalling as well as for music. Most drums are intricately carved out of a solid piece of wood and can be decorated with different woods and hides. Drums are made in all shapes and sizes – this one is almost as tall as the player.

Industry
Oil from the Atlantic Ocean accounts for 90 per cent of Congo's exports, contributing largely to the country's wealth. Fluctuating oil prices have caused some economic problems, but Congo's crop exports have remained strong. The felling of forests to export tropical timber is a pressing environmental concern. Huge barges on the Congo and other rivers carry timber goods as far as Brazzaville; from there the Congo Ocean Railway takes them to Pointe Noire, Congo's only port.

CONGO FACTS

CAPITAL CITY Brazzaville

AREA 341,500 sq km (131,853 sq miles)

POPULATION 2,900,000

MAIN LANGUAGES French, Kongo

MAJOR RELIGIONS Christian, traditional beliefs

CURRENCY CFA franc

Gabon

A palm-fringed sandy coastline 800 km (500 miles) long, and lush tropical vegetation dominate Gabon's landscape. The country earns 80 per cent of its foreign currency from oil and also sells timber, manganese, and uranium ore. Gabon has the potential to be wealthy, but mismanagement by the government has led to continued poverty.

Woman in Libreville, Gabon's capital

Libreville
The bustling port city of Libreville was founded in 1849 by French naval officers. Meaning "free town" in French, Libreville was a new home for liberated slaves. It is now a modern, growing city, and a centre of culture, industry, and government. Many citizens are wealthy, but poverty still exists.

People
Although Gabon is one of Africa's most thinly populated countries, it contains more than 40 different ethnic groups. The indigenous Fang people form the largest group. Once fierce warriors, they now dominate the government. Most Gabonese people are Christians, and about 90 per cent of their children attend primary schools. The Gabonese traditions of dance, song, poetry, and story-telling remain an important social and cultural part of everyday life.

GABON FACTS

CAPITAL CITY Libreville

AREA 257,670 sq km (99,486 sq miles)

POPULATION 1,200,000

MAIN LANGUAGES French, Fang

MAJOR RELIGION Christian

CURRENCY CFA franc

The Trans-Gabon Railway runs from Libreville to Franceville.

Trans-Gabon Railway
Opened in 1986 to transport gold and manganese, the Trans-Gabon Railway has caused much controversy because it cut through rainforest, destroying many valuable and rare trees.

Equatorial Guinea

Two former Spanish colonies make up the country of Equatorial Guinea, located close to the Equator. Río Muni, also called Mbini, is on mainland Africa, and Bioko Island, which has fertile, volcanic soil that is ideal for growing cocoa beans, is situated to the northwest, off the coast of neighbouring Cameroon.

Traditional healing
Like other Africans, many people in Equatorial Guinea believe that illness is due to the influence of bad spirits. Professional healers use dancing and chants to drive out the evil spirits. They keep a range of animal bones, shells, sticks, and other plant parts in their medicine bags for use in group ceremonies.

Hippopotamus tooth

Cowrie shell

Tree root

Animal bone

Extended families
Among the people of Equatorial Guinea there is a strong tradition of large, extended families, who stay together and help one another in times of hardship.

EQUATORIAL GUINEA FACTS

CAPITAL CITY Malabo

AREA 28,050 sq km (10,830 sq miles)

POPULATION 453,000

MAIN LANGUAGES Spanish, Bubi, Fang

MAJOR RELIGION Christian

CURRENCY CFA franc

Dem. Rep. Congo (Zaire)

Formerly known as Belgian Congo and then as Zaire, this country was renamed Democratic Republic of the Congo in 1997 after the overthrow of the corrupt military government. The country consists of a plateau 1,200 m (3,900 ft) above sea-level, through which the River Congo flows. The land is fertile and rich in minerals, but spendthrift governments and civil war, including conflict with Rwanda in 1996–97, have kept it poor.

Cowrie shells are sewn on to decorate the mask.

Mask
Among the many peoples of Dem. Rep. Congo are the Kuba, a small ethnic group who have lived there for many years. Their chief wears a hunting mask, known as a Mashamboy mask, made of shells, beads, and raffia, to symbolize the power of the Great Spirit.

DEM. REP. CONGO FACTS

CAPITAL CITY Kinshasa

AREA 2,267,600 sq km (875,520 sq miles)

POPULATION 51,700,000

MAIN LANGUAGES French, English, Kiswahili, Lingala

MAJOR RELIGIONS Christian, traditional beliefs

CURRENCY Congolese franc

Creole woman selling diamonds

Farming
Dem. Rep. Congo has much potentially cultivable land. Sixty per cent of the population are subsistence farmers, producing palm oil, coffee, tea, rubber, cotton, fruit, vegetables, and rice. Here, on the border of volcanic Virunga National Park, the land is rich and fertile.

Mining
Copper ore, cobalt, and diamonds provide 85 per cent of national exports. Dem. Rep. Congo rates second in world diamond exports, with most mining activity in the Shaba province.

River ports
The River Congo and its tributaries give the country 11,500 km (7,000 miles) of navigable waterways. There are many river ports with boat-building and repair yards, craft shops, and lively markets that sell cassava, fruits, and fish, and delicacies such as monkey and snake meat. Traders take their produce to sell at river markets in dug-out canoes made by local craftsmen.

Ethnic strife
The present country boundaries in Central Africa date back to European colonialism, and cut across logical ethnic groupings. In some places there is actual ethnic warfare, for example that between the Hutus and the Tutsis of Rwanda and Burundi. For hundreds of years, Rwanda was dominated by the Tutsis, who ruled the Hutus. In 1959, the Hutus rebelled, and widespread fighting broke out. In the mid-1990s the violence escalated, resulting in 800,000 Hutu deaths and a massive refugee exodus into other countries.

Refugee camp, Tanzania

Sao Tome and Principe

This tiny country, formed by the main volcanic islands of Sao Tome and Principe, and four smaller islands, lies 200 km (120 miles) off the coast of Gabon. Its mountains are covered with forests, and rich soil supports farms that grow cocoa beans and sugar-cane. Sea fishing has potential for development.

Pepper
The pepper plant's small, green berries redden as they ripen. Harvested straight away, the half-ripe berries are cleaned, dried in the sun, ground, and sifted to make ground black pepper.

Rwanda

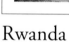

One of Africa's most densely populated countries, Rwanda has been made poor by ethnic strife that forced hundreds of thousands of people to flee to Dem. Rep. Congo for safety. Rwanda makes its money by exporting coffee, tea, and tin and tungsten ores. Most of its people just manage to feed themselves.

Volcanoes Park
The *Parc des volcans* is a scenic reserve dominated by volcanic mountains, two of which are active. The park is the last refuge of the mountain gorillas, which now number around 630.

RWANDA FACTS

CAPITAL CITY Kigali

AREA 24,950 sq km (9633 sq miles)

POPULATION 7,700,000

MAIN LANGUAGES Kinyarwanda, French, Kiswahili

MAJOR RELIGIONS Christian, traditional beliefs

CURRENCY Franc

Burundi

Like Rwanda, its neighbour, Burundi has been torn by conflict between the Tutsis and the Hutus, which has led to riots and thousands of deaths. Burundi has massive oil and nickel reserves beneath Lake Tanganyika, but lacks the funds to begin extraction. Most people are subsistence farmers.

Farming
Most farmers grow cassava and maize to feed their families. Some grow coffee, tea, cotton, and bananas for export. Overplanting fertile land is causing soil erosion.

BURUNDI FACTS

CAPITAL CITY Bujumbura

AREA 25,650 sq km (9903 sq miles)

POPULATION 6,700,000

MAIN LANGUAGES Kirundi, French, Swahili

MAJOR RELIGIONS Christian, traditional beliefs

CURRENCY Franc

Creole culture
Nobody lived on these islands until Portuguese explorers landed in 1470. The Portuguese peopled the islands with slaves from the mainland. Their mixed descendants created a culture called creole, but the creoles now number only ten per cent because more than 4,000 left the country at independence.

SAO TOME AND PRINCIPE FACTS

CAPITAL CITY São Tomé

AREA 960 sq km (371 sq miles)

POPULATION 159,900

MAIN LANGUAGE Portuguese

MAJOR RELIGION Christian

CURRENCY Dobra

FIND OUT MORE   AFRICA, HISTORY OF   EMPIRES   FARMING   FORESTS   MONKEYS AND OTHER PRIMATES   MUSIC   OIL   PORTS AND WATERWAYS   SLAVERY   TRAINS AND RAILWAYS

AFRICA, EAST

ONE OF THE WORLD'S OLDEST civilizations, Egypt, occupies the northeastern corner of East Africa, while Kenya, Tanzania, and Uganda sit farther south. Along the Horn of Africa, a piece of land that juts out into the Indian Ocean, are four of the world's poorest countries – Eritrea, Somalia, Ethiopia, and Djibouti. In recent years, Somalia, Sudan, and Ethiopia have been devastated by drought and war. Most East Africans scrape a living from farming, and some rely on food aid from abroad.

Physical features

Running through eastern Africa is the Great Rift Valley, a huge gash in the Earth that continues north through the Red Sea. Other features include the Nile, the world's longest river, and Lake Victoria, Africa's largest lake. The varied landscape includes deserts, grassland, mountains, and swamps.

River Nile
At 6,695 km (4,160 miles) long, the Nile supports the thousands of people who live on its fertile banks. The river flows north from Lake Victoria to the Mediterranean Sea. The Blue Nile Falls is on an important branch of the Nile in Ethiopia.

Savannah
The southern countries of East Africa contain large areas of savannah, or grassland scattered with acacia and baobab trees. This region is home to much of Africa's wildlife, including antelopes, giraffes, and zebras, and their predators such as lions and hyenas.

Kilimanjaro
Africa's highest peak at 5,895 m (19,341 ft), the snow-capped Mount Kibo is one of the Kilimanjaro group of three volcanoes. The group dominates Arusha National Park in Tanzania, on the border with Kenya. Steam and fumes smoking from Kibo's crater indicate that the volcano is not yet extinct, adding to the attraction for mountaineers.

Regional climate
East Africa's climate is affected by altitude. Dominated by desert, Djibouti, and parts of Egypt, Eritrea, Ethiopia, Sudan, and Somalia are plagued by droughts. South Sudan and western Ethiopia receive seasonal rainfall, while parts of Tanzania, Kenya, and Uganda are hot and dry; their highlands are wet.

23°C (73°F)   20°C (68°F)

580 mm (23 in)

Nomadic herding
Many of the original peoples of eastern Africa, particularly the Dinka of Sudan, are nomads, who move from place to place with their herds of cattle in search of water and grazing land. However, competition for land is forcing many nomads to seek alternative lifestyles. Some men now take occasional work in cities or on construction sites.

Dinka cattle camp, Sudan

Egypt

Today, as throughout its 5,000-year history, Egypt depends on the River Nile for much of its water, food, transport, and energy now generated at the massive Aswan Dam. Egypt controls the Suez Canal, an important shipping route that links Africa, Europe, and Asia, and brings money into the country. About 99 per cent of Egypt's people live along the lush, fertile banks of the river, and most are farmers, although the oil industry and tourist trade provide a growing number of jobs.

Water is drawn up to feed pipes that lead into the fields.

People

Several ethnic groups live in Egypt. Most people speak Arabic, but there are Berber and Nubian minorities. Until recently urban women were among the most liberated in the Arab world, but that may change with the rise of Islamic fundamentalism. In rural families, men go out to work, while women cook and fetch water.

EGYPT FACTS

CAPITAL CITY	Cairo
AREA	995,450 sq km (384,343 sq miles)
POPULATION	68,500,000
DENSITY	69 people per sq km (154 per sq mile)
MAIN LANGUAGE	Arabic
MAJOR RELIGION	Muslim
CURRENCY	Egyptian pound
LIFE EXPECTANCY	67 years
PEOPLE PER DOCTOR	625
GOVERNMENT	Multi-party democracy
ADULT LITERACY	55%

A

Farming

Egypt is one of the world's leading producers of dates, which are mostly grown in oases, along with melons. While some farmers use modern methods, many *fellahin*, or peasant farmers, use centuries-old techniques such as this one, where the donkey drives a wheel that scoops up water for irrigation.

Food

Reputed to be as old as the Pyramids, the traditional Egyptian dish of *ful medames* is made by boiling broad beans with garlic, onion, olive oil, and spices. The beans are served with hard-boiled eggs, lemon, and unleavened bread. Food is often accompanied by sweet tea and coffee.

Ful medames

Ramesses II statue, Temple of Luxor

Tourism

Millions of people flock to Egypt every year to see the Pyramids and other remains of the country's ancient past, such as the tombs in the Valleys of the Kings and Queens, and the temples at Karnak and Luxor. The oldest pyramid is the Step Pyramid at Saqqara, which was built about 2650 BC as a tomb for King Zoser.

Soft dusters on poles are used to clean the delicate sandstone.

Cotton plant

Cairo

Egypt's ancient capital is the largest city in Africa, with a population of more than 7,000,000. It has at least 1,000 mosques, some built with stone looted from the Pyramids. Old Cairo's narrow streets heave with bustling bazaars, while the wealthy west bank has modern casinos and hotels.

The Sultan Hassan Mosque and surrounding area

Suez Canal

More than 20,000 cargo ships sail through the Suez Canal each year. The canal, built by French engineers in 1869, is 190 km (118 miles) long and provides a short cut for ships between the Gulf of Suez and the Mediterranean Sea.

Cotton

Although only five per cent of Egypt's land can be farmed, the country is a leading producer of cotton. Quality cloths are exported or made into cool garments like *jelebas*, or tunics, often worn by locals.

Cotton boll

Sudan

Sudan is the largest country in Africa, measuring 2,050 km (1,274 miles) long from north to south. Desert in the north gives way to a central, grassy plain. Marshland covers much of the south. Two branches of the Nile (the White Nile and the Blue Nile) meet at the capital, Khartoum, providing fertile soil for farming. The country has good oil and mineral resources, but war and drought have weakened it.

People

There are more than 500 Sudanese ethnic groups, speaking about 100 languages and dialects. Some are nomadic herders, many of whom have now settled on farms. Most own their own plots, and live in villages of mud huts along the Nile, where farming is combined with fishing. The produce is sold at markets. Civil war and famine in the south of Sudan have created refugees.

SUDAN FACTS

CAPITAL CITY	Khartoum
AREA	2,376,000 sq km (917,374 sq miles)
POPULATION	29,500,000
MAIN LANGUAGE	Arabic
MAJOR RELIGIONS	Muslim, traditional beliefs, Christian
CURRENCY	Sudanese pound or dinar

Religious conflict

The ruling people of the north are Arab Muslims, and the tall minarets of their beautiful mosques dominate the landscape. Farther south, the majority are divided into many ethnic groups and follow Christianity or traditional African religions. The religious, cultural, and language differences between north and south have caused bitter fighting.

Eritrea

A small, hot country on the Horn of Africa, Eritrea won independence from Ethiopia in 1993 after a 30-year war with Ethiopian troops, which left a legacy of destruction and further war. Vast, but as yet, unexploited copper resources around the rugged mountains have potential for development. Eritrea's strategic Red Sea coastal position gives it access to the sea's oil fields, fishing grounds, and useful trade routes.

Subsistence farming
More than 80 per cent of Eritreans live by subsistence farming, many of them as nomadic herders. Farmers depend on September rains to create seasonal rivers that water the harvest, but recurring droughts have meant that Eritrea has been forced to rely on food aid from overseas.

People
The long war of independence developed a strong sense of nationalism among the people, although they belong to several ethnic groups speaking different languages. Women, 30,000 of whom fought in the war, many at leadership level, have been pressing the government for equal rights in the country's new political constitution.

Somalia

An arid, flat country bordering the Indian Ocean, Somalia has some of the longest beaches in the world. The country gained independence in 1960, but since the late 1980s the south has been in the grip of civil war, waged by wealthy rival warlords, and has had no effective government. Most people are poor, and live in coastal towns in the north and in the south near rivers.

Mogadishu
Conveniently situated on Somalia's coastline, Mogadishu has long been an important port. Arabs founded the capital more than 1,000 years ago, and sold it to the Italians in 1905. In 1960, it was returned to Somalia. The city's buildings are a mixture of older Arab architecture and 20th-century Italian design, but many have been damaged by war.

Civil war
Traditionally, the Somalis were organized in clans, or loyal family groups, that were controlled by elder members. The government destroyed the clan system in the 1980s, provoking bitter wars. Many people are now dependent on overseas aid.

Ethiopia

The Great Rift Valley, a high plateau, and an arid desert dominate Ethiopia. The country has suffered famine, drought, and civil war, but farming reforms and good seasonal rains have enabled Ethiopians to depend less on aid from abroad. Four-fifths of the population make their living through farming. Unique traditions like storytelling, music, and dance are an important part of everyday life.

Food
Spicy foods are standard in Ethiopia. A hot sauce, known as *wat*, is served with beef or chicken, and mopped up with bread. Usually, a soft, flat bread called *enjera* is eaten, which is made from teff, a field crop grown mainly in Ethiopia. A wide range of fish is available to those with money. Ethiopian *kaffa*, coffee flavoured with rye, is known as "health of Adam".

Vegetable dish made from cabbage, carrots, garlic, and red lentils

Hard-boiled egg

Chicken stew with egg, and red peppers

Enjera

A stew of beef, cinnamon, peppers, red chilli, and tomatoes

Red onions, chillies, garlic, and ginger, make wat, *a spicy sauce.*

Orthodox Church
The Ethiopian Orthodox Church is the chief Christian faith in the country. The pilgrimage centre of Lalibela, in Ethiopia's central highlands, is known for its Christian churches, which date from the 10th century. *Timkat*, a yearly festival, is celebrated by many Ethiopian Christians.

Orthodox priests

Djibouti

A desert country on the Gulf of Aden, Djibouti serves as a port for Ethiopia. The two ethnic groups, the Afars and Issas, have a tradition of nomadic herding, but now half of them live in settled homes in the capital, Djibouti.

Shipping and fishing
The 19th-century city of Djibouti is one of the key Red Sea ports in the area, and generates much of the country's income. The fishing industry thrives on its rich waters.

Kenya

Lying on the Equator, Kenya has a varied landscape. The arid north is hot, but there is a rich farming region along the coast, and the southwestern highlands are warm and wet. The country has a stable, prosperous economy based on agriculture. More than 90 per cent of the Kenyan people are under the age of 45 and belong to about 70 ethnic groups. Kenya is noted for its wildlife and its spectacular national parks.

Coffee beans

Tea leaves

KENYA FACTS

CAPTIAL CITY Nairobi

AREA 566,970 sq km (218,907 sq miles)

POPULATION 30,100,000

MAIN LANGUAGES Kiswahili, English

MAJOR RELIGIONS Christian, traditional beliefs, Muslim

CURRENCY Kenya shilling

Nairobi
Founded by British colonists as a railway town in 1899, Nairobi is Kenya's capital and a centre of business and communications. Home to 2,564,500 people, the city's high-rise buildings contrast with the surrounding plains where elephants and lions roam.

Tourism
National parks are the main attraction for the thousands of tourists who visit Kenya every year. Ten per cent of all Kenya is designated parkland, and there are more than 40 major national reserves. Amboseli, where many African animals (including lions, antelopes, and leopards) live, enjoys a spectacular view of Kilimanjaro.

Green beans

Crops
About 85 per cent of the population work on the land. Kenya is the world's fourth largest producer of tea, which, together with coffee, is grown on plantations. Kenya leads the world in the export of pyrethrum, a pink flower that is dried to make insecticides.

Uganda

Independence from Britain in 1962 led to ethnic conflict and poverty in Uganda, but since 1986, when peace was restored, the economy has been recovering slowly. Agriculture is still the main activity, with coffee, cotton, and cane sugar the main exports. Uganda also has good mineral deposits, including copper, gold, and cobalt. Most Ugandans live in rural villages.

UGANDA FACTS

CAPTIAL CITY Kampala

AREA 199,550 sq km (77,046 sq miles)

POPULATION 21,800,000

MAIN LANGUAGES English, Kiswahili

MAJOR RELIGIONS Christian, traditional beliefs, Muslim

CURRENCY New Uganda shilling

Sweet potatoes

Market in Kampala

Farming
About 80 per cent of the work-force farm 43 per cent of the land. Most people own small farms, producing enough cassava, maize, millet, and sweet potatoes for themselves and to trade at market.

Kampala
Uganda's capital, Kampala, stands on hills overlooking Lake Victoria. The ancient palace of the former Buganda kings stands alongside the modern Makerere University. The 953,400 people of Kampala experience violent thunderstorms on an average of 242 days a year, and rain nearly every day.

Lake Victoria
The world's second largest freshwater lake, Victoria lies between Uganda, Kenya, and Tanzania. Giant perch fish have eaten nearly all the lake's natural fish species. A hydroelectricity project at the lake's Owen Falls aims to cut Uganda's oil imports in half.

Tanzania

The islands of Zanzibar united with mainland Tanganyika in 1964, creating Tanzania. More than half the country is covered by forests, and it has a long Indian Ocean coastline. Dar es Salaam, the largest city and chief port, was until recently the capital. Farming is the main activity, but oil, diamonds, and gas have been discovered.

TANZANIA FACTS

CAPTIAL CITY Dodoma

AREA 886,040 sq km (342,100 sq miles)

POPULATION 33,500,000

MAIN LANGUAGES English, Kiswahili

MAJOR RELIGIONS Traditional beliefs, Muslim, Christian

CURRENCY Tanzania shilling

Cotton
Tea, tobacco, and cotton account for two-thirds of Tanzania's exports. Most cotton is produced on government-operated farms in the north and south highlands and around Lake Victoria. Workers carry the cotton to the factory to be spun and woven into cloth.

People
The 120 ethnic groups of Tanzania live together in harmony, as no single group is dominant. More than two thirds of the people live in small, scattered villages, but the state *Ujamaa* policy has tried to resettle them into larger communities to provide more facilities.

Sisal bags

Zanzibar
The island of Zanzibar and its small companion island of Pemba lie off the east coast of Tanzania. Zanzibar is one of the world's leading producers of cloves and sisal, a plant grown for making rope and bags for export.

FIND OUT MORE | AFRICA, HISTORY OF | CHRISTIANITY | DAMS | EGYPT, ANCIENT | EMPIRES | FARMING | ISLAM | PORTS AND WATERWAYS | RIVERS | WARFARE

AFRICA, NORTHWEST

MOROCCO, ALGERIA, TUNISIA, and Libya, plus the disputed territory of Western Sahara, make up the northwest corner of Africa. The region has been dominated by Arabs and their religion, Islam, for more than 1,300 years. Algeria and Libya are huge countries, but much of the land is desert. However, they and Tunisia have abundant reserves of oil and natural gas. Farming, made possible by irrigation projects, is still important to the region. Many people lead nomadic lives roaming the land with their herds of animals.

Mediterranean coast
Once occupied by the Phoenicians, Greeks, and Romans, northwest Africa's Mediterranean coast has many ancient ruins that are particularly popular with tourists in Morocco, Algeria, and Tunisia. Most people live on the coastal plain, which has fertile land and a warm climate.

Physical features

Along the Mediterranean and Atlantic coasts is a fertile strip where most of the people live. The Atlas Mountain chain runs across Morocco and continues as rolling hills in Algeria and Tunisia. The rest of the land is desert, broken by oases and bleak mountain ranges.

25°C (77°F)   12°C (-53°F)

434 mm (17 in)

Regional climate
Along most of the coast and on high ground, summers are hot and dry and winters are warm and wet. Daytime desert temperatures average about 38°C (100°F); at night they are low. Desert rainfall may be as little as 2.5 cm (1 in) a year, and irregular.

Atlas Mountains
The Atlas Mountains consist of several chains of mountains that stretch 2,410 km (1,500 miles) from the Atlantic coast of Morocco to Cape Bon in eastern Tunisia. The highest peak is Djebel Toubkal at 4,167 m (13,665 ft), which lies in the High Atlas range in southern Morocco.

Sahara
The Sahara Desert covers about 9,065,000 sq km (3,263,400 sq miles). Only about one-fifth is sand. The rest includes vast, flat expanses of barren rock and gravel and mountains such as Algeria's Ahaggar range, peaking at 2,918 m (9,573 ft). Crops are grown in 90 large oases.

Berbers

The original people of Northwest Africa are the Berbers. Today, about 15,000,000 Berbers still live in the mountains and deserts of the region. Most are Muslim, but retain their own language and dialects. The Tuareg are a group of nomadic Berber herders who roam the North African desert.

Berber man and child

Morocco

 A mix of African, Islamic, Arab, Berber, and European influences, Morocco attracts more than four million tourists each year. The country's strengths are farming and phosphate mining. Founded in Fès, in AD 859, Karueein University is the oldest in the world.

MOROCCO FACTS

CAPITAL CITY	Rabat
AREA	446,300 sq km (172,316 sq miles)
POPULATION	28,400,000
MAIN LANGUAGES	Arabic, Berber, French
MAJOR RELIGION	Muslim
CURRENCY	Moroccan dirham

Mint tea

The traditional drink in Morocco is a refreshing mint tea, served in glasses or pots, with plenty of sugar and a sprig of mint. It is often offered free of charge in the *souks* (markets), when bargaining is about to begin.

Carpets

Hand-knotted woollen carpets are one of Morocco's great craft industries. The leading carpet factories are in Fès and Rabat. The carpets have bold colours and symbolic, abstract Islamic patterns. Though sold by men, most rugs are made by women.

Western Sahara

Morocco has occupied the ex-Spanish colony of Western Sahara since 1975. Polisario Front guerrillas began fighting for independence in 1983, to resist mass settlement of the area by Moroccans keen to hold on to the phosphate-rich territory.

Polisario soldiers keep watch

Tunisia

A former French colony, Tunisia is the smallest country in the region and one of the more liberal Arab states. Although not admitted into politics, Tunisian women enjoy a high level of equality, making up 31 per cent of the work-force.

TUNISIA FACTS

CAPITAL CITY	Tunis
AREA	155,360 sq km (59,984 sq miles)
POPULATION	9,600,000
MAIN LANGUAGES	Arabic, French
MAJOR RELIGION	Muslim
CURRENCY	Tunisian dinar

Couscous is steamed in a special pot that sits above the stewing meat.

Couscous

The staple food in Tunisia is granules of semolina called couscous. Originally a Berber dish, couscous is served with a meat or vegetable sauce. Tunisians like their food spicy. After this main course, dates stuffed with almond paste, or sweet pastries filled with honey and nuts are served.

Souk

A feature of Tunisian cities – and indeed all northwest African cities – is the *souk*, or market. This is traditionally a tangle of narrow streets flanked by open-fronted stalls, where people can buy anything from food to carpets or hand-made jewellery.

Algeria

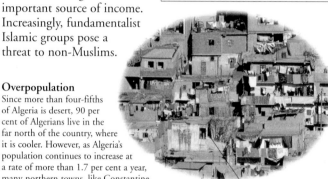

Under French rule from 1830, Algeria won independence in 1962. The country has a high birth rate and a young population: 86 per cent are below the age of 44. Crude oil and natural gas are an important source of income. Increasingly, fundamentalist Islamic groups pose a threat to non-Muslims.

ALGERIA FACTS

CAPITAL CITY	Algiers
AREA	2,381,740 sq km (919,590 sq miles)
POPULATION	31,500,000
MAIN LANGUAGES	Arabic, Berber, French
MAJOR RELIGION	Muslim
CURRENCY	Algerian dinar

Overpopulation

Since more than four-fifths of Algeria is desert, 90 per cent of Algerians live in the far north of the country, where it is cooler. However, as Algeria's population continues to increase at a rate of more than 1.7 per cent a year, many northern towns, like Constantine, are struggling to house everybody, and slum areas are growing.

Houses are built on every available piece of land.

Black dates

Yellow dates

Dates

Algeria is the world's sixth largest producer of dates. They are grown in the fertile north as well as in the many oases of the Sahara, and provide a main source of income. Date palms also yield timber; their leaves are used to thatch buildings.

Libya

Since 95 per cent of Libya is desert, the Great Man-made River Project was set up to irrigate farming land. Water is piped from beneath the Sahara to populated coastal regions.

LIBYA FACTS

CAPITAL CITY	Tripoli
AREA	1,759,540 sq km (679, 358 sq miles)
POPULATION	5,600,000
MAIN LANGUAGES	Arabic, Tuareg
MAJOR RELIGION	Muslim
CURRENCY	Libyan dinar

Oil and gas

The discovery of oil and natural gas in 1959 transformed Libya into a wealthy nation, and many people moved to the towns in search of work. In 1992, trade with the West was severely disrupted when the UN imposed sanctions because of leader Colonel Gaddafi's alleged links with international terrorist groups.

Oil workers at Calanscio

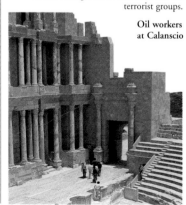

Roman ruins

Libya was abandoned by the Romans after the Arab conquest of AD 643 and was an Italian colony between 1911 and 1951. Today, some of the finest Roman ruins outside Italy can be seen at Leptis Magna, now called Labdah, to the east of the capital, Tripoli.

FIND OUT MORE   AFRICA, HISTORY OF   DESERTS   EMPIRES   FARMING   ISLAM   ISLAMIC EMPIRE   MOUNTAINS AND VALLEYS   OIL   ROMAN EMPIRE   TEXTILES AND WEAVING

A

AFRICA, SOUTHERN CENTRAL

SOUTHERN CENTRAL AFRICA is made up of seven countries that form part of the African mainland, and the islands of Madagascar and Comoros in the Indian Ocean. Farming is still an important source of income in these countries, but major deposits of minerals such as diamonds, copper, uranium, and iron have led many people to move to the towns and cities in search of work. A variety of tribal groups, each with its own language, customs, and beliefs, lives in the southern central region.

Physical features

Although lowlands fringe the coast, most of the region lies 400–1,500 m (1,200–4,500 ft) above sea-level. The landscape includes the Namib and Kalahari deserts in the west and centre, dry savannah and woodland, and humid, subtropical forests in the north.

Acacia trees, Madagascar

Namib Desert
The Namib Desert extends 1,900 km (1,100 miles) in a narrow strip from southwestern Angola, along the Skeleton Coast of Namibia, and down to the border of South Africa. Although it rarely rains, the climate on the coast is humid with cold, morning fogs. Sand dunes reach down to the edge of the Atlantic and the only practical means of transport is the camel.

Savannah
Much of the region is covered by grassland, or savannah. The most common trees in these areas are thorn trees, especially acacias. They are suited to the dry conditions and grow on the edges of the Kalahari and other semi-desert regions.

Regional climate
Most of the region lies in the tropics, where the climate is always hot, but there are two seasons: wet and dry. Rain is heavy in the wet season. Most of Botswana and Namibia has a semi-arid climate, and much of Namibia is desert. Eastern Madagascar has a tropical wet climate.

23°C (74°F) 16°C (61°F)

964 mm (38 in)

Women's role

The traditional role of African women was to look after the home and bring up the children. Many were also expected to cultivate the crops, and some built their own houses. Today, many women in southern central Africa have additional responsibilities, because their husbands are away working in mines and cities. Despite the domestic power of women, few have official jobs or own property.

Zimbabwean woman with her baby

Angola

In 1975, after a long war, Angola became independent of Portuguese colonial rule. With fertile land and huge reserves of diamonds, oil, and natural gas, the country should have become prosperous. However, Angola was torn apart and economic development was restricted by the fighting that continued after independence. Civil war erupted between rival ethnic groups and continues today.

ANGOLA FACTS

CAPITAL CITY Luanda

AREA 1,246,700 sq km (481,351 sq miles)

POPULATION 12,900,000

MAIN LANGUAGE Portuguese

MAJOR RELIGIONS Christian, traditional beliefs

CURRENCY Readjusted kwanza

Oil and diamonds
Most of Angola's oil is produced in Cabinda, a tiny Angolan enclave in Dem. Rep. Congo. Petroleum provides 90 per cent of Angola's exports. Angola also ranks highly in world output of diamonds, its second largest export.

Luanda
Founded by the Portuguese in 1575, Angola's capital and largest city is home to more than 2,500,000 people. Once used for shipping slaves to Brazil, it is still a major seaport. Modern Luanda is an industrial centre with its own oil refinery.

Zambia

Bordered to the south by the Zambezi River, Zambia is a country of upland plateaus, 80 per cent of which are grassland and forest. About 50 per cent of the people live by subsistence farming, constantly threatened by drought. Tobacco is the main exported crop. Hydroelectric power provides much of Zambia's energy. Low copper prices in the 1980s upset finances.

ZAMBIA FACTS

CAPITAL CITY Lusaka

AREA 740,720 sq km (285,992 sq miles)

POPULATION 9,200,000

MAIN LANGUAGES English, Bemba, Tonga, Nyanja, Lozi, Lunda

MAJOR RELIGIONS Christian, traditional beliefs

CURRENCY Zambian kwacha

Cobalt is used in steel production.

Copper forms 90 per cent of exports.

Copper bracelets

Copper and cobalt
Zambia is the world's sixth largest producer of copper. The seam of copper ore where the metal is mined, the Copperbelt, is 320 km (200 miles) long. The second largest producer of cobalt, Zambia also mines lead, silver, and zinc.

Urban living
About half of Zambia's people, a mix of more than 70 different ethnic groups, live in towns and cities. The most populated area is the Copperbelt, where most of them work. The capital, Lusaka, a thriving industrial and business centre, is home to 1,800,000 Zambians.

A

Namibia

An ex-German colony, and ruled for 70 years by South Africa, Namibia won its independence in 1990. Rich mineral resources make mining the country's leading industry. One in seven people lives on the land, mainly rearing livestock, although drought and the expanding desert make farming difficult. Fishing is good off the Atlantic coast.

Himba woman

NAMIBIA FACTS

CAPITAL CITY Windhoek

AREA 823,290 sq km (317,260 sq miles)

POPULATION 1,739,000

MAIN LANGUAGES English, Afrikaans, Ovambo, Kavango

MAJOR RELIGION Christian

CURRENCY Namibian dollar

Uranium
The Rössing Uranium Mine in the Namib Desert is the world's largest, producing 2,000 tonnes (2,200 tons) of uranium every year. Namibia is the world's fifth largest producer of uranium and ranks among the top producers of diamonds.

People
Namibia has a peaceful multiracial society. The white minority lives mostly in Windhoek, in European-style houses. Black Namibians include many groups, the largest of which are the northern Ovambo. To the west, the semi-nomadic Himba raise cattle.

Hair is braided and beaded.

Botswana

Southwest Botswana is covered by the Kalahari Desert. To the north is the marshy delta of the Okavango River, a haven for wildlife. Despite this wetland, however, Botswana suffers droughts. Most people live in the more fertile east. Production of diamonds – the third largest in the world – has helped to stimulate Botswana's economy.

BOTSWANA FACTS

CAPITAL CITY Gaborone

AREA 566,730 sq km (218,814 sq miles)

POPULATION 1,600,000

MAIN LANGUAGES English, Tswana, Shona, Khoikhoi, Ndebele

MAJOR RELIGIONS Traditional beliefs, Christian

CURRENCY Pula

San
The original inhabitants of Botswana are the nomadic San people, once known as Kalahari Bushmen, one of Africa's only remaining groups of hunter-gatherers. There are fewer than 50,000 San today, but small groups still roam the Kalahari Desert hunting small animals and eating edible plants and insects. Many San now work on cattle ranches.

Beef stew with dried spinach   *Savoury porridge*

Food
The Tswana people, who make up the majority of Botswana's population, live mostly by subsistence farming, raising cattle, and growing enough maize, sorghum, and millet for their own use. Their staple diet consists of meat stews served with a kind of porridge made from cereals. Fresh vegetables are rare.

Zimbabwe

 In 1980, the former British colony of Rhodesia became independent and took the name Zimbabwe, after the ancient city of Great Zimbabwe. About 70 per cent of Zimbabweans live from farming. Coal, gold, asbestos, and nickel are mined for export. Zimbabwe has recently suffered great disruption over the issues of government and land re-distribution.

ZIMBABWE FACTS

CAPITAL CITY Harare

AREA 390,580 sq km (150,293 sq miles)

POPULATION 11,700,000

MAIN LANGUAGES English, Shona, Ndebele

MAJOR RELIGIONS Traditional beliefs, Christian

CURRENCY Zimbabwe dollar

Tourism
Zimbabwe's main tourist attractions are the spectacular Victoria Falls, the Kariba Dam, national parks, and the ruins of the city of Great Zimbabwe. Tourists enjoy action holidays, such as canoeing and rafting, on the Zambezi.

Harare
Formerly called Salisbury, the capital is Zimbabwe's commercial and industrial centre and home to almost two million people. It is a clean and sophisticated city that is characterized by flowering trees, colourful parks, and modern buildings.

Madagascar

The fourth largest island in the world, Madagascar is home to some unique wildlife because of its isolated position off Africa's east coast. A high plateau runs the length of the island, dropping to a narrow, fertile strip in the east, where most people live. The country's economy is based on growing crops and raising livestock.

MADAGASCAR FACTS

CAPITAL CITY Antananarivo

AREA 581,540 sq km (224,533 sq miles)

POPULATION 15,900,000

MAIN LANGUAGES Malagasy, French

MAJOR RELIGIONS Traditional beliefs, Christian

CURRENCY Malagasy franc

Vanilla
Madagascar is the world's largest exporter of vanilla. The pods of the plants are used to flavour ice-cream and chocolate. Other important cash crops are cloves, sisal, cocoa, and butter beans.

Vanilla pods grow 25 cm (10 in) long.

Rural society
Most Madagascans are descended from Asians from Malaysia and Indonesia, who began to settle on the island almost 2,000 years ago. Later waves of mainland Africans intermixed to produce a uniquely multiracial society. Three-quarters of the Madagascan labour force works on the land growing subsistence crops, such as cassava and rice.

Mozambique

As a result of years of civil war, flooding, and drought, Mozambique is now one of the world's poorest countries, with a high birth rate. The land, though largely unexploited, is fertile and rich in minerals. The ports and railways provide a trade link for land-locked Swaziland, Malawi, and Zimbabwe.

MOZAMBIQUE FACTS

CAPITAL CITY Maputo

AREA 784,090 sq km (302,737 sq miles)

POPULATION 19,700,000

MAIN LANGUAGE Portuguese

MAJOR RELIGIONS Traditional beliefs, Christian, Muslim

CURRENCY Metical

Fishing
One of Mozambique's key industries is fishing, and shrimps account for more than 40 per cent of export earnings. The country's total annual fish catch averages 24,170 tonnes (26,643 tons). Other exports include cotton, tea, and sugar.

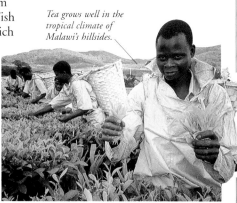

Malawi

With few natural resources, Malawi has a rural society, despite the constant threat of drought. Light industries, such as food processing, textiles, and manufacturing farm tools, are developing. Fish from Lake Malawi, which covers one-quarter of the country, is a source of food.

MALAWI FACTS

CAPITAL CITY Lilongwe

AREA 94,080 sq km (36,324 sq miles)

POPULATION 10,900,000

MAIN LANGUAGES Chewa, English

MAJOR RELIGIONS Christian, Muslim

CURRENCY Malawian kwacha

Tea grows well in the tropical climate of Malawi's hillsides.

Farming
Almost 86 per cent of the Malawi labour force works in agriculture, growing cash crops, such as tea, tobacco, coffee, cotton, and sugar, as well as subsistence crops of maize, rice, cassava, and plantains. The country is self-sufficient in food.

Comoros

 The three islands and few islets of the Comoros archipelago lie north of Madagascar in the Indian Ocean. They were governed by France until 1975. The economy is underdeveloped, and most of the people live by subsistence farming.

COMOROS FACTS

CAPITAL CITY Moroni

AREA 2,230 sq km (861 sq miles)

POPULATION 694,000

MAIN LANGUAGES Arabic, French, local languages

MAJOR RELIGIONS Muslim

CURRENCY Comoros franc

Ylang-ylang
Comoros is the world's largest grower of ylang-ylang, an aromatic tree with greenish-yellow flowers that produce a pleasantly scented oil used to make perfume.

FIND OUT MORE   AFRICA, HISTORY OF   AFRICAN WILDLIFE   DESERTS   EMPIRES   FARMING   FISHING INDUSTRY   GREAT ZIMBABWE   OIL   ROCKS AND MINERALS   SOCIETIES, HUMAN

AFRICA, WEST

THE ATLANTIC OCEAN borders all but three of the 15 countries that make up West Africa. Much of the area is dominated by the Sahara and the Sahel, a vast area of semi-desert, which the Sahara is slowly invading. Despite their potential wealth and rich resources, most of the countries are desperately poor. Long-established trade routes across the Sahara link West Africa with the Mediterranean coast to the north. For millions of West Africans, life is a perpetual struggle against a hostile climate, the threat of drought, and political instability.

Sahel
Immediately south of the Sahara Desert, stretching all the way across West Africa, is a broad band of hot, arid, semi-desert grassland called the Sahel. In Arabic, the word Sahel means "shore" of the desert. Rainfall in this region is sporadic and droughts are common.

Regional climate
Moving from north to south, there are four main climate regions in West Africa: desert, Sahel, grassland, and tropical rainforest. Rain is rare in the northern desert and Sahel regions, yet the south is humid and tropical with a distinct rainy season that can last for four to six months.

25°C (78°F) 26°C (80°F)
1,879 mm (74 in)

Physical features

Most of West Africa lies 200–400 m (600–1200 ft) above sea-level. The Sahara dominates Niger, Mauritania, and Mali, and the Sahel extends south into Senegal, Burkina Faso, and Nigeria. The rivers Senegal, Gambia, Volta, and Niger irrigate the west and south.

River Niger
Africa's third longest river, the Niger flows in a great arc for 4,180 km (2,597 miles) from Guinea through Mali, Niger, Benin, and Nigeria to a vast delta on the Gulf of Guinea. A valuable source of fish and water, it is navigable for more than half its length.

Groundnuts
Also called peanuts, groundnuts develop underground. They are widely grown in West Africa as a source of edible oil, and as a foodstuff that is rich in protein and vitamins. The plants were introduced into West Africa from South America.

Harvesting peanuts

Mauritania

The northern two-thirds of Mauritania are desert. The only farmland lies in a narrow, fertile strip along the bank of the River Senegal in the southwest. This area is scattered with small villages and oases. Nomadic Moors of Arab descent, from the north, live in Mauritania. They have often clashed with black farmers in the south.

Fishing
The waters off Mauritania are said to have the richest fish stocks in the world; they attract many foreign fishing fleets. All catches must be sold through the state fishing company. Fishing provides more than half of Mauritania's export earnings.

Desertification
Successive years of drought and overgrazing in the Sahel region have caused the desert to expand southwards, killing livestock and forcing many nomads to move into towns.

Government schemes are attempting to reclaim the land by reducing soil erosion.

Mineral wealth
The Mauritanian desert contains the largest deposits of gypsum – used for making plaster – and some of the largest reserves of iron ore in the world. The country also exports gold. A single rail line connects mines with Nouakchott, the country's capital and main port.

Gypsum crystal

MAURITANIA FACTS
CAPITAL CITY Nouakchott

AREA 1,025,520 sq km (395,953 sq miles)

POPULATION 2,700,000

MAIN LANGUAGES Arabic, French, Hassaniya, Wolof, Soninké

MAJOR RELIGION Muslim

CURRENCY Ouguiya

Senegal

The flat, semi-desert plains of Senegal are crossed by four rivers – the Senegal, Gambia, Saloum, and Casamance – which provide water for agriculture, the country's main source of income. Tourism is also developing. Senegal has a mix of ethnic groups, the largest of which are the Wolofs.

Dakar
Senegal's capital and major port, Dakar is a bustling industrial centre with good restaurants, shops, and markets. However, many of the 2,500,000 people who live here are poor and live in suburban slums.

Music
At festivals and ceremonies, or *griots*, a mix of historians, musicians, and poets, sing and recite traditional stories, often to the accompaniment of a *kora*.

Kora

Musicians pluck the 21 strings to give a wide range of muted sounds.

Many of Senegal's fruits and vegetables are imported and expensive.

Gourd soundbox

SENEGAL FACTS
CAPITAL CITY Dakar

AREA 192,530 sq km (74,336 sq miles)

POPULATION 9,500,000

MAIN LANGUAGES French, Wolof, Fulani, Sérèr, Diola, Mandinka

MAJOR RELIGIONS Muslim, Christian, traditional beliefs

CURRENCY CFA franc

Farming
About 60 per cent of the Senegalese labour force works on the land growing cotton and sugar-cane for export, and rice, sorghum, and millet for their food. Until droughts in the 1970s damaged yields, groundnuts were the main cash crop. Fish is now the main export.

Gambia

One of the most densely populated countries in Africa, Gambia occupies a narrow strip either side of the River Gambia and is surrounded on three sides by Senegal. With little industry, 80 per cent of the people live off the land. Groundnuts make up 80 per cent of exports. The main ethnic groups are the Mandingo, Fulani, and Wolof.

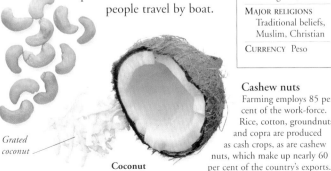

GAMBIA FACTS
CAPITAL CITY Banjul

AREA 10,000 sq km (3,861 sq miles)

POPULATION 1,300,000

MAIN LANGUAGES English, Mandinka

MAJOR RELIGIONS Muslim, Christian, traditional beliefs

CURRENCY Dalasi

Tourism
Gambia is an attractive destination for winter sun-seekers from Europe. Tourism, the country's fastest-growing industry, employs one in ten Gambians. About 10,000 of those work on a seasonal basis.

Guinea-Bissau

Rainfall in Guinea-Bissau is more reliable than in most of the rest of Africa, enabling the country to be self-sufficient in rice. However, flooding is common along the coast because farmers have cut down mangroves to plant rice fields. Most people travel by boat.

Cashew nuts

Grated coconut

Coconut

GUINEA-BISSAU FACTS
CAPITAL CITY Bissau

AREA 28,120 sq km (10,857 sq miles)

POPULATION 1,096,000

MAIN LANGUAGES Portuguese, Crioulo

MAJOR RELIGIONS Traditional beliefs, Muslim, Christian

CURRENCY Peso

Cashew nuts
Farming employs 85 per cent of the work-force. Rice, cotton, groundnuts, and copra are produced as cash crops, as are cashew nuts, which make up nearly 60 per cent of the country's exports.

Guinea

With more than 30 per cent of the world's known reserves of bauxite, and deposits of diamonds, iron, copper, manganese, uranium and gold, Guinea could be a wealthy country. However, years of poor government and lack of support from former French rulers have made Guinea's economic development difficult.

GUINEA FACTS

CAPITAL CITY Conakry

AREA 245,860 sq km (94,926 sq miles)

POPULATION 7,400,000

MAIN LANGUAGES French, Fulani, Malinke, Susu

MAJOR RELIGIONS Muslim, traditional beliefs,

CURRENCY Guinea franc

Coffee beans

Bananas

Pineapple

Fruit growing
Bananas, plantains, and pineapples grow well in the fertile Fouta Djalon hills (Guinea Highlands). Farmers cultivate coffee, palm nuts, and groundnuts as cash crops and sorghum, rice, and cassava for their families.

People
Three-quarters of Guineans belong to one of three main ethnic groups – the Malinke and Fulani who live in the north and centre, and the Susu who live closer to the coast. Two-thirds live in small rural communities, where the standard of living is one of the lowest in the world. Average life expectancy is low, at only 45 years, and only about 35 per cent of people can read.

Sierra Leone

Sierra Leone was founded by the British in the early 1800s as a colony for freed slaves. Its name is Spanish for "Lion Mountains" and refers to the constant roar of thunder. Of the 12 ethnic groups, the biggest are the Mende and the Temne. A ceasefire halted civil war in 2000.

SIERRA LEONE FACTS

CAPITAL CITY Freetown

AREA 71,620 sq km (27,652 sq miles)

POPULATION 4,900,000

MAIN LANGUAGES English, Krio (Creole)

MAJOR RELIGIONS Traditional beliefs, Muslim, Christian

CURRENCY Leone

Industry
Mining is the mainstay of Sierra Leone's economy. The chief exports are diamonds, some of which are still mined by hand, as well as gold, bauxite, and titanium ore. Farming employs more than two-thirds of the work-force, growing coffee, cocoa, palm kernels, ginger, and cassava.

Uncut diamond looks like any other stone.

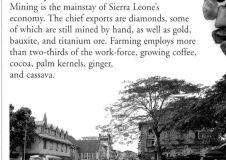

Freetown
Surrounded by green hills, Sierra Leone's capital, Freetown, is a colourful and historic port and home to more than 700,000 people. The name is a reminder of the country's former status as a haven for freed slaves. Among Freetown's attractions are a 500-year-old cotton tree, and West Africa's oldest university, built in 1827.

Ivory Coast

With 600 km (370 miles) of Atlantic coastline, and three main rivers, Ivory Coast is fertile and farming efficient. It is among the world's top producers of coffee and cocoa. Food accounts for half of all exports. Most people work in farming and forestry. Nearly all the forests have been sold off as timber to pay foreign debts.

IVORY COAST FACTS

CAPITAL CITY Yamoussoukro

AREA 318,000 sq km (122,780 sq miles)

POPULATION 14,891,000

MAIN LANGUAGES French, Akan

MAJOR RELIGIONS Muslim, Christian, traditional beliefs

CURRENCY CFA franc

Farmers use pesticides on cocoa plantations, but the lack of protective clothes is a serious health risk.

Yamoussoukro Basilica
Although only 29 per cent of the people of the population are Christian, Ivory Coast has one of the world's largest Christian churches. Able to seat 7,000 people, it dominates the city of Yamoussoukro, which replaced Abidjan as the country's capital in 1983.

Cocoa
Ivory Coast is the world's leading producer of cocoa beans. Cocoa trees need humid conditions, and many cocoa plantations lie in moist, tropical regions where rainforests were felled for timber. Factories have been set up in Ivory Coast to make cocoa butter, which is the basic ingredient of chocolate and some cosmetics.

Liberia

Founded by the USA in the 1820s as a home for freed black slaves, Liberia has never been colonized. About five per cent of the people descend from former slaves and American settlers. The rest are a varied mix of ethnic groups. About 70 per cent of Liberians work on the land, growing oil palms, coffee, and cocoa, and rubber for export. Civil war has damaged trade.

LIBERIA FACTS

CAPITAL CITY Monrovia

AREA 96,320 sq km (37,189 sq miles)

POPULATION 3,200,000

MAIN LANGUAGES English, Kpelle, Bassa Vai, Grebo, Kru, Kissi, Gola

MAJOR RELIGIONS Christian, traditional beliefs, Muslim

CURRENCY Liberian dollar

Civil war
Since 1990, Liberia has been torn by a chaotic and bloody civil war, and its once prosperous economy has collapsed. The war, which began as clashes between various ethnic groups, has made thousands of people homeless and many are forced to live in large refugee camps where food shortages are a part of everyday life.

Monrovia
Reputedly the world's wettest capital city, with more than 4,560 mm (183 in) of rain per year, Monrovia is a sprawling city and major port. Liberia has the world's largest commercial fleet of ships. Almost all are foreign owned, but registered in Monrovia, where taxes are low.

Mali

Desert and semi-desert cover the northern two-thirds of Mali, and only two per cent of the land can be cultivated. Most people live in the south, in farming settlements close to the rivers Niger and Senegal. Droughts, poor food, and an average life expectancy of only 51 years, make Mali one of the world's poorest countries. Some gold is mined, but cotton is the biggest export.

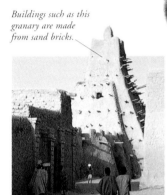

Buildings such as this granary are made from sand bricks.

MALI FACTS

CAPITAL CITY Bamako

AREA 1,220,190 sq km (471,115 sq miles)

POPULATION 11,200,000

MAIN LANGUAGES French, Bambara, Mande, Arabic, Fulani, Senufo, Soninke

MAJOR RELIGIONS Muslim, traditional beliefs

CURRENCY CFA franc

Making "mud cloth"

People

Mali's main peoples are the Bambara, Fulani, Tuareg, and Dogon, with smaller numbers of Songhai and Bozo. Bozo artists, mostly women, are noted for their "mud cloth", made by painting abstract designs on to rough cloth using differently coloured soils.

Tombouctou

Lying on the edge of the desert, Tombouctou is a city of sand still visited by camel caravans carrying salt from mines in the north for shipping up the River Niger to Mopti. This historic city is a centre of Islamic learning.

Burkina

Land-locked in the arid Sahel region and threatened by the Sahara, which is expanding southwards, Burkina (formerly Upper Volta) is one of West Africa's poorest and most overpopulated countries. Faced with droughts and lack of work, many young people are forced to leave to find jobs abroad.

Fulani

The Fulani are nomadic cattle herders who roam West Africa with their animals. In Burkina, where they number about 75,000, they are one of more than 60 ethnic groups. Fulani herders traditionally tend cattle for local farmers in exchange for sacks of rice.

BURKINA FACTS

CAPITAL CITY Ouagadougou

AREA 273,800 sq km (105,714 sq miles)

POPULATION 11,600,000

MAIN LANGUAGES French, Mossi, Mande, Fulani, Lobi, Bobo

MAJOR RELIGIONS Traditional beliefs, Muslim, Christian

CURRENCY CFA franc

Fulani children

Cotton

Burkina's most valuable cash crop is cotton, which brings in about 25 per cent of its export earnings. However, the country's farming is threatened by the mass emigration of young workers, who send money home to their families. The country has deposits of silver and manganese, and exports gold.

Ghana

Once called the "Gold Coast" by Europeans who found gold here 500 years ago, Ghana still has reserves of gold, which has recently replaced cocoa as the country's major source of income. The country is still one of the world's largest cocoa producers. Lake Volta, formed by a dam on the River Volta, is the world's largest artificial lake.

GHANA FACTS

CAPITAL CITY Accra

AREA 230,620 sq km (88,810 sq miles)

POPULATION 20,200,000

MAIN LANGUAGES English, Akan, Mossi, Ewe, Ga, Twi, Fanti, Gurma

MAJOR RELIGIONS Christian, traditional beliefs, Muslim

CURRENCY Cedi

Eseye (a kind of spinach)

Plantains

Food

A popular food in Ghana is *banku*, a mixture of maize dough and cassava. Ghanaians mix leaves of *eseye*, a type of spinach, with palm oil to make a sauce that is eaten with boiled fish or vegetables.

People

Family ties are strong in Ghana, and the extended family is important. About half of Ghanaians are Ashanti people whose ancestors developed one of the richest and most famous civilizations in Africa. Other groups include the Mole-Dagbani, Ewe, and Ga. About 38 per cent of the people live in cities and towns.

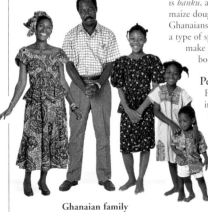

Ghanaian family

Togo

A long, narrow country, just 110 km (68 miles) at its widest point, Togo has a central forested plateau with savannah to the north and south. Nearly half the population is under 15 years of age, and few people are more than 45. Although most people are farmers, Togo's main export is phosphates, used for making fertilizers.

TOGO FACTS

CAPITAL CITY Lomé

AREA 54,390 sq km (21,000 sq miles)

POPULATION 4,600,000

MAIN LANGUAGES French, Kabye, Ewe

MAJOR RELIGIONS Traditional beliefs, Christian, Muslim

CURRENCY CFA franc

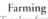

Farming

Togolese farmers produce cocoa, coffee, cotton, copra, and palm kernels mainly for export. New products include herbs, tomatoes, and sugar. For their own use, they grow millet, cassava, and maize. Fishing is important in coastal areas.

Maize

Market women

Although politics and formal employment remain the domain of men, many Togolese women work informally in part-time jobs. The Nana Benz, wealthy women traders so-called because they all seem to own Mercedes Benz cars, dominate Togo's markets and taxi businesses. Based in the market at Lomé, these formidable women fight hard for business and have a legendary capacity for haggling.

Nigeria

With large reserves of oil, natural gas, coal, iron ore, lead, tin, and zinc, and rich, fertile farmland, Nigeria looked set to prosper when it gained independence from Britain in 1960. However, the country's economy has experienced difficulty due to falling oil prices, ethnic conflicts, and corrupt government. After 16 years of military dictatorship, civilian rule was restored in 1999.

Abuja

Begun in 1980, the new, purpose-built city of Abuja replaced Lagos as Nigeria's capital in 1991, because the government believed Lagos was too influenced by the Yoruba people. By the late 1990s, much of Abuja was unfinished as money ran low during construction.

Central mosque, Abuja

People

Nigerian society consists of an uneasy mix of more than 250 ethnic groups. Two-thirds of the population belongs to one of three groups – the Hausa in the north, the Ibo in the east, and the Yoruba in the west. About 57 per cent of people live in small tight-knit villages where communal life is important.

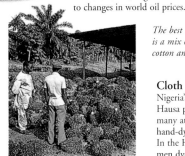

Nigerian oil has a low sulphur content and is ideal for aircraft fuel.

Oil

Nigeria's oil production, which ranks first in Africa and highly in the world, accounts for 95 per cent of all its exports. Almost totally dependent on this new industry, which began in the 1960s, Nigeria is vulnerable to changes in world oil prices.

Plantations

Agriculture employs more than 40 per cent of all Nigerian workers. Although most farmers work on small plots with simple tools, vast plantations have been established to cultivate cash crops on a commercial scale for export, using modern machinery. Crops include cotton, coffee, cocoa beans, and oil palms.

The best cloth is a mix of cotton and silk.

Cloth

Nigeria's Yoruba and Hausa peoples produce many attractive patterned textiles, hand-dyed using natural plant colours. In the Hausa town of Kano, in the north, men dye the cloth in ancient dye pits.

NIGERIA FACTS

CAPITAL CITY	Abuja
AREA	910,770 sq km (351,648 sq miles)
POPULATION	112,000,000
DENSITY	122 per sq km (317 per sq mile)
MAIN LANGUAGES	English, Hausa, Yoruba, Ibo
MAJOR RELIGIONS	Muslim, Christian, traditional beliefs
CURRENCY	Naira
LIFE EXPECTANCY	52 years
PEOPLE PER DOCTOR	5,000
GOVERNMENT	Multiparty democracy
ADULT LITERACY	64%

Benin

A former French colony, Benin took its name from an ancient empire, in 1975, 15 years after becoming independent. It is a long, narrow country with a short coastline on the Gulf of Guinea. Most of the land is flat and forested, with a large marsh in the south. Most people live off the land, producing yams, cassava, and maize. Cotton brings in about three-quarters of the country's export income.

BENIN FACTS

CAPITAL CITY	Porto-Novo
AREA	110,620 sq km (42,710 sq miles)
POPULATION	6,100,000
MAIN LANGUAGES	French, Fon, Bariba, Yoruba, Adja, Fulani
MAJOR RELIGIONS	Traditional beliefs, Muslim, Christian
CURRENCY	CFA franc

Fishing

Every year, fishermen catch about 39,000 tonnes (42,990 tons) of fish in the lagoons along the coast of Benin.

Betamaribé

One of five main ethnic groups in Benin, the Betamaribé, or Somba, live in the northwest near the Atakora Mountains. One of the first peoples to settle in Benin, they have lived free from Western influence for hundreds of years and have managed to keep many of their traditions intact.

Niger

Although it is the largest country in West Africa, Niger is two-thirds desert. The people, who are very poor, live in the dry Sahel region, or in the southwest close to the Niger River, where they plant crops and herd animals. The country is one of the world's top producers of uranium.

NIGER FACTS

CAPITAL CITY	Niamey
AREA	1,267,000 sq km (489,188 sq miles)
POPULATION	10,700,000
MAIN LANGUAGES	French, Hausa, Djerma, Fulani, Tuareg, Teda
MAJOR RELIGION	Muslim
CURRENCY	CFA franc

Fighting the desert

The people of Niger are waging a battle against the advance of the desert into the dry Sahel where they live. They plant trees and grass in an attempt to stop the soil eroding.

Male beauty contest

Every year, in a festival known as the *gerewol*, young Wodaabé men make themselves up to try and attract a wife in an unusual beauty contest. After much dancing, the women make their choice. If a marriage proposal results, the man kidnaps the woman, and they set off into the desert for a nomadic life together.

FIND OUT MORE — AFRICA, HISTORY OF · BENIN EMPIRE · CONSERVATION · DESERTS · FARMING · FISHING INDUSTRY · OIL · ROCKS AND MINERALS · SLAVERY · TEXTILES AND WEAVING

AFRICAN WILDLIFE

NO OTHER CONTINENT matches the wealth of wildlife found in Africa. Covering the full climatic spectrum from intense heat to bitter cold, its varied vegetation has given rise to a wide range of animals, including mammals, birds, reptiles, fish, and insects. Among them are more than 40 species of primate, ranging from tiny galagos to huge gorillas, a great variety of antelopes, gazelles, and other hoofed animals, and 70 species of carnivore. Bird life, too, is extraordinarily rich; more than 1,500 species live south of the Sahara. In addition, Africa is inhabited by the world's fastest land animal, the cheetah; the biggest bird, the ostrich; and the largest land animal, the elephant.

Giraffe
The giraffe's great height – males reach up to 5.5 m (18 ft) – gives it the advantage of being able to spot danger from a distance and then escape at speed. It also enables the giraffe to browse on acacia leaves that are out of the reach of most other grassland animals, giving it a near monopoly of its principal food supply.

Patterned coat provides camouflage.

Long tail with coarse hair is used to deter flies.

Grassland wildlife

African grasslands (savannahs) sustain over 20 species of grazing animals, from the giant sable antelope to the tiny pygmy antelope. The herds of plains game and their predators, including lions, are pursued by scavengers such as hyenas and vultures. Grassland birds include the guineafowl and hornbills.

Long tail feathers help it balance when running.

Secretary bird
Among the most striking of Africa's grassland birds is the secretary bird, with its long legs and feathered crest. It rarely flies, preferring to walk, nodding its head with each step. It attacks snakes, spreading its wings over its body to shield itself from venomous bites, while using its feet to stamp them to death.

Long legs for running through grass after snakes and frogs.

Zebras call to each other while grazing.

Lion
The lion is the principal predator of the African savannah. Lionesses hunt together, preying on large animals, such as buffalo, zebra, and wildebeest.

Aardvark
The aardvark is a solitary, nocturnal animal. It uses its powerful claws to break into the nests of ants and termites, which it extracts with its long, sticky tongue. The aardvark can dig at an astonishing speed – faster than a person with a shovel.

Zebra
Zebras usually live in family groups of 5–20 animals, but in the dry season they may gather in herds of a few hundred, for protection against predators such as lions. Male zebras defend themselves by kicking out with their legs and hooves. Zebras eat the tough tops of the grasses.

Papyrus
The most common plant in African swamps is papyrus. It grows in clumps, often dense enough to support the weight of large animals.

Papyrus may reach 4.5 m (15 ft) in height.

Wetland wildlife

Africa's wetlands are seething with wildlife, such as crocodiles, hippos, floodplain species such as lechwes, and fish, including the Nile perch and tiger fish. The wetlands also provide stopping places for migratory birds flying south to winter in Africa.

Lesser flamingo
Three million flamingos gather at Lake Nakuru, in Kenya, forming an amazing spectacle. They feed on the plentiful algae that flourish in the salty water, sunlight, and high temperatures in and around the lake.

Hippopotamus
Hippos spend most of the day submerged in water, with only their ears, eyes, and nostrils above the surface. They become active at dusk when they emerge from the water to graze on nearby grassland.

Cichlid fish
Lakes Malawi and Tanganyika contain 265 different species of cichlid (mouth-brooding fish); all but five are unique to Africa. Great depth, isolation, and few predators have resulted in this proliferation.

Long legs for wading through water.

Webbed feet

A

Addax

The addax lives in the driest and hottest parts of the Sahara – conditions few other animals could tolerate. It rarely drinks as it obtains all its liquid from the succulent plants and tubers on which it feeds.

Pale coat provides camouflage in the desert.

Desert wildlife

The African deserts include the Sahara, the world's largest desert, and the deserts of the Horn of Africa, Kalahari, and Namib. Though the deserts seem barren, they are home to many animals such as bustards, sandgrouse, and the scimitar-horned oryx.

Fennec fox

The fennec lives in small colonies among sand dunes, into which it burrows to avoid the heat. It burrows so quickly, it disappears from sight in seconds.

Fox obtains all its liquid from its prey.

Sand skink

The sand skink spends most of its life underground in its burrow. It uses its flattened tail to propel itself through the sand. It preys on small mammals such as mice, as well as birds' eggs. If attacked, the sand skink can shed its tail, confusing its attacker and enabling it to get away.

Sandgrouse

Despite living in the open desert, sandgrouse must drink regularly. This often means flying long distances. Sandgrouse obtain water for their young by immersing themselves in water and carrying droplets back to their nests in their feathers.

Rainforest wildlife

Rainforests dominate western Central Africa. The warm, wet environment is home to many animals. Herbivores such as gorillas feed on leaves. Fruit that falls from the canopy provides food for pigs and porcupines, while animals such as tree pangolins forage in the trees.

Yellow-backed duiker

Standing 1 m (3.3 ft) at the shoulder, the yellow-backed duiker is the largest of the forest duikers. In West Africa it lives in the densest parts of the rain forest; in East Africa it lives in bamboo forests.

Yellow back patch

Red colobus monkey

The red colobus is one of five species of specialized leaf-eating primates spread across Africa. It lives in the forest canopy in family groups of about 20 animals, rarely descending to the ground.

Small spotted genet

This cat-like animal spends the day asleep in the branches of a tree, becoming active at night. An agile climber, it stalks its prey – birds, small mammals, and insects – like a cat, before seizing it with a sudden pounce.

Gorillas eat many types of rainforest vegetation.

Mountain gorilla

The mountain gorilla is confined to a small area of rainforest, at a point where the boundaries of Uganda, Zaire, and Rwanda meet. It is a massively built animal, but is not normally aggressive. The females build nests where they sleep with their young.

Gelada

The gelada is the sole survivor of a group of ground-dwelling primates now found only in Ethiopia. It lives in open country at high altitude, close to cliffs and rock faces, where it retreats if alarmed. It eats seeds, roots, grass, and fruit.

Mountain wildlife

The mountains of Ruwenzori, Kenya, and Kilimanjaro have distinctive plants and animals. Rodents inhabit moorland, while the scarlet-tufted malachite sunbird lives in close association with giant lobelias.

Giant plants

Africa's mountain plants include some of the most extraordinary vegetation in the world. Plants small elsewhere have grown into giants, including the giant lobelia, tree heath, and giant groundsel, which reaches 9 m (30 ft) in height.

Flower spikes of the Giant Lobelia are more than 1 m (3.3 ft) tall.

Geladas have a patch of red skin on the chest.

Hyraxes bask in the sun for much of the day.

Rock hyrax

Rock hyraxes live in colonies of 50 or more among rocky outcrops. They remain alert for signs of danger, such as eagles and leopards.

Crowned hawk eagle

One of the largest eagles, the crowned hawk eagle is widely distributed throughout the mountainous regions of East Africa and Zaire, wherever there are suitable forests containing the monkeys that are its chief food.

FIND OUT MORE BIRDS BIRDS OF PREY DEER AND ANTELOPES GIRAFFES HIPPOPOTAMUSES LIONS AND OTHER WILD CATS LIZARDS MONKEYS AND OTHER PRIMATES

AIR

WE LIVE, MOVE, AND BREATHE at the bottom of an immense ocean of air called the atmosphere. Air is an invisible mixture of gases, made up of a teeming mass of millions of tiny gas molecules that move about randomly and at high speed. Without air, the Earth would be a lifeless planet, because the gases air contains are vital to plants and animals.

Carbon dioxide (CO_2)

Carbon dioxide is vital for plant life. Plants absorb carbon dioxide from the air and combine it with water gathered by their roots to form sugars, which they use for growth.

Tablets of nitrogen fertilizer

Nitrogen (N_2)

Every living cell contains nitrogen. Plants cannot take nitrogen from the air, so they get it from the soil. Fertilizers contain nitrogen to replenish what plants remove from the soil.

Fractional distillation

The gases in air have many uses. For example, divers use tanks of oxygen to enable them to breathe underwater, and nitrogen is used in explosives. Gases are extracted from air by a process called fractional distillation. Air is cooled and compressed until it forms a blue liquid. When the liquid expands and warms up, each gas boils off at a different temperature and is collected separately.

Divers with oxygen tanks

Composition of air

Any volume of pure, dry air is 78.09% nitrogen, 20.95% oxygen, 0.93% argon, and 0.03% carbon dioxide and other gases. These coloured balls represent the proportions of the different gases in air.

Red balls represent oxygen.

Green balls represent argon.

Black ball represents carbon dioxide and other gases.

Blue balls represent nitrogen.

Candle burns in jar of air.
Flame goes out and water level rises as the oxygen is used up.

Oxygen (O_2)

Burning is a chemical reaction of a substance with oxygen, as this experiment shows. The candle burns in the jar of air until it has used up all the oxygen. Humans and other animals use oxygen from the air to "burn" food inside their bodies and produce energy.

Argon (Ar)

The gas argon is called an "inert" gas because it is so unreactive. Electric light bulbs are often filled with argon. It prevents the bulb's filament from burning up as it would in air, giving the bulb a much longer life.

Air pollution

Air is not naturally "pure" and contains varying amounts of other substances, such as dust, water vapour, bacteria, pollen, and polluting gases. Air pollution from industry and traffic can cause serious health problems in towns and cities, as well as long-term damage to the environment.

Smog

The hazy air pollution that hangs over an urban area is called smog. Sulphurous smog is the result of burning fuels with a high sulphur content, such as coal. Photochemical smog occurs when sunlight causes car exhaust fumes to react together.

Water vapour

Up to 4 per cent of the volume of air may be water vapour. Warm air can hold more water vapour than cool air. A can of cold drink absorbs heat from the air around it. As the air cools, water vapour condenses out of the air to form droplets on the outside of the can.

Air pressure

Air exerts a force on objects because its moving molecules are constantly colliding with them. Air pressure is a measure of this force. The pressure of the open air is called atmospheric pressure. It is lower at high altitudes, where the air is less dense.

Barometer

A device that measures atmospheric pressure is called a barometer. It can be used to forecast a change in the weather, because air pressure varies slightly from day to day with changes in the air's temperature and humidity.

Sucking

When a person sucks on one end of a drinking straw, the lungs reduce the air pressure inside the straw. Atmospheric pressure on the liquid's surface does the rest, pushing down on the liquid, and making it rise up through the straw.

Compressed air

The pressure of air can be increased by compressing it – that is, pumping more and more of it into a limited space. Bicycle tyres are filled with compressed air to give a smooth, comfortable ride.

Weight of air

Air has weight, as this simple experiment proves. Identical empty balloons are attached to both ends of a stick. The balloons balance when the stick is suspended from its middle. Inflating one of the balloons tips the balance, because the balloon full of compressed air weighs more than the empty balloon.

Balloons balance.

Balance is tipped by inflated balloon.

Inflated balloon contains compressed air.

Joseph Priestley

English scientist and clergyman Joseph Priestley (1733–1804) discovered oxygen in 1774. He also discovered many other gases, including nitrous oxide (laughing gas) and ammonia. Priestley studied carbon dioxide and devised a way to make carbonated (fizzy) water.

FIND OUT MORE — ATOMS AND MOLECULES · CELLS · FRICTION · GASES · LUNGS AND BREATHING · PHOTOSYNTHESIS · POLLUTION · PRESSURE · WEATHER

AIRCRAFT

ANY VEHICLE THAT travels through the air is called an aircraft. The ability to soar over obstacles such as oceans and mountains makes aircraft the fastest form of travel. An airliner (a large passenger plane) can fly a passenger thousands of kilometres in hours. The same journey would take several days by boat or car. Airliners and military aircraft are complex machines. Their frames are built with lightweight metals, such as aluminium, and hi-tech materials, such as plastics. Inside, their sophisticated electronic controls help pilots fly efficiently and safely. Smaller aircraft, such as gliders and hot-air balloons, are often used for sport and leisure.

Types of aircraft

The word aircraft covers all flying machines – from balloons to helicopters. Most aircraft are aeroplanes, which have wings, and jet engines to give them speed. Other types of aircraft are gliders, which have no engines, helicopters, balloons, and airships. An aircraft's function determines its size and shape.

Biplanes
Many planes before World War II (1939–1945) had two pairs of wings, and were called biplanes.

Transport aircraft
Armies need aircraft to transport troops and equipment. Special aircraft are designed to carry very heavy objects, such as tanks.

Balloons
Lighter-than-air craft are known as balloons. A bag is filled with gas or hot air that is lighter than the atmosphere.

Gliders
Currents of air move up and down. A glider has no engine, but flies by the effects of air currents on its wings.

Concorde
Supersonic airliners such as Concorde can travel faster than the speed of sound – about 1,240 kmh (770 mph). They can cross the Atlantic twice as fast as any other airliner, but are very noisy and need lots of fuel.

Anatomy of an airliner

Most airliners, such as this *Boeing 747-400*, have the same basic design. The main part is the fuselage, which is similar to a long, thin, metal tube. The wings are attached to the middle of the fuselage, and the tailplane and fin are attached at the back. A floor separates the passenger cabin from the baggage hold.

The Boeing 747-400 can fly more than 13,600 km (8,451 miles) without stopping for fuel.

Upper deck with business-class seats

Fuselage

Forward cabin with first-class seats

Main cabin, with economy-class seats

Fin

Tailplane

Fuel for engines in fuel tanks inside wings

Engine controls and navigation instruments

Pilot's control column

Turbofan engines hang from wings on pylons.

Freighters
Airplanes that carry cargo are called freighters. The cargo is loaded through a huge door in the aeroplane's nose. The *Boeing 747* can be converted from a passenger plane to a freighter, then back again.

Cockpit
The aircraft is controlled from the cockpit. The pilot and co-pilot fly the plane using control columns, and instruments show the status of all the plane's equipment. The cockpit also contains radar and radio controls.

In-flight food
Pre-prepared meals are stored in trolleys, which lock into spaces in the aircraft's galleys until it is time for the cabin staff to serve them.

Entertainment
Some airliners feature video screens and headphones that can be tuned to music channels.

Howard Hughes
Hughes (1905–76) was an American industrialist, film-maker, and aviation enthusiast. He founded the airline TWA, and broke a number of aviation records in aircraft of his own design. Not all were successful; the *Spruce Goose* (1947) only flew once.

Forces of flight

An aircraft needs two forces to fly: lift to keep it up and thrust to propel it forward. Lift overcomes the plane's weight, and thrust overcomes the drag caused by the air flowing past the plane. When an aircraft is cruising, lift is equal to weight and thrust is equal to drag.

Lift

Thrust

Drag

Weight

Wings

An aircraft's wings create lift. To do this, they need air to flow over them.

The aerofoil shape
If you cut an aircraft wing in two and looked at the end, you would see a special cross-section called an aerofoil. The top surface is longer and more curved than the bottom surface.

The aerofoil at work
The air pressure beneath the wing is greater than above it, and lifts the wing up.

Lift

Angle of attack
Tilting the angle of the blades gives extra lift.

Lift

Flying controls

An aircraft is steered through the air by way of three main control surfaces – the elevators on the tailplane, the ailerons on the wings, and a rudder on the fin.

Elevators make the aircraft's nose tilt up and down.

Ailerons make the aircraft roll from side to side.

The rudder makes the aircraft "yaw" to left or right.

Aero engines

An aircraft's engines drive it through the air by producing thrust. Different types of engine produce thrust in different ways. Piston and turbo-prop engines drive propellers that screw into the air, just as a ship propeller bites into water. Turbo-jet and turbo-fan engines produce a fast-moving stream of gas which pushes the aircraft forwards.

Piston engines
These work in the same way as car engines. Petrol and air vapour are mixed in the engine's cylinders and they cause an explosion. The explosions push pistons, which turn a shaft. The shaft then turns a propeller.

Shaft

Turbo-prop engines
The simplest type of jets – a turbo-jet engine with a propeller is called a turbo-prop engine. A motor turns the compressor and the propeller, which provides the main engine thrust.

Propeller spins to provide engine thrust

Turbo-jet engines
Air is drawn in and compressed, then sent to a chamber where fuel burns. The gases produced are shot out of the back of the engine, which pushes the aircraft forwards, like a deflating balloon.

Gas shoots out

Air drawn in

Turbo-fan engines
A hybrid of turbo-jet and turbo-props, the turbo-fan engine sucks in air, which is combined with the backdraft from a fan, and also sends air around the engine, producing the same effect as a propeller.

Turbo fan

Exhaust

Helicopters

Unlike most aircraft, which have fixed wings, a helicopter has a spinning rotor with two or more long, thin blades attached. When the blades spin round, they lift the helicopter straight up into the air. A helicopter can take off from almost anywhere and does not need to use airport runways. It can hover in one place, and fly backwards, forwards, and sideways. This makes it the most versatile of all aircraft; it is very useful for transport, surveillance, and rescue missions.

Rotor blades twist to control the helicopter's direction.

Turbo-shaft engine

Main rotor

Tail rotor stops fuselage spinning in opposite direction to main rotor.

Landing skids in place of undercarriage

Flying controls
A helicopter pilot has three flying controls. The collective pitch lever changes the amount of lift produced by the main rotor. The cyclic pitch control makes the helicopter move forwards, backwards, or sideways. Rudder pedals make the helicopter turn left or right.

Lifting off
Before take-off, the main and tail rotors are speeded up. When the main rotor is turning fast enough, the pilot lifts the collective pitch lever to increase the tilt of the rotor blades. The tilt produces lift, and the helicopter takes off. The higher the lever is lifted, the faster the aircraft rises.

Moving away
The cyclic pitch control makes the helicopter move in the direction the control is pushed. It tilts the main rotor so that some of the rotor's lift pulls the helicopter along. Here, the pilot has pulled the control back to make the helicopter move backwards.

Igor Ivan Sikorsky
Sikorsky (1889–1972) was born in Ukraine, where he became an aeronautical engineer. In 1919 he moved to the United States where he set up an aircraft factory. He designed the first practical helicopter, the *VS-300*, which first flew in 1939. The design had to be modified many times: at one point, the helicopter flew in every direction except forwards.

FIND OUT MORE   AIRSHIPS AND BALLOONS   ATMOSPHERE   ENGINES AND MOTORS   FLIGHT, HISTORY OF   TRANSPORT, HISTORY OF   WARPLANES   WORLD WAR I   WORLD WAR II

Types of aircraft
Military

Twin tail fins

Harrier can take off and land vertically.

Wings fold back for supersonic flight.

The A-10's huge array of weapons gives it a massive firepower.

Fighter/strike aircraft, McDonnell Douglas F/A-18E Super Hornet

Naval strike aircraft, McDonnell Douglas AV-8B Harrier II

Swing-wing bomber, General Dynamics F-111A Aardvark

Ground-attack "tankbuster" aircraft, Fairchild A-10 Thunderbolt II

Radar dome

Hinged nose is raised to allow loading.

Twin propellers

Extended wings for high-altitude flight.

Radar bulge

Refuelling/electronic counter-measures aircraft, Boeing EC-135 Stratotanker

Heavy transport aircraft, Lockheed C-5A Galaxy – one of the world's largest aircraft

Radar aircraft, Fairey Gannet AEW-3, gives early warning of air attacks.

High-level reconnaissance aircraft, Lockheed U-2

Passenger and cargo aircraft

777's engines are the most powerful aircraft engines ever built.

737 is the world's best-selling jet airliner.

Low-noise engines

More than 1,800 727s were built.

Wide-bodied, long-haul airliner, Boeing 777-200

Medium-range airliner, Boeing 737-300

Short-range airliner, British Aerospace Bae 146-RJ85

Freight transporter aircraft, Boeing 727

Seating for 8–14 passsengers

Turbo-prop engines

Single engine

Cabin holds four people.

Rear-mounted engines

Wing float

Business jet, British Aerospace Bae 125-600

Commuter aircraft, Fairchild Metro II

Leisure aircraft, SOCATA TB-20 Trinidad

Flying boat, Beriev A-50 Mermaid

Helicopters

Wings carry armaments such as rockets and guns.

Five-bladed main rotor

Tail rotor

Radar

Twin rotors

Osprey can fly like both a helicopter and a plane.

Rotors can tilt 90°.

Attack helicopter, Bell AH-1 Cobra

Passenger helicopter, Sikorsky S-61

Transport helicopter, Boeing CH-47 Chinook

Tilt-rotor aircraft, Boeing V-22 Osprey

Sport

Glider soars on warm air currents.

Pilot launches glider by running downhill.

Fabric-covered wings and fuselage

Wing of light woven fabric over metal frame

Propeller

Motor

Hand grip

Wheels allow microlight to take off and land like a normal aircraft.

Hang-glider is like a huge wing with a harness below to hold the pilot.

Biplane training/leisure aircraft, De Havilland Tiger Moth DH8A

Microlight is a kind of motorized hang-glider, with a strong frame and a streamlined fibreglass "tricycle" underneath to carry the pilot.

A

AIRPORTS

TODAY, MORE PEOPLE TRAVEL by air than ever before. Whether they are business people off to visit clients or families going on holiday, all air travellers leave from airports, which range in size from small local facilities to enormous international terminals. A large airport is like a city. It contains shops, offices, and hotels, in addition to all the buildings, runways, and taxiways needed to service the aircraft and their passengers. Airport security is always tight, because airports and aircraft have often been the targets of terrorist attacks.

Features of an airport

Aircraft take off and land on runways, which are linked to the terminal buildings by routes called taxiways. The passengers embark and disembark at the terminal buildings. For the aircraft, the airport has repair workshops, refuelling facilities, and storage hangars.

Runway
To take the biggest jet aircraft, runways have to be 3–4 km (1.8–2.5 miles) long and some 50 m (165 ft) wide. They need a specially toughened surface to take the pounding they get when large jets take off or land.

Terminal building at Kansai International Airport, Japan

"Landside" of terminal

Passengers enter terminal from lower level and leave it from upper level.

Road transport for passengers leaving the airport.

Access area provides escalators to all parts of the terminal building.

International arrivals floor

Curving roof truss

International departures floor

Security area and passport checkpoint

Domestic arrivals and departures are on middle 2 floors.

Boarding gates

"Airside" of terminal

Bridge connects boarding gate to aircraft.

Waiting aircraft

Service area contains boilers, ventilation equipment, and other building services.

Air traffic control

At the heart of an airport is the control tower, where air traffic controllers monitor every moment of an aircraft's arrival and departure. They make sure that each pilot follows the correct flight path, that all aircraft land in the right place, and that there is a safe amount of time between each take-off and landing.

Air traffic controllers in the control tower

Radar display screen
Airport radar tracks each aircraft as it lands, giving the controllers precise details of its position. All aircraft within 20 to 50 km (12 to 30 miles) of the airport can be tracked by radar and shown on the controllers' display screens.

Flight path
Air traffic controllers tell pilots when it is safe to land. They guide a pilot to a specific path, which the pilot must then follow as the aircraft descends to the runway. Navigation aids, such as high-frequency radio beacons, give the pilot accurate bearings.

How an aircraft lands

Fly down and right

Course is correct

Runway (ground level)

Fly up and left

Radar antenna sends out beam to guide plane on to runway.

Flight path

Antenna sends out beam to guide plane's rate of descent.

Radio waves carry information about flight path.

Dials on flight-deck tell pilot whether plane's course is correct.

Security

Airport security staff are always on their guard, trying to spot terrorists or smugglers. Metal detectors and other electronic devices alert staff when a passenger is carrying a gun or other type of weapon. There are also "sniffer" dogs that have been trained to detect the scent of explosives or illegal drugs.

Passports
A person travelling from one country to another usually carries a passport, an official document that identifies the owner and their place of origin. Passports are inspected at international airports.

EU passport

An X-ray reveals a gun.

X-ray scanner
Airport staff use X-ray machines to scan the contents of passengers' luggage. A screen on the side of the X-ray machine shows what is inside each bag. Different materials show up in different colours, enabling items such as guns to be found with ease.

Airports and the environment

A large airport can have a devastating impact on the local environment. Clearing the land to build an airport destroys carefully balanced ecosystems, while the air pollution can harm wildlife, and the noise may scare some animals away.

Airport ecosystems
Since airports cover such vast areas, birds and animals can also move into these areas and establish new ecosystems, undisturbed by people.

Kestrel

Animals can live in the large green spaces around a big airport.

| FIND OUT MORE | AIRCRAFT | ECOLOGY AND ECOSYSTEMS | RADAR AND SONAR | TRAVEL |

AIRSHIPS AND BALLOONS

AIRSHIPS AND BALLOONS are known as lighter-than-air aircraft because, instead of wings, they use a large envelope, or bag, full of gas or hot air that is lighter than the air in the atmosphere around it. The air pushes the envelope upwards, just as water pushes a submerged air-filled ball upwards. In 1783, the Montgolfier brothers achieved the first manned flight ever by sending a hot-air balloon over Paris. Balloons fly where the wind blows them; airships have engines and can be steered. Today, airships are used for aerial filming and coast-guard patrols, and ballooning is a popular sport.

Anatomy of a modern airship

The main part of an airship is its envelope, which contains bags of helium gas. The gas is slightly pressurized to keep the envelope in shape. A fin and tailplane keep the airship steady as it flies slowly along. The crew travels in a gondola attached to the underside of the envelope.

Gas-proof coated polyester envelope *Elevator flaps*

Automatic ballonet valve *Gondola* Skyship 500 HL (semirigid airship) *Rudder to steer the airship.*

The Hindenburg, 1937

Airship disasters
Several terrible disasters made people lose trust in airship travel. Airships were usually lost for two reasons: either they were uncontrollable in bad weather; or the highly inflammable hydrogen gas used inside the envelope exploded. Today, airship pilots use the much safer helium gas in special nylon envelopes. However, they still have to be wary of the weather.

Types of airship

Practical airships could be built only after the lightweight internal combustion engine had been developed. The earliest airships were "nonrigid" (they are still used today). These were followed by the "rigid" and the less usual "semirigid" types of airship.

Nonrigid airships have a flexible fabric envelope, from which the load hangs, suspended by ropes.

Rigid airship's envelope is built around a rigid framework. This skeleton contains bags of the lifting gas – helium.

Balloons

Balloons were first used for aerial reconnaissance during the French Revolution, and used again in the American Civil War. During World Wars I and II, balloons were used to spot targets for artillery attacks, and barrage balloons defended cities against aircraft.

Weather and research balloons
To study what is happening in the upper reaches of the atmosphere, pilots send up helium-filled weather balloons. These carry instruments which measure temperature, wind speed, and so on, and send their results to the ground or to satellites by radio.

Balloon festivals
Today, ballooning is a popular sport. During the summer, ballooning enthusiasts gather at festivals to enjoy the dazzling prospect of dozens of brightly coloured balloons flying together. Some of the balloons are owned by companies, and are made in the shapes of their products, as a form of advertising.

Ferdinand von Zeppelin

German count Ferdinand von Zeppelin (1838–1917) began experimenting with air travel in 1891. In 1900, he devised the first airship, a 128-m (420-ft) rigid craft named the LZ1. During World War I, some 100 Zeppelins were built for military use.

Flight

Hot-air ballooning requires a perfectly clear day with a gentle breeze. Too high a wind puts the balloon at risk on take-off and landing. After take-off, a ground crew follows the balloon in a vehicle to recover both it and the crew after landing.

1 The balloon is laid on the ground. Burners heat air to fill the balloon.

2 The balloon's envelope expands as the hot air starts to fill it

3 The expanding balloon becomes buoyant, and rises into the air.

4 Guy ropes hold the balloon down until the crew boards.

5 The crew blasts hot air into the envelope to keep the balloon afloat.

FIND OUT MORE ATMOSPHERE FLIGHT, HISTORY OF GALILEO GALILEI GASES JOHNSON, AMY RENAISSANCE WEATHER FORECASTING

Airships and balloons

Balloons

Lavishly decorated character from the *Thousand and One Nights*

Easter egg envelope is decorated to celebrate Easter.

Golf ball, an uncomplicated, yet realistic balloon shape

False basket

Upside-down balloon, where a false basket has been attached to the balloon's top.

Fabergé egg, the trademark jewel of a famous Russian jewellers

Basket

Part of this balloon hangs below the basket.

Red, blue, and yellow panels of this balloon's envelope represent the exotic plumage of a parrot.

Modern tractor has its basket hanging where the back axle would be.

Carmen Miranda, a 1940s' singing star

Uncle Sam, a lighthearted symbol of the USA

Moon

A "cow jumps over the moon" is a very complicated balloon shape inspired by the famous nursery rhyme.

Face-shaped balloons are relatively simple to create.

Upturned eaves

Japanese temple; the envelope comes complete with authentic upturned eaves and balcony rails.

Drink can, the first non-traditional balloon shape

Santa Claus, an aerial Christmas decoration

NASA rocket, celebrating space exploration.

Elephant, complete with trunk and a surprised look!

Airships

Spectacular eagle has a very complicated and realistically painted envelope.

Aerial tours are often run by companies that have both airships and balloons.

Modern airships, because of their visibility and size, are often used to advertise products or services.

Rupert the Bear, a favourite fictional character for children all over the world

ALEXANDER THE GREAT

IN LESS THAN FOUR YEARS, a brilliant young general created the largest empire the world had ever seen. The empire was the creation of Alexander the Great of Macedon, a gifted leader who inspired tremendous loyalty from his troops. It stretched from Greece in the west to India in the east. Alexander's sudden death at the age of 33 led to the empire's collapse, but it lived on in a series of towns that spread Greek culture eastwards. These cities, all called Alexandria after their founder, opened up a trade between Asia and Europe that survived for centuries.

Early life
Alexander was born in 356 BC, the son of King Philip II of Macedon (r. 359–336 BC). As a young man he went on military campaigns with his father. Alexander won fame for taming a wild black horse called Bucephalus, which stayed with him throughout his whole life.

Aristotle
Alexander was taught by the Athenian philosopher Aristotle (384–322 BC). Aristotle's interests ranged from politics and morality to biology and literature. He shared his enthusiasm for new ideas with his young pupil.

Alexander's empire

When Alexander became king of Macedon in 336 BC, Greece was dominated by Persia. In a series of brilliant military campaigns, Alexander defeated Persia and created his vast empire.

Greece
The heartland of Alexander's empire was his home state of Macedon, northern Greece. Before Alexander became king, Greece was divided into rival city states, and was threatened by the powerful Persian Empire.

Terracotta figure of the Greek love goddess, Aphrodite

• Gordion
• Issus
• Gaugamela
Alexandria ad Caucasum •
Alexandria Prophthasia •
• Alexandria   Babylon •
• Persepolis

Macedonian Empire

Persia
The rich empire of Persia occupied much of modern Iraq, Turkey, and Iran. After Alexander had conquered the area, he tried to unite Macedonia and Persia by encouraging his generals to marry Persians. Alexander himself married Roxana, a princess from eastern Persia.

Stag comes from palace at Persepolis.

Persian silver stag ornament

Egypt
In 332 BC, Alexander conquered Egypt and was accepted as the new pharaoh. He founded the city of Alexandria, in northern Egypt, which became the most important city of the Greek-speaking world. When Alexander died in 323 BC, he was buried in a vast tomb in the centre of the city.

Alexander wears the pharaoh's crown

Battle of Issus
In 333 BC, the Macedonian army overwhelmed the more powerful Persian army led by Darius III (r. 336–330 BC) at the battle of Issus, Syria. The Persians were defeated again in 331 BC at Gaugamela near the River Tigris. After this battle, the Persian capital, Persepolis, was destroyed and the empire collapsed.

Relief of the Battle of Issus

Eastern empire
By 326 BC, Alexander had marched through Persia and had conquered Afghanistan and the Punjab. Although his troops were very loyal to him, they refused to go further than the River Indus.

Coin from Indus area

Death of Alexander

In 323 BC Alexander caught a fever in the city of Babylon. Although he was only 33, he died. This sudden death meant that Alexander did not have time to consolidate his rule or even name his successor. Within a few years of his death, the huge Macedonian Empire had collapsed.

Alexander's sarcophagus

Carved relief shows Alexander leading his troops.

Sarcophagus from the royal cemetery of Sidon, said to be the tomb of Alexander.

ALEXANDER THE GREAT

356 BC	Born in Macedon
336 BC	Succeeds his father to the Macedonian throne; quells rebellions in Greece
334 BC	Leads his army into Persia and defeats a Persian army at the Granicus River
333 BC	Defeats Darius III at Issus
331 BC	Defeats Darius III again at Gaugamela, completing his conquest of the Persian Empire
326 BC	Reaches the Indus, but is forced to turn back by his troops
323 BC	Dies of fever in Babylon

FIND OUT MORE

ASIA, HISTORY OF	EGYPT, ANCIENT	GREECE, ANCIENT	PERSIAN EMPIRES	PHILOSOPHY

AMERICAN CIVIL WAR

LESS THAN 80 YEARS after independence, the USA split in two over the issue of slavery. The richer, industrial northern states had banned slavery, but slaves were used on plantations in the south. When Abraham Lincoln became president in 1860, the southern states, fearing he would ban slavery, seceded from the Union, and established the Confederate States of America. Fighting began in 1861 and lasted for four years. At first the sides were evenly matched, but the strength of the Union wore down the Confederacy, and it surrendered. Slavery was then abolished throughout the country.

Divided nation

Eleven southern slave states left the Union of states, declaring independence as the Confederacy. Four other slave states refused to break away; West Virginia split from the rest of the state and stayed in the Union.

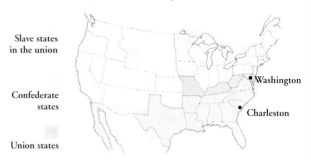

Slave states in the union

Confederate states

Union states

Washington

Charleston

First modern war

The American Civil War was the first recognizably modern war. Railways transported men and supplies to the battlefield, and iron ships were used for the first time. Commanders talked to each other by field telegraph, and the war was photographed and widely reported in newspapers.

Much of the fighting was trench warfare, but troops were also prepared for a pitched battle.

Union soldiers and guns

Gunner

Field gun

Officer

Soldiers
More than three million people fought in the two opposing armies, most of them as infantrymen (foot soldiers).

Percussion musket

Union infantry sergeant

Chevrons

Shell jacket

Sergeant's sash

Sergeant's trouser stripe

Confederate infantryman

Abraham Lincoln
Lincoln was born in Kentucky in 1809. He was elected to the state legislature in 1834, was elected president in 1860, and led the Union states to victory in the civil war. He was assassinated in 1865.

Merrimack and Monitor
The Confederate ironclad ship *Merrimack* (renamed *Virginia*) fought the Union's vessel *Monitor* on 9 March 1862. The battle was inconclusive, but marked the first occasion on which iron ships had been used in naval warfare.

Gettysburg Address
Lincoln's fine speeches helped win the war. In 1863, he dedicated a cemetery on the site of a battlefield in Gettysburg, Pennsylvania. In his speech, he hoped that "these dead shall not have died in vain; that this nation, under God, shall have a new birth of freedom, and that government of the people, by the people, for the people, shall not perish from the earth".

Appomattox
On 9 April 1865, at Appomattox, Virginia, the Confederate general Robert E. Lee surrendered to Union general Ulysses S. Grant. More than 600,000 Americans died in the four years of fighting, and many more were injured.

Signing the surrender documents

Timeline

April 1861 After 11 states leave the Union, war breaks out when Confederate troops fire on the Union garrison at Fort Sumter, South Carolina.

1861 Confederates under generals Jackson and Beauregard win the first major battle against Unionists at Bull Run, near Washington.

Ulysses S. Grant

1862 Confederates win Seven Days' Battle (near Richmond, Virginia) and Battle of Fredericksburg, Virginia.

1863 Union wins its first major battle at Gettysburg; Emancipation Proclamation frees slaves.

1864 Ulysses S. Grant becomes Union commander-in-chief.

1864 General Sherman's Union army marches through Georgia, destroying the state capital and weakening the Confederacy.

Civil War cannon

April 1865 Lee's Confederate army surrenders at Appomattox, Virginia.

May 1865 Last Confederate army surrenders.

December 1865 Slavery is banned throughout the USA by the 13th amendment.

FIND OUT MORE

AMERICAN REVOLUTION   ARMIES   NORTH AMERICA, HISTORY OF   SHIPS AND BOATS   SLAVERY   UNITED STATES, HISTORY OF   WARFARE   WASHINGTON, GEORGE

AMERICAN REVOLUTION

IN 1783, A NEW NATION WAS BORN – the United States of America. Its struggle for independence is called the American Revolution. It began in 1775, when 13 American colonies went to war against Britain. Britain governed the colonies and imposed high taxes. The colonists, who were not represented in the British Parliament, resented the taxes. Protests and demonstrations broke out, and the colonists formed a Continental Congress to negotiate with Britain. A skirmish led to war, and in 1776, the American colonists, inspired by ideals of freedom, declared independence. The British surrendered in 1781, and two years later recognized the new country.

Maine (to Massachusetts)
New Hampshire
Massachusetts
New York
Rhode Island
Pennsylvania
Connecticut
New Jersey
Delaware
Virginia
Maryland
N. Carolina
S. Carolina
Georgia

Thirteen colonies
After the Revolution, Britain's 13 original colonies formed the first 13 states of the new United States.

Stamp tax

The colonists set their own taxes. But in 1765, Britain introduced a stamp tax on legal documents. The angry colonists stated that "taxation without representation is tyranny". They refused to buy British goods.

Boston Tea Party
Britain withdrew the stamp tax, but set others on glass and tea. Three groups of protesters, dressed as Mohawk Indians, boarded tea ships in Boston Harbour and threw their cargo into the water.

Colonists pour tea into Boston Harbour, in protest at British taxes

Lexington and Concord

In April 1775, the war began with skirmishes near Lexington and Concord. American patriots forced the British to withdraw at Lexington. They marched back to Boston under continuous fire.

Paul Revere
Paul Revere (1735–1818) rode through Massachusetts on the night of 18 April 1775, to warn that the British were coming. He was part of an anti-British group called the Sons of Liberty.

Revere on horseback

Thomas Jefferson
A planter from Virginia, Thomas Jefferson (1743–1826) attended the Continental Congress in 1775. He drafted the Declaration of Independence, reformed the laws of his native state, and went on diplomatic missions to Europe. He became the third president of the USA in 1801 and served until 1809.

George Washington
The commander of the colonial army was George Washington (1732–1799). He was an inspiring general, who kept the morale of his troops high in spite of several defeats at the beginning of the war. When France joined the war on the colonial side in 1778, followed by Spain in 1779, victory was assured.

Washington

American soldier
- Cocked hat
- Cartridge box belt
- Knapsack strap
- Brush for musket lock
- Musket
- Gaitered trousers
- Musket

British infantryman
- Cocked hat
- Crossbelt
- Red coat
- Bayonet
- Brush for musket lock
- Breeches
- Leather spatterdash
- Shoe

Surrender at Yorktown
The fighting lasted until spring 1781, when the colonists cut the British off from their supplies at Yorktown. They finally surrendered on 19 October.

Declaration of Independence
On 4 July 1776, the 13 colonies signed the Declaration of Independence. This document stated that "all men are created equal..." and its belief in "Life, Liberty, and the Pursuit of Happiness" later inspired the French Revolution.

Revolutionary war

The war lasted for six years. Washington's leadership played a vital part in the American victory. He led his troops to victories at Brandywine (1777) and Yorktown (1781).

The opposing armies
The British were well trained but poorly led. Their orders came from 4,000 km (2,500 miles) away. The Americans were less well trained and equipped, but knew the terrain and had good leaders.

Timeline
1765 Britain introduces the stamp tax. Protests break out. Britain withdraws the stamp tax, but other taxes remain.

1773 Boston Tea Party. Americans, dressed as Mohawks, dump tea in Boston Harbour as a protest against heavy taxes.

1774–75 Continental Congress. Representatives draft a petition to Britain insisting on no taxation without representation.

1775 Battle of Lexington. Congress takes over government of the colonies, and appoints Washington Commander-in-Chief.

1777 British general John Burgoyne (1722–92) forced to surrender at Saratoga.

1778 France joins the war on the American side.

1781 British surrender at Yorktown.

French private soldier

FIND OUT MORE — FRENCH REVOLUTION — UNITED KINGDOM, HISTORY OF — UNITED STATES, HISTORY OF — WARFARE — WASHINGTON, GEORGE

49

AMPHIBIANS

COLD-BLOODED animals, amphibians are vertebrates (animals with a backbone) that evolved from fish. They are adapted for life on land, but most must return to water in some form to breed. Amphibians undergo a process known as metamorphosis in their development from larvae to adult, hence the Greek origin of their name: *amphi* meaning "double"; *bios* meaning "life". There are three groups of amphibians and more than 3,000 species.

Amphibian features

Apart from the caecilians and a few species of salamander, adult amphibians have four legs, each with four or five digits. Most species take to the water to mate and produce their eggs, but some make nests on land, occasionally in burrows in the ground or in moss.

European common frog

Long legs for leaping.

Frog leaps after prey such as an insect.

Webbed toes for swimming.

Marbled newt

"Marbled" colour extends along the tail.

Newts and salamanders

The tailed amphibians – newts, salamanders, and the eel-like sirens of North America – live in tropical forests, temperate woods, mountain streams, and lakes. Some have very specialized lifestyles: a few even live in the total darkness of caves.

Couch's spadefoot toad

Amphibian groups

There are three groups of amphibians: the worm-like caecilians; the tailed amphibians, including newts and salamanders; and the tail-less frogs and toads, probably the most diverse group.

Caecilians

Caecilians are legless, carnivorous amphibians most of which live in the tropics. Some species burrow in the ground; others are aquatic. They have small eyes and ears and sensory tentacles on the head.

Frogs and toads

In temperate regions, frogs are more aquatic than toads, have slimier skin and longer legs. In the tropics, some species of frog and toad are fully aquatic and live in trees or underground.

Distribution of amphibians
Amphibians live everywhere. Desert species survive the driest season by staying underground inside a membranous sac, which they secrete themselves. Some temperate species hibernate in pond mud in the winter.

Skin

Amphibian skin is thin and scaleless. It is usually kept moist with mucus to increase its ability to allow oxygen through for skin breathing. Skin can be smooth or rough. It secretes certain chemicals: pheromones can attract potential mates, while poisons deter predators. As they grow, amphibians shed the top layer of skin.

White's tree frogs

Colour
Amphibians may have skin colours that absorb or reflect heat. Colour also varies with temperature, becoming pale when warm and darker if cold and damp.

Camouflaged tree frogs

Camouflage
Many frogs and toads are camouflaged to avoid detection by predators. Most have a combination of forest colours and disruptive patterning. Some rainforest species are shaped to look like dead leaves.

Great crested newt   Square marked toad

Mandarin salamander   Tree frog

Texture
Many frogs and toads have smooth skin covered by mucus. Other amphibians, such as the mandarin salamander and many dry-skinned toads, have raised nodules.

Poison-dart tadpoles

Defence
The bright colours of Colombian poison-dart frogs warn predators of their highly toxic skin. The tadpoles develop their skin poisons as their colours develop. Marine toads secrete a strong toxin through large glands behind the head.

Metamorphosis

The development from an aquatic larva that breathes through gills, or spiracles, to an air-breathing adult is called metamorphosis. It involves the growth of legs and the loss of the tail in frogs and toads.

Newt egg

Frog spawn

Eggs
Amphibian eggs are laid singly, in clumps, or in strings of clear "jelly" called spawn. They have no shell and require a moist environment to survive.

Tadpoles
Larvae, or tadpoles, hatch from the eggs. Salamander tadpoles have limbs, but frogs and toads develop these during metamorphosis. Salamander larvae are carnivorous, but most frog and toad tadpoles are herbivorous.

Frog tadpole

Gills

Salamander tadpole

Axolotl
Some salamanders may stay as larvae all their life. The axolotl is a form of the Mexican tiger salamander.

FIND OUT MORE   EVOLUTION   FROGS AND TOADS   POISONOUS ANIMALS   SALAMANDERS AND NEWTS

ANGLO-SAXONS

BY THE END of the 8th century, Britain's people, known as the Anglo-Saxons, had created a rich culture, which included masterpieces of jewellery, architecture, and literature. Originally these people had come from northern Germany and southern Denmark, where they were known as the Angles, Saxons, and Jutes. In the 3rd and 4th centuries, these tribes travelled to various parts of the Roman Empire, including Gaul, or present-day France, where their influence was short-lived. They travelled to Britain in the 5th century, where they settled, and formed several separate kingdoms. Eventually the kingdom of Wessex became the dominant power.

Culture

Cultural life centred on the monasteries and on the royal court. Alfred the Great gathered scholars and artists around him, and he himself translated many of the Latin classics into Anglo-Saxon, or Old English.

Architecture

Anglo-Saxon churches, like the one at Earls Barton, England, often have square towers decorated with stone relief. This pattern may be based on timber buildings of the period, which have all perished.

Decorated manuscripts

Monks produced quality manuscripts. One monk wrote the work, while a second illustrated it with figures, such as St Dunstan (c.909–988) kneeling before Jesus, and a third decorated it.

Kingdoms

There was always a struggle for supremacy among the kingdoms formed by the settlers. Northumbria was the earliest one to dominate under Edwin (d. 633). Then it was Mercia's turn under Aethelbald (d. 757) and Offa (d. 796). Finally, Wessex dominated under Alfred the Great. When Vikings from Denmark attacked and occupied northern England, Alfred stopped them from pushing farther south, and the Anglo-Saxons reconquered the north in the 10th century.

King Canute the Great

By 1016, the Danes ruled all England under the popular Canute (c.995–1035). Canute's sons inherited England, but the Anglo-Saxon Edward the Confessor (c.1003–1066) regained the country in 1042. He had no children and, when he died, an unsettled England was vulnerable to conquest by the Normans.

Edward the Confessor

Canute the Great

Written records

In the 7th century, missionaries from mainland Europe, such as St Augustine of Canterbury, converted the Anglo-Saxons to Christianity. The creation of monasteries meant that more people learned to read and write. Monks produced historical works, such as the *Anglo-Saxon Chronicle*, which today give insights into the events of the period.

Alfred the Great

Ruler of Wessex and Mercia, Alfred (c.849–c.899) was an able soldier who defended his kingdom against the Vikings. He loved learning and education, and arts and crafts flourished in his reign. He could not drive the Vikings from northern England, but most people saw him as their protector. He was the first English king to become a national symbol.

Possible image of Alfred the Great

Jewellery

This jewel is inscribed "Alfred ordered me to be made" and may have belonged to Alfred the Great. The inscription and animal-head decoration are finely worked in gold; the portrait, perhaps of the king himself, is made of enamel.

Anglo-Saxon Chronicle

In the ninth century, Alfred the Great ordered the *Chronicle*, a year-by-year account of the history of England. It covers the lives of kings and church leaders, military history, and major events, such as the Viking invasions, and was last updated in 1154.

Bede (c.673–735)

Bede, an English monk and teacher in Jarrow, wrote *A History of the English Church and People*, one of the most important sources of our knowledge of Anglo-Saxon times.

Timeline

450 Angles, Saxons, and Jutes from northern Germany and Denmark begin to arrive in England. They settle mainly along the eastern coast – East Anglia.

802–39 Reign of Egbert of Wessex. There are many Viking attacks.

871–99 Reign of Alfred the Great, famous for law-making, translating books into Old English, and defeating the Vikings at Edington in 878.

1016 Canute the Great, a Dane, is elected king by the British; he rules until 1035.

1042 Anglo-Saxons regain power under Edward the Confessor.

Anglo-Saxon buckle

1066 Last Anglo-Saxon king, Harold II, is killed by William of Normandy at the Battle of Hastings.

FIND OUT MORE   CELTS   EUROPE, HISTORY OF   MONASTERIES   NORMANS   UNITED KINGDOM, HISTORY OF   VIKINGS

ANIMAL BEHAVIOUR

ALL ANIMALS RESPOND to their surroundings. A cat, for example, will arch its back when threatening a rival, but lower its body when stalking a mouse. Everything that an animal does, and the way in which it does it, makes up its behaviour. An animal's behaviour enables it to increase its chances of survival and find a mate so that it can pass on its genes to the next generation. Some behaviours are inbuilt, or instinctive; others are learned during the animal's lifetime.

Egg-rolling
Greylag geese nest on the ground. If an egg rolls out of the nest, the female goose automatically reaches out with her neck and pulls the egg back in. By being in the wrong place, the egg acts as a sign stimulus that causes the female to carry out the fixed-action pattern of egg-rolling.

Instinctive behaviour

Instinct is a term used to describe behaviours that an animal performs automatically without having to learn them. Instinctive behaviour is programmed by an animal's genes. It consists of unchanging components called fixed-action patterns. The fixed-action pattern often begins when an animal responds to a feature in its surroundings or on another animal, called a sign stimulus.

Web spinning
Many species of spider, including this black widow spider, spin webs in order to trap their insect food. Web spinning is purely instinctive. A spider would not have time in its limited life to learn how to construct such a complex structure.

Sign stimulus
In the spring, when these freshwater fish breed, the male's throat and belly turn red. If one male intrudes into the territory of another male, its red colour acts as a sign stimulus that produces a fixed-action pattern: the occupying fish drives out the intruder.

Bright spring colours

Bright colours fade after the breeding season.

Learned behaviour

Learning occurs when an animal adapts to its surroundings by changing its behaviour. By responding to experiences and adapting to changing conditions, an animal increases its chances of survival. Learning takes time, and animals that are dependent on learned behaviour have long lives and large brains.

Learning tool use
Some animals learn to use simple "tools" in order to feed. Sea otters, found off the coast of California, USA, swim on their backs with a stone on their chests on which they smash the shells of clams and mussels to get at the juicy contents. Young otters learn tool use from their parents.

Trial and error learning
An animal will associate an action it carries out with a successful result, such as getting food or defeating a rival. This "reward" motivates the animal to alter its behaviour to improve the result of future actions.

Puppies play-fight and perfect their hunting skills.

Young ducklings follow their mother.

Imprinting
This is shown by some young animals that make a strong bond with their parent soon after hatching or birth. Young ducklings, for example, stay close to their mother and improve their chances of survival under her protection.

Insight learning
This involves a form of reasoning. Some animals can solve new problems by drawing on past experiences. Chimpanzees, having learned to extract termites or ants from a nest with a stick, can exploit any shape or size of nest.

Communication

Animals communicate by sending out signals that are recognized by other animals and alter their behaviour in some way. The signals can be sights, sounds, or scents. Communication is used, for example, to find a mate, threaten rivals or enemies, defend a territory, warn of danger, or hold a group together.

Song thrush sings from a perch.

Visual signals
Animals may use visual signals as a threat or to attract a mate. This puss moth caterpillar adopts a warning posture if threatened by an enemy. An enemy that ignores the warning is rewarded with a stinging squirt of formic acid.

Puss moth caterpillar

Bright colours add to the warning.

Sound
Many animals, including crickets, bullfrogs, peacocks, and whales, use sound to communicate. This male song thrush sings to proclaim his territory, to warn rivals to stay away, and to attract a female.

Chemicals
Some animals release chemicals called pheromones, which, when detected, affect the behaviour of other members of the same species. Female gypsy moths release pheremones that attract males from several kilometres away.

Gypsy moth

Courtship

Mating in most mammals and birds takes place only at certain times of the year. Courtship describes the behaviour used by male animals to attract a female and mate with her. It informs a potential mate that the intention is breeding and not aggression. During courtship, males usually compete with each other to attract females, advertise that they are ready to mate, and encourage females to be sexually responsive. Females select males by the quality of their courtship display.

Male is aware that the female may lash out at him.

Male is attentive to the female.

Female is sexually responsive and rolls.

Domestic cats
A female cat comes on heat, or is sexually responsive, about twice a year. She produces scents and calls loudly to attract males. Several males may compete for her by fighting. The successful male encourages the female by touching her and calling softly.

Bird of paradise
Most birds have fixed courtship displays that ensure they attract a mate of the same species. Male birds often have brighter plumage than females, and this is especially true of the emperor bird of paradise. Males compete for females by quivering their long feathers and calling loudly.

Territorial behaviour

Many animals defend their territory to maintain access to food, water, shelter, and somewhere to reproduce. Territories can be large or small and held by one animal or by a group. Birdsong or the marking of territorial boundaries may deter rivals from entering a territory and avoid conflict and possible fatal injuries.

Cats
Most cats are solitary and maintain a territory on their own. Cheetahs patrol their territory and mark its boundaries by spraying urine on trees and other landmarks. The scent warns neighbouring cheetahs not to intrude.

Kittiwakes
Like many gull species, kittiwakes nest in colonies on narrow cliff ledges. Each pair of birds defends a small territory on the ledge, just large enough for the female to lay eggs and raise their young.

Aggression

Animals show aggression to other members of their species when competing for food, water, shelter, or mates. Some animals use horns, some use teeth or claws, and others kick. In many cases, animals signal their aggressive intent. This may defuse the situation and prevent injury.

Fighting bighorn sheep

Inflated porcupine fish

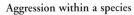

Aggression within a species
These bighorn sheep use their horns to clash head-on in competition for mates. The winner of the fight gains higher social ranking and more females. Aggression like this is highly ritualized, and neither male is likely to be injured.

Aggression between species
Animals may be aggressive towards members of other species that are threatening or attacking them. Some animals use a threat display, often making themselves bigger to deter enemies. This porcupine fish inflates its body like a balloon and erects its spines.

Social behaviour

Social animals live in groups. Individuals co-operate to find food, defend themselves, and look after the young. Social groups range from shoals of fish, which are purely defensive, to societies of honeybees, where social organization affects all aspects of an individual's life.

Helping others
African wild dogs are social animals and often help each other. Male dogs will look after pups that are not their own, but were fathered by a brother or close relative. In this way they help pups to survive.

Living in large numbers
Many fish species swim close together in large numbers called shoals. A shoal moves and turns in a co-ordinated manner that mimics a single large living organism. Predators find it difficult to focus on one individual within the shoal.

Worker bee

Male bee, called a drone

Section of a bees' nest

Konrad Lorenz

Austrian zoologist Konrad Lorenz (1903-89) pioneered the study of animal behaviour. As part of his work on individual and group behaviour, Lorenz discovered imprinting. Lorenz shared a Nobel Prize in 1973 for his work.

Social insects
Within a colony of social insects, such as bees, there are groups that carry out certain tasks. In a bee colony a single queen lays eggs, while sterile female workers look after the young, collect food, and defend the colony. Male bees fertilize the queen.

FIND OUT MORE

BIRDS   FISH   GENETICS   INSECTS   MAMMALS   SONGBIRDS

ANIMALS

MORE THAN a million and a half species of animal have been identified, and there are many millions more yet to be discovered. Animals are living organisms found in nearly all of the Earth's habitats, including the depths of the oceans, the freezing Arctic, and even inside other animals and plants. The animal kingdom is divided into animals without backbones (invertebrates), such as snails and lobsters, and animals with backbones (vertebrates), such as frogs and monkeys. Invertebrates make up 97 per cent of all animal species.

Large eyes enable the leopard to see in dim light.

Body is covered with insulating fur and supported internally by a skeleton.

Long tail is a balancing aid.

Air is breathed in through nostrils.

Black leopard
The leopard is a mammal. Its well-defined head is equipped with sense organs, including eyes, nose, tongue, and whiskers. Sharp teeth in the mouth allow the leopard to kill prey and tear off flesh. Muscular legs enable it to walk, run, and pounce.

What is an animal?

Animals are made up of many cells. Most move actively, and those that are fixed in one place, or sedentary, move their body parts. Animals live by taking food into their bodies. They have sensors and nervous systems that enable them to detect what is happening around them and respond appropriately.

Animal classification

Animals are classified into groups according to their similarities and whether they have common ancestors. There are 35 major groups called phyla (singular phylum). Each phylum is divided into sub-groups. The smallest of these is the species, which contains animals of just one type.

Giant land flatworm

Sponge processed for human use   Sea anemones

Sponges
The simplest animals are sponges (phylum Porifera). There are about 5,000 species, most of which live in the sea attached to rocks and other objects. Water is drawn in through holes, or pores, in the sponge's body wall, and bits of food are filtered out and eaten by the sponge's cells.

Cnidarians
There are more than 9,000 species of cnidarians (phylum Cnidaria), most of which are found in the sea. They include jellyfish, sea anemones, hydras, and corals. Cnidarians catch food using tentacles armed with stinging threads, called nematocysts.

Flatworms
These worms (phylum Platyhelminthes) have a flattened body with one opening, the mouth, on the underside. There are about 18,500 species including those, such as tapeworms, that are parasites of humans and other animals.

Nematodes
Roundworms, or nematodes (phylum Nematoda), have a thin, cylindrical body that is pointed at both ends. Free-living nematodes are found in many habitats and occur in very large numbers in soil. Many nematodes are parasites of plants and animals.

Threadworm

Stalked eye

Coiled shell protects the soft body.

Annelids
Animals in the phylum Annelida include earthworms, marine bristleworms such as ragworms, and leeches. There are about 12,000 species, each of which has a body made up of segments with a mouth at one end and an anus at the other.

King ragworm

Snail emerging from its shell.

Molluscs
Molluscs (phylum Mollusca) form a highly diverse group of about 50,000 species. These include snails and slugs, mussels and clams, and squids and octopuses. They are soft-bodied animals that may be protected by a shell. Most live in water, but some, such as snails, are found on land.

Snail moves on a muscular foot.

Sensory tentacle

Head and foot fully extended

Echinoderms
All echinoderms (phylum Echinodermata) live in the sea. The 6,500 or so species include sea urchins and starfish. Most have five parts radiating from a central point, hard plates under the skin, and many tube-feet.

Cushion star

Bloody Henry starfish

Cushion star

Arthropods have hard, jointed external skeletons.

Arthropods
With at least one million known species, Arthropods (phylum Arthropoda) are the largest group of animals. They include insects, crustaceans (such as crabs), arachnids (such as spiders), and centipedes.

Sharp teeth to grasp food

Chordates
There are about 48,000 species of chordate (phylum Chordata). Most are vertebrates, such as fish, amphibians, reptiles, birds, and mammals. Vertebrates are the most advanced animals.

Tail used for movement or balance is typical of many vertebrates.

Caiman

Tarantula

Animal skeletons

The skeleton is a supportive framework that maintains the shape of an animal and enables it to move. Most skeletons are hard structures, either inside or outside the animal's body, to which muscles are attached. The skeleton may also protect internal organs and, in the case of an insect's external skeleton, prevent the animal from drying out.

Limbs and head attached to backbone

Crab's exoskeleton

Salamander's endoskeleton

Internal skeletons

A skeleton found inside the body is called an endoskeleton. Most vertebrates have a skeleton made of cartilage and bone. Joints between the bones allow the animal to move. The endoskeleton grows with the rest of the body.

External skeletons

A hard outer skeleton that covers all or part of the body is called an exoskeleton. An insect's outer cuticle and a snail's shell are examples of an exoskeleton. An insect's exoskeleton does not grow and must be shed, or moulted, periodically to allow the animal to grow.

Earthworm

Hydrostatic skeleton

The hydrostatic skeleton is an internal skeleton found in soft-bodied animals such as earthworms. It consists of a fluid-filled core surrounded by muscles, and maintains the shape of the worm.

Worm gets longer when it contracts its muscles.

Movement of an eel through water

Eel moves by throwing its body into curves that push against the water.

Animal movement

The ability to move is characteristic of animals, which move to find food, escape from predators, and find a mate. The way in which an animal moves depends on its complexity, lifestyle, and where it lives. The wide range of movement includes swimming through water, walking and creeping on land, and flying or gliding in air.

Wings sweep downward to produce forward thrust.

Movement in air

Insects, birds, and bats are capable of powered flight using wings. Birds have lightweight, streamlined bodies. They use energy to flap their wings, which pushes them forward. As air passes over the wings it creates the lift that keeps the bird in the air.

Young chaffinch in flight

Moving in water

Many aquatic animals are adapted for movement in water by having streamlined bodies. Most fish move by pushing their tail fin from side to side. This pushes the water backward and sideways, and propels the fish forward. Whales move in a similar way, except that the tail moves up and down.

Asian elephant

Feet expand under the elephant's weight as they are put down.

Movement on land

Animals move on land in a variety of ways. Many have limbs that raise the body off the ground, support it, and enable the animal to walk, run, or hop. The animals move forward by pushing the ends of their legs, or feet, backward against the ground.

Animal senses

The main senses are vision, hearing, taste, smell, and touch. Animals use their senses to find out what is going on around them. A stimulus from outside, such as a sound, is detected by a sense organ, such as the ear. Nerve impulses from sense organs are interpreted by the animal's brain which "decides" how to respond.

Eyes

Dragonfly eyes

Eyes contain sensors that are sensitive to light. When stimulated they send nerve impulses to the brain, which enable it to build up a picture. Insects have compound eyes made up of many separate units, or ommatidia.

Antennae

These are found on the head of arthropods such as insects. They are used to detect odours and may detect chemicals called pheromones released by insects to communicate with each other. Antennae also detect vibrations and movements in the air or in water.

Longhorn beetle

External ear flaps channel sounds into the ear.

Ears

Some animals can detect sounds with ears. The ear converts sounds into nerve impulses that can be interpreted by the animal's brain. Animals use sounds to communicate with each other and to detect approaching predators or prey.

Domestic Basenji dog

Feeding

All animals feed by taking in food. They use a range of feeding strategies and can be grouped accordingly. Some animals kill and eat others, some graze or browse on plants, others filter food particles from water. After feeding, or ingestion, food is digested so that it can be used by the body.

Mormon caterpillar consuming a leaf

Herbivores

Animals that feed solely on plants are called herbivores. Many use specialized mouthparts, such as grinding teeth, to break up tough plant tissues. Plant material is not a rich food source, and most herbivores eat a lot to obtain the necessary nutrients.

Giant clam

Filter feeders

These are animals that feed by sieving food particles from water that flows into their body. Many are sedentary and draw in a current of water. Some whales are filter feeders that eat small animals called krill.

Carnivores

These types of feeders are adapted to detect prey animals, to catch and kill them, and to cut them up to eat them. They include cats, eagles, and some insects. Dragonfly larvae live in water and they can catch small fish to eat.

Dragonfly larva with stickleback

FIND OUT MORE   AMPHIBIANS   ANIMAL BEHAVIOUR   BIRDS   FISH   FLIGHT, ANIMAL   INSECTS   MAMMALS   REPTILES   SNAILS AND OTHER MOLLUSCS

ANTARCTICA

WITH THE SOUTH POLE at its heart, Antarctica is the world's windiest, coldest, and most southerly continent. The last region on Earth to be explored, this huge landmass is not divided into countries, but seven countries claimed territories there. In 1959, however, the Antarctic Treaty suspended those claims and stated that the continent is to be used for peaceful purposes only. Antarctica's sole inhabitants are visiting scientists, working in research stations.

Physical features

Antarctica is almost entirely covered by a vast sheet of ice, in places 4.8 km (3 miles) deep. It contains 90 per cent of the Earth's ice, and 80 per cent of the world's fresh water. The vast Ronne and Ross ice shelves are formed where the ice sheet extends over the ocean.

ANTARCTICA FACTS

AREA 13,900,000 sq km (5,366,790 sq miles)

POPULATION 4,000 international researchers

NUMBER OF COUNTRIES None

HIGHEST POINT Vinson Massif, 5,140 m (16,863 ft)

AVERAGE THICKNESS OF ICE CAP 2,450 m (8,000 ft)

Icebergs
Currents beneath Antarctica's vast ice shelves cause giant slabs of ice to break away, the largest of which may be 200 km (124 miles) long. As these enormous icebergs drift north they slowly break up and melt. Only the top third of an iceberg shows above the water.

Mount Erebus
Antarctica has volcanic areas. An active volcano, Mount Erebus, lies on Ross Island on the edge of the Ross Ice Shelf. It forms part of the Transantarctic mountain chain that includes peaks up to 4,570 m (15,000 ft) high.

Tourism
Cruise ships bring around 9,000 people each year to see Antarctica's coastline and wildlife. A hotel now exists on King George Island. Tourists who venture on to the ice must wear insulated clothing and goggles to protect their eyes from the glare.

Tourists shelter in a whale skull

Cross-section through Antarctica
The Transantarctic mountains divide the continent of Antarctica into Greater and Lesser Antarctica. Although the land itself is low, the depth of the ice on top of it makes Antarctica the highest continent, with an average height of 2,100 m (6,900 ft). The ice-cap was formed by the build up of snow over the last 100,000 years and contains 90 per cent of the world's ice.

West Antarctic Ice Sheet (Lesser Antarctica) — Ross Ice Shelf — Transantarctic Mountains — East Antarctic Ice Sheet (Greater Antarctica)

A — Approximately 6,000 km (3,728 miles) from A to B — B

FIND OUT MORE ATLANTIC OCEAN · CLIMATE · GLACIATION · INDIAN OCEAN · PACIFIC OCEAN · POLAR EXPLORATION · POLAR WILDLIFE · POLLUTION · VOLCANOES

ANTEATERS, SLOTHS AND ARMADILLOS

A BIZARRE GROUP of animals make up the order of mammals known as the edentates. They include the anteaters, armadillos, and sloths, all of which, except the nine-banded armadillo, live in the tropical regions of South and Central America. The name "edentate" means "without teeth", but it is a misleading term, as only the anteaters are toothless. In fact, some armadillos have more teeth than any other land mammal.

Young
A female anteater gives birth to a single young. The young anteater travels on its mother's back for the first year of its life, by which time it is almost half the size of its mother.

Anteater
There are four species of anteater. The giant anteater lives in grasslands; the other three species live in forests and have prehensile (grasping) tails with which they hang from trees. Anteaters have long snouts and tongues to enable them to collect the termites and ants on which they feed. They locate their prey with their acute sense of smell. Their foreclaws are so large that they need to walk on their knuckles. The claws are used to break open termite nests and for defence. If threatened, they rear up on their hind legs and try to rip their opponent with their claws.

Giant anteater breaking into a termite mound.

Tongue
Anteaters have long sticky tongues that can be pushed deep into termite nests. The tongue is covered in little spines that point backwards, making it very difficult for ants and termites to escape.

Curved spines on tongue

Long bushy tail

Giant anteater

Armadillo
Of the 21 species of armadillo, the largest is the giant armadillo, which is 91.5 cm (3 ft) in length. It has up to 100 peg-like teeth – twice as many as most mammals – which are shed when the animal reaches adulthood. The smallest species, the fairy armadillo, is less than 15 cm (6 in) long. Armadillos give birth to up to four young. The nine-banded armadillo, from North America, gives birth to quadruplets of the same sex.

Claws
Armadillos have large curved claws. They use them to dig into the ground to make burrows, to escape predators, and to find food. The giant armadillo's middle claw is the largest claw in the animal kingdom, measuring 18 cm (7 in) around the curve.

Nine-banded armadillo

Large claws

Hairy stomach

Nine-banded armadillo

Bony plates

Body armour

Armadillos are encased in "body armour" formed by separate plates made of bone. Soft skin links the plates together, giving them flexibility. In most species the plates cover only the upper part of the body. If threatened, some species, such as the three-banded armadillo, roll into a ball, while others make for their burrow or dig themselves into the ground.

Sloth
Adapted to living upside down, sloths hang by their claws from the branches of trees. They can rotate their heads through a 270° angle, allowing them to keep their head upright while their body remains inverted. They eat, mate, give birth, and spend their entire life-cycle upside down. Sloth's hair lies in the opposite direction from other animals', to allow rain to run off. Only when asleep do they adopt a more normal position, by squatting in the fork of a tree. There are seven species of sloth; all are herbivorous.

Female three-toed sloth with baby

Green algae cover the sloth's coat.

Movement
Sloths are very slow movers. They rarely descend to the ground as they can only just stand, but cannot walk. They drag themselves along with their claws. In water though, they are good swimmers.

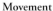

Sloth swimming

Camouflage
Due to the high humidity levels in the rainforest, infestations of green algae grow within a sloth's fur and cover its coat. This acts as a camouflage and makes the sloth less conspicuous. As the seasons change, the algae change colour to match the colour of the trees.

Pangolin
There are seven species of pangolin, or scaly anteater. They have much in common with the edentates, but they belong to a different order called the Pholidota. They are covered with scales attached to the skin. Some species have a long, prehensile tail that is used to grasp branches and also to lash out at predators. They feed on termites, ants, and larvae which they catch with their long tongues.

Malayan pangolin

GIANT ANTEATER

SCIENTIFIC NAME	*Myrmecophaga tridactyla*
ORDER	Edentata
FAMILY	Myrmecophagidae
DISTRIBUTION	South America
HABITAT	Grasslands and savannahs
DIET	Termites, ants, and larvae
SIZE	Length, including tail: 1.83 m (6 ft)
LIFESPAN	25 years (in captivity)

FIND OUT MORE

ASIAN WILDLIFE   CAMOUFLAGE AND COLOUR   CONSERVATION   GRASSLAND WILDLIFE   MAMMALS   RAINFOREST WILDLIFE   SOUTH AMERICAN WILDLIFE

ANTS AND TERMITES

FOR EVERY HUMAN, there are 1,000,000 ants. Ants and termites are social insects that live in large colonies and have developed complex systems of communication. Ants are found worldwide, but, like termites, most of the 9,500 species of ant live in the tropics. There are more than 2,400 types of termite; many are blind, spending their lives inside nests, never seeing the light of day.

Ants

Ants have two pairs of compound eyes, three single eyes, or ocelli, two antennae, and three pairs of legs. Only queens and males have wings. A narrow waist connects the thorax and abdomen. Ants undergo complete metamorphosis, from an egg to larval and pupal stages, before emerging as adults. They live in huge groups and each ant has a particular role. The queen runs the nest and mates with male ants. Workers are female and gather food and nurse the eggs, larvae, and pupae. Soldier ants, also female, guard the nest.

Eyes

Pheromones are released from the abdomen.

Legs are attached to the thorax.

Thorax

Wood ants

Bull ant

Antennae are used to pick up the scent of pheromones.

Eyes

Spiked jaws used to attack prey and predators.

Communication
Ants lay trails of pheromones – chemicals that smell – so that other ants can follow them by using their sensitive antennae to pick up the smell. This helps foraging teams home in on food.

Defence
If a nest is attacked, the ants release pheromones to warn each other. Most run for cover, but soldier ants get aggressive and defend the colony. They attack enemies with their large jaws, or sting them and inject formic acid, which causes extreme pain. Some ants even explode to shower an attacker in venom.

Ant nest
Most ants live in nests or colonies, usually underground. However, weaver ants build nests out of leaves in trees, and army ants build "live nests" of worker ants. Normally, there is one queen in a nest, but there are sometimes several. Nests of Australian bull ants contain up to 600 ants, while some wood ants' nests can house more than 300 million.

"Live nest" made by army ants

Feeding
Many ants are omnivores and eat seeds, nectar, and invertebrates. Army and driver ants are more carnivorous, and kill and eat prey such as worms, spiders, and even some lizards. Leaf-cutting ants are one of a few species of herbivorous ants. They feed on a type of fungus, which grows on the chewed-up remains of leaves and flowers that the ants take back to their nests.

Ants carrying pieces of leaves back to their nest.

Leaf-cutting ants

Termites

Although often called white ants, termites belong to a totally different order, the Isoptera. Like ants, termites live in large colonies. Unlike ants, termites do not have waists, and the male, called a king, does not die after mating, but lives with the queen. They do not go through complete metamorphosis, but grow up gradually through several nymphal stages.

Soldiers
Like ants, termites have soldiers. Termites cannot sting, but defend themselves in other ways. Some soldiers have large jaws that can cut through flesh; others squirt a poisonous sticky liquid from a special nozzle on their heads. Some nests have no soldiers – the termites defend themselves by vibrating their bodies against the side of their nest, making the sound of a hissing snake.

Pincers

Queen and king
A queen termite can reach more than 15 cm (6 in) in length. Her ovaries make her so large. She can lay up to 30,000 eggs a day. The king remains by the queen's side and mates with her several times to fertilize all the eggs.

Fungus
gardens are areas where fungi grow on termites' faeces and break down the cellulose within them. The termites feed on the products released and the fungi itself.

Queen

"Chimneys" allow warm air to rise and escape.

Solid outer walls are up to 50 cm (20 in) thick.

Living quarters

Soft inner walls

Food stores

Termites spread water on walls to cool the nest.

Air channel

Ground level

Nurseries

Royal chamber

Thick pillar supports nest.

Termite mounds
Each species of termite has its own type of nest. Some build towers more than 6 m (20 ft) tall, which help maintain the correct temperature and humidity of the nest at the base. Others build mushroom-shaped mounds – the domed top deflects the rain away from the nest below and has given these insects their name of umbrella termites. Many termites do not build nests above ground, but live below the soil or inside logs. Termites that live in trees build their nests on branches.

Workers
Worker termites build the nest, collect food, and feed the soldiers, king, and queen. The nest is made from saliva, soil, and their own faeces. Most workers feed on wood and have microscopic organisms in their guts to break down the wood into a more easily digested form.

WOOD ANT	
SCIENTIFIC NAME	*Formica rufa*
ORDER	Hymenoptera
FAMILY	Formicidae
DISTRIBUTION	Europe
HABITAT	Woods and forests
DIET	Omnivorous, feeding on seeds and invertebrates
SIZE	Workers 6–8 mm (0.24–0.31 in) in length; queen 10–13 mm (0.4–0.5 in) in length
LIFESPAN	Workers live for 3–4 months; the queen lives for about 15 years

FIND OUT MORE

ANIMAL BEHAVIOUR **ARTHROPODS** **INSECTS** **MONGOOSES AND CIVETS** **MUSHROOMS AND OTHER FUNGI** **NESTS AND BURROWS** **WOODLAND WILDLIFE**

ARCHAEOLOGY

HUMANKIND HAS ALWAYS been fascinated by the question of who we are, where we came from, and how we used to live. Archaeology is the study of our past, from early prehistory onward, using the material remains of our ancestors and the possessions they left behind. Over thousands of years, evidence of human activity, such as camp fires, rubbish tips, and dwellings, become buried. Archaeological teams discover these sites and uncover this evidence by careful excavation. The material is then conserved and studied in order to help the archaeologist piece together a picture of how people lived and died in the past.

Discovery

Iron Age fort, England

Archaeological sites are found during building work, through reading historical documents, geophysical surveys (the study of the soil's structure), and field walking (recording above-ground objects).

Aerial photography
Horizontal and vertical lines seen from the air often show medieval strip fields, ancient roads, walls, and ditches. Aerial photography done when the sun is low shows varying surface levels, moisture levels, and vegetation most clearly.

Excavation

Archaeological sites are excavated by layers. Workers remove the top, most recent layer and work down, uncovering older, deeper levels. The study of these layers and the items they contain is called stratigraphy.

Stratigraphy
By revealing features such as ditches, post holes, and floors, stratigraphy gives information about the history of a site, and the people who lived there. In urban areas, such as London, surface levels rise as debris is shovelled in to level the ground before rebuilding. Because it shows a chrono-logical sequence, stratigraphy was used to date sites before radiocarbon dating was invented.

Cross section through a dig, City of London

17th-century floor · *19th-century drain* · *16th-century chalk floor*

Brick-lined well, c.1800 · *14th-century chalk-lined cesspit* · *Roman tiled floor*

Tools

Pickaxe

Trowel · *Measuring tape*

Archaeologists use shovels and handpicks to remove the topsoil. Then smaller hand tools are used, such as dental picks, teaspoons, and trowels, to excavate delicate objects.

Finds
Archaeologists usually draw or photograph the artefacts (objects) to make a visual record. They carefully measure and record the shapes, colours, decorations, and ages of any artefacts or features. This helps archaeologists link and relate different objects and sites.

Investigation

Buried objects are fragile, and decay quickly after excavation. To stabilize them, they are cleaned and conserved. After conservation, an object can be studied. The material of which it is made, its function, and its date are recorded. It may then be photographed and displayed in a museum.

Salt water has caused corrosion

Pewter jug

Underwater archaeology
Sites beneath the sea or in lakes are more difficult to excavate than those on land because shifting silt or sand causes poor visibility. However, marine sites often preserve materials, such as the wood of the 16th-century ship, the *Mary Rose*, which would usually be lost on dry land. Conservation may involve treatment with water, sealing with chemicals, or careful drying.

A cradle hoisted the ship from the seabed.

To conserve the wood, chilled water is sprayed on the ship 20 hours a day.

The *Mary Rose* in dry dock

Timeline

1748 Pompeii discovered.

1799 An officer in Napoleon's army discovers the Rosetta Stone, which features 6th-century BC hieroglyphs.

1812 Abu Simbel discovered.

1822 Scholars decipher Egyptian hieroglyphs.

1861 Evans and Prestwich confirm the antiquity of humans, and humans' association with extinct animals.

1891 *Homo erectus* material found.

1922 Howard Carter discovers the tomb of Tutankhamun.

1931 Louis Leakey begins excavations at Olduvai Gorge.

1940 Archaeologists discover prehistoric Lascaux cave paintings.

1949 Radiocarbon dating is developed.

1974 Donald Johanson discovers "Lucy", an early hominid.

Australopithecus, an early human ancestor

Mortimer Wheeler

The greatest field archaeo-logist of the day, Wheeler (1890–1976) set up the Institute of Archaeology, London. He developed new excavation methods, and made archaeology popular through TV. In 1944, he became Director-General of Archaeology in India, and investigated the Indus Valley Civilization.

FIND OUT MORE · ASIA, HISTORY OF · BRONZE AGE · EUROPE, HISTORY OF · HUMAN EVOLUTION · PREHISTORIC PEOPLE · STONE AGE

Archaeological finds from the *Mary Rose*

Weapons

Swivel guns

Hailshot pieces

Closed hand

Lint held at this end

Wrought-iron breech chambers

Longbows made of yew

Linstock handle

Demi cannon, a cast bronze muzzle loader

Culverin, a cast bronze muzzle loader

Stone, iron, and lead shot, used for cannon

Wooden linstocks held the slow match (lint), which the crew used to light gunpowder in cannon.

Breech loader gun, made of wrought iron

Shipboard equipment

Wooden razor handles

Apothecary's balance

Deadeye

Personal sundial

Ceramic medicine jar

An angel, a 1545 gold coin

Bronze cooking pot, used for communal meals

Wooden tankard

Pewter spoon and plates were used at the captain's dinner table.

Clothing and personal

Inkpot, made of horn

Manicure set, made of bone

Wooden comb

Leather jerkin

Backgammon set

Yew and spruce inlay

Leather flask for storing wine or water

Leather book cover

ARCHITECTURE

FROM A TOWERING SKYSCRAPER to a functional factory, architecture is the art of planning a building. The word also refers to the different building styles seen throughout history. Looking at changes in architecture tells us about earlier societies: the materials that were available to their builders, the skills mastered by their engineers, and the social ideals that they wished to express in their public buildings.

Ornament
Early in the 20th century, many Western architects rejected all forms of building ornament. This is rare: most buildings from other periods and cultures use it extensively, and even a simple building will usually have some decoration to reflect the taste of its owner. The ancient Greeks, for instance, carved the tops, or capitals, of columns to dignify their most prestigious buildings. The distinct decorations were based on styles called orders.

Doric order

Ionic order

Corinthian order

Architectural features

The main structural and functional features of a building are the roof, arches and walls, doors, and windows. The architect combines the practical knowledge of how to construct these with a sense of how to combine shape, space, and light to suit the function of the building itself.

Groin

Vault

Groin vault, where two barrel vaults intersect

Main arch

Barrel vault

Round arch

Arch and vault
An arch is a curved or pointed structure that bridges a gap; it must carry the weight of the wall, floor, or roof above, and its structure allows it to support greater weight than a flat slab can. A vault is simply an arched ceiling.

Cross and orb

Lantern (turret with windows) provides light

Dome metalling, Church of the Sorbonne, Paris, France, 17th century

Eaves

Round-arched window

Dome on a circular base

Pitched roof, supporting frame

Main rafter (inclined beam)

Horizontal beams add strength to structure.

Dome
Domes – curved, solid roofs – were first built on palaces and religious buildings as striking symbols of the building's status. They are often difficult to build, and have been constructed in various shapes: the Dome of the Rock in Jerusalem is hemispherical; the "onion"-shaped dome is a popular feature of many Russian and Bavarian buildings.

Roof
All roofs are designed for the practical purpose of providing protection from the weather. The design and covering used will reflect the local climate: for instance, in a wet country a sloping (pitched) roof will let rain run off. Roofs can also be ingenious and beautiful, such as when crowning an ornate castle.

Classical Europe

Classical architecture is that of the ancient Greeks and Romans. Both built by laying stones on top of each other, or by resting beams on columns. The Romans also developed the arch, vault, dome, and the use of concrete to develop curved spaces.

Brunelleschi
Italian architect Filippo Brunelleschi (1377–1446) returned to the use of Classical features, rejecting the Gothic style. Architects all across Europe followed his example.

Symbolism
The Pantheon is a temple built to all the Roman gods. Light comes through an opening in its vast dome and moves around the interior, lighting the curved walls. It is as if even the Universe turns around the centre of the building, symbolizing the power of the Roman deities.

Gothic

This distinctive, ornate European style emerged in the 12th century, and was used mainly in cathedrals and churches. Features include pointed arches and windows, and elaborate stone tracery used to divide the openings in window arches.

Eight-sided spire, built using scaffolding and wooden cranes

Turret-like pinnacle

Building innovations
The pointed arch and flying buttress were innovations that allowed Gothic churches to soar higher than had been possible before. Pointed arches can support heavier, taller structures than round arches. The flying buttress is a stone rib which extends down and away from the walls, transferring weight to the ground, and giving extra support to a roof or walls.

Pointed arch

Flying buttress

Pointed arch filled with tracery

Pitched roof

Buttress

Use of concrete
Cheap and durable, this material allowed Roman architects to cover vast curved spaces, which were impossible to construct before.

Opening

Dome, 43 m (142 ft) across

Outer wall faced with brick

Corinthian column

Walls 6 m (21 ft) thick

Entrance porch, or portico

The Pantheon, Rome, Italy, completed c. AD 128

Old St. Paul's Cathedral, London, England, 1087–1666

Southeast Asia and the Middle East

The traditional architectural styles of Asia and the Middle East remained the same for centuries. Both were heavily influenced by religious belief: Buddhism and Hinduism in southern Asia, and Islam in the Middle East. The style of buildings was determined by climate, and the materials available to local builders. As early as the 7th century, wooden temples and monasteries were being built in China and Japan.

Pagoda in Burmese style, 9th–10th century

Gilded crown

Islamic decoration favours geometric patterns and calligraphy.

South and East Asia
Many of the distinctive features of this area's architecture originated in Buddhist India. An example is the multi-storeyed pagoda, a temple which seems to stretch towards Heaven. It was developed initially in Japan and China but was based on the spires found on early Indian temples. An important feature of many traditional Asian buildings is their imaginative roof forms.

Minaret

Islamic architecture
The most important buildings in Islamic countries are usually mosques and tombs. The mosque is the centre of a Muslim community, and provides space for group worship. It contains a prayer hall, often with a domed roof, and may also have a courtyard. A minaret, from which the faithful are called to prayer, is a typical feature.

Early American civilizations

The Aztecs, who ruled in what is now Mexico from the 14th to 16th centuries, built stone pyramids to their gods. The remains of five separate temples have been found at Tenochtitlan, built one on top of the other as new rulers erected bigger temples on the same site.

Shrine to Aztec god

Stone carving of snake's head

Outer stone covering

Remains of different temples

Baroque and Neoclassical

The Baroque style emerged in early 17th-century Europe. It introduced buildings with ornate decoration, complex shapes, and dramatic lighting. It was followed by the Neoclassical style, which revived the more restrained Classical traditions. This was partly as a reaction to Baroque excess.

Greek-style portico

Neoclassical church, France, 1764

The 19th and 20th centuries

The development of new, very strong materials made it possible to construct buildings which were often highly original in style and owed little to the past. Helped by better technology, architects turned to glass, steel, and concrete to express their vision of modern architecture.

Opera House, Sydney, Australia, 1973

Main hall

Ceramic tiles

Interlocked vaults
The dramatic profile of the Opera House dominates Sydney Harbour. The building's roof of interlocked vaults, made from reinforced concrete covered with gleaming tiles, resembles a ship in sail.

Skyscrapers
The invention of the lift during the 19th century made it practical to build skyscrapers, and the first appeared in Chicago, USA, in the 1880s. Today, most are constructed for large businesses: they convey perfectly an image of wealth, size, and strength.

Steel
Following the arrival of reinforced steel, very tall structures could be built for the first time. An internal steel skeleton supports the weight of a skyscraper, such as the 102 storeys of the Empire State Building.

Empire State Building, New York, USA, 1931

Very plain decoration

Limestone and granite facing

Proposed design

Architects
An architect designs a building and oversees its construction. Successful architects become very well-known. Until recently, architects drew large numbers of plans to instruct builders and engineers. Much of this work is now carried out on computer.

Le Corbusier
Le Corbusier was the name used by the Swiss-French Charles Édouard Jeanneret (1887–1965), the most influential 20th-century architect. Le Corbusier promoted the use of new materials and construction techniques. His imaginative buildings favoured plain, often severe, geometric forms.

Timeline

2650 BC The Step Pyramid in Egypt is designed.

c.300 BC Buddhist temple mounds appear in India.

AD 82 Colosseum built in Rome. Dozens of stone arches support the walls of this stone arena.

690–850 Early Islamic buildings are designed around courtyards.

1100–1500 Gothic churches built in Europe.

c.1420 Renaissance begins in Italy; architects return to the elegant, ordered values of Classical builders.

19th century Industrial Revolution: mass-produced materials transform construction.

1920s International Modernism begins, typified by glass-and-steel towers and flat-roofed, white houses.

1970s Postmodernism develops. It refers to past styles, in a humourous way. Strong colours are popular.

1990s Eco-friendly architecture reflects environmental concerns about energy-saving and recycling.

 FIND OUT MORE

BUILDING AND CONSTRUCTION   CHURCHES AND CATHEDRALS   CITIES   MOSQUES

Architecture
Gothic, Renaissance, and Baroque

Carved stone lantern

Magnificent Gothic cathedral

Two lions flank the entrance.

Notre Dame, Paris, France: built from 1163 to 1250.

Palacio de las Cadenas, Ubeda, Spain: built during the mid-16th century. The Classical facade shows the elegance of Renaissance buildings.

St. Paul's Cathedral, London, Britain: built in the Baroque style.

Carved stone figures

Ribbed dome designed by Michelangelo

Facade by Carlo Maderno (c.1556–1629)

135 spires crown the roof.

Capilla del Salvador, Ubeda, Spain: one of Spain's finest Renaissance churches, it was designed by three 16th-century architects.

St. Peter's, Rome, Italy, took over a century to build (1506–1614). It involved all the great architects of the Roman Renaissance and Baroque, including Michelangelo Buonarroti (1475–1564).

Milan Cathedral, Italy, is one of the largest Gothic churches in the world. Building began in the 14th century, but was not completed for 500 years.

Modern architecture

Windows give the effect of glass curtains.

Two towers, linked by means of a central atrium.

Framework

Arched sunburst, typical of 1920's style known as "Art Deco"

Designed in 1942, completed in 1960

Descending spiral gallery

Bauhaus Building, Dessau, Germany: built from steel and concrete in the International Modern Style (1925–26).

Guggenheim Museum, New York, USA: a stunning, innovative design by the great US architect Frank Lloyd Wright (1869–1959).

Steel and concrete structure

Century Tower, Tokyo, Japan, completed in 1991.

Palace of the Statues, Rome, Italy, completed during the 1950s.

Spire of the Chrysler Building, an office block in New York, USA (completed 1930).

Great Arch, Paris, France, completed in 1989, houses an exhibition gallery.

Seagram Building, New York, USA, completed in 1958.

ARCTIC OCEAN

ONE OF THE COLDEST places on Earth, the Arctic Ocean is surrounded by the northern parts of Europe, Asia, North America, and Greenland. These icy lands are rich in minerals and wildlife, but are home to few people. In summer, when temperatures reach 0°C (32°F), warm currents from the Pacific and Atlantic melt some of the ice. With the help of icebreakers to clear their path, ships are able to sail along the coasts of Asia and North America.

Physical features

The Arctic is the smallest and shallowest of the world's oceans. Most of its surface is covered by a frozen mass of floating ice about 2 m (6 ft) thick. The North Pole lies in the centre of the Arctic Ocean on drifting pack ice.

ARCTIC OCEAN FACTS

AREA 14,089,600 sq km (5,440,000 sq miles)

AVERAGE DEPTH 1,330 m (4,360 ft)

AVERAGE ICE THICKNESS 1.5–3 m (4.9–9.8 ft)

LOWEST TEMPERATURE -70°C (-94°F) on northeast tip of Greenland

Icebergs
Giant icebergs break off glaciers in Greenland and drift south into the North Atlantic Ocean. They rise up to 120 m (400 ft) above sea-level. As only a fraction of an iceberg shows above water, they are a shipping hazard.

Northern lights
On dark nights, spectacular coloured lights, or Aurora, can be seen in the sky. Caused by electricity in the upper atmosphere, they are brightest in mid winter when the sun never rises and invisible in summer due to 24-hour sun.

Arctic peoples
About 800,000 indigenous people live in the Arctic. The Yu'pik of Alaska are part of the Eskimo group that includes Inuit in Canada and Greenland and Yuit in Siberia. Many have given up nomadic life and now live in villages. The Arctic is the workplace of about 2,000,000 engineers and traders from the south.

Yu'pik family from Alaska

Greenland

Although Greenland is the world's largest island, its permanent ice cover means few people live there. The most populated area is the southwest coast, where the climate is less extreme than the bleak centre. The island is a self-governing territory of Denmark.

GREENLAND FACTS

CAPITAL CITY Nuuk (Godthaab)

AREA 2,175,600 sq km (840,000 sq miles)

POPULATION 56,000

MAIN LANGUAGES Danish, Greenlandic

MAJOR RELIGION Christian

CURRENCY Danish krone

Halibut

Haddock

Cod

Fishing
Cod, haddock, halibut, and shrimp fishing are the mainstay of Greenland's economy. Fish-processing factories freeze and can the fish for export to Europe and the USA. Much of the cod is made into fish fingers.

FIND OUT MORE   ATMOSPHERE   CLIMATE   FISHING INDUSTRY   GLACIATION   NATIVE AMERICANS   OCEANS AND SEAS   POLAR EXPLORATION   POLAR WILDLIFE   TUNDRA

ARGENTINA, CHILE, AND URUGUAY

THE SOUTHERN PART of South America is occupied by three countries: Argentina, Chile, and Uruguay. Lying between the Pacific and Atlantic Oceans, South America's southernmost point, Cape Horn, lies only about 1,000 km (600 miles) from the northern tip of Antarctica. Once part of the Spanish Empire, all three countries still show strong European influences. Their vast mineral resources have resulted in some prosperity, but all have agricultural economies and have suffered under a series of unstable governments.

Physical features

Dominating the west of the region, the Andes Mountains form a rugged frontier between Chile and Argentina. The hot, humid land of the Gran Chaco covers the northeast, turning to rolling grassland, known as pampas, in the centre. South of this and the arid plateau of Patagonia, lie the windy islands of Tierra del Fuego.

Andes
Forming a barrier between Chile and its eastern neighbours, Bolivia and Argentina, the vast Andes mountain chain stretches for about 8,000 km (5,000 miles). Nearly half of its mighty snow-capped peaks lie along Chile's long eastern border with Argentina, including Mount Aconcagua, an extinct volcano, which, at 6,960 m (22,835 ft), is the highest peak in South America.

Atacama Desert
The hot Atacama Desert is one of the world's driest places. It covers the northern 965 km (600 miles) of Chile's long coastal strip, and receives less than 13 mm (½ in) of rain in a year. By contrast, the Patagonian Desert, in the far south of Argentina, near Antarctica, is a vast, icy-cold expanse of windswept rocks.

Pampas
Also known as the Entre Rios, the natural grasslands of the pampas cover about 20 per cent of Argentina and extend north into Uruguay, where three-quarters of the land is rich pasture. Much of the vast pampas has hot summers, warm winters, plenty of rain, and deep, fertile soil, making the area ideal for growing crops and for raising cattle and sheep.

Mestizos
More than three-quarters of the people in this region descend from Europeans, most of whom moved from Spain or Italy in the 20th century. Many of the Europeans intermarried with Native Americans, giving rise to *mestizos*, people of mixed ancestry. Like their ancestors, most people are Roman Catholics and are close to their extended families. Many of them run successful businesses.

Man and child at an Easter festival

21°C (70°F)   9°C (48°F)

762 mm (30 in)

Regional climate
Chile's long, narrow shape gives it an extremely varied climate. Desert and mountains in the north give way to fertile valleys, with hot, dry summers and mild, moist winters. Argentina's southern Andean peaks and Patagonian glaciers have year-round snow; the north is hotter and wetter. Uruguay is mild and pleasant.

Argentina

After Brazil, Argentina is the second largest country in South America. It is separated from Uruguay by the Río de la Plata estuary, on which its capital, Buenos Aires, stands. Argentina is one of the wealthiest countries in South America, with fertile soils, a wealth of mineral resources, and a skilled work-force. However, years of political instability have left huge overseas debts, which caused the economy to collapse at the end of 2001.

Couple dancing the tango

People
More than 89 per cent of Argentina's people live in towns and cities and most enjoy a high standard of living. However, city slums, or *orillas*, illustrate the sharp contrast between the country's rich and poor. It was in the slums that the tango, the traditional dance of Buenos Aires, originated, in the late 1800s. Many tangos contain lyrics that express the frustrations of the immigrants who came from Spain, Italy, Austria, France, Germany, and Britain. The tango is now famous worldwide.

14 per sq km
(35 per sq mile)

89% Urban

11% Rural

ARGENTINA FACTS

CAPITAL CITY Buenos Aires

AREA 2,736,690 sq km
(1,056,636 sq miles)

POPULATION 37,000,000

MAIN LANGUAGE Spanish

MAJOR RELIGION Christian

CURRENCY Argentinian peso

LIFE EXPECTANCY 73 years

PEOPLE PER DOCTOR 370

GOVERNMENT Multi-party democracy

ADULT LITERACY 97%

Buenos Aires
Situated on the South Atlantic coast, Argentina's capital has been an important trade port since it was founded by the Spanish in 1536. Buenos Aires is a wealthy, sophisticated city, with expensive shops, fine avenues, and modern buildings, as well as a spectacular old cathedral. The city is the centre of government, industry, and culture. Almost 40 per cent of Argentinians, numbering about 14,000,000, live in the metropolitan capital, referring to it as "Baires".

Government buildings

Clarin is Argentina's best-selling newspaper.

Food
High-quality beef, which is produced throughout Argentina, is used as a base for many local dishes, such as *empanadas*, or savoury mince pastries. Every restaurant has a barbeque grill, or *parillada*. As a cheaper alternative to meat, many people eat small potato dumplings called *noquis*, which were introduced by Italian immigrants.

Noquis

Newspapers
More than 180 daily newspapers are published every day in Argentina. Most are in Spanish, but English, French, and German papers are widely available. In the past, dictatorships have imposed censorship on the media, and today's government withdraws advertising from those who do not support its policies.

Schooling
Literacy is high in Argentina, and free-state primary and secondary education is provided. Schooling is compulsory for all children between the ages of six and 14, and more than one-third of all students go on to one of Argentina's 45 universities. Buenos Aires has the largest university in South America, with 140,000 students.

These women work in a fish-packing plant and must wear hats for hygiene.

The Falkland Islands lie 480 km (300 miles) east of Argentina.

Farming
Agriculture accounts for about 60 per cent of Argentina's export earnings. The country is a major producer of wheat, barley, and maize, which flourish on the pampas, and is the world's third largest producer of soya beans. Fruit, especially oranges, grows well in the warm climate, and grapes are produced for wine-making.

Harvesting barley on the fertile pampas

Bolas rope used to slow down cattle

Gauchos
Tough, independent gauchos, or cowhands, have roamed the pampas on horseback for more than 300 years, tending cattle and horses. Modern gauchos work mainly on huge *estancias*, or ranches, owned by wealthy landlords, where they rear animals and mend fences. Gauchos are experts in handling herds and are the national heroes of Argentina.

Woollen poncho, or cloak, for warmth at night

Strong boots have heels to fit into stirrups.

Industry
About 30 per cent of the labour force works in industry. Textiles, food production, and chemical products dominate business. The country is self-sufficient in oil and gas, and rich in minerals.

Falkland Islands
Britain and Argentina have fought over ownership of the Falkland Islands, or Islas Malvinas, since the British claimed the islands from the Spanish in 1833. In 1982, an Argentine invasion of the islands was overthrown, and the British continue to hold them.

Chile

A long and extremely narrow country, Chile measures, at most, only about 430 km (267 miles) wide. Most Chileans live in cities and towns in the Central Valley, between the low coastal mountains to the west and the towering Andes on the east. The cold, stormy southern coast is flanked by thousands of islands, whose waters provide rich fishing grounds. Chile has a strong economy rooted in its natural resources: minerals, fruit, sea products, and timber.

Santiago

Located in the heart of Chile, the capital, Santiago, is a bustling, modern city. The city and suburbs house about five million people. Santiago is known for severe traffic congestion, and has one of the highest taxi densities in the world, with one per 100 inhabitants. About 3,600 km (2,236 miles) of Pan-American Highway runs through Santiago, but high smog levels over the city concern environmentalists.

Some of Santiago's 14,500 buses on Avenue Campama

Mapuche

Descended from the original inhabitants of South America, the Mapuche people are also known as the Araucanians. About 675,000 Mapuche live in the central and southern regions of Chile. They follow the Roman Catholic religion and speak their own language, as well as Spanish. The Mapuche people have fought for independence since the 16th century and are still at odds with the Chilean government. Quechua and Aymara Indians also live in the country, in the north.

20 per sq km
(53 per sq mile)

84% Urban   16% Rural

The Chuquicamata copper mine, 670 m (2,200 ft) deep

Copper

Chile leads the world in the production of copper ore, of which it owns about 20 per cent of known reserves. The Central Valley, which extends for 1,600 km (994 miles), has the world's largest underground copper mine, located at El Teniente. Chuquicamata, in the bleak Atacama Desert, is one of the largest open-cast copper mines in the world. The country also mines iron, gold, and silver.

Wine

Vineyards first planted by Spanish colonists in the 1500s have benefited from the hot, dry summers in the Central Valley. Today, about 320,000 tonnes (350,000 tons) of Chilean wines, red from Cabernet Sauvignon grapes and white from Chardonnay grapes, are exported all over the world.

Cabernet Sauvignon grapes and wine

Crabs are put into small baskets.

Fishing

Although less than one per cent of the people work in the fishing industry, Chile leads the world in fishmeal production. In a good year, around 6,000 tonnes of sardines, anchovetas, mackerel, and salmon are caught and processed. Punta Arenas, on the Strait of Magellan in the south, is the industry's centre.

CHILE FACTS

CAPTIAL CITY	Santiago
AREA	748,800 sq km (289,112 sq miles)
POPULATION	15,200,000
MAIN LANGUAGE	Spanish
MAJOR RELIGION	Christian
CURRENCY	Chilean peso
LIFE EXPECTANCY	75 years
PEOPLE PER DOCTOR	909
GOVERNMENT	Multi-party democracy
ADULT LITERACY	96%

Uruguay

One of the smallest countries in South America, Uruguay is also one of the most prosperous and harmonious. More than 40 per cent of its people, about 1,449,900, live in Montevideo, the capital, chief port, and largest city. The rest are scattered over the vast lowland pastures. Uruguay has a high tourist rate, mainly because of its sandy beaches and fine weather.

People

There are 11 times as many sheep, cattle, and horses as people in Uruguay. Most Uruguayans are of Spanish or Italian descent. They enjoy considerable prosperity, largely due to the wealth from earlier cattle ranching in the country.

Hydroelectricity

More than 90 per cent of Uruguay's power is generated through hydroelectricity. The main hydroelectric plants are situated on the country's major rivers, the Uruguay and its tributary, the Río Negro, which both widen out into the Río de la Plata estuary. Huge turbines have been built across the rivers, so that as the water rushes through, it turns the turbines and makes electricity.

URUGUAY FACTS

CAPITAL CITY	Montevideo
AREA	174,810 sq km (67,494 sq miles)
POPULATION	3,300,000
MAIN LANGUAGE	Spanish
MAJOR RELIGION	Christian
CURRENCY	Uruguayan peso

Wool

Three-quarters of Uruguay is rich, green pasture that provides excellent grazing land for its 25,000,000 sheep and 10,000,000 cattle. The land provides work for nearly half the population. Uruguay is the world's second biggest producer of wool, and textiles made from wool account for about 20 per cent of Uruguayan exports.

Hand-made scarf

FIND OUT MORE   CHRISTIANITY   DANCE   DESERTS   ENERGY   FARMING   GRASSLAND WILDLIFE   NATIVE AMERICANS   SOUTH AMERICA, HISTORY OF   TEXTILES AND WEAVING

ARMIES

FROM ANCIENT TIMES to the present day, the role of an army has always remained the same – to attack enemy territory and defend the country from attack. Armies usually work in close partnership with air and naval forces. Throughout history, foot soldiers called infantry have done most of the fighting, supported by troops on horseback called cavalry. Today, cavalry have been replaced on the battlefield by armoured tank units.

Ancient Greece
Each Greek city-state had its own army. Greek soldiers were so well regarded that other countries hired them to fight on their behalf.

History of armies
The world's first armies, raised in Assyria, Egypt, China, and India, were ill-trained, undisciplined civilians forced to fight for their leaders. The ancient Greeks introduced compulsory military service and rigorous training for their civilian army. Later, the Romans established the first professional (paid) army to protect its empire.

Modern army
Combat troops fighting in the front line need plenty of support. Engineers, for example, repair damaged roads and bridges to help troops cross rough terrain. Other support staff includes doctors and nurses to treat wounded soldiers, caterers to feed the army, and communications experts.

British SAS personal equipment

Gas mask
Knife sheath
Leather glove
Body armour
Grenade pocket
Waist-belt loop
Magazine pouch
Thigh strap
Leather boots
Reinforced toecap

Balaclava
Steel fire lighter
Wire saw
Fire-kindling tin
Miniature harpoons

SAS survival kit

Recruitment
In some countries, the army is made up entirely of volunteer recruits who willingly join the army for a fixed period of time. In other countries, the army is made up largely of conscripts – that is, young people required by law to spend a number of years in the army.

British Army recruitment poster

Training
Modern weapons use advanced technology, so troops need to be not just physically fit but also able to make split-second decisions and operate highly complex computerized equipment. For this reason, technical instruction is just as important a part of a soldier's training as exercise and parade-ground drill.

Specialist units
Most armies have units of troops trained to carry out specialist tasks, such as reconnaissance missions and sabotage raids behind enemy lines, tackling terrorists, and rescuing hostages. These units include the US Army's Green Berets and the British Special Air Service (SAS).

British officer's shoulder strap   **Italian officer's cap badge**

Officers
An army needs a strong chain of command, from the highest to the lowest ranks, so that orders are passed on quickly and clearly. Officers receive training in leading and inspiring their troops. Officers' ranks are shown by special symbols on their uniforms.

Terrorist armies
Sometimes, armies are set up by groups of people struggling to overthrow the existing government or achieve independence for their country or region. Their supporters call them freedom fighters, but those who oppose them call them terrorists. Such groups often stage spectacular bomb attacks to gain publicity for their cause.

Terrorist bomb damage

Non-combat roles
When a nation is at peace, its army still has a vital role to play. For example, when natural disasters occur – such as earthquakes, floods, or famines – an army can bring in medical supplies and food, and restore communications links and electricity and water supplies. Armies can also help to establish peace in other war-torn countries.

Peacekeeping
To separate warring sides in a civil war or to keep the peace once a ceasefire has been negotiated, the United Nations (UN) often sends multinational forces consisting of troops from many different armies.

Crisis response
Armies need to react quickly and efficiently in times of crisis. Huge cargo aircraft carry supplies, trucks, and even small tanks to the crisis area, while passenger planes take troops and other personnel.

ARMS AND ARMOUR

WARRIORS OF THE PAST attacked with slashing swords, sharp spears, flying arrows, deadly axes, and crushing clubs. All of these arms, or weapons, could kill, so fighters protected themselves with armour: tough coverings of wood, leather, or metal. The invention of firearms in the 14th century made armour useless, because metal plates thick enough to deflect bullets were too heavy to wear. By the 16th century, arms and armour were strictly for show. Modern soldiers may still wear shiny breastplates and carry swords or spears on parade, but they swap them for guns and bullet-proof vests on the battlefield.

Arms

The simplest arms – clubs – are extensions of a fighter's fist, delivering a knock-out punch from a greater distance. Most hand arms, however, aim to wound by cutting the body. Swords, daggers, and lances do this for hand-to-hand fighting; arrows and boomerangs do it from afar, killing or injuring foes that may be almost out of sight.

Armour

A suit of armour had to protect against weapons, yet it also had to be comfortable enough to wear all day. Different cultures used various materials, such as leather or metal, to achieve these aims.

Horns
Iron mask

Samurai, 1300s

Pauldron and besagew protect shoulder and armpit.

Bevor protects lower face.

Japanese samurai
Samurai armour was made of many small metal or leather scales laced together with coloured silks. Armour became more decorative when firearms removed its protective value.

A mace was effective against plate armour.

Benin warrior
Soldiers of this great 15th-century African empire wore heavily quilted garments as armour. Light bamboo shields were easy to carry and protected warriors from glancing blows from iron-tipped spears or javelins.

Benin bronze plaque

European knight
Knights wore chain mail (linked metal rings) to protect them. In the 14th century, armourers introduced metal plates (plate armour) for extra protection.

European knight, 1300s

Four circular bosses covered the handle attachment.

Defensive weapons
Shields are used for defence. Prehistoric hunters may have invented them as camouflage when hunting. Later fighters strapped shields to their left arms to fend off sword cuts. Wood and leather shields were light, and strong enough to deflect all but a direct sword thrust.

Indian shield

Boomerang

Parrying shield

Crescent-shaped blade

Tiger heads studded with gems.

Tabars, Indian steel axes

Mughal dagger

Full armour for a horse weighed 34 kg (75 lbs).

Tassles on headpiece protected the horse's face from flies.

Charm made of copper bells.

Spike

Gilt

Italian horse armour, 1570

Leather saddle

Animal armour
African horse armour, such a that of the Fulani people of West Africa, was quilted cotton stuffed with kapok. During battle, horses also wore chain mail across the flanks and around the head. In Europe, metal horse armour was expensive, and knights often armoured only their horses' heads.

Fulani horse armour

Sheath

Attacking weapons
Over the centuries, warriors have used various weapons for different kinds of fighting. Sabres (curved swords) delivered the deadliest cuts, but straight swords were better for thrusting strokes. Clubs and axes had to be heavy and sharp, yet short enough to swing easily. Small, easily hidden daggers were often used for secret assassinations.

Aboriginal weapons

Club

Shamshir, a classic Indian sabre

Modern armour
Artificial fabric, such as nylon, provides soldiers and police officers with more protection than thick metal armour. Bullet-proof vests are made of 16 or more layers of nylon. A bullet flattens when it hits the outer layer; lower layers slow it down so that the wearer is bruised, rather than killed or seriously injured.

Riot police

Arms and Armour

Helmets

Bird feathers

African ceremonial and battle helmet

Embossed designs

Visor to protect face

Close helmet, for use in tournaments, France, 1575

Celtic Bronze helmet, Britain, 1st century AD

Rivets

Comb protects head from sword blade.

Burgonet, an open-faced blackened-steel helmet, 1590

Vents

Italian close helmet, with air vents, 16th century,

Plates lock together.

Morion, the helmet of the Knights of Malta

Italian close helmet, for use in tournaments, 1570

Cheek plates open outwards.

German armet, a helmet with cheek plates, 1535

Gilded close helmet, for use in tournaments, 1555

Decoration imitates ancient Rome.

German burgonet, for use in parades, 1520

Corinthian-type Greek helmet, 7th century BC

Breastplates

Studs for shoulder strap

Steel breastplate "blackened" to withstand rust.

Mail shoulder straps with metal clasps

Cuirass, or breastplate, from the Napoleonic Wars

Lance rest for tilting

Straps for attaching metal skirt

Italian breastplate, made to imitate the doublet, 1570

Indian cuirass, or *char ania* ("four mirrors")

African breastplate, for Fulani cavalryman

Breastplate, specially made for a wealthy boy

Gorget, or neck defence

Skirt

Tassets

Italian cuirass, with skirt and tassets to protect abdomen and thighs

Gauntlets, greaves, and sabatons

Silk overlaid with chain mail

Samurai armoured sleeves, or *kote*, were laced over the arm.

Thumb plate

Gauntlet, with hinged thumb plate, Germany 1515

Indian arm guard, with an extension to protect the hand

Greaves

Sabaton

Left hand carried mace

Gauntlets were riveted on to leather gloves, Italy, late 1300s

Steel mace, c.1520

Pointed cuff

Gothic gauntlet, 15th-century Germany

Articulated (jointed) plates

Italian gauntlets, to protect the hands

German gauntlet, with jointed steel plates attached to a single plate

Greaves and sabatons, for protecting the legs and feet

Manifer, made to fit over the left gauntlet

Sabaton, or foot armour, jointed for maximum movement, c.1550

A

ART, HISTORY OF

FROM THE EARLIEST TIMES, people all over the world have expressed their thoughts and feelings by making art. Over the centuries, styles in the visual arts (sculpture, painting, and drawing) have changed. These differences reflect the changing beliefs and traditions people held as their societies developed. Materials have changed as well, allowing artists to try new ways of reflecting the world around them.

Early art

The earliest works of art usually seem to have had a religious or magical purpose: to represent a god, for example, or to bring a hunter luck as he stalked animals.

Sumerian sculpture
A rich artistic tradition grew up in ancient Sumer (now southern Iraq) during the 3rd millennium BC. This statue, which shows a Sumerian ruler, is carved from hard stone. It represents the strength and dignity of a good leader.

Caves at Lascaux
These extraordinary pictures of wild animals were painted in French caves more than 17,000 years ago. The outlines were painted by hand, and the vivid colours were filled in by spraying pigment through tubes of bone.

Classical art

Western European art stems directly from the traditions of the ancient Mediterranean world, and especially the art of ancient Greece and Rome. In particular, sculpture from these civilizations is remarkably lifelike, or naturalistic, and concentrates on the human figure.

Fresco from Pompeii

Roman wall painting
Most ancient paintings have not survived. This one was preserved by volcanic ash at Pompeii. It shows figures from Roman mythology, and was painted on a wall to decorate the interior of a Roman house.

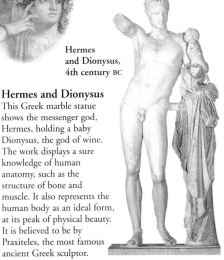

Hermes and Dionysus, 4th century BC

Hermes and Dionysus
This Greek marble statue shows the messenger god, Hermes, holding a baby Dionysus, the god of wine. The work displays a sure knowledge of human anatomy, such as the structure of bone and muscle. It also represents the human body as an ideal form, at its peak of physical beauty. It is believed to be by Praxiteles, the most famous ancient Greek sculptor.

Masaccio, *The Holy Trinity*, 1428

Perspective
The Italian Tomaso Masaccio (1401–28) was the first painter to use perspective since Classical times. Perspective creates the illusion that depth exists behind the flat surface of a painting.

Renaissance

After the fall of the Roman Empire, Classical art was considered too pagan for the Christian civilizations which began to develop in Europe. By the 15th century, painters, sculptors, and architects began to revive a classical tradition in the arts, creating highly lifelike Christian works of art. This revival is called the Renaissance, from the French for "rebirth". It began in Italy and spread through Europe. Influential artists included Michelangelo (1475–1564).

Painted vault gives sense of space.

Skeleton, a symbol of mortality

Non-religious art
During the Renaissance, European painters broke with earlier tradition. Religious subject matter, such as scenes from the Bible, was still important, but artists also began to record everyday events.

Jan Van Eyck, *The Arnolfini Marriage*, 1434

Early paint making

The materials used to produce a painting affect the way it looks. Before oil paints arrived in the 15th century, artists worked straight onto wet plaster with tempera, a mixture of egg and paint pigment. Oil paints, which were more flexible and gave a more realistic finish, soon became the favourite medium.

Mineral, ground into pigment

Egg tempera
Egg (either the yolk or both yolk and white) provides a strong medium for colours, but is sticky and quick-drying, so difficult to apply.

Egg yolk

Oil paint
As a medium, oil has the advantage of being slow to dry, allowing artists to make changes while they work.

Oil for binding paint pigment

Value of colour
Certain colours, such as gold, have always been more expensive than others. Until the 17th century, dark blue was the most costly because it was made from lapis lazuli, a semi-precious stone.

Lapis lazuli

Scales weigh pigment

A

Baroque art

The term "Baroque" describes a style of 17th-century European art. Rome, the centre of the Catholic church, was its birthplace. During the 16th century, the Christian church split into Roman Catholic and Protestant factions. By the 17th century, the Catholic church was using art to spread its teachings. To appeal to the viewer, it promoted a style of art that was theatrical and emotional. Painters were encouraged to use light and shade for dramatic contrasts, sculptors to show figures in dynamic poses. To achieve these effects, artists had to develop great technical skills.

Dramatic facial expression

Arrow is a symbol of God's love.

Bernini, *The ecstasy of St. Teresa*, 1652

Bernini
The Italian painter, sculptor, and architect Gianlorenzo Bernini (1598–1680) was an outstanding influence on Baroque art. He had an exceptional ability to convey great emotion and drama in stone, designed to inspire those who saw his work to greater faith. This sculpture depicts the vision of St. Teresa, in which an angel pierced her with an arrow.

Caravaggio, *The Calling of St. Matthew*, c.1598–99

Light and shade
The Italian painter Michelangelo Caravaggio (1573–1610) shows the moment when Christ calls Matthew to become a disciple. A ray of light illuminates Matthew, but Christ is hidden by shadow.

Friedrich, *Wanderer among the Mists*, 1818

The lonely universe
The German artist Caspar David Friedrich (1774–1840) was spiritually inspired by natural landscapes. There is an intense mysticism to this painting, as a solitary figure contemplates the mighty Alps.

Romanticism

The early 19th century in Europe is known as the Romantic Age. It was, in part, a reaction to 18th-century art, which had emphasized balance and order. Romantic artists questioned the place of human beings in the Universe. They stressed the importance of human emotion and the imagination, and celebrated the wild power of nature in dramatic landscape paintings.

A powerful landscape, shrouded in mist, conveys the strength and mystery of nature.

Change in the 19th century

From the mid-19th century, artists broke with the tradition established by earlier generations. Where they were once told what to depict by patrons, who paid them, they now produced what they wanted, and then tried to sell their work.

Camille Pissarro, *Place du Théâtre Français*, 1898

Selection of colours from Renoir's palette

Lead white *Vermilion* *Emerald green* *Naples yellow* *Cobalt blue*

Impressionism
This school of painting grew up in France in the late 19th century. Artists such as Camille Pissarro (1830–1903), Claude Monet (1840–1926), and Auguste Renoir (1841–1919) painted their impressions of a brief moment in time, in particular, the changing effects of sunlight. They were criticized at first, for viewers expected paintings to look more detailed, but have been very influential.

20th-century art

During the 20th century, artists explored new theories about the world, religion, and the mind. They asked the public to confront things that they might wish to ignore, and explored many different styles. After nearly 2,500 years, the grip of Classical art seemed to have been broken.

Surrealism
During the 1920s, the fantastical art made by the Surrealists explored theories about the way the brain works. New ideas had suggested that people consciously only used a tiny part of their brains, and that they were unaware of subconscious activity, over which they had no rational control. The bizarre, dreamlike paintings of Surrealists, such as the Spanish artist Salvador Dali (1904–89), were inspired by these ideas.

Salvador Dali

Modern art
Much modern art is specially created to be seen in a museum or gallery, and not for houses, palaces, or churches as in the past. It often prefers to baffle, tease, and provoke its audience, rather than make its meaning obvious.

Abstract art
Abstract artists do not represent objects from the everyday world. Colour and shape alone suggest ideas or emotions. In this way, abstract art is like music: neither describe anything that can be defined in words, but both can be expressive and moving. The artists Jackson Pollock (1912–56) and Mark Rothko (1903–70) are two of the most famous abstract painters.

Jackson Pollock, *The Moon, Woman cuts the circle*, 1943

Yoki Terauchi, *Air Castle*, 1994

Ambroise Vollard

The French art dealer Ambroise Vollard (1865–1939) made a living buying, selling, and exhibiting modern art. He gave early 20th-century artists unprecedented financial and creative freedom to paint as they wished. Artists such as Paul Cezanne and Henri Matisse achieved success in Vollard's gallery in Paris in the 1900s.

Art in Africa

African art has a long tradition, although a lack of written records make its history hard to trace. Sculpture and masks are major art forms. Most art seems to have been made for religious or ritual purposes. Wood-carving and bronze-casting techniques were highly developed.

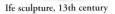

Sculpture
The rich tradition of sculpture in West Africa begins with the pottery figures made by the Nok people from 500 BC. Around the 13th century AD the Ife of Nigeria began to cast outstanding bronze heads and figures in a highly realistic style. These may have influenced sculptures made in Benin, Nigeria, from the 16th to 19th centuries.

Ife sculpture, 13th century

Masks
African masks may represent a spirit or ancestor, or be purely decorative. Their meaning comes from the masquerade (dance, drama, and music) of which they are a part. Wood, beads, ivory, and shells are important materials. This capped mask, carved in a bold, vital style, is from Cameroon.

Wooden mask, 20th century

Asia

Traditionally in Asian art, the symbolic meaning behind the subject of a painting, sculpture, or carving is more important than the illusion of realism. In China, for instance, landscape paintings are stylized to express the ideals of religious thought: natural harmony, peace, and grace. In China and Japan, calligraphy was seen as a high form of art. The inscriptions are usually of short, poetic situations.

T'ang Yin, *Dreaming of Immortality in a Thatched Cottage*, Ming dynasty

Chinese landscape
In China, the art of painting developed from calligraphy. Landscape artists painted on paper or silk, using brush and ink. They did not paint from real life. The flow and vigour of the brush strokes were more important.

16th-century Mughal manuscript

Vividly coloured

High level of detail

Brief poetic description of the scene

Miniatures
During the Mughal Empire (16th–17th centuries), figurative miniature painting flourished in India. These were richly coloured and exceptionally delicate. This illustration comes from a contemporary chronicle of the emperor's exploits.

Hokusai
Katsushika Hokusai (1760–1849) is perhaps the best-known Japanese printmaker. His famous wood-cuts include landscapes as well as scenes of daily life (called ukiyo-e). They are dramatically coloured and composed.

***The Great Wave of Kawagawa*, 1831**

Native American art

Sophisticated Native American societies, such as the Aztec and Maya in Mexico and the Inca in Peru, created distinct artistic and architectural styles. Nearly 3,000 years ago, nomadic peoples in North and South America marked awe-inspiring "sculptures" on to the land, or created vast earthworks whose shapes can only be seen from high in the air.

Tlingit totem pole

Totem poles
Complex in design, and carved with great skill, totem poles showed the status of many Native North American chiefs.

Sand paintings
In the Southwest, Native North Americans trickled coloured sand and ground stones on to a smooth background to create temporary symbolic paintings with a ritual importance.

Navajo sand painting represents figures from Navajo mythology.

Easter Island statues
Between AD 400 and 1680, the people of Easter Island carved huge heads, up to 12 m (40 ft) high, from volcanic rock. They commemorate the divine ancestors of tribal chiefs.

Pacific art

Contact with European Christian cultures from the 18th century onwards had a destructive effect on ancient local lifestyles in the Pacific islands. Much art has been lost, although some remarkable sculptures have survived, due to their durability. Wood and stone carvings, bark cloth paintings, spirit masks, and intricate body tattoos are among the important art forms of the Pacific area.

Statues face out to sea.

Statues, Easter Island

Timeline

30,000 BC Earliest known works of art produced.

30,000–10,000 BC Cave paintings made in France.

c.500 BC Lifelike human figurines produced by the Nok in West Africa.

100 BC–AD 300s Roman empire spreads Classical art around Europe.

Warrior, Greece, 520 BC

618–907 T'ang dynasty, China: great tradition of landscape painting develops.

15th century Beginning of the Renaissance in Europe.

16th century Mughal dynasty holds power in India.

17th century Dutch Golden Age of painting.

19th century Photography invented.

1860s–90s Impressionism develops in France. It is very influential.

Metal tubes are invented in the 1840s.

19th-century oil paints

20th century Time of incredible diversity of styles in the visual arts, including Cubism (1907–1920s), abstract art (1910–50), surrealism (1920s), and Pop Art (mid-1950s).

FIND OUT MORE AFRICA, HISTORY OF   ARCHITECTURE   MONET   NATIVE AMERICANS   PAINTING AND DRAWING   PHOTOGRAPHY   PICASSO   RENAISSANCE   SCULPTURE

ARTHROPODS

MORE THAN ONE MILLION species of arthropod exist, making them the largest group in the animal kingdom. They live in almost all habitats, from mountain tops to the ocean depths. Arthropods are invertebrates – animals without backbones. They come in many shapes and sizes, from tiny mites to large crabs. Their bodies are divided into segments, and they have distinct heads with antennae or eyes. Rigid exoskeletons encase their bodies, but flexible leg joints allow them to move around, and give them their name.

Types of arthropod

Arthropods vary in size, from minute creatures a fraction of a millimetre long to outsized sea dwellers several kilograms in weight. There are four main types of arthropod – insects, arachnids, crustaceans, and myriapods. Insects are the largest group, accounting for almost 90 per cent of all arthropods.

Spiders have 8 legs.

Arachnids
Red-kneed tarantula
Arachnids include spiders, scorpions, and mites. They have eight legs; scorpions use the front pair as claws. Spiders and scorpions are carnivores that live mainly on land. Spiders often kill their prey with poisonous fangs; scorpions use their venom-filled sting.

Delicate wings

Large compound eye helps it to catch prey in flight.

Broad-bodied chaser dragonfly

Insects
Insects are the most diverse group of arthropods. They live in all kinds of land and freshwater habitats. All adult insects have six legs, and most have wings – they are the only arthropods that can fly.

Asian giant millipede
Antenna
Two pairs of legs on each body segment

Myriapods
Myriapods include millipedes and centipedes. They have more legs than other arthropods – as many as 200 in some species. Their bodies are long and tubular. They live in the soil or among leaf debris.

European lobster

Hard exoskeleton

Crustaceans
Crustaceans include crabs, shrimps, and lobsters. Most live in the sea or in freshwater and have five pairs of legs. Lobsters and crabs have very thick exoskeletons and some grow extremely large.

Exoskeletons are made mainly of the substance chitin.

Exoskeleton of a fiddler crab

Exoskeleton

The exoskeleton of an arthropod is a tough outer layer covering the entire body, including the eyes, antennae, and legs. It protects and supports the muscles and soft organs within the body and helps to retain moisture.

Moulting and growth
Exoskeletons are fixed in size. In order to grow, an arthropod must shed, or moult, this rigid layer. Its body then rapidly expands before a new exoskeleton hardens in place of the old one. Moulting is part of a process called "incomplete metamorphosis". This is where the young, called nymphs, emerge from eggs looking like tiny adults. They moult many times before reaching adult size. In "complete metamorphosis", the animal changes form as well as size.

Moulting

1 An emerging adult grasshopper has cracked open its old exoskeleton and is starting to wriggle its body free, headfirst. Before this final moult, the nymph will already have been through four previous moults.

Nymph on twig

Adult is almost free of the nymph's skin.

2 The adult has pulled its legs and most of its body out of the old skin. It is already expanding in size, now that it is free from its confines.

Old, empty exoskeleton

Adult waits as blood pumps into its wings before it flies away.

3 Moulting is now complete. The adult rests while its new exoskeleton hardens and its wings unfurl. Its old exoskeleton, now empty and brittle, still clings to the twig.

Reproduction
Breeding habits are very diverse among arthropods. Fertilization may take place inside or outside the female's body. Normally, eggs are laid; some are guarded, others are hidden and left alone. The young of some arthropods, such as garden spiders, are tiny versions of adults called nymphs; others start life as larvae and look different from the adults.

Cluster of young garden spiders

Feeding

Arthropods feed on all kinds of plant and animal matter, both living and dead. Some arthropods, such as praying mantises, have pincers to gather food; others use their front legs. Many have cutting and chewing mouthparts, while those that feed on fluids, such as true bugs, have mouths modified for sucking. Small aquatic arthropods eat by filtering food particles from water.

Herbivores
Some arthropods, such as chafer beetles, eat only plant matter. Adults feed on stems, leaves, and buds, while larvae eat plant roots.

Field chafer beetle

Carnivores
Many arthropods feed on other animals. Garden spiders, for example, feed mainly on insects. Some meat eaters also eat dead animals and are called scavengers. Sand crabs scavenge on dead birds and other debris found on the beach and seabed.

Web spun around wasp

Garden spider feeding on a wasp

Defence

As arthropods are generally small in size, they are the target for a great many predators. Their hard exoskeleton, which acts as a tiny suit of armour, provides the first line of defence. Some arthropods, such as pill millipedes, take a passive form of defence and roll up into a ball if danger threatens. Other arthropods have special protective weapons; including stings and pincers. Many ant species have glands on their abdomens from which they secrete formic acid to drive off enemies.

Stings and pincers
Some arthropods have pincers and stings which they use to defend themselves against attackers. Scorpions also use their large pincers to catch animals. They then use their venom-filled stings to paralyze their prey.

Sting

Eyes

Fat-tailed scorpion

| **FIND OUT MORE** | ANTS AND TERMITES | BEETLES | CAVE WILDLIFE | CRABS AND OTHER CRUSTACEANS | FLIES | GRASSHOPPERS AND CRICKETS | INSECTS | POISONOUS ANIMALS | SPIDERS AND SCORPIONS |

ASIA

STRETCHING from the frozen Arctic to the equator, Asia is the world's largest continent. It is also a continent of extremes, containing the world's highest point, Mount Everest, as well as its lowest, the Dead Sea. China has the world's greatest population, while Asia's largest country, the Russian Federation, extends into Europe. Asia is separated from North America by the Bering Sea, and from Europe by the Caspian Sea, Turkey, and the Ural Mountains. In the southeast, it breaks into a mass of tiny islands.

Physical features

Much of Southwest and Central Asia is covered with barren desert, such as the Gobi and Syrian deserts. The Himalayan Mountains separate the bleak north from the fierce heat of the Indian subcontinent and the tropical rainforests of Southeast Asia. Asia has many great rivers, including the Huang He, Mekong, and Indus, flanked by fertile plains and valleys.

Lake Baikal
Siberia, the northern region of Asia, has the oldest, deepest, and eighth largest lake in the world. Lake Baikal, which contains more than 20 per cent of the world's unfrozen fresh water, reaches a depth of 1,637 m (5,371 ft). It covers a total area of 31,468 sq km (12,150 sq miles).

A

Himalayas
The snow-capped Himalayan Mountains, the highest range in the world, form a massive natural barrier between the Indian subcontinent and northern Asia. They were pushed up millions of years ago when the Indian plate collided with the Eurasian plate.

Island countries
Two Southeast Asian nations, Indonesia and the Philippines, have more than 20,000 islands between them. Most were formed by volcanic activity in the ocean, and the region has active volcanoes. Southeast Asia is prone to earthquakes.

ASIA FACTS

AREA	44,680, 718 sq km (17,251,315 sq miles)
POPULATION	3,700,700,000
NUMBER OF COUNTRIES	49
BIGGEST COUNTRY	Russian Federation
SMALLEST COUNTRY	Maldives
HIGHEST POINT	Mt. Everest (China/Nepal) 8,848 m (29,029 ft)
LOWEST POINT	Dead Sea shore (Israel) 400 m (1,312 ft) below sea-level
LONGEST RIVER	Yangtze (Chang Jiang) (China) 6,380 km (3,965 miles)
BIGGEST LAKE	Caspian Sea 378,400 sq km (146,100 sq miles)

Cross-section through Asia

From the Indian Ocean, the land rises to the Vindhya Range in central India descending to the Ganges Plain, watered by the Himalayas. In the east, the mountains drop to the Great Plain of China. Across the Yellow Sea, the Korean Peninsula juts out near to Japan in the Pacific Ocean.

Ganges Plain · Mt. Everest · Himalayas, Nepal · Great Plain of China · Red Basin, China · Korean Peninsula · Mt. Fuji, Japan · Sea of Japan · Vindhya Range · Indian Ocean

A — Approximately 6,480 km (4,027 miles) from A to B — B

Climatic zones

Asia has every kind of climate and landscape. In the far north, Siberia is covered in tundra, where part of the ground is permanently frozen. South of the tundra are coniferous forests and open grasslands (steppes). Central and southwest Asia are mostly desert and mountains, while the east has deciduous forests. Tropical rainforests cover much of the south and southeast.

Coniferous forest
Tundra
Mountain
Scrubland
Deciduous forest
Grassland
Desert
Tropical rainforest
Wetland

Tundra

In the bitterly cold and treeless tundra region of Siberia, the subsoil remains frozen – a condition known as permafrost. With temperatures of less than -10°C (14°F) and covered by snow for six to ten months of the year, the topsoil thaws only briefly in the summer. The tundra has rich mineral resources.

Mosses, lichens, and a few flowers appear briefly during the warmer months.

The steppes are the Asian equivalent of the pampas and prairies of the Americas.

Taiga

The Siberian taiga, which lies to the south of the tundra, is the world's largest coniferous forest. The main trees are spruce, fir, larch, and pine. In the spring, much of the taiga becomes flooded as the lower reaches of the north-flowing rivers thaw, while their mouths remain frozen. In summer, some ground remains swampy; in winter it freezes.

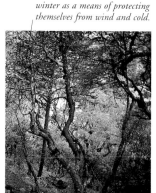

Steppes

The wide, open grasslands that cover Mongolia and southern Siberia are known as the steppes. Livestock is grazed on these broad, treeless plains, which, in places, merge into semi-desert. The soil is mostly fertile and, with irrigation, many areas have become productive farmland.

Harsh conditions make trees stunted and sparse. Ice and snow cover the region for half the year.

Dunes form as sand drifts in the prevailing wind.

Temperatures average 21°C (70°F), with 2,000 mm (79 in) of rain per year.

Trees lose their leaves in winter as a means of protecting themselves from wind and cold.

Taklimakan Desert, China

Deserts

Asia has both hot and cold deserts, as well as many regions of semi-desert where animals can be grazed. Middle Eastern deserts are hot and dry all year, with cold nights. The Gobi and Taklimakan deserts of Central Asia have scorching summers, but are bitterly cold in winter.

Wetlands

Mangrove swamps are found along many coasts of southern Asia, from India to the Philippines. The mangrove trees have long, spreading roots, producing a forest that looks as if it is on stilts. Logging and pollution are destroying many mangroves.

Mangrove roots help stop coast eroding in storms.

Tropical rainforest

There are tropical rainforests in India, Southeast Asia, and the Philippines. They flourish on the southern slopes of the Himalayas, and in Burma (Myanmar), the Malay Peninsula, and the western part of the island of Irian Jaya. Home to 40 per cent of all plant and animal species, the world's rainforests are threatened, as people cut down trees for the timber industry and to clear space for farming.

Deciduous forest

Asia has comparatively few broadleaf forests of deciduous trees that shed their leaves in winter. They occur mainly in eastern Asia, including China, Japan, and the Koreas, or in cooler upland areas, such as the mountains of Nepal.

People

Asia contains two-thirds of the world's population, and the birth rate is still rising in many countries. Most people live in the southern and eastern regions and in the fertile river valleys. Many are farmers, although increasing numbers are moving into expanding cities in search of work.

Israeli boy   Vietnamese girl   Japanese boy

Resources

Asia's natural resources include farmland, which provides work for 60 per cent of the people, and the fishing grounds of the Pacific Ocean. Minerals include oil and natural gas from the Gulf States, as well as bauxite, copper, coal, diamonds, gold, iron, lead, manganese, mercury, tin, and titanium.

Rice

Diamond

Tuna fish

FIND OUT MORE   ASIA, HISTORY OF   ASIAN WILDLIFE   CLIMATE   CONTINENTS   DESERTS   FORESTS   GRASSLAND WILDLIFE   LAKES   MOUNTAINS AND VALLEYS   RAINFOREST WILDLIFE   TUNDRA

ASIA, HISTORY OF

ASIA IS THE WORLD'S LARGEST continent and the birthplace of the world's earliest civilizations, such as those of the Sumerians, China, and India. The emergence of these civilizations had a profound impact on history, both ancient and modern, as did the emergence of three major world religions: Hinduism, Buddhism, and Islam. Colonial interference affected Asia's development over the centuries, but after decades of independent growth, today's Asian economies are booming. There are still conflicts, however, and those in Southeast Asia and the Middle East tend to affect world politics.

Early development
Early civilizations in Asia were largely isolated from each other and from the rest of the world by barriers of deserts, mountains, and oceans. Only the Middle East had strong connections with Europe. Therefore, Asian civilizations and cultures developed independently for thousands of years. Over time, major civilizations, such as those of India and China, began to affect other Asian countries.

Central Asia

For centuries the only travellers in the inhospitable landscape of Central Asia were traders using the Silk Road. In 1398, the Mongolian warrior Timur (1336–1405) swept down from the steppes and founded a Central Asian empire.

Typically tiled Samarkandian roof

Samarkand
In 1369, Timur moved his capital to the prosperous city of Samarkand, in modern Uzbekistan. The city experienced a golden age and became the architectural jewel of Central Asia as Timur and his descendants built palaces, astronomical observatories, and Islamic colleges. In the early 1500s, nomadic Uzbeks attacked the city.

Uleg Beg Medrasa, Uzbekistan

Swat, Pakistan

Kushan Empire
In c.170 BC, a northern Chinese clan, the Yuezhi, moved west to Central Asia. By the 3rd century AD, they had founded an empire that stretched from eastern Iran to the Ganges in India. The Kushans controlled fertile river valleys and were at the centre of the silk trade. They encouraged Buddhism and religious art, but declined in the 4th century.

Padmasambhava

A legendary sage and yoga expert from Swat, modern Pakistan, Padmasambhava founded Tibetan Buddhism. He and his consort, Yeshe Tsogyal, arrived in Tibet in 747, and established the first Buddhist monastery. The sage then spent his life writing and lecturing on the religion.

Semi-precious stones

Ancient civilizations

The Sumerians of western Asia evolved the world's first civilization, but it was the early civilizations of India and China that affected Asia the most. Their religions had special impact: Hinduism (the religion of the people of India) and Buddhism (founded by Siddhartha Gautama and one of the three great religions of China) spread over Asia.

Kogyuro openwork cup

Chola dynasty
From 850–c.1200, a powerful dynasty known as the Cholas began to dominate much of India. They built many Hindu temples and spread their religion to Sri Lanka. They extended their naval power over the seas of Southeast Asia, and this helped spread Hinduism as far as Sumatra and Bali.

Koguryo dynasty
By the 7th century China's influence was increasing, and Chinese monks converted Korea to Buddhism. The Koguryo rulers (1st century BC–AD 7th century) encouraged the spread of Buddhism. From Korea, the missionaries went to Japan, which adopted not only Buddhism but also Chinese script, architecture, and culture.

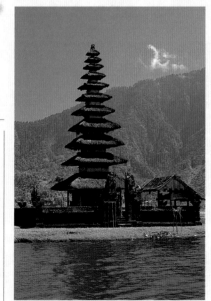

Southeast Asia

For 1,000 years, India was the major shaping force of this region, and provided a mould for Southeast Asian culture, art, and religion. Its influence declined after c.1300.

Siam
Over centuries, waves of migrants from the north entered Siam (Thailand), and inter-married with the native tribes. In the 13th century, one tribe, the Thais, unified Siam into a single nation with one monarch and one religion – Buddhism.

Sea routes
From c.300, Indian traders sailed to Thailand, Malaysia, Indonesia, and the Philippines. From the 1200s, Arabian merchants spread Islam along sea trade routes. From c.1500, the region also traded with Europe.

Dhow leaving Muscat, Oman

Thai tribal woman

A Hindu temple in Bali, Indonesia, attests to the great influence of the Chola dynasty.

A

Trade and culture

During the 17th, 18th, and 19th centuries trade thrived, though some Asian countries were closed to outsiders. Russia and European countries bought silk, tea, and porcelain from China. India traded with the world, and was famous for its handmade textiles, such as "paisley", which was a traditional Indian pattern. During this period, Western powers became increasingly interested in annexing Asian territories for trade purposes.

Manchu Dynasty

China's Manchu Dynasty (1644–1911) was expansionist, and spread its culture by acquiring other territories, such as Mongolia (1697), Tibet (1751), and eastern Turkestan (1760). At home, however, economic conditions worsened.

Yellow lotus is a sacred flower.

A rich woman's silk robe, 19th century

Asian resistance

In the 17th and 18th centuries, China, Japan, Korea, and Siam (Thailand) resisted European expansion. China confined European trade to Macao and Canton, Japan traded only with Holland at Nagasaki, and Korea remained closed to the west. In 1688, a revolution in Siam ended French attempts to gain influence in Bangkok.

Gold-coated roof

Grand Palace, Bangkok

Great Game

During the 1800s, Russia expanded into Central Asia. The British feared the Russians were aiming to take over India, and both sides began to spy on each other. The British called this the Great Game; to the Russians it was known as the Tournament of Shadows.

Mountains of Lake Baikal, Russia

Nineteenth-century colonization

In the 19th century, European powers colonized much of Asia. The British took over Burma, Malaya, North Borneo, and Hong Kong; France dominated Indochina; the Dutch controlled Indonesia; and Russia annexed Central Asian provinces.

Britain
Russia   Netherlands
France   Japan

Conversion of the Philippines

In the late 1500s, the Spanish colonial government encouraged Filipinos to become Roman Catholics, and gave financial support to missionaries. By the 18th century, most Filipinos in towns and lowland areas had converted to Catholicism. The island of Mindanao, however, embraced Islam, which was brought to them by Muslim traders.

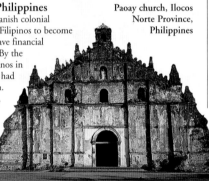

Paoay church, Ilocos Norte Province, Philippines

Engraving of Anglo-Burmese wars, 1824

Anglo-Burmese wars

In 1886, Burma lost its independence to Britain after a series of wars. This takeover was strategic rather than trade-based: the British wanted to prevent the French from gaining too much influence in Asia.

Golden East

As Europe gained in military and industrial strength in the 19th century, it expanded, and Asia became a rich source of food and raw materials. European planters developed tea, coffee, and rubber plantations, founded tin mines, exploited Asian timber, and prospected for gold, silver, and precious stones.

Indian tea

Vietnamese mahogany

Rama V

Chulalonkorn (1853–1910) became Rama V, King of Siam, in 1868. He travelled widely throughout Asia, and was determined to strengthen his country by a process of modernization. In the 1880s, he created a modern army, civil service, and education system. Although Thailand lost some provinces to Britain and France, it managed to preserve its prestige and independence.

The king and queen of Siam

Rebellion

From the 1850s, there were rebellions against European interference in Asian affairs. In 1857, the Sepoy Rebellion took place in India, and, in 1900, there was the Boxer Rebellion in China. Both revolts were protests against western strength and culture. They were crushed by western or colonial government forces.

Cover of *Le Petit Parisien*, 1900, "Death to Foreigners"

Timeline

4000–c.2500 BC The world's earliest civilization flourishes in Sumer, western Asia.

c.2500 BC Indus Valley period, India's earliest civilization.

1800 BC Shang period: China's earliest civilization starts to build its first cities.

c.330 BC Alexander the Great destroys the Persian Empire.

138 BC First recorded journey on the Silk Road.

c.50 Buddhism reaches China from India.

206 BC– AD 220 Height of the Chinese Han Empire.

FIND OUT MORE   ARCHITECTURE   CHINA, HISTORY OF   CONFUCIUS

A

Growth of nationalism

After World War I, Asian nationalism (a belief in independence) grew. In 1918, Arab leaders overthrew Turkish rule. The desire of Jews to create an independent state in Palestine gained support. By 1933, 238,000 Jews had settled in Palestine, and, in 1948, the state of Israel was created.

Living quarters

Jewish settlers in Palestine, 1930s

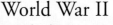

World War II

In 1941–42, Japan occupied Burma, Indochina, and Indonesia. After the horrors of occupation, these areas rejected all foreign rule. In China, communist guerrillas resisting the Japanese, gained popular and political support.

Two war veterans on the Death Railway, River Kwai, Thailand, 1990s

Death Railway

During World War II, the Japanese built a railway to link Burma and Thailand to supply Japanese troops in Burma. Many thousands of Asian labourers and Western prisoners died from malnutrition, disease, and exhaustion building the 420-km (260-mile) railway, and it became known as the Death Railway.

Independence movements

After 1945, many Asian countries threw off colonial rule. In 1947, India and Pakistan struggled for and won independence from Britain. In 1948, a Jewish homeland, Israel, came into being. Indonesia won independence from the Netherlands in 1949, after a four-year battle. France also tried to prevent Vietnamese independence, but was defeated in 1954; the other French colonies, Laos and Cambodia, became independent in 1954 and 1953 respectively.

These territories all gained independence since 1939. There were eventually 48 independent countries in post-war Asia.

Dragon economies

In the 1980s, Singapore, Taiwan, Hong Kong, and South Korea used their well-educated populations and high investment to become prosperous "dragon" economies. In the 1990s, Thailand, Malaysia, and Indonesia also developed rapidly.

Taiwanese factory

Taiwanese exported goods
Taiwan traditionally exported agricultural products, such as sugar, pineapples, and bananas; but by the 1980s it also exported advanced electronic products, such as personal computers, televisions, and portable phones.

Communist Asia

In 1949, the communists established the People's Republic of China – the world's largest communist state. In 1954, the North Vietnamese created an independent communist state. From the 1960s, communist movements in Indonesia and Malaysia threatened to overthrow existing governments.

US troops carrying wounded soldiers from a "chopper"

Khe Sanh, Vietnam

Middle East conflicts
Since 1948, Arab-Israeli territorial conflict, such as the war of 1973 (when Egypt and Syria attacked Israel), has dominated the Middle East. There have also been conflicts between Arab countries, such as the Iran-Iraq war (1980–88). Although the oil boom has helped this situation by lessening poverty, the situation in the Middle East remains unstable.

Oil rigs, Middle East

Vietnam War
From 1954, communist North Vietnam sought to reunite with non-communist South Vietnam by force. Originally a civil war, the Vietnam War escalated into an international conflict with the gradual intervention of the United States in the 1960s. Following defeats and heavy casualties, the USA agreed to withdraw in 1973. In 1975, northern forces unified both halves of Vietnam.

Chaim Weizmann
Weizmann (1874–1952) was born near Pinsk in Belorussia and studied chemistry in Switzerland. In his youth he became a passionate Zionist and eventually was made head of the World Zionist Movement. After World War II, Weizmann campaigned for the creation of Israel, and in 1948, became the state of Israel's first president.

Timeline
c.**618–907** The sophisticated T'ang dynasty dominates China.

1211 Mongol warrior Ghengis Khan invades China.

1300s Silk Road is shut.

1368 Ming dynasty expels Mongols from China.

1397 Mongols invade India.

1350–1460 Collapse of Khmer Empire, Cambodia.

1453 Fall of Constantinople to the Turkish Ottoman Empire.

Toy dog, Thailand, 1926

c.**1488** Ming emperors rebuild the Great Wall of China.

1526–1707 Domination of Mughals in India.

1600–1614 British, French, and Dutch form East India companies.

1757 British take control of Bengal, India.

1839–42 First Opium War.

1736–96 Manchu China prospers under Emperor Qianlong.

c.**1750** Cultural and artistic peak in Japan.

1949 Chinese Revolution.

1950–53 Korean War.

1954–75 Vietnam War.

1907 Anglo-Russian agreement ends the Great Game in Central Asia.

Toy robot, Japan, 1956

FIND OUT MORE

EMPIRES   EXPLORATION   GANDHI, MOHANDAS   INDIA, HISTORY OF   JAPAN, HISTORY OF   MUHAMMAD   PERSIAN EMPIRES   WARFARE

ASIA, CENTRAL

MAINLY ARID DESERT and mountainous, Central Asia is made up of five countries. The Silk Road, an ancient trade route between China, the Middle East, and Europe, once passed through the region, boosting the textile industry, and making handwoven rugs from Central Asia world famous. From 1922 until 1991 the whole area, apart from Afghanistan, was part of the Soviet Union. Under communist rule, the countries were partly modernized. Today, however, as independent nations they face an uncertain future. In 2001 Afghanistan was linked to the terrorist attacks of September 11 in the USA and was devastated by US-led reprisal bombings.

Physical features

Much of Central Asia is covered by two hot, dry deserts: the Karakumy and the Kyzyl Kum. The rest is largely rugged mountain chains. There is a small area of farmland, which has been extended by irrigation.

Kyzyl Kum
The name Kyzyl Kum means "red sands". This desert region lies south of the Aral Sea, between the rivers Syr Daria and Amu Darya, mostly in Uzbekistan. Few people apart from nomads live here. Much of it is covered by low hills and sandy wasteland.

Tien Shan
The literal translation of Tien Shan is "Heavenly Mountains". This range of ice-capped peaks runs for about 3,000 km (1,864 miles) from eastern Kyrgyzstan into China. The highest point is Pobeda Peak, 7,439 m (24,406 ft). Mountain rivers form broad, fertile valleys, which are used for farming.

Karakumskiy Ship Canal
The Karakumskiy Ship Canal is being built from the Amu Darya, one of Central Asia's main rivers, across the Karakumy Desert. It will link the river with the Caspian Sea, 1,400 km (870 miles) away.

Nomads

Many Central Asian people are nomads who roam the land with their animal herds, constantly searching for new pastures. They live in traditional tents usually made of animal skins. Their animals – mainly sheep and goats – provide them with meat, milk, skins, and wool, some of which they sell.

Kyrgyz nomad at home with horse

Regional climate

Most of this region is cold in winter and very hot and dry in summer. Rainfall is uniformly low, which hampers farming. The mountain regions are always cooler than the lowlands, and many of the peaks are permanently covered by snow and ice.

27°C (81°F) −5°C (23°F)
316 mm (12 in)

Turkmenistan

Only two per cent of Turkmenistan's arid land can be farmed. With irrigation, cotton, fruit, wheat, and vegetables are produced. Many people live in nomadic tribes, and there is much intertribal tension. Turkmenistan is the world's fifth largest producer of natural gas.

TURKMENISTAN FACTS

CAPITAL CITY Ashgabat

AREA 488,100 sq km (188,455 sq miles)

POPULATION 4,500,000

MAIN LANGUAGES Turkmen, Russian

MAJOR RELIGION Muslim

CURRENCY Manat

Akhal-Teke
Known as the "wind of heaven", Akhal-Teke race-horses have been bred in the south of the Karakumy Desert for centuries. Fast, hardy, and well suited to the hot, harsh climate, Akhal-Tekes compete in traditional horse races at the Ashgabat hippodrome.

Akhal-Teke

Saddlecloths

Carpets
For centuries, Turkmenistan has produced beautiful, velvety carpets in deep, toning shades of red, brown, and maroon. Women hand-knot each carpet using fine wool from karakul sheep. They make several sizes, including *khali* (large), *ensi* (door rug), as well as weaving curtains, sacks, bags, and pouches.

Uzbekistan

Although 80 per cent of Uzbekistan is covered by dry steppe and desert, its areas of fertile land and resources of oil, gas, gold, copper, and coal make it one of Central Asia's wealthier countries. Fruit, silk cocoons, and vegetables are exported to Moscow. Uzbekistan has the world's largest single gold mine.

UZBEKISTAN FACTS

CAPITAL CITY Tashkent

AREA 447,400 sq km (172,741 sq miles)

POPULATION 24,300,000

MAIN LANGUAGES Uzbek, Russian

MAJOR RELIGION Muslim

CURRENCY Som

The Tillya-Kari is an Islamic seminary in Registan Square.

An intricate mosaic covers building.

Cotton
Uzbekistan is the world's fourth largest producer of cotton. However, the irrigation system used to water crops has seriously depleted the Aral Sea.

Samarkand
Home to 370,000 people, the ancient city of Samarkand was once the centre for trade in silk from China. Today, the manufacture of silk and cotton textiles is still the city's main industry. Samarkand's Registan Square contains some magnificent 14th-century Islamic architecture.

Kyrgyzstan

Dominated by the arid Tian Shan mountains, Kyrgyzstan is a mainly rural country. Only seven per cent of the land is cultivable. Half is used for growing fodder for livestock; the rest supports vegetables, wheat, fruit, cotton, and tobacco.

KYRGYZSTAN FACTS

CAPITAL CITY Bishkek

AREA 198,500 sq km (76,640 sq miles)

POPULATION 4,754,000

MAIN LANGUAGE Kyrgyz, Russian

MAJOR RELIGION Muslim

CURRENCY Som

People
The population of Kyrgyzstan is made up of 57 per cent Kyrgyz people. The rest are mainly Russians and Uzbeks. Many Russians are leaving as a result of the strong nationalist feelings that have grown in the country since the end of Soviet rule. Ethnic tension also exists with the Uzbeks.

Gold

Resources
Gold and mercury are mined for export, as well as smaller amounts of other minerals, including iron ore, tin, lead, copper, zinc, and bauxite. Kyrgyzstan also has reserves of oil, coal, and gas, and its many rivers and lakes give it great potential for hydroelectric power.

Tajikistan

The poorest of the former Soviet republics, Tajikistan has been torn by civil war ever since independence. The main conflict is between ethnic Tajiks, who make up about two-thirds of the population, and Uzbeks, who make up one-quarter. Tajikistan has rich mineral resources.

TAJIKISTAN FACTS

CAPITAL CITY Dushanbe

AREA 143,100 sq km (55,251 sq miles)

POPULATION 6,200,000

MAIN LANGUAGES Tajik, Uzbek

MAJOR RELIGION Muslim

CURRENCY Somoni

Watermelon

Uranium
Tajikistan has 14 per cent of the world's uranium, used as nuclear fuel. It is a major export, but the end of the nuclear arms race has reduced its value.

Farming
Only about six per cent of Tajikistan is suitable for farming. The main farming areas are in the northwest, near Khudzhand, and the southwest, south of Dushanbe. Melons, grapes, and peaches are grown in fertile soils washed down from the mountains into the valleys.

Afghanistan

Afghanistan has a long history of war. After years of civil strife, Afghanistan was further destroyed by a US-led 'war on terrorism' in 2001–02. Pashtuns are the majority ethnic group. Afghanistan is one of the world's poorest countries.

Taliban
An Islamic sect called the Taliban took power in 1996 and created a hardline regime which banned many freedoms. Women suffered heavily under Taliban rule as they were forbidden to receive an education, hold a job, or show their faces in public. The Taliban fled power in 2001 during western war reprisals for the September 11 terrorist attacks.

AFGHANISTAN FACTS

CAPITAL CITY Kabul

AREA 652,090 sq km (251,770 sq miles)

POPULATION 26,800,000

MAIN LANGUAGES Persian, Pashto

MAJOR RELIGION Muslim

CURRENCY Afghani

FIND OUT MORE   ASIA, HISTORY OF   DESERTS   FARMING   HORSES   ISLAM   MOUNTAINS AND VALLEYS   NUCLEAR POWER   ROCKS AND MINERALS   TEXTILES AND WEAVING   TRADE AND INDUSTRY

ASIAN WILDLIFE

ASIA STRETCHES FROM the frozen Arctic in the north to the warm tropics in the south. Although much of Asia is undulating plain, it also boasts the awesome mountain range of the Himalayas. Much of the interior receives little rain, but parts of India hold the world record for annual rainfall. This continent of contrasts provides many habitats, each with its own characteristic plants and animals. Many of the world's best known endangered species, such as giant pandas and tigers, live in Asia. But many less publicized, smaller animals and plants are also threatened by the steady spread of human populations.

Temperate forest wildlife

Asian temperate woodlands are rich in species of broadleaved trees. Summers are mild, but winters can be cold, and after the leaves have fallen, there is little food or shelter. Some animals migrate or hibernate; others, such as the Japanese macaque, are adapted to the cold.

Monkey eating snow

Thick, shaggy coat

Japanese macaque
Living throughout most of Japan, the Japanese macaque lives in a more northerly climate than any other monkey. In winter it grows a thick coat for protection, and some troops sit in hot springs to avoid the chill of a snowstorm. Roots, buds, and shoots form its winter diet.

Japanese emperor butterfly
Only the male Japanese emperor has an iridescent purple sheen, but both sexes have spotted wings. This pattern breaks up their outline, making it difficult to see where they land on sun-flecked foliage. Their caterpillars are leaf green, to camouflage them on the leaves of celtis trees, on which they feed.

Purple iridescence of male

White spots

Rainforest wildlife

Asia's rainforests are warm all year round, but they do have short dry seasons. They are festooned with lianas and epiphytes. The rainforest provides homes for animals at all levels, from fruit bats in the canopy to tigers on the forest floor.

Long aerial roots

Banyan tree
Some fig trees, such as the banyan tree, start life as a tiny seedling that grows in the crown of another rainforest tree. The banyan tree sends aerial roots down to the ground, that enmesh and kill the host tree.

Striped coat provides camouflage in forest.

Tiger
The tiger spends much of its day roaming through its rainforest territory, stalking prey. Tigers love water, and to avoid the heat of the day, they cool down by basking in shallow pools.

Saltwater crocodile
Large reptiles, such as saltwater crocodiles, lie out on the shores of rainforest rivers in the morning sun to warm up their bodies. Later on, when the Sun gets too hot, the crocodiles return to the water to cool down.

Bill is used to kill snakes and scorpions.

Rhinoceros hornbill
With its loud call and noisy wingbeats, the rhinoceros hornbill is a very noticeable rainforest inhabitant. It uses its huge bill with great dexterity to pick fruit and kill prey.

Grassland wildlife

Asia has both tropical savannahs and vast plains of temperate steppes, with hot, dry summers. However, grasses and drought-resistant shrubs do grow there. Large animals have adapted to conserve moisture; smaller ones shelter in burrows.

The papery orange lanterns enclose berries.

Chinese lantern
The Chinese lantern is a drought-resistant plant. Its roots spread deep into the soil to reach any available water. New shoots appear each spring, that bear flowers and edible fruits.

Saiga antelope
Herds of saiga antelopes migrate south in winter to escape severe weather. They return north in summer, when the grasses are more plentiful. Saigas have a mucous-lined sac in the snout that warms inhaled air in winter and filters out dust in the hot, dry summer.

Heavy snout

Tawny eagle
The tawny eagle nests in shrubs and trees by watercourses. It flies long distances over steppes and semi-arid deserts in search of food. The tawny eagle is a skilful hunter, but it increases its chances of getting enough food by feeding on carrion and stealing other predators' prey.

Hooked beak for tearing flesh of prey

Eagle has pushed off ground to launch itself into the air.

A

Mountain wildlife

The steep crags and valleys of the Himalayas provide many refuges for wildlife. Forests on the lower slopes give way to high altitude meadows and snowfields. Animals of the higher slopes, such as the yak, are adapted to survive the winters; others migrate to warmer, lower slopes.

Himalayan griffon
The Himalayan griffon is a large, aggressive vulture that soars over some of the highest mountain slopes in search of food. The diet of vultures is almost entirely restricted to carrion. The Himalayan griffon's powerful hooked bill is strong enough to rip open the leathery hide of a dead yak to feast on the entrails.

Hooked beak helps pull apart prey.

Sharp spines on head and neck provide protection.

Rhododendron
When in flower, rhododendrons set the mountainside ablaze with a riot of colour. Their tiny seeds are readily spread by wind or water.

Yak
Domesticated for centuries, the yak is still found living wild in some parts of its mountain range. With its long, shaggy coat, a yak can survive temperatures as low as -40°C (-40°F). It grazes on whatever plants are available, including mosses and lichens, and can use snow as a source of water.

Armoured pricklenape agama
This lizard lives in the treetops in mountain forests. Its greeny-brown scales conceal it among twigs and leaves. Pricklenape agamas have sharp claws that give them a sure grip, as they run and leap through the branches.

Long toes and claws grip when climbing.

Northern bat
In summer, this hardy bat forages for insects in the forest and even up into the Arctic Circle. To survive the winter it hibernates in caves or buildings. Its distribution is dictated by the availability of suitable roost sites.

Boreal forest wildlife

Just south of the Arctic tundra is a vast forest of conifer trees. In Asia, this boreal forest is called the taiga. Wildflowers, and animals such as the sable, are adapted to exploit the brief summers and withstand the long, harsh winters.

Norway spruce
Narrow-crowned spruces are a characteristic feature of the taiga. Snow slides easily from their curved branches without breaking them. Norway spruce grows at the western reaches of the taiga, soon giving way to Siberian spruce. The seeds of both trees provide food for birds and rodents.

Fur for warmth

Sable
The sable hunts all year round for nestlings and rodents. It also eats shoots and berries if prey is scarce. The sable sleeps, shelters, and gives birth in hollow logs or tree holes.

Thick fur covers the whole body and even the soles of the feet.

Great grey owl
To find enough food, including voles, lemmings, and other small rodents, the great grey owl hunts by day as well as night. It may travel far to a good source of food, but returns to the dense boreal forest to breed. It chooses a secure nest site in a tree, or may use another large bird's old nest.

Desert wildlife

Not all deserts are hot all year round. Temperate deserts, such as the Gobi in Central Asia, have scorching hot summers, but icy cold winters. Nights are cold even in summer, as there is no vegetation to trap the heat. To survive here, animals must be adapted both to the dry environment and extremes of temperature.

Onager
Onagers live in small herds in the desert. There is little vegetation here for grazing animals, but the onager can cope with eating tough desert grasses and straw. Wolves, although uncommon, are their main predators. To defend themselves, onagers can run fast for long distances.

Mongolian gerbil
Like many small desert animals, these gerbils escape from temperature extremes by digging underground burrows. Living below ground also helps to conserve bodily moisture. Gerbils nibble roots, shoots, seeds, and buds, and drink water if it is available. In a drought, they can get sufficient moisture from the early morning dew on their food.

Bactrian camel
Few of these desert creatures remain in the wild. A Bactrian camel has a very thick woolly coat to protect it from severe cold in winter. Fat stored in two humps on its back enables it to survive with little food or water for long periods of time.

Almost all-round vision helps them to spot danger.

Pale fur for camouflage in desert

Cheek pouches stretch so gerbil can carry food in its mouth.

FIND OUT MORE — ASIA · BATS · BIRDS OF PREY · BUFFALO AND OTHER WILD CATTLE · CAMELS · DEER AND ANTELOPES · LIONS AND OTHER WILD CATS · RATS AND OTHER RODENTS · TREES

ASSYRIAN EMPIRE

THE GRAND CITY OF ASHUR, beside the Tigris river in northern Mesopotamia (present-day Iraq), developed as an important trading centre; by 2000 BC, it had become the capital of a great Assyrian kingdom. From 1400 BC, Assyrian armies were marching north and west to secure trade and obtain booty and tribute. Feared for their military strength, they soon came to dominate the Near East. Assyrian kings built several capital cities after Ashur, of which Nimrud and Nineveh were the most magnificent. Assyrian civilization and culture, however, were heavily influenced by Babylonia to the south, and it was the Babylonians who eventually absorbed the Assyrians into their empire.

Extent of the empire
The greatest extent of the empire was reached in the 7th century, when the well-equipped soldiers of King Ashurbanipal conquered and held lands from Egypt to Iran. Assyrian governors controlled the provinces. They were expected to send taxes back to the Assyrian capital and recruit soldiers for the army.

Bronze armour

Army

The Assyrian army was the most efficient fighting machine of its time, and its reputation alone was often enough to frighten rebellious states into surrender. At first, the army consisted of native Assyrians, but Tiglath-Pileser III (745–727 BC) recruited men from other areas of the empire. They were armed with iron helmets, armour, spears, swords, and shields. The Assyrians also used chariots and siege engines (battering rams on wheels), the most advanced weapons of the time.

Assyrian official　　*King Ashurnasirpal II (r.883–859 BC)*　　*Siege engine*

Stone relief of Assyrians attacking a town on the Euphrates river

Nimrud and Nineveh
By 900 BC, the city of Ashur was overcrowded. Nimrud was built in the 9th century BC; Nineveh was constructed in the 7th century BC. These cities were famous for their splendid palaces and temples.

Exotic animals
from all over the empire, such as elephants and lions, filled the wildlife parks and gardens that surrounded the city of Nineveh.

Politics

At his coronation, the Assyrian king swore to expand the empire. The Assyrians believed their god Ashur (after whom the first city was named) chose each king, so he had absolute power. He appointed all the governors of the various parts of his empire, led the army, and was responsible for all the temples. The king demonstrated his power and wealth by many ambitious building projects. A network of spies reported to the king on all matters within the empire.

Gold earrings

Precious stones

Queens of Assyria
Some Assyrian queens were so powerful they became legendary. One such, Sammurammat (Semiramis), dominated court for 42 years in the 9th century BC. Some royal jewellery has been found in tombs at Nimrud.

Art and literature

Brightly painted, stone-relief carvings, the most spectacular of all Assyrian art forms, decorated palace walls from 900 BC. Artists decorated royal furniture with carvings of real or mythical animals, such as sphinxes.

Ivory winged sphinx

Timeline

2400 BC The city of Ashur dominates trade routes.

1900 BC, Assyrians establish trading colonies in Anatolia (modern Turkey).

1250 BC Kings of Assyria campaign as far as the Mediterranean and Babylon.

879 BC Ashurnasirpal II builds a new capital at Kalhu (Nimrud).

744–727 BC King Tiglath-Pileser III creates an empire.

721–705 BC Sargon II builds capital at Khorsabad (Dur-Sharrokin).

Gold earring

701 BC Sennacherib leads his army to Jerusalem from his new capital at Nineveh.

689 BC Sennacherib destroys Babylon.

664 BC Ashurbanipal attacks and conquers Egypt.

612 BC Median and Babylonian armies destroy Nineveh.

609 BC Crown prince Nebuchadnezzar of Babylon finally defeats the Assyrians.

606 BC The Medes from Iran sack Nineveh.

Sennacherib

Sennacherib (r.704–681 BC), a strong king, spent many years building Nineveh. He established control over the coast of the Mediterranean, and destroyed Babylon, but he was murdered by his jealous sons.

FIND OUT MORE　ARMS AND ARMOUR　ASIA, HISTORY OF　BABYLONIAN EMPIRE　HITTITES　PHOENICIANS　SUMERIANS　WARFARE

ASTROLOGY

FOR CENTURIES, people have believed that the position of the stars and planets has an influence on human life. The study of this influence is known as astrology. It began about 4,000 years ago in Mesopotamia (modern Iraq) and eventually spread throughout the ancient world. In most cultures astrology was regarded as a science, and many rulers even used astrology when making important political decisions. Today, although there is no scientific proof for its accuracy, many people still believe in astrology.

Casting a horoscope

To draw up your horoscope, or birth chart, astrologers need to know the exact date, time, and place of your birth. They then use careful calculations to plot the position of the Sun, Moon, and planets. Astrologers claim that they can interpret the finished horoscope to reveal your character.

This line represents the horizon at the time of birth.

The chart is divided into 12 houses, one for each zodiac sign.

Complicated calculations are now done with calculators.

Astrology and astronomy

The scientific study of stars and planets is known as astronomy. For thousands of years, astronomy and astrology were closely linked. From the 17th century onwards, however, leaps in scientific knowledge resulted in astronomy becoming increasingly important, while belief in astrology began to wane.

An early telescope

Astrological map showing the view of the universe in 1660.

Twelve signs of the zodiac

Celestial spheres

Ancient astrologers believed that the Universe was a gigantic sphere, with the Earth at the centre and the stars circling around it. They divided this sphere into 12 sections, each of which was named after a constellation of fixed stars – the signs of the zodiac.

Signs of the zodiac

Each sign of the zodiac takes its name from ancient mythology. Early astrologers chose names to suit the shapes formed by the constellations – the stars that make up Leo, for example, were thought to resemble a lion.

Aries
Taurus
Gemini
Cancer
Leo
Virgo
Libra
Scorpio
Sagittarius
Capricorn
Aquarius
Pisces

Chinese horoscopes

Unlike Western astrology which is based on the movement of the Sun and planets, Chinese horoscopes are based on the cycle of the Moon. Each Chinese year is named after a different animal – the Rat, Ox, Tiger, Rabbit, Dragon, Snake, Horse, Ram, Monkey, Rooster, Dog, and Pig.

The five elements
- Water
- Wood
- Earth
- Fire
- Gold

Astrological wheel
Chinese astrology features 12 animals, and each represents a different personality type. For example, people born in the year of the Snake are said to be sociable, confident, and energetic.

The black and white bands represent the Universe's balancing forces of yin and yang.

Each animal sign is linked to one of the five elements.

Associations

Each astrological animal is associated with a certain food, colour, and symbol. The Rat's symbol is the set of balances, its colour is black, and it is linked with salty-tasting foods.

Fortune telling

People's desire to see into the future has given rise to many different forms of prediction, which vary from culture to culture. They include crystal ball gazing, dream interpretation, palmistry, divination sticks, tarot reading, runes, numerology, and the *I Ching*, an ancient Chinese oracle.

The role of chance

Many fortune-telling systems use dice, coins, or cards to introduce an element of randomness.

Throwing dice is an ancient way of making predictions.

Consulting a fortune teller in Hong Kong

I Ching coins

Palmistry

Each person's palm is unique, with its own distinctive pattern of lines. Palm readers believe these markings reveal the owner's character, past and future. As well as both palms, the palmist examines the fingers and nails.

Palmistry hand

Tarot cards

Tarot cards are found worldwide. They can be dealt in many different ways, and are thought to answer specific questions, or be a guide to the future.

TEMPERANCE.

KING of WANDS

 FIND OUT MORE ASTRONOMY CHINA, HISTORY OF SCIENCE, HISTORY OF STARS SUN AND SOLAR SYSTEM

ASTRONAUTS

MORE THAN 350 PEOPLE have travelled into space; 26 on missions to the Moon and the rest in orbit around Earth. For journeying into space, astronauts must be physically and mentally fit. They must also be trained to prepare them for living and working in the hostile environment of space.

Spacesuit

When astronauts work outside the spacecraft, they need to wear a suit that keeps their body at the correct temperature and protects them from fast-moving micrometeoroids. The suit must also provide oxygen for breathing and be pressurized because there is no air or atmospheric pressure in space.

Yuri Gagarin

The first person to fly into space was a Russian, Yuri Gagarin (1934–68). His flight on 12 April 1961 took him once around the Earth and lasted 108 minutes. No one knew how the space flight would affect a human, so Gagarin's spacecraft, *Vostok 1*, was controlled from the ground.

Pressure helmet

Visor

Cap

Communications headset

Communications input socket

Oxygen inlets and outlets

Liquid-cooled undergarment

Water inlet and outlet

Pressure glove

Wrist clamp

Extravehicular glove

Apollo 9 spacesuit

Urine transfer connection

Snap-on fastening

Integrated thermal micrometeoroid garment

Lunar overshoe

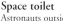

MMU

To fly free from the spacecraft, an astronaut wears a powered backpack, the Manned Manoeuvring Unit (MMU). Mini nitrogen thrusters, operated from arm rests, propel the astronaut at about 20 m/s (65 ft/s).

Living in space

Daily life for an astronaut includes all the usual things, such as breathing, eating, sleeping, and going to the bathroom. The big difference, however, is living in weightless conditions. Sleeping astronauts float around the spacecraft unless tethered down, and using the toilet has to be carefully controlled.

Astronauts need daily exercise to keep fit in the weightless conditions of space.

Meal tray strapped to leg.

Vacuum-wrapped food pack

Rubber grips stop items floating away.

Space food

Meals on the space shuttle are prepared from 70 different foods and 20 drinks. The meal tray is strapped down and the food eaten with the hand or cutlery. Liquids are sucked from cartons or tubes.

Space toilet

Astronauts outside the spacecraft "go to the toilet" in their spacesuit, where the waste materials are collected. Inside the craft, they use a space toilet, making sure they are firmly strapped to the seat. The waste is sucked away by the toilet and collected in a secure unit.

Rubber suction cups

Suction shoes

Staying in one place in a spacecraft can be a problem. Suction-cup shoes allow astronauts to get a better grip.

Working in space

Each member of a space crew has specific tasks. These may include flying the craft, releasing a satellite into orbit, or testing new equipment. The weightless conditions of space mean that astronauts can also perform experiments not possible on Earth.

Repair work

Once a satellite is in space it is left to work on its own. But occasionally one needs repairing. The cargo bay of the space shuttle is equipped with a robotic arm, which specially trained astronauts use to recover the satellite. They can then repair the satellite and release it back into orbit.

Experiments

Astronauts have carried out many experiments in space. These include observing how living things such as bees are affected by weightlessness.

An astronaut, anchored to a foot restraint, works on the *Syncom IV-3* satellite.

Endurance record

Most astronauts spend only a few days in space, but some stay for months. Russian cosmonaut Sergei Avdeyev holds the overall endurance record (748 days). Russian Valeri Poliakov holds the record for longest single stay (438 days).

Valeri Poliakov

Space animals

Humans are not the only space travellers; early ones included dogs, rats, and mice. Animals are no longer sent into space alone, but flies, frogs, and tadpoles occasionally accompany human astronauts.

Chimpanzee Ham returned safely from his 1961 flight.

FIND OUT MORE EXPLORATION GRAVITY HEALTH AND FITNESS MOON ROCKETS SPACE EXPLORATION

ASTRONOMY

ASTRONOMY IS THE STUDY OF SPACE and everything it contains. It is a subject that has been studied since ancient times when humans used their eyes to gaze out at the stars and planets. Today's astronomers use sophisticated equipment to collect information about space and how the Universe as a whole works.

Astronomers' tools

Astronomers collect data from space by analysing a range of electromagnetic radiations; light and radio waves as well as other wavelengths such as X-ray, infrared, and ultraviolet. Astronomers use specialized telescopes with various attachments for collecting and studying the data.

Telescope
The finest and most powerful telescopes use one or more mirrors to collect light from a distant object and form an image. Electronic devices or photographic plates rather than the eye collect the data. Other attachments, such as spectroscopes and photometers, help analyse light emitted by stars.

Kitt Peak Observatory

The largest optical telescope at Kitt Peak is the 4-m (13-ft) Mayall.

Observatories

An astronomer's telescopic equipment is housed and used in an observatory. The atmosphere distorts light and other radiations from space, so many observatories are located at high altitudes.

Optical observatory
The world's biggest optical observatories are on mountaintops, away from city lights and where the atmosphere is clear and dry. The Kitt Peak National Observatory, which has 22 major telescopes, is on a 2,100-m (6,900-ft) mountain in Arizona, USA. Observatories sited in such inaccessible places need support services for the astronomers and their equipment, including accommodation, workshops, and transport.

Radio observatory
Radio waves are largely unaffected by the atmosphere, so radio telescopes can be sited virtually anywhere. The 305-m (1,000-ft) Arecibo radio dish (above) is in a natural hollow on the island of Puerto Rico. It is the world's largest single radio dish.

Space observatory
Telescopes in space collect data 24 hours a day and transmit it back to Earth. The Hubble Space Telescope, launched in 1990, orbits Earth, collecting data from optical and ultraviolet wavelengths.

Cameras and instruments located inside

Hubble Space Telescope

Antenna for sending data

Solar panel

Antenna for sending data

Lander under cover

Solar panel

Viking probe

Space probe
Objects in the Solar System have been studied at close hand by space probes. Instruments perform a host of investigations, including making detailed images of planets and their moons, and analysing what they are made of. Two identical Viking probes investigated Mars in 1976.

Astronomer at work

Most astronomers specialize in one area of research, such as planetary geology, interplanetary dust, stellar development, galaxy formation, or quasars. Whatever the subject, an astronomer can be found in one of two main locations: in universities and observatories.

Observation
Only a fraction of an astronomer's time is spent observing. Instead, most of the data comes from observations made and recorded by other astronomers on big telescopes, or from automatic equipment on space probes. The observations are used to help build theories or to confirm an established theory, such as how stars form.

Data collection
The CCD, an electronic chip that records data from space, can collect enough data in a few hours to keep an astronomer busy for years.

Charge-coupled device (CCD)

Fred Hoyle

The British astronomer Fred Hoyle (1915–2001) helped to solve some of the most baffling questions facing 20th-century astronomers. A major breakthrough was explaining nucleosynthesis – how chemical elements are produced from the hydrogen inside stars. He also wrote science fiction novels.

Analysis
Data can be collected directly on to a computer and then transferred to other computers for analysis. Computers can process images and handle large amounts of information much more quickly than an astronomer.

Timeline
1609 First use of the telescope for the systematic study of space.

1781 Discovery of Uranus doubled the diameter of the known Solar System.

1863 Analysis of starlight shows stars are made of the same elements as those on Earth.

Uranus

Quasar

1963 Quasar is discovered.

1987 Supernova 1987A explodes.

1923 Astronomers observe galaxies other than the Milky Way.

Supernova

1999 Hubble telescope sights 18 other galaxies up to 65 million years away.

FIND OUT MORE   ATMOSPHERE   GALAXIES   SPACE EXPLORATION   STARS   TELESCOPES   UNIVERSE

ATHLETICS

THIS POPULAR SPORT takes place mainly in a stadium where it is divided into two main categories: track and field.
Track includes running and hurdling races; field includes jumping and throwing. Some athletics events involve more than one discipline – 10 in the decathlon for men; seven in the heptathlon for women. Other events are road and cross-country running. Major competitions are the Olympics and world and continental championships.

Water jump for steeplechase · *Pole vault* · *Triple jump* · *Hammer and discus* · *Long jump* · *Shot put* · *Javelin* · *High jump*

Athletics stadium
In an athletics stadium, there is a 400-m (437-yd) running track, usually marked with eight lanes. The field events take place in special areas on the grass area inside the track.

The 100-m sprint, 100-m hurdles, and 110-m hurdles are the only races run in a straight line.

The finish line is in the same place for all races.

Races around bends have a staggered start which means athletes do not start in a straight line.

Track events

Racing takes place on the flat and over hurdles. Competitors in events up to 400 m have to stay in their lane for the whole race. The 800 m is run in lanes until the end of the first bend. A photo-finish camera is used to determine final places, and runners are timed to 0.01 seconds.

Athlete stays in the air as short a time as possible.

Weights in the base of the stand keep the hurdle upright.

Carl Lewis

In 1984, American Carl Lewis (b. 1961) won Olympic golds in the 100 m, 200 m, 4-by-100-m relay, and the long jump. He won five more gold medals in later Olympics and retained his long-jump title three times (1988–96), becoming only the second athlete in history to win four golds in one event.

Hurdling
Athletes have to negotiate 10 hurdles in all the races – 100 m for women, 110 m for men, and 400 m for men and women. In the 3,000-m steeplechase, runners take four hurdles and the water jump on each full lap. They all use the same, fixed hurdles.

Running
Races on the track range from 100 m to the 25-lap 10,000 m. Runners use starting blocks for races from 100 m to 400 m. There are two standard relay races: 4 by 100 m and 4 by 400 m, with team members passing a baton.

Jumping events

There are four jumping events. In the high jump and pole vault, the bar is gradually raised. Competitors are eliminated if they have three consecutive failures. In the long jump and triple jump, competitors have a set number of attempts, the best one counting. The triple jump is a hop, step, and jump.

Pole vault
Poles, usually made of fibreglass, may be of any size. The vaulter plants the pole in a sunken box at the end of the run-up before taking off. The pole bends and then straightens as the vaulter tries to clear the bar feet first, releasing the pole.

Long jump
Competitors must take off before the end of a wooden take-off board sunk into the run-up. The jump is measured from the end of the board to the nearest part of the sand disturbed by the competitor with any part of the body, hands, or legs.

Throwing events

In the shot put, discus, and hammer, competitors throw from special circles. In the javelin, they throw from behind a curved line at the end of a run-up.

Javelin

Javelin distances are measured to where the tip first hits the ground. It does not have to stick.

Shot is a metal sphere weighing 7.26 kg (16 lb) for men and 4 kg (8.8 lb) for women. It is "put" with one pushing action.

Hammer is a metal sphere fixed to a handle by steel wire. Most people turn three or four times before releasing the hammer.

Shot

Discus has a metal rim with a weight at the centre. Like the hammer, the discus is thrown from a cage for safety reasons.

Discus

High jump
Most high jumpers use the Fosbury flop technique, which involves turning at take-off to pass head first and face up over the bar. Competitors are not allowed to take off from both feet together.

The marathon
This road race is 42.195 km (26.2 miles) long. Some major races start and finish in the stadium. It derives from the Battle of Marathon in 490 BC, when a messenger ran to Athens with news of the Athenian victory over the Persians.

FIND OUT MORE

GREECE, ANCIENT · HEALTH AND FITNESS · HUMAN BODY · OLYMPIC GAMES · OWENS, JESSE · SPORT

ATLANTIC OCEAN

THE ATLANTIC IS THE WORLD'S second biggest ocean, covering about one-fifth of the Earth's surface. It separates the Americas in the west from Europe and Africa in the east. The Arctic Ocean lies to the north, and Antarctica to the south. There are several seas around the edges of the Atlantic, including the Baltic and the Mediterranean seas in the east, and the Caribbean Sea in the west. The Atlantic contains some of the world's richest fishing grounds, but is also the most polluted ocean because of the industry around its shores.

ATLANTIC OCEAN FACTS	
AREA 82,442,000 sq km (31,831,000 sq miles)	
AVERAGE DEPTH 3,660 m (12,000 ft)	
GREATEST DEPTH 8,648 m (28,372 ft) Puerto Rico Trench	
LENGTH 16,000 km (9,900 miles)	
GREATEST WIDTH 8,000 km (4,900 miles)	

Physical features

The waters of the Atlantic are never still but move in huge belts of water or currents, such as the Gulf Stream, which affect the world's climate. The currents can be as warm as 30°C (86°F) or as cold as -2°C (30°F). Many of the islands in the Atlantic are volcanic and lie on the Mid-Atlantic Ridge. The largest islands are Greenland and Iceland, bordered by the Greenland Sea in the north Atlantic.

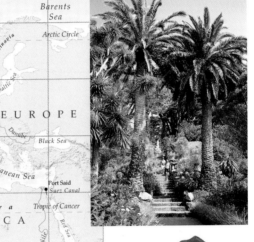

Gulf Stream
Although the Scilly Isles lie just off the coast of Britain, in the northern Atlantic, winters there are mild due to the influence of the Gulf Stream. This warm current, which flows at about 9 kmh (5.6 mph), starts in the Caribbean Sea, circles the Gulf of Mexico, and then heads north and east. Winds that blow over it pick up heat and raise the temperature of northern Europe, keeping ports free of ice in the winter.

Mid-Atlantic Ridge
An underwater mountain chain called the Mid-Atlantic Ridge runs down the middle of the Atlantic, where the ocean floor is splitting. Lava oozes up from the seabed and hardens, forming the mountain range. Many of the peaks surface as mid-ocean islands, such as Ascension Island. The ocean is growing wider at a rate of about 4 cm (1.5 in) a year.

Salmon

Fishing
Although Atlantic fish stocks have run low over the past 20 years because of overfishing, salmon fishing is a thriving industry, and salmon hatcheries are increasingly common.

Iceland

The island country of Iceland lies far north in the Atlantic, midway between Europe and North America, and is increasingly important for international communications. Its position on the Mid-Atlantic Ridge means it has many volcanoes and is prone to earthquakes. Iceland has been a republic since 1944.

Climate

Owing to the Gulf Stream, Iceland's southern lowlands are mild and breezy, and snow is rare. The north is colder, but less windy.

30°C (86°F)   -36°C (-33°F)
11°C (52°F)   1°C (34°F)
860 mm (34 in)

Built-up 1%
Barren 75%
Farmland 24%

Land use

The Icelandic people live in the more fertile coastal areas where 11 per cent are employed in farming, mainly raising sheep. Only about one per cent of the land is used for growing crops. No-one lives in the rocky centre.

Reykjavik

Heated by geothermal water from boreholes, Reykjavik is a clean, modern city, and home to about 100,000 people. It is a bustling hub of culture, industry, commerce, and government.

Brightly coloured houses in Reykjavik's old town

Physical features

Iceland is a land of fire and ice, where steaming hot volcanic springs bubble up through glaciers. The centre consists of uninhabitable plateaus and mountains. In the south are farmlands. There are many rivers, lakes, and spectacular waterfalls.

Volcanoes

The island of Little Surtsey is a volcano that rose from the sea close to Iceland in spring 1965, but disappeared again the following winter. Mainland Iceland has at least 20 active volcanoes that could erupt at any time.

Glaciers

Europe's largest ice-caps cover over one-tenth of Iceland. The biggest is Vatnajökull, which covers an area of 8,133 sq km (3,149 sq miles) in the southeast of the country.

Geothermal power

Every year, thousands of people visit the Blue Lagoon, to swim in this natural pool of healing, geothermal, mineral-rich sea water. Vast resources ensure that hydroelectric and geothermal power stations meet almost all of Iceland's electricity needs.

Fishing

Iceland relies on exporting fish to pay for all the necessities of modern living, which are imported from abroad. Fishing and fish processing are Iceland's leading industries and employ around 20 per cent of the labour force.

People

The first settlers in Iceland arrived from Norway in the 9th century. Today, Iceland boasts a classless society, and around 80 per cent of Icelanders own their own home. Most people live in towns where the standard of living is high, with extensive social security, health services, and free education.

3 per sq km (8 per sq mile)   91% Urban   9% Rural

ICELAND FACTS

CAPITAL CITY	Reykjavik
AREA	100,250 sq km (38,707 sq miles)
POPULATION	281,000
MAIN LANGUAGE	Icelandic
MAJOR RELIGION	Christian
CURRENCY	Icelandic króna
LIFE EXPECTANCY	79 years
PEOPLE PER DOCTOR	307
GOVERNMENT	Multi-party republic
ADULT LITERACY	99%

Cape Verde

The volcanic Cape Verde islands are divided into the Windward and Leeward islands. They lie in the Atlantic, off Africa's west coast. Until 1975, they were a Portuguese colony. Poor soil and lack of fresh water mean that Cape Verde needs to import 90 per cent of its food.

CAPE VERDE FACTS

CAPITAL CITY	Praia
AREA	4,030 sq km (1,556 sq miles)
POPULATION	428,000
MAIN LANGUAGES	Portuguese, Creole
MAJOR RELIGION	Christian
CURRENCY	Cape Verde escudo

São Nicolau

The island of São Nicolau in the Windward Islands has many Portuguese colonial-style buildings. Most of the people here are Portuguese-African Creole. Where they can, they grow bananas and sugar-cane.

Atlantic Islands

The Atlantic Ocean contains hundreds of islands. Some, such as the British Isles, are part of a continent. Others, like the Azores and the Canaries, are volcanic. Ascension, Bermuda, St Helena, and other small islands are the summits of undersea mountains and volcanic in origin.

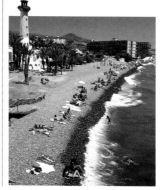

Falkland Islands

The Falklands, with an area of 11,960 sq km (4,617 sq miles), are a British dependent territory off the coast of Argentina – which calls them Las Malvinas, and claims ownership. Until oil was found in their waters, most people were sheep farmers.

Canary Islands

The Canary Islands off northwest Africa are governed as two provinces of Spain. Popular with tourists, the seven islands and six islets have a total area of 7,270 sq km (2,807 sq miles), and a population of 1,630,000.

 FIND OUT MORE   ARGENTINA, CHILE, AND URUGUAY   CLIMATE   CONTINENTS   ENERGY   FISHING INDUSTRY   GLACIATION   ISLANDS   OCEANS AND SEAS   TUNDRA   VOLCANOES

ATMOSPHERE

LIFE ON EARTH could not exist without Earth's atmosphere. The atmosphere is a colourless, tasteless, odourless blanket of gases that surrounds the Earth. It gives us air to breathe and water to drink. As well as keeping us warm by retaining the Sun's heat, it also shields us from the Sun's harmful rays. The atmosphere is approximately 700 km (440 miles) deep, but it has no distinct boundary. As it extends into space, it becomes thinner, eventually fading out. Human activity is upsetting the atmosphere's natural balance, with damaging results.

Composition of the atmosphere

Nitrogen 78%
Oxygen 21%
Argon 0.93%
Carbon dioxide 0.03%
Other gases 0.04%

Pie chart showing the composition of the atmosphere.

Earth's atmosphere is made mainly of two gases – nitrogen and oxygen. It also contains small amounts of argon and carbon dioxide, with tiny traces of other gases. The oxygen is made primarily by green plants, which maintain the balance of gases.

Layers of the atmosphere

The atmosphere is divided into five different layers. The composition of gases varies within these layers, as does the temperature which drops in the troposphere, the lowest layer, and rises in the stratosphere above.

A

Satellite

Exosphere is the outer layer of the atmosphere. Here lighter gases drift into space.

In the thermosphere, gases are very thin but they absorb ultraviolet light from the Sun, raising temperatures to 2,000°C (3,632°F). The ionosphere (layer within the thermosphere) is made of gases electrically charged or ionized by the Sun's light. Radio signals can be bounced off these ionized gases.

Aurora – lights in the night sky, possibly caused by charged particles from the Sun striking atoms.

Space shuttle

Meteorites

Stratopause is the boundary between stratosphere and mesosphere.

In the mesosphere, gases are so thin that temperatures drop rapidly with height to less than -110°C (-166°F), but the air is still thick enough to slow down meteorites.

Sonar balloon

Stratosphere contains 19 per cent of the atmosphere's gases, but little water vapour. It is very calm so airliners fly up here.

Tropopause borders troposphere and stratosphere.

Ozone layer shields the Earth from dangerous radiation.

Sea level

Troposphere extends about 12 km (7.5 miles) above the ground and is the only layer in which living things can survive naturally. It contains 75 per cent of the atmosphere's gases, water vapour, and clouds. Changes here create the weather.

Ozone layer

The thin layer of ozone gas within the stratosphere protects us by absorbing harmful ultraviolet rays from the Sun. But build-up of man-made gases called chlorofluorocarbons (CFCs) has depleted the ozone layer, and holes have started to appear in it every spring over the poles.

Ozone hole over Antarctica is shown as violet and pink

Greenhouse effect
Carbon dioxide and other gases in the atmosphere act like glass in a greenhouse, trapping the Sun's heat. This "greenhouse effect" keeps the Earth warm. But human activity, such as burning forests and running cars, releases too much carbon dioxide into the air and may cause global warming.

Some aerosol sprays use CFC gases.

Oxygen cycle

Gases continually circulate between the atmosphere and living things. Animals breathe in oxygen to help them release energy from food, and breathe out carbon dioxide. Green plants release oxygen back into the air and take in carbon dioxide as they absorb energy from the Sun. Oxygen is also used in the burning of fossil fuels.

Oxygen used in burning fossil fuels

Oxygen given off by marine plants

A large amount of oxygen is stored in the atmosphere.

Oxygen given off by plants and trees

Oxygen used up by marine animals

Oxygen used up by humans and animals

James Glaisher

English meteorologist James Glaisher (1809–1903) was one of the many balloonists who, during the 19th century, took great risks when they ascended to extraordinary heights to discover more about the atmosphere. Glaisher went up almost 12 km (7.5 miles) into the troposphere without oxygen or protective clothing. Such research led to the discovery that air becomes cooler with altitude.

FIND OUT MORE CLIMATE   FORESTS   GASES   LUNGS AND BREATHING   PLANETS   POLLUTION   SUN AND SOLAR SYSTEM   WEATHER

ATOMS AND MOLECULES

Nucleus of carbon-12 atom

Six protons

Six neutrons

 TINY PARTICLES CALLED ATOMS are the basic building blocks that make up everything around us. Forces called bonds effectively "cement" the atoms together. A molecule is a cluster of atoms linked by bonds. There are just over a hundred different types of atom, which are themselves made up of even smaller "subatomic" particles, such as protons, neutrons, and electrons.

Atomic structure

The centre, or nucleus, of an atom contains particles called protons, which carry a positive electric charge, and neutrons, which carry none. Arranged around the nucleus in layers called shells are negatively charged particles called electrons. The atom has no overall charge, because it contains equal numbers of electrons and protons, so the positive and negative charges are balanced.

Isotopes
All the atoms of an element have the same number of protons in the nucleus, but some atoms, called isotopes, have different numbers of neutrons. For example, the carbon isotope carbon-12 has six protons and six neutrons, but the isotope carbon-14 has two extra neutrons.

Quarks
Both neutrons and protons consist of three smaller particles called quarks, stuck together by tiny particles called gluons. Quarks, in turn, may contain even smaller particles.

Electron shells and valency

Atoms can have up to seven shells of electrons. An atom with eight electrons in its outermost shell is very stable. Bonds form when atoms gain, lose, or share electrons in order to achieve this stable arrangement. An atom's valency is the number of bonds it can form with other atoms.

When sodium bonds, it loses an atom, leaving an outer shell of eight electrons.

Sodium
(3 shells, valency 1)

A carbon atom can form up to four bonds with other atoms.

Carbon
(2 shells, valency 4)

Nucleus *Proton (red)* *Neutron (green)*

Electron shells

Electrons move around the nucleus in paths called orbits.

Atom of carbon-12 cut in half

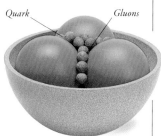

Quark *Gluons*

Inside a neutron

Ionic bonds

When an electron transfers from one atom to another, the atoms become charged particles called ions. The atom losing the electron becomes a positively charged ion, and the atom gaining the electron becomes a negatively charged ion. The force of attraction between the ions' opposite charges is called an ionic bond.

Sodium atom loses electron.

Electron transfers between atoms.

Chlorine atom gains electron.

Formation of ionic bonds in sodium chloride (NaCl)

Covalent bonds

A covalent bond forms when two atoms link up by sharing electrons. Each atom supplies an electron, and the pair of electrons orbits the nuclei of both atoms, holding the atoms together as a molecule.

Double bonds
Sometimes atoms form covalent bonds by sharing two pairs of electrons. This is called a double bond. A triple covalent bond forms when atoms share three pairs of electrons.

Covalent bonds in ammonia molecule (NH₃)

Hydrogen atom

Two shared electrons form covalent bond.

Nitrogen atom

Nitrogen bonds with three hydrogen atoms.

Atoms share four electrons.

Oxygen molecule (O₂)

Double bond links two oxygen atoms.

Chemical formula
Scientists use a kind of code called a chemical formula to describe a substance. The formula uses letters and numbers to show which elements are present in the substance, and in what proportions. Methane, for example, has a chemical formula of CH_4, which shows that it contains carbon (C) and hydrogen (H), combined in the ratio of one carbon atom to every four hydrogen atoms.

Hydrogen atom

Carbon atom

Methane molecule (CH₄)

Linus Pauling
The American chemist Linus Pauling (1901–94) won the 1954 Nobel Prize for Chemistry for his work on chemical bonds and the structure of molecules. He calculated the energies needed to make bonds, the angles at which bonds form, and the distances between atoms. He also won the 1962 Nobel Peace Prize for his efforts to stop the testing of nuclear weapons.

Bonds between molecules
The molecules of covalent compounds are held together by weak bonds called Van der Waal's forces. Some hydrogen-containing compounds, such as water, have stronger forces called hydrogen bonds between their molecules. In water, these bonds form because each oxygen atom in a water molecule is attracted to hydrogen atoms in two nearby molecules.

Covalent bond

Hydrogen bond

Oxygen atom

Hydrogen atom

Hydrogen bonds between water molecules

FIND OUT MORE ELEMENTS | MIXTURES AND COMPOUNDS | NUCLEAR POWER | RADIOACTIVITY

AUSTRALASIA AND OCEANIA

AUSTRALIA, New Zealand, Papua New Guinea, and the nearby islands are collectively called Australasia. The wider area known as Oceania also includes the island groups of Melanesia, Micronesia, and Polynesia and spans a huge area in the South Pacific Ocean. Australia is the largest country and a continent in its own right. Although many Pacific islands were once European colonies, the region now has closer trade links with Asia.

Coral islands
Many of the thousands of tiny islands in Oceania are the peaks of undersea volcanic mountains that are just breaking the surface of the Pacific Ocean. Reefs of coral, teeming with tropical fish, often build up close to the islands' sandy shores.

Physical features

Australasia and Oceania include a wide range of landscapes, from tropical rainforest in northern areas to the arid desert of central Australia. Many islands are volcanic, with sandy beaches, high mountains, and a constant threat of earthquakes.

Geysers
These occur in New Zealand where hot rock heats water in an underground chamber. As the water boils, a fountain of scalding water and steam shoots 500 m (1,640 ft) into the air.

Pinnacles Desert
Tall pinnacles of limestone rise from the sand in parts of Australia's hot, dry Western Desert. These unusually shaped rocks have been sculpted by the eroding action of plant roots and harsh winds over the last 25,000 years.

Cross-section through Australasia

Australia is a largely flat continent, with low mountains in the southwest and a desert centre. The highest mountains are the Great Dividing Range in the east. The Pacific Ocean between Australia and New Zealand dips to 5,000 m (16,405 ft). The Southern Alps run down New Zealand's South Island.

Indian Ocean | Mt. Bruce 1,235 m (4,052 ft) | Great Victoria Desert | Flinders Ranges | Great Dividing Range | South Pacific Ocean | New Zealand Southern Alps | Pacific Ocean

A   Approximately 6,300 km (3,915 miles) from A to B   B

AUSTRALASIA AND OCEANIA FACTS

AREA 8,508,238 sq km (3,285,048 sq miles)

POPULATION 29,700,000

NUMBER OF COUNTRIES 14

HIGHEST POINT Mt. Wilhelm (Papua New Guinea) 4,509 m (14,794 ft)

LONGEST RIVER Murray Darling (Australia) 3,750 km (2,330 miles)

BIGGEST LAKE Lake Eyre (Australia) 9,583 sq km (3,700 miles)

A

Climatic zones

With a wide range of landscapes and spanning such a vast area, Australasia and Oceania experience many different climates. Northern Australia and Papua New Guinea are always hot with wet and dry seasons, the east has hot summers and mild winters, and the centre is dry desert. New Zealand is mild and damp. The most westerly of the Pacific islands have a wet, tropical climate.

Wetland

Desert

Tropical rainforest

Deciduous woodland

Scrub *Grassland* *Mountain*

Many species of insect and animal live in the canopy.

Tropical rainforest

Steamy tropical rainforest covers most of the Solomon Islands, the mountains of Papua New Guinea, and parts of northern Australia. Often shrouded in mist, these dense, lush forests are a haven for wildlife and contain more than 600 species of tree. As a measure to protect the environment, logging is controlled in Queensland.

Scrub

At the edges of the four major deserts that make up the interior of Australia are areas of arid brush where there is little, often unreliable, rainfall. These areas support coarse grass, scattered shrubs, and low trees.

Small, stunted shrubs

After rain, flowers burst into bloom.

Grassland

Australia contains vast areas of dry, open grassland, known as the "outback". The best grazing land for cattle and sheep is in Queensland and New South Wales. Scarce surface water is supplemented by underground water from artesian wells. Lush grassland covers the eastern side of New Zealand's South Island.

Eucalyptus woods

Many kinds of gum tree, also known as eucalyptus, grow in Australia. There is a species of gum tree for virtually every environment, from cold, damp mountain tops to hot, dry inland areas. Gum trees are evergreens, with leathery leaves.

Mountain gum leaves

Narrow leaves hang down to avoid drying out in the hot sun.

Bushes are mostly stunted, evergreen, and spiny.

Sandstone is worn smooth and rounded by erosion.

Coastal climate

The coastal strip between Brisbane and Melbourne in southeast Australia is backed to the west by the peaks of the Great Dividing Range, including the Australian Alps. Warm breezes blow in from the Pacific Ocean, bringing rain to this green and fertile region. The long, sandy beaches and mild, pleasant climate make this the most populated region in Australia.

Powerful waves create long, sandy beaches. **Byron Bay, New South Wales**

Hot desert

The spectacular red Olgas rocks rise unexpectedly out of the arid flat expanse of Australia's scorching central desert. Situated near Uluru (Ayers Rock), this giant mass of boulders formed more than 570 million years ago and gradually eroded during the past 150 million years.

Deciduous woodland

The west coast of New Zealand's South Island is covered with deciduous woodland. Here, oak, beech, and hickory trees thrive in the mild, damp climate.

Beech forest in New Zealand's Fiordland National Park

People

The earliest inhabitants of Australasia were the Aboriginals of Australia, and the Polynesians and Melanesians from the Pacific islands. White Europeans began colonizing Australia and New Zealand in the late 1700s. Since the 1970s, Australia has allowed many other peoples to settle there, including Chinese, Cambodians, and Vietnamese.

Australian schoolchildren

Resources

Land is a major resource for Australia and New Zealand and is used extensively for grazing cattle and sheep, and for growing wheat. Australia is rich in minerals and leads the world in the production of bauxite (aluminium ore), diamonds, and lead ore. The main resources of the Pacific islands are fish and coconut products, such as copra, coir (rope), and matting.

Coconut **Sheep** **Tuna**

FIND OUT MORE ABORIGINAL AUSTRALIANS   AUSTRALIAN WILDLIFE   CLIMATE   CORAL REEFS   DESERTS   EARTHQUAKES   FORESTS   ISLANDS   PACIFIC OCEAN   TREES   VOLCANOES

AUSTRALIA

A COUNTRY and at the same time a continent, Australia is an ancient land mass, and the smallest, flattest, and, after Antarctica, the driest continent. It is the world's sixth largest country yet only 18.9 million people live there, mostly along the coast as the centre of the country consists of desert or semi-desert – the outback. Australia consists of six states and two territories. It has strong trade links with Europe, the USA, and Asia and makes significant contributions to international affairs. The population consists of a wide range of ethnic groups, making Australia a truly multicultural society.

Physical features

The centre of Australia is covered by a vast, flat, arid plain called the outback – one of the hottest places on Earth. Around the coast are tropical rainforests, snow-capped mountains, and magnificent beaches.

Great Barrier Reef
Green Island forms part of the Great Barrier Reef, which stretches 2,000 km (1,243 miles) along the northeast coast of Australia. Its coral is formed by layer upon layer of tiny anemone-like creatures, making it the largest living thing on Earth. Thousands of tourists flock to see it each year, attracted by the clear, warm waters and more than 1,500 species of fish. Recent fears that divers and swimmers may be damaging the reef have led to it becoming a protected World Heritage Area.

Uluru (Ayers Rock)
This giant block of red sandstone that rises from the desert is more than 2.4 km (1.5 miles) long. Once known as Ayers Rock, Uluru, meaning "great pebble", is the original name given to it by the Aboriginal people, who regard it as sacred.

Great Dividing Range
The Great Dividing Range is a series of high plateaus and low mountains that extends down the east of Australia. It shields the arid interior of the country from the rain-bearing clouds that blow in from the Pacific Ocean. In winter, snow covers the higher peaks, and people can ski there.

Land use
Most of Australia's interior is inhospitable desert. Sheep and cattle are reared in the east and north of the country, and wheat is grown in the fertile southwest and southeast. Australia has rich mineral deposits, many of which are in the barren interior.

Desert 47% — Wetland 1% — Forest 5.5% — Built-up 0.5% — Farmland 7.5% — Grassland 38.5%

Canberra
Founded in the early 20th century, Australia's capital, Canberra, is home to about 300,000 people. It is primarily a centre for government and has few industries. Official buildings include Parliament House, the Australian National University, the National Library, and the National Gallery.

Parliament House

Climate
Most people live in the temperate zones that occur within 400 km (249 miles) of the coast in the east and southeast, and around Perth in the west. The interior, west, and south are arid. The north is hot, humid, and tropical.

52°C (126°F) -22°C (-8°F)
20°C (68°F) 6°C (42°F)
629 mm (25 in)

People

Aboriginal people, Australia's first inhabitants, make up only about four per cent of the population. The rest are of mainly European origin, descended either from British settlers, or from Europeans who emigrated to Australia after 1945. Recent years have also seen an influx of Asians.

2 per sq km
(5 per sq mile)

85%
Urban

15%
Rural

Multicultural society
Australian society reflects the many different nationalities who have settled in the country. Aboriginal people, English, Irish, and Central and Eastern Europeans have all made their mark, and since immigration restrictions were lifted in 1972 the arrival of Chinese, Indo-Chinese, and Indonesians has added new influences. Diverse languages, customs, foods, and festivals combine to make Australia a varied and exciting society.

Farming

Less than five per cent of the labour force are farmers, yet over half the land is used for grazing cattle and sheep. Grapes and cereals are also grown.

Livestock
Beef cattle roam the Australian outback, grazing on dry grass and drinking water drawn from artesian wells. They are raised on vast cattle stations mainly for their meat. Australia has seven times more sheep than people. They produce around one-third of the world's wool.

Cereals
Although less than four per cent of the land is suitable for farming cereal crops, Australia grows barley, millet, oats, and rice, and ranks highly in world production of wheat. Other crops include sugar-cane, fruit, and vegetables.

Grapes
The gentle climate of parts of southern Australia is ideally suited to growing grapes for winemaking. The Australian wine industry has grown by leaps and bounds in recent years, now producing about 450,000 tonnes (495,000 tons) of wine a year. Much is exported.

Industry

Australia has a strong mining industry, and is a major exporter of coal, iron ore, bauxite, lead, gold, copper, and diamonds. About 16 per cent of the labour force works in manufacturing, and two-thirds are employed in services such as banks, tourism, and government.

Diamonds

Gold

Quartz

Gold and diamonds
Australia is one of the world's top gold producers and exports more diamonds than any other country. Most of the diamonds are not gem quality and are used to make industrial cutting tools.

Leisure

Australians love the outdoors. Because most live near the coast, many people enjoy water sports such as swimming, skin-diving, surfing, and sailing. Cricket is a popular spectator sport, as are rugby and the unique Australian Football.

Australian Football
One of Australia's national winter sports is Australian Football. It was invented in the 1850s and is based on Gaelic Football. Besides Australia, the only other country where it is played is Papua New Guinea.

Surfing
The crashing waves of Australia's east coast attract thousands to try their luck at riding the surf. The aptly named Surfers' Paradise, in Queensland, is a favourite spot.

Food
Traditionally, Australians are a nation of meat-eaters. They love plain foods, such as fried eggs and grilled steaks that are cooked on the barbecue. But the influx of people from mainland Europe and Asia has brought a wide range of cooking ideas from China, Greece, Indonesia, and Italy.

Barbecued lamb

Grilled pumpkin

Transport

With such a huge territory, and the nearest countries so far away from major population centres, Australians rely heavily on air transport. Buses, cars, and trains are used for short distances in the cities. Trucks carry most intercity freight by road.

Road train
Heavy loads are often transported across the outback by road train. These huge trucks may pull five or six trailers over vast distances, on deserted roads.

Flying Doctor
The Royal Flying Doctor Service was founded in 1928 to bring medical help to people living in lonely homesteads in the outback. Doctors are based at special stations where emergency callers can contact them by radio and receive treatment quickly.

Tourism
The spectacular scenery of the Hamersley Range in Western Australia is popular with tourists, mostly from Japan, New Zealand, and Southeast Asia. About five million visitors visit Australia every year, providing a welcome addition to the country's foreign earnings.

FIND OUT MORE   ABORIGINAL AUSTRALIANS   AUSTRALIA, HISTORY OF   CARS AND TRUCKS   CONTINENTS   CORAL REEFS   DESERTS   FARMING   ROCKS AND MINERALS   SPORTS

AUSTRALIA, HISTORY OF

FOR MOST OF THE LAST 40,000 years, Australia was inhabited only by Aboriginal peoples. The Aboriginals were Asian in origin and created a rich culture based on hunting and food gathering. Their peaceful existence was destroyed by the arrival of Europeans in the late 18th century. The first settlers were convicts sent from crowded British prisons, but later farmers and miners drawn by the wealth of the country joined them. In 1901, Australia became an independent nation, sending troops to fight in both world wars. Today, it is a multicultural country with a rich economy and close ties with Asia, America, and Europe.

Paddles for Aboriginal canoe

First inhabitants

The first people to inhabit Australia were the ancestors of today's Aboriginals. They reached the country about 40,000 years ago after sailing across the shallow seas that then separated Australia from Asia. As sea-levels rose, they moved inland, using stone axes to clear trees to build shelters of wood and bark.

Outrigger canoe from Queensland

Outrigger made from solid wood

Canoe dug out of a whole tree trunk

String made of grass holds the outrigger to the main canoe.

Early sightings

In the 17th century, Spanish sailor Luis Vaez de Torres and Dutchman Willem Jansz explored the islands of Asia and the Pacific. Unplanned landings took place as ships were blown off course. In 1642–43 Dutchman Abel Tasman sailed round Australia without catching sight of it. He landed on an island he named Van Diemen's Land, now called Tasmania.

Early map of Australia

Botany Bay

In 1770, the British explorer Captain James Cook sailed into an inlet in southeastern Australia. He named the place Botany Bay and claimed the entire east coast of Australia for Britain. Joseph Banks, one of the ship's naturalists, sketched and collected hundreds of plants, that had never before been seen by Europeans.

Convict transportation

In 1787, the British decided to transport (ship out) convicts to Australia. The first fleet, containing 759 convicts, arrived in Botany Bay in 1788. A penal settlement was established at nearby Sydney Cove, in Port Jackson. Transportation finally came to an end in 1868.

Convicts were often used as servants.

The 19th century

Some 90 years after the arrival of Cook, the major settlements were all on the coast, and few people travelled inland. The first explorers mapped the Murray and Darling rivers in the southeast, while others tried to reach the heart of Australia.

Crossing the continent

The Royal Society of Victoria decided to send an expedition to cross the continent from south to north. Irishman Robert O'Hara Burke and Englishman William J Wills completed the trip in 1861, but died on the return journey. In July 1862 their rival, John Stuart, completed a similar journey, unaware that Burke and Wills had beaten him to it. He died in the attempt.

Surveyor's chain used to measure land, 1800s

Gold rush

The discovery of gold in 1851 brought a rush of fortune-hunters. By 1860, the population had grown from 200,000 in 1840 to 1.1 million, and Australian gold accounted for 39 per cent of the world's total output.

Prospectors' camp, Victoria

Growth

The colonies prospered in the last years of the 19th century. Industry grew quickly, especially in areas such as construction and manufacturing. Social policies were forward-thinking: for example, education for all was an early goal; trade unions were organized in many areas.

Banner for trade union

Ned Kelly

Throughout the 19th century, parts of Australia were lawless. One of the most notorious outlaws, or bushrangers, was Ned Kelly (1855–80), who led a gang of robbers. The gang killed three policemen in 1878 and robbed several banks before Kelly was caught and hanged in Melbourne in 1880. His fight against the authorities made Kelly a national folk hero.

A

Independent nation

In the early days, Australia consisted of six separate colonies. Each had its own administration but was subject to the sovereignty of Britain. As the agricultural and mining industries grew in strength, the six colonies began to work closely together. In 1901, Australia gained its independence from Britain, and a federal government for the entire country was established with its capital in Melbourne. Today, the federal capital is at Canberra.

Gallipoli

On 25 April, 1915, ANZAC forces landed at Gallipoli at the approaches to the Black Sea, Turkey. They hoped to take Constantinople (modern-day Istanbul) and force Germany's World War I ally, Turkey, out of the war. The men showed extraordinary courage and spirit, but the campaign was a disaster. No important gains were made and more than 11,400 ANZAC troops lost their lives.

Gallipoli memorial

ANZAC forces

Anzac Monument, Sydney

Australian and New Zealand forces fought for Britain in the Boer War (1899–1902) in South Africa and in both world wars. They fought together as the Australia and New Zealand Army Corps (ANZAC), making a contribution out of all proportion to their size. They suffered huge casualties, but the effort forged a strong sense of national identity.

Dominion status

When Australia became independent in 1901, it remained a Dominion of the British Empire and kept close links with its former ruler. But many people had few ties to the old "Mother Country". The threat of Japanese invasion during World War II led to closer links with the USA as the only power that could defend Australia.

The Federation Flag was based on the state flag of New South Wales.

Federation Flag

Immigration

In 1902, the government passed the Immigration Restriction Act to limit Chinese immigration. The act required settlers to speak a European language, and began a White Australia policy that lasted until the 1970s. Britons, Greeks, and Italians flooded into Australia in the 1950s and 1960s, but immigration from Asia later increased.

Scottish emigrants leave for Australia.

Modern Australia

After World War II, Australia continued its military alliance with the USA. The country sent troops to fight with the Americans in Korea during the 1950s and Vietnam in the 1960s. In recent years, those ties have weakened, and Australia has increasingly turned towards Asia, in particular Japan, for trade and investment. Today, Australia is an important trading partner with most of the powerful East Asian economies.

National symbol

Sydney Opera House, with its bold concrete roofs, has become the most widely recognized symbol of Australia.

Australian republic?

In 1992, the prime minister, Paul Keating, said he wanted the country be a republic by the year 2000, with an Australian as the head of state, instead of the British monarch. However, a referendum held in 1999 defeated any such proposals.

Chinese festival, Sydney

Skyscraper, Sydney

Multicultural Australia

Modern Australia is a multi-racial state with large Chinese and Greek populations. However, the Aboriginals are fighting a long campaign to be included in society and to secure their land rights and civil liberties.

Sailing in Sydney Harbour

Sports excellence

One way in which Australia has expressed its national identity is through sporting activities. There have been notable successes in sports as diverse as cricket and yachting. For example, in 1983 Australia overturned a century of US yachting dominance by winning the America's Cup. Sydney was chosen as the site of the Olympic Games in 2000.

Timeline

c.40,000 BC Aboriginals arrive in Australia.

1642–43 Tasman names Van Diemen's Land (Tasmania).

1770 Captain Cook lands at Botany Bay.

1788 First British convicts arrive.

Wallaby

1828 Charles Sturt begins to explore Murray and Darling rivers.

1851 Gold discovered in Victoria and New South Wales.

1860–61 Burke and Wills cross Australia from south to north.

1868 Britain abolishes the transportation of convicts.

Aboriginal digging sticks

1901 Australia becomes self-governing dominion in the British Empire.

1902 Immigration Restriction Act establishes the White Australia policy.

1914–18 60,000 Australians are killed fighting for Britain in World War I.

1927 Parliament meets for the first time in the new federal capital of Canberra.

1970s White Australia policy abolished.

1993 Aboriginal land rights recognized by law.

2000 Olympic Games held in Sydney.

2001 Fierce bush fires cause immense damage.

FIND OUT MORE   ABORIGINAL AUSTRALIANS   CRIME AND PUNISHMENT   COOK, JAMES   EXPLORATION   OPERA   PREHISTORIC PEOPLE   WORLD WAR I   WORLD WAR II

AUSTRALIAN WILDLIFE

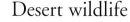

AUSTRALIA HAS BEEN ISOLATED by water for more than 30 million years, resulting in the evolution of many unique animals and plants. Half of all marsupials, such as the koala and kangaroo, live only in Australia, along with the platypus and echidna, the world's only egg-laying mammals, or monotremes. Much of Australia is desert or scrub. The animals and plants that live here are adapted to the hot, dry conditions. There are also areas of tropical and temperate forests, which contain the greatest diversity of life in Australia.

Desert wildlife

Australia's hot, dry, desert interior makes up half the continent. Drought-resistant vegetation, such as porcupine grass and acacias, grow here, providing a refuge for birds and insects. Many desert mammals rest in burrows by day to avoid the heat.

Emu
Emus are large flightless birds that can run at up to 50 kmh (30 mph), although they usually walk. They cover large distances in search of grasses, fruit, and flowers. They also eat insects. Males incubate the eggs and guard the young after they hatch.

Porcupine grass
As its name suggests, porcupine grass is a spiny plant that grows in circular tussocks. It is adapted to dry desert conditions by having a thick outer covering (cuticle) to reduce water loss, and by having deep roots to reach water in the soil.

Galah
The galah, or roseate cockatoo, is one of the most common parrots in Australia. Large flocks of these birds are found not only in dry areas but also in cities. Galahs eat seeds, leaf buds, and insects.

Strong bill is used to dig up insects.

Thorny devil
This lizard's scales are drawn out into long spines. When temperatures fall at night, valuable water condenses on the spines and runs down tiny grooves towards the mouth.

Spines protect against predators.

Mulgara
This carnivorous marsupial (pouched mammal) eats insects and small vertebrates, such as mice and lizards. It bites and shakes its prey to kill it. The mulgara digs burrows in sand, in which it shelters to escape the midday sun.

Mulgara eats prey head first.

Grass forms a refuge for insects, lizards, and birds.

Long, strong legs

Lizard searches for ants.

Scrub and grassland wildlife

Covering about a third of Australia, scrub and grassland are hot and dry in summer and cooler in winter. Occasional downpours of rain are exploited by plants that rapidly bloom and produce seeds, and animals, such as frogs, that emerge to reproduce.

Canopy provides shelter for animals from the midday heat.

Bottle tree
These large trees get their name from their bottle-shaped trunks. The swollen trunk stores water that helps the tree survive periods of drought. The tree also provides food for many animals, including insects, and shelter for some birds and mammals. Other vegetation common in scrubland includes dry grasses and dwarf eucalyptus.

Short-beaked echidna
The short-beaked echidna is an egg-laying mammal found in Australia, Tasmania, and New Guinea. It uses its sticky tongue to extract ants and termites from their nests. If threatened, the echidna rolls into a ball, or digs down into the soil.

Mallee fowl
The male mallee fowl builds a mound of vegetation and soil in which the female lays her eggs. As the vegetation rots, it releases heat that incubates the eggs.

Male checks mound temperature with his beak, and by moving vegetation.

Water-holding frog
This frog survives drought by burrowing into the ground, and forming a thin layer of skin around itself to conserve water. It also stores water in its bladder.

Water is stored in bulbous trunk.

Kultarr
This small, mouse-like marsupial is nocturnal. It has large eyes to help it see in the dark, and to catch insects and spiders. It moves by springing off its long hind feet and tail and landing on its front feet. During the day the kultarr shelters in logs, hollow stumps, and burrows.

Kultarr feeding on a spider.

Temperate forest wildlife

The temperate forests of south and east Australia are hot and dry in summer, and cooler and wetter in winter. They are home to birds, such as parrots and kookaburras, marsupials, including the koala, and a variety of reptiles and insects. Many trees found here, such as eucalyptus and mountain ash, are unique to Australia.

Silver wattle
The silver wattle, also known as mimosa, is a common plant in temperate forests. These trees, with their characteristic silver-grey leaves, can withstand dry periods as well as exploit the wet season.

Bright yellow flowers provide food for insects and other animals.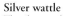

Kookaburra
The kookaburra is the largest member of the kingfisher family. It is rarely found near water, however, preferring open woodland. Kookaburras swoop down from a tree branch perch to pounce on insects, lizards, snakes, and small birds and mammals. They defend their territory by making loud cackling calls that sound like human laughter.

Male lyrebird sings a loud territorial song, mimicking other birds and animals.

Lyrebird
These ground-living birds use their large clawed feet to turn over stones and break open logs, in search of insects. The male lyrebird has a long tail shaped like a lyre, an ancient musical instrument. He performs courtship dances to attract females by vibrating his tail over his back.

Flattened tail helps platypus swim.

Heavy beak to kill reptiles and rodents.

Duck-billed platypus
This unusual-looking animal is an egg-laying mammal, or monotreme, that lives near rivers. The platypus feeds underwater on insect larvae and other food found by probing the stream bottom with its sensitive bill. It hunts mainly at night, spending most of the day in a burrow dug in the stream bank.

Long tail feathers

Koalas spend most of their time in eucalyptus trees, using their sharp claws and strong legs to climb through the branches.

Koala
Koalas are bear-like marsupials that feed on the leaves of eucalyptus trees. They eat mainly at night, spending most of the day resting or sleeping in the fork of a tree.

Tree kangaroo
The tree kangaroo is a marsupial adapted for life in the trees, by having rough paw pads and long claws for gripping. Its diet consists mainly of leaves and bark, but it sometimes descends to the ground to feed on shrubs and seedlings.

Tropical rainforest wildlife

Despite occupying only a tiny part of northeastern Australia, the rainforests contain one-third of Australia's frog and marsupial species, and two-thirds of its butterflies. The wide variety of ferns and trees, such as breadfruit trees, provide shelter and food for these animals, and many birds, bats, and insects.

Long tail for balancing in the trees.

Rainbow lorikeet
These brightly coloured parrots live in screeching flocks of up to 20 birds in the upper rainforest canopy. They feed on pollen, nectar, flowers, seeds, and fruit.

Trigger plant
When a bee lands on a trigger plant flower, the anther – the flower's male part – bends outwards to dust pollen on the bee's hairy back. When the bee visits another flower the pollen sticks to the stigma – the female part of the flower, thereby pollinating it.

Pink flowers attract bees.

Fangs are 1 cm (0.5 in) long so they can inject venom deep into their victims.

Taipan
This forest snake is active in the early morning and evening, and feeds mainly on rats and other small mammals. The taipan is one of the world's most poisonous snakes; a bite from its long fangs is often fatal for humans. Taipans normally retreat and hide when people approach, but they will become aggressive if threatened.

The male is brightly coloured.

Queen Alexandra's birdwing
Found in New Guinea, this is the largest butterfly in the world. The female is larger than the male and has a wingspan of up to 28 cm (11 in). Queen Alexandra's birdwing flies in the sunlight of the upper canopy, where it feeds on flower nectar.

Brown coloration provides camouflage for taipan.

FIND OUT MORE   AUSTRALIA   BIRDS   BUTTERFLIES AND MOTHS   CAMOUFLAGE AND COLOUR   FLIGHTLESS BIRDS   FROGS AND TOADS   KANGAROOS AND OTHER MARSUPIALS   REPTILES   TREES

AZTECS

A GREAT IMPERIAL power, the Aztecs came to dominate the Valley of Mexico in less than a hundred years. Egged on by bloodthirsty gods, they were a warlike people, outstanding for their military skill and well organized society. By the time the Spanish conquistador Hernán Cortés (1485–1547) arrived in 1519, the Aztecs and their allies were rulers of some 25 million people.

Tenochtitlán
Mexico

Rise of the Aztecs

The Aztecs were one of many tribes who invaded the Valley of Mexico soon after the collapse of the Toltecs in the late 12th century. They dominated the valley after 1438.

Human sacrifice
When they won a war, the Aztecs killed many prisoners as offerings to their gods. Aztecs believed that human sacrifices were necessary in order for the universe to continue.

Dish for human heart

Subject peoples
The Aztecs ruled over a network of city states. Subject peoples made regular payments to their Aztec overlords, in the form of maize, cacao, or cotton. As long as this "tribute" was paid, the peoples of the Valley of Mexico were left to govern themselves and to keep their customs.

Shrine of Tlaloc, god of rain
Shrine of Huitzilopochtli, god of war
Quetzalcoatl's temple
Temple plaza

Tenochtitlán

A city of canals and narrow streets, the Aztec capital was built on an island in Lake Texcoco. It was linked to the land by three narrow causeways. The city was home to 200,000 people – four or five times larger than any European city of the time. Most people lived in small houses in the narrow streets surrounding an area of temples – the Great Precinct.

Great Precinct
The centre of Tenochtitlán was dominated by the Great Precinct, surrounded by a wall decorated with huge serpent heads. Inside the enclosure were the temples of the leading gods. A skull rack displayed the heads of countless victims of human sacrifice.

Aztec society

Commoners lived in small mud houses and grew crops on the marshes. They dressed and ate simply. The nobles were warriors, tribute collectors, and judges; they were rewarded for their services with land.

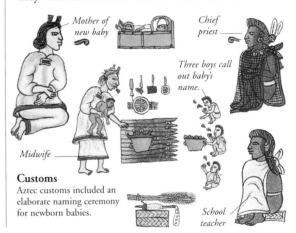

Mother of new baby
Chief priest
Three boys call out baby's name.
Midwife
School teacher

Customs
Aztec customs included an elaborate naming ceremony for newborn babies.

Aztecs on the eve of conquest

By the early 16th century, the Aztec empire was showing signs of weakness. Shortly before the arrival of Cortés, priests and nobles were worried by a series of omens that seemed to forecast Aztec decline. These omens included the rumbling of the volcano Popocatépetl.

Quetzalcoatl
The Aztecs believed that the god Quetzalcoatl had been driven from his kingdom and would return to begin a golden age. When Cortés arrived, they thought he was the god. But the noise of Popocatépetl seemed to be an omen of defeat.

Quetzalcoatl, the feathered serpent

Popocatépetl

Montezuma II

The emperor Montezuma II (c.1466–1520) was unsure if Cortés was Quetzalcoatl, and did not repel the Spanish when they arrived. Cortés and his small army got as far as the capital, and Montezuma welcomed them there. But the Spanish seized the emperor and took him hostage. Montezuma died in prison, the last Aztec ruler.

Conquest of the Aztecs

In April 1519, Cortés founded Veracruz on the coast of the Gulf of Mexico, inside the Aztec empire. With his army of 600 men and 16 horses, he advanced towards Tenochtitlán, forging alliances with Aztec enemies. By August 1521, the Spanish had occupied Tenochtitlán, after laying siege with the help of many local soldiers.

Defeat by Tlaxcala
The growing thirst for human sacrifice led Aztecs to wage constant war on the neighbouring Tlaxcalans. Four years before the arrival of Cortés, the Tlaxcalans inflicted a heavy defeat on the Aztec armies, greatly weakening the empire.

FIND OUT MORE
CENTRAL AMERICA, HISTORY OF   MAYA   MESOAMERICANS   OLMECS

A

Aztec life
Everyday items

Adze was a woodworker's tool.

Chisel used by masons.

Water jar is made of glazed earthenware and has a narrow neck.

Bowl is decorated with bold abstract patterns in two colours.

Axe heads were often made of copper; they originally had wooden handles.

Flute made of bone could play simple tunes.

Ritual items

Tools had blades of flint or obsidian, often with wooden handles.

Flint knives

Obsidian hooked knife

Club with obsidian blades

Spear with obsidian blades

Mask may be made from skull of sacrificial victim.

Greenstone mask was left as an offering to the gods.

Flint knives may have been used to kill sacrificial victims.

Feathered cloak was worn by priest or warrior.

Ritual vessel was used in the temple.

Aztec people

Cleaner with broom

Boy carrying rushes

Mother and babies

Mask in shape of eagle's beak

Sleeves in form of eagle's wings

Eagle's talons on leg-guard

Eagle warrior

Young woman

Weaver

Girl grinding maize

Boatman

Carpenter

Painter

Boatman

Musician   **Schoolmaster**   **Jeweller**

Eagle warrior

Goldsmith   **Featherworker**

Messenger

A

102

BABYLONIAN EMPIRE

ON THE EUPHRATES RIVER, 4,000 years ago, an ancient settlement became the most magnificent city in the Near East. This city was Babylon, and when Hammurabi conquered Mesopotamia, he established his capital there. Over centuries, Babylonian fortunes rose and fell, as the city was invaded by the Hittites, Kassites, and Assyrians. The Assyrians destroyed Babylon in 689 BC. In 612 BC, the Babylonians retaliated by conquering the Assyrians, and again making their city the world's greatest. Babylonia's splendour continued after the Persian Empire absorbed it in 539 BC.

The first Babylonian Empire
By about 1770 BC, Hammurabi had conquered most of Mesopotamia. Babylon was established as the capital of the south for the duration of the Babylonian Empire.

King Hammurabi

Mesopotamia's wisest king, Hammurabi (r.1792–1750 BC), followed ancient tradition by issuing laws to protect his subjects. Using cuneiform script, he had 282 laws carved on a black stone pillar. The empire he founded collapsed in 1595 BC, when Hittites from Anatolia looted it. The Kassites from the mountains to the east of Babylon then invaded and took over.

Kassites
Between 1600 and 1190 BC, people called the Kassites ruled Babylonia. They are best known for their boundary stones (kuddurus), which marked property divisions and recorded gifts of land. These were often decorated with divine symbols. After the end of Kassite rule, Babylonia fell into a long period of chaos.

Kudduru

Persian Empire
In 539 BC, the Persian king Cyrus II took over the Babylonian kingdom, and made Mesopotamia part of his empire. His son Cambyses was usurped by Darius I, also called "the Great", under whom the empire reached its greatest extent.

Darius I (522–486) introduced coinage.

Literature and art

The Babylonian Empire was world-famous for its great artistic and literary achievements. Literature such as the legendary epic of Gilgamesh, a Sumerian hero, was written on clay tablets in cuneiform. Artistic splendours included terracotta plaques, superb sculpture and glassware, and, above all, the lavish and decorative entrance to the city – the Ishtar Gate and Processional Way.

Venus tablet, Kish

Cuneiform script

Science
Babylonia was famous as the home of scientists and scholars. Babylonian astrologers studied the movements of planets and stars, recorded their findings on clay tablets, and used these to predict the future. Many texts are so detailed that modern astronomers can date ancient events from them. Ancient Greeks and Romans used the Babylonian system for naming planets.

Magical spirit

Religion
The Babylonians inherited their religion from the Sumerians. They believed that gods and spirits controlled every aspect of the world. These included Anu, the sky god, who gave birth to some of the most important deities, including Ishtar, goddess of love and war (represented by the planet Venus), and Ea, god of wisdom and fresh water. Ea was the father of Marduk, the god of Babylon, who created the world and made humans by mixing earth with divine blood.

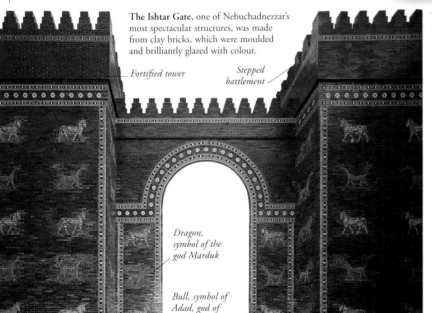

The Ishtar Gate, one of Nebuchadnezzar's most spectacular structures, was made from clay bricks, which were moulded and brilliantly glazed with colour.

Fortified tower

Stepped battlement

Dragon, symbol of the god Marduk

Bull, symbol of Adad, god of the weather

Nebuchadnezzar

After the Babylonian king Nabopolasser defeated the Assyrian enemy, his son Nebuchadnezzar (r.605–562 BC) rebuilt the devastated Babylon on a grand scale. His works included the fabulous Ishtar Gate, and a temple and ziggurat tower. According to Greek tradition, he also built the Hanging Gardens for his homesick wife, and these became one of the Seven Wonders of the World. In 596 BC, Nebuchadnezzar attacked the kingdom of Judah. Ten years later he returned, sacked Jerusalem, and took the Jews into exile in Babylon. They were not released until the reign of Cyrus II.

FIND OUT MORE   ARCHITECTURE   ASIA, HISTORY OF   ASSYRIAN EMPIRE   HITTITES   PERSIAN EMPIRES   SCIENCE, HISTORY OF   SEVEN WONDERS OF THE ANCIENT WORLD   SUMERIANS   WARFARE

BADGERS, OTTERS, AND SKUNKS

THESE THREE GROUPS OF ANIMALS are all members of the weasel family – Mustelidae. Their main characteristics are a long, low-slung body, short legs, and five toes on each foot. They are carnivores, although badgers have a mixed diet. The honey badger is especially fond of honey, as its name suggests. Most mustelids discharge a thick, oily, powerful-smelling fluid called a musk from their anal glands. They use this mostly to send scent messages to other members of the species, usually with their droppings.

Skull
A badger eats meat and plants, and its large canines and broad molar teeth are ideal for this diet. Its jaw muscles are fixed to a rigid bone on the top of the skull, giving the animal a powerful bite.

Badgers

All badgers are thick set with very powerful legs which they use to forage for food and to dig their often extensive burrows. They are nocturnal animals, spending the day underground with others of their social group. There are eight species of true badger, plus the honey badger, which is classed in a sub-family of its own.

Short tail
Long, striped snout

Long coarse hairs over a dense underfur
Badgers have a good sense of smell.

Forepaw print   **Hind paw print**

Paws
A Eurasian badger's track is unmistakable. Each foot has five toes with a kidney-shaped pad behind. The front claws usually leave marks because they are long.

Eurasian badger
This is the largest badger and has the widest distribution. Females give birth to up to four cubs in February. These are weaned at 12 weeks, when they can forage for themselves.

Otters

These semi-aquatic mustelids occur outside the polar regions in every continent except Australia. Some species are exclusively sea creatures, some use only fresh water, and others use both sea and fresh water. Most have sleeping dens, or holts, on land.

European river otter

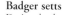

Asian short-clawed otter

Paws
Although all otters swim, not all have webbed feet. For example, the European otter has a large amount of webbing. The Asian short-clawed otter has little webbing and uses its paws to find food by touch.

Fur
An otter's coat consists of two layers. A thick under-layer of fine hairs traps air for warmth, and longer, waterproof guard hairs keep the underfur dry.

Badger setts
During the day, badgers live underground in a complex system of tunnels and chambers called a sett. A main badger sett is easily recognized by the entrances with piles of soil outside.

Honey badger
The African honey badger, also known as the ratel, has a thick, loose skin. Predators can find it difficult to pierce its skin, and the badger can twist around inside its skin and bite back.

Movement

With their long back and heavy tail, otters can look clumsy on land. In the water they are graceful swimmers, propelling themselves forward by moving their hindquarters and tail up and down.

Spraints
Otters secrete a powerful scent. They mark their territory by leaving their droppings, called spraints, which smell of this scent, on high points such as rocks.

Skunks

There are 13 species of skunk, which all occur in the Americas. They are best known for their ability to squirt a foul-smelling fluid from their anal glands. They aim this fluid at the eyes of an enemy, and it can cause temporary blindness. Skunks search for insects and other small animals to eat, mainly at night.

Markings
Skunks have bold black and white coat markings. Like the yellow and black stripes of a wasp, these warn would-be predators of danger.

EURASIAN BADGER

SCIENTIFIC NAME *Meles meles*

ORDER Carnivora

FAMILY Mustelidae

DISTRIBUTION Europe and a wide band across Asia

HABITAT Mainly lowland farmland and woodland

DIET Worms, insects, birds, and other small animals, fruit, cereals, fungi

SIZE Length: 1 m (3.3 ft)

LIFESPAN About 7 years

FIND OUT MORE

ANIMAL BEHAVIOUR   LAKE AND RIVER WILDLIFE   NORTH AMERICAN WILDLIFE   POLLUTION   WEASELS AND MARTENS

Formerly known as **BALKAN STATES**

SOUTHEAST EUROPE

SLOVENIA, CROATIA, Bosnia and Herzegovina, Yugoslavia, Macedonia, and Albania all lie in Southeast Europe. Ruled by Turkey for nearly 500 years, all the countries, with the exception of Albania, were united as Yugoslavia in 1918. It was, however, an uneasy peace, and, in 1991, Yugoslavia split up as a result of rival ethnic and religious tensions. War broke out, lasting until 1995. Since then, fresh conflicts have occurred and the region is still struggling to recover from war.

Physical features
The western region of Southeast Europe is made up of limestone plateaus and steep mountain ranges separated by forested valleys. In the northwest of the region are the flat plains of the River Danube.

23°C (73°F)   1°C (34°F)

870 mm (34 in)

Regional climate
The inland plains and the coastal strip have a temperate continental climate, with hot summers and cold winters. Snow falls in the mountains in winter.

Mountains
Mixed forests of deciduous trees and conifers cover the mountain slopes that dominate the north of the region. The Dinaric Alps are barren limestone ranges, or *karst*, that rise to about 1,800 m (5,905 ft) along the Adriatic Sea coast.

Adriatic coast
The strip of land that runs down the Adriatic coast is narrow, and in places the mountains of the Dinaric Alps rise steeply from the sea. The landscape is mostly barren rock, with sparse vegetation. In winter, snow covers the cliffs, but summers are hot. The coast is prone to the *bora*, a strong, cold wind that blows off the land. More than 600 islands lie along the Croatian part of the coast.

Ethnic groups
Ethnic tensions and religious differences mainly between Christian Serbs and Croats and Muslim Bosnians in the region led to much bloodshed in the war of 1991–95. About 40 per cent of people belong to Eastern Orthodox Churches, and 30 per cent are Roman Catholics. The rest are Muslims, mostly living in Bosnia and Albania.

Bosnian Muslim praying for her son killed in the war.

Iron Gate
The Iron Gate is a 3-km (2-mile) long gorge on the River Danube that runs along the border between the Yugoslavian state of Serbia and Romania. The gate marks the point at which the river breaks through between the Carpathian and Balkan Mountains. In 1896, the Sip Canal was constructed to improve navigation, and, in 1972, a dam for hydroelectric power was completed.

Slovenia

Historically and geographically, Slovenia has more in common with Austria than with other neighbouring states. The country was ruled by Austria for almost a thousand years. Slovenia has many small farms and thriving businesses. Despite economic problems caused by the conflict in areas to the south, it is the region's wealthiest country.

Resources
Slovenia mines mercury, lead, oil, and zinc for export. There are also deposits of brown coal and lignite, but they are poor quality and difficult to extract. One-third of the country's energy comes from a nuclear plant in Krsvo.

Mercury ore

People
About 90 per cent of the population are Slovenes who have kept their language and traditional culture despite centuries of Austrian domination. Wages are higher than in other Balkan states, and standards of education are high. One in seven Slovenes lives in the capital, Ljubljana, which has textile, electronics, chemical, and manufacturing industries.

Tourism
Slovenia is slowly rebuilding its tourist industry, which suffered as a result of the war in Bosnia. Skiing, spa resorts, and lakeside scenery attract many visitors to the Alps in the north of the region.

Lake Bled is a popular tourist destination.

SLOVENIA FACTS	
CAPITAL CITY	Ljubljana
AREA	20,250 sq km (7,820 sq miles)
POPULATION	2,016,000
MAIN LANGUAGE	Slovene
MAJOR RELIGION	Christian
CURRENCY	Tolar

Croatia

Ruled by Hungary for more than 800 years, Croatia became part of Yugoslavia in 1918, gaining independence in 1991. Croatia's economy was damaged by the war with neighbouring Bosnia, but it is fortunate in having important ports and rich resources, including oil, coal, and bauxite. The tourist industry is recovering.

Zagreb
The cultural and industrial capital of Croatia is Zagreb, which grew out of two medieval settlements on the River Sava. The city has museums, art galleries, 13th-century buildings, and cathedrals, such as St Mark's and St Stephen's. Most people travel around by tram and bus.

Adriatic coast
Croatia's Adriatic coast has sandy beaches and hundreds of offshore islands that once attracted up to 12 million tourists every year. However, the outbreak of war in 1991 abruptly halted all tourism. The country still has a thriving fishing industry, with an annual catch of about 25,000 tonnes (27,500 tons).

Flax stalks

Linen fibre

Flax
Fields of flax are cultivated in the fertile river valleys of northern Croatia. Flax fibre, which is obtained by crushing the stalks of the plant, is woven into linen and canvas, and its seeds yield linseed oil. Apricots, grapes, and plums are also grown in northern Croatia.

CROATIA FACTS	
CAPITAL CITY	Zagreb
AREA	56,540 sq km (21,830 sq miles)
POPULATION	4,500,000
MAIN LANGUAGE	Croatian
MAJOR RELIGIONS	Christian
CURRENCY	Kuna

Bosnia and Herzegovina

In 1991, bitter fighting broke out in the twin states of Bosnia and Herzegovina between the Roman Catholic Croats, Muslim Bosnians, and Orthodox Serbs. In all, about 300,000 people were killed, more than 2,000,000 fled the country, and many historic cities were devastated. A delicate peace has prevailed since 1995.

Muslims
During the war, Serbs from Bosnia forced Croats and Muslims out of areas they regarded as their own. Thousands were killed, and many Muslims fled abroad. In 1995, a peace agreement split the country into two provinces: Bosnian-Serb and Muslim-Croat.

Sarajevo
Straddling the River Miljacka, Sarajevo is the capital of Bosnia and Herzegovina. Under communist rule the city was transformed from a sleepy, Islamic town to a bustling, multi-cultural industrial centre. During the civil war, however, it was shattered by 2,000,000 shells, which killed tens of thousands of people. Serbs attacking the city were forced to withdraw in 1995.

BOSNIA AND HERZEGOVINA FACTS	
CAPITAL CITY	Sarajevo
AREA	51,130 sq km (19,741 sq miles)
POPULATION	4,000,000
MAIN LANGUAGE	Serbo-Croat
MAJOR RELIGIONS	Christian, Muslim
CURRENCY	Markar

Farming
Bosnia and Herzegovina's main farming region lies in the southwest. The area has fertile, well-watered soil and hot, dry summers. Crops include citrus fruit, grapes, maize, pomegranates, figs, olives, rice, and tobacco. Sheep are reared on the upland areas.

Figs

Pomegranates

Yugoslavia

Two of the former Yugoslavia's states, Serbia and Montenegro, kept the name Yugoslavia in 1992. As a result of the part Serbia played in helping Serbs fight in Bosnia and Croatia, many countries imposed sanctions and refused to trade with the new Yugoslavia. Its disgraced former president Slobodan Milošević was called to a war crimes tribunal.

Raznjici

Cubes of grilled lamb　　*Skewer*

Food
A favourite Yugoslavian dish is *raznjici*, which is made of cubes of lamb grilled on skewers and served with yoghurt. *Djuvetsch*, meat with rice and vegetables, is also popular. The favourite national drink is *slivovitz*, plum brandy.

People
The people of Yugoslavia speak Serbo-Croat, which they write in the Russian-like Cyrillic alphabet. The largest minority group is Albanian (17 per cent). Most people belong to the Serbian Orthodox Church.

Sveti Stefan was once a popular tourist destination.

Tourism
Before the war, the beautiful beaches and historic towns and villages on Montenegro's coast attracted millions of tourists. However, many beauty spots have been devastated. Yugoslavia only received 150,000 visitors in 2001 and is trying to rebuild its shattered tourist industry.

YUGOSLAVIA FACTS
CAPITAL CITY	Belgrade
AREA	102,350 sq km (39,506 sq miles)
POPULATION	10,600,000
MAIN LANGUAGE	Serbo-Croat
MAJOR RELIGIONS	Christian, Muslim
CURRENCY	Yugoslav dinar

B

Macedonia

The official name of the country is the Former Yugoslav Republic of Macedonia to appease the Greeks, who have a province called Macedonia. Land-locked, it is self-sufficient in energy, with efficient metal, chemical, textile, and food processing industries. Air pollution is a serious problem. Renewed ethnic conflicts broke out in 2001.

Skopje
Despite having been destroyed four times by earthquakes, most recently in 1963, Macedonia's capital, Skopje, is the hub of the country's communications and industry.

Lakes
Lake Ohrid and Lake Prespa in southwestern Macedonia are two of Europe's most beautiful lakes and, in peaceful times, they attract visitors for the scenery and the fishing. Ohrid is 294 m (964 ft) deep. Underground channels link the two lakes.

People
The largest group of people is made up of Eastern Orthodox (Christian) Slav Macedonians who account for two-thirds of the population. Many ethnic Albanian refugees arrived from Kosovo in 1999.

MACEDONIA FACTS
CAPITAL CITY	Skopje
AREA	25,713 sq km (9,925 sq miles)
POPULATION	2,093,000
MAIN LANGUAGES	Macedonian, Serbo-Croat
MAJOR RELIGIONS	Christian, Muslim
CURRENCY	Denar

Albania

From 1944 to 1991, Albania was a one-party state with the most rigid communist regime in the world. It is now a democracy, but in 1997 there was a severe economic crisis. Tirana, the capital, was founded in the 17th century and has light industry as well as government buildings.

Grapes
Tomatoes
Potatoes
Watermelon

Farming
About 24 per cent of Albania is cultivated. Wheat, maize, potatoes and other vegetables, fruit, and sugar beet are the main crops. Sheep, goats, and cattle are reared for meat and milk, and donkeys are bred for transport.

People
As a way of making the population grow rapidly, the communist government encouraged men and women to have large families. Under communism, Albania was the only official atheist state and, even today, many people are non-believers.

ALBANIA FACTS
CAPITAL CITY	Tirana
AREA	28,750 sq km (11,100 sq miles)
POPULATION	3,100,000
MAIN LANGUAGE	Albanian
MAJOR RELIGIONS	Muslim, Christian
CURRENCY	Lek

Transport
Communications are difficult in this rugged land. There are only 440 km (273 miles) of rail lines, and 7,450 km (4,630 miles) of roads, 60 per cent of which are dirt tracks. There is only one car for every 50 people. Horses and carts are the main means of transport.

FIND OUT MORE CHRISTIANITY　EARTHQUAKES　EMPIRES　EUROPE, HISTORY OF　FARMING　FISHING INDUSTRY　ISLAM　LAKES　TEXTILES AND WEAVING　TRADE AND INDUSTRY

BALLET

ONE OF THE MOST beautiful of the arts, ballet is a combination of dance and mime performed to music. Many ballets tell a story; others are abstract and experiment with form and movement. Ballet began in Italy. It was taken to France in 1533 by Catherine de Médicis, a member of a famous Italian family, who married a French prince. In 1661, Louis XIV founded the first ballet school, L'Academie Royale de Danse. Today, children learn the basics in ballet schools around the world.

First position – heels together, feet turned out.

Second position – heels apart, feet turned out.

Third position – one foot crossed halfway in front of the other.

Fourth position (crossed) – one foot in front of the other.

Fifth position – Feet crossed and touching.

Arms open wide

Both arms held in front

One arm in front, the other out to the side

One arm up, the other out to the side

Both arms up

Ballet positions

Every step in ballet makes use of the basic positions. It was at L'Academie Royale de Danse that the five basic positions of the feet were established. To achieve them, the whole leg has to be turned out from the hips. The position of the arms is known as *port de bras*.

Benesh notation

For ballets to survive, the steps must be written down, or notated. One of the most popular notation methods was devised by Rudolf and Joan Benesh in the late 1940s. Symbols represent the position of the hands and feet.

Each line represents a part of the body: top of head; shoulder; waist; knee; floor.

Romantic ballet

In the early 1800s, the Romantic Movement, with its fascination with the supernatural, affected all the arts. One of the most important men in 19th-century ballet was the choreographer August Bournonville. His ballets were influenced by his years in Paris where Romantic ballet began.

Marie Taglione
Taglione (1804–84) was an Italian ballerina who created the role of *La Sylphide,* She perfected the art of dancing on the tips of her toes, or *en pointe.*

Giselle
The ballet *Giselle* is one of the most famous Romantic ballets. The story follows the romance between a peasant girl, Giselle, and Albrecht, a count. Giselle dies, but rises from her grave to dance with her lover.

A scene from Giselle

Nijinsky

The Ballets Russes
Many Russian choreographers and dancers became bored with Classical ballet. Organized by Serge Diaghilev (1872–1929), they formed the Ballets Russes and toured Europe. The dancers included Vaslav Nijinsky (1890–1950), famous for his jumps.

Anna Pavlova
Russian ballerina Anna Pavlova (1881–1931) was the most famous dancer of her time. She danced with the Imperial Ballet, and also toured with the Ballets Russes. She formed her own company and toured all over the world.

Ballet in Russia

In 1847, French dancer Marius Petipa went to Russia to work with the tsar's Imperial Ballet in St Petersburg. With his assistant Lev Ivanov, he created Classical ballets – grand lavish ballets in three or four acts, designed to show off the brilliant techniques of the dancers.

Classical ballets all contain dazzling dances for the hero and heroine to perform together.

Partners have to trust each other.

Tchaikovsky
Russian composer Pëtr Tchaikovsky (1840–93) wrote probably the most famous ballet music of all. He worked with Marius Petipa and Lev Ivanov on the three great classical ballets, *Sleeping Beauty* (1890), *The Nutcracker* (1892), and *Swan Lake* (1895).

Moscow City Ballet in Sleeping Beauty

Ballet today

Almost every country has its own ballet company. The dancers perform Romantic and Classical ballets, ballets created by the Ballets Russes, and the works of more modern and contemporary choreographers.

New York City Ballet
The New York City Ballet (left) was founded by the Russian choreographer George Balanchine (1904–83). This is his ballet *Apollo.*

The Royal Ballet
Britain's Royal Ballet started as the Vic-Wells Ballet in 1931. It often dances works by past artistic directors Frederick Ashton and Kenneth MacMillan.

Jumps require strength.

A character from Ashton's Tales of Beatrix Potter

FIND OUT MORE

ART, HISTORY OF   DANCE   DRAMA   JAZZ   MUSIC   MUSICAL INSTRUMENTS   OPERA   STRAVINSKY, IGOR

BALL GAMES

A WIDE VARIETY OF BALL GAMES is played around the world with all shapes and sizes of ball; on pitches, courts, courses, and tables; by teams and by individuals. As well as various football games and racket games, there are bat-and-ball games such as cricket and baseball, stick-and-ball games such as hockey, hurling, shinty, and golf; and billiard-table games such as pool, snooker, and billiards. Other ball games include basketball, which involves throwing a ball up and into a small hoop, volleyball, in which the ball is hit over a high net, and bowls, in which balls are rolled along the ground.

Batting gloves

Helmet

Bat made of willow

Wicket keeping pads

Wicket-keeping gloves

Leather-cased ball

Wicket

Cricket

This game is played between two teams of 11, one team bowling and fielding against two on the batting side. The batsmen score runs by running between the wickets or hitting the ball over the boundary. The fielding side may dismiss the batsmen in several ways, including bowling at and knocking over the wicket with the ball.

Sightscreen helps the batsman see the ball.

Pitch

Cricket field
The field is usually oval but its size varies. The boundary is marked by a rope or white line. The pitch, situated at or near the middle of the field, measures 20.12 m (22 yd) between wickets and 3.05 m (10 ft) across.

Cricket equipment
Cricket is played with a hard ball, and many players wear protective clothing. The wicket-keeper and batsmen wear special gloves and strapped-on leg-pads. Batsmen and close fielders may wear helmets with face-guards.

Catcher's glove with hard ball

Catcher's mask

Baseball

Baseball is played between two teams of nine which take turns to bat and field. A pitcher throws the ball and the batter attempts to hit it and score runs by progressing around four bases without being tagged or forced out by a fielder. The game has nine innings. An inning is over when six batters – three from each side – are out.

Bat

Baseball equipment
The catcher, who crouches behind the batter, wears a mask and body padding. Batters wear a helmet and fielders wear a catching mitt. The ball is made of cork wrapped in yarn and encased in leather.

Outfield

Home plate

Infield

Baseball field
The field is made up of an infield, or "diamond", and an outfield. A pitcher throws from a mound at the centre of the infield, which has a base at each corner. A batter stands at home base, or plate.

Babe Ruth

The sensational hitting of American baseball player Babe Ruth (1895–1948), brought crowds to baseball in the 1920s. Originally a World Series-winning pitcher with the Boston Red Sox, he joined the New York Yankees in 1920 and slugged record after record, including 60 home runs in 1927 and a lifetime total of 714.

Hockey

This is played between two teams of 11. Each player has a hooked stick, only the flat side of which can be used for playing the ball. The object of the game is to hit the ball into the opponents' goal. Goals may be scored only from inside a semi-circle called the striking, or shooting, circle.

Ball, traditionally white

Goalkeeper's helmet

Stick

Hockey equipment
Players wear guards under their socks to protect their shins and ankles. The goalkeeper wears a helmet with a face mask, shoulder and elbow pads, padded gauntlets, substantial leg guards, and "kickers" over the boots to protect the feet when kicking the ball away.

Hurling
This is a 15-a-side game played with wooden sticks called hurleys, which are used to strike or carry a small, hard ball. Goals are like soccer goals with extended posts. Points are scored for hitting the ball under the crossbar (three points) or over it (one point).

Hockey pitch
The pitch measures 91.4 m x 54.9 m (100 yd x 60 yd). Goals are 3.66 m (12 ft) wide and 2.13 m (7 ft) high. The shooting circles are joined quarter circles drawn from each post.

Basketball

A five-a-side game, basketball allows free substitution from as many as seven other players. The aim is to put the ball into the opposition's basket. Baskets, or field goals, are worth three points when scored from outside the three-point line, and two points when scored from inside the line.

The player holds the ball in both hands when preparing to shoot.

Players can pivot and jump with the ball, as when trying to score a "basket".

Three-point line

A moving player may take one stride with the ball.

High-sided boots are needed to support the ankles when turning and pivoting.

Basketball court
A basketball court is 28 m x 15 m (91.8 ft x 49.2 ft). The baskets stand 3.05 m (10 ft) above the ground.

Basketball

Ball is made of rubber, encased in leather, rubber, or synthetic material.

Basket

Backboard

Basketball equipment
The main equipment needed for basketball is a ball and two baskets. Official time-keepers use clocks to keep track of the many time restrictions in the game, including the five-second limit on a player holding the ball.

Netball
This seven-a-side game is played by women and girls only. The aim is to throw the ball into the opponents' net. Players must stay in certain areas of the court and may not move with the ball. They wear letters to show where they should be.

Volleyball
Teams of six players aim to score points by propelling the ball over a net into the opponents' court so that they cannot return it. Players can play the ball with their hands or any part of the body above the waist. A team is allowed three touches to hit the ball over the net.

Golf

The aim in golf is to take as few strokes as possible to hit a ball a certain distance into a cup set in the ground. Players have a choice of clubs with which to strike the ball. The standard course has 18 holes of various lengths with different hazards.

Starting a swing to hit the ball

Following through after contact

End of follow-through

Tees

Golf balls

Bowls and bowling

Flat-green bowls is played on a flat lawn, or indoors on a carpet. Players roll balls called woods, aiming to get them as close as possible to a smaller white ball called the jack. Tenpin bowling is played on indoor alleys. At each turn, bowlers have two goes to knock down as many pins as possible.

Cue-and-ball games

Games played on billiards and pool tables include snooker and pool. Players use a stick called a cue to propel a white ball on to coloured balls to knock them into a pocket, or pot them. Billiards is played with three balls – one white cue ball for each player and a red ball.

Snooker balls

Playing a hole
Holes range from about 90 m (100 yd) to 550 m (600 yd). The first shot is played from the teeing ground with either a wood, which is used for long shots, or an iron. Irons are used for the next shots until the putting green is reached, when the putter is used.

Wood

Iron

Putter

Flat-green wood

Indoor bowls

Jack

Pool
Eight-ball is the most widely played variety of pool. To win, one player must pot balls 1 to 7 in any order and then the 8, or black ball. The other player tries to pot balls 9 to 15 and then 8. Players take turns, remaining at the table until they fail to pot a ball, or commit a foul.

Snooker
Players pot a red for one point, and then any colour for two to seven points, depending on the colour. The colours are replaced until no reds remain and then potted in order of their value.

Golf equipment
Players are allowed up to 14 clubs, which they carry in a bag or trolley. Most players have three or four woods, nine or ten irons, and one putter. The ball is supported for the first stroke of each hole on a small stand, or tee. Players must wear studded shoes.

Bowling ball

Pins

Equipment
Woods for bowls are weighted on one side so that they curve when rolled. Bowling balls have holes for the thumb and two fingers. The ten pins are cleared and reset automatically.

FIND OUT MORE FOOTBALL HEALTH AND FITNESS OLYMPIC GAMES SPORT TENNIS AND OTHER RACKET SPORTS

Ball games

Balls

Made from waterproofed leather

Pointed ends

Softball

Cricket

Baseball

Rounders

"Dimples" help the ball fly straight.

In bowls the ball is rolled towards the target ball.

Golf

Billiards

Football

Tennis

Table tennis

Squash

Boules

Bowls

American football

Equipment: polo, ice hockey

Mallet held in right hand

Thick and heavy, to help defend goal

Helmet, often with a face guard

Gloves, for grip

Polo players must wear brown boots.

Elbow pad and glove

Rigid plastic, with a foam backing

Chinstrap

Helmet

Made from leather

Mallet is about 1.22 m (48 in) long.

Goaltender's stick

Buckle

Ball often made of willow

Ice hockey puck

Boots

Made from wood

Ice hockey skate

Knee guards are extra thick, for protection.

Polo mallet and ball

Ice hockey sticks

Knee and leg pads, for protection.

Being played

Softball bats must be round, and no longer than 86 cm (34 in).

Boules is also known as petanque.

Players must only shoot, dribble, or throw the ball in basketball.

There are seven players in a netball team; only two may shoot goals.

Boules is a French game.

Golf players use a club to hit a ball into a small hole.

Ball is pitched underarm.

Metal boule

Softball developed in the late 19th-century from indoor baseball.

Netball is a women-only sport.

Boules are aimed towards a target ball.

Basketball is played by two teams of five players each.

Golf is played over a course of 18 holes.

BALTIC STATES AND BELARUS

THE THREE Baltic states of Estonia, Latvia, and Lithuania occupy a small area on the Baltic Sea coast to the west of the Russian Federation. Belarus, formerly known as "White Russia", sits between Russia, Poland, and Ukraine. All four countries were former Soviet republics; in 1991, after the break-up of the Soviet Union, they declared independence. Since then, they have suffered high inflation and environmental problems, but are now working to form a trade link between eastern and western Europe.

Physical features

The Baltic states have a flat landscape of plains and low hills, with forests and swampy marshes. There are thousands of rivers and lakes, of which the largest is Peipus, at 3,626 sq km (1,400 sq miles), shared between Estonia and Russia.

Baltic coast and islands
Estonia, Latvia, and Lithuania all have coasts and ports on the Baltic Sea, and ice covers much of the sea in winter. Estonia has the longest coastline, and the country includes more than 1,500 islands that form a barrier protecting the Gulf of Riga.

Forests
Dense deciduous and coniferous forests cover between 30 and 40 per cent of the Baltic region. Belarus is dominated by lakes and thick forests full of wildlife such as deer and mink. The east of Latvia is forested.

Forested Ganja River valley, Latvia

Pripet Marshes
Covering a vast area of southern Belarus, the Pripet Marshes are the biggest wetland area in Europe. They stretch for 40,000 sq km (15,000 sq miles), and are fed by several rivers including the Byerazino and Dnieper. The soils of the Pripet are clay or sandy, and large areas are waterlogged.

Regional climate
Estonia, Lithuania, Latvia, and Belarus have cold winters and cool, wet summers, because of their location on the Baltic Sea. Heavy snow falls during the winter throughout the region, particularly in Belarus.

17°C (63°F)   -5°C (23°F)

668 mm (26 in)

Cultural diversity
Estonia, Latvia, and Belarus have large Russian populations, who were resettled in the Baltic states under communist rule. This has caused some racial tension with ethnic peoples in Estonia and Latvia. In Belarus, where most people are Russian speakers, and Lithuania, where 80 per cent are ethnic Lithuanians, there is social harmony.

Folk dancer, Estonia

Estonia

The smallest and most northerly of the Baltic states, Estonia has a long coastline and beautiful scenery that attracts many tourists from Finland and Scandinavia. Under Soviet rule, its rural economy was transformed. It is now an industrial nation, and most people live in towns. Estonians are closely related to Finns and speak a similar language.

ESTONIA FACTS

CAPITAL CITY Tallinn

AREA 45,125 sq km (17,423 sq miles)

POPULATION 1,400,000

MAIN LANGUAGES Estonian, Russian

MAJOR RELIGION Christian

CURRENCY Kroon

Tourism
More than one million tourists visit Estonia every year. The medieval buildings of Tallinn, Estonia's capital, are a major attraction, with a wealth of historical monuments. Summer regattas and boating and yachting in the sheltered waters of the Gulf of Riga are also popular.

Flax stems are used to make linen fabric and ropes.

Flax
Textiles made from flax and cotton are among Estonia's leading exports. Flax is harvested at different times for various purposes: young green stems make fine cloth called linen; tougher fibres are used for ropes and mats.

Latvia

Sandwiched in a central position between Estonia and Lithuania, Latvia is a flat country with about 12,000 rivers. Manufacturing, encouraged under Soviet rule, is the basis of the economy. Like the other states in this region, Latvia suffered high inflation during the 1990s. Farming, fishing, and timber are valuable sources of income.

LATVIA FACTS

CAPITAL CITY Riga

AREA 64,589 sq km (24,938 sq miles)

POPULATION 2,400,000

MAIN LANGUAGES Latvian, Russian

MAJOR RELIGION Christian

CURRENCY Lat

B

Farming
Latvia has a larger area of fertile land than the other Baltic states. Since independence, the huge state farms introduced by the Russians have been dismantled and are now privately owned. Most are dairy farms.

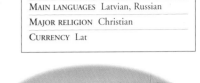

Women wear traditional costumes in Latvia's Rites of Spring Festival.

People
About one-third of Latvians are of Russian origin and there are smaller numbers of Ukrainians and Belarussians. Just over half the population are ethnic Letts, or Latvians, who cling to their cultural heritage. They celebrate many traditional and religious festivals.

Lithuania

Once a powerful nation, ruling lands that extended to the Black Sea, Lithuania sits south of Latvia. Most people live in the interior of the country, working in industry or farming. The short coastline, fringed with sand dunes and pine forests, is famous for amber. Since 1991, there have been disputes with Latvia over Baltic Sea oil.

LITHUANIA FACTS

CAPITAL CITY Vilnius

AREA 65,200 sq km (25,174 sq miles)

POPULATION 3,782,000

MAIN LANGUAGES Lithuanian, Russian

MAJOR RELIGION Christian

CURRENCY Litas

Hill of Crosses, near Siauliai, a shrine to honour the dead.

Yellow amber

Amber
The Baltic states produce two-thirds of the world's amber, the fossilized sap of pine trees. Amber is used to make jewellery in shades of yellow, orange, and deep gold.

Religion
By contrast to Estonians and Latvians, who are mainly Protestants, Lithuanians are mostly Roman Catholics. They managed to keep their faith even under Soviet rule, which discouraged religion.

Belarus

Land-locked, and with few natural resources, Belarus suffers great poverty. In 1986, an accident at the Chernobyl nuclear reactor in the Ukraine severely contaminated farmland. Many areas remain unsafe. The shaky economy is based on the manufacture of machines, cars, chemicals, and a large farming sector. Unlike the other Baltic states, Belarus has maintained close political and economic ties with Russia and is taking steps to set up a union.

BELARUS FACTS

CAPITAL CITY Minsk

AREA 207,600 sq km (80,154 sq miles)

POPULATION 10,320,000

MAIN LANGUAGES Belarussian, Russian

MAJOR RELIGION Christian

CURRENCY Belarussian rouble

Ceramics
Belarus produces many beautifully crafted ceramic and porcelain items, such as vases and ornaments. The country is also known for its high-quality decorated glassware, made by heating sand with salt, limestone, and old glass, then moulding the molten liquid glass.

Draniki   **Sour cream**

Food
The national dish of Belorussia is *draniki*, made from fried, grated potatoes, and served with sour cream and pickled berries or beetroot. Soup made from beetroot is also a popular dish.

 FIND OUT MORE CHRISTIANITY FARMING FESTIVALS FORESTS FOSSILS GLASS LAKES NUCLEAR POWER RIVERS SOVIET UNION TEXTILES AND WEAVING

BANGLADESH AND NEPAL

NORTH OF THE BAY OF BENGAL, between India and Burma (Myanmar), is Bangladesh, a poor but fertile country whose low-lying land and repeated flooding has largely dictated its fortunes. Nepal and Bhutan are small Himalayan states, ruled by kings, but slowly adopting democratic ideas. All three countries have a subsistence farming economy, and the majority of the people, who are a mix of Muslims, Hindus, and Buddhists, live in small, rural villages. Manufacturing industries are being developed.

Physical features

Bangladesh is dominated by a low-lying plain created by soil caught up and carried on the great Ganges River and its tributaries. Much of the land is less than 15 m (50 ft) above sea-level. By contrast, Nepal and Bhutan sit high in the mountains, with plunging forested valleys watered by many rapid streams.

Himalayas
Nepal lies in the highest part of the Himalayas, a vast mountain range that stretches 2,400 km (1500 miles) between India and China. Mount Everest, the world's highest peak at 8,848 m (29,029 ft), is part of the range and several other peaks are more than 6,000 m (19,685 ft) high, including Ama Dablam in Nepal, at 6,856 m (22,493 ft).

23°C (73°F)   11°C (52°F)

1,901 mm (75 in)

Regional climate
Bangladesh has a hot tropical climate, and monsoon winds bring heavy floods to 67 per cent of the country. Southern Nepal and Bhutan are hot and wet, but the Himalayas are cold and harsh, with much snow.

Forests
About 70 per cent of Bhutan is forested. Deciduous forests, which include hardwoods such as teak, grow in the south, while thick pine forests cover the steep mountains of central Bhutan. Bangladesh's flat landscape rises in the north and southeast to form wooded hills.

Delta
Large parts of central and southern Bangladesh are made up of the flat low-lying plains, formed by the delta of the rivers Ganges, Brahmaputra (Jamuna), and Meghna. As the rivers split continually in their journey south towards the Bay of Bengal, they become a maze of channels that often flood.

Hydroelectricity
Bangladesh, Bhutan, and Nepal share vast natural water resources in the form of hundreds of tributaries of the Ganges River system. All three countries have harnessed their waters for hydroelectricity. Bhutan's Chhukha Dam exports power to India, and there are plans to construct more dams in the region. Nepal's Arun III hydroelectric project was approved in 2001.

Welding turbine wheel for hydroelectric plant, Nepal

Bangladesh

Formed in 1971 when it became independent of Pakistan, Bangladesh has a troubled political history. Democracy was restored in 1991, after a period of military rule. Bangladesh has one of the world's highest population densities and half of its people live in poverty. The country's vast water resources provide good farming conditions, but floods and cyclones wreak seasonal havoc.

BANGLADESH FACTS

CAPITAL CITY	Dhaka
AREA	143,998 sq km (55,598 sq miles)
POPULATION	129,000,000
MAIN LANGUAGE	Bengali
MAJOR RELIGIONS	Muslim, Hindu
CURRENCY	Taka

Stilt houses
Many people live in houses that are built on stilts to protect them from the frequent floods. The country is overcrowded, and about 75 per cent of the people live in rural communities. Most grow just enough rice to live on, and fish in the Ganges.

Jute rope

Jute
Bangladesh is second only to India in the production of jute, a tough fibre used for sacking, rope, and carpeting. The country provides about 80 per cent of the world's jute fibre. Jute products make up 13 per cent of Bangladesh's exports.

Silkworms spin a silky thread up to 1 km (0.6 miles) long.

Dhaka
The capital, Dhaka, lies on the Buriganga River, which links ports around the country. This has made it a centre of trade and commerce. The city contains more than eight million people, many of whom live in overcrowded slums.

Textiles
Many Bangladeshis work in the textile industry, with cotton and silk the country's leading fabrics. Ready-made garments are the main product, totalling 60 per cent of exports. Women are the backbone of the textile industry.

Nepal

The Himalayas and their forested foothills cover most of this land-locked country. Nepal was an absolute monarchy until 1991, but now has a multi-party constitution. It is one of the world's poorest countries; the people are mostly farmers whose crops depend on the monsoon rains.

People
There is a wide variety of peoples in Nepal, and most are of Indian or Tibetan descent. The Sherpas of the north are skilled, tough mountaineers. About 90 per cent of Nepalese people are Hindus, who combine their religion with Buddhism.

Hindu holy man

NEPAL FACTS

CAPITAL CITY	Katmandu
AREA	140,800 sq km (54,363 sq miles)
POPULATION	23,900,000
MAIN LANGUAGE	Nepali
MAJOR RELIGIONS	Hindu, Buddhist, Muslim
CURRENCY	Nepalese rupee

Farming
Nepal is dependent on farming, which, with forestry, employs 90 per cent of the work-force. Rice, maize, and sugar are grown on terraces cut into the mountainsides.

Katmandu
Lying in a valley 1,370 m (4,500 ft) above sea-level, Nepal's capital, Katmandu, is a city full of ornate temples and shrines. About 400,000 people live in the city, including the Newars of the valley who are famed for their wood carving.

Buddhist temple overlooking Katmandu.

Trekking
Mountain climbing and trekking in the Himalayas attract 450,000 visitors to Nepal each year. Tourism attracts much-needed income, but threatens the ecology.

Bhutan

A small, isolated country, Bhutan is covered in forests and snow-capped mountains. Ruled by a monarch, known as the Dragon King, it is an isolated state, though there are plans for modernization. Three-quarters of the people are of Tibetan descent; the rest are Nepalese or Hindus. Farming, fishing, forestry, and small-scale industry provide jobs.

Apricot

Cardamom seeds

Crops
Less than ten per cent of Bhutan's land can be cultivated, but 90 per cent of the people make a living from farming. Rice, maize, and potatoes are the staple foods, and cash crops, such as apricots, apples, chillies, cardamom, and oranges, for export to other Asian countries, are being developed in the fertile central valleys.

Apple

Orange

Chilli peppers

BHUTAN FACTS

CAPITAL CITY	Thimphu
AREA	47,000 sq km (18,147 sq miles)
POPULATION	2,100,000
MAIN LANGUAGE	Dzongkha
MAJOR RELIGIONS	Buddhist, Hindu
CURRENCY	Ngultrum

FIND OUT MORE   ASIA, HISTORY OF   BUDDHISM   DAMS   ENERGY   FARMING   HINDUISM   INDIA   ISLAM   MOUNTAINS AND VALLEYS   RIVERS   TEXTILES AND WEAVING

BARBARIANS

To the ancient Greeks, all foreigners or outsiders were known as barbarians, but from the 3rd century on, this term was increasingly applied to nomadic mounted tribespeople from Asia, eastern Europe, and parts of Germany, such as the Huns and Goths. Organized into fearsome cavalry armies, these so-called barbarians caused havoc in their search for land, and were finally responsible for the collapse of the western Roman Empire.

Who were the barbarians?
To most Europeans, barbarian tribes included Huns and Avars (from Asia), and Saxons, Vandals, and Goths (from Germany). Huns migrating from Asia into Europe caused fear among the resident Germanic tribes, who then poured in huge numbers across the Roman Empire's frontiers. In a short time, this migration led to the fall of the empire.

Huns

The Huns were a nomadic Mongol people from the high plains, or steppes, of Central Asia who invaded southeastern Europe in c.370. Fierce in battle and famous for their skill on horseback, they conquered the Ostrogoths and drove the Vandals and other tribes westward. Under the leadership of Attila they reached their zenith, ravaging the Byzantine Empire and invading Gaul (modern France). In the 5th and 6th centuries, the White Huns, a related people, raided Persia (Iran) and northern India.

Huns made bows and arrows out of strips of bone.

Horse saddle

*Hunting on the Steppes
by Chen Chii-Chung (Sung dynasty)*

Catalaunian Plains
The Huns were deadly in battle as mounted archers. They made short bows of bone, which were light and easy to use while on horseback. They also fought with sabres at close quarters. Under Attila, the Huns were victorious many times, but in 451, they were finally defeated by the Romans and their allies at the Catalaunian Plains, Gaul (now Chalons-sur-Marne, France).

Attila the Hun
Attila (c.406–453) became king of the Huns in 434 jointly with his brother Bleda, whom he murdered in 445. Attila united his people into a vast horde based in Hungary, then waged campaigns to win land and tribute from the Roman and Byzantine empires. Short and crafty, the so-called "Scourge of God" was cruel to his enemies but fair to his own people. He died – possibly of poison – on his wedding night.

Ostrogoths and Visigoths

The Ostrogoths were a Germanic tribe on the Black Sea who were related to the Visigoths from the Danube area. After the Roman Empire fell in 476, the Visigoths adopted Christianity, and translated the Bible from Latin into a "Gothic" script, which was used for centuries in German printing.

Gothic architecture
Many medieval churches and cathedrals were built in the Gothic style. The highly decorative details, such as gargoyles, were believed by Renaissance artists to be "barbarous" when compared with the simplicity of older Roman buildings. So the artists named them after the Gothic tribes that overran Rome.

Notre-Dame gargoyles, Paris, France

Saxons

Saxon shoulder clasp

Gold and enamel

Gold and garnet

Etched snake designs

Gold

Mosaic glass

Saxon purse lid

Saxon buckle

"The barbarians drive us to the sea, and the sea drives us back to the barbarians; one way or another we die." So wrote a group of 5th-century Britons to their former masters in Rome. The seafaring barbarians threatening them were Saxons, Angles, and Jutes – Germanic tribes of skilled craftworkers and farmers who conquered and settled stretches of fertile Britain from c.500.

Richborough Fort
The Romans built bases at Richborough and elsewhere on the southeastern English coast in the 3rd and 4th centuries. From these forts they could see and try to intercept Saxon raiders.

Walls were 1.2 m (4 ft) thick.

British ships destroying Chinese junks

Barbarians in the East
People beyond Europe also believed that outsiders were barbarians. The 18th-century Chinese looked down on "foreign devils", and insisted that all trade between China and the west took place only in the port of Canton. The Japanese actually stopped any foreigners from entering Japan for more than 200 years, until 1854.

FIND OUT MORE   ARCHITECTURE   ANGLO-SAXONS   ROMAN EMPIRE   WARFARE

BATS

WITH ALMOST 1,000 species, bats are the second largest order of mammals after the rodents. They are the only mammals that can truly fly. The name given to their order is Chiroptera, meaning "hand wings". When bats are resting, they hang upside-down. Most bats are nocturnal. They eat a variety of food, which they find either by scent and sight, as fruit bats do, or by using sound waves, a process called echolocation, as insect-eating bats do.

Bat features

A bat's wing consists of an elastic membrane of skin that is stretched between the elongated fingers of its front limb, and back to its hind limb. Bats have lightweight bodies and strong, clawed toes with which they cling to a suitable support.

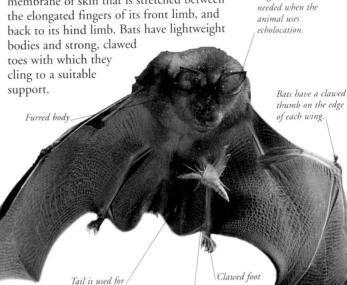

Insect-eating bats have large ears, which are needed when the animal uses echolocation.

Bats have a clawed thumb on the edge of each wing.

Furred body

Wing is formed by a membrane stretched over the bones of the fingers and forelimb.

Tail is used for balance and for braking in flight.

Bat catches insect in midair.

Clawed foot

"Fingers"

Greater horseshoe bat

Types of bat

Bats are divided into two groups. These are the Megachiroptera, or megabats, which are the old world fruit bats, and the Microchiroptera, or microbats, sometimes called insect-eating bats.

Megabats

Fruit bats, or megabats, are also sometimes called flying foxes. They live in the tropical and subtropical parts of Africa, Asia, and Australasia. Most megabats eat fruit, but some also feed on flowers, nectar, and pollen.

Large eyes and nose

Epauletted fruit bat

Ears are almost as long as the bat's head and body combined.

Long-eared bat

Microbats

The term insect-eating bats is a misleading name for these bats. Many feed on fruit, meat, fish, pollen, and even blood, as well as insects. Microbats live in both temperate and tropical regions, but in cooler climates they hibernate or migrate for the winter.

Roosts

Bats need a variety of places to roost, or rest. At night they rest between bouts of feeding and often settle to eat large prey. During the day, they need somewhere to sleep and groom. Females choose a safe, warm place to give birth.

Tent bats

Cave habitats

In warm climates, caves provide daytime and nursery roosts, where females give birth and look after their young. Bracken Cave in Texas, USA, has the largest colony in the world with up to 20 million bats.

Free-tailed bats in Bracken Cave

Tree habitats

Microbats often roost in tree holes, such as old woodpecker nests, or cracks caused by storm damage. These Honduran white bats, also called tent bats, build a tent from large leaves.

Hibernation

Bats need to hibernate somewhere cold but where they will be protected from frost, which would kill them. The place where they roost, called a hibernaculum, also has to be damp so that the bats do not dry out. Suitable sites include caves, loft spaces, and tree holes.

Natterer's bat

Echolocation

To find objects in the dark, a microbat makes bursts of high-frequency sound. The sound bounces off objects, such as a moth, and the bat pinpoints the moth's position by listening to the returning echoes.

Insect prey

Horseshoe bat

Returning echoes

How a horseshoe bat catches prey

Horseshoe bats emit sounds through their noses.

1 The "horseshoe" on the bat's nose focuses the sound into a narrow beam. The bat sweeps its head from side to side as it flies along, scanning for insects.

Small eyes

2 The bat's large, mobile ears pick up vibrations made by the movement of an insect's wings. The bat can tell the size of an insect from the vibrations.

Broad, rounded wings

3 When the bat has located its prey, it scoops up the insect in its wings, often eating in midair.

The bat uses its wing membrane to put food in its mouth.

Feeding

Bats have a wide variety of food sources. Most bats eat insects and can consume huge amounts in one night. The smaller bats, such as pipistrelles, catch tiny gnats and mosquitoes. Larger bats, such as noctules and serotines, feed on cockchafers and dung beetles. Some bats pounce on prey that is on the ground, and pick insects off leaves. Fruit-eating bats live mostly in the tropics, where they have a year-round supply of food.

Bulldog bat

Fishing bats trail their long legs in the water to catch a fish.

False vampire bat

The bat finds its prey using echolocation.

Fishing bats
Some bats use echolocation to detect fish just below the water's surface. Fishing bats have long legs and they fly along the surface and catch the fish with long, sharp claws.

Meat-eating bats
Many larger microbats catch and eat mice, rats, frogs, and lizards. False vampire bats from Asia and America carry their catch to a suitable perch to devour it, using their thumbs and wing membranes to hold the heavy prey.

Vampire bats
True vampire bats feed on the blood of mammals or birds. Using their razor-like incisor teeth, they make a wound on an ear or ankle. As the blood flows, the vampire bat drinks it with a grooved tongue that acts like a drinking straw.

Bat drinking from a donkey.

Incisor teeth

Bats will only eat the pulp of the fruit.

Spectacled flying fox

Fruit bats
These bats squash ripe fruit against ridges on the roof of their mouth. They spit out the rind and large seeds that are difficult to digest. Fruit bats sometimes eat the fruit in the tree where they pick it, but they may carry it to a safe roost to eat.

Some nectar-feeding bats hover above the flower.

Glossophagine bat

Nectar feeders
Trees that are pollinated by bats provide the animals with nectar and pollen as a reward for their services. The tongues of nectar-feeding bats have a brush-like tip which the bats use to lap up the nectar and pollen inside the flowers.

Nursery

Like all true mammals, a female bat carries her young inside her womb until she gives birth. Usually, only one bat is born at a time to minimize the extra weight a pregnant female has to carry in flight. Females gather, often in large numbers, to give birth in a nursery roost.

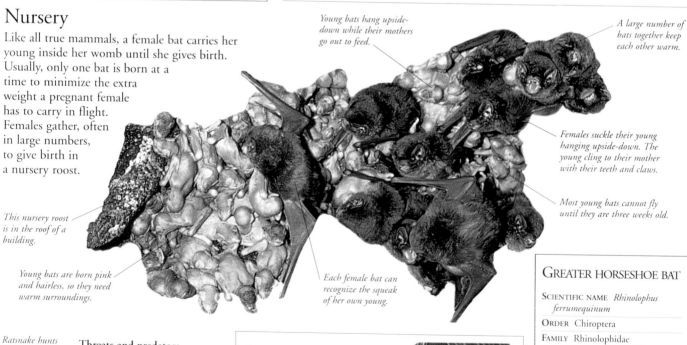

Young bats hang upside-down while their mothers go out to feed.

A large number of bats together keep each other warm.

Females suckle their young hanging upside-down. The young cling to their mother with their teeth and claws.

Most young bats cannot fly until they are three weeks old.

This nursery roost is in the roof of a building.

Young bats are born pink and hairless, so they need warm surroundings.

Each female bat can recognize the squeak of her own young.

Ratsnake hunts at night.

Threats and predators
This red-tailed racer from Southeast Asia, also known as a mangrove ratsnake, catches bats in the tops of mangrove trees. Other animals that prey on bats include bat hawks, owls, and cats. Some of the greatest threats to the survival of bats around the world are habitat destruction, pesticides, and human vandalism. Many species are in danger of extinction.

Largest and smallest
The largest bat is a Malaysian flying fox which can have a wingspan of up to 1.7 m (5.6 ft). The smallest bat is the bumblebee bat, also known as Kitti's hog-nosed bat. This tiny animal is only about 30 mm (1 in) long and weighs only 2 g (0.07 oz).

GREATER HORSESHOE BAT

SCIENTIFIC NAME *Rhinolophus ferrumequinum*

ORDER Chiroptera

FAMILY Rhinolophidae

DISTRIBUTION Central and southern Europe, North Africa across to Japan

HABITAT Woodland, pasture, human settlements

DIET Insects

SIZE Length: 6–7cm (2.4–2.75 in)

LIFESPAN Up to 30 years

FIND OUT MORE   CAVE WILDLIFE   CONSERVATION   HIBERNATION   MAMMALS   WHALES AND DOLPHINS

B

Bats

During sleep, toes have special locking mechanism to prevent falling.

The bat hangs from a branch with its strong, hooked claws.

Bats can grip many types of surfaces.

Wings are made of skin and bone.

Clawed thumb on the edge of the wing

Mexican fruit bat eats mostly fruit but will also eat insects.

Funnel-eared bat lives in South America and roosts in caves.

Mouse-tailed bat lives in Africa and Asia.

Short-tailed leaf-nosed bat eats bananas in South America.

New World fruit bat helps to spread American tree seeds.

Short-tailed leaf-nosed bat has an acute sense of smell.

Franquet's fruit bat is an African bat that eats ripe fruit.

Yellow-shouldered bat feeds on nectar, pollen, and fruit.

Lesser horseshoe bat feeds exclusively on insects.

Proboscis bat roosts in trees by streams; its fur looks like lichen.

Spear-nosed bat has a well-developed sense of smell.

Common vampire bat has saliva that prevents its host's blood clotting.

New World fruit bat can produce young twice a year.

This species of bat uses its wings just two weeks after birth.

White line, which helps to disguise bat in foliage.

Wings are folded in while the bat hangs upside down on branch.

Borneo fruit bat has a distinct long and fox-like muzzle.

Noctule bat flies over fields and meadows, hunting for large beetles.

White-lined bat often roosts in the trunks of trees.

White-lined bat hanging

This bat has a strong sense of smell to locate fruit to eat. It also eats insects.

BEARS

THERE ARE SEVEN different species of bear, plus the giant panda which has recently been classified as a primitive bear. The polar and brown bears are the largest meat-eating land animals alive today. All bears rely heavily on their acute senses of smell and hearing to find food and to locate predators. Bears that live in cool climates hibernate in dens during the winter, but those in warmer areas are active all year round.

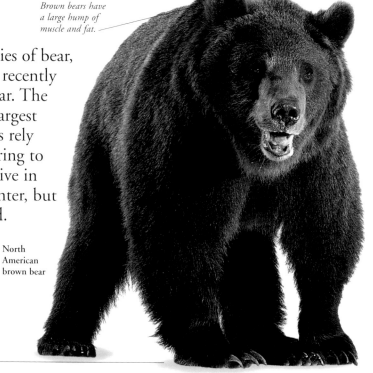

Brown bears have a large hump of muscle and fat.

North American brown bear

Brown bears

There are nine subspecies of brown bear. The largest is the Kodiak bear found on islands in Alaska. It may stand 3.5 m (12 ft) tall on its hind legs and is one of the most powerful animals in North America. The grizzly bear, also of North America, has white-tipped fur, giving it a "grizzled" look. The other brown bears live in Europe and temperate Asia.

Large canine teeth and powerful jaws

Fishing
Bears of North America have a rich source of salmon when the fish swim up rivers to spawn. The bears may stand in the water and catch fish in the air as they leap up a waterfall.

Asian black bear feeding

Diet

Bears belong to the order of mammals called carnivores, meaning meat-eaters. They catch and kill other animals for food and eat carrion, but they will take almost any kind of food they can find, including insects. About three-quarters of most bears' diet is plant material, such as fruits, nuts, roots, and shoots.

Paws
There are five clawed toes on a bear's paws. The animals use their forepaws to gather food and manipulate small food items. They can kill another animal with one blow from a paw, or use their long claws to dig up roots, and open insects' nests.

Kermodes bear
Most American black bears are black, but some are brown, beige, or blue-black. Small isolated populations of white black bears, called Kermodes bears, live on the coast of British Columbia, Canada.

Types of bear

Brown bear This bear lives across the northern hemisphere, but in small populations only. It has disappeared from many areas.

Shaggy black fur

Sloth bear A long-coated bear from India and Sri Lanka, the sloth bear eats mainly termites, which it sucks up through its lips.

Sun bear This bear from south-eastern Asia is the smallest bear. It has short, dense fur, with a yellow mark on its chest. It has a long tongue with which it licks up ants and termites.

Spectacled bear The only South American bear, this rare animal lives on the wooded slopes of the Andes. It eats mostly plant material, especially fruit, but will eat meat if it is available.

A crescent of white fur accounts for this bear's other name of moon bear.

Polar bear This white-coated bear is the most carnivorous, eating mainly seals and fish. It lives on the Arctic coast.

Asian black bear An agile climber, this bear lives in woods of south-eastern Asia, from Afghanistan to China and Japan.

American black bear Found across North America, this bear will raid tents, cars, and dustbins for food.

Cubs' games are practice for adult conflicts.

Cubs
A female bear gives birth to her cubs in a den, where she stays with them for up to two or three months. Each litter usually contains one to three cubs, which are born helpless and weigh only a tiny percentage of their mother's weight. They develop quickly but will stay with their mother until nearly full-grown. This may be for as long as two or three years in the case of the larger bears. Female bears make good mothers and will defend their cubs ferociously.

GRIZZLY BEAR

SCIENTIFIC NAME *Ursos arctos horribilis*

ORDER Carnivora

FAMILY Ursidae

DISTRIBUTION Northwestern North America

HABITAT Mountains, forests, wilderness

DIET Almost anything, including berries, leaves, roots, small animals, fish, and carrion

SIZE Length: 1.8–2.8 m (6–9 ft)
Weight: 160–230 kg (350–500 lb)

LIFESPAN 25–30 years

FIND OUT MORE

ASIAN WILDLIFE   HIBERNATION   NORTH AMERICAN WILDLIFE   PANDAS AND RACCOONS   POLAR WILDLIFE

BEATLES, THE

JOHN LENNON PLAYED rhythm guitar, Paul McCartney played bass, George Harrison played lead guitar, and Ringo Starr played the drums. Together they formed The Beatles – the most famous and influential group in the history of popular music. Their songs dominated the 1960s, when people believed that music could change the world, and the songwriting skills of Lennon and McCartney have ensured that their music lives on. Their songs still influence many musicians today.

Early life
All four Beatles were born in the English port of Liverpool and played in various rock and roll groups in the late 1950s. In 1960–61 John, Paul, George, and drummer Pete Best played at the Star Club in the German port of Hamburg, which taught them much about live performance. Back in England, The Beatles played regularly at Liverpool's Cavern Club. In 1962 their manager, Brian Epstein (1934–67), replaced Best with Ringo Starr as drummer.

Live performances
The Beatles began by playing live in clubs in and around Liverpool, UK. Their lively performances were an exciting contrast to the staid and solid players who dominated popular music at the time. The Beatles' reputation was based on the songwriting abilities of John Lennon and Paul McCartney. At first they both wrote traditional rock and roll songs about friendship and love, but as the pair developed, their subjects became more varied.

The Beatles play a football stadium in the USA

Beatlemania
In January 1964 , "I Want To Hold Your Hand" reached the top of the American music charts. A new word, "Beatlemania", entered the language as thousands of screaming fans mobbed the group wherever they went. Within months, The Beatles were the biggest music group in the world.

Recording
In 1966 The Beatles stopped performing live, and spent more time in the studio. There they experimented with different instruments, such as string orchestras and sitars, and with new recording techniques. Their masterpiece, *Sgt. Pepper's Lonely Hearts Club Band*, took many months to produce and made use of techniques such as tape-splicing and multi-track recording.

Plates with pictures of The Beatles

Memorabilia
The Beatles were one of the first bands to be featured on a host of souvenirs and memorabilia. The four were immortalized on everything from mugs and T-shirts to buttons, badges, posters, and other souvenirs. Many fans bought everything that featured their four favourite musicians.

Toy guitar with pictures of The Beatles

Please Please Me

Sgt. Pepper's

The last albums
By 1969 the group was falling apart as conflicts grew between the four members and their musical interests took different directions. Their last albums to appear were *Abbey Road* (1969) and *Let It Be*, which was released in 1970 but recorded before *Abbey Road*. The Beatles disbanded later that year. All four continued their careers as solo musicians.

The Beatles recording tracks for *Let It Be*

George Martin

British producer George Martin (b.1926) produced almost all The Beatles' records, having accepted their first demonstration tapes at EMI in 1962. Martin was a record producer with a background in both classical and popular music. He helped The Beatles get the most out of the recording studio and the wide range of instruments used in their records, translating many of their ideas into polished musical form.

THE BEATLES

1940	John Lennon and Richard Starkey (Ringo Starr) born.
1942	Paul McCartney born.
1943	George Harrison born.
1957	John and Paul form first group, The Quarrymen.
1962	First record with EMI; Ringo Starr joins as drummer.
1964	Beatles head charts in USA.
1967	*Sgt. Pepper's Lonely Hearts Club Band* released.
1970	*Let It Be* released; Beatles disband.
1980	John Lennon shot dead.
1997	Paul McCartney knighted.
2001	George Harrison dies.

FIND OUT MORE   MUSIC   ORCHESTRAS   ROCK AND POP   SOUND RECORDING

B

BEES AND WASPS

THEIR STINGS USUALLY bring these insects to our attention. However, by pollinating crops and killing pests, bees and wasps play vital roles in the world we live in. There are 115,000 species of bees and wasps. Most, such as carpenter bees, are solitary, but some, including the honeybee and common wasp, are social insects, living in complex colonies. People keep honeybees in hives for their honey and wax.

Features of bees and wasps

Bees and wasps are similar in appearance, with narrow waists between the thorax and abdomen. Most species have two pairs of wings and are excellent fliers. They have two compound eyes and three small eyes, giving them good eyesight. Bees are hairier than wasps, and are normally herbivores, while wasps are generally carnivores.

Two pairs of wings for rapid flight

Compound eye

Waist

Pointed abdomen

Claws **Common wasp**

Antenna

Jointed legs with claws **Honeybee**

Stings

Only the females of most species of bees and wasps have stings. The sting evolved from the egg-laying tube. Wasps have unbarbed stings that they can use repeatedly for defence or to kill prey. Bees have barbed stings that cannot be extracted, causing the bee to die. Consequently, bees only sting if provoked.

Bee sting

Abdomen

Poison sac

The sting may be painful and, in rare cases, fatal.

Queen

Social bees and wasps have a queen in their colonies which lays eggs and runs the colony. Honeybees have one queen per hive; if two appear at the same time they fight to the death. Queens produce queen substance, a chemical that stops full sexual development of the workers.

Worker

Queen is larger than workers.

Life cycle of a honeybee

1 The queen bee spends most of her day checking cells and laying single eggs in them. She lays more than 2,000 eggs a day when there is a plentiful food supply. After 1–2 days, larvae hatch from the eggs.

2 Workers feed the larvae honey, pollen, and royal jelly. If fed extra royal jelly, larvae become queens. The larvae grow and moult, and on day 5 they spin a silk cocoon and pupate. Workers seal the cell with wax.

3 By about day 21 pupation is complete and the new adult bees have to chew their way out of the cell. Once the external skeleton has hardened and they are able to walk, the bees begin their tasks within the nest.

Food supplies

Wasps eat fruit and insects, which they also feed to their young. Adult and larval bees feed on nectar and pollen that the adults collect. Bees do a dance to tell other bees the location of the flowers, and navigate there by using the Sun.

Pollen carried on legs

Pollen, nectar, and honey

Bees carry pollen on hairs on their legs and store nectar in their stomachs. At the nest, they regurgitate the nectar. Water evaporates, concentrating the nectar to form honey. Honey and royal jelly, a high-protein substance made by workers, are also fed to the larvae.

Common wasp's nest

Protective layers of paper

Pupae in cocoons

Hole in nest is repaired.

Fertilized eggs develop into workers and queens.

Unfertilized eggs become drones.

Old worker wasps gather wood, chew it up, mix in saliva, and use the mixture to build nest walls.

Worker wasps spend the first week of their adult life cleaning the nest. Once able to fly, they leave the nest and hunt for insects to feed to the grubs (larvae) in the nest.

Eggs are glued into cells, as the cells face downwards.

Entrance is below.

Nest walls are striped because the wood is collected from many sources.

Nests

Common wasps' nests have the texture of paper and are made of chewed-up wood, saliva, and water. They are usually built in hollow trees or below ground. Other wasps, such as oriental stenogaster wasps, build nests out of mud. Honeybee nests are made of wax produced from glands on the bees' abdomens. Wasp and bee nests usually contain combs – layers of six-sided cells in which the young grow.

Colonies

Social wasps and bees live in large groups called colonies. Each member of the colony has a specific duty and works for the benefit of the whole nest. Wasp colonies may contain more than one million individuals; bees' nests can exceed 70,000 in number, consisting of one queen, about 69,000 workers, and 300 drones. Both queen wasps and queen bees run their nests; drones are fertile males who mate with the queen and die soon after; workers perform many tasks from building the nest to foraging for food. Drones appear before swarming time. This is when new queens leave the nest, mate with the drones, and set up nests on their own.

Types of bee and wasp

Parasitic bees

These solitary bees abandon their eggs in other bees' nests. The young then destroy the original eggs and wait to be fed by the host.

Hornets

Hornets are among the largest of the social wasps. They live in large colonies and defend their nests aggressively.

Hunting wasps

These solitary wasps paralyse other insects with a sting and lay their eggs on them. The young hatch and feed on the live host.

HONEYBEE

SCIENTIFIC NAME	*Apis mellifera*
ORDER	Hymenoptera
FAMILY	Apidae
DISTRIBUTION	Worldwide
HABITAT	Nests are built in hollow trees in the wild; also cultivated in hives
DIET	Pollen and nectar from flowers
SIZE	Length: workers: 10–15 mm (0.4–0.6 in); queen: 15–20 mm (0.6–0.8 in)
LIFESPAN	Workers live for 2–3 months; queen lives for 3–5 years

FIND OUT MORE

ANIMAL BEHAVIOUR • ANTS AND TERMITES • ARTHROPODS • EGGS • FLIGHT, ANIMAL • FLOWERS • INSECTS • NESTS AND BURROWS • WOODLAND WILDLIFE

BEETHOVEN, LUDWIG VAN

FROM HIS BIRTH in Bonn in 1770 to his death in Vienna in 1827, Ludwig van Beethoven's lifetime spanned a period of revolution and transformation. Despite a tragically unhappy life, beset with family problems and deafness, he became the major composer of his time. His symphonies, sonatas, and chamber music expanded the Classical forms, introducing exciting new musical ideas that ushered in the fiery Romantic style. Unlike previous composers, Beethoven tried to remain independent, writing for himself rather than for a single rich patron. Independence allowed him to develop his own personal expressive musical style.

Beethoven's birthplace

Early life
Beethoven was born in Bonn, Germany. His childhood was not a happy one. His father, himself a musician, forced Ludwig to practise and perform in public at an early age, hoping he would become a child prodigy. When his mother died and his father lost his job, young Ludwig had to provide for the whole family.

Vienna

Beethoven's first visit to Vienna was cut short by his mother's illness, but he returned in 1792 to study with the composer Haydn. He soon established himself as a pianist and teacher, and settled there for the rest of his life. However, as his deafness worsened, he suffered from depressions and raging tempers, and withdrew from social life. He found consolation in composing music which expressed both his despair and his optimism and joy.

Performance
Until the onset of deafness, Beethoven earned his living as a teacher and performer. He was a superb pianist, whose emotional performances could move his audience to tears. Many of his piano compositions, especially the sonatas and concertos, explore the expressive capabilities of the instrument and are amongst his finest works.

Deafness
In his late twenties, Beethoven's hearing began to fail. By 1820, he was almost totally deaf. Unable to hear what he was playing, he could not earn a living from performing. Instead, he concentrated on composing.

Ear trumpets

Notebooks
We can get a good idea of how Beethoven worked by looking at his manuscripts and notebooks. They show how he revised his work until he was completely satisfied with it. He wrote quickly and furiously, often crossing out and rewriting whole sections of the music.

Beethoven's Broadwood grand piano

The symphonies

Symphonies before Beethoven's time were orchestral works that followed a fairly set pattern, but, in his nine symphonies, Beethoven developed the form into a large and expressive work. From the third symphony, the *Eroica*, on, these works became longer and more adventurous, using new instruments and even vocalists and a choir in the ninth symphony.

Manuscript of the *Pastoral* symphony

Chamber music
Much of Beethoven's music is for small groups, such as the string quartet. This chamber music was often written for amateur players, but Beethoven found it provided an ideal way of expressing his new musical ideas.

Pastoral symphony
This symphony is unusual because it describes a scene: the countryside around Vienna where Beethoven loved to walk. It is full of the sounds of the country, including imitations of birdsong and a thunderstorm.

Eroica symphony
Beethoven originally dedicated this symphony to his hero Napoleon, but was disgusted when Napoleon proclaimed himself emperor. He scratched out the dedication, but kept the title *Eroica* (heroic).

LUDWIG VAN BEETHOVEN

1770	Born in Bonn, Germany
1792	Moves to Vienna, studies with Joseph Haydn
1796	Begins to go deaf
1802	Writes a letter, known as the "Heiligenstadt Testament", to his brothers, describing his unhappiness about his deafness
1803	*Eroica* symphony
1808	*Pastoral* symphony
1809	Piano Concerto No 5, "The Emperor"
1824	*Choral* symphony
1827	Dies in Vienna, Austria; some 10,000 people attend his funeral

FIND OUT MORE   MOZART, WOLFGANG AMADEUS   MUSIC   MUSICAL INSTRUMENTS   NAPOLEON   ORCHESTRAS

BEETLES

THERE ARE AT LEAST 350,000 types of beetle. They make up 30 per cent of all animals and 40 per cent of all insects. They range in size from the 2 mm (0.08 in) long battle d'or beetle to the giant timber beetles, which grow up to 150 mm (6 in) long. Beetles live almost everywhere, from hot deserts to snowy mountain tops, but they are most numerous in the tropics. They eat a wide range of food, including crops, and are considered pests, but they perform a valuable role by breaking down dead animals and plants and returning the nutrients to the soil.

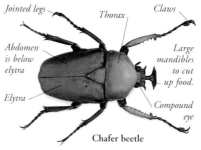

Jointed legs · *Thorax* · *Claws* · *Abdomen is below elytra* · *Large mandibles to cut up food.* · *Elytra* · *Compound eye*

Chafer beetle

Features of a beetle

Beetles have three body parts – the head, thorax, and abdomen. They have compound eyes, and antennae used for touch and smell. Their forewings have developed into hard wing cases, or elytra, which protect the hind wings. The wings, elytra, and six legs are fixed to the thorax.

2 The beetle opens its wing cases. These act as stabilizers, similar to the tail wings of an aeroplane. The delicate hind wings unfold and provide the main force in flight.

Elytra raised · *Feathery antennae spread to sense the air currents.*

Beetle often opens and shuts elytra several times before taking off.

Cockchafer beetle

Wings beat during flight.

Outstretched hind legs help streamline the beetle.

How a beetle flies

1 Large beetles, such as this cockchafer beetle, take a few seconds to get airborne. First the beetle pumps air into its body by expanding its abdomen.

Wings unfurling, ready to beat.

3 The cockchafer beetle pushes off with its legs and starts to beat its hind wings. Within a few seconds the hind wings reach the 200 beats per second needed for take-off, and the wing cases help to provide lift. During flight, the beetle uses 100 times more oxygen than it does at rest.

Wood-boring beetles

Some beetles remain as larvae for many years. Jewel beetle larvae may live in wood for over 40 years. They eat the wood, making tunnels through it, leaving small holes.

Jewel beetle

Reproduction

Most beetles undergo complete metamorphosis. Larvae hatch from eggs laid by an adult female and are the main feeding stage in a beetle's development. Once the larvae have finished growing, they turn into pupae. Inside, they change, or metamorphose, into the adult beetle that will eventually emerge from the pupa.

Mealworm beetle larva · *Inside – the larva's body breaks down and changes into the adult.* · *Pupa develops for about 6 weeks.* · *Adult beetle has emerged.*

Giant mealworm beetle

Fighting

Male beetles often fight with each other over a possible mate. They use their mandibles (mouthparts) as weapons. Stag beetles have huge, but not very powerful mandibles, which they use mainly to impress rivals. Despite their size, the mandibles do little harm. In this way, fighting is more symbolic, and both beetles live to fight and mate again.

The beetle clasps his rival in his huge jaws and tries to throw it on its back.

Stag beetles fighting

Feeding

Beetles' feeding habits, like beetles themselves, are diverse. Many, including spider beetles, feed on decaying leaf litter; others consume both living and dead wood. Some beetles, such as tiger beetles, actively hunt for live food. Scavengers, such as hide beetles, feed on rotting vegetation, dead animals, and dung. Some beetles, for example, rove beetles, are even parasites, living on creatures such as bats.

Ladybirds

Ladybirds are found worldwide. They prey on small insects, such as aphids and scale bugs. In this way they are helpful animals to have in the garden and can be used to control pests instead of using polluting chemicals.

Ladybird feeding on an aphid.

Defence

Well-armoured external skeletons and camouflage protect many beetles from predators. The bombardier beetle has an ingenious method of defence. It ejects a hot mixture of potent chemicals from its rear with an audible pop.

Bombardier beetle

Water beetles

Many beetles live in water. Diving beetles use their oar-like legs to push themselves through the water after their prey. Whirligig beetles scavenge for food that floats on the water's surface. They have special eyes that are split in two. One half looks downwards for fish, while the top half scans the air for predatory birds.

Whirligig beetle

COCKCHAFER BEETLE

SCIENTIFIC NAME Melolontha melolontha

ORDER Coleoptera

FAMILY Scarabaeidae

DISTRIBUTION Europe and western Asia

HABITAT Gardens and woods

DIET Adult feeds on sap and nectar; the larvae feed on the roots of plants, such as rose and oak

SIZE Larvae: 4 cm (1.6 in) in length; adults: 2–3 cm (0.8–1.2 in) long

LIFESPAN Larvae take about 2 years to become adults; adults live for about 2–3 months

 FIND OUT MORE · ARTHROPODS · DESERT WILDLIFE · GRASSLAND WILDLIFE · INSECTS · WOODLAND WILDLIFE

Beetles
Carnivores

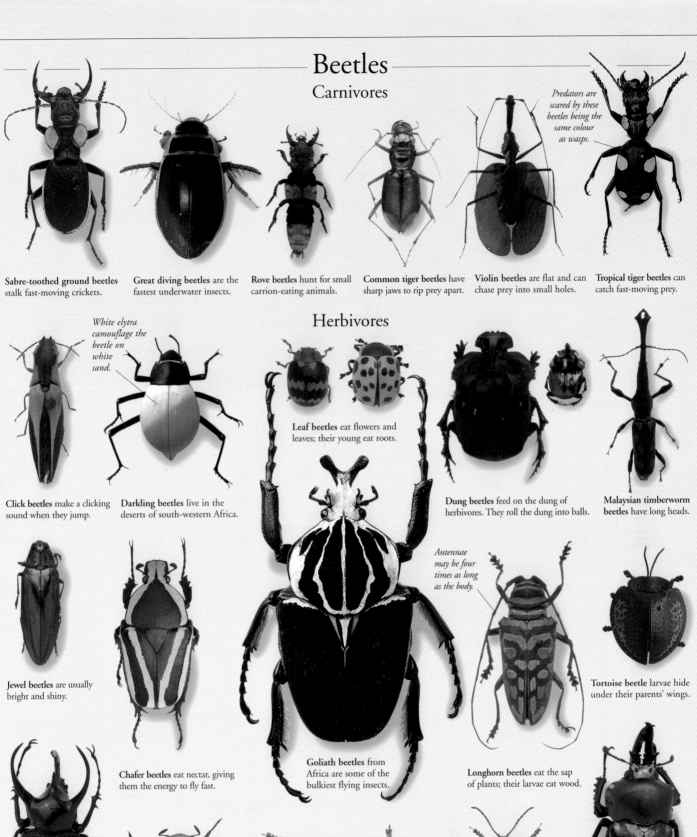

Predators are scared by these beetles being the same colour as wasps.

Sabre-toothed ground beetles stalk fast-moving crickets.

Great diving beetles are the fastest underwater insects.

Rove beetles hunt for small carrion-eating animals.

Common tiger beetles have sharp jaws to rip prey apart.

Violin beetles are flat and can chase prey into small holes.

Tropical tiger beetles can catch fast-moving prey.

Herbivores

White elytra camouflage the beetle on white sand.

Leaf beetles eat flowers and leaves; their young eat roots.

Click beetles make a clicking sound when they jump.

Darkling beetles live in the deserts of south-western Africa.

Dung beetles feed on the dung of herbivores. They roll the dung into balls.

Malaysian timberworm beetles have long heads.

Jewel beetles are usually bright and shiny.

Antennae may be four times as long as the body.

Tortoise beetle larvae hide under their parents' wings.

Chafer beetles eat nectar, giving them the energy to fly fast.

Goliath beetles from Africa are some of the bulkiest flying insects.

Longhorn beetles eat the sap of plants; their larvae eat wood.

Strong legs help them cling to mate.

Lamellicorn beetles eat nectar and sap, despite their huge jaws.

Golden beetles live only in Costa Rica in Central America.

Weevils are beetles that have a snout, or rostrum, with small biting jaws at the tip.

Malaysian frog beetles feed on sweet plants.

Stag beetles are the largest British beetles.

BELGIUM

THIS SMALL, DENSELY POPULATED country in northwest Europe borders France, Germany, and the Netherlands. Its current borders were settled in 1919, after World War I (1914–18). Today, Belgium is a highly developed industrial nation with a thriving economy. As a founder member of the European Union since 1957, and of the Benelux alliance (with the Netherlands and Luxembourg), Belgium plays an important role in European and international affairs.

BELGIUM FACTS

CAPITAL CITY Brussels

AREA 32,820 sq km (12,672 sq miles)

POPULATION 10,200,000

MAIN LANGUAGES Dutch, French, German

MAJOR RELIGION Christian

CURRENCY Euro

LIFE EXPECTANCY 78 years

PEOPLE PER DOCTOR 294

GOVERNMENT Multi-party democracy

ADULT LITERACY 99%

Physical features

In the north of Belgium is a flat plain stretching from Flanders to the Dutch border. The central plateau is bounded to the south by the Meuse and Sambre rivers. The Ardennes Plateau extends into Luxembourg and France.

Ardennes Plateau
The Ardennes Plateau covers 10,000 sq km (3,860 sq miles) in southern Belgium, Luxembourg, and northern France. Crossed by deep river valleys such as the Semois and Meuse, this upland area is rocky and heavily wooded and has spectacular limestone caves.

River Meuse
The Meuse flows slowly through gentle farmland and steep-sided valleys for 950 km (590 miles) from its source in France, west to east across Belgium, to the Dutch coast.

37°C (99°F) -18°C (0°F)
18°C (64°F) 2°C (36°F)
825 mm (32 in)

Climate
The Belgian climate is generally mild, but the skies are often cloudy. Rainfall is plentiful, especially in the mountains of the Ardennes where winter snow lingers. Summers tend to be short.

Land use
Much of Belgium is built-up and densely populated. Farmers produce cereals, fruit, vegetables, and sugar beet and raise cattle, sheep, and horses. Belgium has few natural resources and uses over 60 per cent nuclear power.

Forest 35%   Farmland 58%

Built-up 7%

People
In southern Belgium people speak Walloon, a dialect of French. In the north people speak Dutch, formerly called Flemish. A few people in the east speak German.

311 per sq km (805 per sq mile)

97% Urban   3% Rural

Brussels
With about a million inhabitants, Belgium's capital, Brussels, is the centre of government and trade. With three languages – Dutch, French, and German – it is a truly international city and the administrative headquarters of the European Union.

Gothic buildings in Brussels' Grand Place

Industry
Belgium has highly developed business and service industries, such as banking and insurance. The once-thriving coal and steel industries on the rivers Meuse and Sambre are now in crisis and are being rapidly replaced by new industries producing pharmaceuticals, chemicals, electrical equipment, and textiles. Belgium is one of the world's largest exporters of chocolate, and produces fine beers.

Belgian chocolates

Luxembourg

This tiny country shares borders with Belgium, Germany, and France. Its people enjoy low unemployment and Europe's highest living standards. It is known as a banking centre.

Finance centre
Despite its tiny size, Luxembourg is a key member of the European Union. The headquarters of the European Parliament and the European Court of Justice are based in Luxembourg City.

LUXEMBOURG FACTS

CAPITAL CITY Luxembourg

AREA 2,585 sq km (998 sq miles)

POPULATION 431,000

MAIN LANGUAGES French, German, Letzeburgish

MAJOR RELIGION Christian

CURRENCY Euro

FIND OUT MORE

EUROPE   EUROPE, HISTORY OF   EUROPEAN UNION   FARMING   NETHERLANDS   TRADE AND INDUSTRY   WORLD WAR I

BENIN EMPIRE

ESTABLISHED IN THE 11TH CENTURY, Benin was a powerful West African kingdom which flourished in the forests west of the River Niger. The wealth of Benin was based on trading: trans-Saharan trade with African savannah kingdoms, which linked the Benin Empire with the Mediterranean and the Middle East, and, coastal trade with Europeans. Benin's obas, or kings, controlled the trade networks. Immensely powerful, they lived in the royal palace in the capital city of Benin. In 1897, the British conquered Benin and ended the empire.

Empire boundaries

The Benin Empire was in modern Nigeria, where Benin City now stands. Both it and the modern republic west of Nigeria take their name from the old empire.

Sahara Desert

Benin City

Benin City

The empire of Benin was centred on the impressive capital, Benin City. A wide road ran through the centre, and a huge earthenwork wall surrounded the city. The wall acted as a defence and would have taken some considerable time to build. Its size stood as a symbol of the influence held by Benin's oba. The city housed the oba's royal palace, and areas called wards where the craftspeople lived.

Engraving of Benin City

Craft guilds

Guilds of craftspeople, such as leather workers, blacksmiths, drummers, weavers, carpenters, ivory carvers, and brass casters lived in Benin City. The brass casters formed one of the most important guilds. They made the distinctive "bronze" heads and plaques for the royal palace.

Spikes to support ivory carving

Only obas wore neck rings.

Bronze head

Benin "bronze" heads are actually made of brass. They commemorated dead obas and their family members, court ceremonies – even European traders. Carved ivory adorned the heads, which were kept in shrines in the royal palace.

Memorial head of an oba

Obas and courtiers wore ornamental weapons on ceremonial occasions.

Oba flanked by two courtiers

Brass plaques

Carved plaques decorated the wooden pillars that supported the oba's palace roof. They depicted court life and important events, such as the presentation of gifts from the oba to his courtiers.

Ivory carving

Ornately carved ivory tusks were among Benin's luxury goods. All trade in ivory was controlled by the oba. If elephant hunters killed an elephant, they had to give one tusk to the oba before they could sell the other.

Carved human figures

Carvings often told of the oba's wealth and military strength.

Carved elephant's tusk

Trade

For centuries, Benin traded with African kingdoms to the north, including the Songhai Empire. The arrival of the Europeans in the 1400s disrupted these traditional relationships and established new trading outlets.

Brass manilla

Brass manillas

In Benin, merchants used bracelet-shaped objects called manillas to buy expensive purchases, but they used tiny, white cowrie shells for smaller items.

Merchants

Travelling by sea, Portuguese traders bought slaves, peppers, cloth, gold, and ivory from Benin, and paid with manillas, cowrie shells, and guns.

Portuguese flag

Ship, called a caravel

British conquest

In 1897, in revenge for an attack on a British party, the British burnt and looted Benin City, exiled the oba, and brought Benin under colonial rule.

Oba Ewuare the Great

The warrior-king Ewuare (r.1440–80) rebuilt Benin City and, under his rule, the surrounding territory reached its greatest extent. Ewuare also established a tradition of secure hereditary successsion.

Ewuare's leopard-shaped arm ornament

Timeline

11th century Benin Empire founded in the forests of Nigeria.

1450 Peak of Benin Empire.

1486 First European to visit Benin is Portuguese explorer, Afonso d'Aveiro; shortly afterward a Benin chief establishes a trading store for the Portuguese.

Benin ornamental sword

1500s English, Dutch, and French merchants start to trade with Benin Empire.

Early to mid-16th century King of Portugal sends Christian missionaries to Benin to convert Oba Esigie, and build churches.

1688 Dutchman Olfert Dapper writes a history of Benin.

1700s Empire weakened by succession struggles.

1897 Britain takes Benin City by force.

1960 Nigeria, including the old Benin Empire, gains independence.

FIND OUT MORE

AFRICA, HISTORY OF   EMPIRES   EXPLORATION   METALS   SONGHAI EMPIRE

BICYCLES AND MOTORCYCLES

FUN, AND ENVIRONMENTALLY friendly, the bicycle is the simplest form of mechanical transport. A bicycle, or bike, is a two-wheeled machine that converts human energy into propulsion; a motorcycle, or motorbike, is a bicycle with an engine. Modern motorcycles are complex, with engine sizes ranging from 50cc (cubic centimetres) to more than 1,000cc. In many countries, such as China, most people travel or transport goods by bicycle. Across the world, bicycles and motorcycles are used for sport and leisure.

Parts of a bicycle

From a mountain bike to a racing bike, or a hybrid (a cross between the two), all bicycles are built in a similar way. Designed to be easy to pedal and comfortable, the weight is also important, as it affects the speed at which the bike can be propelled.

Saddles are adjustable, moving up and down to accommodate different riders.

Gears, operated by levers, move the chain between different-sized gear wheels, to change the speed at which the wheels turn.

Handlebars may be dropped for riding crouched.

Seat post slides in and out of frame to adjust seat level.

Frame, made from metal tubes, to support the rider.

Brakes are controlled by pulling levers on handlebars, which force brake blocks against wheel rims to slow the bicycle down.

Brake cable

Chain wheel

Cannondale SH600, hybrid

Reducing drag

Drag is the resistance of air that can slow down a bicycle or motorcycle and its rider. It is reduced by creating a streamlined shape for the air to flow around – some competitive bicycle riders even shave their legs to achieve this streamlined effect.

Spokes are arranged to create a strong but lightweight wheel.

Time-trial bike

Tyres fitted on a metal wheel rim give a smooth, quiet ride over small bumps; mountain bikes have fatter tyres to handle rough and rocky terrain.

Pedals, attached to the chain wheel, are pushed to turn the wheel.

Wheel hub secures the wheel to frame.

Parts of a motorcycle

Like a bicycle, a motorcycle has a frame, a rear wheel that drives it along, a front wheel for steering, and controls on the handlebars. Like a car, it has an internal combustion engine and suspension. The suspension supports the motorcycle's body on the wheels, and stops it being affected by the bumping of the wheels on the road.

Speedometer

Indicator and warning lights

Ignition switch

Engine rev counter

Motorcycle instrument panel
Motorcycles have an instrument panel in the centre of the handlebars. Control switches for lights and indicators can be operated with hands on the handlebars.

Riding a motorcycle
A motorcycle rider changes speed by twisting the right-hand handlebar grip, and changes gear by flicking a foot lever up or down. The front brakes are operated by hand, and the rear brakes by foot. To go round a corner, the rider turns the handlebars and leans the motorcycle over.

Small engine for speed and economy

Open "step in" frame

SFX moped

Mopeds and scooters
Small motorcycles used for short journeys in towns and cities are called mopeds or scooters. They have small engines, so they cannot go very fast, but are very economical. Mopeds, restricted to a 50cc engine, have pedals which the rider can use on steep hills.

Two-stroke engine with one cylinder. Larger motorcycles have more cylinders.

Lightweight frame

Fuel tank

1992 Yamaha FZR1000 Exup

Front suspension

Three-spoke alloy rear wheel, supported by suspension strut.

Motorcycle tyres grip the road even when the motorcycle leans over at corners. These are smooth, treadless, "slick" racing tyres.

Timeline

1839 Kirkpatrick MacMillan, a Scot, invents a lever-driven bicycle.

1863 The French Michaux brothers build the first pedal-powered bike, a velocipede.

1868 The Michaux brothers add a steam engine to a bike, creating the first motorcycle.

1885 In England, James Starley makes modern-style bicycles.

1885 German Gottlieb Daimler builds an engine-powered tricycle (below).

1901 The 1901 Werner is the first practical road-going motorcycle.

1914–18 Motorcycles used extensively in World War I.

1963 Dutchman Van Wijnen designs what will become the Ecocar – covered pedal-powered transport.

| FIND OUT MORE | AIR | CARS AND TRUCKS | ENGINES AND MOTORS | ENERGY | FORCE AND MOTION | MACHINES, SIMPLE | MOTOR SPORTS | POLLUTION | SPORTS | TRANSPORT, HISTORY OF |

Bicycles

Criterium racer allows the rider to pedal round corners easily, especially in races.

5-speed Peugeot is a traditional "ladies" bike – without a crossbar.

Mountain bikes, ideal for off-road cycling, have rugged frames and fat tyres.

BMX (Bicycle Motocross) bikes are used for rough terrain and tricks, such as "wheelies".

Tricycles have three wheels for additional balance.

Triple tandems have three sets of pedals for three riders, linked by a chain to the back wheel.

Pedicabs are pedal-powered taxis. This one was made in 1980, in Bangladesh.

Kingcycle Bean, 1990, is designed to reduce drag for extra speed.

French Velocar, 1933, is a recumbent, which allows the rider to sit back while pedalling.

Motorcycles

Harley Davidson, 1942, was adapted for military use, but was based on the civilian model.

Harley Davidson Knucklehead 61E, 1936, took the lead in American design; its engine resembled a clenched fist.

Harley Davidson Hydra Glide, 1951, has a classic chopper look with the machine stripped down to the bare essentials.

Heinkel Perle, 1956, has all the wires and cables running from the handlebars through the frame.

BMW R/60, 1956, has links to vary the angle between the "Steib" sidecar and the bike.

"Mod" scooters were popular in the 1960s: the more mirrors and lights, the more fashionable they were.

BMW R75/5, 1971, is a touring bike that combines reliability with comfort.

Honda GL1500/6 Gold Wing, 1991, has a 1500cc engine, an extra pair of cylinders, and luxuries such as a cassette player.

Husqvarna Motocross TC610, 1992, is a racing motorcyle, for driving through fields or mud.

BIG BANG

AN INCREDIBLE EXPLOSION called the Big Bang is believed to have created the Universe. Observations of galaxies and heat radiation from space have helped confirm this theory. Astronomers are now working to explain exactly what happened from the point of the Big Bang explosion which created everything in today's Universe – matter, energy, space, and time – to the present Universe with its galaxies, stars, planets, and us.

Steady State theory

In the late 1940s and the 1950s, the Steady State theory was as popular as the Big Bang theory. It proposed that the Universe looked the same at any place and at any time. Although expanding, it would stay unchanged and in perfect balance. Material was being continuously created to keep the density of the Universe constant. As scientists found proof for the Big Bang, the Steady State theory was largely abandoned.

A Steady-State universe now (left) and later in time (right). The galaxies have moved apart, but new ones (coded orange) have been created to take their place. The density stays the same.

Georges Lemaître

In 1931, Belgian cosmologist Georges Lemaître (1894–1966) was the first to put forward the theory that the Universe started from a dense, single unit of material in a big explosion. The name Big Bang followed in 1950, introduced by Fred Hoyle, a British astronomer and supporter of the Steady State theory.

Origin of the Universe

One of the most difficult problems facing scientists in the 20th century was to explain how the Universe was created. The Universe is changing, but from what and to what? The Steady State theory suggested that the Universe had no beginning or end. The alternative, and now generally accepted, theory is the Big Bang. It proposes that the Universe was created in an explosion 15 billion years ago. From very small and simple beginnings it has grown vast and complex.

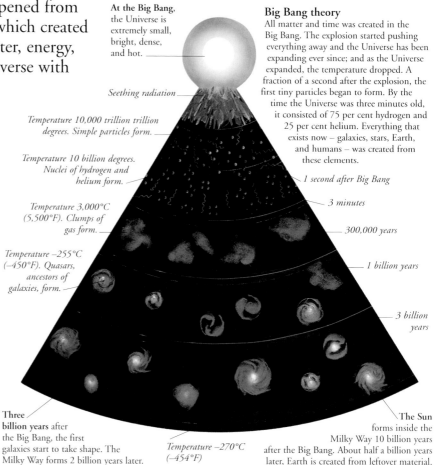

At the Big Bang, the Universe is extremely small, bright, dense, and hot.

Seething radiation

Temperature 10,000 trillion trillion degrees. Simple particles form.

Temperature 10 billion degrees. Nuclei of hydrogen and helium form.

Temperature 3,000°C (5,500°F). Clumps of gas form.

Temperature –255°C (–450°F). Quasars, ancestors of galaxies, form.

Three billion years after the Big Bang, the first galaxies start to take shape. The Milky Way forms 2 billion years later.

Temperature –270°C (–454°F)

Big Bang theory
All matter and time was created in the Big Bang. The explosion started pushing everything away and the Universe has been expanding ever since; and as the Universe expanded, the temperature dropped. A fraction of a second after the explosion, the first tiny particles began to form. By the time the Universe was three minutes old, it consisted of 75 per cent hydrogen and 25 per cent helium. Everything that exists now – galaxies, stars, Earth, and humans – was created from these elements.

1 second after Big Bang

3 minutes

300,000 years

1 billion years

3 billion years

The Sun forms inside the Milky Way 10 billion years after the Big Bang. About half a billion years later, Earth is created from leftover material.

Expanding Universe

In the 1920s, analysing starlight from galaxies showed that the galaxies are moving away from Earth. This is true of galaxies in every direction from Earth. Over time, the Universe is becoming larger and less dense. The idea that the Universe started in an explosion from a single point grew out of observations that the Universe is expanding.

Background radiation
The heat produced by the Big Bang has been cooling ever since. It now has a temperature of –270°C (–454°F), detected as microwave radiation from all over the sky. The false-colour map shows variations in the temperature 300,000 years after the Big Bang. The blue (cooler) patches are gas clouds, from which the galaxies formed.

Redshift: The faster a galaxy is moving away, the more the wavelength of its starlight is stretched, or redshifted.

The lines are shifted towards the red end of the spectrum.

Lines on the spectrum reveal a galaxy's speed.

More distant galaxies are speeding away faster than closer ones. Their light has a greater redshift.

Future of the Universe

Nobody knows for certain what is going to happen to the Universe. At present, it is getting larger and less dense. Most astronomers believe there will be a time when it stops expanding. But there is disagreement about what happens then: will the Universe live on for ever, wither and die, or start to contract?

Big Crunch
The Universe may end in a Big Crunch if it starts to contract until it is hot and dense once more. But even this may not mean the end of the Universe. The Big Crunch might be followed by another Big Bang explosion, and the whole process could start over again.

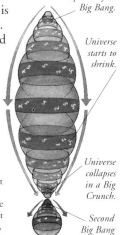

Universe expands after Big Bang.

Universe starts to shrink.

Universe collapses in a Big Crunch.

Second Big Bang

FIND OUT MORE   ASTRONOMY   BLACK HOLES   GALAXIES   GRAVITY   STARS   TIME   UNIVERSE

BIOLOGY

WHEN YOU LOOK at a running horse, you know immediately that it is alive; a beach pebble, by contrast, is non-living. What distinguishes the two is life, or the state of being alive. Biology is the study of life and living things, and it can be divided into two main fields: zoology and botany. People who study biology are known as biologists; the living organisms they study range from animals such as horses to micro-organisms such as green algae. All use energy obtained from food and released by respiration in order to fulfil their natural processes.

Classifying living things

There are around 2 million species of living organisms, and biologists classify them into groups. The largest and most general group is called a kingdom. There are five kingdoms: Monera (bacteria), Protista (protozoa and algae), Fungi, Plantae (plants), and Animalia (animals).

Number of lifeforms in the world

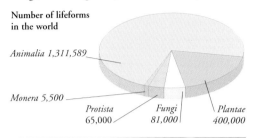

Animalia 1,311,589

Monera 5,500

Protista 65,000

Fungi 81,000

Plantae 400,000

Branches of biology

Biology covers a number of different studies. Ecology examines how living things interact and where they live. Physiology looks at how organisms work. Genetics is concerned with how characteristics inherited from one generation pass to the next. Other branches include anatomy, taxonomy, microbiology, and parasitology.

Bird skeleton

Anatomists study skeletons to understand how an organism functions.

Anatomy
Anatomy is the study of the structure of living organisms. Anatomists investigate the shape and form of the parts that make up organisms. This analysis allows them to work out things such as how bats and birds are able to fly.

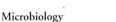

Case displays butterflies and moths

Taxonomy
The science of classifying the millions of living things into groups of related organisms is called taxonomy. Scientists called taxonomists identify and name organisms, and then group them together according to the characteristics they share and their common ancestry.

Microbiology
Micro-organisms are living things that are too small to be seen without a microscope. Microbiology is the study of all aspects of the biology of these tiny organisms, which include bacteria, viruses, protists, and some types of fungi such as yeasts.

Parasitology
Parasites live in or on another organism and exist at its expense; the study of parasites is called parasitology. Fleas are parasites that suck blood from their host. Tapeworms live and feed in their host's intestine.

Compound microscope

Magnified flea image

Flea uses needle-like mouth part to suck blood.

Zoology

Zoology is the branch of biology that is concerned with the study of animals. Animals are an amazingly diverse group of living organisms and encompass everything from sponges, spiders, and earthworms to lobsters, cats, and chimpanzees. Zoologists study the structure of animals, how their bodies function, and how they live and behave in their natural environment.

Lorenz

Ducklings imprinted on Lorenz instead of their mother.

Ethology
The study of animal behaviour is called ethology. Austrian zoologist Konrad Lorenz (1903–89) helped establish the science of ethology. He discovered imprinting, a rapid learning process that occurs early in life. Imprinting to food, surroundings, or mother, happens instinctively during a short, fixed timespan early in life.

Kew Gardens, London, England

Work of a biologist
Biologists are trained in all branches of biology, but usually focus on one specific area. Their research might involve observing animal behaviour, investigating plant photosynthesis, or studying ecosystems.

Petri dishes contain control samples.

Biologist at work in a laboratory

Botany

Botany is the study of plants. Plants are diverse organisms, encompassing everything from mosses and ferns to trees, cacti, and flowers. They make their own food by a process called photosynthesis which transforms sunlight into energy. Botanists are concerned with all aspects of the structure, function, and ecology of plants.

Rachel Carson
In 1962, the American marine biologist and writer Rachel Carson (1907–64) published a book called *The Silent Spring*. In it, she warned that the indiscriminate use of pesticides and weedkillers was poisoning the natural world. Her pioneering book was fundamental in starting the environmental movement and in making ecological information accessible to the public.

| FIND OUT MORE | ANIMAL BEHAVIOUR | ANIMALS | ECOLOGY AND ECOSYSTEMS | GENETICS | MICROSCOPIC LIFE | PARASITES | PHOTOSYNTHESIS | PLANTS |

B

BIRDS

IN THE LIVING WORLD, only birds, insects, and bats are capable of powered flight. Birds are the largest and fastest of these flying animals, and are the only ones that have feathers. There are about 9,000 species of bird, and they live in a huge range of different habitats – from deserts to the open oceans. They eat a variety of food, which they find mainly by sight. All birds reproduce by laying eggs. Most look after their young until they can fend for themselves.

Wings almost touch during the upstroke.

Pigeon in flight

Fanned tail feathers act as a brake.

Flight feathers are spread out as the bird prepares to land.

Feet are held against the body during flight.

Bird features

Birds have a lightweight skeleton and their feathers give them a smooth outline, which helps them move easily through the air. They do not have any teeth, but they have a hard beak instead. Birds use their beaks for eating, and also for many tasks that other animals carry out with their front legs and feet, such as grasping items, or tearing up food.

Internal air space with reinforcing struts

Legs and feet
A bird's feet and lower legs are usually covered with scales. Muscles that move them are close to the body. The feet are shaped according to their use.

Beak
A bird's beak is covered with keratin – the same substance that makes up human fingernails. The keratin keeps growing so that the edges of the beak do not wear away.

Bone structure
Most of the larger bones of a bird are hollow, which saves weight. They contain air spaces that connect to the special air sacs the bird uses when it breathes. Some diving birds have solid bones to make diving easier.

Skeleton
Birds have fewer bones than reptiles or mammals, and many of the bones are fused together. A large flap called the keel sticks out of the breastbone and anchors the muscles that power the wings.

Wings
The bones in a bird's wing are similar to those in a human arm. Most birds use their wings to fly. Strong muscles pull the wings downward when the bird flies; other muscles fold them up when not in use.

Feathers

Birds use their feathers to fly, and also to keep warm and dry. Each feather is made of fine strands called barbs that carry rows of smaller barbules. In some feathers, the barbules lock together with hooks to produce a smooth surface needed for flying through the air. In others, they stay partly or fully separate. These feathers are soft and fluffy for warmth.

Microscopic hooks lock barbules together.

Macaw flight feather

Curved tip with interlocking barbules

Continuous curved surface

Central quill

Breeding colours
Male birds often have bright colours which attract mates. In some species, these colours disappear at the end of the breeding season when the birds moult and a new set of feathers grows. In other species, such as pheasants, the colours are permanent.

A hollow quill anchors the feather in the bird's skin.

Down feathers
These short fluffy feathers do not have hooked barbs. They form an insulating layer next to a bird's skin. They trap air, which helps to stop heat from escaping from the bird's body.

Body feathers
The tips of these feathers overlap like tiles on a roof, giving the bird a smooth shape. The fluffy base of each feather is close to the body and helps to save heat.

Flight feathers
These feathers are strong but flexible. They provide lift when the bird is airborne. Birds have to preen them carefully to keep them in good condition.

Tail feathers
A bird uses its tail feathers for steering and braking. Some male birds have long or brightly coloured tail feathers. These play an important part in courtship.

Breeding

Birds lay their eggs either directly on the ground or in a nest. One parent – or both – keep the eggs warm by sitting on them, or incubating them. Young birds hatch from eggs at different stages of development. Some can look after themselves almost immediately; others rely on their parents for food and protection.

Eggs
Birds' eggs have a hard shell. Ground-nesting birds often lay eggs that match their background. Birds that nest in trees often lay plain eggs.

Helpless young
Tree-nesting birds usually produce poorly developed young without feathers. The young stay in the nest until they are ready to feed themselves.

Well-developed young
The young of most ground-nesting birds can feed within hours of hatching. They soon leave the nest and follow their mother.

Foster parents
Brood parasites are birds that trick others into raising their young. Here a reed warbler is feeding a cuckoo that hatched in its nest.

Monocular vision
Binocular vision

Owl

Raven *Most birds have a field of view like that of a raven.*

Snipe

Blind spot

Vision
Birds that hunt, such as owls, have eyes at the front. This restricts their field of view, but they can judge distances accurately. Shorebirds, such as the snipe, have eyes at the side. They can spot danger in any direction, including behind.

Senses

For most birds, vision is by far the most important sense. It guides them to their food and helps them to avoid their many enemies. Hearing plays a part in helping birds to communicate, and is important to birds that hunt in the dark. The sense of smell is far less vital to birds than it is to many other animals, although some birds, such as the kiwi, use it to find food.

Crane

Like most birds, a crowned crane has keen eyesight. Its eyes are so big that they almost meet in the centre of the skull. Its ear openings are at the base of its crown, but they are hidden by short feathers. Its nostrils are in its beak.

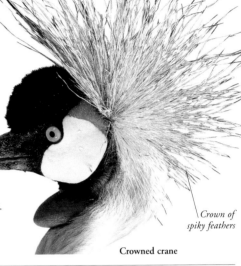

Crown of spiky feathers

Crowned crane

Flight

This complex way of moving requires superb co-ordination. Some birds stay airborne almost entirely by flapping, but others hold their wings out and glide through the air, using the natural curve of their wings to provide lift. During flight, a bird adjusts the shape of its wings to alter its speed and height.

A pigeon's wings allow good manoeuvrability when extended, and fast flight when partly closed.

A kestrel's large wings provide lift as the bird flaps them non-stop while it hovers in the air.

A grouse's wings are shaped for load-bearing rather than speed. A grouse flies only in short bursts.

A peregrine falcon's slender wings partly fold up when it dives out of the sky on to its prey.

Largest and smallest

The world's heaviest bird is the ostrich. It weighs up to 125 kg (275 lb). This is about 80,000 times heavier than the rare bee hummingbird, the smallest bird. This tiny bird's eggs are the size of peas.

Wing shapes

Birds have evolved a variety of wing shapes that enable them to fly in different ways. Some wings provide lots of lift but do not work well at speed. Others create as little friction as possible when they cut through the air, allowing a bird to fly faster.

Flightless birds

During the course of evolution, some birds have given up being able to fly. Flightless birds do not need a light body, and although some are quite small, they include the biggest birds that have ever lived.

The flightless rhea comes from South America.

Feeding and diet

Birds spend much of the time looking for food. To be able to fly, birds need food that provides them with lots of energy. Many of them eat small animals, which they catch either on land, in the air, or in water. Others visit plants and eat fruits, seeds, nectar, and pollen. Some have a mixed diet. Unlike mammals, only a few birds eat grass or the leaves of other plants.

Fish eaters
The great blue heron catches fish by stabbing them with its beak. Other fish eaters snatch their prey with talons, dive-bomb them from above, or chase them through the water.

Seed eaters
Different birds eat different seeds. They usually crack open the seed's husk before eating the food inside. The goldfinch is a typical seed eater. It feeds on thistles.

Insect eaters
Insect-eating birds search for their food on the ground or on plants, or snap it up in mid-air. The goldcrest often feeds high up in trees. Like other small insect eaters, it is expert at spotting insects hidden on leaves or bark.

Meat eaters
Many birds eat small animals, but owls and birds of prey specialize in hunting larger animals, such as mammals, reptiles, and other birds. A hooked beak allows them to tear up their food before swallowing it.

FIND OUT MORE

ANIMAL BEHAVIOUR • BIRDS OF PREY • EGGS • FLIGHT, ANIMAL • FLIGHTLESS BIRDS • NESTS AND BURROWS • OWLS AND NIGHTJARS • SKELETON • SONGBIRDS

B

Birds

Fish and meat eaters

Large eyes

Black-crowned night heron hunts for fish mainly after dark.

Inca tern flutters in the air before diving down to snatch fish from the surface of the sea.

Spectacled owl has keen eyesight and hearing for catching small animals.

Harris's hawk uses its hooked beak to tear off meat before swallowing it.

Flamingo feeds with its head down, trailing its beak through the water.

Kookaburra is a member of the kingfisher family and feeds in woodland and forests.

Seed eaters

Scarlet eyestripe

African pygmy goose uses its broad beak to collect seeds floating on the water.

Patagonian conure lives in open grasslands of Argentina and Chile.

Mourning dove feeds on the ground in North America.

Eurasian goldfinch has a fine beak and extracts seeds from flowers.

Common waxbill is a common African finch that feeds in open grassland.

Sparrows have short, stout beaks that can crack the husks from small seeds.

Insect eaters

Bushy crest

Kentucky warbler has a narrow beak, ideally shaped for picking up small insects.

Ochre-bellied flycatcher chases after insects and catches them on the wing.

Flycatchers wait on a perch for insects to fly by that they can catch.

Didric cuckoo of Africa specializes in feeding on hairy caterpillars.

Striated yuhina of Asia picks insects off leaves, and often searches under the leaves.

Racquet-tailed roller often feeds on ants and termites from the ground.

Nectar eaters

Bright yellow throat

Blue-crowned hanging parrot has a brush-tipped tongue that helps it to collect nectar and pollen.

Duyvenbode's lory feeds on flowers of New Guinea forest trees, lapping up nectar with its tongue.

Yellow-fronted woodpecker feeds on fruit, probing deep into flowers to reach their nectar.

Rufous hummingbird pumps nectar into its mouth with its tongue.

Booted racquet-tail has quite a short beak, and feeds at flowers with spreading petals.

Fruit eaters

Bill has serrated edges.

Eurasian bullfinch feeds on buds as well as fruit, using its short powerful beak.

Bearded barbet feeds mainly on figs, and uses its heavy bill to dig nest holes in wood.

Chestnut-eared aracari uses its long bill to reach for fruit on the end of long branches.

Fire-tufted barbet of Malaysia eats insects as well as fruit.

Splendid glossy starling gathers in isolated trees that carry ripe fruits.

Long-tailed starling searches for fruit in trees along forest edges.

Mixed food eaters

Eurasian jay feeds on acorns in autumn and winter, but many foods during the rest of the year.

Alpine chough eats small animals and seeds, and also scavenges animal remains.

Blue magpie eats seeds and fruits, and small animals including lizards and snakes.

Swainson's thrush eats insects, spiders, and fruit, particularly in winter.

Red-capped manakin hovers in front of plants to eat the fruit, and also eats insects.

Red-throated ant tanager catches flying insects, and also eats fruit.

B

BIRDS OF PREY

At the end of a dive, the falcon opens its wings to slow down.

MOST BIRDS OF PREY, INCLUDING EAGLES, hawks, and falcons, kill and eat live animals. They soar high above the ground or dart among trees, using their excellent eyesight to search for their prey. Once they spot a victim, they attack with their sharp talons, then tear up their food with their hooked beaks. Not all birds of prey feed in this way. A few species eat unusual foods, such as snails or nuts. Vultures eat carrion – animals that are already dead. They often wait for another animal to make a kill and then swoop down to the ground to feed on the remains of the carcass.

Long broad wings with finger-like tips

The falcon controls its flight by moving its long wing feathers.

Eyes
Birds of prey have superb eyesight for spotting prey on the ground from high up. Their eyes face forwards, which makes the birds good at judging distances. This is essential for a bird such as the lanner falcon, because it has to know exactly when to brake as it hurtles toward its prey.

Beak
Birds do not have teeth, so they cannot cut meat into pieces before they swallow it. Instead, birds of prey tear up their food with their beaks. Despite the ferocious appearance of a bird of prey's beak, it is hardly ever used as a weapon.

Widely spread flight feathers brake the falcon's flight as it makes an attack.

Bird of prey features
With their forward-facing eyes, sharp claws, or talons, and hooked beak, birds of prey are perfectly adapted for hunting and feeding on meat. Most species have feathers covering the upper legs. These are for warmth and protection.

Lanner falcon
This falcon lives in desert and savannah areas of southern Europe, Africa, and the Middle East. Like other falcons, it catches prey by folding its wings back and falling on it in a steep dive. Falcons also attack birds in mid-air by diving on them from above.

Tail feathers are used to steer in flight.

Talons
Birds of prey have large feet with long toes. Each toe ends in a talon, which stays sharp by flaking into a point as it grows. The birds use their talons to kill food, and carry it away. Many species can lift more than half their own weight.

Chukar partridge is prey of the falcon.

Flying styles
Most large birds of prey, such as eagles, look for food while soaring on currents of rising air. This uses little energy, allowing the birds to fly long distances every day. Smaller species, such as hawks, usually fly in short bursts. Kestrels are unusual in being able to hover in the air.

Splayed feathers reduce air turbulence.

Flight path of kestrel

Kestrel can see small animals on the ground.

Long, narrow wings

Hovering
Kestrels hover close to the ground while looking for prey. This uses a lot of energy, but the kestrels can dive quickly on anything that moves below them.

Flight path of goshawk

Broad, rounded wings

Long, broad wings

Soaring
Eagles, buzzards, and vultures soar by riding on currents of rising air. They spiral around slowly as they soar upwards, keeping their wings straight and steady.

Low-level flight
Hawks usually hunt by flying in short bursts. They are highly manoeuvrable, and can swerve between trees and over hedges, using surprise to catch small birds.

Flight path of eagle

B

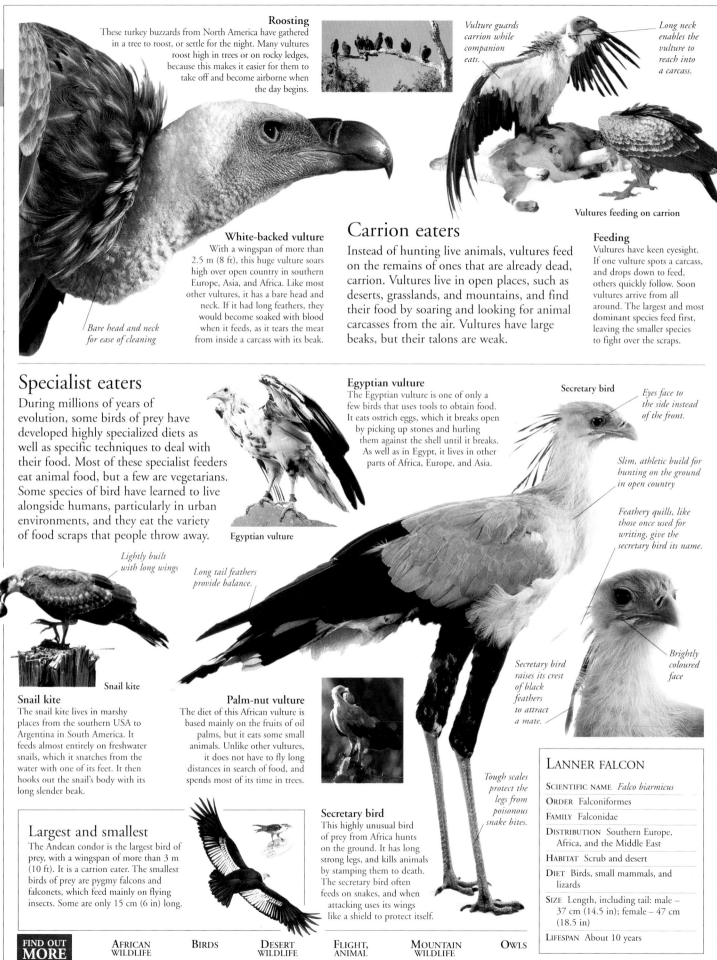

Roosting

These turkey buzzards from North America have gathered in a tree to roost, or settle for the night. Many vultures roost high in trees or on rocky ledges, because this makes it easier for them to take off and become airborne when the day begins.

Vulture guards carrion while companion eats.

Long neck enables the vulture to reach into a carcass.

Vultures feeding on carrion

White-backed vulture

With a wingspan of more than 2.5 m (8 ft), this huge vulture soars high over open country in southern Europe, Asia, and Africa. Like most other vultures, it has a bare head and neck. If it had long feathers, they would become soaked with blood when it feeds, as it tears the meat from inside a carcass with its beak.

Bare head and neck for ease of cleaning

Carrion eaters

Instead of hunting live animals, vultures feed on the remains of ones that are already dead, carrion. Vultures live in open places, such as deserts, grasslands, and mountains, and find their food by soaring and looking for animal carcasses from the air. Vultures have large beaks, but their talons are weak.

Feeding

Vultures have keen eyesight. If one vulture spots a carcass, and drops down to feed, others quickly follow. Soon vultures arrive from all around. The largest and most dominant species feed first, leaving the smaller species to fight over the scraps.

Specialist eaters

During millions of years of evolution, some birds of prey have developed highly specialized diets as well as specific techniques to deal with their food. Most of these specialist feeders eat animal food, but a few are vegetarians. Some species of bird have learned to live alongside humans, particularly in urban environments, and they eat the variety of food scraps that people throw away.

Egyptian vulture

The Egyptian vulture is one of only a few birds that uses tools to obtain food. It eats ostrich eggs, which it breaks open by picking up stones and hurling them against the shell until it breaks. As well as in Egypt, it lives in other parts of Africa, Europe, and Asia.

Egyptian vulture

Secretary bird

Eyes face to the side instead of the front.

Slim, athletic build for hunting on the ground in open country

Feathery quills, like those once used for writing, give the secretary bird its name.

Brightly coloured face

Lightly built with long wings

Long tail feathers provide balance.

Snail kite

The snail kite lives in marshy places from the southern USA to Argentina in South America. It feeds almost entirely on freshwater snails, which it snatches from the water with one of its feet. It then hooks out the snail's body with its long slender beak.

Snail kite

Palm-nut vulture

The diet of this African vulture is based mainly on the fruits of oil palms, but it eats some small animals. Unlike other vultures, it does not have to fly long distances in search of food, and spends most of its time in trees.

Secretary bird raises its crest of black feathers to attract a mate.

Tough scales protect the legs from poisonous snake bites.

Largest and smallest

The Andean condor is the largest bird of prey, with a wingspan of more than 3 m (10 ft). It is a carrion eater. The smallest birds of prey are pygmy falcons and falconets, which feed mainly on flying insects. Some are only 15 cm (6 in) long.

Secretary bird

This highly unusual bird of prey from Africa hunts on the ground. It has long strong legs, and kills animals by stamping them to death. The secretary bird often feeds on snakes, and when attacking uses its wings like a shield to protect itself.

LANNER FALCON

SCIENTIFIC NAME *Falco biarmicus*

ORDER Falconiformes

FAMILY Falconidae

DISTRIBUTION Southern Europe, Africa, and the Middle East

HABITAT Scrub and desert

DIET Birds, small mammals, and lizards

SIZE Length, including tail: male – 37 cm (14.5 in); female – 47 cm (18.5 in)

LIFESPAN About 10 years

FIND OUT MORE	AFRICAN WILDLIFE	BIRDS	DESERT WILDLIFE	FLIGHT, ANIMAL	MOUNTAIN WILDLIFE	OWLS

Birds of prey
Eagles, hawks, and falcons

Large broad wings

Tail is fanned out to provide lift as the kestrel hovers.

Common kestrel hovers to find its prey, instead of chasing it like other falcons.

Tawny eagle is a scavenger, feeding on carcasses, and even human rubbish. It also steals from other birds of prey.

Goshawk hunts in forests and often catches birds in mid-air.

Black eagle is from southern Asia. It flies over forests and often snatches birds from their nests.

Feathers down to the toes as in all true eagles

American kestrel is a small falcon. It often feeds on insects.

Golden eagle lives in remote places throughout the northern hemisphere.

Harris's hawk sometimes hunts in groups, which is unusual for a bird of prey.

Imperial eagle is rare. It lives in Spain, eastern Europe, and Asia.

Caracara has long legs and toes that enable it to hunt on the ground.

Peregrine falcon is the fastest bird in the world.

Bateleur is almost tailless. This African eagle has an unusual zigzagging flight.

Vultures

Black vulture lives in the Americas. Like the turkey vulture, it has slender legs and toes.

Turkey vulture has an immense range, stretching from Canada to Tierra del Fuego at the tip of South America.

Collar of white feathers around the base of the neck

Huge flight feathers allow effortless soaring.

Worn feathers will be replaced when the vulture moults.

Andean condor is the largest bird of prey. As its name suggests, it lives in the Andes Mountains of South America.

Feet are too weak for catching food.

White-backed vulture has only a few feathers on its neck and a bare head like all vultures.

A bare neck is easy for the vulture to clean after feeding.

BLACK DEATH

IN THE 14TH CENTURY, a deadly epidemic swept the world. The Black Death, as it became known, was bubonic plague, a terrible disease that begins with fever, causes agonizing black swellings in the glands, and leads to death, usually within a few days of infection. Millions died. Terrified people fled infected areas and carried the plague with them. In towns the doors of plague carriers were marked with crosses to warn others to keep away. The dead were collected in carts and buried in mass graves. In Europe about one-third of the population died; a similar number probably died in Asia.

Progress of the plague

The plague reached the Black Sea from Asia in 1346. From there, it was carried by Italian traders to ports on the Mediterranean. It then spread up rivers and land routes into northern Europe. By 1350, most of Europe was affected.

Plague-free areas

Black Sea

Prague
Paris •
Milan
Genoa• Florence • Constantinople
Bordeaux

c.1351
Dec 1350
June 1350
Dec 1349
June 1349
Dec 1348
June 1348
Dec 1347

Plague-free areas
Some areas, such as modern-day Poland and Milan, escaped the plague, but the reason for this is still a mystery.

Disease carriers

Plague is caused by a bacterium that lives on rodents. The disease was caught by black rats in Asia, which then colonized ships to Europe and spread the disease among people there. An infected person could also pass the plague through the air, by coughing.

Plague bacterium
The bacterium is called *Yersinia pestis,* after the Swiss biologist Alexander Yersin, who discovered it. It is common in wild animals such as field mice, ground squirrels, and marmots.

Flea carriers
The plague bacterium lives in the digestive system of a flea, and causes a blockage there. When the flea feeds, the blockage makes it vomit the newly eaten blood back onto its host, along with plague bacteria, which then infect the host.

Animal carriers
The black rat lived in towns and on ships and scavenged in food stores and rubbish heaps. Rats carry fleas, and when plague-carrying rats died of the disease, their fleas searched for other hosts. If these new hosts were people, they, too, caught the plague.

Human carriers
The plague turned into an epidemic so rapidly because human travellers helped spread it. Mongol nomads and Asian merchants carried it across Asia. The traders of the great Italian cities, such as Genoa and Venice, carried it around Europe in their ships.

Effects of the plague

The disease was so widespread that many left their families and took to the road to try to escape death. Some thought the plague was God's punishment for the sins of people, and mercilessly whipped themselves in the streets to show repentance.

Labour force
By the end of the 14th century, the smaller population of Europe meant that life was better for those who had survived. Because there were fewer peasants, they got higher wages and there was more food to go around. But recurring peasant rebellions showed that they still had grievances.

20M

Population decline
When Pope Clement VI asked how many people had died from the plague, he was told at least 20 million people in Europe, and 17 million in Asia. In comparison, around 8 million soldiers died in World War I.

8M

💀 = **2 million dead**

Black Death   World War I

Dealing with the plague

Some people tried to fend off the plague by using herbal remedies, bleeding by leeches, fumigation, and even bathing in urine. A 14th-century poem, called the Dance of Death (which states that death comes for people of every rank) was often enacted and painted, to remind people that death – and the plague – could strike at any time.

Lungwort   Mint   Rose

Simple lead crosses were placed on corpses in mass graves.

Tombs
During the plague, people faced death every day. Death is often realistically shown on 14th-century tombs, where images of skeletons and decaying corpses are common.

Chantries
People often left money for masses to be said for their souls. These masses were said in special chapels inside churches known as chantries. This chantry is at Winchester, England.

FIND OUT MORE

ASIA, HISTORY OF   DISEASES   EUROPE, HISTORY OF   MEDIEVAL EUROPE   MICROSCOPIC LIFE

BLACK HOLES

ASTRONOMERS HAVE SPENT much time analysing how stars form and how they develop. One problem was to explain what happened to a massive star at the end of its life. In 1967, the term "black hole" was used to describe one type of object that is left when a massive star dies. Four years later, Cygnus X-1 was found, the first candidate for a black hole.

A massive star ends its days in an explosion, leaving a very dense core that then collapses.

Detecting a black hole

Black holes appear black because nothing, not even light, can escape from their powerful gravity. Astronomers cannot detect them directly, but can "see" them because of the effect their gravity has on everything around them, such as gas from a nearby star. The boundary of the black hole is called the event horizon. Material pulled in towards the hole is swirled around by the gravity, forming a disc, before crossing the horizon.

Event horizon

Gravity increases as the core of the dying star shrinks.

Anything trying to escape the gravity must travel almost at the speed of light, as the core approaches the size of the event horizon.

Once the core is smaller than the event horizon, not even light can escape.

The core continues collapsing until it takes up virtually no space. The star is a singularity, a point mass of infinitely high density inside a black hole.

Stellar collapse

Massive stars can end their lives in an explosion, called a supernova, that leaves behind a central core. If the core's mass is more than that of three Suns, it becomes a black hole. Gravity forces the core to collapse. As the core shrinks, its gravity increases. At a certain point it reaches a critical size, that of the event horizon.

Gas is torn from a nearby star.

Close to the black hole, the gas glows with heat.

Black hole

Gravity pulls the gas towards the black hole.

Accretion disc

Accretion disc
The material that swirls around a black hole forms a rapidly spinning accretion disc. As the material is pulled closer to the hole, it travels faster and faster, and becomes very hot from friction. Close to the hole, the material is so hot it emits X-rays before crossing the event horizon and disappearing forever.

Black holes are black because no light or other radiation can escape, and a hole because nothing that crosses the event horizon can get out.

Event horizon **Gravity**
Black holes have incredibly strong gravity which pulls in anything that comes close enough. Anything pulled in beyond the event horizon will be squashed to near infinite density and never escapes.

Entering a black hole

1 At the start of the fall, everything appears normal.

Astronaut becomes distorted.

2 As the astronaut approaches the hole, he starts to be stretched.

3 Light is also stretched to a longer wavelength so the astronaut appears redder.

Galaxy NGC 4261 in the constellation of Virgo has what appears to be a huge accretion disc – 30 million light years across – swirling around a huge black hole.

Supermassive holes

Some galaxies have very active centres that give out large amounts of energy. An object of powerful gravity, such as a supermassive black hole, could be the cause of the activity. Such a hole would be a hundred million times more massive than the Sun.

Inside a black hole

Space and time are highly distorted inside a black hole. Anyone unlucky enough to fall into one would be stretched to resemble spaghetti, as gravity pulled more on the feet than the head. An observer watching the person fall would also see time running slower as the person fell towards the event horizon.

4 Gravity stretches the astronaut. Close to the hole, he is torn apart.

Roger Penrose

The English mathematician Roger Penrose (b. 1931) theorizes on the nature of space and time. He has shown that a massive collapsing star inevitably becomes a black hole, and that all black holes have a singularity – a point, occupying virtually no space, that contains the entire mass of the dead star. Penrose believes the singularity is always hidden by an event horizon.

FIND OUT MORE   FRICTION   GALAXIES   GRAVITY   STARS   SUN AND SOLAR SYSTEM   UNIVERSE

BOLÍVAR, SIMÓN

SIMÓN BOLÍVAR WAS the brilliant and charismatic leader who led South America to independence from 400 years of foreign rule. Together with other generals, he overthrew the Spanish in just 12 years. As president of the federation of Gran Colombia, he wanted to rule the whole continent, but this dream came to nothing. To this day, he is still known as "The Liberator", and one of the South American nations, Bolivia, is named after him.

Early life

Bolívar was born into a rich family in Caracas, Venezuela, in 1783. His parents died when he was young, and he was educated by private tutors, such as Simón Rodríguez, a teacher who taught him about European ideas, such as liberty.

Bolívar in Europe

In 1799, Bolívar was sent to Madrid to live with relatives and improve his education. While in Europe, Bolívar learned of an attempt in 1806 by Francisco de Miranda to liberate Venezuela from Spanish rule. The rebellion failed, but inspired Bolívar to fight for independence.

Ferdinand VII of Spain

Fighting for independence

At the start of the 19th century, all of South America, except Brazil and Guiana, was under the rule of the Spanish king Ferdinand VII. Many South Americans resented this and wanted to govern themselves. In response, independence movements broke out all over South America. Bolívar, keen to work in the independence movement, returned to South America and fought the Spanish in Venezuela.

Bolívar's storms to victory at the Battle of Carabobo

First republic

In 1810, Francisco de Miranda returned from exile in Europe and was made president of the new republic of Venezuela. In 1811, it became the first South American country to declare independence from foreign rule. Bolívar joined the rebel army, but the republic collapsed. He carried on the struggle, going to Colombia to fight the Spanish there.

Francisco de Miranda in prison

The Liberator

From 1811 onwards, Bolívar was the focus of independence movements across South America. In 1813, he defeated the Spanish and entered Caracas, where he was given the title of "The Liberator". In 1819, he put together an army of 2,500 men and marched them across the continent to Boyacá, Colombia. He won the resulting battle, and Colombia gained its independence.

Angostura Congress

At a congress held at Angostura, now Ciudad Bolívar, Bolívar was elected president of Venezuela. The congress also proposed the formation of Gran Colombia, a federation that included present-day Venezuela, Colombia, Ecuador, and Panama. Between 1819 and 1822, Bolívar won a series of victories against Spain, confirming the independence of Colombia and Venezuela, and liberating Peru.

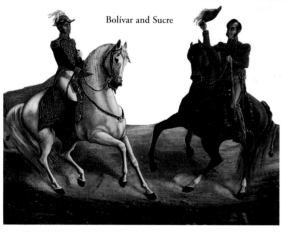

Bolívar and Sucre

Ecuador and Peru

In 1822, one of Bolívar's most talented generals, Antonio José de Sucre, defeated the Spanish at Pichincha to win Ecuador's independence. Two years later, Bolívar made a deal with the Argentinian liberator José de San Martín, whose forces were active in Peru. As a result, Sucre defeated the Spanish at Ayacucho, bringing independence to Peru. As a result of Bolívar's influence, another large area of South America was liberated.

Bolivia

In 1825, Bolívar dispatched Sucre to conquer Alto Perú, in west central South America, which was still under Spanish control. Once the Spanish were defeated, the newly independent country was named Bolivia in honour of the Liberator. By now, every South American state except Uruguay had won its independence.

Bolívar's statue at government buildings, La Paz, Bolivia

SIMÓN BOLÍVAR

1783	Born in Caracas, Venezuela.
1799	Sent to Europe.
1811	Venezuela declares its independence; Bolívar becomes a military leader.
1812	First republic is defeated.
1813	Bolívar enters Caracas as "The Liberator", but is soon defeated.
1819	Angostura Congress.
1819	Bolívar wins Battle of Boyacá to win Colombian independence.
1821	Bolívar wins Battle of Carabobo to win Venezuelan independence.
1822	Ecuador wins independence.
1825	Bolivia named in his honour.
1830	Dies of tuberculosis.

FIND OUT MORE   CENTRAL AMERICA, HISTORY OF   NAPOLEON BONAPARTE   SOUTH AMERICA, HISTORY OF   SPAIN, HISTORY OF

BOLIVIA AND PARAGUAY

BOLIVIA AND PARAGUAY are the only land-locked countries in South America. They are also two of the poorest in the continent, reliant on their neighbours for access to the sea. In a bitter war (1932–35) between them over ownership of the Gran Chaco, Bolivia lost, but both countries suffered political turmoil. Under Spanish rule between the 1530s and 1820s, Bolivia and Paraguay still bear its legacy: Spanish is an official language, and more than 90 per cent of the region's population is Roman Catholic. Many people farm and, in Bolivia, some grow and sell coca for cocaine, a drug that the government has taken steps to banish.

Aymara

The Aymara are a group of native South Americans who have farmed on the Bolivian Altiplano for hundreds of years, strongly resisting cultural change. With the Quechua, another native group, they make up more than half of Bolivia's population, but suffer discrimination and do not contribute to politics or the economy. The state has successfully persuaded many Aymara to move into towns.

Aymara farmers, Altiplano, Bolivia

Physical features

The Altiplano dominates the west of Bolivia, while the east is covered by a lowland plain called the Oriente. Paraguay is divided north to south by the Paraguay River. In the west is the Gran Chaco, a region of grass and scrub; the east is covered in grassy plains and forests, and drained by the mighty Paraná River.

Altiplano
At about 3,800 m (12,467 ft) above sea-level, the Altiplano, a vast, windswept, almost treeless plateau, lies between two ranges of the Bolivian Andes. Despite its cold, arid climate, more than half of Bolivia's population lives here, growing a few crops and rearing animals such as llamas and alpacas.

Lake Titicaca
The clear blue waters of Lake Titicaca cover 8,288 sq km (3,200 sq miles) at a height of 3,810 m (12,500 ft) above sea-level, making it the highest navigable lake in the world. It is the last surviving stretch of an ancient inland sea known as Lago Ballivián.

Gran Chaco
The flat, dry plain that covers southeastern Bolivia and northwest Paraguay is called the Gran Chaco. Since so few people live in this region of coarse grass, thorny shrubs, and cactus, a wide range of plants and animals thrives here.

Regional climate
Bolivia's Altiplano has a cool, crisp, dry climate. The eastern part of the country is warm and humid, as is most of Paraguay. The Chaco is hot, with 50–100 cm (20–40 in) of rain a year, although it often has droughts in winter.

19°C
(67°F)

12°C
(55°F)

1,890 mm
(74 in)

Bolivia

The highest and most isolated nation in South America, Bolivia is named after Simón Bolívar, who, in the 1800s, led wars of independence against the Spaniards. Despite rich natural resources, exporting is difficult because of Bolivia's position. About half the people are Native Americans; the rest are Spanish or of mixed blood.

Chuqui

Pipes are made from a local reed. The longer the reed, the deeper the sound.

La Paz
Although Sucre is Bolivia's official capital, the country is governed from La Paz, which also has capital status. At 3,631 m (11,913 ft) above sea-level, La Paz is the world's highest capital and Bolivia's largest city, with a population of about 2,515,000, of whom over half are Native Americans. La Paz has chemical and textile industries, but unemployment is generally high.

Music
Bolivian music has Incan, Amazonian, Spanish, and African influences. Rural Aymara orchestras are often composed entirely of panpipes, called *chuqui*. Other instruments include drums, flutes, and the *phututu*, made from a cow's horn.

Deforestation
Tropical rainforests in Bolivia are being cut down at the rate of 2,000 sq km (772 sq miles) a year, mostly for cattle ranching or growing coca for cocaine. Chemicals used in the manufacture of cocaine are discharged directly into the rivers of Amazonia, many of which have high pollution levels that damage plant and tree life.

Tin

Metal mining
Bolivia is rich in mineral deposits. Its tin mines lie high in the Andes mountains and it is the world's largest producer of tin. It is also a leading exporter of antimony and silver. Other mineral deposits include zinc, gold, and lead.

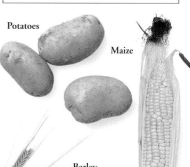

Potatoes

Maize

Barley

Crops
Bolivian farmers living on the Altiplano grow potatoes, soya beans, barley, and wheat for themselves and their families. Rice, maize, bananas, and plantains are grown in the lowlands. Cash crops include sugar-cane, cocoa beans, and coffee, although the profits from illegal coca crops greatly exceed all legal farming produce combined.

Paraguay

The Paraguay River, from which the country takes its name, divides the land in two. To the east lie the fertile hills and plains that are home to 90 per cent of the people. The vast majority are *mestizos,* people of mixed European and Native American ancestry; the rest are Guaraní or Europeans. To the northwest is the Gran Chaco, large areas of which Paraguay won from Bolivia in the 1930s. Only five per cent of the people live in the Chaco, including 10,000 Mennonites, farmers of German descent who retain their culture.

Beef
The main industry in Paraguay's Gran Chaco is cattle ranching. Herds of animals roam the flat grasslands, tended by skilled Paraguayan cowboys called *gauchos* who round the cattle up on horseback. The farms are called *estancias* and are some of the only buildings in this open landscape.

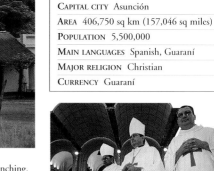

Jesuits
In 1588, Spanish missionaries from the Jesuit order of the Roman Catholic Church arrived in Asunción. They converted the local Guaraní people to Christianity, and taught them trades such as weaving. The Jesuits built large stone churches.

Macá bag

Macá
The Macá are a small ethnic group who follow a traditional lifestyle in the Gran Chaco. They make a living from farming. Macá women also weave bags and cloth for the tourist trade.

Itaipu Dam
With a reservoir 3,250 sq km (1,255 sq miles) and 220 m (722 ft) deep, the Itaipu Dam, on the Paraná River, was undertaken as a joint project with Brazil. It provides water for the world's largest hydroelectric plant and generates enough electricity to make Paraguay self-sufficient in energy.

Dam generates 13,320 megawatts of electricity – enough to supply New York City.

Exports
Soya-bean flour and cotton make up around 50 per cent of Paraguay's exports. The country also sells timber from its forests, vegetable oils, and processed meat. Leading trading partners include Brazil, Argentina, and the Netherlands.

FIND OUT MORE   BOLÍVAR, SIMÓN   CHRISTIANITY   DAMS   DRUGS   ENERGY   FARMING   MUSIC   NATIVE AMERICANS   ROCKS AND MINERALS   SOUTH AMERICA, HISTORY OF   TEXTILES AND WEAVING

BOOKS

FROM ENCYCLOPEDIAS TO NOVELS, books are a vital record of human life and achievement. They store the thoughts, beliefs, and experiences of individuals and societies, preserving them after the author's death. There are many kinds of books, from religious works, such as the Qur'an, and non-fiction, such as dictionaries and educational books, to fiction such as plays and stories. The Chinese invented printing in the 9th century; it arrived in Europe during the 15th century. Printing made it possible to mass-produce books, and knowledge was spread more widely. Today, publishing is a global industry.

Early Chinese book, made of fragile bamboo strips

Early books

The first books were not made of paper. Long before 3000 BC, the Sumerians wrote on clay tablets. Around 1300 BC, the Chinese began making books from bamboo strips bound together with cord.

Making books

Much preparation goes into making books and some take several years to produce. For example, making an encyclopedia will involve a team of people that includes authors, editors, designers, picture researchers, illustrators, photographers, and IT experts, as well as printers.

Artist's pencil roughs
Finished pieces of colour artwork
The colour proof before text is added to page
Transparencies are a high-quality image format.

Illustration
The designer draws a detailed plan, showing the position of each illustration. The artist makes rough sketches, which are checked, then paints each picture separately. The artwork is photographed, and carefully positioned on the page using a computer, until the design is perfect.

Author
The author is the first person to start work, researching and writing the contents of the book. The author advises the designer on suitable images for the book and works closely with the editorial team throughout the project.

The printed colour matches the original artwork as closely as possible.

The spine of the book holds the pages in place.
The editor checks the author's text for mistakes and adjusts length of text if necessary.
Pictures and text are perfectly integrated.

Text
The text is edited on a computer screen, and then produced as a page called a proof. The proof is matched with the artwork to make sure that words and images fit exactly, before going to the printer.

Finished book
At last the book is finished, and fitted with a hard cover and a protective jacket. It is now ready to sell. An illustrated book may take several years to make, although new technology is speeding up this process.

Paper

Papyrus plants grow by the Nile.

The ancient Egyptians wrote on scrolls made from papyrus, which grew by the River Nile. Later civilizations in the Middle East wrote on parchment made from animal skin. Modern paper was probably invented in China around AD 150. It was made by pulping flax fibres, then flattening and drying them in the sun. The Chinese kept this process a secret for 500 years before they passed it on to the rest of the world.

CD Roms

There is a limit to how big any book can grow before it becomes too heavy and cumbersome to be practical. Now, modern technology is developing compact alternatives to traditional books. One CD Rom can contain as much text as a shelf of encyclopedias. Text and pictures from CD Roms can be read and transmitted by computer.

CD Rom

Paperbacks
A paperback book contains the same text as a hardback, but has a soft cover. The first modern paperback books were published in London by Penguin, in 1935, priced sixpence. They are far cheaper than hardbacks, and many more people can buy them.

Timeline
c. 285 BC Egyptian pharaoh Ptolemy I establishes a library at Alexandria, Egypt.

AD 300s Books with pages first invented.

Gutenberg Bible

c.1440 Johannes Gutenberg invents the metal type.

1789 French Revolutionaries proclaim the fundamental public right to print without fear of censorship.

1796 Lithography (a technique for printing illustrations) invented.

1811 First totally mechanized printing press invented, USA.

1935 First paperback books published for mass market by Penguin in UK.

1980s Electronic books for the computer published in CD Rom format.

1990s Books first published on the Internet.

FIND OUT MORE — CHILDREN'S LITERATURE · COMPUTERS · DRAMA · EGYPT, ANCIENT · LITERATURE · POETRY · PRINTING · WRITING

BRAIN AND NERVOUS SYSTEM

EVERY THOUGHT YOU HAVE, every emotion you feel, and every action you take is a reflection of the nervous system at work. At the core of the nervous system are the brain and spinal cord, known as the central nervous system (CNS). The most complex part of the CNS is the brain; this constantly receives information from the body, processes it, and sends out instructions telling the body what to do. The CNS communicates with every part of the body through an extensive network of nerves. The nerves and the CNS are both constructed from billions of nerve cells called neurons.

Nerves

Nerves form the "wiring" of the nervous system. Each nerve consists of a bundle of neurons (nerve cells) held together by a tough outer sheath. Nerves spread out from the brain and spinal cord and branch repeatedly to reach all parts of the body. Most nerves contain sensory neurons that carry nerve impulses towards the CNS, and motor neurons that carry nerve impulses away from the CNS.

Inside a nerve

Sensory neuron

Motor neuron

Bundle of neurons

Blood vessels

Outer sheath of the nerve

Nerve endings
At the ends of sensory neurons there are nerve endings called sensory receptors. If you touch an object, a sensory receptor in the skin is stimulated, nerve impulses travel to the brain along the sensory neuron, and you feel the object. In this way, visually impaired people can "read" the Braille language with their fingertips.

Brain is the body's control and co-ordination centre.

Cranial nerves

Cervical nerves

Brachial plexus

Spinal cord relays information to and from the brain and the rest of the body.

Radial nerve controls the muscles in the arm and hand.

Lumbar plexus

Sacral plexus

Thoracic nerves

Lumbar nerves

Sacral nerves

Sciatic nerve controls the muscles in the leg and foot.

Tibial nerve controls the muscles of the calf and foot.

Nervous system

The nervous system is made up of the CNS and the peripheral nervous system, which consists of the nerves. The peripheral nervous system has two sections: the somatic system which controls voluntary actions, and the autonomic nervous system which controls automatic functions such as heart rate.

Neurons

Neurons are long, thin cells adapted to carry electrical signals called nerve impulses. There are three types of neurons: sensory neurons, motor neurons, and association neurons. The most numerous are association neurons, which transmit signals from one neuron to another and are found only inside the CNS.

Nerve impulses

Nerve impulses are the "messages" that travel at high speed along neurons. Impulses are weak electrical signals that are generated and transmitted by neurons when they are stimulated. The stimulus may come from a sensory nerve ending, or from an adjacent neuron. Nerve impulses travel in one direction along the neuron.

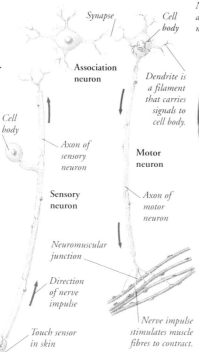

Synapse

Cell body

Association neuron

Dendrite is a filament that carries signals to cell body.

Cell body

Axon of sensory neuron

Motor neuron

Sensory neuron

Axon of motor neuron

Neuromuscular junction

Direction of nerve impulse

Touch sensor in skin

Nerve impulse stimulates muscle fibres to contract.

Neuromuscular junction is a synapse between a motor neuron and muscle fibre.

Synapses

A synapse is a junction between two neurons. At a synapse, neurons do not touch. Instead, there is a tiny gap. When a nerve impulse reaches a synapse it triggers the release of chemicals, which travel across the gap and stimulate the second neuron to generate a nerve impulse.

Reflex actions

If you touch something sharp, you automatically pull your hand away without thinking about it. This is a reflex action. A sensory neuron carries impulses to the spinal cord, where an association neuron transmits impulses to a motor neuron, and the arm muscle contracts.

Receptors in hand detect the prick of a pin and send signal to spinal cord.

Brain

Sensory receptors

Motor neuron

Muscle

Sensory neuron

Santiago Ramón y Cajal

Spanish anatomist Santiago Ramón y Cajal (1852–1934) pioneered the study of the cells that make up the brain and nerves. He developed methods for staining nerve cells so they could be seen clearly under the microscope. His work revolutionized the examination of brain tissue.

Brain

The brain is the body's control centre. Your brain enables you to think and to have a personality, and also regulates all your body processes. It has three main regions: the forebrain, the cerebellum, and the brain stem. The forebrain consists of the cerebrum (which is made up of two halves or hemispheres), the thalamus, hypothalamus, and the limbic system, which controls emotions and instinctive behaviour.

White matter *Grey matter*

Section through brain tissue

Grey and white matter

Each cerebral hemisphere has two layers. The outer layer, the cerebral cortex, consists of grey matter containing cell bodies of neurons that form a communication network. The inner layer, or white matter, consists of nerve fibres that link the cerebral cortex to the other parts of the brain.

B

Thalamus relays information about the senses to the cerebrum.

Cerebrum is the site of conscious thought.

The two cerebral hemispheres are joined by a band called the corpus callosum.

Hypothalamus regulates body temperature, thirst, and appetite.

Cerebellum co-ordinates movement and balance.

Spinal cord

Frontal lobe

Pituitary gland

Brain stem controls essential automatic functions, such as breathing and heart rate.

Left and right brains

The left cerebral hemisphere controls the right side of the body, and the right cerebral hemisphere controls the left side of the body. Although both hemispheres are used for almost every activity, each hemisphere has its own specialist skills. In most people, the left hemisphere is involved in spoken and written language, mathematical ability, and reasoning, while the right hemisphere controls the appreciation of art and music, insight and imagination, and shape recognition.

Right cerebral hemisphere

Left cerebral hemisphere

Cerebral cortex is the outer layer of the cerebral hemisphere.

Facial skeleton

Brain cells

The brain consists of hundreds of billions of nerve cells. Many of these are association neurons that are constantly receiving and transmitting nerve impulses. Any one of these neurons can have links to over 1,000 other neurons, producing a complex network. The brain also contains other nerve cells, called glial cells, which hold the neurons in place.

Association neuron in brain *Glial cell*

Brain areas

Certain areas of the cerebrum are involved with particular body functions. These areas can be highlighted on a brain map. Motor areas of the brain, such as the speech and basic movement areas, send out instructions to control voluntary movement. Sensory areas, such as the hearing, taste, smell, touch, and vision areas, receive information from sensory receptors around the body. Association areas, such as the frontal lobe, deal with thoughts, personality, and emotions, analyse experiences, and give you consciousness and awareness.

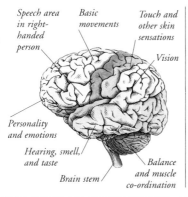

Speech area in right-handed person *Basic movements* *Touch and other skin sensations* *Vision* *Personality and emotions* *Hearing, smell, and taste* *Brain stem* *Balance and muscle co-ordination*

Brain waves

The brain's neurons are constantly sending out and receiving nerve impulses. This process produces electrical signals that can be detected using a machine called an electroencephalograph (EEG). Electrodes linked to the EEG can be attached to a person's scalp in order to record the brain's electrical activities as a series of patterns called brain waves.

Sleep and dreams

As you sleep, you move repeatedly between phases of light REM (rapid eye movement) sleep and phases of deeper NREM sleep. These shifts can be detected using an EEG.

Metal rod

Skull of Phineas Gage

Personality

The frontal lobe of the brain plays a major role in deciding personality. This was shown by the case of an American worker called Phineas Gage. In 1848, an accident sent a metal rod through Gage's cheek and frontal lobe. He survived but his personality changed from being friendly to being aggressive.

Spinal cord

The spinal cord relays information between the brain and the rest of the body, and is involved in many reflex actions. It is a flattened cylinder of nervous tissue, about 43 cm (17 in) long and as thick as a finger. It runs from the base of the brain to the lower back, surrounded by the backbone.

Grey matter relays information between spinal cord and spinal nerves.

Section of spinal cord

Spinal nerve relays nerve impulses to and from all parts of body.

Spinal ganglion

White matter carries signals up and down spinal column.

Pierre Paul Broca

French anatomist and surgeon Pierre Paul Broca (1824–80) demonstrated that a specific region of the brain controlled a particular body function. Broca found that a small area co-ordinated the muscles in the mouth and throat that produce speech. This area is now called Broca's area, or the speech area. Broca made his discovery when treating a patient who could not talk after damage to part of his brain.

FIND OUT **MORE** | CELLS | EYES AND SEEING | HORMONES AND ENDOCRINE SYSTEM | HUMAN BODY | MUSCLES AND MOVEMENT | SKIN, HAIR, AND NAILS | SMELL AND TASTE

BRAZIL

THE LARGEST COUNTRY in South America, Brazil is a land of opposites. Watered by the second longest river in the world, the Amazon, it has the world's largest rainforest, arid deserts in the northeast, and rolling grassland in the south. Crowded cities contrast with remote areas that have never been explored. The country has many well-developed industries and a huge, successful agricultural base, but many people live in poverty. Brazilian society is a vibrant, diverse mix of cultures.

Physical features

The Amazon Basin and its forests, some mountainous, occupy northern Brazil. The southeast is a region of plateaus that vary from sunburnt arid scrublands to rich fields and pastures.

BRAZIL FACTS

CAPITAL CITY	Brasília
AREA	8,511,970 sq km (3,286,472 sq miles)
POPULATION	170,000,000
MAIN LANGUAGE	Portuguese
MAJOR RELIGION	Christian
CURRENCY	Réal
LIFE EXPECTANCY	68 years
PEOPLE PER DOCTOR	769
GOVERNMENT	Multi-party democracy
ADULT LITERACY	85%

Highlands
The Brazilian Highlands extend from the Amazon Basin to the coast, rising to 3,000 m (10,000 ft). About 60 per cent of the country is dominated by the plateau, where landscape ranges from tropical forest to dry, rocky desert.

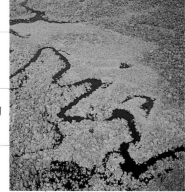

Amazonian rainforest
Around half of Brazil is cloaked in dense rainforest. The River Amazon, 6,448 km (4,007 miles) long, runs through the north of Brazil, giving life to more than 40,000 different species of plants and animals in the forests.

Brasília
Brazil's modern capital city, Brasília, lies on the extreme northern edge of the plateau region. Purpose-built in the 1950s on the site of a felled rainforest, the city replaced Rio de Janeiro as capital. Its inland position has helped to develop new areas away from the coast. There are many imaginative, futuristic buildings, including the spectacular cathedral.

Brasília Cathedral

41°C (106°F)   -4°C (25°F)
18°C (64°F)   22°C (72°F)
1,600 mm (63 in)

Climate
All except the extreme south of Brazil lies in the tropics, so temperatures are always high. The Amazonian rainforest receives about 4,000 mm (157 in) every year. By contrast, droughts are common in the northeast corner. Farther south, summers are hot and winters can be cold with frosts.

Built-up 0.3%   Farmland 10%
Desert 29.7%
Forests 59.5%   Wetland 0.5%

Land use
Thick forests cover the majority of the land, but are being cleared at an alarming rate to make way for farmland and roads. The fertile southeast, especially around São Paulo, is permanently farmed. Much of the land is desert.

B

People

The Brazilian people have a wide ethnic background, and there are large groups of African, European, and Asian origin. The original inhabitants of Brazil form only a tiny percentage of the population. Many families are tight knit, fiercely loyal, and strict Roman Catholics. The majority live in towns clustered along the southeastern coast.

20 per sq km (52 per sq mile)   **81% Urban**   **19% Rural**

Indian groups
Some native Brazilians still live in the rainforests, following traditional ways of life. However, about 14 groups now shelter in Xingu National Park, set up when their forest home was destroyed.

Leisure

The mainly Roman Catholic people of Brazil celebrate many religious festivals, such as the Rio and Bahía carnivals. Sports, including football, basketball, and water sports along the coast, are the chief leisure activities for millions of Brazilians. The samba, one of the world's most popular dances, originated in Brazil.

Rio Carnival
Known as one of the world's largest and most spectacular festivals, the Rio Carnival, in Rio de Janeiro, is held just before Lent every year. During the carnival, processions of brightly decorated floats, and a myriad of colourful singers, musicians, and dancers with imaginative costumes, fill the streets.

Football
Many Brazilians have a passion for football, either as players or spectators. The national team has won the World Cup more times than any other team. Its star player, Edson Arantes do Nascimento, known as Pelé, was the world's leading player in the 1960s and is regarded by fans as a living legend.

Farming

Brazil has immense natural resources. About 22 per cent of the labour force works on the land, growing all Brazil's own food, with a vast surplus for export. The best farmland is around Rio de Janeiro and São Paulo, where water is plentiful and the climate is frost-free. About 150 million cattle are reared on large ranches in this region.

Cattle ranch, São Paulo

Orange

Coffee leaves and berries

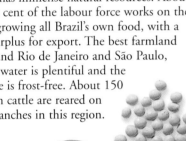

Soya beans
Each berry contains two beans, which are washed, dried, and roasted.

Meat production
Brazil is one of the world's largest producers of beef and veal. Cows graze on the rich, green pastures of central Brazil. Large areas of tropical rainforest are cleared to create new cattle ranches, but the soil is soon exhausted and more forest has to be felled.

Bananas

Crops
Brazil is a leading producer of cocoa beans, coffee, oranges, and sugar-cane, and one of the world's largest growers of soya beans and bananas. About 22 per cent of the world's coffee comes from Brazil, and millions of oranges are picked every year. These crops grow successfully in the warm, fertile soils of central and southern Brazil.

Forest products

The plants and trees of the Amazonian rainforest have long been used for food, housing, and medicine by the people who live there. Some of these, such as rubber and Brazil nuts, are now known world-wide. Other lesser-known plants are quinine, taken from chinchona bark and used to treat malaria; ipecacuanha, an ingredient of cough medicines; and curare, once part of an arrow poison, now a life-saving muscle relaxant used in operations.

Brazil nuts

Transport

A vast network links Brazil's main centres, but of the 1,660,352 km (1,031,693 miles) of roads, only nine per cent are paved. Brazil has one of the world's largest national air networks. Cities with rapid growth, such as São Paulo, are expanding their subways.

Industry

The manufacturing industry employs about 15 per cent of the Brazilian work-force. Machinery, textiles, cars, food products, industrial chemicals, and footwear are the main export products. Brazil has large mining, oil, and steel industries, but has suffered high inflation.

Mining
Brazil is a leading producer of gold, manganese, and tin ore. The country is noted for its precious stones, such as amethysts, diamonds, and topaz, but the quest for mineral wealth has led to much forest destruction.

Steel
South America's top steel maker, Brazil ranks highly in world production. This, and cheap labour, have attracted many car makers to invest in the country.

"Green" cars
About one-third of all Brazil's cars are run on so-called "green petrol", or ethanol, which is made from fermented sugar-cane. Because it produces less carbon monoxide than petrol when it is burned, it is less harmful to the environment and is reducing pollution.

 FIND OUT MORE   CHRISTIANITY   CRYSTALS AND GEMS   FARMING   FESTIVALS   FOOTBALL   FORESTS   NATIVE AMERICANS   RIVERS   ROCKS AND MINERALS   SOUTH AMERICA, HISTORY OF

BRIDGES

B

CURVING MAJESTICALLY across rivers and valleys, bridges are some of the most spectacular structures engineers have ever created. They are also some of the most useful, because bridges can speed up journeys by cutting out ferry crossings, long detours, steep hills, and busy junctions. The first bridges were probably tree trunks laid across streams. Wooden beam bridges and stone or brick arches were the main types of bridge from Roman times until the 18th century, when iron became available to engineers. Most modern bridges are made of steel and concrete, making them both strong and flexible.

Types of bridges

On a journey, you may see many different shapes and sizes of bridge, but there are really only a few main types: arch bridges, beam bridges, cantilever bridges, suspension bridges, and cable-stay bridges. The type of bridge used depends on the size of the gap it must span, the landscape, and traffic that will cross it.

Arch bridge
The arch is used to build bridges because it is a strong shape that can bear a lot of weight. To bridge a wide gap, several arches of stone or brick are linked together.

Beam bridge
In a beam bridge, the central span (or beam) is supported at both ends. Very long beams are impractical, because they would be liable to collapse under their own weight.

Cantilever bridge
A beam fixed at one end and stretching out over a gap is a cantilever. Balanced cantilever bridges have several supports, each with two beams that reach out from either side.

Suspension bridge
The deck of a suspension bridge hangs from cables slung over towers and anchored to the ground at each end of the bridge. Such bridges have spans of up to 1 km (0.62 miles).

Pylon

1 The foundations are laid, and the two pylons are erected. The concrete side spans, which will link the bridge to the shore, are assembled.

Side span

2 The deck sections are hung from cables attached to the pylons, and the bridge begins to stretch across the river from each shore.

Cables

3 The central deck spans are lifted by crane off river barges, welded into place, and attached to cables.

Crane

4 When the last deck section is in place, the bridge is complete. The cables transfer the weight of the deck to the pylons.

Building a bridge

A cable-stay bridge is a type of suspension bridge with a deck hung from slanting cables that are fixed to pylons instead of the ground. Once the pylons are in place, the bridge is built outwards in both directions from each pylon. This ensures that the forces on the pylons balance, so that there is no danger of the pylons collapsing.

23 pairs of cables attach to either side of pylon.

Model of the Pont de Normandie

Bridge carries 4 lanes of traffic.

Pylon of reinforced concrete

Piers support side spans.

Deck is 52 m (170 ft) above water.

Steel cables are coated in plastic to prevent rusting.

Foundations of pylons extend 50–60 m (164–197 ft) below ground.

Isambard Kingdom Brunel

English engineer Isambard Kingdom Brunel (1806–59) was a genius of bridge design. Brunel designed and built two of the earliest suspension bridges. He also planned and built railways and several huge steamships.

Aqueducts

Not all bridges carry roads or railway tracks. An aqueduct is a bridge that carries water. The Romans built aqueducts to supply water to the baths and drinking fountains in their cities. More recent aqueducts carry canals over steep-sided valleys in order to keep the canal level. This avoids having to build long flights of locks.

Aqueduct on the River Dee, Wales

Timeline

200 BC Roman engineers build arch bridges of stone or wood, and aqueducts.

1779 The first bridge made of cast iron is built at Ironbridge, England.

1883 In the USA, New York's Brooklyn Bridge is the first bridge to be supported by steel suspension cables.

1930 Switzerland's Salginatobel Bridge is constructed of reinforced concrete (concrete strengthened with steel).

Sydney Harbour Bridge, Australia

1932 Australia's Sydney Harbour Bridge opens, carrying a road and rail tracks suspended from a huge steel arch.

1998 The Akashi Kaikyo suspension bridge over Japan's Akashi Strait has the longest main span in the world.

FIND OUT MORE BUILDING AND CONSTRUCTION IRON AND STEEL RIVERS ROADS ROMAN EMPIRE SHIPS AND BOATS TRAINS AND RAILWAYS TRANSPORT, HISTORY OF TUNNELS

BRONTË SISTERS

THREE OF THE FINEST writers of the 19th century, Charlotte, Anne, and Emily Brontë, were brought up in solitude in a small town in northern England. In spite of many difficulties, including being far away from the world of publishing in London, they produced some of the most popular novels of the period. The books portrayed characters with a new frankness and showed how difficult life could be for women of that era. Their stories still enthral readers of today.

Haworth parsonage

The Brontë sisters were brought up in the small town of Haworth in Yorkshire, northern England. Their father was the curate (priest) at the local church, so they lived at the parsonage (clergyman's house). It was a grim stone building, with a view over the graveyard.

Brontë family
Charlotte, Emily, and Anne lived with their father, Patrick Brontë and their brother, Branwell. Their mother, Maria, died when the children were young and two other children died in infancy, so the sisters were brought up by their aunt. They had a lonely life. They mixed little with other children and had to make their own entertainment.

Education

Charlotte and Emily were sent away to Cowan Bridge school. The conditions were poor and made Charlotte ill. Lowood school, in *Jane Eyre*, is based on her time there. All three sisters later worked as teachers, or governesses – one of the few jobs then open to educated young women.

Manuscripts are still preserved at Haworth parsonage.

Cowan Bridge school

Poetry manuscript by Charlotte Brontë at around the age of 14

Manuscripts and illustrations completed by the Brontë sisters in their teenage years.

Angria and Gondal

To amuse themselves in the bleak moorland rectory, the Brontë children invented two imaginary lands, called Angria and Gondal. They wrote many stories and poems about these lands, which were peopled with heroes and heroines who lived exciting and tragic lives.

Novelists

In 1846, the Brontës started to get their works published. They began with a volume of poems, but only two copies were sold. In the following two years Emily's *Wuthering Heights*, Charlotte's *Jane Eyre*, and Anne's *Agnes Grey* were published. At the time it was not thought proper for the daughters of clergymen to write fiction, so the sisters used pseudonyms (false names), to keep their identities secret. Many people bought the books and wanted to know more about the authors.

Bell brothers

The Brontë sisters published their books under three male names – Acton, Currer, and Ellis Bell, the initials of which matched those of the sisters' own names. To begin with, even their publishers did not know who the "Bell brothers" really were.

WUTHERING HEIGHTS

A NOVEL.

BY

ELLIS BELL.

IN THREE VOLUMES.

VOL. II.

LONDON:
THOMAS CAUTLEY NEWBY, PUBLISHER,
72, MORTIMER St.,—CAVENDISH Sq.

1847.

Jane Eyre
Charlotte Brontë's first novel tells the story of Jane Eyre and her struggle to be an independent woman in a hostile society. Working as a governess, she falls in love with her employer, Mr Rochester, only to discover terrible secrets in his past. The novel was considered radical in its time.

Wuthering Heights
Emily Brontë's novel follows a series of tragic relationships through different generations and is especially famous for its depiction of Catherine and Heathcliff. Set against the Yorkshire countryside, the novel deals with contemporary issues of social change and industrialization.

CHARLOTTE BRONTË

1816	Born Yorkshire, England.
1822–32	Educated at Cowan Bridge School and Miss Wooler's School, Roe Head, Yorkshire.
1846	Publishes her poems.
1847	Publishes *Jane Eyre*.
1849	Publishes *Shirley*.
1853	Publishes *Villette*.
1854	Marries Arthur Nicholls.
1855	Dies.

FIND OUT MORE   BOOKS   CHRISTIANITY   DICKENS, CHARLES   FILM AND FILM-MAKING   LITERATURE   UNITED KINGDOM, HISTORY OF   WRITING

BRONZE AGE

IN ABOUT 3000 BC, prehistoric people began to use bronze – an alloy of copper and tin – instead of stone, to make weapons and ornaments. The dates for this development, which is known as the Bronze Age, vary from culture to culture, but the earliest bronze workers probably lived in Mesopotamia (modern Iraq). These people initially used pure gold and copper, which were easy to hammer into shape, before discovering how to make bronze. They were also responsible for developing the world's first civilizations. The Bronze Age was followed by a time when people learned to smelt and shape iron ore to produce stronger tools and weapons. This period is known as the Iron Age.

Stone wristguard with gold screws

Copper dagger blade

The first metalworkers

In the early days of the Bronze Age, metalworkers used gold, copper, and bronze for luxury items, or for high-status weapons, such as the dagger in the Barnack grave, England. People still made tools from stone, because stone was harder than bronze.

Pottery beaker for use in the afterlife

The Barnack grave, c.1800 BC

Prongs for lifting meat from a cauldron

Flesh hook

Making bronze

People learned how to extract metal from ores by heating the rock. The metal could then be used to make useful or decorative objects.

Ore

This common type of copper ore was fairly easy for people to spot on the ground.

Yellow chalcopyrite

Blue bornite

Smelting

To extract the metal, Bronze Age people heated the ore to a high temperature. When the metal in the ore reached melting point, they collected it in a round, stone crucible.

Casting

Bronze Age people cast objects by pouring hot, molten bronze into a mould. When the metal had cooled and set, the mould was opened, revealing the finished item. Casting was used to produce decorative items.

Molten metal was poured through holes.

The mould was carved to the shape of the item.

Cast pin

Stone mould

Mould

This is one half of a stone mould for casting pins. It was made in Switzerland, c.1000 BC. To use the mould, the two halves were fastened together, and metal poured in through the holes at the top.

Cast pin

Bronze pins like this were cast in the stone mould. The mould used to make this pin was carved to create the delicate pattern on the pin-head.

Copper

The royal family of the city of Ur in Mesopotamia used copper for jewellery, as well as for everyday items, such as this flesh hook. They used gold to make beautiful vessels for special occasions.

Ornate French sword

Bronze swords were sometimes cast, although they were stronger when the bronze was beaten into shape. This Danish sword is polished to show the original golden colour of bronze.

Bronze axe head

Pins fastened clothing before buttons were invented

Danish bronze sword

Bronze bangle

Bronzeware

Bronze was prized for its beauty. In Europe, the nobles liked to wear bronze jewellery, such as bangles and pendants, and bronze pins in their clothing. Bronze swords were high-status weapons.

Bronze pendant

Trace of an ingot

Ingots

Early metalworkers discovered how to add molten tin to copper to make bronze. Liquid bronze was poured into round moulds and left to set. The blocks of bronze were called ingots.

Timeline

3800 BC The earliest known metal objects are produced by smelting. Copper is the main metal smelted in Tepe Yahya, Iran.

3000 BC Bronze objects are used throughout western Asia, where copper is being combined with tin.

2500 BC Bronze is used in the cities of Mohenjo-Daro and Harappa, Indus Valley.

2000 BC Bronze-working comes to the civilizations of the Minoans on Crete and the Myceneans in mainland Greece. These Aegean cultures trade in Europe for copper and tin.

1900 BC Iron Age starts in western Asian areas such as Turkey, Iran, and Iraq.

Shaft-tube axe, Hungary

1800 BC Bronze Age reaches European areas, such as modern Slovakia.

800 BC Early Iron Age starts in central Europe.

FIND OUT MORE GREECE, ANCIENT INDUS VALLEY CIVILIZATION METALS MINOANS POTTERY AND CERAMICS STONE AGE SUMERIANS

BUDDHA

BUDDHISM IS A WORLD faith that has changed the lives of millions of people. It began in Sakya, a small kingdom in northeast India. The founder of Buddhism was a prince, called Siddhartha Gautama, but today he is known simply as the Buddha, a title meaning "the enlightened one". When he was a young man, Siddhartha began a search for an understanding of suffering. By the end of his life he had become the Buddha, founded the Buddhist faith and already had many followers.

Early life
According to tradition, Siddhartha was born while his mother, Maya, was on her way to visit her parents. She died soon afterwards. His father was told that the boy would become either a great ruler or a Buddha. The king was afraid that Siddhartha would leave the court to become a holy beggar, so confined him to the palace grounds. But eventually he left to search for the true meaning of suffering.

Siddhartha, later called the Buddha

Maya, mother of the Buddha

The Buddha meditating

Buddha sat under a holy fig or bo tree

Enlightenment
When Siddhartha left the palace, the suffering he saw around him made him decide to become a holy man. He spent six years depriving himself of food and sleep, and learning about spiritual matters. Eventually he realized that this made him too weak for deep reflection, so he meditated under a tree. Here he made the breakthrough to an understanding of the truth known as enlightenment.

Teaching
After experiencing enlightenment, the Buddha set out to teach others what he had learned. Many were converted, and the Buddha sent them away as wandering missionaries. Later, the Buddha returned to his father's court to teach his own people what he had learned. His father was among the first to be converted.

Sarnath
At Sarnath, near Varanasi, the Buddha preached his first sermon to five men who had previously sought enlightenment with him. He taught them that suffering is caused by desire, and to end suffering they must give up desire. Sarnath became the site of one of the greatest Buddhist shrines.

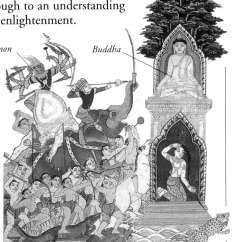

Mara, the demon

Buddha

Temptations
While Siddhartha was meditating, a demon named Mara sent his beautiful daughters to tempt him from his chosen path. Mara also whipped up a storm and hurled thunderbolts at Siddhartha. But the young man carried on meditating, unmoved. He meditated for a whole night before understanding the truth, which he called *dharma*, and reaching peace, or *nirvana*, in his heart.

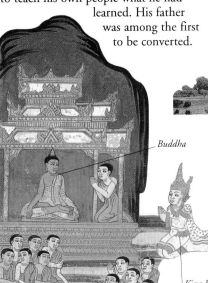

Buddha

Bimbisara
Even during his own lifetime, the Buddha commanded so much respect that many people left their homes to follow him and form orders of monks and nuns. When King Bimbisara gave the Buddha a generous gift of land – "the gift of the bamboo grove" – Buddha's followers built the first Buddhist monastery there.

King Bimbisara

THE BUDDHA

Earliest records of Buddha's life were written more than 200 years after he died, so details are hard to verify. The following dates are accepted by most authorities.

563 BC Siddhartha Gautama, son of King Suddhodana of the Sakya, born in northeast India.

533 BC Siddhartha leaves his father's court to become a holy man.

527 BC Siddhartha attains enlightenment, and becomes the Buddha.

483 BC Buddha dies at Kusinagara, in Oudh, India.

Death of Buddha

Pilgrim

Later life
When the Buddha was 80 years old, he ate some food that had been accidentally poisoned, and died at Kusinagara in India amongst his disciples. Many people came to pay homage to him. His body was cremated and the remaining bones were placed under stone mounds that have since became holy places of pilgrimage for Buddhists.

| FIND OUT MORE | BUDDHISM | CHINA | INDIA, HISTORY OF | MAURYAN EMPIRE | MONASTERIES | SHRINES |

BUDDHISM

THE BUDDHIST FAITH was founded by an Indian nobleman called Gautama Siddhartha in the 6th century BC. Gautama, who became known as the Buddha, or the "Awakened One", told people how to achieve fulfilment. He taught that fulfilment is reached by meditation, wisdom, and correct behaviour in all aspects of life. Buddhists also believe in reincarnation, in other words that a person can be reborn after death. The Buddha is revered by his followers, but not worshipped as a god. For this reason, Buddhism exists side-by-side with other religions in many countries. There are probably some 320 million Buddhists worldwide, although the majority are in Asia.

Rites and ceremonies

Ceremonies at Buddhist temples are usually simple. They involve reciting extracts from Buddhist scriptures and making offerings to the Buddha. A monk may give a sermon. Some Buddhist rituals also involve candle-lit processions and music-making. The Buddhist year is enlivened with festivals, most of which take place at full Moon. The most famous festival is Wesak, at New Year, which celebrates the birth, enlightenment, and death of the Buddha.

Hand gestures on a statue of the Buddha

The Buddha touches earth as witness to his worthiness for Buddhahood.

This gesture shows the Buddha actively turning the Wheel of Law.

The Buddha reassures an approaching person.

The Buddha

Statues of the Buddha are kept in temples and homes to inspire Buddhists to live as he did. Buddhists bow before the statue to show their respect. They also carry out the ceremony called "Going for refuge", in which they recite texts that show their dedication to the Buddha, to his teaching (the Dharma), and to the community of Buddhists (the Sangha).

Teachings

The Buddha taught the Four Noble Truths, which explain the Buddhist attitude to suffering and how fulfilment can be achieved. The Truths say that suffering is always present in the world; that the human search for pleasure is the source of suffering; that it is possible to be free from these desires by achieving a state called nirvana; and that the way to nirvana is through the Eightfold Path.

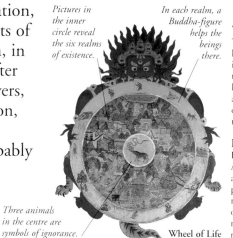

Pictures in the inner circle reveal the six realms of existence.

In each realm, a Buddha-figure helps the beings there.

Three animals in the centre are symbols of ignorance.

Wheel of Life

Wheel of Law

The Eightfold Path

The Path teaches that the way Buddhists lead their lives should be correct in eight important aspects: understanding, thought, speech, action, means of livelihood (work), effort, recollection, and meditation. The eight-spoked Wheel of Law shown above represents each of the eight stages of the Path.

Karma

Buddhists believe in the law of karma. According to this law, good and bad actions result in fitting rewards and punishments, both in this life and in later rebirths. The Wheel of Life is a symbol of rebirth. When people die, they are reborn into one of its six realms of existence.

Offerings

Buddhists regularly make offerings to the Buddha, such as flowers and food. Burning incense or candles and scattering petals around the Buddha's statue are ways of making an offering that also beautifies the temple. The light of the candles is the light of the Buddha's great wisdom, and the smoke from incense wafts the truth of the doctrine towards the devotees.

The Buddha's topknot is a sign of his princely wisdom.

His face has the serene expression of meditation.

Long ear lobes symbolize his nobility.

Eyes cast down show that he is meditating.

Coloured sash is changed for each season.

Candles

Incense

Lotus flowers

Meditation

Buddhists meditate in order to purify their minds and free themselves from thoughts about material things. In this way they hope to achieve "perfect mindfulness", one of the stages in the Eightfold Path. One way in which they meditate is to concentrate on feeling their breath going in and out. This empties the mind of selfish thoughts, making the person calmer and the mind clearer.

Buddha's cross-legged position is called the lotus position.

Branches of Buddhism

From its beginnings in India, Buddhism spread around eastern and Southeast Asia, where the majority of the world's Buddhists still live. There are also Buddhist communities in other parts of Asia, and in the West. Buddhism has two main strands – Mahayana and Theravada – but other forms of Buddhism with distinctive features have also developed.

Theravada

This branch of Buddhism is closest to the teachings of the Buddha himself. It is dominant in Southeast Asia (Burma, Cambodia, Laos, Sri Lanka, and Thailand). Theravada Buddhists revere the Buddha and do not worship other figures. They aim to become "perfected saints" by following the Eightfold Path and tend to believe that people can reach the state of nirvana only through their own efforts.

Mahayana

This form of Buddhism prevails in China, Korea, Japan, Mongolia, Nepal, and Tibet. A follower's first aim is to become a Bodhisattva, an enlightened being who does not pass into nirvana but remains in this world in order to help others to enlightenment. Mahayana Buddhists therefore place a high value on charity.

Monks are given offerings of food by locals.

Almsgiving emphasizes the close relationship between monks and lay people.

Chinese Bodhisattva head

Zen

This form of Buddhism originated in China and spread to Japan in about the 13th century. Zen Buddhists aim to lead a simple life, close to nature, using everyday actions as a means of meditation. Zen Buddhists meditate in a way that tries to see beyond logical patterns of thought and preconceived ideas.

Tibetan Buddhism

A form of Mahayana Buddhism is found in Tibet. Here, special value is placed on the Buddhist virtues of meditation and wisdom. Tibetan Buddhists have their own rituals, such as repeating sacred sayings, or mantras. Since the Chinese invasion of Tibet in the 1950s, few Buddhist monasteries remain in Tibet.

Mantra

Inside a prayer wheel is a mantra that the monk repeats while spinning the wheel.

A Zen monk tidies a garden.

Monasticism

Buddhist monasteries began when the Buddha's followers built permanent settlements to live in together during the rainy season. Today there are many monks (and some nuns) who devote their lives to explaining the Buddha's teachings and setting an example by the way they lead their lives.

Shaven head shows the monk has renounced worldly vanities.

The monk's meditative pose suggests peace and stability.

Living as a monk

Monks live apart from their families and have few personal possessions. They rely on gifts for survival, carrying alms bowls into which people place food. They obey strict rules. They must avoid entertainments in which there is singing or dancing, give up decorative clothes, and eat only at set times.

Sharpening stone

Needle and thread   **Razor**   **Water strainer**

Alms bowl lid is also used as a plate.

Alms bowl lid

Alms bowl   **Belt or girdle**

Sacred texts

Buddhism has sacred texts made up of sayings and sermons, many of them attributed to the Buddha. One of the most important books of writings is the Dharmapada, which forms part of the Pali Canon, the oldest collection of Buddhist scriptures.

In Tibetan-style libraries, manuscripts are wrapped in cloth and placed between boards.

Library in Shey Monastery, Ladakh, India

Temples

The religious buildings of Buddhism vary widely in their shape and decoration, from Japanese pagodas to Thai wats. But all contain statues of the Buddha. The statues act as a focus for devotion and for offerings. People go to the temples to carry out acts of private worship and for special ceremonies.

Devotees gather with their offerings in the grounds of the temple.

Wat Benchamabophit, in Thailand's capital, Bangkok, is known as the marble temple.

Stepped roofs symbolize stages of spiritual development.

Dalai Lama

The Dalai Lama is the spiritual and political leader of Buddhists in Tibet, who believe that each Dalai Lama is a reincarnation of the previous one. The present Dalai Lama, Tenzin Gyatso, was born in 1935. In exile since 1959 following the Chinese takeover, he is still Tibet's most important leader.

FIND OUT MORE   ASIA, HISTORY OF   BUDDHA   CHINA, HISTORY OF   FESTIVALS   MAURYAN EMPIRE   RELIGIONS   SHRINES   SIGNS AND SYMBOLS   THAILAND AND BURMA

B

BUFFALO AND OTHER WILD CATTLE

THE FIVE SPECIES OF BUFFALO, and all other cattle, are members of the family Bovidae. They have split, or cloven, hooves, and both sexes have horns which they can use to defend themselves. The animals also gain some protection from living together in herds. Only the anoas are solitary animals. Cattle were among the earliest animals to be domesticated. The Asiatic buffalo, yak, banteng, and gaur all have a domesticated version. Loss of habitat, hunting, and diseases have drastically reduced the world's wild cattle. No fewer than nine of the eleven species are in danger of extinction.

Broad hooves support the weight of the buffalo.

Bison

Plains bison

Often wrongly called buffalo, there are two species of bison. The American bison is a grassland animal which appears in two forms – the plains bison and the woods bison. The European bison, or wisent, is a forest dweller. Bison are massive animals standing more than 1.5 m (5 ft) tall and weighing more than 910 kg (2,000 lb).

American bison
The head, neck, and forequarters of the American bison are covered with long hair, which, with the large hump, makes the forequarters appear much bigger than the hindquarters. The horns are short and curved, and are grown by both sexes.

European bison
The wisent lives in Poland's Bialowieza Forest. It is taller than the American bison and has a longer, less barrel-like body, and longer legs. Its hindquarters are also more powerfully built.

Oxen

The group of wild cattle commonly called oxen contains four species – the yak, the banteng, the gaur, and the kouprey. Domestic cattle also belong to this group. Most breeds of domestic cattle are descended from the now-extinct aurochs, which at one time inhabited the plains and woodlands of Europe and Asia in great numbers.

Yak
Largest of the wild cattle, the wild yak lives in herds high up on the Tibetan Plateau in Central Asia. To protect them against the bitterly cold climate, yaks have long, shaggy black hair reaching almost to the ground, with a thick undercoat.

Banteng
Found in Southeast Asia, Java, and Borneo, the banteng is a shy animal. Females and young are a brick-red colour; adult males are black.

African buffalo

The buffalo is the only species of wild cattle found in Africa. Cape buffalo bulls are up to 1.5 m (5 ft) at the shoulder and weigh more than 816 kg (1,800 lb). Their horns have a span of up to 1.5 m (5 ft) and form a massive helmet, or boss, across the head. A smaller subspecies, the forest buffalo, lives in equatorial forests.

Asiatic buffalo
There are four species of Asiatic buffalo – the water buffalo (shown here), the lowland and mountain anoa, and the tamarau. The water buffalo occurs in a domestic and a wild form, but only a few wild herds survive. Its horns are semi-circular and sweep outward and backward.

Largest and smallest
Wild cattle range in size from the wild yak, which is more than 2 m (6.5 ft) high at the shoulder, to the mountain anoa, which is no more than 76 cm (30 in) high.

Mountain anoa

Wild yak

Endangered tamarau
Confined to the highlands on the island of Mindoro in the Philippines, this dwarf buffalo has been relentlessly hunted. Only about 100 survive today.

CAPE BUFFALO

SCIENTIFIC NAME	*Syncerus caffer*
ORDER	Artiodactyla
FAMILY	Bovidae
DISTRIBUTION	Africa, south of the Sahara
HABITAT	Grassland and woodland savannahs, but seldom far from water
DIET	Mainly grass, occasionally supplemented with foliage
SIZE	1.5 m (5 ft) at the shoulder
LIFESPAN	About 20 years

FIND OUT MORE   DEER AND ANTELOPES   FARMING   NORTH AMERICAN WILDLIFE   SHEEP AND GOATS

BUGS

THE WORD BUG is often used to describe any crawling insect or a disease-causing germ. The true bugs are a group of insects that have long feeding tubes specially adapted for sucking fluids out of plants and animals. Bugs, such as shield bugs, are often brightly coloured, and, as a group, they are remarkably varied in shape. There are about 55,000 species of bug, including large solitary insects, such as giant water bugs and cicadas, and tiny creatures, such as scale insects, bedbugs, and aphids. It is the smaller bugs, such as greenfly and leaf hoppers, that create problems for farmers because of the severe damage they cause to crops.

Features of a bug

All bugs have specialized mouthparts with cutting implements for piercing, and needle-like sucking tubes held within a protective sheath. Some bugs, such as lantern bugs, have their membranous wings exposed when at rest; others have forewings that are partially thickened and used not for flight, but as a protective cover for the delicate hind wings.

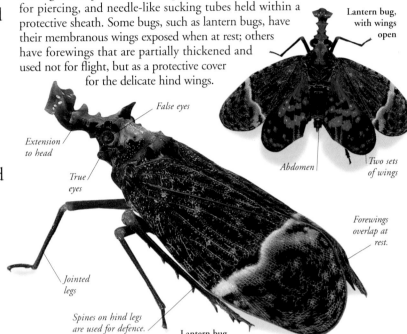

Lantern bug, with wings open

False eyes

Extension to head

True eyes

Abdomen

Two sets of wings

Forewings overlap at rest.

Jointed legs

Spines on hind legs are used for defence.

Lantern bug

Reproduction

Bugs attract a mate in many ways, such as giving off scent, or vibrating the surface of water. Male cicadas attract females with their loud song, produced by drum-like organs on the abdomen. During mating, male and female bugs are often attached for hours. Females usually lay hundreds of eggs. These hatch into nymphs – tiny versions of their parents – and moult many times before reaching adult size.

Parthenogenesis

Aphids such as greenfly and blackfly, multiply rapidly, because they can reproduce without mating. Females produce a succession of identical female offspring from unfertilized eggs, each of which later produces more of the same. This is called parthenogenesis.

Shield bugs

Shield bugs are found virtually worldwide. They are also called stink bugs, as they can give off a bad smell. Females protect their eggs and young from attack.

Young shield bug nymphs being guarded by their mother.

Feeding

Bugs use their mouthparts to cut a hole in their food and pierce the soft parts inside. They inject enzymes and digestive juices through a pair of tiny tubes to break down solids and suck up the resulting fluids. In this way, predatory bugs, such as assassin bugs, can suck their victims dry. Bedbugs are parasites that suck the blood of birds and mammals, including humans. Some bugs feed only on plant juices.

Assassin bugs

Assassin bugs are carnivores. Most prey on other invertebrates, such as millipedes. Some steal prey already caught in spiders' webs. Assassin bugs can squirt toxic saliva at would-be predators.

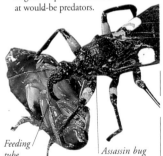

Feeding tube

Assassin bug feeding on a cockroach.

Leaf hoppers

Leaf hoppers are herbivores. They are often considered pests as they cut holes in the leaves of plants, such as cotton plants, to suck out the sap, thereby weakening the plants.

Defence

Small bugs face many enemies from ladybirds to birds. To deter would-be attackers, bugs have evolved a range of defences. Some bugs, such as tree hoppers, have developed elaborate camouflage; others, such as stink bugs, give off bad smells. The larvae of spittle bugs, also known as frog hoppers, hide within a frothy substance called cuckoo spit. Aphids employ ants to protect them by providing their guardians with a nutritious sugary secretion.

Tree hoppers

Tree hoppers camouflage themselves with projections of cuticle that resemble thorns.

Water bugs

Some bugs live in water. Pond skaters skim over water on their dainty legs, while water boatmen dart below the water using paddle-shaped limbs. Underwater bugs come to the surface to breathe, or carry around an air bubble.

Pond skater

RED-BANDED LEAF HOPPER	
SCIENTIFIC NAME	*Graphocephala coccinea*
ORDER	Homoptera
FAMILY	Cicadellidae
DISTRIBUTION	Eastern USA and eastern Canada
HABITAT	Meadows and gardens
DIET	Plant juices
SIZE	Length 8–11 mm (0.4–0.5 in); wingspan 12–16 mm (0.5–0.6 in)
LIFESPAN	Adults: up to 4 months

FIND OUT MORE | ARTHROPODS | CAMOUFLAGE AND COLOUR | FARMING | FLIGHT, ANIMAL | INSECTS | LAKE AND RIVER WILDLIFE | PARASITES | PLANTS, DEFENCE

BUILDING AND CONSTRUCTION

THE SIMPLEST BUILDING is a permanent structure with a roof and four walls. Buildings come in a huge variety of shapes, sizes, and appearances – from skyscrapers and factories to schools, hospitals, houses, and garden sheds. Despite these differences, all buildings have the same basic purpose – to provide a sheltered area in which people can live, work, or store belongings. The engineers, surveyors, and construction workers who plan and build these structures also work on other projects, such as roads, bridges, dams, and tunnels.

Early building
Since the beginning of history, people have built shelters to protect themselves from the weather, wild animals, and their enemies. The first buildings were simple, single-storey structures made of materials such as wood, stone, and dried grass and mud. The first large-scale stone constructions were temples for the worship of gods and goddesses, and palaces in which powerful leaders lived. About 6,000 years ago, people discovered how to bake clay bricks. In time, engineers developed new building methods that enabled them to build higher and lighter structures.

Walls are made from mud and bricks dried in the Sun's heat.

Ancient tower-house, Sana, Yemen

Anatomy of a building

Most buildings have certain features in common, such as walls, a roof, and floors. A large modern building, such as this airport terminal, also has a strong internal frame. Underneath this are the solid foundations on which the whole structure rests. The building is equipped with services, such as electricity and water supplies, as well as escalators, stairs, or elevators to give access to different storeys, and fire escapes that enable people to leave the building rapidly in the event of an emergency.

Roof
A roof is a protective covering over a building. Roofing materials include thatch, clay tiles, slate, glass, and steel. Roofs in wet climates are shaped to make rainwater run off; in cold countries, they slope steeply to stop snow from building up; and in dry climates, they are often flat. Sloping roofs are held up by supports called roof trusses.

Steel beams | **Overhead cutaway of roof**

Kansai Airport, Japan

Glass wall lets in a lot of light.

Roof trusses sit on frame. | *Roof truss*

Roof is clad with shiny steel panels.

Floor rests on columns, which are part of frame.

Foundations
A building's foundations spread its huge load evenly into the ground, stopping the building from sinking under its own weight. Pile foundations are columns that rest on hard rock; raft foundations are concrete platforms that rest on soft rock. The foundations form the base on which the building's frame is constructed.

Internal frame
The "skeleton" of a large building is its internal frame, which supports the roof, the walls, and the floors. Frames can be made of wood, steel, or reinforced-concrete columns and beams joined together.

Foundations extend underground.

Basement houses service machinery.

Walls and floors
In a house, the walls – which may be made of wood, stone, or brick – are strong enough to hold up the floors, ceilings, and roof trusses. In a larger structure, however, the frame supports the building's weight, and the walls simply hang from the frame. The floors in a large modern building are reinforced-concrete slabs.

Structural engineers

Long before the construction of a building is underway, structural engineers begin working on the design of the building with an architect. They calculate how strong the building's structure needs to be and draw up detailed plans, usually on a computer. When the building work commences, they make sure that everything happens safely, on time, and within the financial budget.

Structural engineer on a building site

Surveyors
Accuracy is extremely important in construction work if the completed building is to have vertical sides and level walls, and be structurally safe. Even small errors in the design or assembly can result in parts not fitting together properly. People called surveyors check the building at every stage of its construction, using special instruments, such as theodolites and spirit levels, to take accurate measurements.

Hard hat

Theodolite is an instrument that measures angles to find distances, lengths, and heights.

Surveyor using theodolite

B

Building sites

The different stages in the construction of a large building must always take place in a certain order, starting with the preparation of the site. Materials and machinery must arrive just when they are needed: if they are too early, the site may get too crowded; if they are too late, the building work may be delayed.

Site clearance and excavation
The building site must first be cleared, which may involve demolishing other buildings, removing vegetation, and levelling the site. Holes are excavated (dug) for the foundations and basement.

Foundation laying
The next stage is to build the foundations. This involves driving steel beams, called piles, into the ground, or pouring liquid concrete into a deep pit to form a solid base that will support the building.

Frame building
The building's frame soon rises from the foundations. The frame is built either by bolting together steel beams, or by pouring concrete into moulds crossed by steel rods. A shell of metal poles and wooden planks, called scaffolding, is temporarily erected around the building so that workers can reach all parts.

Completed building is ready for use.

Completion
With the frame in place, work starts on the floors, walls, and roof. Services such as water and waste pipes, heating and air-conditioning ducts, and electricity and telephone cables are installed on each storey. Finally, the windows are inserted, and the interior is decorated.

Equipment

Some of the tasks on a building site, such as plastering a wall or laying bricks, are done by tradespeople using hand tools. Other tasks, such as erecting the building's frame or lifting heavy objects, may require large, specialized machines. Together, these machines are known as construction plant.

Plumbline

Set square

Spirit level

Trowel

Bricklayer's tools

Hand tools
Each tradesperson involved in building and construction uses special tools. A bricklayer, for example, uses a trowel to spread mortar on to bricks, a plumbline to ensure that a wall is vertical, and a spirit level and a set square to check that it is horizontal.

Construction plant
Powerful machines, such as cranes and cement mixers, can do jobs in a few minutes that would take manual workers hours or even days. Other machines include pile-drivers to hammer steel piles into the ground, bulldozers to level building sites, and excavating diggers.

Backhoe digger

Trench-digging bucket

Hydraulic jacks steady digger.

Wide shovel tool scoops up soil.

Building materials

Some building materials, such as steel, concrete, and bricks, are structural – that is, they make up the basic structure of the building. Other materials, such as ceramics and glass, are mainly decorative. Traditional materials, such as stone and wood, have been used for many centuries and are often found locally.

Building site materials

Steel rods for reinforced concrete

Wooden planks for scaffolding

Steel girders for frame

Concrete and steel
Most modern buildings contain concrete, steel, or a combination of both. Concrete is a mixture of cement, water, and small stones (called aggregate) that hardens like rock when it sets. Steel is iron that contains a tiny amount of carbon. Concrete strengthened by steel rods is called reinforced concrete.

Types of concrete

Wood
Some houses have floors made of wooden planks and wooden beams for roof trusses. Scaffolding may have walkways of wooden planks.

Bricks
Blocks of hardened clay, called bricks, are laid in rows and joined together with mortar – a mixture of cement and sand.

Local materials
Many buildings throughout the world are built from materials that occur naturally in the surrounding area. These local materials may include straw, mud, stone, wood, and even animal dung. They can do just as good a job as modern manufactured materials, which are usually more expensive and have to be imported from elsewhere.

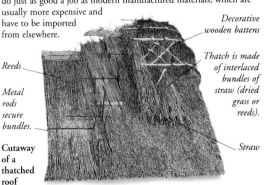

Decorative wooden battens

Reeds

Thatch is made of interlaced bundles of straw (dried grass or reeds).

Metal rods secure bundles.

Cutaway of a thatched roof

Straw

Construction workers
People from a wide range of trades with many different skills will work on a building before it is finished. These tradespeople include welders, bricklayers, electricians, carpenters, plasterers, and plumbers. For safety reasons, construction workers often wear hard hats and other protective clothing, such as goggles.

Welder wearing safety visor and gloves

FIND OUT MORE   ARCHITECTURE   BRIDGES   CHURCHES AND CATHEDRALS   DAMS   HOUSES AND HOMES   IRON AND STEEL   ROADS   TUNNELS

BUTTERFLIES AND MOTHS

SCALY WINGS AND A COILED feeding tube set butterflies and moths apart from other insects. Together, they form a single group of about 170,000 species, of which 90 per cent are moths. Both have four stages to their life cycle in which they change from a caterpillar to an adult with wings. They feed on plants, and rely on camouflage, irritating hairs or spines, or poisons in their body for protection against predators.

Wing scales
Scales on the wings contain coloured pigments. Some scales produce colours by reflecting the light.

Scales overlap like the tiles on a roof.

The front and back wings of a moth are hooked together.

Moth's bright colouring indicates it is poisonous

Zygaenid moth

Moths

Most moths fly at night. They tend to have drab colours, and have a fatter body and longer, narrower wings than butterflies. When resting, moths usually hold their wings open or fold them flat over their back.

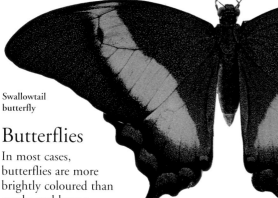

Swallowtail butterfly

Butterflies

In most cases, butterflies are more brightly coloured than moths and have a thinner body. Unlike moths, they hold their wings upright when resting. The front and back wings are loosely joined together by a lobe on the back wing that grips the front wing. Butterflies are usually active by day rather than by night.

Wings are made of a tough membrane supported by a network of rigid veins.

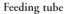

Proboscis is rolled up when not in use.

Moth antennae have a large surface area for picking up scents.

Feeding tube
Adult butterflies and moths suck up liquid food, such as flower nectar, through a tube called a proboscis. A few moths have no proboscis because they do not feed as adults.

Antennae
Insects use their antennae for smelling, touching, and tasting. Butterfly antennae are clubbed; moth antennae range from single strands to feathery branches.

Life cycle
Butterflies and moths start life as an egg, which hatches into a caterpillar. This feeds and grows until it turns into a pupa. The adult develops inside the pupa. This process of change is called metamorphosis.

Pupa protects developing adult.

Adult butterfly emerges.

Butterfly pumps blood into its wings to expand and stiffen them.

Adult Blue Morpho

Defence

To escape from predators, butterflies and moths often fly away or hide. Some have irritating hairs or spines, or are poisonous. Bright colours may warn predators that a butterfly or moth is poisonous. Poisons often build up in a caterpillar from the plant it eats. These then remain in the adult.

Camouflage
Many butterflies and moths blend in with their surroundings at some stage of their life cycle. Camouflaged like this, they may escape predators.

Eyespots
False eyes on the wings can startle predators or stop them from pecking the real eyes. A damaged wing is not as serious as an injury to the head.

Mimicry
Some butterflies and moths gain protection by looking like another species of butterfly or moth. The top butterfly shown here is poisonous; the bottom one is not.

Wing colour
When a butterfly is resting, only the underside of its wings shows. This is often coloured for camouflage. The colours of the upper side help to attract a mate.

SWALLOWTAIL BUTTERFLY

SCIENTIFIC NAME	*Papilio palinurus*
ORDER	Lepidoptera
FAMILY	Papilionidae
DISTRIBUTION	From Burma to the islands of Borneo and the Philippines in Southeast Asia
HABITAT	Tropical rainforest
DIET	Flower nectar
SIZE	Wing span: 9.5 cm (3.75 in)
LIFESPAN	Varies (The adults of most butterflies live for only a few weeks or months)

FIND OUT MORE

CAMOUFLAGE AND COLOUR   INSECTS   FLIGHT, ANIMAL

Butterflies

Owl butterfly

Japanese emperor

Brown-veined white

Orange-barred giant sulphur

Great spangled fritillary

Viceroy

Great orange tip

Common opal

Blue morpho

Peacock

African giant swallowtail

Common blue

Chequered skipper

Swallowtail

Cairns birdwing

Small copper

Hewitson's blue hairstreak

Moths

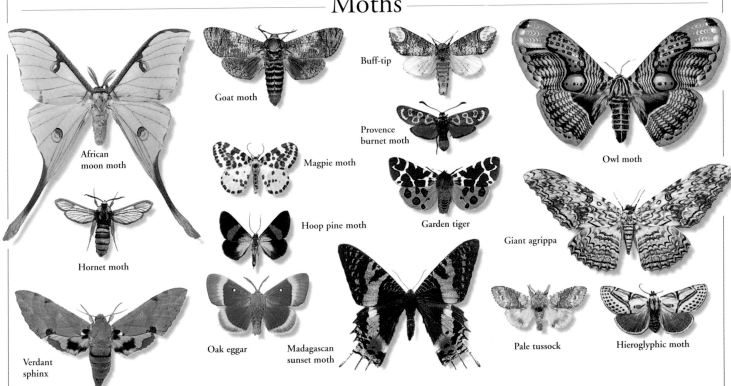

African moon moth

Goat moth

Buff-tip

Owl moth

Hornet moth

Magpie moth

Provence burnet moth

Hoop pine moth

Garden tiger

Giant agrippa

Verdant sphinx

Oak eggar

Madagascan sunset moth

Pale tussock

Hieroglyphic moth

BYZANTINE EMPIRE

IN 395, THE GREAT ROMAN EMPIRE split into eastern and western sections. The western half – still called the Roman Empire – was centred on Rome. The eastern half became the Byzantine Empire with its centre at Constantinople. The Greek character – in language, customs, and dress – of Constantinople contrasted with Latin Rome. Despite efforts on the part of emperors to reunite the two halves of the old empire, the Byzantine Empire gradually grew away from Rome. The Roman Empire collapsed in 410, but the Byzantine Empire existed until 1453 when the Ottoman Turks captured it.

Extent of Byzantine Empire, c.565
Because of its fabulous wealth, superb shipbuilding facilities, and strategic position between Asia and Europe, the Byzantine Empire was under almost constant siege by its powerful neighbours – Persia, Arabia, Turkey, and some states of the Christian west.

Mosque

Byzantium to Constantinople

The ancient Greek port of Byzantium stood on the Golden Horn, a strip of land surrounded by sea on three sides. Constantine the Great (c.274–337) re-designed the city and re-named it Constantinople in 330 AD. Soon it was one of the world's most beautiful cities.

Bridge over the Bosporus Strait, linking Asia and Europe

Art and religion

Byzantine churches were famous for their interiors, which were lavishly decorated on a huge scale, with painted icons and intricate mosaic images of Christ, the Virgin, and saints.

Icons
In the 8th century, the empire was racked by arguments over whether it was idolatrous to worship beautiful religious statues and paintings, known as icons. Finally in 843, it was declared to be legitimate, and their production increased. Later, icons were portable, and collected by Renaissance artists.

East versus west

By the 9th century, the Byzantine form of Christianity was changing from the western, or Roman, form. Greek had replaced Latin as the official language, and the Roman pope and Byzantine patriarch argued over church ritual. However, they were united in their fear and hatred of the non-Christian Turks and Arabs.

Great Schism
In 1054, representatives of the Roman and Byzantine churches excommunicated each other. This religious split, or schism, destabilized political links between east and west, and caused mutual suspicion and hostility.

Orthodox priest

St Gregory of Nazianzus *Virgin and Child* *St John Chrysostom*
Triptych icon, 12th century *Gilt covering*

Hagia Sophia
The biggest church in the eastern empire, Hagia Sophia was built in only five years (532–37). The Ottomans converted it into a mosque in the 16th century, and today it is a museum.

Fall of Constantinople
Constantinople was conquered twice: once by the west and once by the east. In 1204, it was ransacked by Christians on their way to the Holy Land. In 1453, Ottoman Turks overran it, and it became a Muslim stronghold.

Fall of Constantinople, 1453

Mosaics
Byzantine artists pressed cubes of tinted glass, marble, or precious stones into beeswax or lime plaster to make a mosaic. The artists often decorated the images with gold and silver leaf.
Christ Pantokrator, 11th century

Timeline

395 Roman Empire divided into west (Roman) and east (Byzantine).

867–1056 Empire reaches its peak.

The Good Shepherd mosaic, 5th century

529–34 Justinian I introduces his Roman Law Code.

1054 Great Schism: Byzantine church breaks with the Roman church and forms the Eastern Orthodox church.

976–1025 Basil II, known as "the Bulgar-slayer", gains more land than any emperor since Justinian I.

1096 First Crusade: European army joins Byzantine army at Constantinople.

1204 Fourth Crusaders sack Constantinople.

1453 Ottoman Turks capture Constantinople, ending the empire.

Emperor Justinian I
Justinian I (r.527–565), expanded the empire in the west by conquering North Africa, southern Spain, and Italy, while holding off the Persian threat in the east. In addition Justinian built Hagia Sophia, and his Codex Justinianus, or Roman Law Code, still forms the basis of the legal system in many European countries.

 FIND OUT MORE ART, HISTORY OF   CHRISTIANITY   OTTOMAN EMPIRE   PERSIAN EMPIRE   ROMAN EMPIRE

CAESAR, JULIUS

JULIUS CAESAR WAS A BRILLIANT general and ruler of the Roman world. He is one of the most famous, and controversial, figures in history. He transformed the Roman world, expanding Rome's territory into Gaul and suppressing many revolts. He was a fine administrator, reforming the Roman calendar and Roman law and bringing strong government to the republic. Caesar was also a great writer and orator. But he could be unscrupulous in pursuit of his own interests, and made many enemies during his career.

Early life
Caesar was born in Rome in about 100 BC. A member of a rich family, he had a successful military and political career, rising through various offices to become Pontifex Maximus, or high priest, in 64 BC. In 61 BC he became Governor of Further Spain, one of the most important jobs in the Roman republic.

Triumvirate

In the years leading up to 60 BC, rival politicians competed to gain power. Order was restored when Caesar, the financier Marcus Crassus, and the army commander Pompey set up a three-man committee, or triumvirate, to rule Rome. In 59 BC, the triumvirate allowed Caesar to be elected consul, one of the two magistrates who held supreme power. As consul, Caesar strengthened and reformed the government.

Pompey
Gnaeus Pompeius Magnus (106–48 BC), known in English as Pompey, was a Roman general who conquered Palestine and Syria, and did much to get rid of opposition to Roman rule in Spain and Sicily. Although he was a member of the triumvirate and he married Caesar's daughter, he was always Caesar's rival.

Pompey the Great

Gallic wars

From 58–50 BC, Caesar waged a series of wars which led to the incorporation of Gaul (modern France and Belgium) into the Roman republic. Caesar displayed great military ability in the Gallic Wars, and was ruthless with any tribes who tried to resist conquest. Caesar recorded his achievements in his famous memoirs of the campaign.

Roman legionary's helmet

Civil war

After the death of Crassus in 53 BC, rivalry between Caesar and Pompey reached new heights. Pompey became sole consul in 52 BC and, with the support of the Roman senate (parliament), declared Caesar an enemy of the people. In 49 BC, Caesar crossed the Rubicon, the river dividing Italy from Gaul, and marched on Rome in triumph. In 48 BC he defeated Pompey. By 45 BC, Caesar had removed all opposition, becoming master of the Roman world.

Roman catapult bolts

Roman cavalry spur

Cleopatra
Caesar followed Pompey to Egypt and remained in the country after Pompey's death. He befriended and lived with Cleopatra, queen of Egypt, and helped establish her firmly on the throne. When Caesar returned to Rome in 47 BC, Cleopatra came with him. After Caesar's death, the Egyptian queen had twin sons with the Roman soldier and politician Mark Antony (c.82–30 BC).

Caesar as soldier — Caesar crosses the Rubicon.

Pharsalus
Caesar showed his military skills when, in 48 BC, he defeated the much larger army of Pompey near the Greek town of Pharsalus. Caesar's strategic sense and better location enabled his small force to overwhelm Pompey's army, which was routed. Pompey himself fled to Egypt, where he died.

Battle of Pharsalus

Antony and Cleopatra

Dictator

In 45 BC, Caesar was appointed dictator for life. He reformed the living conditions of the Roman people by passing new agricultural laws and improving housing. He also made the republic more secure from its enemies.

Assassination
Despite his reforms, Caesar's dictatorial rule made him enemies in Rome. On 15 March 44 BC – the Ides of March – Caesar was stabbed to death in the senate house by rival senators, including Cassius and Brutus. But his work lived on in his great-nephew and adopted son, Octavian, who became emperor.

Assassination of Caesar

JULIUS CAESAR

c.100 BC Born in Rome.

80 BC First military service in Turkey.

60 BC Forms triumvirate with Crassus and Pompey.

59 BC Elected consul.

58–50 BC Conquers Gaul.

50 BC Roman senate declares him an enemy of the people.

49 BC Starts civil war against Pompey.

48 BC Defeats Pompey and follows him to Egypt.

44 BC Assassinated in the senate in Rome by rival senators.

FIND OUT MORE ARMIES FRANCE, HISTORY OF ITALY, HISTORY OF ROMAN EMPIRE UNITED KINGDOM, HISTORY OF

CAMELS

WELL-SUITED TO DESERT LIFE, camels can withstand extreme conditions. There are two main types: the one-humped dromedary, which lives in Africa and Arabia, and is usually domesticated; and the two-humped Asian Bactrian, some of which still roam wild in the Gobi Desert. Closely related to camels are four animals without humps – llamas, alpacas, guanacos, and vicunas. All six species, called camelids, belong to the artiodactyls, a group of herbivorous, even-toed mammals that also includes cattle.

Features of a camel

Camels are the largest of the even-toed mammals, standing up to 2.4 m (8 ft) at the shoulder. They have long legs, and walk at an ambling pace. Camels have a split upper lip, which allows them to eat dry, spiky plants. Their lips and upright heads have given camels a reputation for arrogance. In reality this is nonsense. However, camels may spit at, or bite, humans if annoyed or frightened. During the mating season, male camels often fight, biting their rivals when competing for females.

Hump
Contrary to popular belief, the camel's hump is not filled with water, but is a fat store that provides the camel with energy when food is scarce. Because fat is stored in the hump, there is less fat under the rest of the skin enabling the camel to lose heat more easily in hot conditions.

Thick fur keeps camel warm during cold desert nights, and helps prevent overheating in the day.

Long eye lashes

Slit-like nostrils

Split upper lip

Head of dromedary camel

Feet
Camels' feet have two toes joined by a web of skin; underneath is a soft, flexible pad that splays out when the camel walks. The camel's feet are very wide, and this, together with the pad, prevents the camel from sinking into soft sand and enables it to walk over rough terrain.

Web of skin

Foot of dromedary

Large, wide feet with soft pads allow camel to walk on sand.

Shaggy fur

Bactrian camel

Long legs help camel walk long distances.

Dromedary camel

Long, curved neck, allows camel to reach desert vegetation.

Eyes and nostrils
Camels have long eyelashes that protect their eyes from fierce sandstorms and enable them to see under difficult conditions. They can close their slit-like nostrils to reduce the amount of sand and dust blowing up the nose, and minimize moisture loss from the nasal cavity.

Ships of the desert
Camels are the only animals that can carry heavy loads long distances in extreme heat and with little water. Nomadic peoples survive in deserts by using camels as pack animals, as well as for meat, milk, and skins.

Salt-laden caravan, Taoudenni, Mali

Water loss
Camels can exist for long periods without water, but make up the loss quickly when water is available. Camels are also adapted to reduce water loss by producing dry faeces and small amounts of syrupy urine. In addition, their body temperature can rise to 40.5°C (104.9°F) during the day, reducing the need to keep cool by sweating, a process that also causes water loss.

During long periods without drinking, a camel can lose 40 per cent of its body mass as water.

Within 10 minutes, camels can drink sufficient water to make up huge losses.

Types of camelid
Related to camels are two species of domesticated camelid, the llama and alpaca, and two wild species, the vicuna and guanaco; all live in or near the Andes mountains in South America. Small herds of guanaco feed on grass and shrubs in shrubland and savannah up to heights of 4,250 m (13,900 ft), from southern Peru to southern Argentina.

Vicunas are a protected species.

Alpacas' wool may be black, brown, or white.

The wool, milk, and meat of llamas are all used.

Vicuna
Vicunas, the smallest of the camelids, live in family groups at high altitudes.

Alpaca
The highland peoples of Peru and Bolivia breed alpacas for their long, soft wool.

Llama
Llamas are used as pack animals to carry loads of up to 100 kg (220 lb), at altitudes of 5,000 m (16,400 ft) over long distances.

DROMEDARY CAMEL

SCIENTIFIC NAME *Camelus dromedarius*

ORDER Artiodactyla

FAMILY Camelidae

DISTRIBUTION Domesticated in North Africa, Middle East, southwestern Asia; feral populations in Australia

HABITAT Desert

DIET Any type of desert vegetation, including thorny twigs and salty plants that other animals avoid

SIZE Head and body length 3 m (10 ft); shoulder height 2 m (6.5 ft); weight up to 600 kg (1,320 lb)

LIFESPAN Up to 50 years

 FIND OUT MORE • ANIMALS • ASIAN WILDLIFE • DESERTS • DESERT WILDLIFE • MAMMALS • PIGS AND PECCARIES • SOUTH AMERICAN WILDLIFE

CAMERAS

A LIGHTPROOF BOX with a hole or lens at one end, and a strip of light-sensitive film at the other, is the basic component of a traditional camera. To take a photograph, the photographer points the camera at an object and presses a button. This button very briefly opens a shutter behind the lens. Light reflected from the object passes through the lens and on to traditional film or a digital chip to produce an image.

Digital cameras

Digital cameras contain no film. Instead, the image is captured on a photosensitive chip. Photos are displayed instantly on a screen on the camera and can be deleted if not liked. Images can be loaded into a computer and printed out.

Computer imaging
After an image has been stored on a digital camera, it can then be fed into a computer. From here it is printed out on photo paper or sent over the Internet. Special software allows the picture to be manipulated and gives the photographer a lot of control over the image.

Images are set to high or low quality.

Some cameras can also record tiny video clips.

Batteries inside supply power.

Digital camera

Parts of a camera

Shutter release button

Shutter and film speed dial

Self-timer lever

Lens

Shutter and film speed dial

Connection for flash

Film rewind knob

Shutter release button

Aperture scale

Distance scale

Lens

Movable flash head

Flash light sensor

Flashes
A flash provides the extra light needed for taking pictures after dark, or in dim conditions. The flash is electronically controlled to go off at the moment the shutter opens.

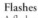

A mirror sends light from the lens to the viewfinder while the shutter is closed.

Light enters the lens

Single-lens reflex camera
Unlike other cameras, the view through a single-lens reflex (SLR) camera is that of the actual image that is recorded on the film. Mirrors in the viewfinder correct the upside-down image sent from the lens.

The quality of a photograph is controlled by adjusting the film and shutter speed dials, flash, and aperture scales. This is because the final image will depend on the type of film in the camera, the amount of light that enters the lens, and the length of time that the film is exposed to light.

35mm cameras
The most popular cameras are the 35mm, named after the width of the film they use. These cameras are small and easy to manage. They often have in-built features, which adjust automatically to variations in light and distance, to ensure that a clear photograph is taken every time.

Shutter release button

Viewfinder

Shutter

Film

As the shutter is released, the mirror slips up allowing the light to reach the film (shown by the dotted line).

Lenses

Different lenses achieve different visual effects. A wide-angle lens allows more of the scene to appear in a photograph than a normal lens. A telephoto zoom lens can take a close-up shot of a distant object. The fisheye lens distorts images for dramatic effect. These lenses are detachable from the camera.

Normal lens

Wide-angle lens

Telephoto zoom lens

Fisheye lens

Film types
Today, plastic film comes in various sizes and speeds, in a colour or a black and white format, packaged as rolls or plates. The speed, given in ASA/ISO or DIN numbers, indicates how quickly the film reacts to light. A new device, the Electronic Film System, fits into a 35mm camera and holds up to 30 digital images which can be transferred to a computer.

110mm film

35mm film

Plate film

George Eastman
An American inventor, George Eastman (1854–1932), formed the Kodak company. In 1884, he produced the first roll film and in 1888 the first box camera, making photography an accessible hobby. In 1889, he used clear celluloid film on which the first movie pictures were taken.

Timeline
4th century BC The "camera obscura" is developed; it consists of a darkened room into which an image is projected.

1822 Frenchman Joseph Niepce takes the first photograph on a sheet of pewter, coated with bitumen.

1839 Niepce's colleague, Louis Daguerre, announces process for recording images on copper.

1839 William Fox Talbot, an Englishman, invents a process that allows photographs to be copied.

1895 The Lumière brothers of France patent their original camera/projector using celluloid film with sprocket holes at the edge.

1948 American inventor Edwin Land develops the first instant camera, which is marketed by the Polaroid Corporation.

1956 A camera that records onto reel-to-reel magnetic videotape, rather than plastic film, is invented.

1980s First digital cameras prototyped.

1986 Disposable camera launched.

1992 The jpeg, a compressed file format for storing digital images, is introduced.

FIND OUT MORE   COLOUR   FILMS AND FILM-MAKING   GLASS   INVENTIONS   LIGHT   PHOTOGRAPHY   PLASTICS AND RUBBER   TELEVISION   VIDEO

Stills cameras

Early cameras

Image projected upside down

Fox Talbot's camera of 1835 required exposure times of over an hour.

Daguerreotype camera of mid-1800s was the first model sold to the public.

Shutter operated by a cord

Kodak Autographic Special of 1918 was an early roll-film camera.

Ensign of the 1930s, with a side viewfinder: was popular in sports photography.

Box made camera sturdy

Brownie Hawkeye of the 1940s reflected the new use of plastic in design.

Upper lens is for viewing

1950s Duaflex was modelled on the superior twin-lens cameras of the time.

35mm cameras

Shutter and film speed dial

Manual SLR camera needs to be focused and wound on manually.

Shutter release button

Automatic SLR camera has an automatic film-loading and wind-on mechanism.

Basic compact camera has a fixed length lens and built-in flash.

Advanced compacts are often fitted with a zoom lens, giving extra flexibility.

Zoom controlled by motor

Leica cameras were the first to use the small-format, 35mm film.

Image is seen here

Waist-level viewer attachment allows photos to be taken from waist height.

Medium- and large-format cameras

6 x 4.5 cm camera is a small, light, medium-format camera.

6 x 6 cm camera produces a square image and is used by many professionals.

Direct vision camera has rangefinder focusing lenses, reducing size and weight.

6 x 7 cm camera produces a rectangular image ideal for landscape photography.

6 x 9 cm camera produces large images that make very clear enlargements.

Large-format camera uses individual sheets of film for each image.

Special cameras

Large viewfinder

Underwater camera has large easy-to-read dials for use deep underwater.

Panoramic camera rotates to take a view of up to 360° in one exposure.

Bellows camera allows for a very wide range of image magnifications.

Moving bellows along track alters magnification

Film exit slot

Polaroid camera produces a finished photo seconds after taking the picture.

Built in flash

Disposable camera is simple and light, and is used only once.

Movie cameras

Debro pavro was an early movie camera. The handle was turned to start filming.

Marey's rifle is a camera shaped like a rifle, with the lens in the barrel.

Trigger works like a shutter release

Magazines hold three strips of film separately

Technicolor three-strip camera produces good, but expensive films.

Matt-box keeps stray light out of the lens

Cine 8 takes still photographs in rapid succession.

Camcorders are hand-held video cameras, used by many individuals.

Images are recorded directly on video tape

CAMOUFLAGE AND COLOUR

ANIMALS HAVE EVOLVED different colours, shapes, and patterns that help them survive. Some, such as birds-of-paradise, are brightly coloured to attract a mate; others, such as the fire salamander, use colour to advertise that they are poisonous to eat. Animals, such as lapwings and polar bears, are camouflaged – coloured or patterned – in such a way that they blend with their surroundings. Camouflage helps animals to hide from predators, but it can also help predators to creep up on their prey.

Types of coloration

Coloration falls into two main categories: cryptic and phaneric. Cryptic colours and patterns help an animal to remain concealed, thus helping protect it from enemies, or assisting in the capture of its prey. The factors that cryptic species suppress – colour, movement, and relief – are exaggerated in phaneric species. Phaneric coloration makes an animal stand out. It can include the conspicuous display of brilliant colours, shapes, and actions, as demonstrated by birds-of-paradise.

Bright colours of male make him stand out and attract females.

Cryptic coloration

Cryptic coloration is common among birds. The plumage of many desert species blends perfectly with the ground colour of their habitat. Birds of the forest canopy, such as parrots, are frequently green to match the dense foliage in which they live. Not all members of the same species are of cryptic colours. Sometimes the female or nestlings, which are generally in greater need of concealment, may be of cryptic colour, while the male is conspicuously coloured to attract a mate.

Newly hatched lapwings match colour of straw.

Young lapwings in nest

Red-headed gouldian finch

Phaneric coloration

Phaneric coloration used by animals such as macaws and mandrills makes them stand out and be noticed. It is used between male and female in courtship displays, between parent and young and members of a group for purposes of recognition, between rival males in threat displays, and between predators and prey as warning signals, bluff, or to deflect attack. Long ear- and head-plumes, fans, elongated tail feathers, wattles, and inflatable air sacs are all used to attract attention.

Camouflage

For concealment to be effective, the colour and pattern of an animal's coat or skin must relate closely to its background. A bird's colour often harmonizes with its nesting requirements; some ground-nesting birds choose a nest site with surroundings of similar colour to their eggs as an aid to concealment. Colour and posture can be a highly effective form of camouflage. The many types of concealment include disruptive coloration, disguise, and immobility.

Disruptive coloration

Irregular patches of contrasting colours and tones of an animal's coat divert attention away from the shape of the animal, making it harder to recognize. Tigers and giraffes show disruptive coloration.

Tiger camouflaged in long grass

Giant spiny stick insect

Disguise

Cryptic coloration aims to disguise rather than conceal. The combination of colour, form, and posture can produce an almost exact replica of a commonplace object associated with the habitat. Stick insects, for example, resemble small twigs, while nightjars, when lying down, look like stones or wood fragments.

Mimicry

Mimicry is an extreme form of concealment. It occurs when a relatively defenceless or edible species looks like an aggressive or dangerous species. The mimic not only takes on the appearance of the object it is mimicking, but also adopts its behaviour, assuming characteristics that are completely alien to it. For example, harmless milk snakes resemble poisonous coral snakes so that other animals will not attack them. The monarch, a poisonous butterfly, is mimicked by a non-poisonous species, *Hypolimnus*, which is indistinguishable from it.

Coral snake

Milk snake

Milk snakes have stripes of the same colour as coral snakes, but in a different order.

Immobility

Effective camouflage is possible only if an animal remains still. Many animals react to danger by freezing. For example, if confronted with danger, reedbuck crouch down with their necks outstretched, and by remaining motionless, become hard to distinguish from their surroundings. Some birds, particularly ground-nesting birds such as nightjars, squat down to reduce the shadow they make.

Reedbuck

Assassin bug

Many species of assassin bugs resemble the insects on which they feed. This enables them to get close to their prey without being detected, before seizing it and injecting a toxic fluid. One species of assassin bug, *Salyavata variegata*, lives in termite nests. It camouflages itself by covering its body in debris, including the bodies of termites, and then enters the nest, unnoticed, to feed on the inhabitants.

Assassin bug covered in debris by termites' nest

Termite

Social displays

Social displays take many different forms, from threat display to courtship and bonding. Both cuttlefish and octopuses can change colour; they darken and flash different colours to intimidate rivals or enemies. The male Uganda kob, a type of antelope, establishes territorial breeding grounds by displaying along the boundary of his territory. Lowering his head, he makes a mock attack with his horns. This warns rival males to keep out of his territory, while at the same time, induces other females to join his harem.

Ring-tailed lemurs signalling with raised tails

Signalling

Signs and signals help animals to maintain contact, preserve the social hierarchy, and intimidate rivals and enemies. The signals have to be conspicuous and unmistakable. The ring-tailed lemurs of Madagascar raise their long black-and-white tails to waft scent at their rivals, and to enable all members of a group to maintain contact. The black rings encircling the cheetah's white-tipped tail enable the cubs to follow their parent, which would otherwise be invisible in the long grass. The young of ringed plovers have a white neck-band which helps the parents keep the brood together.

Courtship

Many animals use courtship displays to attract a mate. The fiddler crab, for example, waves its outsize claw, the elephant seal inflates its nose, and the grouse spreads its tail and inflates its air sacs. Among the most impressive courtship displays are that of the male peacock, which spreads his brilliantly coloured tail plumage, and the elaborate rituals of birds-of-paradise and bowerbirds. These involve vibrating the body, fanning feathers, puffing out plumage, decorating nesting areas, and calling loudly.

Tail feathers overlap and rest on the ground when relaxed.

Peacock

Strong feathers at the rear, attached to muscles, are used to raise the long feathers.

Peacock with tail feathers raised

Peacock starting to erect tail plumage.

Male calls as he starts to display.

Henry Walter Bates

The English naturalist and explorer, Henry Bates (1825–92) spent 11 years exploring the Amazon, returning with 8,000 species of previously unknown insects. In 1861, he published a paper on mimicry which made an important contribution to the theory of natural selection. He suggested that some harmless insects looked like harmful ones to discourage predators from attacking them.

Red and black froghopper

Warning signals

Animals use many methods to frighten off other animals. Warning colours make prey appear unpalatable to discourage predators. Many poisonous and venomous animals do not need to be camouflaged; they advertise themselves with bright coloured patterns of red, yellow, and black, which are recognized warning colours. Skunks' black and white coats warn they can squirt foul-smelling spray.

False warning

Many animals employ bluff as a means of defence. In birds, this may take the form of fluffing up feathers, spreading wings, and clacking beaks. Many frogs and toads blow themselves up, to make them appear larger; the hawkmoth caterpillar looks like a snake to intimidate enemies; and the Australian frilled lizard erects its frill and hisses loudly to intimidate intruders.

The toad raises itself on its legs to make itself appear bigger.

European common toad

The caterpillar looks like a small pit viper snake to scare predators.

Hawkmoth caterpillar

Seasonal change

Some Arctic animals, such as the polar bear and snowy owl, remain white throughout the year; others undergo a seasonal change. In far-northern latitudes, the stoat becomes completely white in winter, except for the tip of its tail, which remains black. In the warmer parts of its habitat, it can retain its russet coloration, become part-coloured, or change to white as needed. This ability to change colour provides the stoat with effective camouflage throughout the year.

Stoat with dark summer coat

Stoat with pale winter coat

FIND OUT MORE BIRDS BUGS DEER AND ANTELOPES FROGS AND TOADS LIONS AND OTHER WILD CATS MONKEYS AND OTHER PRIMATES OWLS AND NIGHTJARS POISONOUS ANIMALS SNAKES

CAMPING AND HIKING

ONE OF THE MOST popular types of holiday, camping offers people the chance to enjoy the great outdoors at close quarters. For many people, their first experience of camping is as children, setting up a tent in their own back yard. But it is also a popular activity with adults, who enjoy getting away from cities to explore the countryside, and perhaps even learning survival skills in the wild. Camping offers the freedom to choose to stay at one campsite through a holiday, or to set up camp at a different site each night. Whatever the type of holiday, it is important to take the appropriate clothing, food, and equipment.

An ideal campsite

Prevailing winds

Trees provide shelter from the wind.

River is a source of water for drinking and washing.

Ground is level and there is no danger of flooding.

Choosing a campsite

Many campers stay on organized campsites with shared cooking and washing facilities. Those who prefer to camp "in the wild" look for high, level, dry ground on which to pitch a tent. The best campsites are sheltered from the wind, and not too close to any rivers or dams.

Fire ingredients

Tinder

Kindling

Small fuel

Main fuel

Large fuel

Making a teepee fire
Fires provide warmth and a means of cooking, but they can also be dangerous. Campers must make certain that a fire is permitted, safe, and will not harm their tent or the surroundings. They are especially careful if a strong wind is blowing.

1 The camper gathers the fuel he or she needs (ranging in size from twigs to branches), cuts out a square of turf, and puts a layers of sticks in the hole.

Make sure the fuel is dry.

2 The camper then balances four sticks to meet at the top in a teepee shape, making sure the teepee has enough space for tinder inside the sticks.

3 Gradually, the camper adds more sticks, making the teepee as sturdy as possible, and puts some tinder, such as leaves and dry grass, inside.

Hole for putting in tinder

4 Having set light to the tinder, the camper gradually adds more tinder, then twigs and larger pieces of fuel. He or she takes care not to knock the teepee over. When the teepee burns, it will collapse and create embers that can be used for cooking.

Keep a torch at the head of the sleeping bag.

Unpack things only as needed.

The head of a sleeping bag should face the door.

Living in your tent
There is very little room inside a tent, so campers need to be well organized, or they may lose things and be uncomfortable. To stop damp seeping in from the soil under a sleeping bag, campers put a waterproof sheet on the ground beneath the tent.

Things to take camping

It is better to take only the basic items of equipment camping. These include all the tools needed to set up a camp, as well as cooking and eating utensils. In addition, campers should take hard-wearing clothes to protect them against all types of weather.

First-aid kit

Survival kit

Binoculars

Torch

Swiss army knife

Wash kit

Sewing kit   *Matches*

Plastic Mug

Lip salve

Compass

Plastic plate and bowl

Cutlery

Food and water

For healthy eating, campers aim to maintain a balanced diet, including fruit and vegetables, bread, and food containing protein, such as fish and meat. If it is difficult or impossible for campers to buy food while they are away, they take tinned or freeze-dried foods, which will not perish. Campers should only drink water from approved sources. If necessary, they take water purifiers or a portable water filter.

Keep water containers spotlessly clean.

Water

Meals for a day on the trail

When campers are going on a long hike, they plan their meals before they set out, sorting food into labelled plastic bags. They eats main meals at the start and end of the day, and nibble snacks during the day for energy.

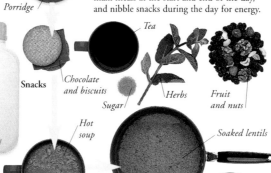

Hot drink

Breakfast *Porridge*

Tea

Snacks *Chocolate and biscuits*

Sugar

Herbs

Fruit and nuts

Hot soup

Lunch

Soaked lentils

Soup

Stew

Evening meal

Peach juice

Peaches

Frankfurters and baked beans

Freeze-dried meal is dehydrated, leaving the texture of food intact.

Dried foods

Dried meals are useful for hikers. They are portable and are prepared simply by adding hot water. This saves time and fuel. If meals are prepared in their bags and resealed, hikers can eat them on the trail.

Rice

Curry

Foil bags

Egg

Food for travelling

Boiled sweets   **Kidney beans**   **Gravy cubes**

Portable foods

To keep their backpack easy to carry, experienced campers put as much of their food as possible into bags. When they do take tins, these are small enough for the camper to eat the contents in one go.

Salami   **Pasta meal**

Sardines

Canoe hiking

In some parts of the world, people can go hiking in canoes. They travel along rivers and spend the nights camping on the riverbank. Where the river is too dangerous for canoeing, they move to the land and carry their canoes. The canoes used are light and easy to carry.

Caravanning

A popular alternative to camping is caravanning. Caravans are small, compact homes on wheels, which can be towed by a car to a campsite. They are more comfortable to live in than tents. Most have stoves, beds, and toilets, and some may even have refrigerators and showers. Some campsites have permanent, fixed caravans that you can rent for a holiday if you do not have your own.

Using a compass

Hikers take a map and a compass when they go on a long walk, so that they can follow the route and not get lost. A protractor compass, shown here, is popular because it is light, reliable, and accurate.

Hiking

Walking through the countryside, for a few hours or for up to several weeks, is a form of exercise enjoyed by people of all ages. Hikers walk in groups, so that if an accident occurs, at least two can go for help together, and one can stay with the injured member of the party. Hikers should be fully equipped for the sort of journey they are making and should tell someone where they are going.

Shoulder straps can be adjusted to fit.

Ice pick

Windproof jacket with a hood.

Ice hammer

Backpacking

A comfortable way to carry belongings, backpacks range from light day packs to large packs that have space for everything needed for several days' hiking. They sit as high as possible on the shoulders, to distribute weight.

Mountain walking

The most difficult and dangerous form of hiking is mountain climbing. Mountain climbers enjoy testing their strength and skill on steep rock faces. They need to be particularly fit, and use special climbing equipment.

Crampon

Tent poles and pegs in the same bag

The pack is kept full so heavy items stay at the top.

Sleeping bag at the bottom.

How to pack a backpack

To keep the contents of a backpack dry, line it with a plastic bag and put everything in separate plastic bags. Pack the lighter, bulkier things at the bottom and the heavier things at the top. Spare clothes can be packed down the back to protect the spine.

FIND OUT MORE   ENERGY   EXPLORATION   FIRE   FIRST AID   FOOD   HEALTH AND FITNESS

CANADA

THE WORLD'S SECOND LARGEST country, Canada covers the northern part of the North American continent and is made up of ten provinces and three territories. Canada borders Alaska and the Pacific Ocean to the west, and the Atlantic Ocean to the east. Winters in the northern third of the country, much of which lies within the Arctic Circle, are so severe that very few people can live there. About 80 per cent of Canadians live within 320 km (200 miles) of the US border. Canada has huge forests, rich mineral resources, and open, fertile farmland.

CANADA FACTS

CAPITAL CITY Ottawa

AREA 9,220,970 sq km (3,560,217 sq miles)

POPULATION 31,100,000

MAIN LANGUAGES English, French, Chinese, Italian, Native American

MAJOR RELIGION Christian

CURRENCY Canadian dollar

LIFE EXPECTANCY 79 years

PEOPLE PER DOCTOR 476

GOVERNMENT Multi-party democracy

ADULT LITERACY 99%

Ottawa

Canada's capital sits on the south bank of the Ottawa River, and has a population of 921,000. The city has clean, wide streets, many lined with parks. The Rideau Canal, part of a complex of lakes and canals linking Ottawa with Lake Ontario, freezes in winter, becoming the world's longest skating rink.

Skating on the Rideau Canal

Physical features

Covered in lakes, rivers, and forests, Canada has one-third of the world's fresh water. Frozen islands lie in the Arctic, high mountains in the west, and vast prairies in the south.

45°C (113°F)   -63°C (-81°F)
21°C (70°F)   -11°C (12°F)
871 mm (34 in)

Climate

Most of Canada has a continental climate with long, bitterly cold winters and hot, humid summers. Coastal areas are generally mild, especially the Pacific west coast. The glaciers and ice-caps of the north are permanently frozen.

Built-up 0.5%   Wetland 2%   Grassland 1%
Forest 59%
Barren 5.5%
Tundra 27%
Farmland 5%

Land use

Canada's vast prairies are used for growing wheat. The forests support a thriving timber industry. Only five per cent of Canada's land area is cultivated.

Rocky Mountains

The snow-capped Rocky Mountains dominate western Canada, extending south into the USA. Canada's highest mountain is Logan, at 5,959 m (19,551 ft).

People

Most Canadians have European ancestors who emigrated to Canada from the UK, France, Germany, Scandinavia, and Italy. There are large numbers of Ukrainians, Indians, and Chinese. The indigenous peoples of Canada form about four per cent.

3 per sq km
(8 per sq mile)

77% **23%**
Urban **Rural**

Inuit
The Inuit are one of the country's indigenous groups, and almost 50,000 Inuits live in northern Canada. One-quarter are settled on Baffin Island, in the east Arctic, and speak their own language, *Inuktitut*. In 1999 the Inuit homeland of Nunavut was made a territory.

Leisure

Many Canadians enjoy outdoor activities. In the summer, people sail, raft, canoe, or simply enjoy one of Canada's many well-kept parks. The major spectator sports are hockey, baseball, and football.

Winter sports
Plentiful snow makes skiing and ice-skating popular with many Canadians. Ice hockey is played everywhere, from frozen backyards to national stadiums. Calgary hosted the 1988 Winter Olympics.

Hardwood stick

Calgary Stampede
One of the world's largest rodeos, the Calgary Stampede attracts one million visitors every year. Held in July, the 10-day rodeo is an exciting recreation of the Wild West. People dress up in cowboy outfits and try their luck at calf roping, chuck wagon racing, and bronco riding.

Tough rubber puck is hit into the goal.

Farming

Five per cent of Canada's land is arable, and the country is a top exporter of wheat, oats, maize, and barley. Forest products and fish are also key exports. Cattle and pigs are raised on the pastures of the southeast. Three per cent of the work-force are farmers.

Apple

Cranberries

Niagara Fruit Belt
The land between Lakes Ontario and Erie is called the "Niagara Fruit Belt" because the soil and climate are ideal for growing soft fruit, such as cherries and peaches. Apples and cranberries flourish in British Columbia. In the east, the maple tree, whose leaf is Canada's national emblem, yields rich syrup, a favourite served with sweet pancakes.

Maple leaves

Wheat
Canada's main cereal crop is wheat, and on the eastern prairies, around Saskatchewan, wheat farming is a way of life. About half of the 29,870,000 tonnes (32,930,000 tons) grown every year are exported.

Transport

The 8,000-km (5,000-mile) Trans-Canada Highway links the east and west coasts. The St Lawrence Seaway provides trade links for the eastern provinces. A vast air network, railways, rivers, and the lakes are also used for transport.

St Lawrence Seaway
Opened in 1959, the St Lawrence Seaway links the Great Lakes with the St Lawrence River and the Atlantic. Over 725 km (450 miles), a series of locks enables ocean-going ships, from all over the world, to sail inland.

Industry

The centre of Canada's industry is at the western end of Lake Ontario, a region known as "the Golden Horseshoe". Canadian factories process foods, assemble cars, and make steel, chemical products, and paper. The service industries are thriving, and tourism now employs one in ten Canadians.

Nickel

Zinc

Mining
Minerals have been one of the major factors in the growth of Canada's economy. The country is the world's largest producer of zinc ore and uranium, and second of nickel and asbestos.

Forestry
Canada's abundant forests have made it the world's second largest exporter of softwood (fir and pine) and wood pulp. Ten per cent of Canada's labour force work in the lumber industry, where timber is used as a raw material. British Columbia, Québec, and Ontario are the major timber-producing provinces.

Snowplough
Canada's long, cold winters bring heavy snow and ice to the country, making travelling by road difficult and dangerous. Snowploughs work through the day and night to keep roads clear. Most Canadian roads are wide to allow room for snow to be piled up on either side.

Québec

At the heart of French Canada, Québec City has many stone houses and 17th-century buildings, and its old town was declared a World Heritage Site in 1985. The province of Québec is home to nearly 7,500,000 people. More than three-quarters of the people are of French descent, and keep the French language and culture alive. There have been many attempts by the province to claim independence from Canada.

Château Frontenac, Québec old town

FIND OUT MORE

CANADA, HISTORY OF   FARMING   FISHING INDUSTRY   FORESTS   LAKES   NATIVE AMERICANS   PORTS AND WATERWAYS   ROCKS AND MINERALS   TUNDRA   WINTER SPORTS

CANADA, HISTORY OF

FOR MOST OF ITS history, Canada has been home to Native Americans and Inuits. They were descendants of the first people to settle there during the Ice Age, and built advanced cultures based on hunting and trapping fish and animals. In 1497, the first Europeans visited the country, establishing settlements in the early 1600s. In the 18th century, French and British armies fought for control of the entire country. The British won, but a sizeable French community has remained in Québec to this day.

First Canadians

The first inhabitants of Canada were peoples from northern Asia who crossed a land bridge from Siberia and moved south through America more than 20,000 years ago. The Inuits lived in the Arctic regions, while other Native American peoples occupied the plains and coastal areas. They all developed their own distinctive cultures. For example, the tribes of the northwest coast recorded their family history on totem poles, carving out representations of the family spirits on the trunks of cedar trees.

Fur trading

European settlers were attracted to Canada by the wealth to be made from furs and skins of animals trapped in the forests. The English-owned Hudson's Bay Company, established in 1670, and other trading companies set up fortified trading posts to trade furs and other goods with local Indian tribes. Québec (established 1608) and Montreal (1642) became important centres of the fur trade.

Traders travelled by canoe in order to reach the trading post.

Missionaries built churches to convert Native Americans.

Wigwams made of birch wood covered with skins or bark.

Trading post

Houses and walls were built of wood from the forests.

Jacques Cartier

The French sea captain Jacques Cartier (1491–1557) was hired by Francis I of France, to look for a northwest passage to China round the north of America. In 1534, he sailed into the Gulf of St Lawrence, and, in 1535, discovered the St Lawrence River. As he sailed up the river, he stopped at two Indian villages – Stadacona (modern Québec) and Hochelaga (Montreal). As a result, French immigrants began to settle by the St Lawrence River.

Capture of Québec

In 1759, British forces led by General James Wolfe attacked Québec, capital of the French colony of New France. Wolfe captured the city arriving from the Gulf of St. Lawrence with a flotilla of 168 ships that carried over 30,000 men. However, both he and the French commander, Louis, Marquis de Montcalm, were killed. All of French North America came under British control.

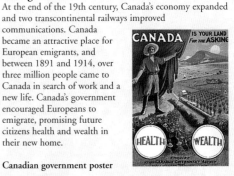

Wolfe's flotilla arrives in Québec.

Northwest Territories, 1870

Saskatchewan, 1905

Canadian provinces

Nunavut 1999

Ontario, 1867

Québec, 1867

New Brunswick, 1867

Newfoundland 1949

Nova Scotia, 1867

Alaska

Yukon Territory, 1898

British Columbia, 1871

Alberta, 1905

Manitoba, 1870

Independence

In 1867, Canada became an independent dominion (nation) within the British Empire. At first, the new country consisted only of parts of Ontario, Quebec, and two provinces on the Atlantic coast. Gradually, the other provinces joined. By 1905, most of Canada had joined the Dominion.

Immigration

At the end of the 19th century, Canada's economy expanded and two transcontinental railways improved communications. Canada became an attractive place for European emigrants, and between 1891 and 1914, over three million people came to Canada in search of work and a new life. Canada's government encouraged Europeans to emigrate, promising future citizens health and wealth in their new home.

Canadian government poster

Timeline

1497 John Cabot, an Italian sailor, claims Newfoundland for Britain.

1534–35 Jacques Cartier explores the Gulf of St. Lawrence for France; then discovers the St. Lawrence River.

1605 French establish the first European colony at Port Royal, Nova Scotia.

1754 French and Indian War between Britain and France. France forced to relinquish Québec to Britain.

1846 Oregon Treaty confirms present borders with USA

1949 Founder member of NATO

1968 Québec Party formed to demand independence for Québec.

1989 UK transfers all power relating to Canada in British law.

1998 Government apologises to Native Americans over land.

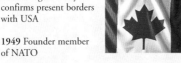

Canadian flag

Québec

Canada recognized both its English- and French-speakers as equal, but in the 1960s, many people in French-speaking Québec began to press for their province to become independent. In 1982, Québec was given the status of a "distinct society", but referendums seeking independence were defeated in 1980 and 1995.

FIND OUT MORE

EXPLORATION   FRANCE, HISTORY OF   NATIVE AMERICANS   NORTH AMERICA, HISTORY OF   UNITED KINGDOM, HISTORY OF   UNITED STATES, HISTORY OF

CARIBBEAN

HUNDREDS OF ISLANDS lie in the Caribbean Sea, east of the USA and Central America, and stretching west into the Atlantic Ocean. These Caribbean islands, also known as the West Indies, take their name from the Caribs, the original inhabitants of the region, until the Spanish arrived in 1492. Most islanders today are descendents of African slaves brought to work in plantations between the 16th and 19th centuries. The islands have a tropical climate, turquoise waters, and fine beaches, and have developed a booming tourist industry. However, many people are poor and live by farming.

Volcanic islands
Many Caribbean islands are made of volcanic rocks that emerged from the ocean millions of years ago. Some, such as the St Lucian Gros Piton, 798 m (2,619 ft), and the Petit Piton, 750 m (2,461 ft), are the remains of ancient volcanoes that rise up from the sea on the west coast, near the town of Soufrière. One or two are still active, such as La Soufrière, at 1,219 m (4,000 ft) on St Vincent.

Physical features

Long, sandy beaches, tropical seas, and fine natural harbours have earned the Caribbean islands a reputation for beauty. Most of the islands are forested and mountainous. Some are volcanic in origin, others are founded on coral reefs. Hurricanes, earthquakes, and active volcanoes shake parts of the region from time to time.

Coral islands
The warm, tropical seas of the Caribbean provide ideal conditions for corals. Some of the Caribbean's volcanic islands, such as Barbados and the Cayman Islands, are fringed with coral reefs, which protect them against the lashing waves. The 700 islands and 2,300 islets of the Bahamas are entirely built up of coral, which can be viewed from the bridge that links Nassau with Paradise Island.

Hurricanes
Powerful tropical storms called hurricanes sweep the Caribbean between May and October every year, often causing great damage and economic hardship. They begin as thunderstorms that are whipped up by high winds and warm waters to form destructive stormclouds, swirling around a single centre at up to 360 kmh (220 mph). The violent winds and torrential rain can last for 18 hours.

Regional climate
The countries of the Caribbean all enjoy a warm, tropical climate. Mountainous islands, such as the Windwards, receive three times as much rainfall as lower areas. Most islands have a wet, hurricane-prone season between June and November. From January to March, it is generally dry and pleasant.

28°C (82°F)   23°C (73°F)

1,167 mm (46 in)

Ethnic mix
The earliest inhabitants of the Caribbean islands were the Siboneys, who migrated from Florida to the Bahamas, and the Native Americans of the Carib and Arawak groups. Some Caribs survive in Dominica, but most people are descended from black African slaves, or from the white Spanish settlers of the 16th century, or a mix of the two.

Cuban women of mixed race

Cuba

The largest island in the Caribbean, Cuba has fertile lowlands set between three large mountainous regions. Sugar, rice, tobacco, and coffee are grown on the lowlands, and chromium and nickel are mined. Formerly a Spanish colony, Cuba has been a communist state since 1959. Hostile politics caused the USA to impose a trade embargo, which has disabled Cuba's economy and kept it agricultural.

Sugar is extracted from the cane.

Sugar

With an annual production of 50,000,000 tonnes (55,000,000 tons), sugar-cane is Cuba's largest crop. It is grown around Havana and processed in the city's factories. Cuba is one of the world's largest producers but suffered a decline in the 1990s following the collapse of one of its main customers, the Soviet Union.

Communism

The only communist state in the Caribbean, Cuba is led by Fidel Castro (b. 1926), who led the revolution in 1959. Under Castro, and with Soviet help, Cuba made considerable social and economic progress, although living standards suffered with the breakup of Soviet communism in 1991. US policies remain hostile.

CUBA FACTS

CAPITAL CITY	Havana
AREA	110,860 sq km (42,803 sq miles)
POPULATION	11,200,000
MAIN LANGUAGE	Spanish
MAJOR RELIGION	Christian
CURRENCY	Peso

Havana

Situated in a natural harbour, Cuba's chief port and capital, Havana, was founded by the Spanish in 1515. Its old town has many ancient buildings and cobbled streets. There are no shanty towns here, unlike many capitals in the region, but of its 2,328,000 people, half live in sub-standard houses.

Cigars

Cuba's fertile soil and warm climate are ideal for growing high-quality tobacco. Havana cigars are popular all over the world and are made from a blend of at least five different types of tobacco. Cigars are still rolled by hand at long wooden tables.

Bahamas

Located to the northeast of Cuba, the Bahamas extend south for about 965 km (600 miles). Of the 3,000 coral islands and islets, only 30 are inhabited. Most of the people are black, but on Spanish Wells island, there are around 1,200 white descendants of Puritan settlers. Tourism, fishing, and financial services flourish on the islands.

Festival

Music and dancing are everywhere in the Caribbean, but especially so at the Junkanoo Festival on the Bahamas islands. Held at the end of every year, Junkanoo is a lively celebration with street dancing, music, and colourful parades where people wear wild costumes and blow whistles. The festival has roots in the celebrations of a slave leader called John Canoe, and slaves' days off at Christmas.

BAHAMAS FACTS

CAPITAL CITY	Nassau
AREA	10,010 sq km (3,864 sq miles)
POPULATION	307,000
MAIN LANGUAGE	English
MAJOR RELIGION	Christian
CURRENCY	Bahamian dollar

Jamaica

The third largest island of the Caribbean, Jamaica is a land of springs, rivers, waterfalls, and sandy beaches. A few wealthy families dominate the island, but the slum areas around Kingston are controlled by violent gangs. Many of the people of those areas are Rastafarians, worshippers of the former Emperor of Ethiopia. Jamaica is a prosperous country, with booming tourist, mining, and farming industries. Cricket is a popular game.

Reggae

Jamaica's distinctive form of popular music, reggae, began in the 1960s as an offshoot of rhythm and blues, with songs calling for social and political change. Bob Marley (1945–81), whose band won world fame in the 1970s, is a reggae icon, and his birthday is celebrated by all Jamaicans.

JAMAICA FACTS

CAPITAL CITY	Kingston
AREA	10,990 sq km (4,243 sq miles)
POPULATION	2,600,000
MAIN LANGUAGE	English
MAJOR RELIGIONS	Christian, Rastafarian
CURRENCY	Jamaican dollar

Women

The Caribbean women's rights movement began in Jamaica, and many Jamaican women hold senior posts in economic and political life. An increasing number of women prefer to be single mothers, especially those who have careers. Women also dominate the growing data-processing industry, largely because they work for lower wages than men.

Okra (Lady's fingers)

Breadfruit

Dasheen, or taro

Vegetables

Jamaicans grow a wide range of vegetables. *Dasheen*, or *taro*, is a staple vegetable whose root and leaves are eaten. There are more than 1,000 varieties of *dasheen*, and it is also used for medicinal purposes. Okra, or lady's fingers, are green pods that are used in "pepperpot stews". Breadfruit, with a creamy, pulpy texture, grow to 13 cm (5 in) wide, and are eaten baked or roasted.

Bauxite

Jamaica is the world's third largest producer of bauxite, the ore from which aluminium is made. Refineries produce alumina, the next stage in producing the metal, worth ten times as much as the ore. This provides about half of Jamaica's export income, and accounts for 10 per cent of global output.

Haiti

Occupying the western third of the island of Hispaniola, Haiti is one of the most mountainous countries in the Caribbean. It is also the poorest. About 95 per cent of its people are descendents of black slaves. The country is overcrowded, and has suffered deforestation, soil erosion, and desertification, as well as a turbulent political history.

Port-au-Prince

Smart modern hotels have lured many visitors to Haiti's capital, Port-au-Prince. The city has two cathedrals, a university, and many government buildings. However, it also has the worst slums in the Caribbean, most of which are found to the north of the centre. They have no water facilities and are overcrowded.

Voodoo

A Haitian blend of West African religions and Christianity, voodoo uses drums, singing, and dance. Its followers believe that through worship of spirits, they can live in harmony with nature and their dead. Many celebrations coincide with Christmas and the Mexican Day of the Dead.

Voodooists on Gede, or All Saint's Day

HAITI FACTS

CAPITAL CITY Port-au-Prince

AREA 27,750 sq km (10,714 sq miles)

POPULATION 8,200,000

MAIN LANGUAGES French, French Creole

MAJOR RELIGIONS Christian, Voodoo

CURRENCY Gourde

Puerto Rico

About 1,600 km (994 miles) southeast of Miami, the crowded island of Puerto Rico is a self-governing territory of the USA. It is home to more than 3.8 million people, of African and Spanish descent, of whom half live in the capital, San Juan. An old walled city, it has colonial buildings.

Balconies, old San Juan

Dominican Republic

Lying 966 km (600 miles) southeast of Florida, the Dominican Republic spreads across the eastern two-thirds of Hispaniola. It has the Caribbean's highest peak, Pico Duarte, 3,175 m (10,417 ft), and also its lowest point, crocodile-infested Lake Enriquillo, 44 m (144 ft) below sea-level. Nickel, amber, and gold mining are important industries, and holidaymakers flock to the island for its long, pearly beaches, modern hotels, and wildlife.

People

With a higher standard of living than neighbouring Haiti, the Dominican Republic provides good healthcare for its people. The mixed race middle classes form about 73 per cent of the population. The minority of blacks work as farmers, selling their produce at market.

Farming

About 24 per cent of the labour force work on farms, which are mostly in the north and east of the country, and in the San Juan valley. Sugar, tobacco, and cocoa are main crops, and, although the market has slowed, most are exported to the USA.

Tobacco leaves are hung upside down to dry and then made into cigars and cigarettes.

DOMINICAN REPUBLIC FACTS

CAPITAL CITY Santo Domingo

AREA 48,730 sq km (18,815 sq miles)

POPULATION 8,500,000

MAIN LANGUAGES Spanish, French Creole

MAJOR RELIGION Christian

CURRENCY Dominican Republic peso

Tourism

The Dominican Republic is the largest tourist destination in the Caribbean, attracting two million each year. The industry brings in half of the country's earnings and provides much-needed jobs.

St Kitts and Nevis

The two islands of St Kitts (or St Christopher) and Nevis sit in the northern part of the Leeward Islands. Both are mountainous, and their idyllic, palm-fringed beaches attract many tourists. Most people are descendents of black Africans, and nearly all work in farming or tourism.

ST KITTS AND NEVIS FACTS

CAPITAL CITY Basseterre

AREA 360 sq km (139 sq miles)

POPULATION 41,000

MAIN LANGUAGE English

MAJOR RELIGION Christian

CURRENCY Eastern Caribbean dollar

Sugar-cane

The main crop on St Kitts is sugar-cane, which accounts for 25 per cent of exports and provides 12 per cent of jobs. Low world prices and hurricane damage have created problems.

Antigua and Barbuda

The largest of the Leeward Islands, Antigua has two dependencies: Barbuda, a small, coral island bursting with wildlife, and Redonda, an uninhabited rock with its own king. The blue lagoons and corals that surround Antigua teem with tropical fish.

ANTIGUA AND BARBUDA FACTS

CAPITAL CITY St John's

AREA 440 sq km (170 sq miles)

POPULATION 66,400

MAIN LANGUAGE English

MAJOR RELIGION Christian

CURRENCY Eastern Caribbean dollar

Yachting

The harbour at St John's has an annual Sailing Week that attracts many visitors and rich yachtspeople. Cruise ships and luxury boats call at the 18th-century Nelson's Dockyard.

Dominica

The largest and most mountainous of the Windward Islands, Dominica has some of the finest scenery in the Caribbean, with rainforests containing 200 wildlife species. Bananas and coconuts are principal exports; prawn farming is proving successful.

DOMINICA FACTS

CAPITAL CITY Roseau

AREA 750 sq km (290 sq miles)

POPULATION 73,000

MAIN LANGUAGES English, French

MAJOR RELIGION Christian

CURRENCY Eastern Caribbean dollar

Carib Reservation
In the 1900s, the British forced the Caribs to move to a reservation. Today, the Carib reservation, on the east coast of the island, is home to more than 2,000 Caribs, descendants of the original inhabitants. Within the reservation – a popular tourist attraction – Caribs follow traditional lifestyles although their language has died out. Many Carib craftspeople make a living selling bags made from banana leaves and grasses.

St Lucia

The beautiful island of St Lucia has clear seas, sandy beaches, and striking volcanic mountains. Most people work in farming, tourism, or industry. Each year, 150,000 tonnes (165,000 tons) of bananas are exported.

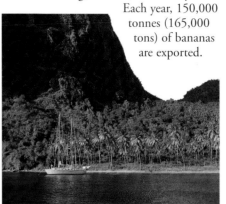

ST LUCIA FACTS

CAPITAL CITY Castries

AREA 620 sq km (239 sq miles)

POPULATION 156,300

MAIN LANGUAGE English

MAJOR RELIGION Christian

CURRENCY Eastern Caribbean dollar

Ecotourism
St Lucia's lush rainforests, boiling springs, and twin Piton peaks are attractions that lure visitors to the island. Aromatic tropical plants, trees, and flowers grow everywhere.

Barbados

Known as the "singular island", Barbados lies 160 km (100 miles) east of the Caribbean chain. Barbados retains a strong English influence, and many Britons retire to the island. The people of Barbados, called Bajans, enjoy some of the Caribbean's highest living standards.

BARBADOS FACTS

CAPITAL CITY Bridgetown

AREA 430 sq km (166 sq miles)

POPULATION 270,000

MAIN LANGUAGE English

MAJOR RELIGION Christian

CURRENCY Barbados dollar

Tourism
Barbados has one of the Caribbean's most well-developed and lucrative tourist industries. About 556,000 people visit the island every year.

St Vincent and the Grenadines

The quiet island of St Vincent is fertile and volcanic, while its 100 tiny sister islands of the Grenadines are flat coral reefs. Both are exclusive holiday resorts, and their waters are popular with yachtspeople. Bananas are the main export.

Arrowroot
St Vincent is the world's largest producer of arrowroot, a starchy liquid that is removed from the arrowroot plant. It is used as a thickening agent in foods, and more recently, as a fine finish for computer paper. Arrowroot is St Vincent's second largest export.

Arrowroot

Arrowroot powder

ST VINCENT AND THE GRENADINES FACTS

CAPITAL CITY Kingstown

AREA 340 sq km (131 sq miles)

POPULATION 115,500

MAIN LANGUAGE English

MAJOR RELIGION Christian

CURRENCY Eastern Caribbean dollar

Grenada

The most southerly of the Windwards, Grenada rises from a rugged coast to a high, forested interior. A former British colony, Grenada has built its economy on agriculture and tourism. Its people are of African or mixed origin.

Nutmeg

Ginger

Cinnamon

GRENADA FACTS

CAPITAL CITY St George's

AREA 340 sq km (131 sq miles)

POPULATION 99,500

MAIN LANGUAGE English

MAJOR RELIGION Christian

CURRENCY Eastern Caribbean dollar

Spices
Grenada is described as the "spice island". It grows about two-thirds of the world's nutmeg, and, with Indonesia, dominates the market. Large quantities of cloves, mace, cinnamon, ginger, bay leaves, saffron, and pepper are also cultivated on the island.

Trinidad and Tobago

The low-lying island of Trinidad and its smaller partner, Tobago, lie just off the coast of Venezuela. The islands have a vivid, cosmopolitan culture, home to people from every continent. Both have fertile farmland, fine beaches, and abundant wildlife.

TRINIDAD AND TOBAGO FACTS

CAPITAL CITY Port-of-Spain

AREA 5,130 sq km (1,981 sq miles)

POPULATION 1,317,000

MAIN LANGUAGE English

MAJOR RELIGIONS Christian, Hindu, Muslim

CURRENCY Trinidad and Tobago dollar

Steel bands
Trinidad and Tobago are the home of steel bands, calypso, and limbo dancing. The first drums, or *pans*, began as empty oil containers. Today, drums are hand-decorated and tuned so that melodies can be played on them. They provide the beat for lively calypso songs.

FIND OUT MORE

CARIBBEAN, HISTORY OF   CHRISTIANITY   FARMING   FESTIVALS   ISLANDS   MUSIC   RELIGIONS   ROCKS AND MINERALS   SLAVERY   VOLCANOES

CARIBBEAN, HISTORY OF

FOR CENTURIES, the Caribbean islands were home to the Carib and Arawak peoples. Their way of life was abruptly disturbed when Europeans arrived in the 1490s. Within 100 years, most had been wiped out by new European rulers who brought thousands of Africans into the Caribbean to work on sugar plantations. The sugar-based economy continued until its decline in the late 19th century. From the mid-1960s, the islands gradually gained independence from European control.

Original inhabitants

The Caribs were expert navigators, travelling great distances in wooden canoes. The Arawaks were skilled craftworkers, who produced baskets and furniture.

Arawak-style wooden seat from the Bahamas

Spanish conquest

The arrival of the Spanish-sponsored navigator Christopher Columbus in the Caribbean in 1492 transformed the region. Convoys of galleons laden with gold and other treasures from the Spanish empire in South America soon crossed the sea on their way back to Spain. Within a few years, Spanish armies had conquered and settled almost every island. Most of the Caribs were killed by the invaders.

Columbus's ship, the *Santa Maria*

European settlement

In the 16th century, with unofficial government backing, English, French, and Dutch pirates raided Spanish treasure ships. They also captured many of the smaller islands. Settlers from Europe arrived, and by 1750, most of the islands were under British, French, or Dutch rule.

— Route of trading ships

NORTH AMERICA

EUROPE

Crops taken to England

Manufactured goods taken to Africa

CARIBBEAN

AFRICA

Slaves taken to Caribbean

Plantations

Europeans set up plantations to satisfy demand for sugar and tobacco in Europe. African slaves worked on the plantations. By 1750, the Caribbean produced most of the world's sugar.

Sugar cane

Tobacco

Slave trade

Most of the Caribbean slave trade was controlled from English ports. Ships left England for West Africa with goods to barter for slaves. The slaves were shipped across the Atlantic. Sugar, tobacco, and other crops were then taken back to England for sale.

Toussaint L'Ouverture

Ex-slave Toussaint L'Ouverture (1743–1803) led a revolt of slaves in French-ruled Haiti in the 1790s. He declared the country a republic, but the French regained control and took him to France, where he died.

Rastafarians

Many Jamaicans are Rastafarians. They believe that the last emperor of Ethiopia, Ras Tafari, or Haile Selassie, was the new messiah who would lead his people back to Africa.

Cuban War

In 1895, following an earlier, unsuccessful uprising, the Cubans rose in revolt against their Spanish rulers. In 1898, the USA declared war on Spain, and freed Cuba.

Emigration

After World War II, many people left the Caribbean in search of work and a better standard of living in Europe. In 1948, the *Empire Windrush* took 492 emigrants from Kingston, Jamaica to London, UK. Over the next 20 years, thousands of Caribbean islanders emigrated to Britain.

Fidel Castro

In 1959, Fidel Castro (b.1927) became the President of Cuba and introduced many social reforms. The US government tried to depose him in 1961, and he turned to the USSR for help. When Soviet nuclear missiles were installed in Cuba in 1962, the world came close to nuclear war.

Timeline

1300s Caribs drive out Arawak people from the eastern Caribbean islands.

1492 Christopher Columbus lands in the Bahamas.

1500s The Spanish take control of the Caribbean.

1700s French, British, Dutch, and Danes capture many islands.

1804 Haiti becomes first Caribbean island to achieve independence from European rule.

1898–1902 Cuba under rule of USA.

1933 Fulgencio Batista becomes ruler of Cuba.

1948 *Empire Windrush* takes first emigrants to Britain.

Capturing a slave

1959 Cuban Revolution; Fidel Castro takes power.

1962 Cuban missile crisis brings the USA and the USSR to the brink of nuclear war.

1962 Jamaica becomes the first British Caribbean colony to win independence.

1962–83 Most British islands win independence; Dutch and French islands remain tied to Europeans.

1983 USA overthrows left-wing regime in Grenada.

Flag of Jamaica

1994 USA intervenes to secure democracy in Haiti, after years of dictatorship on the island.

FIND OUT MORE

AFRICA, EAST   COLUMBUS, CHRISTOPHER   EMPIRES   EXPLORATION   FRANCE, HISTORY OF   GOVERNMENTS AND POLITICS   SLAVERY   SPAIN, HISTORY OF

CARNIVOROUS PLANTS

PLANTS THAT catch and "eat" insects are called carnivorous plants. These plants fall into two groups. Some species, such as the Venus flytrap, have active traps with moving parts. Other species have passive traps, catching their victims on a sticky surface or drowning them in a pool of fluid. Carnivorous plants live in areas where the soil is poor in nitrates and other nutrients, such as bogs, peatlands, and swamps. They obtain extra nutrients by catching insects, which are digested by special juices.

Monkey-cup pitcher plant

Tendril

Pitcher plants from Southeast Asia form traps that hang from their leaves.

Hanging pitcher

The lid and the smooth rim are often brightly coloured to attract insects.

Passive traps

Most carnivorous plants have passive traps. Usually the leaves of these plants have evolved to catch insects in a variety of ways. Some are sticky, others form pit-fall traps with fluid at the bottom and are called pitcher plants.

Rim of the pitcher contains nectar.

The lid stays closed while the pitcher develops.

Mouth of pitcher

Insects fall into the liquid and are digested.

Development of a pitcher plant

1 A young leaf tip extends into a tendril.

2 An upturned swelling appears at the end.

3 The swelling develops into a pitcher.

4 The lid opens when the pitcher is mature.

American pitcher plants

Although they catch their prey in the same way as other pitcher plants, American pitcher plants grow up from the ground rather than hanging from leaves. The inside of the pitcher is slippery and lined with downward pointing hairs which prevent the insects from escaping. The liquid below drowns and slowly digests them.

Pitcher plant

Pitcher is made of leaves joined at the edges.

Butterworts

These small plants have sticky leaves. Small flies are attracted to their smell and get stuck. The leaves slowly roll up, and the insects are digested by juices that ooze out of the leaf.

Common butterwort

Leaf

Sundew flowers develop at the end of a long stalk.

A fly stuck to the hairs on a sundew leaf

Cape sundew

Active traps

Any trap with moving parts is called an active trap. These include plants such as sundews and butterworts, and the Venus flytrap.

Sundews

The upper surface of a sundew leaf is covered with red hairs that secrete drops of clear, sticky liquid. Insects get stuck, then the edges of the leaf slowly roll inward enclosing the insect, and the plant secretes juices that digest it.

Sticky leaf

Venus flytrap

The most spectacular of all the carnivorous plants is the Venus flytrap. It is related to the sundews but has evolved a more elaborate trap. The Venus flytrap grows wild only in one small patch of marshy ground on the border of North and South Carolina, USA. Its trap springs closed when an insect touches the hairs on its surface.

Closed trap

Venus flytrap

Bladderworts

These are rootless water plants. Their leaves and stems bear tiny bladders with a lid covered in sensitive hairs. If a creature brushes the hairs, the lid of the bladder flips open. Water rushes in, carrying the victim with it.

Greater bladderwort

Stimulation of at least three trigger hairs sets off the mechanism that closes the trap.

Surface of the trap

Magnified view of a trigger hair

How a Venus flytrap works

1 An insect lands on a leaf, touching the sensitive trigger hairs.

2 The leaf closes, and the spines interlock, trapping the insect.

3 The trap is fully closed in 30 minutes, and digestion begins.

Trigger hair

Trap is fringed with long spines.

Insect is trapped in one-fifth of a second.

FIND OUT MORE

ASIAN WILDLIFE · FLOWERS · INSECTS · NORTH AMERICAN WILDLIFE · PLANTS · PLANTS, ANATOMY · PLANTS, DEFENCE · PLANTS, REPRODUCTION · SOUTH AMERICAN WILDLIFE

CARS AND TRUCKS

OF ALL THE DIFFERENT FORMS of transport, cars have the biggest effect on our lives. Cars give people the freedom to go where they like, when they like – with some types of car you don't even need a road. Trucks are used for long-distance haulage and for performing many specialized tasks, such as fire-fighting. In parts of the world where there are no railways, trucks offer the only way of transporting goods. But cars and trucks create pollution. Because there are now so many of them on the roads, the world's cities have become clogged with traffic, and the air that many of us breathe is poisoned with traffic fumes.

A Benz Motor Wagen of 1886

Early cars

Early cars were called "horseless carriages". They were made by manufacturers of horse-drawn carriages and coaches, and had the same large wheels, high driver's seat, and suspension. They were powered by a single-cylinder petrol engine, which could reach a top speed of 15 kmh (9 mph).

Modern cars

Efficiency, safety, and comfort are the most important features of a modern car, as well as minimal air pollution from exhaust fumes. To be efficient, cars need engines that use as little fuel as possible, and a streamlined shape to reduce air resistance. In some cars electronics help efficiency and safety. Modern cars are built with the help of computers and robots in high-tech, automated car plants.

Henry Ford

American engineer Henry Ford (1863–1947) formed the Ford Motor Company in 1903. In 1908, Ford launched the Model T. It was made cheaply on a factory assembly line and sold by the million.

Stiff bodyshell is made from thin sheets of steel pressed into shape and welded together. It is chemically treated and painted to protect against rusting.

Windscreen of toughened glass protects driver and passengers from wind and rain. If hit by a stone, the windscreen cracks but does not shatter.

Side windows can be lowered.

Padded seats

Engine burns fuel and uses the energy stored within the fuel to propel the car along.

Bonnet is raised to examine engine.

Radiator circulates water around the engine to cool it.

Luggage is stored in boot.

Rear bumper

Exhaust pipe carries waste gases away from the engine and expels them at the rear of the car.

Hub-cap covers the centre of the wheel.

Suspension spring allows the wheel to move up and down as the car travels over bumps in the road, protecting passengers against uncomfortable jolting.

Driveshaft (or prop shaft) connects the gearbox to the rear wheels, which are driven round by the engine.

Gearbox contains intermeshing **gear** wheels that change the amount of power going to a car's wheels.

Pneumatic (air-filled) **tyres** grip the road and help give a smooth ride.

Front bumper

Luggage is carried in the boot.

Family saloon

Aerodynamic design enhances speed performance.

Sports car

People carrier/MPV

Three rows of detachable seats

Formula 1 racer

Wing

Driver's cockpit

Types of cars

The most popular car is the saloon, which has an enclosed passenger compartment and a separate rear space for luggage. Hatchbacks are saloons with a large rear door and a folding back seat for extra luggage space.

Sports cars

Sports cars are designed to be stylish, fast, and fun. Some sports cars are convertibles, which have a flexible roof that can be folded down so that passengers can enjoy driving in the open air. Luxury convertibles have roofs that open and close automatically.

People carrier

One of the latest types of car is the people carrier, or multi-purpose vehicle (MPV). This vehicle is a cross between a saloon car and a minibus. People carriers are very versatile, with at least six seats and plenty of space for luggage. They are perfect for outings or holidays.

Racing car

Some cars are purpose-built for racing. They have a very powerful engine, wide tyres, and a low, wide body for stability around fast corners. An aerodynamic "wing" on the back helps keep the car on the road at high speeds. Saloons can be converted into racing or rallying cars.

Trucks

Trucks are used for carrying cargo along roads. Their journeys can range from a few kilometres on local deliveries to thousands of kilometres across continents. The first trucks were built in the 1890s, and were driven by steam engines. Since then, trucks have grown ever larger. In Australia, trucks called road trains tow hundreds of tonnes of cargo across long distances in several full-sized trailers. Some trucks are "rigid", that is, built in one piece. Articulated lorries are built in two sections: a tractor unit and a semi-trailer, which is designed to carry specialized loads. Great skill is required to drive an articulated lorry.

Modern trucks

At the heart of most modern trucks is a powerful diesel engine, using diesel oil, a type of petroleum. Some diesel engines are turbocharged for extra power. The engine powers the truck, and operates any hydraulic parts, such as the lifting arms of a dumper. Some trucks, such as military vehicles, have chunky tyres and strong suspensions, to enable them to travel off-road in rough terrain.

Some trucks have up to 20 forward and 10 reverse gears.

A tractor unit and semi-trailer

Inside a truck cab

Long-distance truck drivers spend many hours in the cabs of their trucks. Cabs are designed for comfort, and some of the controls, such as the steering and brakes, are power-assisted to make them easy to use. Many cabs have a small rear room, with a bunk, washing facilities, and television. To help prevent accidents, some countries have introduced tachometers to record how many hours the truck is on the road. It is illegal for the driver to go beyond a certain number of hours.

Heating controls (temperature selector and fan speed selector) keep cab at a comfortable temperature in hot or cold weather.

Cassette, radio, and CB (citizens' band) radio provide entertainment on the road. Drivers may use CB to warn each other of traffic jams.

Adjustable nozzles allow fresh air into the cab.

Warning indicators light up if anything goes wrong with the truck.

Gauges, such as the speedometer, show speed, engine temperature, and the amount of fuel left.

Large diameter steering wheel is easy to turn with power assistance. This is known as power steering.

Gear selector   *Clutch pedal controls gears.*   *Brake pedal*   *Accelerator pedal*

Karl Benz

In 1886, German engineer Karl Benz (1844–1929) patented his first car, using an internal combustion engine. The car had electric ignition, three wheels, differential gears, and was water-cooled. In 1926, his company merged with Daimler to become one of the leading car and truck producers in the world.

Research and development

Modern research aims at improving car economy, safety, and ecology. Because petroleum reserves are limited and its use is environmentally unsound, research is taking place into new fuels from sustainable sources, such as plant oils. Researchers are also experimenting with new materials for car parts, including plastics for car bodies. Car manufacturers are aware that making cars cleaner and safer is likely to improve sales.

Crash test dummy

Testing airbag inflation

Catalytic converter

Cars and trucks are gradually becoming "cleaner", which means they create less pollution. Most new cars have a catalytic converter, which removes carbon monoxide, nitrogen oxides, and other poisonous chemicals from the exhaust gases.

A catalytic converter from a car exhaust

Safety features

Manufacturers are constantly developing new safety features, such as airbags that inflate automatically in the event of an accident. They are also working on new ways of preventing accidents, such as anti-lock brakes.

Types of truck

Most trucks start life as a standard chassis and cab. Car manufacturers can then add the body, which determines the function of the truck. Common specialized trucks include rubbish trucks, flat trailers to transport large items, such as cars, tankers, fire engines, and vehicles modified to carry animals, such as horse boxes.

Rubbish truck

This truck has a closed container for rubbish and a rubbish-bin lift that empties a bin into the body through a protective shield.

Car transporter

A car transporter is used to convey cars to showrooms. There are ramps at the back which fold down at the rear so that the cars can be driven on and off. The trailer of a car transporter can carry up to 18 vehicles.

Storage space above the cab

Horse box

This truck carries horses to shows. The horse enters the truck via a door at the rear, which folds down to make a loading ramp.

FIND OUT MORE   BICYCLES AND MOTORBIKES   ENGINES AND MOTORS   FORCE AND MOTION   OIL   POLLUTION   ROADS   TRANSPORT, HISTORY OF   TRAVEL   UNITED STATES, HISTORY OF

Cars

Known as the "Silver Ghost"

Introduced front wheel drive

Rolls Royce 40/50, UK; launched 1907; top speed 88 kmh (55 mph)

Model T Ford, USA; launched 1908; top speed 68 kmh (42 mph)

Citroën Traction Avant, France; launched 1934; top speed 113 kmh (70 mph)

Best-selling car ever produced

An icon of 1950s' America

Volkswagon Beetle, Germany; launched 1939; top speed 132 kmh (82 mph)

Jaguar XK120, UK; launched 1949; top speed 203 kmh (126 mph)

Ford Thunderbird, USA; launched 1955; top speed 183 kmh (114 mph)

Famous "gullwing" doors

Nicknamed "the shark"

Mercedes-Benz 300SL, Germany; launched 1954; top speed 265 kmh (165 mph)

Fiat 500 D, Italy; launched 1957; top speed 95 kmh (59 mph)

Citroën DS, France; launched 1960; top speed 187 kmh (116 mph)

A sporty, compact car

Won the Le Mans 24-hour race four times in a row

Austin Mini Cooper, UK; launched 1963; top speed 161 kmh (100 mph)

Ford Mustang, USA; launched 1964; top speed 204 kmh (127 mph)

Ford GT40, USA; launched 1964; top speed 322 kmh (200 mph)

Streamlined shape

Classed as a passenger van

Micro-car is ecologically designed and easy to park.

Porsche Carrera 911 RS, Germany; launched 1972; top speed 243 kmh (150 mph)

Toyota Previa, Japan; launched 1990; top speed 180 kmh (111 mph)

Smart car, France/Germany; launched 1998; top speed 139 kmh (87 mph)

Trucks

Front, tractor section

So heavy and wide, it can use only major roads

Pickup or utilities truck: useful for carrying small loads, these popular trucks have open, flat backs

Semitrailer: a monster truck suitable for a wide range of bulk or heavy goods

18 wheels

CARTOONS AND ANIMATION

CARTOONS, OR ANIMATED FILMS, are movies in which drawings or models seem to come to life. The effect is achieved by slight changes to the drawing or model between each frame of film. Animated films first appeared in the 1900s, and the art has developed alongside motion pictures; computer animation is now used to create amazing special effects in movies. Cartoons usually have a comic theme, although animation can also be a thought-provoking medium for a serious message.

Hanna-Barbera
The US animators Bill Hanna (1910–2001) and Joe Barbera (b.1911) created many of the most popular TV cartoon characters. Their first film, called *Puss Gets the Boot*, was released in 1940 and starred Tom and Jerry, the cat and mouse rivals. Other Hanna-Barbera characters include Yogi Bear and the Flintstones.

Cel animation
In cel animation, animators produce at least 12 drawings for each second of action. The background, which usually does not move, is drawn on paper. The animator draws the moving characters on layers of cel (clear plastic film), so there is no need to redraw the parts that do not move between frames. The background shows through the clear areas of cel.

Paints used to add colour

Background is drawn on paper.

Boy is drawn onto cel.

Clear cel strip

Direct animation
With this method the animator creates characters from clay or other media. The characters are slightly repositioned before the camera between each frame of film, creating the effect of movement.

Scene from A Close Shave (1995)

Clay model in an animated sequence

Step 1: figure starts out with his back to the camera.

Step 2: position is manually altered before next frame is shot.

Step 3: a sequence has been created which shows him turning around.

Wallace & Gromit
Wallace & Gromit are the creations of British animator Nick Park and have starred in several award-winning films. The plasticine puppets are less than 15 cm (6 in) high. It took a budget of £1.3 million and a crew of 25 animators, modelmakers, and camera operators to make *A Close Shave*.

Key shapes
Traditionally, one of the most difficult areas of direct animation has been to show a character talking. Specific mouth and lip positions, called "key shapes", must be created for every word spoken. Today, computers can aid this process.

Chuck Jones
US animator Chuck Jones (1912–2002) drew the rabbit Bugs Bunny and many other famous characters in Warner Brothers' "Looney Tunes" cartoons. He directed his first animated film in 1938 and made 300 films in his lifetime, winning three Academy Awards.

Computer animation
Animators use computers to draw the images between the start and end of an action, or to improve or alter hand-drawn images. Computers can now generate an entire film, as in *Toy Story* (1996), as well as breathtaking special effects.

Aladdin
Aladdin (1992) was one of Disney's first major computer-animated films. Although the characters were hand-drawn, three-dimensional software was used to create dramatic effects in lighting, texture, and movement, such as the lava sequence.

© Disney

The Simpsons
Matt Groening created *The Simpsons* while still at school, publishing them as a newspaper comic strip. The animated series made its debut on US television in 1989 and has since become one of the world's most popular shows. The quirky storylines centre on Bart and his family.

Homer

Marg

Maggie

Lisa

Bart

MATT GROENING

The Simpson family

FIND OUT MORE — CAMERAS • DISNEY, WALT • FILMS AND FILM-MAKING • NEWSPAPERS AND MAGAZINES • PAINTING AND DRAWING

C

CASTLES

IN MEDIEVAL EUROPE, castles acted as both home and military stronghold. They were occupied by a lord, his family, servants, and sometimes an army of professional soldiers. They provided refuge for local people in times of war. Local lords could control the surrounding land from their castles, hence they were a very important part of feudalism. Castles were built to be defended, with walls strong enough to keep out an enemy, while allowing the occupants to shoot at any attackers. Designs changed as builders invented better methods of defence, or adapted new ideas from castles in the Islamic world.

The Chapel
Every castle had its own chapel. It was usually in an upper room in one of the towers. This is the chancel of the chapel at Conwy. The altar would have been beneath the windows, and there would have been enough room for everyone in the castle to gather together.

North-west Tower

Outer Ward

The Great Hall was the centre of activity. There was a high table for the lord and lady, and lower tables for everyone else.

The Kitchen was where food for the whole castle was prepared. There were wood fires, oak tables, and alcoves.

The Stockhouse Tower got its name when stocks for prisoners were made here in the 1500s.

The Inner Ward was the last refuge in time of attack.

Machicolations, or overhanging parapets, allowed defenders to pour boiling water on their opponents.

Chapel Tower

The Prison Tower had a deep, dark dungeon.

Bakehouse Tower

King's Tower

The King's Tower
This room on the first floor, close to the royal apartments has a stone fireplace and a recessed window. The recess means a person looking out remains safe from any enemy fire. The original floors have been removed.

Conwy Castle, Wales, in the 13th century

The East Barbican was the first line of defence against attack by sea, and was also a good position from which to fire. Defenders could isolate the enemy in this area.

Lookout Tower

Parts of a castle

Chapel

King's Tower

Early castles had a keep, which contained the lord's rooms, hall, chapel, storerooms, and a well-defended gatehouse. Later castles abandoned the keep, and replaced it with a Great Hall, which was built against the castle walls. The lord's rooms were sometimes built into the gatehouse, but in Conwy they are in the Inner Ward, which was the heart of the castle, and most easily defended.

Timeline

1066 The Normans erect wooden motte-and-bailey castles during the conquest of England. These are quick to build, and the motte, or tower on top of a mound, is easy to defend. Most buildings are in the bailey, or courtyard.

Krak des Chevaliers, Syria

1142 Krak des Chevaliers built in Syria; one of the most easy-to-defend crusader castles, has concentric stone walls.

1127 Rochester Castle built: includes a great hall, chapel, and storerooms. The entrance is well protected, and defenders can shoot at attackers.

Great Tower, Rochester, England

1150 Many French lords build castles along the River Loire. Examples built (or extended) during this period include Loches, Chinon, and Montreuil-Bellay.

1200 The German lords of Liechtenstein build their castle on a high crag for extra defence.

Caerphilly, Wales

1238 The Muslim rulers of medieval Spain begin the castle-palace of the Alhambra.

1271 Concentric castles, like Caerphilly, become popular. They have rings of walls and sometimes water defences (moats).

C

How castles were built

Building a castle required many skilled workers. A master mason drew up plans and supervised the work, and less senior masons carried out the building. Carpenters did the woodwork, and metalworkers made hinges and door fasteners. In a large castle, some specialists stayed on permanently to do the maintenance work.

Wood and earthwork

The Normans chose a site where there was a water supply, built a mound and a wooden castle on top, and surrounded the structure with a wooden fence, or palisade. Most were replaced with stone constructions.

Motte-and-bailey

Stonework

Building a stone castle took decades, but the result was a strong castle that would withstand attack well. The important structures, such as the outer walls, mural towers, and keep, were all made of stone. Buildings in the castle courtyard were still made of timber and had thatched roofs.

Attack and defence

Attackers could fire arrows, hurl missiles using catapults, break down doors or walls with battering rams, climb the walls using ladders, or try to demolish the walls by tunnelling under them (mining). As well as defence features, such as thick walls and doors, moats, and machicolations, a castle also needed plenty of storage space for food so that the stronghold could withstand a long siege.

Arm

Sling pouch

Rope to pull arm down again

Hauling rope

Ropes to winch arm down

Throwing arm

Wooden cup for missile

Handle to turn ropes

Crossbow

Crossbows were powerful but slow to reload. Despite this they could be useful in defending castles, where they could be reloaded behind the safety of the stone walls.

Catapult

The soldiers used a handle attached to a rope (made from a skein of twisted rope) to winch the throwing arm down. They then released it, and the arm flew up, releasing its missile, usually a rock, from a wooden cup.

Traction trebuchet

This siege engine was like a giant catapult. When soldiers pulled down on the ropes, the end of the arm flew upward, and the sling opened to release a missile, which usually weighed about 45–90 kg (100–200 lb).

Windows

Most castle windows were narrow or cross-shaped slits. They usually had a large alcove on the inside of the wall. This allowed an archer to stand to one side and avoid missiles while preparing to shoot.

Fishtail bottoms   *Rectangular opening*   *Crosslet*   *Round ended cross*   *Gun loop*

Arrow slits developed that were large enough for a defender to shoot an arrow out, but too small for an attacker's missiles. Later, the gun loop developed with a circular hole to fit a gun barrel.

Edward I

In the early years of his reign, Edward I (r.1272–1307) conquered Wales, and built an "iron ring" of castles in strategic Welsh towns to keep the country under his control. Many of these Welsh castles, such as Harlech and Beaumaris, were built on the concentric plan, which meant they had both inner and outer walls for defence. Concentric castles were very difficult to attack successfully.

Asian and African castles

Castles have been built in many different places. There was a strong tradition of castle-building in the Islamic world, and medieval soldiers took Muslim ideas about fortification to western Europe when they returned from the crusades.

Himeji Castle, Japan

Seventeenth-century Japan had a feudal system similar to that of medieval Europe, and Japanese lords also lived in castles. Tall towers with pagoda-like roofs had narrow window openings through which soldiers could shoot. The towers were surrounded by courtyards and walls.

Fasilidas Castle, Ethiopia

The central stronghold shows many features in common with western castles, including thick walls of stone, round corner towers, and battlements. The remains of the outer curtain wall can be seen in the foreground to the right.

Van Castle, Turkey

Built on a rocky outcrop, Van Castle was begun in 750. It was later extended, and was occupied by the Seljuk and Ottoman Turks before being taken over by Armenian Christians.

Pfalzgrafenstein, Germany

1338 Many German castles are built on the Rhine because of the river's importance as a trade route.

Bodiam, England

1385 Bodiam Castle has a curtain wall around a court-yard, which contains the hall and chapel.

Real de Manzanares, Spain

1416 By this time many French castles, such as Saumur on the River Loire, have conical towers, strong defensive walls, and luxurious rooms.

1435 The elaborate Real de Manzanares is built.

1642 In Traquair, a Scottish tower-house, turrets and battlements are more for decoration than defence.

1600s Many castles were built by local lords in Japan, like Himeji.

Traquair House, Scotland

FIND OUT MORE   ARCHITECTURE   EUROPE, HISTORY OF   FEUDALISM   MEDIEVAL EUROPE   NORMANS

CATS

DOMESTIC CATS are related to wild cats, such as lions and tigers, and they are able to fend well for themselves. They are excellent hunters, and their eyes, ears, nose, and whiskers are well adapted for their natural preference for hunting at night. Cats are affectionate and respond well to humans. They were domesticated about 4,000 years ago to keep people company and to destroy pests.

Kittens
Cats have an average of four or five kittens in a litter. Kittens love to stalk, chase, and pounce on things. This helps to make them strong, and develops the skills they will need as adults.

Domestic cats
There are more than 100 recognized breeds of domestic cat. They are distinguished mainly by their body shape. People started to breed cats for their looks between 100 and 150 years ago.

| White | Lilac | Red | Blue | Chocolate |

Fur
Cats can be divided into long- and short-haired breeds. Fur is of various textures. Common coat colours are grey-blue, black, brown, white, red, and mixtures of these, such as silver and lilac.

| Siamese | British shorthair | Persian longhair | Devon Rex |

Head shapes
Cat head shapes range from large and round, like that of the British shorthair, to wedge-shaped, like that of the Siamese. Some breeds have special characteristics, such as the Scottish fold, which has the tip of its ears bent forward.

Games enable kittens to practise hunting skills, such as stalking and catching.

Loose-fitting skin gives freedom of movement.

Flexible spine allows the cat to twist its body.

1 If a cat suddenly falls, balance organs in its ears tell it which way is up.

Grooming
Cats are very clean animals and spend at least an hour a day grooming, using their tongue as a "comb". The tongue has tiny hard spines, called papillae, on its surface. The licking helps to keep the fur clean and waterproof, and also spreads the cat's scent all over its body.

Papillae

2 The cat turns its head around first so that it can see where it is falling, and where it is going to land.

3 Then the cat turns the rest of its body. By the time it reaches the ground, it will be the right way round.

Balance
A cat's long flexible tail helps it to balance. Cats will almost always land on their feet, even when falling from a great height. They have very quick reflexes and can twist and turn their body the right way up in a fraction of a second.

Back paws are brought forward.

Senses
Cats can see well in low light and can focus on small objects a long way away. Their super-sensitive hearing picks up sounds that we cannot hear and can also take in two sounds at once, such as a mouse in a thunderstorm. Whiskers are sensitive to touch. Cats use them to feel their way in the dark, and to measure whether spaces are wide enough for them to go through.

Ears are funnel-shaped to draw sounds inside the ear.

Long, flexible ears can turn toward sounds.

Cats rely more on eyesight than smell when hunting. They have the largest eyes in relation to their size of any animal.

Cats use their sense of smell to identify objects, other cats and animals, and food.

Sense of taste is important for distinguishing any food that may be harmful.

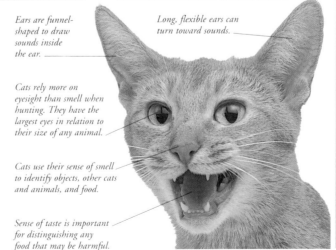

4 The cat stretches out its front legs to absorb the impact of landing.

Claws
Cats use their claws to defend themselves and to climb. At other times, the claws are drawn in, or retracted, for protection. They are covered by a bony sheath that is an extension of the last bone of each toe and fit inside pockets in the skin.

Narrow pupils in the light

Large pupils in the dark

Changing pupils
A cat's pupils expand enormously in the dark to let in as much light as possible. A layer of cells at the back of the eyes, called the tapetum, reflects light back into the eye which helps cats see in the dark.

FIND OUT MORE

| ANIMAL BEHAVIOUR | EYES AND SEEING | LIONS AND OTHER WILD CATS | MAMMALS | MOUNTAIN WILDLIFE |

Cats
Long-haired

Long silky fur

Flattish, round face

M-shaped tabby marking

Matching mittens

Tufted ears

Turkish van (auburn) has a chalky white coat.

Persian longhair (blue) has a short, bushy tail.

Birman (seal tabby point) has pure white paws.

Somali (sorrel) was bred from the Abyssinian.

Ragdoll (blue mitted) goes limp when it is stroked.

Turkish angora (blue-cream) has fine, silky fur.

Longer fur forms a ruff.

Balinese (blue tabby point) has a long, well-plumed tail.

Javanese (cinnamon) is graceful and lithe – a typical Oriental cat.

Somali (silver) has ticking (bands of colour) on each hair.

Maine coon (brown classic tabby) is a large, hardy cat.

Colour pointed longhair (chocolate point) has thick fur.

Short-haired

Crimped coarse fur feels like lamb's wool.

Ears are folded forward and downward.

Massive round head on a thick neck

Thick undercoat with longer top coat

Widely spaced ears with rounded tips

American wirehair (brown mackerel tabby) is active.

Burmese (chocolate) has glossy fur with a satin feel.

Scottish fold (tortie and white) has folded ears.

Exotic (blue) is playful and affectionate.

Manx (red classic tabby) is bred to have no tail.

American shorthair (silver classic tabby) has thick fur.

Muscular body

10-cm- (4-in-) long inflexible tail

Dorsal stripe

Colour gets darker with age.

Small rounded ears and rounded head

Korat (blue) is a playful cat. It has close-lying fur.

Japanese bobtail (red and white) is usually patterned.

Egyptian mau (silver) has a spotted coat.

Siamese (seal point) has an angular face and large ears.

California spangled (gold) has well-defined spots.

Colour pointed British shorthair (cream point).

Flat skull and large ears

Oriental shorthair (foreign red) is a sleek, slender cat with fine glossy fur.

British shorthair (chocolate) has a solid build with a round face and short nose.

Cornish rex (cinnamon silver) has a short wavy coat, patterned over the whole body.

Chartreux (blue-grey) is an old French breed. All Chartreux are this colour.

Large pricked ears

Coat has a silvery sheen.

Tonkinese (cream) is a Burmese and Siamese cross. It is active and affectionate.

Abyssinian (usual) is an elegant cat, and looks similar to the cats of ancient Egypt.

Russian shorthair (blue) has a graceful, long body with thick, fine fur.

Oriental shorthair (Havana) was developed from a chocolate point Siamese.

CAUCASUS REPUBLICS

THE COUNTRIES of Georgia, Armenia, and Azerbaijan lie just within Asia, on a narrow plateau sandwiched between the Greater and Lesser Caucasus mountains. They are often collectively called Transcaucasia or the Caucasus Republics. To the west of the region lies the Black Sea, and to the east, the land-locked Caspian Sea. All three countries were part of the former Soviet Union and only gained their independence in 1991. Since the end of communist rule, growing ethnic and religious tensions have caused civil unrest throughout much of the region.

Physical features

Much of the land is mountainous and rugged, with large expanses of semi-desert in the Armenian uplands. The Kura is the longest river, flowing 1,364 km (848 miles) from central Georgia, through the fertile lowlands of Azerbaijan to the Caspian Sea. The low Black Sea coastal area in western Georgia is lush and green. The area suffers earthquakes.

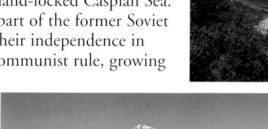

26°C (79°F)   0°C (32°F)

375 mm (15 in)

Regional climate
The varied landscape of this region gives rise to a wide range of climates. Georgia's Black Sea coast is warm and humid, while Armenia is generally dry with long, cold winters. The lowland areas of Azerbaijan have long, hot summers and cool winters. Winters in the mountains are bitterly cold.

Ararat Plains
Most of Armenia is a high plateau with large expanses of semi-desert. In the southwest, the land drops towards the River Aras, which forms the border with Turkey and drains most of Armenia. Known as the Ararat Plains, this fertile, sheltered strip is used for growing vegetables and vines.

Lake Sevan
Once valued for its pure waters and stunning setting, Armenia's Lake Sevan is at the centre of an ecological crisis. Tragically, irrigation and hydroelectric projects begun in the 1970s have caused the water level to drop by up to 16 m (52 ft).

Greater Caucasus Mountains
The Greater Caucasus range stretches for about 1,200 km (745 miles) from the Black Sea to the Caspian Sea, effectively separating Europe from Asia. Rich in copper, iron, and lead, the mountains also shelter the Caucasus Republics from the icy winds that blow down from Russia in the north. The highest mountain is Mount El'brus at 5,633 m (18,481 ft), just over the Russian border.

People
More than 50 ethnic groups live in the Caucasus Republics. Most people speak the first language of their country, but retain their own customs and culture. Communist efforts to end ethnic differences failed, and racial tension is a major problem in the region.

Refugees of the war over Nagorno-Karabakh

Georgia

Georgia is the westernmost of the three republics. About 70 per cent of the people are ethnic Georgians, most of whom belong to the Christian Georgian Orthodox Church. In recent years, the economy has suffered as a result of civil wars and ethnic disputes in the regions of Abkhazia and South Ossetia, which are trying to break away. This has damaged the Black Sea tourist industry.

Gold threads enhance bright patterns.

Textiles
Georgia produces fine silk cloth, and mulberry bushes, used to feed silkworms, grow well. Bright cotton fabrics are used to make the headscarves worn by so many of the Georgian women.

C

People
More Georgians claim to live for over 100 years than any other nationality in the world. Contributing factors are thought to be a healthy diet, regular exercise, a clean environment – and a genetic predisposition to longevity. Claims for ages over 120 have not so far been proved.

Tbilisi
Situated on the banks of the River Kura, Tbilisi, Georgia's capital since the 5th century, is a multicultural city of 1,200,000. Home to most of Georgia's Armenian minority, it has places of worship for many religions.

Tea and wine
More than 90 per cent of the tea sold in Russia is grown in Georgia, which produces about 250,000 tonnes each year. Georgia also has extensive vineyards and produces excellent red wines.

Armenia

Land-locked and isolated from its neighbours, Armenia is the smallest of the Caucasus Republics. The only way out of the country is by difficult road and rail links over the mountains to Georgia. The people, mostly ethnic Armenians, speak a unique language. The country exports fruit, brandy, and minerals such as copper.

Azerbaijan

The largest of the Caucasus Republics, Azerbaijan also has the most extensive area of farmland. Around 93 per cent of the population are Muslims. Most other people are Christian Armenians and Russians. Naxçivan, a separate part of Azerbaijan, lies within Armenian territory.

Cubes of meat are separated by peppers and onions for flavour.

Metal skewer allows cooking meat to be turned.

Food
Lamb is the main meat, often served as kebabs, with a variety of vegetables. Cooks use pine-nuts and almonds for flavouring. Local cheeses and rich desserts are specialities.

Oil industry
Natural gas and oil are extracted from the Caspian Sea. Pipelines link Baku, which is the centre of the industry, with Iran, Russia, Kazakhstan, and Turkmenistan. Other oil-related industries include the manufacture of chemicals and oil-drilling equipment.

Yerevan
Armenia's capital, Yerevan, is also its largest city. Situated on the River Razdan, it is a major cultural and industrial centre. Market traders sell fruit, vegetables, and rich, colourful rugs woven locally from silk and wool.

Territorial conflict
Nagorno-Karabakh, an enclave in southern Azerbaijan, has been the subject of armed conflict with Armenia since 1988. Most of the people here are Armenians, and Armenia claims the territory. A ceasefire was negotiated in 1994, but dispute over the area continues today.

Farming
Agriculture, mainly in the Aras river valley, employs 30 per cent of the work-force and is the country's main source of wealth. Crops include cereals and fruit such as apricots, grapes, olives, and peaches.

Soldiers on parade, Karabakh

People
Communal drinking of hot, sweet tea from tiny glasses is a typically male ceremony. As in neighbouring Georgia, the Azerbaijanis have a reputation for longevity, and it is not uncommon for people to continue working into their eighties.

FIND OUT MORE | ASIA, HISTORY OF | CHRISTIANITY | ENERGY | FARMING | ISLAM | MOUNTAINS AND VALLEYS | OIL | SOVIET UNION | TEXTILES AND WEAVING | TRADE AND INDUSTRY

CAVES

BENEATH THE GROUND, there is a network of large holes, or caves. Caves are naturally occurring chambers, formed out of rock. There are many different cave types, some housing hidden lakes and waterfalls; caverns are extensive networks of giant caves. Some caves are no bigger than a cupboard, but others are huge. The Sarawak Chamber in Malaysia is 700 m (2,296 ft) long and 50 m (164 ft) high; the world's biggest sports stadium, the Louisiana Superdome, could fit into it three times over. Damp and dark, caves have distinctive features, such as stalactites and stalagmites.

Types of cave

The biggest and most common cave systems are found in carbonate rocks, such as dolomite and limestone, but small caves form in all kinds of rock. Caves are found in many terrains, from the sea to glaciers, and can have different formations.

Sea cave
Small caves form in sea cliffs; waves force water into cracks, blasting the rock apart. The hole may emerge as a blow-hole on the cliff-top.

Fissure cave
The movement and force of an earthquake can create deep fissures, long, narrow openings, and caves.

Ice cave
Greeny-blue tunnel caves form under glaciers after spring meltwater carves out passages under the ice.

Lava cave
Tunnel-like caves form in lava – surface layers harden, and molten lava flows underneath.

Limestone cave
Most caves form in limestone. This rock has many joints and its calcium content is vulnerable to the acid in rainwater.

How a cave forms

Most of the world's biggest caves are formed by water trickling down through soluble rocks, such as limestone. The water widens joints or cracks by dissolving the rock. Rainwater is dilute carbonic acid and wears away the rock, creating a cave.

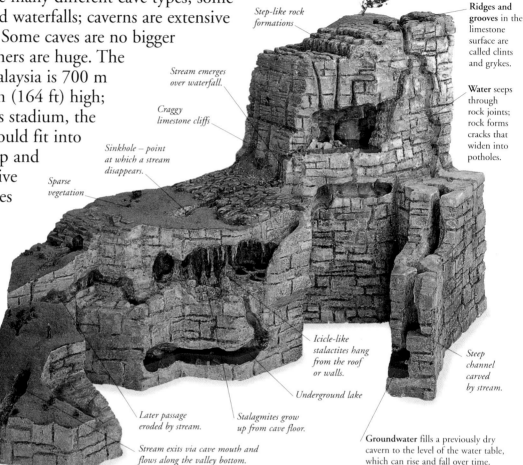

Step-like rock formations

Stream emerges over waterfall.

Craggy limestone cliffs

Sinkhole – point at which a stream disappears.

Sparse vegetation

Ridges and grooves in the limestone surface are called clints and grykes.

Water seeps through rock joints; rock forms cracks that widen into potholes.

Icicle-like stalactites hang from the roof or walls.

Underground lake

Steep channel carved by stream.

Later passage eroded by stream.

Stalagmites grow up from cave floor.

Stream exits via cave mouth and flows along the valley bottom.

Groundwater fills a previously dry cavern to the level of the water table, which can rise and fall over time.

Cave features

Formed over thousands of years, stalactites and stalagmites are found in caves. Droplets of water partially evaporate to form calcium deposits (calcite); drips create hanging stalactites on the roof, and upright stalagmites where they fall to the floor. Spiralling drips form twisted helictites. Flowstone is solidified calcite on the cave floor or walls.

Stalagmite

Stalagmites and stalactites
Stalactites can form in different ways – a long, thin curtain stalactite is formed when water runs along the cave roof. When stalactites and stalagmites meet in the middle, they form a column. The biggest stalactite, 10 m (33 ft) long, is in Pruta do Janelão, Minas Gerais, Brazil; the biggest stalagmite is over 32 m (105 ft) tall in the Krasnohorska Cave in Slovakia.

Merged stalactites

Stalactite

Stalactite with ring marks

Curtain stalactite

Potholing

Potholes are the vertical pipes that lead down to many extensive cave networks. Today, potholing is a popular but dangerous sport. Exploring and discovering caves can unearth historic treasures. The caves at Lascaux, France, for instance, which contain a wealth of prehistoric wall paintings and tools, were discovered by potholers.

FIND OUT MORE CAVE WILDLIFE COASTLINES EARTHQUAKES FOSSILS PREHISTORIC PEOPLES ROCKS AND MINERALS SPORT

CAVE WILDLIFE

A DEEP CAVE is a world of its own, with conditions far removed from those outside. Deep within a cave there is no light at all. No day and night pass, and temperatures change little with the seasons. Without light plants cannot grow, yet animal life exists even here. Some creatures enter caves for shelter or to hunt for prey; others spend their entire lives in this dark, dank environment and have adapted to move about and sense food in the dark.

Caves

Caves occur in sea cliffs, around volcanoes, and under glaciers, but the most spectacular are those formed when rainwater hollows out fissures in limestone rock. Limestone caves contain various habitats for wildlife, including narrow tunnels, chambers, streams, pools, and the partly lit entrance. Some caves, especially those in the tropics, are teeming with life. Bat colonies live in the roof, and an army of invertebrates consumes their droppings on the floor below.

Limestone cave

Plants

No plants can grow deep in a cave due to lack of light. But the cave entrance is often framed by a fringe of plants, such as liverworts, mosses, ferns, and algae, that have adapted to damp, shady conditions. Many of these plants grow without soil, sending out small roots that grip the bare rock.

Fern
Moss

Invertebrates

Caves are often full of invertebrate life. Beetles, spiders, snails, worms, and crayfish survive in large numbers in caves. They feed on debris brought in by running water or dropped by animals that feed outside.

Touch-sensitive spikes
Long antennae

Cave cricket
Scavenging cave crickets use their long, wiry antennae to feel their way past objects in the dark and towards food on the cave floor. Alert for the merest brush against them, they try to out-manoeuvre prey such as cave centipedes. Cave crickets, like cockroaches and other invertebrates, feed on debris dropped by bats and cave birds. They also eat the fallen carcasses of these animals when they die.

New Zealand glow-worm
These glow-worms are gnat larvae that live at the entrances to caves. They have evolved an ingenious method of catching food. The larvae spin dangling sticky threads that they illuminate with a light produced from their own bodies. In the darkness of a cave, the glowing threads lure and ensnare small flying insects that the larvae haul up and devour.

Larvae hauling up an insect.
Trapped insect

Eyes
Transparent legs

Cave crab
Tropical caves are often home to some small species of crab that use their pincers to pick food debris from underground streams or the cave floor. Like many cave dwellers – among them millipedes, spiders, salamanders, and shrimps – cave crabs are ghostly pale in colour. In the total darkness of deep caves, skin pigmentaion is of no value. Some animals also lose their sight due to the lack of natural light.

Birds

Some birds, such as barn owls and swifts, make nests within caves. The oilbird of South America nests deep within caves and uses rapid tongue clicks to navigate by echolocation. Colonies of oilbirds fly outside the cave at night to feed on fruit in the surrounding forests. The birds' droppings litter the cave floor below the birds' roosting ledges, and bring nutrients into the cave from far and wide.

Oilbird

Mammals

Some mammals make temporary or permanent homes in caves. The American black bear sometimes shelters in caves during the winter months, as do some foxes. Many species of bat roost, rear their young, or hibernate in the security of caves, some forming colonies thousands strong. Hanging from the roof by their hind feet, the bats are out of reach of almost all predators.

Lesser horseshoe bat
The lesser horseshoe bat is found in large numbers in caves all over Europe, Asia, and northern Africa, where it hibernates during the winter months. Like other bats, it navigates in the dark by using echolocation. It emits high-pitched calls and listens for the echoes that bounce back from the cave walls, stalactites, and other obstructions.

Wings made of elastic skin supported by bones.

Fish

A number of fish species have adapted to living in subterranean streams that flow inside cave systems throughout the world. Most are sightless, with only remnants of eyes underneath their lids, because nothing can be seen underground.

Blind cave characin
Sightless cave animals compensate for their lack of vision with a highly refined sense of touch. Most fish have a lateral line along their sides – a row of sense organs containing nerve endings. The blind cave characin of Mexico has a very prominent lateral line with which it can sense vibrations from passing prey.

Row of dark scales is the lateral line.

FIND OUT MORE BATS BIRDS CAVES CRABS AND OTHER CRUSTACEANS FERNS FLIES FISH GRASSHOPPERS AND CRICKETS HIBERNATION MOSSES AND LIVERWORTS

CELLS

ALL LIVING ORGANISMS are made of self-contained units of life called cells. Some, such as the amoeba, consist of a single cell, while others, such as humans, are made up of billions of cells. Each cell has a nucleus that contains the genetic material DNA, which provides the instructions the cell needs to maintain itself. Surrounding the nucleus is the cytoplasm, which contains the matter that makes the cell function. Forming a layer around the cytoplasm is the cell membrane, which forms the cell's boundary.

Specialized cells

Nerve cell

Sperm cell

White blood cell

Muscle cell

Most plants and animals consist of many cell types, each specialized to perform a specific task. Neurones are long cells that carry nerve impulses around an animal's body; guard cells are rigid box-like structures filled with fluid. They open and close pores on the surface of plant leaves.

Palisade mesophyll cell

These cells are found in the upper layer of the middle part, or mesophyll, of plant leaves. They are packed with chloroplasts, which contain the green pigment chlorophyll that harnesses the energy in sunlight.

Palisade mesophyll cell

Liver cells

The human liver has over 500 functions related to controlling the chemical balance of the body. These functions are carried out by cells called hepatocytes. For instance, some liver cells remove poisons from blood.

Liver cell

Abnormal cells

When cells divide inside an organism they do so in a controlled way. Sometimes, cells become abnormal and start dividing uncontrollably, leading to the production of growths called tumours. The presence of these abnormal cells and tumours causes a number of different forms of a disease called cancer.

Cancer tumour cell (yellow) being attacked by a T-lymphocyte cell (green).

Marie-François Bichat

French pathologist Marie-François Bichat (1771–1802) showed that an organ, whether a leaf of a plant or a kidney of an animal, is made of different groups of cells. He called each group a tissue, and showed that the same tissues could appear in different organs. His research formed the basis of histology – the study of organs and tissues.

Cell structure

Most cells have similar structures. They consist of a fluid called cytoplasm, a surrounding cell membrane, and a nucleus. Cytoplasm contains structures known as organelles. Plant cells, unlike animal cells, have a tough outer wall and chloroplasts.

Model of an animal cell

Endoplasmic reticulum is a maze-like network of membranes that make and store chemicals.

Golgi apparatus sorts and stores proteins.

Nucleus is the cell's control centre.

Vacuole is a small and temporary space where food and waste is stored.

Glycogen granules are food reserves or insoluble waste.

Pinocyte allows substances to filter in and out of cell.

Plasma membrane is the thin flexible layer surrounding the cytoplasm.

Mitochondrion generates energy from sugars and fatty acids.

Cytoplasm forms the bulk of the cell and gives it its shape.

Organelles are any structures that live in the cytoplasm and control special functions.

Model of a plant cell

Cellulose cell wall is a tough outer jacket mainly made of cellulose.

Plasma membrane is selectively permeable or semi-permeable and is concerned with receiving stimuli.

Chloroplast is an organelle present in green plants; it converts light energy into food by photosynthesis.

Nucleolus, centre of nucleus

Cytoplasm

Vacuole is a clear space filled with fluid.

Cell division

Cells reproduce by dividing. During cell division the nucleus divides first, followed by the cytoplasm. There are two kinds of cell division: mitosis and meiosis. Mitosis produces cells needed for growth and to replace dead cells. Meiosis produces sex cells for reproduction.

Mitosis

This produces two daughter cells that are identical to the parent cell. The cell's chromosomes (genetic material) make copies of themselves. These separate and move to opposite ends of the cell to form two new nuclei. The cytoplast splits and two new cells are formed.

Mitosis

Meiosis

This takes place in sex organs and involves two cell divisions. It makes four sex cells that differ from the parent cells because they have half the normal number of chromosomes. These sex cells are called sperm in males and ova in females.

Meiosis

Studying cells

Cells are so small they need to be studied with a microscope. Both the light microscope and the electron microscope have revealed cells' external and internal structure. For this study cells must be carefully prepared to see their details clearly.

Chemical dyes used for staining cells

Staining cells

When cells are seen under a microscope they are often transparent, showing little detail. For that reason, they are coloured with chemical stains to pick out details such as the nucleus.

FIND OUT MORE

BIOLOGY GENETICS HUMAN BODY MICROSCOPES MICROSCOPIC LIFE PHOTOSYNTHESIS PLANTS, REPRODUCTION REPRODUCTION

CELTS

PROUD WARRIORS AND SKILLED METALWORKERS, the Celts were among Europe's oldest peoples. The first tribes lived in central European hillforts, but by 400 BC, they also dominated the British Isles, Spain, Italy, and France, and even pushed on into western Asia. Unique and decorative Celtic arts spread with their mythology and religion via trade routes, but the Celts showed no interest in building an empire, or even unifying all their territories. By 50 BC, the mighty Romans and Germanic peoples had squeezed the Celts into Europe's fringes, where they converted to Christianity. Today, Celtic culture and languages survive in Ireland, Scotland, Wales, and parts of France and England.

Celtic world c.200 BC
The first phase of Celtic society probably developed around Hallstatt (now in Austria) between 1200 and 750 BC. From 500 to 50 BC there was a second phase known as La Tène, after its centre in modern France.

Celtic society

Celtic tribes were made up of three main classes: warriors, druids, and farmers. Warfare was an important part of life, so the warriors, armed with their sophisticated iron weaponry, formed an aristocracy. Druids were religious leaders, who often held the power of life and death over other tribe members. Farmers, who reared cattle and cultivated crops using iron tools, kept the economy going. Celts lived in fortified camps called hillforts. Though built for defence, hillforts were also places of trade and religious worship – some even grew into towns. Each pagan Celtic tribe had its own king, and maybe even its own gods. Skilled metalworkers probably had high status.

Thatched roof

Timber fence

Wooden frame supports roof.

Ditch

Earthen bank

Souterrain, or underground passage, used for storage or defence

Celtic hillfort

Celtic horse
The horse played a major part in early Celtic warfare and religion. A horse-goddess called Peon was worshipped first by the Celts, but then also by cavalrymen in the Roman army. There are several chalk figures cut into the rock in former Celtic areas. Some resemble the horse figures that appear on surviving Celtic coins.

Chalk bedrock

Uffington horse, England

Druids

The druids were holy men in pagan Celtic society. The earliest record of them was made by Julius Caesar, who reported that they acted as judges, led rituals in forest clearings, and used golden sickles to cut mistletoe from sacred oak trees. Druids were skilled in herbalism, and kept oral records of their tribe's history. Occasionally, they performed human and animal sacrifices. Those wanting to become druids had to study for up to 20 years.

Oak leaves

Ritual
The druids left no written records, so their rituals are shrouded in mystery. Celts worshipped many gods and spirits, particularly of trees, rocks, and mountains. One of the oldest gods, Cernunnos, is known as the lord of the beasts. He is often portrayed either wearing antlers or with horned animals, such as stags. He is also often shown wearing golden torcs, and seems to represent fertility and abundance.

Stags are often shown with Cernunnos.

Horned animals symbolize aggression and vitality.

Detail from Gundestrup Cauldron

A stone head with three faces is called a triple head.

Cult of the head
The human head was very important to the pagan Celts, as was the number "3". One custom was to cut the head off a dead enemy, hang it from a horse bridle, then put it on public display. This may have been because the druids believed that a person's soul was in his head, and had to be mastered.

Boudicca

Boudicca (d.61 AD) was queen of the Iceni, one of Britain's Celtic tribes. When the Romans conquered Britain after 43 AD, the Iceni joined forces with them to defeat a rival tribe. However, the Romans then seized Iceni lands and flogged Boudicca. She led a huge revolt, destroying the Roman settlements at St. Albans, Colchester, and London. The Romans finally defeated the rebels, and Queen Boudicca killed herself by taking poison rather than risk being captured.

Red glass
inlay

Circular
boss

Curved
patterns

Curves
(made
with
compasses)

Battersea shield

Art and decoration

The Celts were a warlike people, but they were gifted craftworkers and artists too. Celtic metalworkers excelled at decorated weaponry, jewellery, vessels, and mirrors. After the conversion to Christianity, Celtic monks in the British Isles made illustrated holy books of awesome detail. The Lindisfarne Gospels (c.700) feature 45 different colours – all made from finely ground minerals or vegetable dyes.

Battersea shield

Many of the most beautiful bronze Celtic shields were too thin for use in battle, and were purely ornamental. The Battersea shield was probably used only for military parades. It was found in the River Thames, London, in 1857.

Torc

According to the ancient Greek writer, Strabo, Celts loved to dress in colourful clothes and wear jewellery in gold, silver, or electrum (an alloy of gold and silver): "They wear torcs around their necks, and bracelets on their arms and wrists," he wrote. Many gold, bronze, and silver torcs have been found in Celtic graves.

Electrum torc

Amber

Gold
wire

Enamel

Tara brooch

Tara brooch

Brooches, such as the Tara, date from the 8th century – the early Christian era in Celtic Ireland. Only 9 cms (3.5 inches) in diameter, the Tara brooch is a magnificently detailed piece of jewellery, featuring filigree, gilt chip-carvings, enamelled glass, amber, and gold wire.

Sculpture

Animals and birds often figured in Celtic art and decoration, and certain animals were sacred, such as pigs or boars, which often appear in Celtic legend. The legendary King Arthur himself was known as "the Boar of Cornwall".

The boar
was an
important
symbol for
the Celts.

Bronze boar

Metalworking

As well as sophisticated iron weaponry and farming tools, skilled Celtic metalworkers produced high-status goods for chieftains, and elaborately decorated items for trade throughout Europe. In Gaul (modern France) the smiths even had their own god – a smith-god known as Sucellos.

Sword and
shield

Swirling
abstract
pattern

Chieftain's bronze couch, Germany

Wagon pulled
by horses

Wheel

Female
figure

Celtic
cross

Christianity

During the Roman occupation, Christianity came to Britain – but failed to take deep root. However one convert, St Patrick, went on to convert pagan Celtic Ireland in the 5th century. After this, the Celts adopted the religion with gusto and Ireland became a Christian stronghold for the next three centuries.

Monks

Celtic Christianity was famous for the harshness of the monks' lives, and the enthusiasm of their devotions. From c.500, monasteries ranged from simple cells for single monks to communities the size of towns.

Early Christian church, Ireland

Missionaries

After Irish Christians set up monasteries in Britain, France, and northern Italy, they started to convert the native peoples. The monks loved learning and helped to keep culture alive in Europe, during the chaos that followed the decline of the Roman Empire. Irish monks operating from the island of Iona, off western Scotland, produced the beautiful *Book of Kells*, c.800, with its extraordinary illuminated (decorated) lettering.

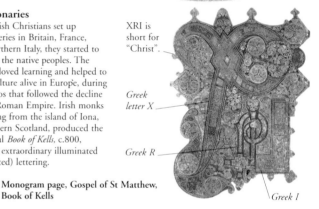

XRI is
short for
"Christ".

Greek
letter X

Greek R

Greek I

Monogram page, Gospel of St Matthew, Book of Kells

Myths

The pagan Celts had a rich oral tradition. Their stories included myths about mighty gods, such as the Welsh Bran the Blessed, and the Irish Dagda (Father of All); legends about fearless warrior-heroes, such as Cuchulain and King Arthur; and tales of the "shape-changers" – magical creatures from the Underworld. Since the Celts had no written language, monks later wrote down the stories for future generations.

Merlin

The first written legends of the Welsh wizard, Merlin, said that he was a Celtic boy whose father was the devil. At an early age, he found he could foretell the future. In later stories, he appeared as the wizard and mentor of King Arthur of England.

Engraving of the wizard Merlin

Languages

Two types of Celtic language continue to be spoken and written today: Brythonic (Breton, Welsh, Cornish) and Gaelic (Irish, Scots Gaelic, Manx). They may all be traced back to a common ancient Indo-European language.

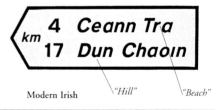

km

4 Ceann Tra
17 Dun Chaoin

Modern Irish

"Hill"

"Beach"

FIND OUT MORE

BARBARIANS   CHRISTIANITY   EUROPE, HISTORY OF   IRELAND, HISTORY OF   METAL   MYTHS AND LEGENDS   RELIGIONS

CENTRAL AMERICA

SEVEN SMALL COUNTRIES make up Central America, a tapering neck of land that connects northern North America to South America. The Pacific Ocean lies to the west, and the Caribbean Sea, an arm of the Atlantic Ocean, lies to the east. The two oceans are connected by the Panama Canal, a short cut that saves ships months of sailing time. The original peoples of Central America were Native Americans, conquered by the Spaniards in the 1500s. Since gaining independence, these countries have had periods of turbulent politics and unstable economies.

Tropical rainforest
The hot, tropical climate and high rainfall of Central America's Caribbean coast gives rise to vast areas of dense rainforest, particularly in Belize and Guatemala, and on Nicaragua's Mosquito Coast. Economic pressure is forcing people to cut and clear parts of the forest for crops.

Physical features

Central America has a backbone of rugged volcanic peaks and massive crater lakes that run from Guatemala down to Costa Rica. The Pacific coast is flat and fertile, and the eastern lowlands, stretching to the Caribbean Sea, are wild, empty swamps and rainforests, with little cultivation.

Sierra Madre
The Sierra Madre is the highland region of Guatemala and El Salvador, and is a continuation of the Sierra Madre of Mexico. It includes Tajumulco, an extinct volcano, which, at 4,220 m (13,845 ft), is the highest peak in Central America. Most Guatemalans live in this cooler region.

Lake Nicaragua
Covering an area of 7,925 sq km (3,060 sq miles), Lake Nicaragua is the only freshwater lake in the world to contain sea fish, including sharks, which swim up the San Juan River from the Caribbean Sea. The lake is dotted with 310 islands, the largest of which is Ometepe.

Regional climate

25°C (77°F) 22°C (72°F)

1,615 mm (63 in)

Throughout Central America the climate is tropical and hot, with a distinct rainy season from May until November or December. Mountain and upland areas are cooler. Rainfall is higher along the Caribbean coast than on the Pacific side, and can be as high as 6,600 mm (260 in) per year.

Pan-American Highway

The Pan-American Highway runs the length of Central America, providing an important road link between North and South America. In the north, the road connects with the US highway network, and in the south, it extends as far as Chile – a total distance of about 9,000 km (5,593 miles) from the Mexican border.

Pan-American Highway, Costa Rica

Guatemala

Once the hub of the Mayan civilization, modern Guatemala is Central America's largest and most populated country, and has the biggest manufacturing sector. Guatemalan factories produce foods, textiles, paper, pharmaceuticals, and rubber goods. Plantations in the south grow coffee, bananas, cotton, and sugar-cane for export.

GUATEMALA FACTS

CAPITAL CITY Guatemala City

AREA 108,890 sq km (42,043 sq miles)

POPULATION 11,400,000

MAIN LANGUAGES Spanish, Quiché, Mam, Kekchí, Cakchiquel

MAJOR RELIGION Christian

CURRENCY Quetzal

Farming

About half of Guatemala's people are of Mayan descent. Most live in the western highlands, growing crops and rearing animals, which they trade at local markets. People from distant hamlets use weekly markets as a chance to socialize and keep abreast of local news.

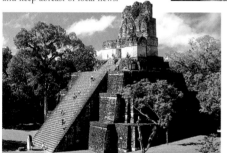

Tikal

Tourism is a growing industry in Guatemala, and each year about 500,000 people visit the country's Mayan ruins. Tikal, once a great Mayan city, was founded in 600 BC and flourished until about AD 890, when it was suddenly deserted. The city once had about 40,000 inhabitants.

Honduras

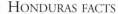

A small, poor country, Honduras relied for many years on bananas and timber as its main sources of income. However, since the banana industry was devastated by Hurricane Mitch in 1998, coffee, flowers, and fruit now supply the country's income. Unemployment is high, and most people live in small villages.

HONDURAS FACTS

CAPITAL CITY Tegucigalpa

AREA 112,090 sq km (43,278 sq miles)

POPULATION 6,350,000

MAIN LANGUAGES Spanish, English Creole, Garifuna

MAJOR RELIGION Christian

CURRENCY Lempira

People

About 90 per cent of Hondurans are *mestizos*, of mixed European and Native American descent. Along the Caribbean coast are settlements of the Garifuna, descendants of black slaves who swam ashore more than 350 years ago when slave ships from Nigeria were shipwrecked off the Honduran coast.

Hurricane Mitch

The vast banana plantations in the northeast of the Honduras were wiped out by Hurricane Mitch in 1998. The storms caused £2 million ($3 billion) worth of damage and the deaths of 5,600 people. Bananas comprised 40 per cent of the country's exports, but have been replaced by coffee, shrimp, and melon.

El Salvador

The smallest country in Central America, El Salvador has a rugged landscape that includes more than 20 volcanoes. A thick layer of volcanic ash and lava provide ideal conditions for growing coffee. Economically, El Salvador is still recovering from a civil war that raged between 1979 and 1992 and major earthquakes in 2001.

EL SALVADOR FACTS

CAPITAL CITY San Salvador

AREA 21,040 sq km (8,124 sq miles)

POPULATION 6,300,000

MAIN LANGUAGE Spanish

MAJOR RELIGION Christian

CURRENCY Colón and US dollar

People

El Salvador is Central America's most densely populated country. There are about 304 people per sq km (788 per sq mile) and the population is growing at about two-and-a-half per cent a year. Almost 90 per cent are *mestizos*, and three-quarters are Roman Catholics. More than one-third are farmers who scrape a living in the highlands.

Deforestation

Today, only about five per cent of El Salvador is still forested. Vast tracts of forest, including cedar, oak, and mahogany, have been felled for export and to clear land for farming cash crops such as coffee.

Belize

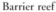

As most of Belize is dense rainforest, most of its small population live along the Caribbean coast. The two largest groups are the *mestizos* and Creoles, who also have African blood, and are descended from black slaves who were marooned in Belize in the 17th century.

BELIZE FACTS

CAPITAL CITY Belmopan

AREA 22,960 sq km (8,865 sq miles)

POPULATION 200,000

MAIN LANGUAGES English, English Creole, Spanish, Maya, Garifuna

MAJOR RELIGION Christian

CURRENCY Belizean dollar

Barrier reef

Protecting Belize's swampy coastal plains from flooding is the world's second largest barrier reef, 290 km (190 miles) long. The reef supports a wide variety of colourful fish.

Belmopan

Belize City, the country's chief port, was the capital for many years. In 1960, a hurricane and tidal wave caused severe damage, so in 1970, a new capital, Belmopan, was built in the centre of the country, far from coastal storms. Its population is only 4,000, mostly civil servants.

C

Nicaragua

Occasionally called the land of lakes and volcanoes, Nicaragua lies at the heart of Central America. Volcanoes and earthquakes frequently shake the country, and Hurricane Mitch caused great damage in 1998. In 1978, Nicaragua experienced a civil war between the left-wing Sandinista government and right-wing "contras", backed by the USA. The war ended in 1990.

Delivery of sugar-cane

Farming
Agriculture employs about one-quarter of the work-force, growing cotton, coffee, sugar, bananas, and meat for export. The country has also developed related industries, such as sugar refineries and canning factories that process agricultural produce.

People
Mestizos make up 70 per cent of Nicaraguans. The rest are whites or blacks, descended from Africans who were taken to Nicaragua as plantation workers in the 18th century. Three-quarters of the population is below the age of 30. Families are tight-knit, and up to three generations may live together.

Chilli pepper
Garlic
Black pepper
Onion
Spring onion
Hot chilli sauce

Food
Nicaraguans enjoy maize roasted on the cob. Meat and bean dishes are spiced with pepper and garlic and scooped up in thin pancakes called tortillas, which are made from maize flour. Food is often topped with hot chilli sauce.

NICARAGUA FACTS
CAPITAL CITY	Managua
AREA	130,000 sq km (50,193 sq miles)
POPULATION	5,100,000
MAIN LANGUAGES	Spanish, English Creole, Miskito
MAJOR RELIGION	Christian
CURRENCY	Córdoba oro

Costa Rica

Unlike its neighbours, Costa Rica is a stable and peaceful country with a democratically elected government. The army was abolished in 1949. Costa Ricans enjoy excellent schools and hospitals. Most people are *mestizos* of Spanish origin. In the Puerto Limón area on the east coast, one-third are English-speaking blacks, descended from plantation

Costa Rica has some 750 species of bird – more than the whole of the USA.

COSTA RICA FACTS
CAPITAL CITY	San José
AREA	51,100 sq km (19,730 sq miles)
POPULATION	4,000,000
MAIN LANGUAGES	Spanish, English Creole, Bribri, Cabecar
MAJOR RELIGION	Christian
CURRENCY	Colón

San José
Founded in 1737, San José became Costa Rica's capital in 1823. With many parks and a mix of traditional and modern Spanish architecture, San José is a commercial centre and has food-processing factories. It has rail links with Pacific and Caribbean ports and lies on the Pan-American Highway.

Tourism
More than 20 per cent of Costa Rica has been set aside to create a network of national parks, including volcanic peaks and undisturbed tropical forest rich in plant and animal species. Many ecotourists are attracted by the country's resident wildlife, such as jaguars, giant sea turtles, crocodiles, and armadillos.

Coffee
Costa Rican coffee is some of the world's finest, and fetches a high price. It grows in the rich black volcanic soils near the capital, San José. Costa Rica was the first Central American country to grow the beans. Bananas are the other leading cash crop.

Dark-roasted coffee beans have a deep, rich taste.

Panama

Occupying the southernmost and narrowest part of Central America, Panama is cut in two by the Panama Canal, which links the Atlantic and Pacific Oceans. A country of swamps, mountains, and grassy plains, Panama has some of Central America's wildest rainforest.

Some 14,000 ships pass through the canal every year, earning Panama valuable toll fees.

PANAMA FACTS
CAPITAL CITY	Panama City
AREA	77,080 sq km (29,761 sq miles)
POPULATION	2,900,000
MAIN LANGUAGES	Spanish, English, Creole, Indian languages
MAJOR RELIGION	Christian
CURRENCY	Balboa

Financial centres
At opposite ends of the Panama Canal, Colón and Panama City are important business centres, providing banking, financial, and insurance services. A free trade zone in Colón enables goods to be imported and exported free of duty.

Panama Canal
Linking the Caribbean Sea with the Pacific Ocean, the Panama Canal was built by the USA, and opened in 1914. It is more than 65 km (40 miles) long, and passes through three sets of locks. The length, which is the distance between deep-water points of entry, is 82 km (51 miles).

Shrimps
Panama has a busy and important fishing fleet. The leading catch is shrimps, which form 11 per cent of the country's exports. Anchovetas, small fishes used for fish meal, make up three per cent of exports. Other catches include herrings and lobsters.

CENTRAL AMERICA, HISTORY OF

RICHLY ENDOWED WITH natural resources, Central America has had a violent history, with civil wars, revolutions, and terrible repression. The area was home to the great Maya civilization, but the Spanish arrived in the 16th century and began to conquer and settle Mexico and the lands to the southeast. As a Spanish colony, the area was called the Captaincy General of Guatemala and had its capital in Guatemala City. After gaining independence in the 1820s, the region split into separate nations ruled by a few rich families. During the 20th century, the United States often intervened in Central American politics with aid and arms.

Maya

Maya civilization was at its peak in the tropical forest lowland area of Guatemala from about AD 250 to 900. Here the Maya built cities, with step pyramids. Around AD 900, the Toltecs from the north conquered the Maya. The Maya revived around 1200, but were in decline by the time of the Spanish conquest.

Maya pottery bowl

Captaincy General

A small group of wealthy Spanish merchants born in Central America dominated the rich trade in indigo dye, and also the political life of the colony. The area was ruled by a Captain General of Guatemala and his council at Guatemala City.

Independence

In 1821, following the example of Mexico, Central America declared independence. A federation of new states was proposed, but politicians disagreed over what form it should take. The disputes led to war and the break-up of the area into five self-governing republics in 1838.

Panama Canal

With military support from the USA, Panama separated from Colombia in 1903. US engineers built a great canal linking the Atlantic and the Pacific. The Panama Canal, which runs across the south of the country, opened in 1914. After this, the Panamanian economy came to depend almost entirely on the USA.

Coffee

In the 1850s, there was a high world demand for coffee. Rich landowners began to grow coffee in large quantities, forcing local people off their land. Coffee export enabled Costa Rica and El Salvador to achieve some stability in the late 19th century, but changes in coffee prices brought problems later.

Coffee growing, El Salvador

Coffee beans

Modern Central America

Immense differences between rich and poor, combined with the strong economic, political, and cultural influence of the United States, made Central America a turbulent region in the 20th century. Many rulers were dictators and governments changed rapidly, giving little chance of political stability. There were many revolutions, which were often suppressed with huge loss of life.

US intervention

During the 20th century, the United States was closely involved in the affairs of Central America. In 1909, the US supported a right-wing revolution in Nicaragua, and US marines occupied the country until 1933 when, after a guerilla war, Augusto Sandino (1895–1934) forced them to withdraw. Later, the US intervened to stop left-wing revolutions and to prevent the spread of communism during the Cold War. More recently, the US supported the Contras (right-wing guerillas) in Nicaragua and, in 1989, invaded Panama to oust corrupt ruler General Manuel Noriega.

Students in El Salvador erect a statue of Augusto Sandino.

Somoza family

Anastasio Somoza and his sons ruled Nicaragua from 1937–79. The economy grew under their rule, but there was widespread corruption. In 1979, an uprising led by the Sandinistas (a left-wing group named after the former socialist leader Augusto Sandino), ousted the Somozas from power.

Daniel Ortega

Socialist politician Daniel Ortega (b.1945) became the Nicaraguan head of state in 1981 and won free elections in 1984. But he failed to free his country from the conflict between the right-wing politicians backed by the USA and his own left-wing allies.

Oscar Romero

Archbishop Oscar Romero (1917–80) was head of the Catholic church in El Salvador. His reading of the Bible led him to demand better conditions for the poor. Many Catholics began to get involved in social activism in the 1970s. This annoyed the government, which employed death squads to kill priests. When Romero declared that armed struggle was the only option left, he too was shot dead.

CHARLEMAGNE

ON CHRISTMAS DAY, 800, a remarkable emperor was crowned in Europe. His name was Charles, and he was known as Charles the Great, or Charlemagne. He was king of the Franks of northern France, and managed to create a large empire after the turmoil that followed the fall of Rome. Under Charlemagne, Europe enjoyed a period of peace and unity it had not had for 400 years. Yet the king was illiterate and brutal, and held his empire together only by force.

Early life
Charlemagne was born in Aachen in what is now Germany in about 742. He was the oldest son of Pepin, king of the Franks, and inherited his kingdom in 768, jointly with his brother, Carloman. When Carloman died in 771, Charlemagne became sole ruler of the Franks.

Carolingian Empire

In order to control his vast territory, Charlemagne installed bishops and counts in each district to run both the religious and the secular affairs of the empire. He supported an educational system based on the monasteries, and introduced a legal system that owed much to the Roman Empire.

Marches
In order to protect his vast empire, Charlemagne established marches, or buffer zones, along the southern border with Muslim Spain and the eastern border with the various Germanic tribes. Troops of armoured horsemen patrolled the marches to protect the empire against raids across its lengthy borders.

Extent of the empire
By the time of his death in 814, Charlemagne controlled an empire that stretched from Hamburg in northern Germany to south of Rome, and from the Atlantic Ocean to the River Danube. He converted the warlike Saxons to Christianity, and subdued the Lombard kingdom of northern Italy.

Charlemagne's realm

  Frankish lands, 714

  Adjoining territories

— Empire of Charlemagne

Charlemagne used cavalrymen to protect the borders of his empire.

Double-edged blade

Socket to attach shaft

Carolingian spearhead

A new Roman emperor

In the 8th century, the Pope's security as head of the Christian church was threatened by the Lombards from northern Italy. In 773, Charlemagne conquered Lombardy. To recognize his support, the Pope gave Charlemagne the title of Emperor of the Romans.

Coin of Charlemagne

Coronation
Charlemagne visited Rome in 800, and Pope Leo III crowned him and paid him homage. For the first time since the Roman Empire, Christian Europe was united, and the idea of a Holy Roman Empire was born.

Dark Ages

For centuries, historians talked of the time after the fall of the Roman Empire as the Dark Ages. But we now know that the period was a time of great achievement in scholarship and the arts. This activity reached its height under Charlemagne.

Aachen
At his capital of Aachen (Aix-la-Chapelle), Charlemagne created a brilliant court where art flourished. He built a vast palace and chapel which some visitors thought was like a "second Rome".

Scholarship
Scholars came from all over Europe to Aachen to work for Charlemagne. They rescued classical Latin learning from oblivion, and ensured that future generations could learn about the Roman Empire.

CHARLEMAGNE

c.742 Born in Aachen.

768 Succeeds to Frankish Empire with his brother Carloman.

771 Takes sole control of empire.

772 Begins conquest of Saxony in northern Germany.

773 Subdues Lombards in Italy.

778 Conquers Bavaria in southern Germany.

795 Establishes Spanish march to protect his kingdom from Muslim Spain.

800 Crowned emperor of the Romans by Pope Leo III.

814 Dies and is buried at Aachen.

FIND OUT MORE   FEUDALISM   FRANCE, HISTORY OF   GERMANY, HISTORY OF   HOLY ROMAN EMPIRE   KNIGHTS AND HERALDRY   ROMAN EMPIRE   SPAIN, HISTORY OF   WRITING

CHAVÍN

FROM THE 10TH to the 1st centuries BC, a brilliant civilization flourished in Peru. It is known today as Chavín, after the important town of Chavín de Huántar in central Peru. Its people produced large temples, fine textiles, and created religious art in a distinctive style. They were also the first people to unify the flat coastal region of Peru with the high Andes Mountains beyond. By doing this, they prepared the way for other important Peruvian civilizations, such as the Incas.

Chimú
Huari
Tiahuanaco
Chimú and Huari

Civilizations
Other cultures, such as the Chimú, grew up in the Andes region after the Chavín declined.

Chavín de Huántar
The main city of the Chavín civilization was built at a natural transport interchange. It lay on the Mosna River next to two passes into the mountains. The city was therefore well placed for trade, with food such as chillies and salt coming down to the city through the mountain passes.

Castillo
The people of Chavín de Huántar built stone temples at the centre of their city. The famous Old Temple or Castillo was a complex stone structure, containing many intricate passages. Some of these were probably drainage ducts, designed to channel away water from the temple. The adjoining rooms may have been storerooms for offerings and religious equipment.

Art
Chavín art was highly elaborate. Chavín artists made carved stone reliefs, statuettes in precious metals, and beautiful textiles, some of which have survived. Their favourite subjects were gods and goddesses, and the priests, birds, and animals that attended them. Many works of art, such as the textiles and gold statuettes, were small and easily portable. They were traded far and wide in South America, and later cultures copied their styles.

Kennings
Chavín sculptors liked to use the kenning, a type of visual pun, to represent parts of the body. Instead of carving a person's face realistically, they made up their features using repeated elements such as eyes or snakes. Many Chavín carvings, like this stone relief of a god, are therefore intriguing but difficult to understand.

Jaguar vessel

Animal-figure bowl

Pottery vessel
Andean peoples, such as the Chavín, made highly decorated pottery vessels with tall, curved handles. This example, from Chavín de Huántar, has the face of a jaguar god with a gold nose ornament and large, dangling earrings.

Ornate bowl
This bowl in the shape of an animal is another example of the skill of the Chavín potters' art. It may have been used in a religious ceremony, or adorned the table of a wealthy member of the Chavín nobility.

God carries staff in his right hand.

God carries shield with cross design in his left hand.

El Lanzón
This was probably the main god of the Old Temple. Its statue is found in one of the innermost rooms in the building. It was a human figure that had cat-like teeth, suggesting that it was part-human, part-jaguar, like many ancient gods of South and Central America.

Religion
The Chavín people had several gods, including a creature called El Lanzón, or "the smiling god". His statue was placed in a central room in the temple at Chavín de Huántar. Above the statue was a hole. A hidden person could speak through this hole, giving the impression that the god himself was speaking.

The staff god
Another important Chavín deity is known as the staff god. This figure is shown in carved reliefs waving a long staff. He was often shown with crops such as manioc, gourds, and peppers, and was thought to be the provider and protector of these valuable foodstuffs.

After the Chavín
Several civilizations dominated the Andes after Chavín declined. Tiahuanaco, another highland culture, and their neighbours the Huari, flourished from AD 500 to 900. On the coast, the Chimú were the dominant people from the 10th to 15th centuries, until they were conquered by the Incas.

Vessel from Tiahuanaco

Tiahuanaco
This highland empire was a strong, centralized state based in a city on a high plain some 4,000 m (13,100 ft) above sea-level. Its monuments included the Gateway of the Sun, which was carved out of a single block of stone.

Face of Sun god

Carved lintel

Typical square-headed opening

Gateway of the Sun

FIND OUT MORE

GODS AND GODDESSES

INCAS

POTTERY AND CERAMICS

SOUTH AMERICA, HISTORY OF

CHEMISTRY

THERE IS MORE TO CHEMISTRY than messy experiments in laboratories – doctors use it to fight diseases, chefs use it to cook food, and farmers use it to increase the growth of their crops. Chemistry is the branch of science that studies the structure of different elements and compounds. It also investigates how they change and interact with each other during processes called chemical reactions.

Chemical change

When a pile of orange ammonium dichromate crystals is heated by a flame, a chemical reaction occurs. Heat, light, and gases are given off, and a mound of grey-green ash is left behind. The ash not only looks different from the crystals, but it also has a different chemical make-up – it has changed into the substance chromium oxide.

The reaction is so vigorous that a cloud of ash is hurled into the air.

Pile of crystals is lit by a flame.

Ash

Ammonium dichromate crystals

Antoine and Marie Lavoisier

The French chemist Antoine Lavoisier (1743–94) showed that burning is a chemical reaction, that air is a mixture of gases, and that water is a compound of hydrogen and oxygen. His wife, Marie (1758–1836), translated and illustrated many of his scientific works.

$$2H_2 \quad + \quad O_2 \quad \longrightarrow \quad 2H_2O$$

Chemical equations

Scientists write equations to describe what happens during reactions. The equation above shows how hydrogen (H_2) and oxygen (O_2) react in the ratio of 2 to 1 to make water (H_2O).

Rates of reaction

Reactions can be speeded up by making the reacting particles come into contact with each other more often. One way of doing this is by increasing a reactant's surface area. Sulphuric acid reacts more rapidly with powdered chalk than with chalk pieces, because the powder has a greater surface area.

There is a gentle fizzing as carbon dioxide gas is given off.

Faster rate of reaction causes reactants to spill out of beaker.

Dilute sulphuric acid on powdered chalk

Dilute sulphuric acid on chalk pieces

Catalysts

Compounds called catalysts speed up a chemical reaction by helping substances react together. The catalysts are left unchanged by the reaction. Many cars are fitted with a catalytic converter to remove polluting gases from engine fumes. The converter forces the gases into close contact with catalysts. The catalysts make the gases react rapidly with each other, producing less harmful gases that escape out of the exhaust.

Chemical reactions

During a chemical reaction, substances called reactants break apart and new substances called products form. Energy is taken in to break the bonds between the reactants' atoms. As the atoms link up again in different combinations to make the products, new bonds form and energy is given out.

Exothermic reactions
In an exothermic reaction, such as burning, more energy is given out than is taken in from the surroundings.

Endothermic reactions
Most of the reactions that occur in cooking are endothermic, which means that more energy is taken in than is given out.

Oxidation and reduction

When iron rusts, a reaction occurs between the iron and oxygen in the air. The iron gains oxygen, and an orange-brown compound called iron oxide forms. A reaction in which a substance gains oxygen is called oxidation. When oxidation occurs, there is a simultaneous reaction called reduction, in which a substance loses oxygen. When iron oxidizes, the air is reduced as it loses oxygen to the iron.

Coating of iron oxide forms on the metal.

Rusting iron

Reversible reactions

Many chemical reactions permanently change the reactants, but reversible reactions can go both forwards and backwards. For example, when nitrogen dioxide is heated, it breaks down into nitrogen monoxide and oxygen. Cooling this mixture makes the two gases react to form nitrogen dioxide again.

Nitrogen dioxide gas is brown.

Heating

Cooling

Symbol for reversible reaction

Nitrogen monoxide and oxygen are both colourless gases.

Nitrogen dioxide

Nitrogen monoxide and oxygen

Chemical industry

The chemical industry is one of the world's largest and most important industries. It involves taking raw materials – such as air, oil, water, coal, metal ores, limestone, and plants – and using chemical reactions to change them into useful products. These products include food, clothing, medicine, pesticides and fertilizers, paints and dyes, soaps and detergents, plastics, and glassware.

1 A container of full-cream milk is allowed to stand for a day or so. The curds are removed and then heated.

Acetic acid

2 Acetic acid is added to the warm curds. This causes a white, rubbery material called casein to form in the liquid.

Organic chemistry

The study of carbon compounds is called organic chemistry, because all living organisms depend on carbon compounds for their existence. Today, chemists can also create synthetic carbon compounds. Natural and synthetic carbon compounds occur in a wide range of materials, such as food, fuel, paint, textiles, and plastics. This experiment shows how paint can be made from casein – an organic compound derived from milk.

Casein forms in curds.

3 The casein is removed by straining the liquid, It is kneaded in warm water and then dried.

Casein hardens as it dries.

4 Casein can then be mixed with other materials to form paint. The casein is used to bind the pigment to the surface.

Casein-based paint

Aliphatics

Organic compounds containing a chain of carbon atoms linked by single, double, or triple bonds are called aliphatics. The aliphatic ethane occurs in natural gas, and ethene is used to make plastics.

Ethane (C_2H_6)

Double bond

Single bond

Ethene (C_2H_4)

Aromatics

The strong-smelling organic compounds called aromatics contain a ring of six carbon atoms. Benzene, the simplest aromatic, is a colourless liquid obtained from coal, natural gas, and petroleum. Aromatics are used to make vivid dyes called anilines.

Carbon atoms (black)

Benzene (C_6H_6)

Hydrogen atoms (white)

Fats and oils

Liquid vegetable oil is an unsaturated fat – a type of fat in which some of the carbon atoms are linked by double bonds. When the oil reacts with hydrogen, the double bonds break and the carbon atoms link up with extra hydrogen atoms, forming a solid fat such as margarine. Solid fats contain only single bonds between their carbon atoms. These fats are said to be saturated because they cannot bond with more hydrogen atoms.

Liquid oil **Solid fat**

Polymers

Polymers are giant molecules that consist of winding chains of thousands of small organic molecules called monomers. Fats, starches, and proteins are natural polymers; plastics and artificial fibres are made of synthetic polymers. Polythene contains polymers made of many ethene monomers joined together.

Plastics, such as polythene and PVC, are made up of polymers.

Plastic products

Electrochemistry

The study of the relationship between electricity and chemical substances is called electrochemistry. Many compounds consist of electrically charged particles called ions, which form when atoms lose or gain electrons. A battery uses a chemical reaction to generate an electric current.

Electrons flow towards copper plate.

Simple battery

As the zinc dissolves in the acid, the zinc atoms lose electrons and become ions.

Dilute sulphuric acid

Current lights bulb.

Electrons flow through wire as an electric current.

Electrolysis

The process of splitting up a compound by passing an electric current through it is known as electrolysis. Two metal or carbon rods called electrodes are placed in the compound and connected to a battery. As electricity flows through the compound, positive ions are attracted to the negative electrode (the cathode), and negative ions are attracted to the positive electrode (the anode), causing the compound to split apart.

Chlorine gas collects at top of tube.

Deposits of copper metal form as copper ions move to cathode.

Chlorine ions move to anode and form chlorine gas.

Electrolysis of copper chloride solution

Research into respiration

Geochemist examining rocks

Biochemistry

The study of the chemistry of living organisms and the chemical processes, such as respiration, that take place within them is called biochemistry. The discoveries of biochemists are used in industry, medicine, and agriculture.

Geochemistry

The Earth's composition and the chemical structure of rocks are studied in geochemistry. The findings of geochemists give us a greater knowledge of the Earth's history and help us to find ores, minerals, and other resources.

Alfred Nobel

The Swedish chemist Alfred Nobel (1833–96) invented the explosives dynamite in 1867 and gelignite in 1875, which made him very rich. On his death, he left his vast wealth to pay for a series of annual awards – the Nobel Prizes – for achievements in science, art, and medicine.

Timeline

2 BC Egyptian alchemists try to change "base" metals, such as lead, into gold.

1661 Robert Boyle, an Irish scientist, realizes that chemical reactions can be explained by the existence of small particles.

1770s Antoine Lavoisier investigates compounds such as air and water.

1807 Englishman Humphry Davy uses electrolysis to discover the element sodium.

Davy's equipment

1808 English scientist John Dalton proposes that each element has its own unique type of atom.

1830s German chemists focus on studying carbon and its compounds.

1909 American Leo Baekeland makes the first fully synthetic plastic – Bakelite.

1939 Linus Pauling, an American chemist, explains the nature of chemical bonds between atoms and molecules.

Bakelite radio set

FIND OUT MORE

ACIDS AND ALKALIS   ATOMS AND MOLECULES   DYES AND PAINTS   ELECTRICITY   ELEMENTS   GLASS   MEDICINE   MIXTURES AND COMPOUNDS   PLASTICS AND RUBBER

CHESS AND OTHER BOARD GAMES

BOTH CHILDREN AND ADULTS enjoy games, whether for the challenge of perfecting a skill, the excitement of competition, or simply for fun. Board games, in which competing players move pieces on a special board following rules agreed in advance, are particularly popular. They have a long history, and exist in every culture. They range from demanding games of skill and strategy, such as the ancient game of chess, to more simple games of chance, like snakes and ladders, where a throw of the dice determines the winner.

Strategy games

Games of strategy are challenging, for superior skill, concentration, and tactics decide the winner. Chance plays no part. In most strategy games two players aim to cross the board, or to encircle or capture their opponent's pieces.

Go
Go, also known as *wei-ch'i*, is at least 4,300 years old. It is extremely popular in China, Japan, and Korea. Players capture areas of the board by surrounding them with their own pieces.

Chess

Chess is a war-game. Two players aim to capture, or take, the other's pieces, ultimately trapping the opponent's king. This situation, known as checkmate, occurs when the king cannot be protected by his own pieces, and cannot move without being taken. The word checkmate comes from the Persian *shah-mat* (the king is dead). Chess can be enjoyed at all levels: by beginners, or contested by grandmasters in international competition.

The board has 64 squares.

Each player starts with 16 pieces.

Illumination from Persian treatise on chess, undated

Kasparov plays the computer

History of chess
It is thought that chess originated in China or India more than 1,400 years ago. It spread to North Africa and was introduced to Europe after the Muslim conquest of Spain. Early pieces were based on an Asian army, with elephants, chariots, and footsoldiers.

Pieces
Chess pieces consist of eight pawns, two bishops, knights, and rooks (castles), a king, and a queen. Each piece has its distinctive moves: pawns, for instance, can only move one space forward, while the queen can move in any direction, as far as is needed.

Computer chess
Computers can be programmed to play chess against humans. In 1997, the chess world was shocked when a supercomputer beat the Russian world champion Gary Kasparov (b.1963) in a match. A vast memory for the tactics of past games gives computers an edge.

Race games

Many board games are races, where the winner is the first player to reach a certain part of the board or remove all their pieces. Some race games depend on luck, when a throw of the dice decides how quickly a player moves. This allows players of different ages or levels to compete fairly against each other.

Starting position for mancalah

Mancalah
There are many varieties of this ancient game of skill from Africa. Two or more players compete to clear their side of the board. Each takes turns to pick up a pile of pebbles, dropping them one by one in the hollows.

Pachisi
In India, pachisi is a popular game. Four players race counters around a cross-shaped board; they throw dice or shells to see how many spaces to move. Many other games, such as ludo, are based on pachisi.

Starting position for backgammon

Men playing pachisi in India.

Backgammon
Invented 5,000 years ago in Asia, backgammon is a fast-paced game for two players. It draws on both skill and chance, and is most popular around the Mediterranean. The first player to remove all his or her "men" from the board wins.

Playing cards

Card games do not need a special board, but must be played on a flat surface. Generally, games are for two or four players. Some games, such as bridge, require concentration and skill, and are played at international competition level; games such as poker, which rely more on luck, are often played by gamblers for money.

A pack of cards contains 52 cards, divided into four groups, known as suits.

Hearts

Diamonds   Spades   Clubs

FIND OUT MORE   CHINA AND TAIWAN   COMPUTERS   INDIA AND SRI LANKA   JAPAN   SPAIN, HISTORY OF

C

Chess and other board games
Chess pieces

King moves one square at a time in any direction.

Bishop moves diagonally across the board.

Rook travels in straight lines but not diagonally.

Pawn moves forward one square at a time.

Knight can jump over other pieces to new position.

Queen can move in any direction, but cannot jump.

Board games

Game accessories

Draught piece

Draughts is a game of skill that was played in ancient Egypt.

Monopoly, patented in 1935, can be adapted to show streets of any major city in the world.

Pieces move around board collecting pies.

Monopoly tokens

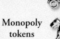

Trivial Pursuit, introduced in 1982, is available in a range of editions.

Players build up words from letter blocks.

Each player chooses a character.

Harry Potter, launched in 2000, is based on JK Rowling's children's book series of the same title.

Marbles are used as pieces.

Scrabble, originally known as Criss-Cross, is a word game that was devised in 1931.

Scrabble letters

Solitare is game of skill that is played by only one person.

Cluedo, a detective game played around the world, was created in 1944.

Ludo, a game for two to four players, originated from an ancient Indian game called pachisi.

A compendium is a collection of different board games contained in one box.

Snakes and Ladders is a game of chance. Players move their pieces up ladders or down snakes.

C

CHILDREN'S LITERATURE

WRITTEN LITERATURE has existed for more than 3,000 years, but it is only in the last 300 years that literature has been created especially for children. Before then, children listened to oral fables and folk tales. Early children's books were educational, but in the 19th century many new forms, or genres, developed such as adventure and fantasy stories, and picture books.

Books

Finnish
French
German
Japanese
Russian
Swedish
Italian
Iranian

Children's books are produced in more styles, shapes, and sizes than any other form of literature. They range from pop-up books to picture books and novels. Books for younger readers have large type, and use pictures to help explain the story. As readers get older, their books become longer and the stories more complex.

Fables

A short story which illustrates a moral or lesson is called a fable. Fables usually feature animals with human characteristics, such as wisdom or carelessness, and have traditionally been read or told to children in order to encourage good behaviour. A fable may, therefore, end with a proverb such as "look before you leap".

Aesop's Fables

The most famous collection of fables are attributed to a Greek called Aesop who is thought to have lived in the 6th century BC. There are many stories about him; he is often described as a slave who gained freedom to become a royal adviser. The stories attributed to Aesop were first passed on orally, then written down in the 4th century BC.

The *Tortoise and the Hare* is one of Aesop's most famous fables.

Modern fables

Some modern children's stories have been strongly influenced by ancient fables. English author Beatrix Potter (1866–1943) wrote a story about a squirrel called Nutkin whose naughty behaviour ended in punishment.

Uncle Remus

The *Uncle Remus* stories by American author Joel Chandler Harris (1848–1908) are fables based on the stories of plantation slaves in the United States. Told in African-American dialect, the tales are narrated by a wise, genial black man to the son of a plantation owner, and feature characters such as the trickster Brer Rabbit.

Brer Rabbit and Brer Fox

James Thurber (1894–1961)

In *Fables for Our Time* (1940), American author James Thurber reworked traditional stories, such as fairy tales, into fables that were relevant to the 20th century. For example, in Thurber's reworking of the tale of *Little Red Riding Hood*, the girl recognizes the wolf and shoots him dead.

Folk and fairy tales

These are among the most popular types of stories, particularly for young children. All cultures have created their own stories about magical beings and events, and the same folk story may occur in many places. For instance, the tale of an orphaned girl with a wicked stepmother is found in most societies.

A scene from *Cinderella*, by the London City Ballet

An illustration from Andersen's *The Snow Queen*

Hans Christian Andersen

Danish writer Hans Christian Andersen (1805–75) was one of the first authors to write new fairy tales. His first collection, *Fairy Tales*, was published in 1835. By the time of his death, he had published more than 160 stories; most of them, such as *The Ugly Duckling*, are still read today.

Charles Perrault

Frenchman Charles Perrault (1628–1703) was the first person to write down oral folk tales. His *Tales of Past Times* (1697) included *Cinderella*, but his version was less violent and bloody than the original.

Monkey King

The daring Monkey King is one of the best known folk heroes in Chinese literature. The Chinese writer Wu Cheng'en used many oral folk tales as source material in his novel about the Monkey King's adventures, *Journey to the West* (1500s).

Monkey battles with the White-Bone Demon

Brothers Grimm

German brothers Jakob (1785–1863) and Wilhelm (1786–1859) Grimm were the editors of *Grimm's Fairy Tales*, which included *Snow White*, and *Hansel and Gretel*. Their scholarly approach to collecting folk tales from Europe means that their versions of these ancient tales are often seen as the definitive versions.

Wilhelm Grimm   **Jakob Grimm**

Fantasy stories

Until the mid-19th century, most of the stories written for children were concerned with the teaching of morals and good behaviour. However, the enormous success of Hans Christian Andersen's fairy tales encouraged many writers to produce wild fantastic stories which celebrated the imagination above all else.

Tenniel illustration of the Mad Hatter

Alice in Wonderland
Written in 1865, English author Lewis Carroll's (1832–98) fantasy revolutionized children's literature with its fantastic plot, bizarre characters, and absence of any moral. The half dream, half nightmare world that Alice encounters when she plunges down the rabbit hole shows the limitless possibilities of the fantasy story.

Peter Pan
English author JM Barrie (1860–1937) originally wrote *Peter Pan* as a play in 1904. Peter, a motherless half-magical boy, takes the Darling children to Never Land.

Wonderful Wizard of Oz
American author L Frank Baum (1856–1919) wrote this fantasy in 1900. Dorothy is carried by a whirlwind out of Kansas to the magical Land of Oz, where she befriends the Scarecrow, Tin Woodman, and Cowardly Lion. In 1938, it was made into a popular film, ensuring that people world-wide know the story, even if they have never read the book.

The Hobbit
JRR Tolkien (1892–1973) published the tale of the Hobbit, Bilbo Baggins, in 1937. The trilogy that followed it, *The Lord of the Rings,* is one of the most popular stories ever published.

Peter Pan

Still from the 1938 film of *The Wizard of Oz*

The Hobbit

Adventure stories

The 19th century saw the beginning of great adventure stories for children. The books celebrated bravery, daring, and excitement, although the heroes were often boys rather than girls. Some books, such as *Treasure Island*, described imaginary lands while others, such as *Huckleberry Finn*, were about adventures close to home.

Huck and Jim

Treasure Island
Scottish author Robert Louis Stevenson (1850–94) told a story of piracy. The tale is told by Jim Hawkins, who acquires a map showing hidden pirate gold. He has to defeat the pirates before he can claim the treasure.

Huckleberry Finn
American author Mark Twain (1835–1910) set his novel on the banks of the Mississippi River. One of its themes, black slavery, is illustrated by Huck's friendship with the runaway slave Jim.

A scene from the 1950 film of *Treasure Island*

School stories

School is part of children's experience, and often features in literature. The first and most famous school story was called *Tom Brown's Schooldays* (1857) by Thomas Hughes (1822–96). It was based on the author's own time at boarding school in England. Today's school stories usually reflect the experiences of most children.

Harry Potter
Author JK Rowling published the first in the Harry Potter series in 1997, *Harry Potter and the Philosopher's Stone*. The book won several literary awards and was followed by equally popular sequels. The stories centre on Harry, an orphan who is sent to live with his aunt and uncle and discovers the Hogwarts School of Witchcraft and Wizardry. By 2002 the series had sold 100 million books in 46 languages.

Daniel Radcliffe played Harry Potter on screen.

Roald Dahl

British author Roald Dahl (1916–90) is known for his fantasy stories, which include *James and the Giant Peach* (1961), *Charlie and the Chocolate Factory* (1964), *Matilda* (1988), and *The BFG* (1989). His popularity is partly due to his skill in describing adults' frightening peculiarities in such a way as to make them laughable.

Illustration from *Tom Brown's Schooldays*

Family stories

Children's literature often takes as its theme family life. Stories of family life date back to the 19th century; one of the first was *Little Women* (1869) by Louisa May Alcott. Today's family-based stories look at the difficulties that children may experience, such as divorced parents, bereavement, or abuse.

Little Women
Louisa May Alcott's (1832–88) novel about life in a small town in New England, was one of the first books that presented children in a realistic fashion. The story of the March family, Meg, Jo, Beth, Amy, and their mother, Marmee, was in part autobiographical. It inspired many other American writers to produce stories about family life. Alcott wrote several sequels to *Little Women* including *Little Men* and *Good Wives*.

A scene from the 1949 film of *Little Women*

Picture books

Children's picture books have a long history; from the *Orbis Pictus* in 1658 there have been picture books for children. Babies and young children can enjoy books in which pictures are just as important as words. The illustrations tell stories and help teach concepts such as colours, shapes, and the names of things. Many talented artists now make books for children.

Visible world

Even the earliest books included illustrations. However, the first picture book that was specially designed for children was called *Orbis Pictus*, or *Visible World* (1658), by John Amos Comenius. It used pictures in order to help the translation of German into Latin.

Merchandising

Successful children's books are now big business. Popular characters soon appear as toys, games, and even crockery. The image of the characters can be found printed on clothing and books.

Beatrix Potter books are printed in many languages.

Beatrix Potter

The first master of the picture story book was Beatrix Potter (1866–1943). She was a lonely child who taught herself to draw and became skillful at painting animals. Her first book, *The Tale of Peter Rabbit,* was published in 1901. The books of Beatrix Potter are still popular throughout the world.

Beatrix Potter merchandise

Cuddly Peter Rabbit toy

Teapot

Jug

Mug

Board game

Where the Wild Things Are

When this book was published by the American writer Maurice Sendak (b.1928) in 1963, many people thought it was too scary for children. It tells the story of a boy called Max, who sails away to the land of the Wild Things, where after many adventures, he becomes their king.

Dr Seuss

The American artist Dr Seuss (Theodore Geisel 1904–90) created many classic picture books. Stories such as *The 500 Hats of Bartholomew Cubbins* (1938) are built around strange and improbable situations. Dr Seuss was one of the first authors to make rhyming storybooks that helped teach children to read. In *The Cat in the Hat* (1958), a cat visits two children and creates rhyming chaos while their mother is away.

Children's poetry

Verse for children dates back to the songs and ballads of the oral tradition, and children still memorize rhymes and songs and pass them on among themselves. Children's poetry has been written in every style imaginable, from humorous fantasies and nonsense limericks to powerful social commentary.

Nursery rhymes

Spoken rhymes are found all over the world, and many are ancient. Little Bo Peep is linked to a hide-and-seek game called Bo-Pepe, which is more than 600 years old. Ring A Ring O' Roses describes the symptoms of the plague, which left rose-like marks on its victims.

Limericks

The English artist Edward Lear (1812–88) wrote many nonsense rhymes. His limericks generally involve all sorts of people in very odd situations.

"There was an old man of Whitehaven, who danced a quadrille with a raven."

Prizes

Today, more children's books are being published than ever before. To encourage good writing and illustration, prizes are awarded for the best books. There are awards for everything from teenage fiction to picture books. Some prizes are nominated by children.

Newbery Medal

The American Library Association awards this prize for the year's best children's book. It is named after John Newbery (1713–67), who opened the world's first children's bookshop in 1745.

Carnegie Medal

This prize has been awarded by the British Library Association since 1936. It takes its name from American millionaire Andrew Carnegie (1835–1919), who founded libraries in Britain and the United States.

Timeline

15th century Chapbooks (crime and miracle stories) published. Courtesy books tell children how to behave.

1745 John Newbery sells *Little Goody Two-Shoe*s in the first children's bookshop.

Little Goody Two-shoes

1877 English author Anna Sewell publishes *Black Beauty*.

1883 *Pinochio*, by Italian author Carlo Collodi (1826–1890) published.

1894 *The Jungle Book*, by Rudyard Kipling (1865–1936) published.

1908 Kenneth Grahame (1859–1932) publishes *The Wind in the Willow*s.

1922 The first Newbery Medal for children's literature awarded.

1926 *Winnie-the-Pooh*, by AA Milne (1882–1956) published.

1929 *Emil and the Detectives* by German author Eric Kästner (1899–1974) published.

1931 French artist Jean de Brunhoff publishes *The Story of Babar*.

1952 EB White (1899–1985) publishes *Charlotte's Web*.

1968 *The Pigman* by Paul Zindel (b.1936) published.

1975 *Forever*, one of the first books for teenagers, by American author Judy Blume (b.1938) published.

1997 JK Rowling publishes the first book in the *Harry Potter* series.

FIND OUT MORE   BOOKS   DRAMA   EDUCATION   LITERATURE   MYTHS AND LEGENDS   POETRY   PRINTING   WRITING

CHINA AND TAIWAN

THE WORLD'S THIRD LARGEST COUNTRY, after Russia and Canada, China covers a vast area of eastern Asia. It has, by far, the largest population in the world and contains about 36 per cent of Asia's people. China has a long Pacific coastline to the southeast, but also borders 14 countries inland. Closely associated with China are Taiwan, an independent island, and the two former European colonies of Hong Kong and Macao. China is ruled by a communist government, which is working to continue the country's economic boom of the 1990s.

Great Wall

More than 2,200 years ago, about 300,000 slaves built the Great Wall of China to keep out invaders from the north. Stretching from Central Asia to the Yellow Sea, the wall's total length is 6,400 km (3,980 miles), and is the world's longest human-made structure.

Soldiers walking along the Great Wall

Physical features

China's vast land area includes rugged hills, subarctic regions, deserts, and tropical plains, and is watered by many river systems. High mountains, mainly in the north and west, dominate one-third of China's land.

Huang He

Two mighty rivers flow in eastern China, the Chang Jiang and the Huang He. At 5,464 km (3,395 miles), the Huang He is known in English as the Yellow River, or "China's Sorrow", after the yellow soil left behind by its devastating floods.

Guilin Hills

China's agricultural heartland lies in the south and centre of the country. The Li river is used to irrigate land that can be intensively farmed. Here at Guilin, the river supports fishermen and their families who make a living from its rich waters. The steep Guilin Hills rise up behind the river.

Climate

China has two main climates. More than half of the country is arid or semi-arid, and in the north and west, deserts and mountains experience extreme temperature variations. The winters are bitterly cold and summers are hot and dry. The summer monsoon brings rain from the Pacific to areas nearer the sea, particularly the south and east, where conditions are wet, warm, and often humid.

44°C (111°F)   -34°C (-30°F)
26°C (79°F)   -4°C (24°F)
623 mm (24 in)

206

China

Ruled by the Communist Party since 1949, China is divided into 22 provinces, five autonomous regions, and three special municipalities. Although technically governed from Beijing, many of these are becoming increasingly independent. About 93 per cent of China's people are Han Chinese, and around 60 per cent follow no religion, because the communist rulers discourage religious beliefs. Although fertile land is in short supply, farming is often intensive and employs two-thirds of the work-force. The Olympic Games will be held in Beijing in 2008.

Built-up 1.5%
Farming 36%
Wetland 2%
Barren 6.5%
Forest 9%
Grassland 24%
Desert 21%

Land use

The majority of China's farmland is in the east and south of the country. Much of the desert and mountain regions is uninhabitable. China has large mining areas in the Shaanxi and Sichuan basins, and is the world's largest coal producer.

CHINA FACTS

CAPITAL CITY Beijing

AREA 9,596,961 sq km (3,705,406 sq miles)

POPULATION 1,300,000,000

MAIN LANGUAGE Mandarin Chinese

MAJOR RELIGIONS Traditional beliefs, Buddhist

CURRENCY Renminbi (known as yuan)

LIFE EXPECTANCY 70 years

PEOPLE PER DOCTOR 500

GOVERNMENT One-party state

ADULT LITERACY 84%

C

People

Around 80 per cent of Chinese live in less than half the country's land area, mostly in small villages. However, more than 30 of China's cities have more than one million inhabitants. China's population is growing by 15 million a year, so the government has asked families to have just one child, and fines those who have more. Known as "Little Emperors", single boy children are often spoiled.

Schoolchildren in Beijing

137 per sq km (335 per sq mile)

Urban 32% Rural 68%

New Year

China's most important festival is the celebration of New Year, which begins in January or February, at the second new Moon of winter. People celebrate with colourful processions and dragon dances and close all shops and offices. Each year is named after an animal.

Food

Chinese food varies greatly from region to region. Rice is the basis of all dishes in the south, where it grows, whilst in the north, wheat noodles are the staple food. Both noodles and rice are usually served with stir-fried vegetables and meat. Cantonese food is reputed to be the most exotic in China, using rare meats such as snake and turtle. Fish and duck are also served frequently. The Chinese eat with chopsticks held in one hand.

Chopsticks

Dry-braised noodles

Beijing

For more than 2,000 years, Beijing has been a capital city, either of all China or part of it. Built symmetrically within three rectangles, it is a bustling city of historical buildings, temples, and beautiful parks. The Forbidden City lies at its heart, home to the 15th-century emperor's Imperial Palace. Also from that period is the Temple of Heaven, designed in the Chinese pagoda style.

Temple of Heaven, Beijing

Leisure

City-dwellers, who have no gardens, are encouraged to take exercise in the well-kept parks. At weekends and on summer evenings, neighbours meet to play board games such as *mah jong*.

Xi'an bicycle factory, Shaanxi

Handle-bars

Industry

China has well-developed heavy industries such as iron and steel. Since the late 1970s, growth has been concentrated in Special Economic Zones in eastern China, where joint Chinese and foreign trade and enterprise are encouraged.

Shanghai

A leading centre of trade and industry and a busy harbour, Shanghai is China's largest city and home to about 16,000,000 people. The city has traditional pagodas and glittering skyscrapers alongside the Chang Jiang River.

Rice farming

Many women work in flooded paddy fields in southern China. Rice is the main crop, and in a good year two yields can be harvested as well as one of vegetables. When the crop is ready for harvesting, it turns golden. The women cut and tie the stalks into bundles for threshing, which separates the grain and its protective husk from the stalk.

Tibetan monk pours Chang beer at hosar festival.

Tibet

The mountainous region of Tibet became a part of China in 1965. Most Tibetans are devout Buddhists, but under Chinese rule their religious and civil liberties were taken away. Opponents of the government were exiled, and some Han Chinese were resettled in the area, causing tension. The monks still practise their faith and carry out ceremonies, such as offering beer to Buddha in a *hosar*, or New Year, ritual.

Hong Kong

Hong Kong is a special administrative region in southeast China, made up of 236 islands and a mainland area. It has a busy port and is a leading financial centre. More than six million people live there. A former British colony, Hong Kong was returned to China in 1997. It experienced economic setbacks after the transition, but is now recovering.

Gambling
Gambling is a popular activity in Hong Kong. Playing mahjong, a traditional game, with friends and family is a way of socializing. Horse racing is a big industry, with many people placing bets online.

Houseboats
Some Hong Kong fishing families live in houseboats called sampans, which are moored in the harbours. The fishermen are now facing increasing competition from more efficient deep-sea trawlers.

Macao

A tiny peninsula in southeast China, Macao became a Portuguese colony nearly 450 years ago and was returned to China in 1999. Situated about 64 km (40 miles) west of Hong Kong, Macao is a popular tourist destination, with fragrant woods, and a sandy coastline onto the South China Sea.

Tourism
Macao has a strong tourist industry due to historical attractions such as the ruins of St. Paul's Church, built by the Portuguese in 1602. Macao's greatest attraction, however, are the casinos that bring the territory about one third of its total income. The economy has been in decline since the handover to China.

Taiwan

Often referred to as a "Little Dragon", Taiwan has one of Asia's most rapidly expanding economies. However, it is not recognized by the UN and lies at the centre of a debate over ruling rights. China claims Taiwan to be a province of Beijing, although the Taiwanese have governed here since the communists gained control of China in 1949. Despite this tension, Taiwan has established global trading markets, and its people enjoy high living standards.

People
About 84 per cent of Taiwanese are Han Chinese, who moved to Taiwan when the communists took power in 1949. They live in extended family groups, following traditional customs. Taiwan's native peoples of Indonesian origin now make up only two per cent of the population. The Ami, of the eastern mountains, are the largest group. Expert potters and farmers, their women rule the household.

TAIWAN FACTS

CAPITAL CITY	Taipei
AREA	32,260 sq km (12,456 sq miles)
POPULATION	22,200,000
MAIN LANGUAGE	Mandarin Chinese
MAJOR RELIGIONS	Buddhist, traditional beliefs
CURRENCY	Taiwan dollar
LIFE EXPECTANCY	76 years
PEOPLE PER DOCTOR	894
GOVERNMENT	Multi-party democracy
ADULT LITERACY	94%

Opera
Traditional Chinese opera was brought to the island with settlers from China. The operas are based on traditional stories. Stage sets are basic, but the costumes are elaborate, made from richly coloured silks with delicate embroidery. Make-up is used to highlight emotions.

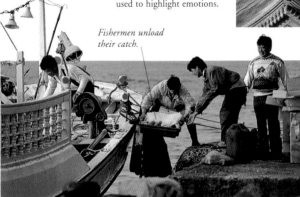

Fishermen unload their catch.

Fishing
Taiwan's fishermen land 1,171,000 tonnes (1,290,793 tons) of fish annually from the rich fishing grounds surrounding the island. Some Taiwanese fishermen have been accused of plundering Atlantic fishing grounds. Much of the catch goes to supply the huge Japanese market. Freshwater ponds are used for farming carp.

Sun Moon Lake
Taiwan's scenic Sun Moon Lake, known as *Jih-yüeh Tan*, is surrounded by the Central Mountains. The two parts of the lake, Sun Lake and Moon Lake, supply a hydroelectric plant that produces four per cent of the country's power. The tranquil, forested area is known for its ornate buildings, including the Buddhist Wen Wu Temple.

Taipei
The high-tech capital in the north of the island is the fastest growing city in Asia, having expanded to four times its original size. Many of the three million inhabitants ride to work on motor scooters, causing pollution and jams.

Industry
Few natural resources have forced Taiwan to develop a booming, highly specialized industry. Backed by an educated, ambitious work-force, the country exports electronic equipment, such as computers and television sets, machinery, textiles, sports equipment, toys, and watches. Profits are invested, or used to buy oil for energy. Farming and fishing ensure self-sufficiency in food.

FIND OUT MORE   ASIA, HISTORY OF   BUDDHISM   CHESS AND OTHER BOARD GAMES   CHINA, HISTORY OF   FESTIVALS   FISHING INDUSTRY   GARDENS   OPERA   PORTS AND WATERWAYS   TRADE AND INDUSTRY

CHINA, HISTORY OF

CHINA IS THE WORLD'S oldest continuous civilization. For more than 2,000 years, from 221 BC to AD 1911, it was united as a single vast empire under a series of all-powerful rulers. During this period, borders changed, capitals shifted, and the country was invaded by fierce tribes, including the Mongols. However, for most of its history, China led the world in art and technology, with inventions including paper, porcelain, and gunpowder. Despite its huge size, a unique system of government and a strong sense of national identity have helped to maintain a united China.

Shang bronze ritual cauldron

Shang bronze staff-head

Ancient China
The first known Chinese dynasty, the Shang, ruled from about 1500 to 1027 BC. The Shang rulers were believed to be semi-divine, and wre called the Sons of Heaven. It was their duty to maintain good relations between earth and the heavenly realm.

Qin Shi Huangdi
When Zheng (258–210 BC), the leader of the victorious Qin army, took control of China in 221 BC, he took the title of First Sovereign Qin Emperor, or Qin Shi Huangdi. The First Emperor treated his subjects harshly, and his dynasty was overthrown by a peasant rebellion in 207 BC. The name China comes from Qin.

Each soldier has a different face and is modelled on a real soldier.

Hollow body

Unification
By 400 BC, central government had broken down, and many small kingdoms fought among themselves. In 221 BC, the state of Qin emerged victorious, uniting all the rival kingdoms under the rule of the First Emperor. The Great Wall was built at this time, using slave labour.

Chinese civil service exam paper

Han Dynasty
In 207 BC, a new dynasty took power. The Han emperors, who ruled until AD 220, set up a national civil service to run the country. Officials studied the teachings of the philosopher Confucius (551–479 BC), and were selected by a rigorous examination system. The structure of the civil service remained largely unchanged for 2,000 years. The Han reign marked a period of peace and prosperity.

Characters are read vertically.

Terracotta army
The First Emperor's tomb was guarded by thousands of life-sized terracotta warriors with horses and chariots, whose job was to protect the emperor in the afterlife. This terracotta army was found in 1974 by men digging a well. The tomb lies near to the modern-day city of Xian.

The soldiers once carried real weapons made of bronze, but these were stolen by grave robbers.

Great Wall

Qin Empire

First empire
Protected by the Great Wall, the Qin empire covered what is now northern and eastern China. The wall was built as a defence against hostile tribes from Central Asia.

Solid legs

Inventions
Throughout Chinese history, emperors encouraged the development of science and technology. Paper and printing, gunpowder, harnesses for animals, the magnetic compass and stern rudder, and the wheelbarrow were all invented in China.

15th-century gun

Shield protects soldier.

Bronze "knife coins"

Multiple gun fires a hail of bullets.

Paper money
The Chinese perfected paper-making in about AD 105, using pulped silk waste. In later years, hemp, bark, or bamboo were used. The development of printing followed, and paper money was first circulated in China in the 9th century. By this time, the Chinese were also printing books using carved wooden blocks.

Gunpowder
Chinese scientists first produced gunpowder in the 9th century, and soon adapted their technology to make fireworks and weapons. Early Chinese rockets, fuelled by gunpowder, were in use by the 13th century. The Chinese also invented the gun, the bomb, and the mine.

Chinese character, or symbol, which translates to mean "happiness and good fortune".

Three perfections
The Chinese call calligraphy, poetry, and painting "the three perfections". From the Song dynasty (960–1279) onwards, the combination of these three disciplines in a single work of art was considered to be the height of artistic expression, and to be skilled in them was seen as the greatest accomplishment of an educated person. Calligraphers spent many months practising the brushwork of just one or two characters.

Ming roof tile
decorated
with horse

Ming dynasty

In 1368, Hong Wu, a peasant who had led
revolts against China's Mongol rulers, managed
to drive the Mongols out and create a new
dynasty, the Ming. He built a new capital at Beijing
and established peace, prosperity, and good government.
To make society more equal, he abolished slavery, confiscated
big estates, gave land to the poor, and taxed the rich.

Admiral Zheng

As part of the policy of
restoring Chinese prestige,
the Ming emperors sent
Admiral Zheng He
(1371–1433) to visit foreign
rulers. Zheng made seven
voyages in Southeast
Asia and the Indian
Ocean, sailing as far west
as East Africa. He was
accompanied by a fleet
of 317 ocean-going junks.

Ocean-going junk

*Tile would have
decorated the ridge of a roof.*

Foot binding

The Chinese believed that tiny feet
were a vital part of female beauty.
Young girls from rich families had
their feet tightly bound to prevent
them from growing. This process
was very painful. Adult women
were also forced to wear platform
shoes. In 1902, the emperor issued
an order banning foot binding,
although it continued for many years.

*Platform shoes
made the wearer take tiny steps.*

Opium
pipe

Decline of the empire

During the last 250 years of the Chinese
empire, the throne was occupied by the
Manchus, a non-Chinese people from north of
the Great Wall. The first Manchus were
enlightened rulers, but later emperors
feared that change might lead to
rebellion and they clung to old
traditions. In 1911, the Chinese
overthrew the feeble Manchus,
and established a republic.

Boxer rebels

Boxer Rebellion

In 1900 a secret group called the Society of Harmonious Fists
(Boxers) rose up in protest at European involvement in China.
The rising was swiftly put down when an international force
captured Beijing, but it weakened China's government.

*Japanese
troops in
Manchuria*

Opium wars

In 1839, the Chinese tried to stop the British
opium trade in Canton. The British went to
war, forcing the Chinese to open ports to
foreign trade and to cede Hong Kong to the
British. France, Russia, and later Japan, made
similar demands.

Japanese invasion

Civil war and a communist uprising weakened the
new republican government. In 1931 the Japanese
took advantage of the chaos to invade the northern
province of Manchuria. Six years later they invaded
the rest of China, capturing cities and ports.

Communist China

In 1949, the communist party led by Mao
Zedong (1893–1976) finally took control of
China after years of civil war. The new
government nationalized industry and the
land, and began a series of five-year
plans to transform the country
into a major industrial power.

Red star, symbol from the Communist
Chinese flag

Modern China

After the death of Mao Zedong
in 1976, the Chinese began
to modernize their economy by
introducing western ideas and
technology. Central government
control over the economy
relaxed, and this led to an
economic boom as new
industries were established.

Tiananmen Square

In 1989, students took
to the streets of Beijing
demanding democratic
reform. Many students
occupied Tiananmen
Square, Beijing. On 4
June, the army entered
the square, killing more
than 3,000 people. After
the Tiananmen massacre
the pro-democracy
movement was
ruthlessly suppressed.

Troops in Tiananmen Square

Timeline

c.1650–1027 BC Shang dynasty rules
northern China; bronzeworking and
writing are developed.

221 BC First Emperor, Qin Shi
Huangdi, founds the Qin dynasty
and unites the country.

Shang bronze halberd (dagger)

221 BC–AD 618 Great Wall of
China built.

589–618 Short-lived Sui dynasty
builds the Grand Canal linking
major rivers.

618–906 Tang dynasty brings
great prosperity to China; art
and trade flourish.

960–1279 Industrial revolution
occurs under the Song dynasty.

1279 Mongols under Kublai Khan
conquer China; trade with Europe
flourishes along the Silk Road.

1368–1644 Ming dynasty
establishes China as world power.

1644–1911 Manchu dynasty.

Mao Zedong

1911 Chinese republic declared.

1949 Communists declare the People's
Republic of China.

1966 Mao Zedong heads Cultural Revolution.

1997 Deng Xiaoping dies. Hong Kong
handed back to China by the UK.

1999 Portugal hands back Macao to China.

FIND OUT MORE   ASIA, HISTORY OF   CHINESE REVOLUTION   GUNS   INVENTIONS   MONGOL EMPIRE   POTTERY AND CERAMICS   WRITING

Chinese arts and crafts
Jewellery and adornment

Belt and garment hooks, worn by men, could be beautifully decorated.

Gilded hair comb has prongs of silver; it was probably used by a high-ranking woman.

Gilded sleeve weight helped wide sleeves hang properly.

Gold buckle is decorated with carved patterns.

Belt and garment hooks were sometimes inlaid with turquoise and gold.

Silver and gilt belt plaque is decorated with a pattern of fruit.

Gold and silver nail guards were used to decorate and protect the long fingernails of rich men and women.

Status artifacts

Jade buckle plaque with dragon design

Rich, gilded decoration

Fish is Buddhist symbol representing spiritual freedom.

Decoration made by pushing enamel paste into gaps between metal.

Box is made of lacquer, carved with leaves.

Cup carved from jade, a precious gemstone.

Jade pot was used for washing writing brushes.

Jade pot is adorned with carving of man and house.

Camel ornament is made of glazed earthenware.

Elephant ornament is made of gold and ivory, inlaid with gems.

Box is made of lacquer, carved with peony flowers.

Fish vase is decorated with enamel paste and gilded metal.

Inlaid lid for writing brush

Writing brush has wolf-hair tip and is inlaid with mother-of-pearl.

Extremely detailed work

CHINESE REVOLUTION

THE CHINESE REVOLUTION refers to the bitter struggle
for control of China between the Kuomintang, or
Nationalists, led by Chiang Kai-shek, and the
Communists, led by Mao Zedong. The struggle
began in the 1920s, when the Nationalists expelled the
Communists from their movement; it ended in 1949,
when the Communist Party took power, and
Chairman Mao proclaimed that China was a People's
Republic. Under Mao's leadership, China was
transformed from a backward peasant society into
one of the most powerful nations in the world.

1911 Revolution
In 1911, a Nationalist revolution
overthrew the Manchu dynasty, and
created a republic in southern China.
Sun Yat-sen (1866–1925) was elected
provisional president of the republic,
but the lives of the peasants did not
improve, and real power remained
with warlords (military leaders).

Kuomintang
In 1926, a Kuomintang general named
Chiang Kai-shek (1887–1975) defeated
the warlords, helped by the Communist
Party. Chiang set up a government in
Nanking but, once in power, he threw
the Communists out of the government
and massacred many Communist leaders.

Long March
In 1931 Mao and a small band of
Communists set up China's first
communist state in Jiangxi, southern
China. The Kuomintang attacked them
constantly, and in 1934 Mao was forced
to withdraw. The following year he led
100,000 people, mostly peasants, over
9,000 km (6,000 miles) of some of the
world's roughest terrain, to a new base in
Shaanxi province in the north. The Long
March crossed 18 mountain ranges, 24
rivers, and passed through 11 provinces
and 62 cities.

Only 30,000 marchers out of the original
100,000 reached their destination.

Mao Zedong addressing
followers at the Yan'an
soviet during the early
days of the revolution.

Liberation Army
Mao's Liberation (Red) Army was
made up of peasant militia. It had
an enormous amount of support;
numbers rose from 150,000 in 1938
to 3 million in 1945.

Yan'an soviet
In 1935, Mao set up new headquarters in
northern China – his Yan'an soviet, or base. He and
his followers lived in caves around the city of Yan'an,
and went into the countryside where they recruited a
huge following among the peasantry.

*Cap featuring
red star*

*Epaulettes
show rank*

*Green
wool
trousers*

**Red Army
uniform**

Mao Zedong
The son of a peasant, Mao (1893–1976)
followed the nationalist ideals of Sun
Yat-sen. In 1921, he helped found the
Chinese Communist Party. Convinced
that revolution should come from the
peasants, not the industrial workers, he
built a huge following. After victory
against Chiang Kai-shek, he became
chairman of the new republic.

Little Red Book

Cultural Revolution
In 1966, in an attempt to
introduce revolutionary
zeal, Mao introduced a
socialist cultural revolution
to attack the four "olds":
old ideas, old culture, old customs, and
old habits. Those accused of "revisionism"
(rejecting the revolution) were publicly
humiliated in "struggle meetings". The
Cultural Revolution ended in 1969, but
its excesses nearly led to civil war.

Red Guard
Radical students, trained as Red Guards,
were the main participants in the Cultural
Revolution. Using the *Little Red Book*,
containing the thoughts of Chairman
Mao, the Red Guard attacked anyone they
believed guilty of betraying the revolution.

Timeline
1911 Nationalist
revolution ends rule
of the Manchu
dynasty. A republic
is formed.

1921 Chinese
Communist Party
formed.

1926 Northern Expedition:
Communists and
Nationalists unite to
fight warlords.

1927 Kuomintang
under Chiang Kai-shek
attacks and executes
hundreds of Communists.

Chairman Mao

1931 Japan
invades
Manchuria.

1934–35
Long March.
Communists
march to
Shaanxi.

1937–45 Japan invades
China. Communist
guerillas harass Japanese
and liberate most of
northern China by 1945.

1945–48 Civil war
between Kuomintang
and Communists after
Japanese surrender in
World War II. Mao's

Communists gain
control, and set up
government in
Beijing (Peking).
Nationalists and
Chiang Kai-shek
flee to Taiwan.

1 October 1949
People's Republic of
China is declared.

FIND OUT MORE	CHINA, HISTORY OF	COLD WAR	GOVERNMENTS AND POLITICS	JAPAN, HISTORY OF	RUSSIAN REVOLUTION	SOVIET UNION

CHRISTIANITY

CHRISTIANS BELIEVE that Jesus of Nazareth was the son of God, who came to Earth as promised in the Old Testament, and through whose life, death, and resurrection believers are freed from their sinful state. Christianity began in the first century AD in the area now known as Israel and Palestine, which was then a part of the Roman empire. The faith was gradually spread around the Mediterranean by followers of Christ, such as Saint Paul.

Christian world

In the early years there were few Christians, and they were persecuted by the Romans because they refused to worship the Roman gods. But in AD 394, Christianity became the official religion of the Roman empire after the conversion of the emperor Constantine. The faith spread quickly through the empire. Today's Catholic Church is still based in Rome and claims to be the descendant of the early Church in the Mediterranean. There are now nearly 1.6 billion Christians worldwide.

Shading shows worldwide distribution of Christians.

Christianity is the largest world religion.

Cross

Christ's death on the cross, and his resurrection, were the two key events in his life on Earth. The cross has therefore become the most important Christian symbol. Every church is marked by a cross, and crosses are placed on altars and in other prominent places inside. During worship, some Christians make the sign of the cross.

The cross symbolizes Christ's resurrection from the dead.

This elaborate gold cross is ornamented with precious stones.

Stained glass window showing St Luke and St John teaching the gospel.

Spreading the word

Jesus preached the coming of God's kingdom, but his message was rejected and he was put to death. On the third day after Christ's death, God brought him back to life. Christ met his followers and told them to spread the word. Since then, Christianity has been spread by preachers and missionaries. From Europe, colonists took the faith with them to Africa, the Americas, and Australasia.

God the Father

The Holy Spirit is shown as a white dove, the symbol of peace.

Christ on the cross is a symbol of death and salvation.

Beneath Christ's feet is a globe representing the Earth.

Holy Trinity

Christians believe that God exists as three persons: God the Father is the creator; God the Son is Jesus Christ; and God the Holy Spirit is the presence of God on Earth. It is the Holy Spirit that inspires prophets and that acts as a means of divine revelation. Although there are three persons in the Holy Trinity, they exist as one substance, so Christians believe in one God.

Branches of Christianity

Two important groups have split from the Roman Catholic Church: the Protestant Churches, which broke away during the Reformation of the 16th century; and the Eastern Orthodox Church, which is strong in eastern Europe and western Asia.

Roman Catholicism

Catholics make up the largest Christian denomination. They stress the importance of the Church's role in interpreting the scriptures and the authority of the Pope as the leader of the Church. They believe in the doctrine of transubstantiation, in other words that the bread and wine used in the Mass are actually converted into the body and blood of Christ.

In Catholic churches, incense is burnt to release scented smoke.

Charcoal is put into the censer and lit to heat the incense.

Medieval censer

A Protestant service in London, UK

Bare walls without paintings or statues

Protestantism

There are many different Protestant Churches based around the world, but especially in North America. To a greater or lesser extent, they all stress the authority of scripture itself, rather than the clergy's interpretation of the text of the Bible. They do not believe in the doctrine of transubstantiation. Although there is great variation in their rituals, Protestants have simpler church buildings and less elaborate ceremonies than the Catholic and Orthodox Churches.

Orthodox Christians pray to icons, such as this image of St George.

Orthodoxy

Like the Roman Church, the Eastern Orthodox Church stresses the importance of the sacraments. Orthodox Christians do not recognize the authority of the Pope: the highest authority is the Church's Ecumenical Council.

C

Ceremonies

The most important Christian ceremonies are the sacred rites known as sacraments. The Roman Catholic and Orthodox Churches recognize seven sacraments: baptism (the rite of entry into the Church); confirmation (a further initiation ceremony); the Eucharist (Mass); penance (turning to God after sin); extreme unction (preparation for death); ordination (becoming a priest); and marriage. The Protestant Churches recognize baptism and the Eucharist.

Baptism
This ritual is an act of ceremonial cleansing before becoming a member of the Church. In some cases, holy water is splashed on the head of the infant. In other cases, an adult entering the Church is totally immersed in water.

Marriage
Christians believe that marriage symbolizes the relationship of Christ with his Church. It marks the beginning of a new family and a new generation.

Eucharist
At his last supper with his disciples, Christ identified the bread and wine as his body and blood. Christians remember this at the Eucharist (or Mass), at which a priest consecrates bread and wine and distributes it among the worshippers.

Head of saint

A priest blesses the wine in a chalice.

Sixteenth-century silver chalice

An Amish couple in Pennsylvania travel in a horse-drawn carriage.

Amish
The Amish are a Protestant sect founded in the 17th century. Its followers live separately from the rest of society and believe that salvation can only be reached within the community. In the United States, Amish communities follow a simple lifestyle with strict rules. They reject modern technology and wear traditional dress, such as waistcoats and hats and bonnets and capes.

Festivals

The most important Christian festival is Easter, when believers commemorate Christ's crucifixion and resurrection. The celebration of Christ's birth, Christmas, is an important festival. Ancient pagan festivals merged with Christian festivals, so that old fertility rites are linked with Easter and winter festivals with Christmas.

In the Middle Ages, saints' relics were kept in reliquaries.

The Adoration of the Magi by Botticelli (1444–1510)

Saints' days
Christians who have lived outstanding lives, or who were killed for their beliefs, are revered as saints. Each saint has his or her own special day, and these are often marked with processions, celebrations, and church services. Festivals on saints' days are particularly popular in Catholic countries.

Reliquary of St Eustace, an early Roman Christian martyr

Easter
The celebration of Easter can involve many moods, from the solemn prayers of Good Friday, when the crucifixion is remembered, to joy at the resurrection three days later. A spring festival, Easter is a time when new life is celebrated. Christ's resurrection is reflected in the new growth of plants and crops, and is celebrated in the giving of Easter eggs.

Christmas
Christ's nativity (birth) is traditionally celebrated in December. The Christmas story tells of his birth in a stable in Bethlehem. The many Christmas customs include giving presents, decorating trees, lighting candles, singing special hymns (or carols), and eating elaborate meals.

This nativity painting shows the worship of the Magi, the three Wise Men who came bearing gifts.

An Easter procession in Granada, Spain

Christians carry a statue to symbolize Christ carrying the cross.

Bible

The sacred text of the Christian religion is the Bible. Its first part is the Old Testament, a group of books inherited from the Jews, among whom Christianity originally grew up. Second comes the New Testament, which is made up of books dealing with the early history of Christianity. The New Testament includes the four Gospels, the Acts and Epistles (giving details of the spread of Christianity), and the Book of Revelation (containing prophecies for the future).

The Dead Sea Scrolls

Gospels
The first four books of the New Testament are called the Gospels, from a word meaning "good news". They tell the story of the life of Christ. Three of the four Gospels (those of Matthew, Mark, and Luke) are very similar and are known as the Synoptic Gospels. John's gospel is quite different from the others, and its author may not have known the other three texts.

Dead Sea Scrolls
These scrolls of parchment were discovered in caves near Qumran on the Dead Sea in the 1940s and 1950s. They contain writings which include texts of parts of the Old Testament in versions earlier than any previously discovered. They were hidden in AD 68.

St Paul
Originally opposed to Christianity, Paul (d. AD 64) converted when he had a vision of Christ. He began to preach Christianity and spread the faith on four arduous missionary journeys through Greece and Asia Minor. His role was central to the early development of the Church. He wrote several of the New Testament books in the form of letters to the Christian communities he visited.

FIND OUT MORE CHURCHES AND CATHEDRALS   CRUSADES   EUROPE, HISTORY OF   FESTIVALS   HOLY LAND, HISTORY OF   JESUS CHRIST   MONASTERIES   MOTHER TERESA   REFORMATION   RELIGIONS

CHURCHES AND CATHEDRALS

CHURCHES AND CATHEDRALS are Christian places of worship. Early churches were small, with only enough room for an altar and a small congregation. As Christianity spread, larger churches, with separate areas for the clergy and the followers, were built. A cathedral is a church in which a bishop presides; he organizes the day-to-day running of local parishes.

The first churches

Christianity began in the Mediterranean during the time of the Roman Empire. Early churches were modelled on the public buildings of ancient Rome, especially basilicas, where meetings and law courts were held. The congregation sat in an area called the nave, and the altar was housed in a smaller area, the sanctuary.

St Sabina, Rome
Founded in AD 422, this early church has a wide nave and small, semi-circular sanctuary.

Parts of a cathedral

Many cathedrals and churches are designed in the shape of a cross. The "arms" of the cross, the transepts, contain small chapels. The altar lies to the east to face the rising sun; the nave lies towards the west.

123-m (404-ft) spire

Columns and vaults
The interior has decorative stone ceilings, called ribbed vaults, supported on columns of local Purbeck marble. Each column is surrounded by four shafts (smaller columns), which create a light, delicate effect.

Bell towers have openings to allow the sound of the bells to escape.

The large nave can accommodate big congregations.

Intricately carved west front

Cathedral interior
The great nave, with its high, vaulted ceiling, is made to appear larger still by aisles on either side. Light comes in through stained-glass windows.

Main entrance

Salisbury Cathedral
This 13th-century Gothic cathedral has slender walls and pointed arches and windows. These features help make it elegant and delicate in spite of its huge size. The 14th-century spire is the tallest in England and can be seen from far away.

Western transept

Eastern transept

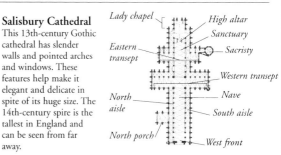

Lady chapel — *High altar* — *Sanctuary*

Eastern transept — *Sacristy*

Western transept

North aisle — *Nave*

South aisle

North porch — *West front*

Floor plan
The cross shape symbolizes the wooden cross on which Christ died.

Sanctuary

Pointed arches are a typical feature of Gothic architecture.

Lady chapel

Buttresses (supports) help bear the weight of heavy vaults.

Church decoration

Many churches and cathedrals are richly decorated with symbols of the Christian religion, including images of Christ, angels, the saints, and crosses. Protestant churches tend to be less elaborately decorated than Roman Catholic and Eastern Orthodox churches.

Fan vaulting
This delicate fan vault can be found at Canterbury Cathedral, England.

Gargoyle
Devils and grotesques were carved on church exteriors during the Middle Ages to represent evil outside the church.

Triptych
The finest decoration of all is usually close to the altar, such as this triptych in St Peter's Basilica, Rome.

Mosaic
Mosaics were an early form of decoration in Mediterranean churches. This 9th-century mosaic is in the Santi Nereo e Achilleo, Rome.

Stained-glass windows
Beautiful coloured windows that decorate churches often illustrate Bible stories told by Jesus and his disciples.

Statuary
Representations of the Madonna and Child are found in Roman Catholic churches. This Renaissance-style statue, which was finished in 1896, is in the church of the Sacré-Coeur, Paris.

Churchyards

Churchyards separate a church from noisy streets and provide land to bury the dead. Burials also take place in purpose built cemeteries.

Celtic cross
This cross in Ireland combines two Christian symbols: the cross and the circle, a symbol of eternity.

Columbarium
A Columbarium houses the ashes of cremated people.

Tombs
Some tombs tell the lives of those buried inside. This tomb of much-imprisoned French revolutionary Raspail, is in the form of a prison.

FIND OUT MORE

ARCHITECTURE   CHRISTIANITY   FESTIVALS   GLASS   MEDIEVAL EUROPE   RELIGIONS

CITIES

LESS THAN 200 YEARS AGO most people lived in villages. Today, around one-half of the world's population lives in cities. During the 19th century, towns and cities expanded as people moved away from rural areas to work in new industries. Cities have continued to grow, but haphazardly, in contrast to the carefully-planned cities of the ancient world.

Hole in roof instead of door

Walls made of mud

Çatal Hüyük

Early cities had no streets.

First cities

Settlements in western Asia, such as Jericho (Israel), Çatal Hüyük (Turkey), and Ur (Iraq), started to expand around 4000 BC. At this time, craftworkers began to trade goods outside their local areas, creating new wealth that was used to build palaces, large temples, and strong, defensive walls. These towns grew in importance and emerged as the first cities.

Modern cities

The world's cities have grown rapidly in modern times but inadequate planning has contributed to poor living conditions and poverty in many urban centres. Poor areas, wealthy neighbourhoods, and areas dominated by one particular ethnic group are all features of city life. Most cities offer many people a wide choice of jobs, houses, and recreational facilities.

Gardens, parks, and squares give people the chance to escape the bustle of city streets.

Entertainment is a feature of most cities. Cities are usually cultural centres with theatres, museums, galleries, and music venues, such as Sydney's striking Opera House.

Residential
There are different residential areas in cities. Older houses and flats are close to the city centre, while modern developments extend outwards, clustering around railway lines and major roads.

Business is always located close to the heart of the city. Nowadays, the business area is usually dominated by tall office blocks.

Apartment building

Skyscraper

Converted loft

Brownstone

Underground

Services

Sydney, Australia

Roads, railways, boats, and airlines bring people into the city centre.

Manufacturing
Small factories and workshops were once at the heart of cities. Today, large industrial complexes are usually built further out, reducing pollution.

New York
The city of New York in the USA contains some of the world's tallest skyscraper office blocks. It also has large apartment buildings, low-rise commercial sites (some of which have been converted into homes called lofts), tall, 19th-century brownstone (a type of sandstone) houses, and smaller, modern houses. Steps lead to underground trains and shops.

Villages

A traditional village is a small, rural settlement, often by a stream or river. In most parts of the world, people still live and work in villages, farming the surrounding countryside, and trading with nearby settlements.

Maasai village, Kenya
Many of the Maasai people live in groups of thatched, mud houses surrounding a central cattle enclosure.

Stilt village, Sumatra
In many Southeast Asian villages, houses are raised on stilts to keep out unwanted animals, like snakes.

Gold rush town
Towns grew around 19th century gold mines. Abandoned as the gold ran out, some still stand as "ghost towns".

Forbidden City

The Forbidden City in Beijing, China, was built in the 15th century. Only the emperor, his family, and his officials were allowed in.

Timeline

8000 BC Strong walls and a stone tower are built at Jericho.

3500 BC City-states such as Ur, develop in Mesopotamia (modern-day Iraq).

5th century BC Greeks plan and build the elegant city of Athens.

1st century BC The Roman Empire expands, and new European cities are built.

12th century AD Stone walls, such as those at Carcassonne, France, are built to protect medieval towns and cities.

1421 Construction starts on Forbidden City, Beijing, China.

15th century Renaissance architects lay out classical cities, such as Florence and Siena in Italy.

19th century Industrialization stimulates growth of towns and cities in Europe and America.

Siena, Italy

1950s Brasilia designed and constructed as new capital of Brazil.

1990s Skyscrapers dominate most city skylines.

FIND OUT MORE | ARCHAEOLOGY | ARCHITECTURE | BUILDING AND CONSTRUCTION | INDUSTRIAL REVOLUTION | IRON AND STEEL | RENAISSANCE | SOCIETIES, HUMAN | TRAINS AND RAILWAYS

CLIMATE

WEATHER CAN CHANGE from moment to moment. Over a long period of time, a region's characteristic weather – however changeable – is called its climate. Climates are generally warm near the Equator, the imaginary line around the middle of the Earth, and cool towards the poles. Other influences on the three broad climate types – warm tropical, cold polar, and mild temperate – include the distance from sea and the position within a continent. The climate determines a region's animal and plant life.

Polar
Mountain
Tundra
Temperate
Mediterranean
Dry grassland
Desert
Subtropical
Tropical

Climate zones
Close to the Equator, the Sun's warmth is strong – it climbs high in the sky at midday: closer to the poles, the Sun's warmth is weaker – it climbs less high. Climatic zones, which effect vegetation, can be further classified by physical features.

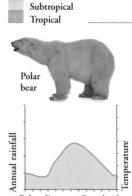

Polar bear

Polar climate – Greenland

Annual rainfall / Temperature

Polar climate
Towards the ice-capped poles, the Sun is always low in the sky, and in winter barely rises at all: summers are brief. Winter temperatures in the tundra regions around the North Pole are below -60°C (-76°F).

Tropical climate

Weather in a tropical climate, such as Brazil, is always warm, often with heavy rainfall. Some tropical climates, such as deserts, are hot and dry; others, such as rain-forests, are warm and moist.

Parrots

Oak sprig

Temperate climate – Seattle, USA

Annual rainfall / Temperature

Temperate climate
In mid-latitude (imaginary lines parallel to the Equator) areas such as the USA, summers are warm, and winters cool, with regular rain. A Mediterranean climate with dry summers and warm, damp winters is a type of temperate climate.

Oceanic and continental climate zones

Tropical climate – Brazil

Annual rainfall / Temperature

Monsoons
These are warm, tropical climates with wet and dry seasons. In India, it is dry from October to May as the winds blow out to sea, and very wet from June to September as the monsoon winds blow inland.

Mountain climate
High altitude causes the air to cool, thus creating a cold climate. Exposed mountain tops also make mountain climates very wet and windy. Above a certain height called the snow-line, there is always snow.

Oceanic and continental climate
Coastal regions have wet, changeable weather. The summers are cooler and the winters are warmer, because the ocean heats up and cools down more slowly than the land. Places in the continental interior, such as Moscow, have cold winters.

Continental climate – Moscow

Annual rainfall / Temperature

Desert climate
Over a fifth of the world's land surface is desert, where there is typically an annual rainfall of less than 100 mm (4 in). In the tropics, desert temperatures frequently climb above 50°C (122°F).

Each tree ring shows one year's growth: a wide ring means the weather was warm and the tree grew well.

Climate change
Over long periods of time, climate fluctuates. Signs of widespread glaciation, for instance, show that the world was once much colder. We now live in an interglacial period. Subtle changes in the climate's recent past are revealed by such things as variations in the sizes of tree rings.

Global warming
Pollution may be warming the world up. Certain gases trap the Sun's heat in the Earth's atmosphere. Rising levels of these "greenhouse gases", such as carbon dioxide, which come from burning oil or forest land, may trap so much heat that the Earth could warm up by 4°C (7.2°F) over the next 50 years.

| FIND OUT MORE | DESERTS | MOUNTAINS AND VALLEYS | OCEANS AND SEAS | POLLUTION | RAIN | WEATHER | WEATHER FORECASTING | WINDS |

CLOTHES AND FASHION

PEOPLE HAVE ALWAYS WORN CLOTHES, either as protection from the weather or for modesty. Yet through history, people have also chosen clothes to impress or attract others, or to reflect their job, social status, or religious beliefs. Clothes send out signals about the wearer's lifestyle and the type of society they live in: for instance, during the 20th century, the emancipation of women was reflected in the kind of clothes they wore, such as practical trousers.

Hats
In the early and mid-20th century, adults usually wore hats in public. The way people dress has become less formal since then, and the hat's importance as a smart accesssory has declined.

Sports cap is now casual everyday wear

Belt

Shirts
In medieval Europe, shirts were worn beneath a tunic. Over the years, more and more of the shirt was allowed to show, and now it is regarded as an outer garment. Everyday shirts need to be hard-wearing and easy to put on.

Clothing design

Designers choose the fabric, colour, and shape of a garment. Their decisions are influenced by the function of the item, and who will eventually wear it. A work shirt, for example, must be made from durable fabric; a high-fashion shirt can be made from less practical silk or linen.

Sample of fabric

Sketched design

Design
Some designers sketch their ideas for a new style onto paper. Others work directly with the fabric, draping it over a dressmaker's dummy, and pinning it until the right shape emerges.

Pattern
Once the design has been decided, it is translated into pattern pieces, made from paper or card. These are used as a guide for cutting out the fabric. The pattern pieces are made in different sizes, and sent to the cutting room.

Daily wear

The popular informal outfit of shirt, jeans, and trainers can be seen in many parts of the world, worn by both sexes of all ages. This casual outfit is an example of the changing attitudes to clothes seen in the 20th century. For the first time, everyday clothing crossed barriers of age, gender, and social class.

Sample pattern

Sleeve

Back section

Cutting instructions

Jeans
Bavarian-born retailer Levi Strauss (1829–1902) sold the first blue jeans – Levis – to miners in the 1850s. They have been popular ever since, because they are hard-wearing, and easily adapted to changes in fashion.

Trainers
Trainers were originally made for tennis or basketball players – the rubber soles stopped them from slipping. They have since become fashionable "street" wear.

Rubber sole

Leather or fabric upper

Cotton

Clothing manufacture

The clothes manufacturing industry is massive, and employs millions of people worldwide. Some designs are exclusive, produced by the great fashion houses. Most clothes however are manufactured in standard sizes and, from cutting to pressing, are mass-produced in factories.

Cutting
Up to 150 layers of fabric are spread out on long tables. The pattern pieces are then laid on top and the material is cut, using either a mechanical knife or a laser.

Computerized control panel

Needle

Sewing machine
To make a stitch, a sewing machine must loop one thread around another. The latest models are computerized: touching a panel changes the type of stitch. Domestic machines perform about 1,000 stitches a minute; industrial machines are ten times faster.

Sewing
The cut pieces are carried to the person whose job it is to match them up for the sewing machinist. Each machinist concentrates on a particular part of the garment, such as the sleeves.

Pressing
Once the clothes are sewn together, they are laid on large, flat tables to be pressed. Then a final inspection is held to check the quality of the finished garment, before it is sold to a wholesaler.

Thread loop catches on bobbin hook.

Stitched fabric

Hook spins around.

1 As the needle pierces the fabric, it makes a loop of thread, which is picked up by a bobbin hook beneath the needle plate.

Needle moves upwards.

Bobbin thread joins top loop.

2 The loop is pulled around thread drawn from within the bobbin, joining the top thread as a stitch. Both threads are then released.

Traditional clothing

The clothes worn in some parts of the world combine modern lifestyles and traditions thousands of years old. Traditional national costumes often reflect the dress of peasants, whose garments were suited to the local climate and the kind of work they performed.

Traditional jacket (parka) in modern fabric
Insulated boots

Shaved head
Silk jacket
Rubeka

Headscarf
Embroidery
Hang pen
Sports shoes (not traditional)

Canada
Inuit people dress to protect themselves against cold weather: in northern Canada, it snows from October to May.

Tanzania
The Maasai wear vivid pieces of cloth called *rubeka*. Young women who are old enough to marry wear special headdresses.

South Korea
This traditional silk costume is called *hanbok*, meaning "Korean clothing". It is worn on special occasions.

Vietnam
The traditional outfit of the Dao people, a hill tribe, is a *lamchu*: a scarf, skirt, jacket, and *hang pen* wound around the legs.

India
The most popular dress for Indian women is the *sari*, which is usually made from a length of silk or cotton.

Elegantly draped sari

Tying a sari
The sari is a length of material, between 5 and 9 metres long, and just over a metre wide. It is worn over a tight-fitting bodice, called a *choli*, and a long petticoat. When the weather gets hot, the sari can be adjusted to let in cool air.

Choli
Sari fabric

1 First, the material is wrapped round once, and tucked into the petticoat.

2 The sari fabric is pleated, then tucked into the petticoat again.

3 The spare fabric is draped over the shoulder.

Coco Chanel
The French designer Gabrielle "Coco" Chanel (1883–1971) had a powerful influence on Parisian and world fashion for almost 60 years. Her designs stressed simplicity and comfort at a time when clothes tended to be restrictive and uncomfortable. Many of her innovations are now fashion classics, such as bell-bottomed trousers, bobbed hair, and the so-called "little black dress".

Body decoration

Every culture has practised some form of body decoration, ranging from scarring and tattooing, which are permanent, to make-up and body paint, which last for only a few hours. One of the oldest forms of body decoration is jewellery, worn to show wealth and status, for protection and healing, or for beauty. Examples include rings, necklaces, earrings, bracelets, and brooches.

Glass necklace
Dress clips
Bracelet

Jewellery
Beads, berries, feathers, shells, bone, glass, precious stones, and metals have all been used to make jewellery. Most fashion jewellery is made from cheap materials, such as plastic, because it is only worn for a short time.

Plastic brooch

Body painting
People paint their faces and bodies to mark a religious occasion, celebrate important events in their community, or ward off illness. Sikh brides, for example, paint ornate, beautiful patterns on their hands using dye from the henna plant.

Body paint in Papua New Guinea

High-fashion wedding dress

Fashion

Following fashion (the changing trends in clothing) was once so expensive that only the wealthy could afford it. Today, however, advances in manufacturing, and the invention of synthetic fabrics, allow more people to follow fashion. Styles have changed faster than ever before, and fashion has become big business. Shows by fashion houses such as Dior (France) or Ralph Lauren (USA) attract buyers from all over the world.

Hats and shoes

Through the ages, hats and shoes have come in many styles: hats have ranged from headdresses to berets, shoes from simple leather sandals to chunky platform boots.

Riding hat
Chin strap

Badge

Police officer's cap
Hats may stand for authority, as with the police officers' cap, which is part of their uniform.

Hard hat
People who are especially at risk of head injuries, such as riders or construction workers, wear hard hats to protect themselves.

Shoe
Shoes must suit people in different climates, as well as follow fashions. They are commonly made from durable leather, but rubber, plastic, silk, and canvas are also used.

Lining
Tongue
Thin upper encloses foot
Steel shank supports arch of foot

Cross-section of shoe

FIND OUT MORE   DYES AND PAINTS   GLASS   INDIA AND SRI LANKA   METALS   PLANT USES   TEXTILES AND WEAVING

Fashion in the 20th century

Corset pushes chest forward and hips back

Daywear, typical S-bend silhouette, 1900s

Daywear, narrow, tailored line, 1910s

Shirt collar is turned down, a recent development in fashion

Wrapover skirt

Lounge suit, single-breasted, 1910s

Orange-blossom headdress

Wedding dress, with new, shorter skirt, 1920s

Wide knicker-bockers, or "plus-twos"

Three-piece suit, for country wear, 1920s

"Modesty" skirts on both costumes

Wool bathing costumes (knitted one-piece), 1930s

Boxy style, economical with fabric

Bias cut fabric clings to the body

Crepe evening dress, full-length, 1930s

Felt trilby

Daywear from World War II, 1939–45

Tightly fitted bodice

Long, full skirt

Suit, in style of French designer Christian Dior, 1950s

Thigh-high hem

Mini dress, "Space Age" influence, 1960s

"Ethnic" styles influence fashion

Flared (wide-leg) trousers

"Hippy" fashion, 1970s

Trousers

Day wear, 1990s

Underwear, hats, and shoes

Cotton camisole with lace inserts, 1900s

Brassieres from the 1920s and 1930s

Corset, worn from the 1930s to the 1950s

Underwear in easy-care nylon, 1960s

One piece in polyester, 1980s

1920s "Long Johns"

Aertex cotton shorts, 1950s

Brief cotton pants, 1980s

Men's underwear

Boater, worn on the river and as informal wear, 1900s

Silk hat on wire-frame base, 1920s

Cloche, bell-shaped hat with small brim, 1920s

Bowler, worn horse-riding, 1920s

Felt hat, with shallow crown, 1930s

Silk hat, with glass berries, 1950s

Shoes with steel beading, early 1900s

Kid boots, possibly worn for cycling, early 1900s

Reptile-skin shoes, popular in the late 1920s

Lace-up shoes with a wedge sole, 1940

Boots with black and gold thread woven into fabric, 1960s

Platform soles, high fashion in the 1970s

CLOUDS

WHEN YOU LOOK UP at the sky, you may see clouds. In temperate or mild climates, there are usually at least a few clouds and, sometimes, cloud cover is total. Clouds are dense masses of water drops or ice crystals so light and small that they float on the air. Clouds form when rising air cools to a point where it can no longer contain its water vapour, and so the vapour condenses. There are three basic forms, or shapes, of cloud – puffy cumulus, layered stratus, and feathery cirrus – but each form can vary to make many different cloud types. The type of cloud depends on how high the air rises, and its temperature.

Cloud formation

Clouds form by the condensation or freezing of water vapour. The way they form depends on their height and on the speed of upward air movement. When pockets of warm air rise rapidly, clouds form in heaped shapes (cumulus). When air rises slowly and evenly over a large area, clouds form in layers (stratus).

Making a cumulus

The sun-warmed ground creates thermals – rising currents of warm air. The air cools as it rises. Eventually, it becomes so cool that water droplets condense and a cloud forms. The cloud continues to build up as long as the· thermal continues to supply water vapour.

Formation of a cumulus cloud in three stages

Luke Howard

A keen amateur meteorologist, but a pharmacist by profession, British-born Luke Howard (1772–1864) kept detailed weather diaries. These provided valuable meteorological data, before official records were kept. Howard used Latin names to identify each cloud by shape. His classification of clouds is still used today.

Cloud types

There are 10 distinct types of cloud. Cirrus, cirrostratus, and cirrocumulus clouds form 5–11 km (3–7 miles) above sea-level. Altocumulus, altostratus, and nimbostratus clouds form 2–7 km (1–4 miles) above sea-level. Stratocumulus and stratus form at 2 km (1 mile) or under above sea-level. Cumulus and cumulonimbus clouds form over a wide range of heights.

Cirrus clouds form at high altitude where air is cold and strong.

Cirrostratus is a high level veil of cirrus cloud.

Altostratus is a thin watery sheet of cloud.

Cirrocumulus are clouds of ice crystals with a dappled appearance.

Clear	1	2	3	4

5	6	7	8	Cloudy

Cloud cover

The amount of sunlight reaching the ground depends on how much sky is covered by cloud. This is measured in "oktas" (eighths). One okta means one-eighth of the sky is covered in cloud; two oktas equals two-eighths of cloud cover in the sky, and so on.

Cumulonimbus is created by strong updraughts, bringing heavy thunder and rain.

Fog and mist

When water vapour in the air condenses near the ground it forms fog and mist. "Radiation" fog forms on cold, clear, calm nights, when the ground rapidly loses the heat it has absorbed during the day and cools the air above to its dew point. "Advection" fog forms when warm, moist air flows over a surface so cold that the water vapour in the air condenses.

Altocumulus are puffs or rolls of clouds at medium height.

Cumulus are fluffy white clouds, often short-lived.

A cloud plume floating around a mountain-top is called a banner cloud.

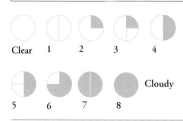

Sea mist

When warm moist air flows over cold water, water vapour in the air may condense to form a kind of advection fog called a sea mist. These mists are most common on early summer mornings, when the air is calm.

Beachy Head, Sussex, England

Nimbostratus are layers of dark rain clouds.   **Stratus** are cloud layers, often giving long periods of rain.

FIND OUT MORE   ATMOSPHERE   CLIMATE   RAIN   STORMS   WEATHER   WEATHER FORECASTING   WINDS

COAL

MORE THAN two hundred million years ago huge trees grew in the warm, humid swamps that covered vast regions of the world. They captured the Sun's energy to make their wood. When they died, their trunks became buried and gradually changed into coal. When we burn coal today, we release the energy the trees captured all those years ago. Because of its origin, coal is called a fossil fuel. It was the first fossil fuel to be used by people, and is still today second only to petroleum in importance for energy production worldwide.

Coal mining

Almost 5 billion tonnes of coal are mined a year. China and the United States mine the most coal, with annual outputs exceeding 1.6 billion tonnes. Coal deposits can be up to about 20 m (66 ft) thick, but they average less than 3 m (10 ft). Some deposits are found on the surface, but most lie underground, sandwiched between rock layers.

Piles of dead plant material accumulate in swampy regions

How coal is formed

Coal began to form in swampy forests about 350 million years ago, during the Carboniferous period. Decaying plants were buried under layers of mud. As heat and pressure increased, plant remains slowly converted into coal. Today, there are three main grades of coal – lignite, bituminous coal, and anthracite.

Peat represents an early stage in coal-formation. It is soft, fibrous, and moist, but still gives off heat when burned.

Lignite, or brown coal, is a low-grade fuel containing up to about 60 per cent carbon, along with plant remains and moisture. It is soft and crumbly.

Bituminous coal is a better quality fuel, comprising more than 80 per cent carbon. It is the most common solid fuel used in industry. It is hard, but dirty to the touch.

Anthracite is the highest grade coal, containing more than 90 per cent carbon. It is shiny black, clean to touch, and burns with little smoke.

Collecting coal at a strip mine

Strip mining

One method of surface, or opencast, mining is called strip mining. The coal is excavated in a series of long strips. Any soil above each strip is used to fill in the trench created when the coal has been removed from a previous strip.

Drilling coal in a shaft mine

Shaft mining

Coal seams deep below the surface are reached by a system of vertical shafts and horizontal tunnels. The coal is dug out by powered coal-cutters and hydraulic tools.

Coal products

Coal can be processed into valuable products, by a method called destructive distillation. Coal is heated in coke ovens at up to 1,300 °C (2,400 °F) without air. A mixture of liquid vapours and gases escapes and is then separated into coal gas, ammonia liquid, and coal tar. The solid left behind is called coke.

Coke

This solid, porous substance is, like coal, an excellent fuel, which contains more than 80 per cent carbon. It is widely used in industry, mostly in blast furnaces for making iron. In the furnace, it also acts as a chemical agent in the iron-extraction reaction.

Coal tar

Coal tar is a black oily liquid that is a rich source of mostly organic chemicals, such as benzene, phenol, and creosote. These can be processed into a variety of materials including dyes, paints, and drugs.

Coal tar soap

Mine safety

Mines are dangerous places because of the risk of rock falls and the build-up of explosive gases, such as methane. One safety device was invented by an English scientist, Humphry Davy, in 1815. His safety lamp was able to detect dangerous levels of poison gases.

Davy lamp

Power

About 25 per cent of the world's energy supply is generated from coal. In coal-fired power stations, the coal is first pulverized (powdered) and then burned in a furnace. The hot gases produced pass over tubes containing water and turn it into steam. The steam drives powerful turbogenerators, which produce electricity. The electricity is then transmitted through a national grid network.

Coal-fired power station, Germany

Domestic fuel

Until the mid 1900s, coal was the fuel most used in Western homes. Each room was heated by open coal fires, and cooking was usually done on a coal-burning stove. Today, few modern homes have coal fires, as people tend to use other forms of heating. Some cities and towns allow only smokeless fuels to be used for energy.

Burning smokeless fuels keeps pollution low

FIND OUT MORE | CHEMISTRY | DYES AND PAINTS | ELECTRICITY | ENERGY | FIRE | INDUSTRIAL REVOLUTION | IRON AND STEEL | OIL | PLASTICS AND RUBBER

COASTS

A COAST IS SIMPLY defined as the boundary between the land and sea – an area that may range from a rocky cliff to a sandy beach. This boundary is always shifting as the sea continues its relentless assault on the land – waves roll up and down, and tides ebb and flow. The action of the sea creates distinctive landforms, such as a cliff, created by eroding (wearing away) rock; a shore (an area between low tide levels and the highest storm waves); or a beach, built up by shore deposits. Wind and rain erosion also contribute to the changing aspect of coastlines.

Evolution of a coast

Waves crash against a shore with great force, wearing away rocks by pounding them with water, and hurling rocks and stones at them. On high coasts, the waves undercut the foot of the slope, creating a cliff. The model below shows the gradual effect of waves and seawater on the coast.

Beaches and sandbars
Material worn away from rocky coasts is pounded by waves into sand and shingle and deposited elsewhere as beaches and sandbars – an offshore strip of sand or shingle. A spit resembles a sandbar, with one end attached to the land; a tombolo is a spit that links an island to the mainland.

Sea erodes into the cliffs, sculpting patterns of rock, such as this arch.

Waves eat back inland, leaving a wave-cut platform which juts out beyond the cliff.

Eroded material accumulates at the shoreline, forming beaches.

Stack or lone pillar

Cliffs are attacked by storms; sea arch roof collapses, leaving a stack; another arch appears behind.

Cliff retreats further as rocks fall.

Rough seas continue to erode coastline, spurting through a blowhole, a crack in the cliff.

Storm waves eat away at cliff base.

Stack is worn down.

Cave mouth

Cliff face marked with crags and gulleys where boulders fall.

Coastline has moved backwards with erosion of cliffs.

Types of coasts

Coasts vary according to their composition and structure. Whether the coast is high or low, and made of soft or hard rock, affects whether it has been formed largely as a result of erosion or by deposition.

Bay-head beach
This is formed when material eroded from headlands (high land jutting into the sea) is washed into a bay, a coastal inlet between the headlands.

Wave direction

Drowned coast
Where the sea-level has risen or the land sunk, valleys are flooded to form narrow inlets, or rias. Where the valleys are glacial, the inlets are called fjords.

Wave direction

Highland coast
Where the sea meets a highland coast, it generally wears away the rocks, creating cliffs, small coves, and wave-cut rock platforms.

Raised beach

River slopes towards new sea level.

Lowland coast
Broad beaches, salt marshes, and estuaries are features of lowland coasts.

Waves

The wind whips the sea's surface into waves. Waves travel across the water, but the water in them circulates on the spot. When waves reach the shore, the bottom touches the beach and slows down; the top spills on, causing the wave to "break".

Wave formation

Top spills over; wave breaks.

Circular motion is upset as the wave hits the beach.

Waves grow steeper as they approach the shore.

Water circulates in the wave in orbital paths.

Coastal protection
When waves strike a beach, they wash sand or pebbles across the beach at an angle,. This repeated process is known as longshore drift. Fences or groynes may be built, to slow down such reshaping of the beach.

Coastal fences

Beach material
Fine sand and silt are usually found lower down a beach; bigger storm waves wash gravel and pebbles higher up. On some beaches, there is a ridge of pebbles, called a storm beach, which has been flung up beyond the high-tide mark by violent storms.

Pebbles and stones

Fine sand

Gritty sand

FIND OUT MORE   CAVES   CORAL REEFS   GLACIATION   MOUNTAINS AND VALLEYS   OCEANS AND SEAS   ROCKS AND MINERALS   SEASHORE WILDLIFE

CODES AND CIPHERS

A CODE IS ANY SYSTEM of prearranged symbols, words, or numbers that is used in communication. For example, the flags that are used to send messages at sea are a naval code. We use codes to simplify, organize, and communicate complex information, for instance, in dialling and postal codes, or bar codes that describe goods in a way that machines can read. Not all codes have an everyday use. Ciphers (secret codes) hide the true meaning of a message. Banks use them to keep financial deals private, and spies or criminals to avoid capture.

Ciphers

In a cipher, each letter is represented by a different letter or symbol. For instance, it is easy to encipher a message by jumbling the alphabet, changing C into M and M to C. It is easy to break such a simple cipher, but computers can create ciphers that are impossible to read without the key (a long number that unlocks the meaning).

Spies
A spy is a secret agent, who collects information for a government or organization. A spy's work often involves stealing the secrets of rival governments. Spies use ciphers to scramble data when they send it to their employers.

Spy codesheet

Cipher discs
These devices create ciphers by replacing letters of the message on the outer ring with the letters alongside them on the inner ring.

Cipher disc

Cipher machines
The Enigma cipher machine was used during World War II. It had a typewriter keyboard with electrical connections that scrambled the letters. Each letter was coded separately, making the cipher hard to break.

Metal cover plate fits over rotor cylinders

Viewing window shows code letters

Rotor cylinder

Coding rotor

Plugboard setting is altered to change cipher

Keyboard

Filter to dim lights

German Enigma cipher machine, World War II

Smoke signals

Fire beacons and smoke codes were used to send signals by the people of ancient China, Egypt, and Greece. Native Americans, such as the Cheyenne, Comanche, and Sioux, communicated over distances using smoke signals, shaping smoke with an animal hide or blanket. There were a few generally understood signals – two puffs meant "all's well" – but each group also had secret codes which they shared only with people they wanted to read the messages.

Frederic Remington, Smoke Signals

Uses of code

Codes make messages quicker to send. They have been used for many reasons. Sailors, for example, used flag codes to communicate for more than 1,000 years. By flying the three flags standing for the letters NKA, a warship could send a message meaning "I have not sighted any vessels since leaving my last port". A code book carried on every ship translated the codes.

Computer codes
Special codes are used to program information inside computers, where letters and punctuation marks are represented by binary numbers. Ciphers can also be also used to protect e-mail (mail sent between computers), so that it can only be understood by the sender and the addressee.

E-mail can be encrypted so that only the addressee, who holds a secret "key" (a long number), can read it.

The alphabet in Morse code

A	•_	N	_•
B	_•••	O	_ _ _
C	_•_•	P	•_ _•
D	_••	Q	_ _•_
E	•	R	•_•
F	••_•	S	•••
G	_ _•	T	_
H	••••	U	••_
I	••	V	•••_
J	•_ _ _	W	•_ _
K	_•_	X	_••_
L	•_••	Y	_•_ _
M	_ _	Z	_ _••

Morse code
The telegraph was invented in the 19th century; it used electricity to send messages quickly over long distances for the first time. The system could not transmit speech, so to communicate operators used an alphabetic code devised by US artist Samuel Morse (1791–1872). Letters were represented by dots and dashes (long and short pulses of power). Operators tapped a key to turn the electric current in the telegraph wires on and off. Morse code is still in use.

Prototype telegraph key, 1840s

William Friedman
Russian-born American William Friedman (1891–1969) decrypted secret messages for the US government in World Wars I and II. In 1940, William led the team that discovered the key to the Japanese Purple cipher. A message in this cipher warned of the Pearl Harbor attack.

FIND OUT MORE   FLAGS   INFORMATION TECHNOLOGY   LANGUAGES   NATIVE AMERICANS   SIGNS AND SYMBOLS   WORLD WAR II

COLD WAR

IN 1945, THE ALLIED FORCES of the USA, Britain, France, and the USSR – now known once again as Russia – gained victory over Germany in World War II. Within four years, the allies had become enemies, and a new war had broken out. This was not a military war, but a "cold" war – a political and diplomatic battle between communist Eastern Europe and capitalist Western Europe. The rival blocks expressed hostility by backing opposing sides in conflicts such as Korea and Vietnam. The Cold War ended in 1990, when Eastern Europe's communist governments fell.

Winston Churchill, FD Roosevelt, and Josef Stalin, Yalta Conference

Yalta Conference
In 1945, the British, American, and Soviet leaders Churchill, Roosevelt, and Stalin met in the Russian resort of Yalta to determine the shape of post-war Europe. The conference agreed Soviet control over Eastern Europe. This started the political division of Europe into east and west that was to last until 1990.

Iron Curtain

By 1949, there was a clear division in Europe between the communist states in the east that followed Russia, and the capitalist states in the west that followed the USA. Both east and west became secretive and hostile. In 1946, the British Prime Minister Winston Churchill famously described this polarization as "an iron curtain ... (descending) across the continent."

Iron Curtain

Austria was divided until 1955.

Switzerland was neutral during the war.

Capitalist   Communist

Mig-15 jet

Korean War
In 1945, Korea was divided between a communist north and an American-backed south. In 1950, North Korea invaded the south; the USA supported South Korea, while the USSR and China supported North Korea. War raged until an armistice was agreed in 1953. Korea remains divided to this day.

Red Scare
In the early 1950s, fear of Communism in the USA led to a witch-hunt against known Communist Party members and possible sympathizers. Senator Joe McCarthy led a government committee that created a "Red Scare" in the USA, and caused hundreds of innocent people to lose their jobs.

Spies

Technological information was very important during the Cold War. In order to find out what the other side was planning, both sides of the Iron Curtain employed spies. Spies worked undercover in civilian and defence jobs, passing vital military secrets back to their own governments.

Invisible powder stuck to a spy's body and was detectable under ultraviolet light.

Chemical detection kit

Soviet ship returning to the USSR

Cuban missile crisis

In 1962 Soviet ships delivered nuclear weapons to the Cuban government. The US – only 90 miles (145 km) from Cuba – blockaded the island, which caused a crisis between the USA and the USSR. After several days of tension, the USSR withdrew its missiles.

Détente

In the 1960s, tension between east and west began to ease. In the 1970s, Willy Brandt, West Germany's leader, negotiated treaties with Poland and the USSR. In the late 1980s, Mikhail Gorbachev began to reform the USSR, which eventually led to the fall of communism in Eastern Europe.

Berlin Wall is dismantled, 1989

Anti-communist poster

Timeline

1945 Europe divides into eastern and western blocks.

1949 Western nations set up NATO (North Atlantic Treaty Organization).

1950–54 McCarthy era, USA.

1950–53 Korean War.

NATO symbol

1955 Warsaw Pact establishes military alliances between communist countries.

1961 Berlin Wall divides East from West Berlin (and East from West Germany).

1962 Cuban missile crisis marks the peak of the Cold War; its resolution slowly leads to détente.

1989 Fall of the Berlin Wall begins the fall of communist governments throughout Eastern Europe.

1990 Re-unification of East and West Germany.

1991 Gorbachev resigns; collapse of communism in USSR.

Mikhail Gorbachev

Gorbachev (b.1931) became leader of the USSR in 1985. He attempted to reform the USSR, and negotiated arms reduction agreements with US President Reagan. Despite his success, he failed to improve the living standards of the Soviet people, and resigned in 1991.

 FIND OUT MORE   EUROPE, HISTORY OF   RUSSIA, HISTORY OF   SOVIET UNION   UNITED STATES, HISTORY OF   WARFARE   WEAPONS   WORLD WAR II

COLOUR

A WORLD WITHOUT COLOUR would be dull and uninspiring. Colour is a form of light. Light is made up of electromagnetic waves of varying lengths. The human eye detects these different wavelengths and sees them as different colours. White light – like that from the Sun – is a mixture of all the different wavelengths. Objects look coloured because they give out or reflect only certain wavelengths of light.

White light spectrum

Passing white light through a transparent triangular block called a prism separates out the different wavelengths of light. The prism refracts (bends) each wavelength by a different amount, forming a band of colours called a white light spectrum, or a visible spectrum. The seven main colours are red, orange, yellow, green, blue, indigo, and violet. Red has the longest wavelength and violet the shortest. Here, a convex lens combines the colours back into white light.

Rainbow

A rainbow at dawn

If it rains on a sunny day, you may well see a rainbow if you stand with your back to the Sun. A rainbow is a curved white light spectrum that forms when light is reflected and refracted by raindrops in the sky.

How a rainbow forms

When white sunlight passes through a raindrop, the raindrop acts like a tiny prism. The raindrop refracts the light and splits it up into its separate colours. The colours fan out and emerge as a spectrum. A rainbow is made up of spectra from millions of raindrops.

Sunlight

Colours refract again.

Spectrum

Light refracts.

Colours reflect off back surface.

Colour and temperature

Objects at room temperature emit (give out) electromagnetic waves, but these waves are too long for human eyes to see. Heating an object, such as this steel bar, gives the waves it emits more energy and makes them shorter. The waves eventually become short enough to be seen, and the bar begins to glow. As the bar's temperature rises, it glows with different colours.

Steel bar at 630°C (1,170°F)

Steel bar at 1,530°C (2,790°F)

Spectroscope

Light source

Diffraction grating

An instrument called a spectroscope is used to analyze the light given out by hot substances. Inside the spectroscope, a prism or diffraction grating (a glass slide scored with fine lines) splits light from a glowing substance into its component wavelengths.

Emission spectrum

Each chemical element gives out a unique range of light wavelengths when heated. Seen through a spectroscope, these wavelengths appear as a set of bright lines on a dark background. This is the element's emission spectrum. A compound's emission spectrum is a combination of spectra from the elements that make up the compound.

Emission spectrum of a sodium flame

Sodium flame

Cone cells

Cone cells

At the back of the eye there are special cells called cones that enable humans to see colours. There are three types of cone, called red, green, and blue cones. Each type of cone is sensitive to a different range of light wavelengths. White light stimulates all three types of cone.

Sensitivity of red cones

Sensitivity of green cones

Sensitivity of blue cones

Visible spectrum

Sensitivity of cone cells in the human eye

Glowing white

Glowing red

Visible spectrum

Red hot and white hot

As the steel bar gets hotter, it emits more and more of the visible spectrum. At about 630°C (1,170°F), it is "red hot" and emits light from the red end of the spectrum. At about 1,530°C (2,790°F), the "white hot" bar emits the entire white light spectrum.

Hot stars

The colour of a star gives a clue to its age. To the naked eye, most stars look white, but their true colours can be seen using a telescope. Young stars are hot and glow with white light. Older stars are relatively cool and glow red or orange.

A cluster of young stars

Joseph von Fraunhofer

The German physicist Joseph von Fraunhofer (1787–1826) became interested in the nature of light while training as a mirror maker and lens polisher. His training enabled him to make spectroscopes of great precision. From 1814–17, he used them to make the first scientific study of the Sun's emission spectrum.

Munsell colour system

Describing colours exactly using words alone is not easy. To avoid confusion, manufacturing industries use standard colour-identification systems. The Munsell system is used to specify colours for dyes and pigments. It defines a colour by its value (brightness), its chroma (strength), and its hue (position in the spectrum).

Colour matching systems

Graphic designers use swatches of colour cards to match the colours in their work with those available from printers. The designer supplies the printer with the reference number of the colour, so the printer knows exactly what is wanted.

Each colour has a reference number.

Green

Red and green light mix to give yellow.

Green and blue light mix to give cyan.

Red, green, and blue light mix to give white.

Red

Blue

Red and blue light mix to give magenta.

Coloured lights

Different amounts of red, green, and blue light can be mixed to form light of any other colour. This process is called colour addition. Unlike paints, red, green, and blue are the primary colours of light. Equal amounts of any two primary colours give a secondary colour (yellow, cyan, or magenta). When all three primaries are mixed in equal amounts, white light is produced.

Image is formed by tiny glowing strips.

Colour television

The principle of adding coloured lights is used in colour television. The screen is covered with tiny strips that glow with red, green, or blue light. They are so small that, at a normal viewing distance, the human eye mixes the light coming from them. By adjusting the intensities of these three colours, the sensation of any other colour can be produced.

Painting with dots

"Pointillism" is a style of painting in which an artist uses thousands of tiny coloured dots to build up a picture. When viewed close up, the colours of the individual dots are clearly visible. Like the coloured strips on a television screen, the dots are too small to be seen from farther away. When viewed from a distance, the dots seem to merge, giving areas a single colour.

Pigments

A pigment is a chemical that absorbs only certain colours from white light. This process is called colour subtraction. Yellow, magenta, and cyan are primary pigments. Each absorbs one of the primary colours of light and reflects the other two. For example, a yellow pigment absorbs blue light but reflects green and red, which mix to give yellow. An equal mix of all three pigments absorbs all the colours from white light, giving black.

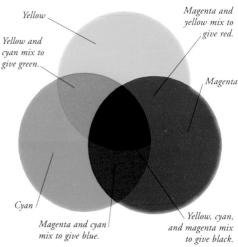

Yellow

Yellow and cyan mix to give green.

Magenta and yellow mix to give red.

Magenta

Cyan

Magenta and cyan mix to give blue.

Yellow, cyan, and magenta mix to give black.

Colour printing

To print a full-colour picture, three single-colour images are printed on top of each other – one in cyan, one in magenta, and one in yellow. Each picture is made up of tiny coloured dots. The dots overlap and absorb the right wavelengths of light to give all the other colours required. A black image is then added to make the picture sharper.

Picture is made up of tiny ink dots.

Mixing paints

Paints are pigments mixed with water or oil. Any colour except white can be made by mixing the three primary pigments. Mixing paints has the effect of evenly mixing the pigments, and absorbing more of the white light spectrum.

Scattering and interference

Two other processes, called scattering and interference, can remove colours from the spectrum. Interference occurs when light from two sources meets and combines. In scattering, some parts of the spectrum are briefly absorbed by particles of matter and then radiated out again in all directions.

Blue sky

Sunlight includes all the colours of the spectrum. The sky appears blue during the day because air molecules in the atmosphere scatter light from the blue end of the spectrum in all directions.

Soap bubble

When white light strikes a soap bubble, it reflects off both the inner and outer surfaces of the bubble. The reflected light rays interfere, making some colours cancel each other out but others appear bright.

Interference creates a pattern of bright colours and dark bands.

Using interference

Stress is a force that can stretch or bend objects. Engineers shine light through plastic models of their designs to test their ability to withstand stress. The plastic molecules make the light rays split up and interfere. The interference patterns show the points of greatest stress.

High stress

Reflecting colours

Objects have colour only when light falls upon them, because colours do not exist in total darkness. An object that appears one colour in white light may look different when illuminated by coloured light. The yellow pot in this sequence of pictures appears yellow only in white light.

White light

The yellow pot reflects the red and green parts of the white light spectrum, but absorbs the blue part.

Red light

The yellow pot reflects red light, and therefore appears red when illuminated by red light.

Green light

When illuminated by green light, the yellow pigment reflects the green light and so appears green.

Blue light

When only blue light is available, the yellow pot absorbs the blue light, making it look black.

FIND OUT MORE

DYES AND PAINTS   EYES AND SEEING   LIGHT   PHOTOGRAPHY   PRINTING   TELEVISION

COLUMBUS, CHRISTOPHER

CHRISTOPHER COLUMBUS was the first European since the Vikings to visit America. In the 1400s, Europeans did not know that America existed – they thought that Asia faced Europe across the Atlantic Ocean. In 1492, Columbus set sail from Spain across the Atlantic. He hoped to open up a trade route to Asia that would be quicker than the old land journey. He found some islands he believed were the East Indies, off what was presumed to be the Asian mainland. What he had really discovered was a continent soon to be known as America by the Europeans.

The port of Genoa in the 16th century

Early life
Columbus was born in the port of Genoa, Italy in 1451 and was named after St Christopher, the patron saint of travellers. His father was a weaver, and Christopher had little formal education. As a boy, he went to sea, and later worked in Lisbon, Portugal, where he drew sea charts for Portuguese sailors.

Crossing the Atlantic

While the Portuguese and other sailors were trying to find a sea route to Asia by sailing south and east round Africa, Columbus believed that, since the world was round, he could reach Asia from the opposite direction by sailing west across the Atlantic. In 1492, he persuaded the king and queen of Spain to finance his voyage, and set sail with three ships, the largest of which was the three-masted *Santa Maria*. At his first attempt, he landed in the Bahamas. Columbus, however, thought these islands were off the coast of Asia.

The *Santa Maria*

Royal flag of Spain

Main mast

Mizzen mast

Square-rigged sails

Room for 40 crew below deck

Columbus' four voyages
— 1492
→ 1493
— 1498
→ 1502

Four voyages
Columbus made four voyages across the Atlantic between 1492 and 1504. On the first, he reached Cuba, the Bahamas, and Hispaniola; on the second, he explored Jamaica; on the third he reached Trinidad and the South American coast. On his fourth voyage he actually set foot on the mainland of the "new" continent.

Foremast

Because accommodation was so cramped, food was often cooked on deck.

Navigation
Columbus had few instruments to help him navigate across the ocean. He used a crosstaff and astrolabe to calculate the ship's latitude, but had no way of knowing its longitude. Despite this lack of information, he managed to navigate successfully back home to Europe.

Astrolabe

Using the crosstaff

Crosstaff

West Indies

Columbus was amazed by the beauty and lush vegetation of the Caribbean islands, but he was disappointed that he had not found the rich trading cities of Asia. However, his discoveries encouraged other Europeans to visit the area in the coming centuries, founding colonies and opening up new trade links between Europe and the Caribbean.

Columbus arriving at the island of Hispaniola

New discoveries
While in the West Indies, Columbus and his crew tasted new foods, such as pineapple, potatoes, and sweetcorn. They saw people sleeping in hammocks, and observed the Arawak peoples of Cuba rolling up dried tobacco leaves and smoking them.

Later life
In 1493, Columbus was made governor-general of all the lands he discovered, but he was a poor administrator. In 1500, there were complaints about his rule of Hispaniola. As a result, Columbus was arrested and sent back to Spain in chains. He retired to Seville, where he died in 1506.

CHRISTOPHER COLUMBUS

1451 Born in Genoa, Italy

1476 Becomes a chartmaker in Lisbon, Portugal

1479 Marries Filipa de Perestrello e Moniz

1484 Becomes master mariner in Portuguese merchant service

1492 First voyage: sails across Atlantic Ocean in search of new route to Asia

1493–96 Second voyage

1493 Establishes European colony on Hispaniola

1498–1500 Third voyage

1502–04 Fourth and final voyage

1506 Dies in Seville, Spain

 FIND OUT MORE   CENTRAL AMERICA, HISTORY OF   EXPLORATION   NAVIGATION   SHIPS AND BOATS   SOUTH AMERICA, HISTORY OF   SPAIN, HISTORY OF

COMBAT SPORTS

FIGHTING SPORTS, which had their origins in ancient Greece, developed in different ways. Judo and the other martial arts, such as karate, kung-fu, taekwondo, and aikido, evolved in the East, often as a way of life or connected with religion. Only since the 1950s have their secrets become known in the West and their popularity as sports spread. The chief Western combat sports are boxing, wrestling, and fencing. These have Eastern counterparts – kick boxing, sumo, and kendo respectively.

The judo suit, or "judogi", is a loose-fitting cotton jacket and trousers.

Players grip an opponent by the jacket.

	Red
	Black
	Brown
	Blue
	Green
	Orange
	Yellow

Belts
The colour of the belt a player wears around the jacket indicates his or her grade. Judo grades range from *kyu*, meaning student, to the advanced *dan* grades when the player wears a black belt, or red for ninth or tenth dan.

Performing a hip throw

Judo

Judo means "the gentle way", and players try to use their opponent's weight and strength against them. Players can use more than 40 recognized throws to put their opponent on their back. Or, in groundwork, they try to pin their opponent's back on the mat with a hold. In competition, a referee awards points for throws and holds.

The arm is used to absorb the impact of a throw.

The shoulder is pinned to the ground during groundwork.

Scoring
A perfect throw or 30-second hold-down earns *ippon*, worth ten points, and wins the contest outright. Near-perfect throws or shorter hold-downs earn *waza-ari*, worth seven points, and two of these win a contest. If the contest goes its full length, other scores and penalties count.

Fencing

In fencing, points are scored by registering "hits" on the opponent's target areas. These vary according to the weapon used: the upper body including the arms for a sabre; the trunk only for a foil; and the whole body for an épée. A bout lasts until one player has scored the agreed number of hits or the time limit has been reached.

Scoring a hit

Weapons
A foil and sabre must not weigh more than 500 g (17.5 oz), an épée not more than 770 g (26.9 oz). The foil and épée have a 90-cm (35.4-in) blade and must strike the target with the point. The edges of a sabre's 88-cm (34.7-in) blade may be used for a hit.

Gauntlet *Mask*

Wired-up over-jacket

Foil

Épée

Sabre

Fencing kit
Fencers wear protective clothing on the body, a mask of steel or plastic mesh, and a padded gauntlet on the sword hand. In competition, target areas may be electrically wired to register hits, signalled by lights.

Boxing

Boxers fight in a raised, square "ring" bounded by ropes. Amateur boxing is staged over three three-minute rounds. Professional fights last up to 12 rounds (15 in title fights). Fights may be won by a knock-out, by the referee stopping the fight, or on points.

Amateur's headgear

Padded gloves

High-sided boots

Muhammad Ali

Arguably the most colourful figure in sport, Muhammad Ali (b.1942) was the first boxer to regain the world heavyweight title three times. Born Cassius Clay, he won the Olympic light-heavyweight title in 1960, turned professional, then gained the world heavyweight crown with a shock win over Sonny Liston in 1964. He changed his name when he joined the Black Muslims.

Other combat sports

Like judo, most of the other Eastern combat sports come from Japan, including karate, sumo wrestling, and kendo.

Karate, meaning "empty hands", uses kicks and strikes by the hands, elbows, and head.

Sumo wrestling is steeped in the ritual of the Shinto religion. Each contestant tries to throw his opponent or push him out of the ring.

Kendo pays tribute to the samurai fighters of feudal times. "Swords" are bamboo sticks.

FIND OUT MORE GREECE, ANCIENT   JAPAN, HISTORY OF   OLYMPIC GAMES   RELIGIONS   WEAPONS

COMETS AND ASTEROIDS

COMETS AND ASTEROIDS ARE LEFTOVERS from when the nine planets formed in the Solar System 4.6 billion years ago. Comets are fragile balls of snow and dust found at the edge of the Solar System in the Oort Cloud. Some leave the cloud and travel towards the Sun. The Sun's heat melts the snow and the comet appears to grow in size many times over. Asteroids are made of rock and are found mainly between the orbits of Mars and Jupiter.

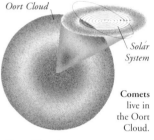

For most of its orbit, a comet is a dirty snowball.

Tail develops as comet approaches Sun.

Tail is longest near Sun.

Tail shrinks as comet moves away from Sun.

Thin, straight gas tail

Anatomy of a comet

At the centre of a comet is the nucleus – a dirty ball of snow and dust that is just a few kilometres across. If a comet is close to the Sun, the snow becomes gas, and gas and dust are released, forming a vast cloud of material – the coma – and one or two tails.

Comet West passed Earth in 1976. It had two distinctive tails.

Broad dust tail

Nucleus *Coma*

Halley's Comet
Halley's Comet is the only comet that has been seen up close. Five spacecraft went to investigate when it travelled through the inner Solar System in 1986. The space probe *Giotto* took this image of its dark, potato-shaped nucleus.

Edmond Halley
Comets are usually named after their discoverer, but one is named after the English scientist, Edmond Halley (1656–1742). He was the first person to show that comets can be periodic and follow orbits that return them again and again to Earth's sky.

Periodic comets
When a comet leaves the Oort Cloud it can travel on an orbit which returns it again and again to the inner Solar System. This is a periodic comet. About 150 are short-period comets; they return to appear in Earth's sky in periods of less than 200 years. Halley's Comet passes Earth every 76 years.

Oort Cloud

Solar System

Comets live in the Oort Cloud.

Oort Cloud
Surrounding the Solar System is the Oort Cloud, made up of 10 trillion comets. Although the cloud is large, it is so distant that the comets cannot be seen. Comets only become visible when they travel within the inner Solar System. Astronomers have seen about 700 comets in Earth's sky.

Meteoroids

Tiny pieces of dust and chunks of rock travel through space. They are meteoroids and originate from two main sources: comets and asteroids. About 220,000 tonnes of such material enter Earth's atmosphere a year. The smallest meteoroids produce meteors. Larger pieces reach Earth and land on its surface. These are meteorites.

Meteors
Tiny meteoroids burn up as they travel through Earth's atmosphere, producing streaks of light known as meteors. When Earth travels through a concentration of meteoroids, a meteor shower is produced. The meteoroid material is left by comets as they pass close to the Sun.

Meteorites
More than 3,000 meteorites land on Earth every year. Most fall in the sea, but a handful are seen to fall on land. There are three main types of meteorites: stony, iron, or stony-iron.

Stony-iron meteorite

Fragment of nickel-iron

Nakhla meteorite

Rock from Mars
Eight meteorites are known to have come to Earth from Mars. The Nakhla meteorite fell in Egypt in 1911. It is 13 million years old. Such meteorites tells us that Mars once had running water.

Impact crater
When a meteorite lands on Earth, it can create a crater. Earth was once bombarded by meteorites but its surface has since changed, removing the evidence. Today, about 150 impact craters can be identified, including Wolfe Crater in Australia.

Wolfe Crater

Asteroid belt

Between the orbits of Mars and Jupiter is the asteroid belt – a doughnut-shaped ring made of millions of asteroids, pieces of rock, and metal. The smallest are specks of dust; the biggest, Ceres, is more than 900 km (550 miles) across.

Gaspra
About 5,000 asteroids have been identified, but only about 10 are spherical and larger than 250 km (150 miles) across. The smaller ones, such as the stony asteroid Gaspra, are irregular in shape.

Asteroid belt

Jupiter

Mars

Trojan asteroids

Asteroid groups
Not all asteroids are in the asteroid belt. About 10 per cent travel in groups away from the belt. The Trojans travel along Jupiter's orbit, one group in front and one group behind the planet. The Amor, Apollo, and Aten groups all follow orbits closer to Earth.

FIND OUT MORE ASTRONOMY PLANETS SPACE EXPLORATION SUN AND SOLAR SYSTEM UNIVERSE

COMPUTERS

WITH LIGHTNING SPEED, a computer carries out millions of calculations each second. Sets of instructions called programs tell the computer what to do. The hard-disk unit is the heart of a computer. It contains the central processing unit (CPU), which controls all of the operations of the computer. The hard-disk unit, monitor, keyboard, and other connected devices are called hardware. The programs that enable it to function and carry out specific tasks are known as software.

Personal computer

A personal computer (PC) is a compact computer that can be operated by only one person at a time. It consists of a hard-disk unit, to which hardware called peripherals is connected so that data can be either input or output. Keyboards and printers are examples of peripherals. Interfaces are electronic circuits that allow the hard-disk unit to communicate with each peripheral.

Hard-disk unit contains the memory, the CPU, and the disk drives.

Personal computer (PC) with peripherals

Monitor receives signals from the hard disk and forms images of text and graphics in a similar way to a TV set.

Right loudspeaker with controls

Left loudspeaker

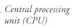

Mouse mat

Keyboard consists of numbers, letters, and special function keys that allow data to be typed directly into the computer.

Printer receives data from hard disk and produces print-out of documents and graphics.

Graphics tablet enables images to be "drawn" on the monitor screen, as a pen-like device moves over its surface.

Mouse controls pointer on screen; inside the mouse is a ball that rotates as the mouse moves, and the ball's movement sends signals to the computer.

Scanner copies an image and translates it into on-off pulses of electricity that are fed into the computer, so that the image can be displayed on the monitor screen.

Motherboard

A motherboard is a large circuit board in the hard-disk unit to which the computer's key electronic components are attached. These components are linked together by strips of metal called "buses" on the underside of the motherboard. Also attached to the motherboard are the interfaces that link the hard-disk unit to the peripherals, as well as expansion slots, to which other circuit boards can be added to improve the computer's performance or capabilities.

Memory

A computer's electronic memory allows it to "remember" how to function. There are two parts to the memory: the random access memory (RAM) and the read-only memory (ROM). Both consist of circuits called microprocessors, or silicon chips.

PC motherboard

Expansion slots for extra circuit boards

Video card controls operation of monitor screen.

Sockets called ports allow peripherals such as a modem or printer to connect to the hard disk.

Buses carry signals around the computer.

Battery controls computer's internal clock.

Central processing unit (CPU)

ROM (read-only memory) chips store important programs, such as the disk-operating system, whose content cannot be changed.

RAM (random-access memory) chips store data fed into the computer on disks or via the keyboard, which can then be retrieved and changed as desired.

Charles Babbage

English mathematician Charles Babbage (1791–1871) built a mechanical computer called the Difference Engine that consisted of hundreds of gear wheels. It could do complicated sums more quickly than doing the same calculations by hand.

Monitor screen displays data.

RAM

CPU

Data input via a keyboard.

ROM

Central processing unit (CPU)

The CPU is a single microprocessor that holds a large number of circuits. The CPU receives data from the ROM, RAM, and keyboard. It sends data to the RAM for storage, and to output devices, such as the monitor.

C

Computer disks

Programs and data can be stored on computer disks. Magnetic disks record data as magnetic patterns in tiny iron particles that coat the disks' surfaces. A hard disk is a stack of magnetic disks inside a computer. Other types of disk include compact discs (CDs) and magneto-optical disks. A device called a disk drive is used to store data on disks and retrieve it.

Sector boundary — *Concentric tracks*

Floppy disk — *Sector*

Recording surface

How a disk drive works

Disks arrange data into divisions called tracks and sectors. A disk drive has a magnetic read-write head that "reads" data from, or "writes" data to, a specific sector and track on the disk. In CD and optical disk drives, the read-write head is a laser beam.

Types of computer disk

Floppy disks are small magnetic disks.

Optical mini-disks are small magneto-optical disks.

SyQuest disks are large magnetic disks able to store more data than floppies.

Magneto-optical disks store data magnetically, but are read by a laser beam.

Compact discs (CDs) store data as tiny pits in the surface of the disk.

Operating system allows this girl to use a program for learning Spanish.

Operating system

Every computer has a program called an operating system (OS) that controls its basic functions. The OS is always at work "behind the scenes" when other applications are running. A graphical user interface (GUI) often forms part of a computer's OS. The GUI allows the computer operator to use a mouse to move information or to run programs.

Steve Jobs and Steve Wozniak

The Apple Computer company – one of the world's largest – was founded in 1976 by Steve Jobs (b. 1955) and Steve Wozniak (b. 1950), who wanted to make computers affordable to ordinary people. Their 1977 Apple II computer was the first PC made for the mass market. It was hugely successful, because users of the Apple II needed no prior knowledge of electronics or computing.

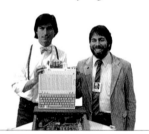

Types of computer

Most schools and many homes have personal computers, but there are many other types of computer, both larger and smaller than a PC. Some computers enable people to work while they are travelling; others are designed purely for entertainment. Large, powerful, high-speed computers are often used to process information for many people at once, or perform many tasks simultaneously.

Dedicated computer
While some computers can carry out many different tasks, others are "dedicated", meaning that they are designed for one specific purpose. A familiar example of a dedicated computer system is a games computer.

Laptop
Many business people take small, portable PCs called laptops with them when they travel. A laptop contains rechargeable batteries that allow it to function on trains, buses, outdoors – in fact, almost anywhere.

Mainframe
Most large organizations have a mainframe computer that can be used by many people at once, each working at a separate monitor, or terminal. A mainframe must be kept in a cold, dry environment.

Supercomputer
The most powerful computers are supercomputers. They are used to perform very complex tasks, such as forecasting future weather systems or analysing gravity and black holes in space. The first supercomputer was launched in 1976 by Cray.

Timeline

1642 Blaise Pascal invents the first mechanical adding machine.

1834 Charles Babbage designs a mechanical computer, which he calls the Difference Engine.

1939 John Atanasoff, an American, completes the first electronic computer.

Commodore personal computer, 1970

1945 ENIAC, the world's first automatic computer, is built in the USA.

1967 Keyboards are used for data entry.

1970 Floppy disks appear.

Late 1970s Mass-produced PCs are introduced.

1975 The first portable computer is introduced.

Late 1970s The Xerox Corporation invents the graphical user interface.

1983 The mouse is first used on an Apple computer.

1985 Computer CDs appear.

Assorted software programs

1980s Sales of PCs soar.

1990 IBM Pentium PC performs 112 million instructions per second.

2000 Mobile phones and other hand-held devices are designed to include computing facilities, software, and Internet.

 FIND OUT MORE   ATOMS AND MOLECULES   ELECTRONICS   INFORMATION TECHNOLOGY   LASERS AND HOLOGRAMS   MATHEMATICS   NUMBERS   SOUND RECORDING   WEATHER FORECASTING

CONFUCIUS

TWO THOUSAND YEARS AGO, China was in a state of turmoil and warfare. Strong imperial government had collapsed, and civil order had broken down. One man learned the lessons of this disorder. Confucius devised a moral code based on respect, kindness, and the strength of the family. He believed people could be taught to behave themselves as members of a well-ordered community. This vision, although based on a traditional view of Chinese society, is still influential in China today.

Early life

Confucius was born in Lu province in northeast China in about 551 BC. His name was Kong Qiu. His father died when he was three, leaving his mother to bring him up. He became known as K'ung Fu-tse, or "great master kong". In the West he was called Confucius, the Latin form of this title.

Confucius' teaching

Confucius learned to develop his new moral outlook from his experience in government. He taught that a good ruler should set an example by dealing fairly with his subjects, using force only as a last resort. In return, subjects had a duty to respect and obey their ruler.

Ancestor worship

In all his teachings, Confucius encouraged ancestor worship because it strengthened family ties. As a result, the Chinese people came to see themselves as part of a great national family that included not only living people but also the dead and those people who were still to be born. Many of the traditional Chinese gods and goddesses were believed to be ancestors who once lived as ordinary people in China and who, after their death, could influence everyday life.

Chün-tzu

According to the writings of Confucius, the ideal gentleman, or Chün-tzu, was a person who was compassionate, self-controlled, respectful of superiors, and concerned for the welfare of others. As a result, he was against slavery and human or animal sacrifices. Under the influence of Confucius it became common to bury pottery figures in tombs, rather than living animals or slaves.

Bronze tomb model of a rhinoceros

Traditional goddess, Kuan Yin

Zhou dynasty

Between 1027–256 BC, most of northern China was ruled by the Zhou dynasty. The early Zhou emperors ruled well, but later, as a result of pressure from powerful local lords, China split into a number of warring states. Confucius looked on the early years of the Zhou as a golden age of social harmony.

Handle in the form of mythical beast

Ritual vessel, Zhou period

Political career

For some years, Confucius worked as an adviser to the Duke of Lu and other local rulers. He attempted to promote good government by advising respect for the existing social order and fostering political stability. But his severe lifestyle and strict views were not popular, and Confucius eventually left Lu province.

Analects

Most of what we know about the teachings of Confucius can be found in a book of his sayings, the *Lun Yü*, or Analects. These sayings were collected by the followers of Confucius after his death. Confucius is also said to have compiled or edited five classic books known as the *Wu Ching*. The most famous of these is the *I Ching*, or Book of Changes. The *I Ching* provides a method of revealing the future through the use of 64 patterns of broken and unbroken lines.

Chinese characters written by a later follower of Confucius

Mencius

After Confucius' death, a number of his followers carried on his work. The most famous was Mencius (c.371–c.288). He believed that people are basically good, and that it is the duty of the ruler to ensure the prosperity, education, and moral well-being of his subjects. His pupils wrote down his thoughts and sayings in *The Book of Mencius*.

Impact

Although Confucius did not found a religion, his teachings are still influential throughout the world, especially in China, where the traditional values of the family are still based heavily on his views. The moral code taught by Confucius fits well with such established religions as Buddhism, Taoism, and Shinto, while his writings and classic texts are still widely studied in the West.

Chinese family, 19th century

CONFUCIUS

1027 BC	Zhou dynasty takes control of northern China.
c.551 BC	Confucius born in Lu.
532 BC	Confucius marries.
531 BC	Confucius' son born.
517 BC	Confucius goes into exile for the first time.
501–496 BC	Holds important post in Lu province.
483 BC	Returns to Lu province after many years of wandering.
c.481–221 BC	China splits into seven warring states.
c.479 BC	Death of Confucius.

 FIND OUT MORE   BOOKS   CHINA, HISTORY OF   PHILOSOPHY   RELIGIONS   SOCIETIES, HUMAN   WRITING

CONSERVATION

THE PRINCIPLE AIM of conservation is to ensure the survival of life in all its forms and variety, and to make certain that natural resources are not used beyond their capacity for renewal but continue for the benefit of future generations. Conservation requires an understanding of ecology – the interrelationships of the different plants and animals (including our own species) with each other, and with their environment. Concern for the health of the environment is steadily increasing, as can be seen from the growth of conservation organizations on almost every continent.

Why we need conservation

Ever increasing human populations lead to an increase in the demand for natural resources. This has many effects including deforestation, habitat loss, pollution of air and water, and extermination of species. Poaching of animals for meat, fur, and the medicine trade also reduces animal numbers. Conservation is an active means of slowing down or reversing these trends, in an attempt to safeguard the environment and all living things within it.

Endangered species
As human numbers increase, more land is needed to grow food, so forests are cut down and habitats destroyed. Without its habitat, wildlife cannot survive. Human pressure and hunting is causing many species, such as the white rhino, to become rare or endangered, some to the point of extinction. It is too late for animals such as the Tasmanian wolf, but others, such as the grey whale, have been saved from extinction.

Rhinos are hunted for their horns.

White rhino

Grizzly bears stand 3 m (10 ft) high.

Grizzly bears are the largest and most powerful of the animals living in Yellowstone National Park.

Males use antlers to fight.

Wapitis live in the forests of Yellowstone. They are larger than the red deer of Eurasia, but their behaviour is similar.

When displaying, male lifts tail into a fan.

Sage grouse are the most spectacular of the North American grouse. When displaying, the male struts around vibrating his wings and emits a booming sound.

Wingspan may reach 9 cm (3.5 in).

Phoebus butterflies appear in the Rockies in mid-summer.

Conservation

Conservation means wise use of resources, thus recognizing that to use natural resources is perfectly acceptable, as long as they are not exploited beyond their capacity for renewal. Conservation is concerned with the survival of life in all its forms, and with maintaining organic life at the optimum rate of productivity.

Forests are home to wapitis.

Preservation
Preservation differs from conservation in that preservation means strict protection as an end in itself, without regard for the consequences. The first area of land to be preserved was Yellowstone National Park in the USA, where animals such as grizzly bears and wapitis thrive in this undisturbed environment. Over-protection can lead to a build-up of the animal numbers, causing habitat destruction and the starvation and decline of the animals. This can be avoided by good management and by culling excess numbers of animals.

Yellowstone National Park, USA

Environmental organizations
Hundreds of organizations are concerned with safeguarding the Earth's resources. The International Union for Conservation of Nature and Natural Resources (IUCN), and the Worldwide Fund for Nature (WWF), carry out conservation projects worldwide.

Park rangers, WWF, Tsavo National Park

Methods of conservation
The establishment of national parks and wildlife sanctuaries is a very effective method of conserving natural areas and their wildlife. Other methods include education, breeding programmes, using renewable energy such as solar, wind, and wave power, and legislation. Some developing countries have agreed to safeguard areas of natural habitat in return for a reduction in their foreign debt.

Legislation
The Convention on International Trade in Endangered Species (CITES) controls trade in rare species, such as tigers; other groups control fishing and pollution.

Tiger bones are used to make oriental medicines.

Siberian tiger remains

Education
The importance of educating young people about conservation and the effect it has on their lives cannot be overstated. The need for education is as vital in the west as in the developing world. For conservation to be effective, it must have the support of the local people.

Game ranger teaching children

Breeding programmes
The best chance of survival for some animals close to extinction lies in breeding them in captivity for eventual return to their natural habitat. In one of the earliest breeding programmes, the few remaining Arabian oryx were captured, bred in the USA, and later successfully re-introduced to Oman.

Pale fur helps conceal oryx in the desert.

Arabian oryx

 FIND OUT MORE   BEARS   DEER AND ANTELOPES   ECOLOGY AND ECOSYSTEMS   ENERGY   LIONS AND OTHER WILD CATS   POLLUTION   RHINOCEROSES AND TAPIRS   ZOOS

Endangered animals

Dugongs live in tropical oceans, where they feed on sea grass.

Blue whales are the largest animals ever to have lived, reaching a length of 30 m (100 ft) or more.

Great white sharks are man-eating sharks, found in warm seas worldwide.

Cuvier's beaked whales are widely distributed, except in polar seas.

Giant pandas are bears that feed exclusively on bamboo.

Tigers are hunted for their fur and their bones, which are used in Chinese medicine.

Jaguars are endangered, due to habitat destruction and hunting for their fur.

These are among the world's largest butterflies.

Queen Alexandra's birdwings live only in Papua New Guinea.

Daubenton's bats hunt for insects over ponds and rivers.

St Vincent parrots live on the island of St Vincent.

Kakapos are preyed on by introduced rats and stoats.

Kakapos are nocturnal, flightless birds from New Zealand.

Wingspan may reach 2.7 m (9 ft).

Californian condors are among the largest living birds.

Great crested newts are the largest of the European newts, at up to 15 cm (6 in) long.

Golden mantellas from Madagascar are threatened by habitat destruction.

This weta is among the largest insects in the world.

Stephen's Island weta is confined to a small island off the coast of New Zealand.

Przewalski's horses are extinct in the wild, but captive bred animals have been re-introduced.

Gorillas are endangered, due to destruction of their rainforest habitat.

Père David's deer, extinct in its native China, has been bred in captivity.

White rhinos are scarce in Zaïre, but more abundant in South Africa.

Endangered plants

Dawn redwoods were rediscovered in China.

Insects are trapped when the two lobes of the leaf snap shut.

Venus's flytraps feed on insects.

This plant is threatened by introduced goats.

Silverswords live on the volcanic islands of Hawaii.

Knowlton cacti are among the world's rarest cacti.

Cactus shrinks back into the ground for part of the year.

New Zealand brush lilies are eaten by introduced possums.

Japanese sago palms are slow-growing evergreens.

CONTINENTS

THE WORLD'S SEVEN great land masses are known as continents. The seven continents are North America, South America, Africa, Europe, Asia, Antarctica, and Australia. Although you may not realize it, the continents are crunching together and drifting apart even as you read this page. This is because the Earth's outer shell, or crust, is made up of a number of vast, ever-moving slabs of rock called tectonic plates. The continents are embedded in these plates, which move very slowly – Europe and North America, for example, are drifting apart by just 4 cm (1.5 in) each year. Over millions of years, however, the continents have shifted this way and that across the globe, dramatically changing the face of the planet time and time again.

Continental drift

If you study a world map, you will notice that the east coast of South America looks as if it would fit neatly into Africa's west coast. This is because 220 million years ago Africa, South America, and all the other continents formed a single giant "supercontinent", now called Pangaea. Eventually, Pangaea split up into smaller land masses that drifted over the Earth's surface, giving the arrangement of continents that appears on your map today. Earth scientists call this theory continental drift.

200 million years ago: Pangaea, the single land mass, begins to break up.

Asia

135 million years ago: the South Atlantic opens up, pulling Africa and South America apart; India moves towards Asia.

Africa

South America

India *Europe* *Australia*

South Atlantic *North Atlantic*

North America

10 million years ago: Antarctica and Australia drift apart; the North Atlantic opens up, moving North America away from Europe.

Antarctica

Tectonic plates

There are nine major tectonic plates and a number of smaller ones. They fit together like the pieces of a jigsaw, covering the whole of the Earth's surface. The continents are carried by continental plates, such as the Eurasian plate. Oceanic plates, such as the Pacific plate, form most of the seafloor; the rest is made up of the fringes of the continental plates, which lie underwater.

Glossopteris fossil

Fossilized *Lystrosaurus* skull

Evidence for continental drift

Identical fossils of land-based plants and animals, such as the fern *Glossopteris* and the mammal *Lystrosaurus*, have been found in continents now widely separated by the sea. The only plausible explanation is that the continents were once linked together.

Alfred Wegener

German meteorologist and geophysicist Alfred Wegener (1880–1930) devised the theory of continental drift. As evidence, he cited the continents' matching coastlines, similar rock strata in continents separated by huge oceans, and fossil discoveries. Although widely accepted now, his ideas were ridiculed at the time.

Eurasian plate	Anatolian plate	Iranian plate	Phillippines plate	Plate boundary	Pacific plate	North American plate

Caribbean plate

South American plate

African plate	Arabian plate	Indo-Australian plate	Antarctic plate	Cocos plate	Nazca plate	Scotia plate

The major plates of the Earth's crust

Triple junctions

At places called triple junctions, a column of magma – hot, molten rock from the Earth's interior – burns its way through a continental plate. This splits the plate three ways, producing huge rift valleys between the fragments of the plate. The Great Rift Valley in East Africa was formed in this way. The fragments of the plate are forced further apart over millions of years, creating new continental land masses. As the rift valleys widen, new oceans form between the pieces of the fragmented plate.

Satellite image of Africa's Great Rift Valley

Diverging plates

At some places beneath the world's great oceans, the tectonic plates that make up the Earth's surface are slowly diverging. These places are called constructive margins. As the plates pull apart, molten rock called magma wells up through the crack between the plates and emerges as lava. When the lava cools, it adds new material to the sea floor. This process is known as sea-floor spreading.

Mid-ocean ridge

As two plates pull apart, the lava emerging from the Earth's interior solidifies and builds a line of undersea mountains along the crack. This is called a mid-ocean ridge. There is such a ridge beneath each of the world's great oceans. In Iceland, the North Atlantic Ridge rises above sea level and can be seen as a long gash in the landscape.

North Atlantic Ridge, Thingvellir, Iceland

Model of the North Atlantic

Mohorovicic discontinuity – boundary between crust and mantle

Continental crust

Iceland sits on top of the ridge.

Mid-ocean ridge

North American plate

Direction of plate movement

Eurasian plate

Continental crust

Rigid part of mantle

Transform faults are sideways tears along a mid-ocean ridge caused by the curve in the Earth's surface.

Rising magma

Sediments

Oceanic crust

Median valley is a long trough, or rift, which runs along the ridge.

Converging plates

In many places the tectonic plates are converging, or moving against one another. In places known as destructive margins, oceanic plates are drawn underneath the continental plates. The oceanic plate is pulled down into the layer of the Earth's interior called the mantle, where it is destroyed by intense heat. This process is called subduction. In other places called collision zones, the edges of two continental plates may crumple as they collide. This process creates great mountain ranges such as the Alps and the Himalayas.

Transform

In some places where tectonic plates meet, the plates neither collide nor pull apart, but simply slide past each other in opposite directions. These places are called transforms, or conservative margins. Perhaps the most famous transform is the San Andreas Fault in California, USA, where the Pacific and North American plates grind slowly past one another. As the plates move, they often snag and judder, setting off violent earthquakes.

San Andreas Fault, California, USA

Model of subduction zone around Japan

Magma burns through the crust to form an arc of volcanic islands.

Japan is an island arc created by subduction.

Eurasian plate

Plate boundaries

Direction of plate movement

Pacific plate

Philippine plate

Continental crust

Magma rises as plate melts in the Earth's interior.

Ocean trench is a long, deep dip in the ocean floor that forms where one plate is forced beneath another.

Mohorovicic discontinuity

Wedge of sediments builds up where subduction occurs.

Ocean trench

Oceanic crust

Rigid part of mantle

Ocean-floor sediment

FIND OUT MORE   EARTH   EARTHQUAKES   FOSSILS   GEOLOGY   MAGNETISM   MOUNTAINS AND VALLEYS   OCEAN FLOOR   OCEANS AND SEAS   VOLCANOES

237

COOK, JAMES

UNTIL THE MID-18TH CENTURY, European explorers were motivated by trade or plunder. James Cook, a British naval captain, began a new form of exploration – he was more interested in scientific research. From 1768 to 1779, he made three voyages to the South Pacific, applying scientific methods to navigation for the first time, and making astronomical observations that would help future sailors. He also carefully recorded everything he saw, bringing back many specimens and drawings of previously unknown flora and fauna.

Early life
James Cook was born in the town of Marton-in-Cleveland near Whitby, England in 1728. He went to sea as a boy, sailing in the Baltic before joining the British Royal Navy in 1755. Cook rose quickly through the ranks and was given command of his first ship in 1759, during the Seven Years' War with France.

Port of Whitby, England

The Endeavour
During the 1760s, Cook mastered the skills of navigation. These were put to good use when he was asked in 1768 to sail to Tahiti in the South Seas to observe the transit of the planet Venus across the sky. His choice of ship was unusual: the *Endeavour*, a converted collier familiar to Cook, and known for its toughness and ability to carry a heavy cargo.

The *Endeavour*

Main mast

Mizzen mast

Cook's explorations

Fore mast

Red ensign (British naval flag)

Large hold for supplies

Cook's sextant

Navigation
Navigation during Cook's time was primitive but effective. Cook used a chronometer to determine longitude (position east-west) and a quadrant or sextant to determine latitude (position north-south).

Lemons and limes

Diet
Cook was the first sea captain to take measures against scurvy – a disease caused by lack of vitamins – and supplied his crew with fresh fruit, meat, and vegetables wherever possible.

Mapping the Pacific
Cook made three voyages around the Pacific, circumnavigating New Zealand, mapping the east coast of Australia, and exploring many islands. He guessed correctly that there was an area of frozen land around the South Pole, and confirmed that Australia was a large island and not part of any southern continent.

Joseph Banks
Cook took with him botanist Joseph Banks, artist Sydney Parkinson, and a team of scientists. They discovered many species, such as the breadfruit and the kangaroo, previously unknown to Europeans. One area yielded so many new species that they called it Botany Bay. It is now a suburb of Sydney, Australia.

Joseph Banks

Some of Parkinson's illustrations

Death of Cook
On his third voyage, which started in 1776, Cook came across the Hawaiian Islands, which he named the Sandwich Islands. He spent the winter of 1778–79 in Hawaii, learning much about the inhabitants, and he returned in the spring of 1779, after exploring the west coast of America. This time, however, the local people were less friendly, and after a quarrel broke out, Cook was stabbed to death.

Cook is killed fighting the Hawaiian islanders.

Hawaiian clubs, used against Cook

JAMES COOK

1728	Born in Marton-in-Cleveland, Yorkshire, England
1755	Joins Royal Navy
1759	Takes command of his first ship
1768–71	Sails to the Pacific Ocean to observe the transit of Venus; explores Tahiti, New Zealand, and Australia
1772–75	Second voyage: maps many of the Pacific islands and sails south towards Antarctica
1776–79	Third voyage: sails into North Pacific; looks for inlet into Arctic Ocean
1779	Stabbed to death in Hawaii

FIND OUT MORE AUSTRALIA   AUSTRALIA, HISTORY OF   EXPLORATION   NAVIGATION   SHIPS AND BOATS

CORAL REEFS

TEEMING WITH WILDLIFE from shrimps to sharks, coral reefs are some of the most beautiful underwater structures. A coral reef takes thousands of years to form; it is composed of the living and dead skeletons of colonies of tiny animals called corals. Corals have flourished and built reefs in shallow, tropical seas for more than 440 million years. Corals are related to sea anemones and jellyfish, and belong to the group of animals called coelenterates. Australia's Great Barrier Reef is 2,000 km (1,240 miles) in length but is under serious threat from increased pollution.

Corals compete for light and food-bearing water currents.

Coral reefs

Coral reefs cover 619,000 sq km (239,015 sq miles) of the Earth's surface. Fringing reefs grow along coastlines, atolls are reefs that grow around extinct volcanoes, and cays are complete islands made of coral. Coral comes in all colours from red and yellow to blue and green, and grows in a variety of shapes and sizes including delicate fan corals, upright staghorn corals, and dome-shaped brain corals. Many animals hide in the holes and crevices within the reef.

Staghorn coral releasing eggs

Reproduction
Corals reproduce asexually to form colonies of genetically identical polyps. They also reproduce sexually, releasing eggs and sperm into the water. The fertilized eggs turn into larvae that join the plankton, which is carried on the currents, ensuring wide distribution.

Symbiotic algae live within corals and give them their bright colours.

Coral polyps open at night

Coral polyps close in the day

Coral polyp
Coral reefs are made up of many individual animals called coral polyps. They normally live in large colonies, but a few species are solitary. Soft corals have a rigid inner layer for support; hard corals secrete a cup-shaped chalky skeleton from their jelly-like bodies. A circle of tentacles, armed with stinging cells, immobilizes prey and pushes it through the mouth into the stomach. Coral polyps close up during the day, but at night the reef comes to life when the corals extend their tentacles into the water currents ready to trap prey.

Fish

Coral reefs are home to fish of all shapes and sizes, from solitary giant groupers and wrasse, at up to 1.8 m (6 ft) long, which lurk in reef caves and recesses, to shoals of tiny damselfish, which graze the fronds of seaweed on the top of the reef. Some, such as the moray eel, are vicious predators; others such as parrot fish, feed on coral.

Tubular mouth

Seahorses often hide within seaweed.

Prehensile tail grasps seaweed.

Seahorse
Seahorses are pipe fish with upright S-shaped bodies and prehensile tails. They eat small crustaceans, such as shrimps, and suck them into their tubular mouths. Females lay eggs in the males' brood pouches; the young develop and later emerge.

Spine can be raised.

Mandarin fish
The most poisonous fish of the reef are the various scorpion fish, such as the mandarin. Their bodies are protected by bony plates and poison-tipped spines. Mandarin fish swim slowly. They live near the seabed, waiting to pounce on their prey.

Black tip reefshark
The largest inhabitants of the reef are the black tip reefshark and its distant relative, the giant manta ray. They patrol the seaward drop-off flank of reefs, on the lookout for potential fish prey that stray too far from the protection of the reef. By contrast, mantas are filter feeders attracted to the reef by the upwelling of plankton.

Eyes close when eating.

Black tip of fin

Jaws contain sharp teeth.

Gills

Streamlined body for speed

Powerful tail

Reptiles

Flippers

Wide feet help it paddle in water.

Green turtle

Reptiles
Sea turtles and sea snakes are reptilian inhabitants of reefs. Both need to surface to breathe air, but while turtles have to move onto land such as oceanic island reefs to breed, sea snakes can give birth to live young at sea. Some turtles prey on other animals, while others feed on grass. Sea snakes are good swimmers and are the most venomous snakes in the world. They prey on the abundant reef fish.

Invertebrates

Reefs provide a variety of habitats for invertebrates such as sea slugs, sea cucumbers, and sea urchins. The reef protects delicate filter feeders, such as sponges, from the impact of the waves. Some bivalve molluscs nestle in crevices; others such as mussels, anchor themselves to the coral with root-like hairs. Many crustaceans, such as shrimps, scavenge amongst the corals.

Strong suckers help octopus grip rocks.

Common octopus
The reef is an ideal environment for the octopus to hide – its soft body slips easily into crevices. A stealthy hunter, it grabs prey with sucker-covered tentacles. When out in the open, its ability to change the texture and tone of its skin provides excellent camouflage.

Giant clam
This biggest living shellfish grows to 1 m (3 ft) long and, like corals, is inhabited by symbiotic algae. A clam opens its shell to feed on plankton and closes it if danger threatens. Giant clams remain stationary once they are adult.

Shell is made of two halves.

Siphon for waste

Algae

FIND OUT MORE

AUSTRALIA FISH OCEAN WILDLIFE OCTOPUSES AND SQUIDS SHARKS AND RAYS TURTLES AND TORTOISES

CRABS AND OTHER CRUSTACEANS

THERE ARE SOME 30,000 SPECIES in the crustacean class, including crabs, barnacles, copepods, krill, lobsters, prawns, shrimps, and woodlice. Crabs and other crustaceans share characteristics including two pairs of antennae, mandibles, and a shell. In size they can range from microscopic freshwater fleas to giant Japanese spider crabs, which have a claw-to-claw span of 3.6m (11 ft). Most crustaceans live in the sea, others prefer fresh water, and a few, such as the woodlouse, live on land. Some are parasitic – they live on or in other animals.

Pincers

Smooth legs

Bumps on front legs

Carapace, or hard shell

Spikes protecting carapace

Mouth and eyes under edge of carapace

Jointed legs

Walking legs

Spiny spider crab

Defence

Apart from the protection they get from their shells, crabs can also defend themselves using their enlarged claws, or pincers, which often have a sharp serrated (toothed) edge. Some crabs, such as the decorator crabs, camouflage themselves by fixing seaweed to their shells, and blending into their surroundings. However, even with these methods of defence, crabs are still eaten by octopuses, fish such as bass, shore birds, and mammals.

Teeth

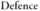

Claw of Japanese spider crab

Features of a crab

Crabs belong to the order Decopoda (10-legged). They have four pairs of jointed walking or swimming legs, plus an extra modified pair, called pincers. They have two pairs of antennae, gills, and a segmented, calcareous shell, or carapace. As they grow, crabs shed the carapace and grow a new one.

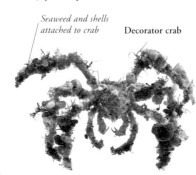

Seaweed and shells attached to crab

Decorator crab

Feeding

Crabs, such as the hermit crab, are generally omnivorous, and can be either predators or scavengers. Hermit crabs catch their prey in their pincers. The crab then uses the pincers like a fork, to pass the food to its mandibles (specialized jaws). The crab chews its food, then uses two pairs of adapted limbs to push the food further into the mouth.

Fish **Hermit crab**

Breeding

After the male has fertilized the female's eggs, she may carry them in a brood pouch until ready to hatch, or release them into the sea. Some crustaceans hatch as tiny adults, but crabs go through a larval stage, and spend their early life as plankton.

Eyes on stalks

A colourfully enlarged pincer attracts females.

Fiddler crab

How a crab moves

Crabs walk slowly forwards or backwards on their jointed legs when exploring their surroundings under water, but scuttle sideways across the ground when threatened. Some crabs, such as velvet crabs, are able to swim because their hind legs have been adapted into flattened paddles, also known as swimmerets.

Pincers

Crab crouching in defence.

Crab starts to turn to its left.

Shore crab turning. *Missing limb* *Small flap-like abdomen* *Fully turned crab can scuttle away.*

Barnacles

Young barnacles float in the sea until they find any stable surface, such as a rocky shore. They then attach themselves to a rock, and secrete a calcium-based substance that forms protective plates around them. They leave an opening for feeding, which closes when the animal is exposed to the air at low tide. Barnacles are hermaphrodites – that is, both sexes exist in one individual.

Goose barnacles attach themselves to driftwood with long stalks.

Goose barnacles

Feeding

Most barnacles feed themselves using their feet! When covered by water, these fine, feathery, curly limbs protrude from the barnacle's opening. The feet trap food as it floats past, filter it from the seawater, and transfer it into the barnacle's mouth. Goose barnacles do this while floating in the sea.

Woodlice

Woodlice are the only true land-living crustaceans. A woodlouse's "shell" consists of flat, waterproof plates that protect its back. Woodlice can dry out, so some species, such as the pill bug, have developed the ability to roll up and reduce water loss.

Waterproof plates

Lobsters

Lobsters, together with crabs, shrimps, prawns, and crayfish, are all known as crawlers, because of their movement. They live on the seashore, seabed, and in streams. Lobsters have large pincers for defence and feeding. The male's pincers are usually larger than the female's. The biggest species is the blue lobster, which weighs up to 25 kg (55 lb). Crayfish, close relatives of the lobster, live in freshwater and tend to be smaller.

Defence

Lobsters can evade capture by discarding a limb. There is a special "breaking plane" near the base of the leg that, when twisted, causes the leg to snap off. The wound soon heals and a new limb starts growing immediately.

Common lobster adopting a defensive pose

Small antennae *Eyes*

Lobster march

In an extraordinary event known as the lobster march, hundreds of lobsters gather and walk one after the other for more than 100 km (60 miles) across the seabed. It is possible that they are looking for a suitable area to settle, with an adequate supply of food. The lobsters make sounds during their migration and it is thought that these are noises of communication that help co-ordinate the journey. This event has not been seen in any of the other larger crustacean groups.

Environments

Lobsters prefer an environment featuring many nooks and crannies. Their ideal hiding place is a sandy burrow under a rock.

Lobster backing into its burrow.

Second pair of legs has claws.

Large antennae sense food and danger.

When threatened, the lobster's large pincers open.

Spiny lobsters

Cleaner-shrimps

Brightly coloured and easily recognizable cleaner-shrimps remove external scale and gill parasites from passing fish, such as the goby – and even remove unswallowed food particles from within the fish's mouth. Both animals benefit from this association, which is known as "cleaner symbiosis". Other symbiotic relationships exist between shrimps and sponges, sea anemones, and corals.

Cleaner-shrimp

Shrimps

The world's seas are full of scavenging shrimps and prawns. They look similar but prawns have a pointed rostrum (a saw-like structure at the front of the body) and two pairs of pincers, while shrimps have only one pair. Krill, small shrimp-like animals that live in the Antarctic seas, form the main food of whales.

Growth of shrimps

Most crustaceans, including shrimps, are unable to increase in size because their exoskeleton (shell) is inflexible. Therefore, they moult their shells at regular intervals. The new soft exposed skin underneath hardens quickly to form another, larger shell.

Shrimps have flatter bodies than prawns.

Strawberry shrimp

Water fleas

Water fleas, a group that includes brine and fairy shrimp, all breathe through leaf-shaped gills on their feet. Apart from brine shrimp (which live in saline pools), water fleas inhabit freshwater. Fairy shrimp live in temporary puddles. When these dry up, their eggs become airborne until they fall into another pool.

Daphnia water flea

Mussel shrimp

The tiny mussel or seed shrimp (so-called because its carapace is made up of two shells, like that of a mussel) produces the largest sperms in the animal kingdom. The 0.3-mm (0.01-in) long male of one species produces sperms 20 times its own length.

Copepods

These tiny creatures are an important part of plankton, which provides most of the world's fish with food. One species, *Calanus finmarchicus,* forms the staple diet of open-sea fishes, such as herring, sprat, and mackerel. Others, however, are parasitic and live in or on worms, molluscs, other crustaceans, fish, and whales.

Long fringed tentacles

Legs are extended for food gathering.

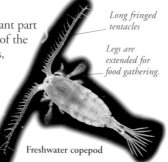

Freshwater copepod

Gribble

Able to digest wood, the gribble bores into the submerged wooden supports of jetties, wharfs, bridges, and pilings. It can turn these structures into a pulpy mass, causing them to collapse.

Segmented shell

SPINY SPIDER CRAB

SCIENTIFIC NAME *Machrocheira kaempferi*

SUBCLASS Malacostraca

ORDER Decapoda

DISTRIBUTION Seas around Japan

HABITAT On the seabed

DIET Scavenges anything edible from the seabed – an omnivore, it eats meat and plant matter

SIZE Span claw-to-claw 3.6 m (11 ft)

LIFESPAN Unknown, but lobsters, a relative, have lived up to 70 years in captivity

FIND OUT MORE   ARTHROPODS   CAVE WILDLIFE   CORAL REEFS   OCEAN LIFE   OCEANS AND SEAS   SEASHORE WILDLIFE

CRAFTS

BASKETMAKERS, WOODCARVERS, and stone masons are craftspeople; they handmake objects that are both useful and attractive. Unlike other art forms, crafts are concerned with function as well as beauty: they are made to be used. Before the Industrial Revolution, craftspeople made the furniture for the home and tools for the workplace. Today these items are mass-produced in factories, so hand-crafted objects are valued for their individuality, and because they often come from a tradition that is centuries old.

Stone carver at work

Goggles for protection

Carver taps chisel gently to cut stone to pattern.

Carpet to protect edges of stone

Plaster-of-Paris holds stonework steady

Banker, or workbench

Early craftspeople

Medieval craftspeople made their living from being skilled in one particular craft, such as coopering (barrel making), dyeing cloth, leather work, or goldsmithing. Each craft had its own guild, which was an association of the workers. The guilds fixed prices and standards of work, and supported members who fell on hard times.

Dyers

Judging a masterpiece

Apprentices
Boys aged between 10 and 15, who wanted to learn a trade, would pay to start work as an apprentice to a craftsman. They spent between four and seven years learning every aspect of their craft from a master.

Masterpieces
At the end of his term as apprentice, each boy was required to produce an object that showed he had learned his craft. It was called a masterpiece, because it was judged by a master craftsman.

Mallet

Hammer-head chisel

Mallet-head chisels

Types of crafts

Almost any material can be used in craft, from wood, stone, and metal, to beads, reeds, and shells. A craftsperson may sell work to earn a living, but craft is also a popular leisure activity.

Traditional weaving technique

Basketwork
From prehistoric times, basketmakers worldwide have woven materials, such as leaves, twigs, grass, and bark, to make unbreakable containers, to build boats and houses, and to make shoes and hats. Machines cannot yet match the fine technique displayed in a hand-woven basket.

Basketmaker, Spain

Finished baskets

Craft workshop

Many craftspeople have a workshop where they keep tools and materials. People who produce crafts objects for a living often sell goods from their workshop, so they can work when they are not helping customers.

Stonework
The craft of cutting and shaping stone for building is centuries old. Medieval masons prepared the stone to build churches, dams, and bridges; stone carvers, also known as banker masons, prepared ornamental finishes.

Shaping the stone
The carver begins by drawing a design onto a piece of acetate. This is then transferred to a block of stone as a guideline for cutting or carving. The stone carver then uses a toothed tool (a claw) to gouge out the basic design.

Stone, trimmed (cut) into a small block

Marked out design

Finished article
A variety of chisels and carving gouges further define the shape of the carving, removing the worst of the marks left by the claw in the process. Finally, a double-ended file, called a riffler, is used to smooth out the marks left by the chisels. It takes years to master ornamental carving.

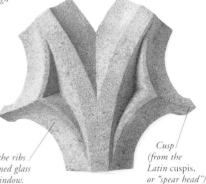

This piece links the ribs that support stained glass in a cathedral window.

Cusp (from the Latin cuspis, or "spear head")

Silk thread used for wings

Gold thread used for outline

Embroidery
Embroidery, where designs are stitched onto fabric, decorates everyday clothing and furnishings, as well as garments for festive occasions. The embroiderer either draws the design onto the fabric before stitching into the cloth, or develops it while she or he is working on the embroidery.

Butterfly detail, embroidered sleeve, China

African beadwork

Beadwork
Beads, made from materials such as wood, bone, shell, seeds, plastic, and glass, have been used to decorate material for centuries. The geometrical designs of Native North American beadworkers feature on clothing, bags, and shoes. African beadwork decorates vessels, festive garments, and jewellery.

Papier-mâché items, such as this bowl, can be simple to make.

Papier-mâché
Some people take up a craft as a hobby. One popular example is papier-mâché. Named after the French word meaning "chewed paper", it involves building up layers of paper and paste over a mould. When the paste dries, the paper is firm and can be painted and varnished.

FIND OUT MORE

INDUSTRIAL REVOLUTION

MEDIEVAL EUROPE

POTTERY AND CERAMICS

UNIONS, TRADE

TEXTILES AND WEAVING

Crafts
Basketwork

Shopping basket, rope detail decoration, England

Sewing basket, bamboo handles, Canada

Basket, traditional design, Thailand

Sisal basket, Kenya

Willow potato basket, wire base, France

Stone and woodcarving

Mason's tools

Decorated vault, Italy

Roof decoration, carved fruit and leaves, Britain

Ballflowers decoration, Britain

Flowing tracery, medieval Britain

Wall ornament, medieval Britain

Carved panel, 16th-century Britain

Church roof detail, medieval Britain

Embroidery and beadwork

Tobacco pouch, North America

Beaded gourd, Africa

Necklace, South Africa

Metal fringe

Tobacco pouch, North America

Zulu beadwork, Africa

Flask, made from gourd fruit, Africa

Charm to ward off evil

Amulet, North America

Imported glass beads

Traditional design

Colourful embroidery

Colourful geometric pattern

Cradleboard, North America

Child's coat, North America

Masquerade costume, Africa

Deerskin moccasin, North America

Embroidered sandals, North Africa

CRIME AND PUNISHMENT

A CRIME IS A FORBIDDEN ACT, punished by law because it may harm a society or injure its members. The type of act that is considered a crime varies from culture to culture, changing as societies and attitudes develop. For example, in some parts of the Middle East, it is a crime to drink alcohol, but a man may have more than one wife. In the United States, alcohol is not illegal, but having more than one wife is against the law.

Bronze cat from ancient Egypt, dedicated to the cat goddess Bastet.

Killing cats
The ancient Egyptians honoured cats as sacred animals, depicting them in paintings and sculptures. As a result, killing a cat was seen as a serious crime. The punishment was usually instant execution.

Types of crimes

Some acts, such as murder and theft, have been crimes in all civilized societies for thousands of years, and are known as *malum in se* (the Latin phrase for "bad in themselves"). Other crimes, such as driving an unregistered or untaxed car, are known as *malum prohibitum* (bad because the law says so).

Murder

Crime against the person
When one person intentionally kills another, this is known as murder. It is a crime against the person, and does not respect the individual's right to live his or her life without fear of attack and violence. Assault, rape, and kidnapping are other such crimes. Killing someone in self-defence (to protect your own life), or killing an enemy of one's country in times of war, is not considered to be murder.

Crime against property
Laws exist to protect people's right to own property. It is a criminal act to take or damage the property of another against the owner's wishes. Examples of such crimes include theft, forgery, arson, and vandalism.

Electrical goods

Silverware   Antiques   Jewellery   Stolen property

Organized crime

Organized crime consists of large-scale activities by groups of gangsters, sometimes known as the underworld. They make much of their money by providing illegal goods, including drugs, and services, such as gambling or prostitution.

Crime syndicates
Secret criminal organizations exist across the world, such as the Mafia, which first originated centuries ago in Sicily. During the 1920s a powerful crime syndicate grew up in Chicago, USA, run by brutal gangsters, such as the notorious Al Capone (1899–1947).

Al Capone

Prison

Someone who commits a crime may be sent to prison for a length of time which reflects the seriousness of the offence. Prison is mainly a punishment, but it also offers criminals a chance to reform. It acts to deter other people from crime and keeps dangerous criminals away from the public.

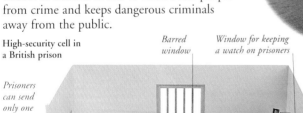

High-security cell in a British prison

Prisoners can send only one letter a week.

Simply furnished

Inmates can bring only a few personal belongings to prison.

Barred window

Window for keeping a watch on prisoners

Men and women go to separate prisons. As inmates, they may spend as much as 23 hours a day locked in their cells, which they usually share with one or two others. They must wear prison uniforms.

Alcatraz
A maximum-security prison was built on the island of Alcatraz in San Francisco Bay, USA. It was in use from 1933 to 1963; in that time, not one prisoner escaped alive. Of the 23 that tried, five were shot dead, six drowned, and 12 were recaptured.

High-security cell
Criminals convicted of serious crimes are sent to high-security prisons. Inmates are only allowed to leave their cells to eat, work, or for study programmes. People who commit lesser crimes may be sent to open prisons, where they have more freedom.

Punishment

Theories about punishment have developed since the 18th century when even minor offences were harshly punished to deter others from committing crime. Around the world, law-breakers are punished in various ways: in the UK, for instance, criminals are usually fined, or sent to prison.

Cat-o'-nine tails whip

Each strand is knotted

Corporal punishment
In some countries, people are whipped for certain minor crimes. This is corporal punishment. It was once common, and beatings took place in public as a warning to deter others from crime.

Capital punishment
The ultimate penalty for a crime is death, or capital punishment. Hanging, gassing, and the electric chair are some of the methods that have been used. Many people now argue that mistakes can be made and that capital punishment is morally wrong. In the USA, this issue is hotly debated; many other Western nations have abolished the death penalty.

Electric chair

FIND OUT MORE | EGYPT, ANCIENT | HUMAN RIGHTS | LAW | POLICE | SOCIETIES, HUMAN

CROCODILES

SUBMERGED BELOW water, crocodiles lie in wait ready to attack almost any animal that strays too close. Crocodiles belong to the group of reptiles, called the crocodilians, which has remained largely unchanged for more than 140 million years. This group contains crocodiles, alligators, caimans, and gharials which are all very similar apart from small differences, such as snout shape and arrangement of teeth. All are effective freshwater predators and are well adapted to a semi-aquatic way of life.

Eyes

A crocodile's eyes protrude above its snout providing 25° overlapping vision to judge distance. A third eyelid slides across from the side to allow underwater vision. Special pupils allow more light to reach the retina in low light levels and protect the retina from bright light. The retina itself has a layer of night-seeing cells that glow red in torchlight.

Third eyelid moves across from side.

Transparent eyelid converts eye for underwater vision.

Nostrils and eyes are high on head so crocodile can breathe and see when almost submerged in water.

Crocodiles

Crocodiles are tropical reptiles found in freshwater habitats around the world. There are 14 species ranging from the 2 m (7 ft) long dwarf crocodiles of western Africa to the huge man-eating 7.5 m (25 ft) long Indo-Pacific crocodiles. The American, Nile, and Indo-Pacific crocodiles can live equally as well in the sea as in freshwater. The Cuban and Siamese crocodiles are endangered due to habitat destruction and hunting.

Huge cone-shaped teeth line the long jaw.

Nile crocodile

Snout shape

Alligators and caimans have broad, rounded snouts, while gharials have very narrow snouts. Crocodiles have broad or narrow snouts. They also have an externally visible fourth tooth. This distinguishes them from alligators in which this tooth is concealed.

Caiman

Alligator

Crocodile

Gharial

Breeding

Loud bellowing preceeds mating under water. One month later females lay up to 90 leathery-shelled eggs that they incubate for 2–3 months in nests. Some species lay eggs in several locations to avoid total loss by flooding or predation. High temperatures during incubation result in more males than females. A hatchling calls its mother with squeaks and breaks out of the eggshell by "pipping" with an egg tooth on the tip of its snout.

Mother carries young to a crèche where she will guard them until they become independent.

Baby crocodile pushing itself out of its egg.

Nile crocodile with eggs

Movement

On land crocodiles may slide along on their bellies, scooting with their feet. Sometimes they adopt the "high walk" and raise their bodies fully off the ground. The "gallop" is when crocodiles run with their tails in the air, usually when being chased. The "tail walk" is used to snatch prey from branches above the water.
In water, crocodiles swim using powerful sweeps of their tails.

High walking

Dwarf crocodile

Tail walking involves pushing the body up using the tail.

Feeding

After lying hidden for hours, a crocodile suddenly seizes prey from riverbanks and drags it below water until it drowns. Crocodiles cannot chew, so prey is dismembered by shaking and spinning. The whole animal is eaten. Strong juices and pebbles in the stomach help break down the food.

Topi

The jaws close with tremendous force, splintering bone and crushing tissue.

Alligators

There are two true alligators. The American alligator from south-east United States is up to 5.5 m (18 ft) long. It is the only crocodilian that is not endangered. The Chinese alligator from the Yangtze River, eastern China, is smaller at up to 2 m (7 ft). Alligators are subtropical, and are more widely distributed than other crocodilians.

Regular-sized scales

American alligator

Thick muscular tail

Caimans

Caimans are South American alligators. There are six species ranging from the 1.5 m (5 ft) long dwarf caiman that lives in forest creeks to the 4.5 m (15 ft) long black caiman of larger rivers. The spectacled caiman has ridges around the eyes resembling spectacle frames.

Spectacled caiman

Stocky body

Gharials

There are two species of gharial, which have long narrow snouts. The Ganges gharial lives in India, Bangladesh, Pakistan, Nepal, and Burma. It reaches 7 m (23 ft) in length. Some males have a bulbous swelling on the end of their snout. The other species, the tomistoma, lives in Indonesia and Malaysia. It reaches a length of 4.7 m (15.5 ft).

Widely spaced teeth line the forcep-like jaw

Ganges gharial

NILE CROCODILE

SCIENTIFIC NAME	*Crocodylus niloticus*
ORDER	Crocodylia
FAMILY	Crocodylidae
DISTRIBUTION	Africa south of the Sahara, excluding the Kalahari; Madagascar. Now largely exterminated from the River Nile in Egypt
HABITAT	River systems, lakes, marshes, estuaries, and mangrove habitats. Also able to swim out to sea
DIET	Fish, frogs, reptiles, wading birds, and mammals up to the size of water buffalo. Humans are also sometimes victims
SIZE	Length: 6 m (20 ft)
LIFESPAN	25–100 years

FIND OUT MORE | CONSERVATION | EGGS | LAKE AND RIVER WILDLIFE | MARSH AND SWAMP WILDLIFE | REPTILES | RIVERS

CROWS

CROWS AND THEIR RELATIVES are intelligent and noisy birds that are sometimes found in flocks. They are most widespread in the northern hemisphere and are often common in woods and farmland. Some species can be found in gardens and backyards. Birds in the crow family are not specialized for one particular way of life and this allows them to make the most of different kinds of food. Many of them will eat almost any kind of food that they come across, including young birds.

The crow family

There are about 113 species in the crow family. These include ravens, jays, magpies, rooks, and jackdaws. Most species are almost jet black, but many jays and magpies are brightly coloured. Members of the crow family are classified as songbirds, but they communicate mainly by harsh chattering calls or croaks.

Carrion crow
This widespread crow lives throughout Europe and much of Asia. Like most crows, it is a great opportunist, and often feeds on the remains of dead animals that have been run over on roads.

Glossy black plumage

Broad wings used for soaring high.

Blue jay
Measuring 28 cm (11 in) long, this brightly coloured bird is one of the smallest species in the crow family. It lives in eastern North America.

Common raven
Ravens are the largest members of the crow family. They live in remote places, such as mountains and rocky coasts, and have a deep, croaking call.

Powerful beak can tear open the bodies of dead animals.

Powerful legs covered with large scales.

Feeding

Crows have strong beaks, but compared to many birds they are not fussy about what they eat. They are fond of seeds, worms, and insects, and in spring they sometimes eat the eggs and nestlings of other birds. They are determined feeders. Farmers try to scare them off with scarecrows or shotguns; small birds have more difficulty keeping them away.

Seed eaters
Unlike most members of the crow family, some jays live mostly on the seeds of oaks, pines, and other trees. They collect seeds during the autumn, and then bury them. These seed stores provide food for the winter.

Nest robbers
Magpies make life difficult for small birds by raiding their nests. Magpies are cumbersome and, despite their large size, quite timid. They rarely plunder nests that are constantly guarded.

Jackdaw hierarchy
These small but boisterous crows come from Europe and western Asia. They live in groups in which there is a strict hierarchy. They are good at living near humans and often nest on buildings.

Social groups

Ravens, jays, and magpies often live on their own or in pairs, but some members of the crow family spend their lives in large flocks. This way of living makes it easier for the birds to defend themselves against predators, and also increases their chances of finding food.

Carrion eaters
Ravens search for food by flying high over open ground, just like birds of prey. Instead of killing animals, they usually eat ones that are already dead.

Rooks
These birds build their nests at the top of high trees, and they gather together as the sun begins to set. These nesting sites are called rookeries. The same name is used to describe breeding groups of many other animals, from penguins to seals.

Azure-winged magpie
This magpie lives in two different areas of the world: China and Japan, and Spain and Portugal. Some people think it was brought to Europe from Asia long ago. Others think it once lived all over Europe and Asia, but disappeared from many areas because of climate changes.

Long tail gives the magpie manoeuvrability in the air.

COMMON RAVEN

SCIENTIFIC NAME *Corvus corax*

ORDER Passeriformes

FAMILY Corvidae

DISTRIBUTION North America, Europe, northern and central Asia

HABITAT Mountains, moorland, and rocky coasts

DIET Seeds, small animals, and animal remains

SIZE Length: 64 cm (25 in)

 FIND OUT MORE | ANIMAL BEHAVIOUR | BIRDS | BIRDS OF PREY | FLIGHT, ANIMAL | PENGUINS | SEALS | SONGBIRDS

CRUSADES

JERUSALEM HAD LONG been a place of pilgrimage for Christians from Europe, but by the 11th century the area was ruled by devoutly Muslim Turks, and pilgrims were often attacked. In 1095, Pope Urban II called for a crusade, or Holy War, to conquer Jerusalem for the Christians – the First Crusade. Over the next two centuries, a pattern emerged: Christians attacked and captured cities such as Jerusalem and Damascus, and the Muslims recaptured each one, until finally the crusaders lost all their territory and retreated from the Holy Land (Palestine) for the last time.

Crusaders

Crusaders came from all walks of life. They ranged from poor, badly equipped pilgrims, who joined the First Crusade under the preacher Peter the Hermit, to well-equipped mounted knights. In between were thousands of foot soldiers. Only the better-equipped soldiers stood a chance against the strong forces of the Seljuk Turks.

Crusading knight
With his shield, flat-topped helm, and coat of mail, the crusading knight was well protected against enemy swordsmen.

Turkish warrior
One dynasty of Turks, the Seljuks, were formidable defenders of Muslim lands, helped by expert marksmen.

Land and sea routes

The route from western Europe to Syria and Palestine was long and hazardous. Many travellers died from disease and hunger, and never saw the Holy Land. Sea travellers relied on trading cities, such as Venice and Genoa, to provide ships. The sea route was also far from safe – the Holy Roman Emperor Frederick I drowned while leading the Third Crusade.

Children's Crusade
In 1212, thousands of children marched from the Rhineland to the Mediterranean. Most died of hunger or disease, and were caught and sold as slaves.

→ 1096–99
→ 1147–49
→ 1189–92
→ 1202–1204

Paris
Bruges
Vienna
Genoa
Rome
Constantinople
Damascus
Toulouse
Marseilles
Acre
Jerusalem

First Crusade
The crusaders journeyed across Europe, and took Antioch and Jerusalem. They then claimed lands throughout the area.

Second Crusade
After their earlier defeat, the united Muslims attacked Christians in the east. They captured Damascus, and routed the new French and German crusaders.

Third Crusade
In 1187, the great Saladin reconquered Jerusalem. Crusaders from England, France, and the Holy Roman Empire retaliated, but achieved only the capture of Acre.

Fourth Crusade
Sponsored by the pope, crusaders sailed to Constantinople, looted the city, and installed Baldwin of Flanders as emperor. They did not carry on to the Holy Land.

Military orders

The military orders were founded during the 12th century. They were monks who took religious vows but, unlike other monks, also bore arms and fought against Muslims. They included the Knights of St John, the Templars, and the Teutonic Knights (a German order).

Knights of St John
The Knights of St John, or the Hospitallers, used their medical skills to care for wounded crusaders and sick pilgrims. They eventually settled on Malta, where they continued to fight for the Christian cause.

The spread of knowledge

The crusades increased contact between East and West, and helped take Islamic science and technology to Europe. Western medicine and architecture improved, although this may also have been due to contact with Muslims living in Spain.

Windmills
Wind power was used in the eastern Mediterranean to provide power to grind corn, and crusaders may have taken the idea back to Europe with them. The first European windmills appeared in France in 1180.

Islamic medicine
Islamic medicine was well developed, and the writings of the Arabian physician Avicenna, or Ibn Sina (980–1037), were influential. Herbs were used as medicines. Myrrh was used for various infections, while balm of Gilead was used for chest and throat diseases.

Balm of Gilead

Myrrh

Templars
Originally a group of knights who protected Christian pilgrims, these men were given a base in the Holy Land in 1118. They became a religious order and took their name from their base near the Temple of Jerusalem.

Saladin

The brave Salah-ed-din (1138–1193) ruled Syria and part of northern Africa. He expelled the crusaders from Jerusalem in 1187, and ruled most of Palestine (modern Israel) from then on.

Richard I

King Richard I of England (the Lionheart) spent most of his reign (1187–1199) abroad. Despite victories on the Third Crusade, he never captured Jerusalem. After the Crusades, he was put in prison, ransomed, and spent his last years in France.

Timeline
1096–99
First Crusade: The victorious armies establish first bases in the Holy Land.

1147–49 Second Crusade: Muslims retake Damascus; crusaders fail to retrieve it.

1189–92 Third Crusade: Christians take Acre, but Muslims keep Jerusalem.

1202–1204 Fourth Crusade: armies conquer Egypt, and loot Constantinople.

1218–21 Fifth Crusade: Crusaders capture land in Egypt, but fail to keep it.

1228–29 Muslims and Christians negotiate a truce which lasts 10 years.

1248–70 Seventh and Eighth Crusades.

1291 Muslims recapture the city of Acre, which is the last Christian stronghold in the Holy Land.

FIND OUT MORE   BYZANTINE EMPIRE   HOLY LAND, HISTORY OF   KNIGHTS AND HERALDRY   MEDICINE, HISTORY OF   MEDIEVAL EUROPE

CRYSTALS AND GEMS

THE WORLD AROUND US is made of tiny crystals. Much of the Earth's surface is made of rocks that contain minerals which are, in turn, formed from crystalline particles. A crystal is a solid substance that has grown in a regular, geometric form, with a smooth, plane surface, or face, and straight edges. Crystals have many different properties, and are used in industry, and for decoration. Most gemstones are crystals prized for their beauty; they are usually cut and polished to enhance their appearance.

Crystal structure
Crystals are usually made from a single mineral. They are built up from a regular lattice, or framework, of atoms. Each atom has its own special position and is tied to others by bonding forces. The atoms of each mineral always bond together in the same way to form crystals of that mineral.

Limescale crystals that form in a kettle

Crystal systems

Well-formed crystals have regular, symmetrical shapes. The geometrical shapes in which minerals crystallize are grouped into seven crystal systems. Within each of these systems many different forms are possible, but all the forms can be related to the symmetry of that system.

Cubic system contains cube-shaped crystals, and also includes 8- and 12-sided crystals.

Hexagonal and trigonal are two systems with similar symmetry.

Tetragonal systems are generally more elongated than the cube.

Triclinic is one of the least symmetrical of the crystal systems.

Orthorhombic system has prisms and flattened tabular forms as its most typical features.

Monoclinic has less symmetry than the cubic system.

Cecil Rhodes

Known as the "King of Diamonds", British imperialist and businessman Cecil Rhodes (1853–1902) made his fortune after staking a claim in a diamond mine in Africa in 1871. By 1888 he had secured a virtual monopoly of the African diamond industry.

Cartoon of Rhodes as "King of Diamonds"

Crystal habit
Crystals form as molten magma cools, or as a liquid evaporates from a solution containing a dissolved mineral. Crystals rarely form perfectly. The conditions under which crystals grow affect their shape. The general shape of crystals is called their habit.

Prismatic crystals are prism-shaped.

Massive crystals grow in a mass in which individual crystals cannot be seen.

Acicular crystals have slender, fragile, needle-like masses.

Dendritic crystals have tree or plant shapes.

Aggregates are groups of crystals. This is an aggregate of prismatic crystals.

Bladed crystals look like the blade of a knife.

Gems

Highly valued and used in jewellery, most gemstones are beautiful, rare, and durable inorganic crystals. A few gems are organic, such as amber, jet, and pearls. Others, called synthetics, are produced in laboratories. They have similar appearances and properties to natural gemstones, but are cheaper to buy.

Diamond in kimberlite

Diamonds
The world's hardest substance, diamonds are sought after not only for their unique lustre, but also for use in drill bits and glass cutters.

Gem cutting
Most rough crystals have to be cut and polished to remove surface imperfections and to reveal their true brilliance. Before this happens the lapidary, or cutter, studies the rough stone through a loupe (lens) to see if it is suitable for cutting.

1 The cutter identifies the natural grain and flaws, then marks where the diamond should be cut and ground.

2 The diamond is sawn in two to remove the top pyramid, then rounded by grinding it against another diamond.

3 The stone is mounted on a dop (stick) and several flat facets, or faces, are ground on a cast-iron wheel called a scaife.

Quartz
Quartz is "piezo-electric". This means that when an electric current passes through quartz, it resonates at such regular intervals that it can be used to keep time very accurately.

Quartz watch

Geode
Many gemstones are found in geodes, round rock-hollows lined with crystals. These are formed from the bubbles of hot gas and mineral-rich fluids in magma. They are prized by collectors.

Amethyst crystals in geode

4 Slanted side facets called bezels are ground between the table facet (the flat top) and the girdle (the rim).

5 The stone is turned over and faceted in the same way. It is then finished by a brillianteer who adds 40 small facets.

FIND OUT MORE | ATOMS AND MOLECULES | CLOTHES AND FASHION | ROCKS AND MINERALS | SOLIDS | TIME

Gems

Precious stones

Drop-shaped morganite

Black precious opal

Sapphire

Brilliant cut diamond

Pendeloque emerald

Octagonal aquamarine

Cushion cut ruby

Morganite, which is coloured by manganese, is the pink form of beryl.

Opal is hardened silica gel. Precious opal is iridescent.

Sapphire is a precious form of corundum. It is usually blue.

Diamonds are made from carbon placed under extreme pressure.

Emerald is a green variety of beryl.

Aquamarines are a blue-green variety of beryl.

Ruby is the red, precious form of corundum.

Semi-precious stones

Crystallization progresses towards centre of cavity

Quartz crystals are built-up in layers.

Smoky quartz crystals joined together in a twisted group.

Amazonstone is a blue-green type of microline.

Amethyst is a purple form of quartz.

Rose quartz is best used for carvings and making into beads.

Calcite is the main component of limestone and marble.

Chalcedony is a massive variety of quartz made from tiny fibres, or grains, of silicon dioxide.

Rose quartz is usually found in great lumps – single crystals are very rare.

Turquoise is usually intense blue or green.

Some people believe crystals have healing properties.

Labradorite can be multi-coloured and has a sheen.

Rhodochrosite gets its colour from manganese.

Turquoise is sought after for its amazing colours.

Rock crystal is an almost colourless form of quartz.

Lapis lazuli contains several different minerals.

Carnelian is a red variety of chalcedony.

Organic gems

Coral carving

Polished amber bead

Ivory relief

Shell pill box

Cut and polished jet

Jet containing fossils

Pearls

Coral is the calcium carbonate skeleton of colony-living sea creatures. It is usually pink.

Amber is the fossilized resin, or sap, of trees. It is usually translucent.

Ivory comes from the teeth and tusks of mammals. The best ivory comes from the African elephant.

Mother-of-pearl lining of shells is prized for its iridescence.

Jet is a fine-grained black stone formed from very hard coal.

Pearls are tiny pellets of calcium carbonate that form inside some shellfish.

CURIE, MARIE

THE PHYSICIST MARIE CURIE was a pioneer in the science of radioactivity – the study of powerful rays emitted by certain rare materials. Her work changed physics and chemistry and formed a basis for later research in nuclear physics. She discovered two previously unknown elements and also founded an important research institute. In 1903, she shared the Nobel prize for physics with her husband Pierre, with whom she worked, and French scientist Henri Becquerel. In 1911, she was awarded the Nobel prize for chemistry. She died after suffering for years from an illness caused by exposure to radiation.

Early life
Marie Curie was born in Warsaw, Poland. After finishing school, she worked as a governess to save up money to go to university in Paris. In 1891, she left to study at the Sorbonne. She was top of her year there, in spite of being so hungry sometimes that she fainted during classes.

Poland
At the time that Marie was born, Poland was under the rule of neighbouring Russia, and the best jobs and education went to Russians. After she had finished her schooling, Marie began to go to secret meetings of the "Floating University", a group of Polish people who met to read books that the Russians banned in case they might stir up rebellious ideas.

Radioactivity

In 1895, the German physicist Wilhelm Röntgen discovered invisible "penetrating rays", which he called X-rays, coming from an electric tube in one of his experiments. The following year Becquerel discovered similar rays coming from the metal uranium. The Curies devoted the rest of their lives to studying these rays.

Equipment
For much of her life, Marie Curie worked under difficult conditions. Her laboratory was in an unheated shed and much equipment was home-made. Pierre helped her design and build some of her equipment, including a device called an electrometer, which measured the strength of radiation coming from uranium compounds.

Electrometer measures electric current.

Piezo-electric quartz plate measures radioactivity.

Pierre Curie
Born in Paris and educated by his father, Pierre Curie (1859–1906) began work as a laboratory assistant in Paris. He made several important discoveries before he met Marie in 1894. After they married he spent the rest of his life working with her. He made some of her equipment and worked beside her in the laboratory. He was killed in a street accident in 1906.

Ionization chamber contains radioactive substance.

Tripod stand

Isolating radiation
The Curies noticed that pitchblende, the ore from which uranium is extracted, was many times more radioactive than uranium itself. They realized that pitchblende must contain other radioactive substances, so they processed tonnes of pitchblende to extract these other radioactive elements.

Pitchblende
The Curies spent about 12 years separating out the radioactive elements in pitchblende. They found there were two substances. One they named polonium, after Marie's home country, and the other they called radium.

X-rays
When World War I (1914–18) broke out, Marie Curie raised funds to set up mobile X-ray units to be used on the battle front. She supervised the conversion of around 200 vans for this purpose. These became known as "Little Curies".

Radium Institute

In 1912, the Sorbonne and the Pasteur Institute decided to found a Radium Institute in Paris, devoted to research into radiation and the medical uses of radioactivity. Marie became a director of the Institute and spent much of her time supporting scientists in their work and raising money for research.

The Joliots
Marie Curie's daughter, Irène, was also a scientist. She and her husband, Frédéric Joliot, worked together, much like Marie and Pierre. They discovered how to make non-radioactive substances radioactive, by bombarding them with radioactive rays. In 1935 they were awarded the Nobel prize for chemistry.

MARIE CURIE

1867 Born Manya Sklodowska in Warsaw, Poland

1891 Goes to the Sorbonne, Paris; changes first name to Marie

1895 Marries Pierre Curie

1898 Discovers the elements polonium and radium

1903 Awarded Nobel prize for physics

1910 After 12 years of work on pitchblende, she produces pure radium for the first time

1911 Awarded Nobel prize for chemistry

1918 Radium Institute opens after delay owing to World War I; Marie becomes research director

1934 Dies in France

FIND OUT MORE CHEMISTRY ELEMENTS MEDICINE, HISTORY OF PASTEUR, LOUIS RADIOACTIVITY WORLD WAR I X RAYS AND THE ELECTROMAGNETIC SPECTRUM

CYCLING

CYCLE SPORTS are held on tracks, roads, and cross-country circuits. Races range from 1,000-m (1,094-yd) sprints on an indoor track to multi-stage events over hundreds of kilometres that last a week or more. Special courses are prepared for off-road racing, which includes cyclocross and mountain-bike racing. Racers ride specialized bikes for the different races. Some need to be be as light as possible; others need to be strong, and the top riders have bicycles made for them to their own specifications.

Track racing

Track races take place on wooden indoor tracks, with banked sides, or flat asphalt outdoor tracks. Races include sprints, in which riders jockey for position before making a last-lap dash, and pursuits, in which riders start on opposite sides of the track, the race won by the fastest rider or when one catches the other.

Riders crouch over the handlebars in a streamlined position.

Disc wheels are more efficient indoors because there is no cross-wind.

Track bicycles have no gears or brakes.

Pursuit bicycle

Road racing

Races take place on courses set along ordinary roads. There are single-stage races and multi-stage events such as the Tour de France, in which the total time determines placings. In individual and team time-trials on the road, the riders start at intervals. Criterium races are 40–100 km (25–62 miles) long. They take place over short courses with many laps, along city streets and through parks.

Saddle is set high for more pedalling power.

Criterium bicycle

Composite wheel

Types of wheel
The design and material of wheels are constantly being improved to suit particular uses. Weight and shape are the important factors. Using spokes saves weight, but increases drag.

Spoked wheel

Team pursuit
In team pursuit, riders take turns to lead their group of four. The time of the third rider in each team determines the result. One rider usually makes an all-out effort near the finish before trailing off.

British cyclist Chris Boardman on his revolutionary Lotus bike

Time-trials
In time-trials, competitors ride as fast as possible, on their own, over a set distance or for a fixed time. Time-trials are some of the hardest races and require continuous effort.

Tour de France
The world's leading road race is the Tour de France which lasts about three weeks. The overall leader on total time wears the famous yellow jersey for the next stage.

Off-road racing

Bicycles for off-road races have chunky tyres for the rough terrain. Cyclocross is the original form of cross-country cycling, with world championships since 1950. Mountain biking is now the most popular form, with world championships since 1990 and Olympic recognition in 1996.

Cyclocross
In cyclocross, races take place over laps of a cross-country course. Riders often find it quicker to dismount and carry their bikes over obstacles such as fences, gates, and ditches, and may have to run up steep hills or wade through water with them.

For log hopping, the rider must learn to shift her weight.

Mountain biking
Mountain bikes are built to survive rough handling. Most have steel-alloy frames, straight handlebars, and flat knobbly tyres. Courses for races have many climbs and descents, with routes over fields and gravel pits.

Rider brings her weight over the front wheel.

Weight is kept over the front wheel until the hop has been completed.

Weight over the rear wheel

Miguel Indurain

Spanish road racer Miguel Indurain (b. 1964) became the first cyclist to win the Tour de France in five successive years (1991–95), equalling the record number of wins. In 1996, he took first place in the Olympic road time trial.

FIND OUT MORE

BICYCLES AND MOTORCYCLES   FRANCE   HEALTH AND FITNESS   MOTOR SPORTS   OLYMPIC GAMES   SPORT

D

DAMS

IN MANY AREAS of the world, people rely on dams for their water and electricity supplies. A dam is a barrier that holds back water. The dam itself and the surrounding hills form a bowl in which water collects to form an artificial lake called a reservoir. Most dams are built across a river valley to catch the river's flow, but some dams create reservoirs into which water is pumped for storage. How strong a dam needs to be depends on the depth of the water in the reservoir. Some dams are enormous: the Grand Coulee Dam in the USA weighs nearly 10 million tonnes.

Types of dam

There are three main types of dam: arch dams, gravity dams, and buttress dams. The type of dam that engineers decide to build depends on the geography of the location. Factors affecting the decision include the width and depth of the river valley and the type of rock around the site.

Buttress dam
A buttress dam is a huge concrete wall that leans into a reservoir of water. The wall is made up of concrete slabs that are supported on the downstream side of the dam by concrete projections known as buttresses.

Arch dam
An arch dam is built across the entrance to a narrow valley, so that the height of the dam is greater than its width. The dam's curved shape holds back water because it transfers the push of the water to the rock of the valley sides.

Gravity dam
A gravity dam is a huge embankment of earth or rock. Leakage is prevented by a waterproof clay core or a concrete skin on the upstream side of the dam. The dam's immense weight prevents the water from pushing it over.

Water from reservoir enters intake towers.

Arched concrete wall

Sides of river valley

Reservoir

Roadway across top of dam

Water flows through pipes in dam to hydroelectric power station.

Model of an arch dam

Spillway lets excess water flow into river, so that dam does not overflow.

Anatomy of a dam

This model shows an arch dam that creates a reservoir for supplying water and electricity to nearby towns and cities. The dam is made of thin concrete strengthened by thousands of steel bars. Water flowing through pipes in the dam drives electricity generators in the hydroelectric power station at the foot of the dam.

Flood control

On large rivers, dams help prevent flooding by holding back surges of flood water and releasing them downstream slowly. A flood barrier is a movable dam built across a tidal river. The barrier has gates that are usually open to allow the river to flow freely, but which can be closed when dangerously high tides threaten to surge upstream.

Environmental effects

A river dam and the reservoir it forms can harm the environment. Huge areas of countryside are drowned by the reservoir, and the dam disrupts the river's natural flow, affecting wildlife and irrigation downstream. A dam also prevents fish from moving freely up and down the river.

Tidal barrage

A barrage is a dam across a river estuary that generates hydroelectric power. The dam holds back the tide as it ebbs and flows. The water is forced through pipes inside the barrage, where it drives electricity generators.

La Rance barrage, France

Weir

A weir is a low river dam that controls the flow of water by creating a stretch of deeper water upstream. Deep water makes the river navigable for boats.

Weir in Middlesex, England

Model of Thames Flood Barrier, UK

Hydraulic rockers turn the gate arm.

Circular gate arm opens and closes gate.

Steel-plated roof

Water level

Concrete pier

Gate open; when gate closes, it rotates into its vertical position, blocking the flow of water.

Barrier gate is a hollow semi-circle plated with high-strength steel.

Steel piles sunk into riverbed.

FIND OUT MORE · BUILDING AND CONSTRUCTION · ELECTRICITY · ENERGY · FARMING · LAKES · RAIN · ROADS · OCEANS AND SEAS · RIVERS

DANCE

WHEN PEOPLE MOVE in time to music they are dancing. People have a natural urge to move in time to rhythms. Children jump up and down when they are excited; babies move naturally to rhythms they hear or feel. In dancing, these natural movements are organized into rhythmic and visual patterns. Different dances have developed all over the world, and are performed for different reasons. Dancing can be both an art form and recreation. It can express an emotion, tell a story, or set a mood.

Origins

Dancing is one of the oldest art forms. The first dances may have evolved from spontaneous stamping steps. These steps were later given rhythms and shapes and accompanied by grunts and shouts.

Ceremonial dance
Early people found that rhythmic movements had a strong effect on the mind, and felt that dancing must have magical powers. They began to dance to ward off evil spirits, heal people, and ensure good crops.

Australian Aboriginals performing the corroboree

Dance as entertainment
The ancient Egyptians were the first people known to use dancing simply as a form of entertainment. Professional dancing girls entertained the pharaoh and his guests at banquets, performing dances that included running, high kicks, and sensual hip movements.

Ancient Egyptian dancing girls

Chorus depicted on a Greek vase

Dance as theatre
The ancient Greeks made dance the basis of all their theatre. The chorus in a Greek play was a group of actors who danced and sang a commentary on the action.

Maasai dancers
The Maasai of East Africa move in straight lines as they dance, and include high jumps in their routines. As happens in all African dance, they are accompanied by rhythmic, exhilarating drumbeats.

Asian dancing
The main influence on dance styles in Asia comes from India. Many Asian dances make use of stylized hand movements, particularly those from countries such as India, Sri Lanka, Burma, Thailand, and Cambodia.

Bent-back fingers

Dragon
The mythical dragon is a very important symbol in Chinese culture. Dragon dances are performed to celebrate festivals such as the Chinese New Year.

Dancers wear a dragon costume.

Head-dress

Indian dances
Indian classical dancers mime out stories from Indian mythology, and include sequences of more abstract dance movements.

There are six styles of Indian classical dance.

Southeast Asian dances
Classical dance in Southeast Asia typically includes slow, controlled movements, with many graceful hand and arm gestures. Dance-dramas, performed by highly trained dancers, are particularly popular in Indonesia and Thailand. Throughout the region there is a wide variety of traditional folk dances.

Royal Thai classical dancer

European folk dancing
Every European country has its folk dances, which are now essentially social. Some of them have been taken to other countries by settlers. The dances are often performed in traditional costumes, and many of them involve people forming simple patterns, such as lines and circles.

African dance
Dancing is an essential part of life to many Africans, and important events, such as births, deaths, and initiation to adulthood, are all observed by dancing. African dances can last for many hours. The dances for men are usually very energetic, and include a lot of stamping and leaping. Women tend to do more gentle dances, clapping and swaying to the music or rhythm.

Flamenco
Perhaps the most famous of all Spanish dances is the flamenco. This dance is a mixture of both the Spanish and Arab cultures. The men use complicated footwork, while the women weave patterns with their arms. The dancers are accompanied by fast, dramatic guitar music.

Flamenco dancers also use their voices.

Irish dancing
Irish jigs are usually performed either by pairs or by individuals, but large groups also perform Irish dances. The jig is based on simple steps, but the dancers can elaborate and perform complicated leaping steps. They hold their upper body still and their arms straight down at their sides or holding hands. The dances are usually accompanied by the fiddle or bagpipes.

South American dancing

The dances of Central and South America reflect the cultures not only of the native peoples who have long occupied the region, but also of the European colonists and their African slaves. Many dances that originated in this region, such as the tango and samba, have become popular all over the world.

Macumba

The Macumba dance was taken to Brazil by African slaves as a form of voodoo-worship in which the dancer is believed to be possessed by a god. Macumba dancers worship Yemannjah, a goddess of the sea. Like all voodoo dances it involves shaking of the head and shoulders.

Tango

This dance originated in Argentina about 200 years ago. It had to be "cleaned up" before it became fashionable in Europe in the 1900s, because it was considered too immodest for the dance halls.

Contemporary dance

This style has no fixed technique. Dancers express their feelings in their movements. Contemporary dance began at the start of the 20th century, when US dancer Isadora Duncan broke away from ballet and developed her own style.

Samba

The samba was first danced in Brazil, especially at Carnival time, and became extremely popular in the United States and Europe in the early 1940s. It is danced by couples who perform simple backward and forward steps, swaying their bodies. In Brazil, there are many versions of the dance, each with a different rhythm, tempo, and mood.

Ballroom dancing

Developed in the courts of Europe, many ballroom dances, such as the waltz and samba, were adapted from folk dances. They were danced on flat, polished floors, which allowed for elegant gliding movements, rather than the jumping and stamping which folk dancers developed to cope with the rough floors or grass on which they danced.

Dancing the waltz

In competitions, dancers dress formally.

Partners dance in close contact with each other.

The couple progress around the dance floor in an anticlockwise direction.

Waltz

When the waltz first became popular with the aristocracy, in the 1700s, it caused a scandal because the couple was expected to dance close together. It was originally a simple Austrian peasant dance, but by the 19th century it was highly fashionable and composers such as Austrian Johann Strauss the younger (1825–99) specialized in writing waltz music.

Top-class dancers require strong ankles and a fit body.

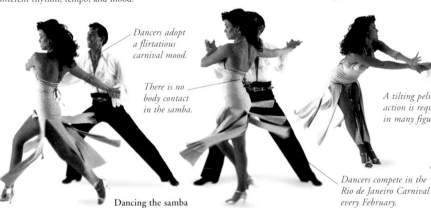

Dancers adopt a flirtatious carnival mood.

There is no body contact in the samba.

A tilting pelvic action is required in many figures.

Dancers compete in the Rio de Janeiro Carnival every February.

Couples progress in an anti-clockwise direction.

Dancing the samba

Gene Kelly

American dancer Gene Kelly (1912–96) made film musicals popular with his athletic dance style. His best known films include *For Me and My Gal* (1942), *An American in Paris* (1951), and *Singin' in the Rain* (1952).

US dancer and actor Fred Astaire

Tap dance

In 19th-century America, black slaves combined African rhythms with the jigs of English and Irish settlers. Tap dance was thus created and became very popular.

Jazz dance

When jazz music became popular in the 1920s, an energetic, expressive form of dance developed with it. Today, jazz dancing is the main form of dancing in musicals and films.

Disco

Disco dancing became popular in the 1970s. The name comes from the clubs called discotheques, in which records were played for dancing. Couples usually dance facing, but not touching, each other, using simple repetitive movements.

FIND OUT MORE BALLET DRAMA FILMS AND FILM-MAKING JAZZ MUSIC OPERA ROCK AND POP

DARWIN, CHARLES

THE BRITISH NATURALIST Charles Darwin is best known as the man who developed the remarkable theory of evolution by natural selection. The theory, which describes how one species can develop or evolve into another, caused a revolution in biological science. Darwin was not the first person to suggest a theory of evolution, but was the first to present a solid body of evidence for the idea. He also wrote books about his travels, coral reefs, barnacles, the pollination of flowers, and insect-eating plants.

Early life
Darwin was born in 1809, in Shrewsbury, England. His grandfather, Erasmus Darwin, had put forward his own theory of evolution in the 1790s. At first, Charles Darwin did not believe in the idea of evolution. He trained as a priest before studying geology and biology.

D

Galápagos Islands
Darwin studied thousands of plants and animals all around the world on the *Beagle*'s journey. The most interesting part was the few weeks spent in the Galápagos Islands, about 1,000 km (600 miles) from the coast of South America. Darwin noticed that the species there were different from those elsewhere in the world.

Notebooks used by Darwin in Galápagos

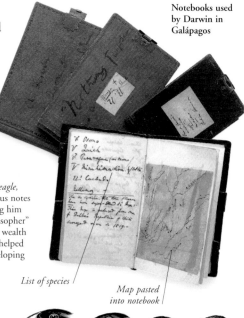

The Beagle
At Cambridge, Darwin made friends with John Henslow, the professor of botany. Henslow suggested that Darwin would be a good choice as official naturalist on the naval survey ship HMS *Beagle*, which was about to sail around the world on a five-year scientific cruise. The trip lasted from 1831 to 1836.

Darwin's watch   Darwin's telescope

Galápagos Islands

Notebooks
During his voyage on the *Beagle*, Darwin made careful, copious notes of everything he saw, gaining him the nickname "the old philosopher" from the ship's officers. The wealth of information he gathered helped him later, when he was developing his theory of evolution.

List of species

Map pasted into notebook

Darwin's finches
When he got home, Darwin realized that the finches on the Galápagos Islands had different beaks, depending on which island they inhabited. He decided that the birds had developed beaks that were best suited to the diet on their particular island.

Fossil finds
When he landed in South America, Darwin found fossils of extinct animals, such as the giant sloth (now called *Mylodon darwini*), that closely resembled modern species. This suggested that animals had gradually changed to suit their environments.

Bones of Macrauchenia, *a prehistoric mammal found by Darwin*

Rock hammers

The Origin of Species
Darwin returned to England and wrote an account of his travels. He spent years studying the specimens he had collected and the notes he had made. Gradually, he developed his idea that species evolved as animals adapted to suit their environments. He published his findings in his book *On the Origin of Species by Means of Natural Selection*. The work caused an outcry among Christians because it challenged the creation story in the Bible.

Wallace
The British naturalist Alfred Russel Wallace (1823–1913) drew up a theory of evolution by natural selection quite independently of Darwin. He wrote to Darwin for advice, and the men wrote a paper about evolution together.

CHARLES DARWIN

1809 Born in Shrewsbury, England.

1831 Sets sail on the *Beagle*.

1836 Returns to England.

1858 Wallace writes to Darwin about his evolutionary theory; they produce a paper on evolution together.

1859 Darwin publishes his *Origin of Species*.

1871 Publishes *The Descent of Man*, on human evolution.

1875 Publishes *Insectivorous Plants*, which describes how the sundew traps insects.

1880 Publishes *The Power of Movement in Plants*, which shows how light influences the direction of plant growth.

1882 Dies at Downe, England.

The naturalist
After his voyage, Darwin spent the rest of his life studying specimens, doing experiments, and writing up his findings. He never left England again, and for much of the rest of his life he was too ill to leave his home. Illness did not stop him working on subjects ranging from earthworms to the pollination of plants.

Some of Darwin's equipment

Scissors for dissection

Hand lens

Specimen boxes, one containing butterfly

Seeds sent to Darwin

Slide

Natural selection
Parents produce many offspring, all different from each other. Only those best suited to their environment will survive, passing on some of their features to their offspring.

Lesser black-backed gull

Herring gull has same ancestor as Lesser black-backed, but has evolved separately.

 FIND OUT MORE   BIOLOGY   DINOSAURS   EVOLUTION   EXPLORATION   FOSSILS   GEOLOGY   HUMAN EVOLUTION   SCIENCE, HISTORY OF

DEER AND ANTELOPES

THE MOST noticeable difference between deer and antelopes is in their headgear. Deer have branched antlers that are shed, whereas antelopes have unbranched horns that are permanent. Both deer and antelopes are herbivorous hoofed mammals. They look similar to each other, but belong to different families. Deer are in a family of their own, while antelopes belong to the cattle family. They include gazelles, duikers, and spiral-horned antelopes.

Female red deer have no antlers.

Fringe-eared oryx
Oryx live in the arid grasslands of Tanzania and Kenya, in Africa. They obtain water from roots and tubers.

Red deer
This is the most widespread deer. It is found across Europe and Asia, and as far as Japan, the Himalayas, and Australia.

Both sexes have long, straight horns.

Stages of antler growth in a fallow deer

Growing antlers

Fully grown antlers

Peeling velvet

Antlers
The larger a stag's antlers, the more females it will attract. While the antlers are growing, they are protected by a velvety skin, richly supplied with blood vessels and nerves. At the end of the deer's breeding season, the blood supply to the antlers is cut off, causing the velvet to dry out and peel off in strips.

Deer

There are 38 species of deer spread over most of Europe, as well as Asia, North Africa, and the Americas. Some have been introduced into Australasia. Most species live in herds that split up in the breeding season. Most male deer, or stags, bear multi-branched antlers, which are shed and regrown every year.

Antelopes

Most of the 60 species of antelope live in Africa. Some, such as the blackbuck and the Tibetan antelope, are Asian. A few species have been introduced to other countries. Antelopes range in size from the giant Derby eland to the pygmy and royal antelopes, which are no bigger than hares.

Antelope horns

All male antelopes have horns, but only some females. The males use their horns to intimidate their rivals and to defend their territory.

Horns are hollow.

Front view of hartebeest horns

Front view of greater kudu horns

Browsing antelope

Grazing gazelles

Four-horned antelope
Males have two pairs of horns, making the deer a sought-after trophy for hunters. The front pair of horns is smaller than the back pair.

Nyala
The nyala, found in southeast African forests, has dark brown horns with a white tip. These can be up to 78 cm (31 in) long, with usually one open curve.

Hartebeest
Both male and female hartebeests have curved horns. Each has about 12 ridges but a smooth tip. Seen from the front, the horns are angular.

Greater kudu
The triple-spiralled horns of the male greater kudu are among the most imposing horns of any living animal. They grow up to 1.5 m (5 ft) long.

Roan antelope
Males and females have horns. About 55 cm (22 in) long, they are strongly ridged and curve gradually backward.

Browsers and grazers
The antelopes include both grazing and browsing species. In Africa, for example, some species, such as Thomson's gazelle, graze on grass. Other species, such as the gerenuk, browse the leaves and shoots of trees. Grant's and dorcas gazelles browse and graze, according to what is available.

Largest and smallest deer

The largest of all deer is the moose of North America, known as the elk in Europe. An adult male moose may stand 1.8 m (6 ft) at the shoulder and weigh 545 kg (1,200 lbs). The smallest deer is the South American pudu, which stands only about 40 cm (16 in) at the shoulder and weighs about 9 kg (20 lbs).

Père David's deer
This deer once lived wild in China. Then, for 3,000 years, it existed only in parks. In 1865, the missionary Père David saw the last surviving herd. This herd was later wiped out, but the Duke of Bedford established a herd in England. In recent years, deer bred in captivity have been sent to China and reintroduced into a special reserve.

Rutting

For most of the year, red deer stags remain apart from the females, or hinds, and their young. During the breeding season, known as the rut, males collect harems of hinds which they vigorously defend by roaring or, if necessary, by fighting.

Breeding

Most species of antelope and deer give birth when the weather is fine and food is abundant. Young caribou are born in early June when the herd is migrating. The calves can follow their mother within minutes of birth. The young of some species are left alone. Their mothers come to suckle and clean them several times a day, until they are strong enough to join the herd.

Caribou

The Eurasian reindeer and the North American caribou are the same species. They live in large herds and migrate long distances every year to find food. The reindeer has been semi-domesticated by, among others, the Lapps of north Europe.

Female reindeer are the only female deer that grow antlers.

Females in a herd give birth within two weeks of each other.

A calf can run with the herd when only an hour old.

A reindeer calf weighs about 4 kg (9 lb) at birth.

Reindeer with calf

Antelope habitats

Antelopes are found in most kinds of tropical and subtropical habitats. Most are creatures of the open plains and forests, but others have adapted to live in deserts, wetlands, and mountains. Grazing antelopes live where there is plenty of grass, whereas the browsers tend to inhabit woodlands and forests.

Woodland inhabitant

Also called the chousingha, the shy, solitary four-horned antelope lives in wooded, hilly country. Hunting has greatly reduced its numbers, but it still survives in several wildlife reserves in India, and one reserve in Nepal.

Sitatunga hoof

Swamp inhabitant

The sitatunga lives only in swamps and marshes. It has evolved long hooves that help it to walk on marshy ground. When danger threatens, it submerges itself in water leaving only its nostrils exposed.

Defence

Some deer and antelope, the larger species in particular, may sometimes use their antlers and horns to defend themselves, although generally antlers and horns are not strong enough for defence. Most deer and antelopes rely on their excellent eyesight and acute sense of hearing to detect potential enemies, and on speed to escape from any predators that attack.

Pointed antler

Muntjak head

Tusk-like teeth

Muntjak skull

Self-defence

If attacked, a muntjak's first defence is to run away. If this fails, males thrash with their antlers. These are mounted on "stalks" of bone as long as the antlers themselves. Males also have two tusk-like teeth used mainly in fighting rivals.

Camouflage

Some deer and antelope avoid predators because they blend into their surroundings. Kirk's dik-dik is an African antelope that lives in dry bush country, where the thorny thickets protect it.

Pronking

The springbok of Africa can run fast to escape a predator. Like most gazelles, it will often leap high into the air, with legs stiff, hooves close together, and back arched. Called pronking, or stotting, this action may confuse predators, raise the alarm, or simply give the gazelle a better view.

RED DEER	
SCIENTIFIC NAME	*Cervus elaphus*
ORDER	Artiodactyla
FAMILY	Cervidae
DISTRIBUTION	Europe and Asia. Introduced into Australia, New Zealand, and South America
HABITAT	Woodland and open country
DIET	Grass, leaves, shoots, flowers (it both grazes and browses)
SIZE	Height at the shoulder: 1.4 m (4 ft 6 in)
LIFESPAN	12–15 years

FIND OUT MORE   AFRICAN WILDLIFE   BUFFALO AND OTHER WILD CATTLE   GRASSLAND WILDLIFE

DENMARK

THE SMALLEST, flattest, and most southerly country in Scandinavia, Denmark occupies the Jylland peninsula, the islands of Sjaelland, Lolland, Falster, and Fyn, and more than 500 smaller islands. The Faeroe Islands and Greenland in the North Atlantic are self-governing Danish territories. A prosperous, environmentally conscious, and liberal nation, Denmark offers its people a high standard of living and was one of the first countries to set up a welfare system in the 1930s.

DENMARK FACTS

CAPITAL CITY	Copenhagen
AREA	43,069 sq km (16,629 sq miles)
POPULATION	5,300,000
MAIN LANGUAGE	Danish
MAJOR RELIGION	Christian
CURRENCY	Danish krone
LIFE EXPECTANCY	76 years
PEOPLE PER DOCTOR	345
GOVERNMENT	Multi-party democracy
ADULT LITERACY	99%

Physical features

Denmark's flat landscape is broken by low, rolling hills and gentle valleys with shady beech forests. There are also extensive areas of heathland, a beautiful lake district, and a coastline of cliffs, dunes, and broad sandy beaches.

Jylland (Jutland)
The Jylland peninsula makes up about 70 per cent of Denmark's land. Its west coast is edged with beaches and the southwest has a sandy plain. Strong winds sweeping across the land drive windmills for generating electricity.

Baltic islands
The steep, chalk cliffs on the Baltic island of Møn contrast with the gentle dunes on other islands. The Danish take great care of their environment and beaches.

Climate
Denmark's usually mild and damp climate is dominated by stiff westerly winds. In many coastal areas, to prevent sand from the dunes from blowing over the land, the Danes have planted conifers as windbreaks.

Land use
Over four-fifths of Denmark is farmland, including lush pasture for grazing cattle and for raising pigs. Denmark's land yields few natural resources, although high winds are harnessed to produce power.

People
Only four per cent of the population is foreign – mainly Europeans. The only minority groups are Turks and Inuits from Greenland. The Danish have liberal policies on homosexuality and marriage, with a high divorce rate. Today, 47 per cent of all children are raised by unmarried couples or single parents. Three-quarters of all women work, and Denmark has the best child-support system in the world.

Danish pigs

Danish family visiting Legoland on Jylland

125 per sq km (324 per sq mile)

85% Urban   15% Rural

Farming and industry
Danish farming is efficient and often run by co-operatives. Only about four per cent of the work-force is employed in farming, mainly of dairy cattle and pigs, yet agriculture accounts for much of the country's export income. Denmark also has successful fishing, manufacturing, and food industries for processing bacon and dairy products. Service industries employ 79 per cent of workers.

Copenhagen
Denmark's capital is also its most important port and Scandinavia's largest city. Criss-crossed with a network of canals, quaint alleys, and cycle paths, Copenhagen has many historic buildings and churches. It also boasts the Tivoli Gardens, an amusement park that attracts millions every year.

Tourist boat on canal

| FIND OUT MORE | ATLANTIC OCEAN | ENERGY | EUROPE | EUROPE, HISTORY OF | EUROPEAN UNION | FARMING | FOOD | SCANDINAVIA, HISTORY OF | TRADE AND INDUSTRY | VIKINGS |

DESERTS

FEW PLACES ON EARTH are as stark and hostile as a desert. Deserts are vast areas where very little rain falls – typically under 100 mm (3.9 inches) a year. Any rain that does fall quickly evaporates. Few plants can survive, and soil cannot develop in such a dry and barren or arid environment. The landscape is bare sand, gravel, or rock. Clear skies and sparse vegetation leave the ground exposed to extremes of temperature. In the tropics, cloudless skies create hot deserts with daytime temperatures which are often over 50°C (122°F). Deserts at higher latitudes can be extremely cold.

Areas thought to be at risk of desertification (shown in orange)

Twelve per cent of land is desert.

Desert regions
The world's great deserts lie deep within continents far from the moisture of the oceans. They are also along the Tropics of Cancer and Capricorn, on either side of the Equator, where sinking air creates stable dry weather.

D

Desert landforms and dunes
Strong winds, sudden flash floods, and exposure to extreme temperatures create distinctive desert features. The wind piles sand up in dunes or sand-blasts rocks. Flash floods carve canyon-like valleys. The desert heat creates corrosive chemicals which sculpt rocks into bizarre shapes.

Mesa – isolated, flat-topped, steep-sided mountain

Parabolic dunes are also common on coasts.

Wadi – gorge-like, generally dry valley

Butte – eroded mesa

Zeugen rocks are produced by weathering.

Hamada is an area strewn with boulders and stones.

Eroded arch

Playa is a dry lake bed of salt.

Bolson is a drainage basin.

Barchan dune is shaped like a crescent and its tips usually point downwind.

Transverse dune – ridge lying across the wind

Bajada is a slope of sand deposited by rivers along mountain edges.

Oasis
An oasis, such as the Azraq oasis in Jordan (above), is a fertile area within a desert that lies near an underground stream or a spring. Crops such as date palms can grow and desert dwellers can live supported by the land. Artificial oases can be created through irrigation.

Seif dunes form where sand is sparse and wind comes from two directions.

Oasis is a pocket of water.

Mirage
Sometimes the desert heat is so intense that desert travellers believe that they can see water. This is an optical illusion (a trick of the eye), caused by the reflection of a faraway object, which may give the false appearance of a sheet of water.

Types of deserts
Climatic conditions create different types of deserts. In Africa, the Sahara has vast areas of erg (sand seas), hamada (stony plateaus), reg (pebble plains), rocky deserts, canyons, and cliff deserts. In the Antarctic there are ice deserts, while in the deserts of the western USA the heat evaporates rain so quickly that it leaves behind dissolved minerals in a hard, salty crust.

Rocks brought to desert by flood water.

Sandy desert
In flat areas, vast sand seas, or ergs, develop. After a rainfall, water rushes along a wadi, a dry river bed. The sandstone cliffs on either side are gradually worn away by the heat, wind, and rain.

Rocky desert
Many of the world's deserts are strewn with boulders that have been washed there by flash flooding. These rocks are gradually broken down by the action of wind and weather.

The shifting desert
As climatic conditions change, deserts shrink and expand. In the past, the Sahel, the southern margin of the Sahara, was watered by summer rains moving up from the south. In recent years, the lack of rain in the Sahel has caused drought and famine in places such as Sudan and Ethiopia.

Desertification
The effect of drought and heavy grazing by cattle, sheep, and goats destroys vegetation cover, turning the area permanently to desert. This process is known as desertification.

FIND OUT MORE   CLIMATE   DESERT WILDLIFE   ECOLOGY AND ECOSYSTEMS   ROCKS AND MINERALS   WEATHER

DESERT WILDLIFE

THE DRIEST PLACES ON EARTH are known as deserts. Food is scarce, and there is little shelter from the sun and wind. Deserts are among the most inhospitable of all places in which to live. In spite of this, many remarkable animals survive and even thrive in these hostile surroundings. Birds, mammals, insects, arachnids, amphibians, and reptiles are all represented, together with some equally remarkable plants.

Sahara
Stretching across North Africa, the Sahara is the greatest of all deserts. It is a vast wilderness of sand and rock, with only scattered palms and bushes to offer shade from the searing daytime sun. Most of the animals that live there find shelter under rocks or in burrows.

Oases
Oases provide reliable sources of drinking water for wildlife in the desert. They form in the few places where springs bubble up from underground, or where rainwater from neighbouring mountains collects in hollows.

Deserts
Many different types of desert exist in different parts of the world. Some are mountainous and rocky; others are pebbly or full of sand dunes. Some become baking hot by day; others have bitterly cold winters.

Birds

Though some desert-dwelling doves and finches forage for seeds, the most well-known birds of arid lands are predators. They probe vegetation and scour the ground for prey, obtaining all the moisture they need from the bodies of their victims.

Gila woodpecker
The Gila woodpecker forages for insects in the deserts of Mexico and the USA. Typically, it hammers out nest-holes in the stems of large cacti.

Roadrunner
Roadrunners seldom fly, but they are extremely fast, agile runners. They often prey on desert snakes, which they subdue with a series of lethal stabs from their sharp beaks.

Lanner falcon
This darting bird of prey nests among rocks and cliffs in the Sahara. It hunts small birds, which it chases and snatches in mid-air or on the ground. It also preys on smaller animals, such as gerbils, lizards, and locusts.

Falcons can spot prey from a great height.

Dwarf hamster
Only about 8.5 cm (3.3 in) long, this hamster lives in the deserts of Mongolia, Siberia, and China. It has thick fur, which helps to keep it warm in the bitterly cold winters.

Long, bushy tail can be curled around the body to keep it warm during the night.

Red kangaroo
In Australian deserts, red kangaroos browse on bushes. They produce dry dung as a way of saving moisture, but still make regular trips to waterholes to replace moisture lost through sweating.

Kalahari ground squirrel
These burrowing rodents eat seeds and other plant material in the Kalahari Desert of Africa. During the day, they hold their bushy tails over their bodies for shade.

Mammals

Desert mammals show a remarkable ability to cope with conditions that would be dangerously hot and dry for most animals. Some, such as camels, can tolerate steep rises in their body temperature and long periods of dehydration. Others have special means of securing shade, obtaining moisture, finding food, and avoiding danger in the wide-open terrain.

Pale-coloured fur reflects heat.

Large erect ears help the fox to hear the slightest sound of prey and tell from where it is coming.

Fennec fox
The fennec fox is small with large pointed ears. The large size of the ears helps the fox lose excess heat from its body during the heat of the day. The fox has dense fur, which keeps it warm on cold nights.

Bactrian camel
Camels are perfectly adapted for life in deserts. They can roam about for days without drinking or sweating. The two humps of the Bactrian camel act as fat reserves, off which the animal can live. The shaggy coat protects the camel during the cold winters in Asia's Gobi Desert.

Humps flop over when the fat is depleted.

Long fur covers the upper surface of the feet.

Reptiles and amphibians

Both snakes and lizards are tolerant of dry climates, and these reptiles are among the most common of desert animals. Amphibians are much more in danger of drying out, but a few species do appear on the desert surface, especially after rare bouts of rain.

Snake descends vertically into the sand.

Sand viper buries itself tail first.

Sand viper
The sand viper has perfected an efficient way of disappearing on desert dunes. It wriggles down into the loose sand, becoming buried within seconds. It does this to escape danger and to be ready to attack prey.

Fringe-toed lizard
This lizard forages in sandy deserts. When the surface becomes too hot, it stands on two legs to help keep cool. Projections between its toes spread its weight and stop it from sinking into the sand.

Lizard can close its nostrils to prevent sand getting into its air passsages.

Smooth scales

Water-holding frog
For months, this frog lies dormant underground in a waterproof cocoon. It emerges to feed and breed only after heavy rains, swelling its body with water before it returns into the soil.

Sandfish
The sandfish is a lizard that makes its home on desert sand dunes. It is named after the way it moves across and through the sand, pushing sideways with its flattened toes as if it were swimming. Like other small lizards, it hunts mainly for insects.

Gila monster
The Gila monster is a fearsome lizard. Large, with a venomous bite, it leaves its burrow at dawn to hunt rodents and raid birds' nests. Fat stored in its thick tail provides nourishment when prey is scarce.

Yucca moth
The yucca moth of American deserts has evolved a close relationship with the yucca plant. The moth pollinates the plant; the yucca flowers give shelter to the moth larvae.

Desert cricket
An inhabitant of the deserts of India and Pakistan, the desert cricket can bury itself quickly in the sand. It digs a hole directly beneath itself with its star-shaped feet and sinks down.

Invertebrates

Few insects and other invertebrates can withstand the full force of the desert Sun. Those that can have an especially tough, waxy covering, or cuticle, that prevents them from drying out. Other invertebrates take shelter during the day.

White spots warn off predators.

Domino beetle
This domino beetle lives in the dry lands of northern Africa through to the Middle East. During the day, it hides under rocks and in holes made by other animals. At night, it emerges to hunt insects and other small prey.

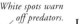

Scorpion
Scorpions are among the hardiest of desert invertebrates, able to tolerate strong sunshine though they normally hunt at night. Armed with strong claws and a lethal sting, they ambush foraging insects such as locusts, as well as spiders and other scorpions.

The venom of this scorpion is strong enough to kill a person.

The scorpion holds its prey in its large claws.

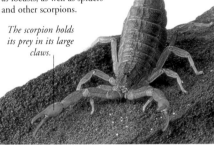

Plants

Only the hardiest of drought-resistant plants can survive all year in the desert. Among these are cacti and yuccas. Seeds of more fragile plants lie dormant in the soil. After a rainburst, they sprout and flower before the moisture evaporates.

Desert holly
Some desert plants, such as the desert holly, have dusty-looking leaves. Salt secreted through leaf pores forms a fine whitish powder. This reflects some of the Sun's rays, helping to keep the leaves cool and preventing excessive evaporation of moisture.

Cacti
Many different kinds of cactus grow in American deserts. All store water in their green swollen stems. They do not have leaves, and this prevents excess moisture loss. Sharp spines deter animals from biting the succulent stems.

Seeds develop after the vine's flower has been pollinated by insects.

A welwitschia plant may live for 1,000 years or more.

Welwitschia
This plant has two ribbon-like leaves that trail across the sand. Each leaf has millions of pores that extract moisture from the sea fogs that sweep the Namib Desert in Africa.

Little snapdragon vine
Rains in the Mexican desert bring the seeds of snapdragon vines to life. The vines quickly grow, trailing over the soil and curling around other plants. They flower and set new seed before they die as the conditions get dry again.

Each leaf grows up to 2 m (6.5 ft) long.

Leaves usually split into several strips.

FIND OUT MORE   AFRICAN WILDLIFE   AMPHIBIANS   ASIAN WILDLIFE   BIRDS   BIRDS OF PREY   DESERTS   INSECTS   MAMMALS   PLANTS   REPTILES

DESIGN

ORIGINALLY A DESIGN was an artist's first sketch for a work of art; today, design plays a broader role in our lives. Before any object can be made, it must be designed. Most things around us have been designed to carry out a particular job. The design of objects is known as product design. There are also many other areas of design, such as fashion, garden, interior, and graphic design. Changing tastes can result in popular design movements, such as art nouveau and Bauhaus.

Product design

In order to design an object, the designer has several factors to consider. He or she must select a shape that suits the object's purpose but also consider other factors, such as the material to be used, the cost of manufacture, the safety and durability of the product, and how it will finally look. Product design usually aims to be both functional and stylish.

This bottle's shape is easily recognizable.

A can's ringpull opening is designed to open easily.

Classic design
Some product designs so successfully combine functionality with a strong sense of style that they are timeless. The distinctive shape of the Coca-Cola bottle, for example, is a classic design that has hardly changed since 1915.

Coca-Cola bottle

Headlamps and bumpers are chrome.

Large steering wheel

The MGB is compact but stylish.

MGB Tourer

Classic cars
Some classic designs express certain ideals perfectly. The sleek lines of a sports-car's body, such as this MGB, are intended to suggest speed and freedom. Launched in 1962, the MGB became the best-selling single model sports car ever, with 512,000 owners worldwide.

The design process

The first stage in the design process is writing a design brief which details the functions and features to be achieved in the finished object. The designer then does a first sketch. This is translated into a rough model, or prototype, which is repeatedly tested and revised as needed. The design process of making numerous small amendments is called an iterative process. Finally, the actual product is made.

1 The designer does a first sketch on a drawing board or computer. This sketch shows a vacuum cleaner.

This prototype is shaped out of hard foam.

The plastic casing is very strong and light.

Large back wheels for manoeuvring

Dust collects in this area.

Long nozzle

Early prototype

Vacuum cleaner

This vacuum cleaner uses a unique cyclone system to pick up dirt.

2 A series of prototypes is made out of different materials to test aspects of the design. The final prototype is handmade and painted to look identical to the final product.

3 The final product is made to the revised design brief. Designs can be patented (protected by copyright law) to prevent someone copying an original design.

Graphic design

Graphic designers use words and images to communicate a strong visual message. We are surrounded by graphic design, in magazines and books, on posters, on street signs. Designers use letters in different sizes and typefaces, often with colours and patterns, to make an impact.

London Underground map
The London Underground map is a brilliant piece of design. By distorting the distances between stations, it is possible to see the entire London Underground at a glance.

Shell Oil logo

Logos
Logos are graphic designs that aim to communicate a message without words. Companies design logos to be easily recognized by the public. The simple shape and strong colours of the logo shown above advertise the Shell Oil Company worldwide.

Computer-aided design
Increasingly, much of the design process is carried out on computer. Using computer-aided design, the designer creates a three-dimensional model, such as a car, on screen which can then be rotated and viewed from all angles.

Walter Gropius
In 1919, the German architect Walter Gropius (1883–1969) founded the Bauhaus design school. It taught the importance of functional design and of using materials such as steel, glass, and concrete. Bauhaus influenced the development of the arts. Gropius (on right) is shown with the French architect, Le Corbusier (1887–1965).

Art Nouveau
Design movements are trends in design, some of which have a lasting influence. Art Nouveau was a design movement beginning in Europe in the 1880s that aimed to make ordinary objects, such as buildings, furniture, and jewellery, beautiful.

This Art Nouveau window in Paris, France, shows typical decorative curves based on organic forms.

FIND OUT MORE ARCHITECTURE   ART, HISTORY OF   BUILDING AND CONSTRUCTION   CARS AND TRUCKS   CLOTHES AND FASHION   FURNITURE   GARDENS   PAINTING AND DRAWING   PRINTING   TRADE AND INDUSTRY

DICKENS, CHARLES

CHARLES DICKENS IS one of the greatest writers in the English language. He was a household name in his own lifetime. His lively descriptions of 19th-century Britain combine with a superb gift for depicting people and their eccentricities, a social conscience, and compassion for the problems faced by ordinary people. He brought to the English novel the ability to portray an entire society in one book. His novels are still loved by readers of all ages.

Early life
Charles Dickens was born in Portsmouth, England, in 1812. His father was a clerk in the Royal Navy pay office and worked for a time in the royal dockyards in Chatham, Kent, where Charles spent much of his childhood. When his father was imprisoned for debt in London's Marshalsea Prison, Charles, then aged 12, had to take a series of menial jobs in factories and offices. He later used these painful experiences in some of his novels.

"Boz"

As a young man, Dickens was a journalist, covering Parliament for the *Morning Chronicle*. In 1833 he began to write a series of articles, mostly about London life, using the pseudonym "Boz". These were collected together in *Sketches by Boz* in 1836. Following their success, he was commissioned to write some humorous sporting stories. These appeared in 1836–37 as *The Posthumous Papers of the Pickwick Club* and made Dickens the most famous writer of his day.

Scrooge meets the Ghost of Christmas Past

David Copperfield

David Copperfield
In 1849–50 Dickens wrote *David Copperfield*, a partly autobiographical novel in which he used his own experiences of an impoverished childhood and menial employment to great effect. Of all his books, it was Dickens' favourite. The novel features Mr Micawber, who is loosely based on Dickens' father. Always in debt, and always waiting for "something to turn up", Micawber is one of the great characters of English literature.

Household Words
From 1850, Dickens edited and contributed first to the magazine *Household Words*, and then, from 1859, to *All The Year Round*. He used these monthly magazines to publish his latest novel in instalments, reaching a far wider readership than he would have done by simply publishing a book. Both magazines featured works by other famous writers of the time, such as Elizabeth Gaskell and Wilkie Collins. Dickens also included articles about the social problems of his time, such as poor housing and factory accidents.

A Christmas Carol
Ebenezer Scrooge, who refused to celebrate Christmas, and his impoverished clerk Bob Cratchit make *A Christmas Carol* (published in 1843) one of Dickens's most popular novels. Scrooge changes his ways when he witnesses a series of visions, including his own death and the ghosts of Christmas Past, Present, and Future.

In a scene from *Oliver Twist*, Oliver asks for more porridge.

Oliver Twist
The story of Oliver tells of a pauper child of unknown parentage who was brought up in a workhouse and dared to ask for more food. *Oliver Twist* was first published as a book in 1838. The book was later made into a successful musical and film. The story was the first by Dickens to explore the dark side of London life in the 19th century, and the fact that thousands of children were living rough on the streets or in inhuman workhouses.

Dickensian London

In Dickens's time, London was a rich city at the centre of the biggest empire the world had ever seen. But many people lived in poverty, making a living from whatever work they could find. Dickens described their suffering, but he loved London – its sights, sounds, and smells feature in all his books.

Social reforms
Dickens often spoke in public about the plight of the poor, the need for educational reform, and the importance of good sanitation to remove the threat of disease. His speeches and novels helped to raise awareness of the need for radical reform, and led to many changes in the law.

London street, 19th century

Public readings
Dickens went on three tours of Britain and one of America, reading selections from his novels. He put vast amounts of energy into these readings, adapting his works specially for public performance, and reading aloud all the parts himself. In 1869, he began a fourth British tour, but his health began to fail, and he died the following year.

CHARLES DICKENS

1812	Born in Portsmouth, England.
1824	Father imprisoned for debt.
1836	Marries Catherine Hogarth; publishes *Sketches by Boz*.
1836–7	*Pickwick Papers*
1838	*Oliver Twist*
1839	*Nicholas Nickleby*
1850	*David Copperfield*
1853	*Bleak House*
1857	*Little Dorrit*
1858	First reading tour
1859	*A Tale of Two Cities*
1861	*Great Expectations*
1864	*Our Mutual Friend*
1870	Dies and is buried in Westminster Abbey.

 FIND OUT MORE   BOOKS   EMPIRES   INDUSTRIAL REVOLUTION   LITERATURE   UNITED KINGDOM, HISTORY OF   WRITING

DIGESTION

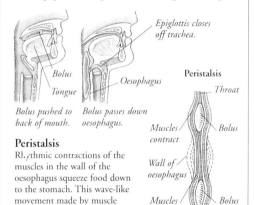

THE BODY NEEDS THE **nutrients** in food to grow, maintain its structure, and provide energy. But the food we eat cannot be used by the body until it is processed by the digestive system. This is essentially a long tube, running from mouth to anus. As food passes along the digestive system it is chewed, and crushed, and then broken down chemically by enzymes. As it passes along the small intestine, food resembles a thin soup, and simple food molecules can be absorbed into the body itself by way of the bloodstream.

Swallowing

Once food is chewed, the tongue pushes the ball of food, or bolus, to the back of the mouth. As it touches the throat, the bolus triggers a reflex action and passes into the oesophagus. A flap called the epiglottis closes the entrance to the trachea (windpipe) to stop food entering the lungs.

Epiglottis closes off trachea.

Bolus
Tongue
Oesophagus

Bolus pushed to back of mouth.
Bolus passes down oesophagus.

Peristalsis

Throat
Muscles contract
Bolus
Wall of oesophagus
Muscles relax
Bolus

Peristalsis
Rhythmic contractions of the muscles in the wall of the oesophagus squeeze food down to the stomach. This wave-like movement made by muscle contraction is called peristalsis. It also occurs in the small intestine.

Digestive process
The digestive process has four stages: ingestion, digestion, absorption, and egestion. Ingestion happens when you eat food and is followed by digestion. Absorption is the transfer of food molecules into the bloodstream and egestion is the removal of waste as faeces.

Mouth

Teeth and tongue break food up into small pieces.

Throat

Epiglotis

Pancreas produces digestive enzymes that are released into duodenum.

Duodenum

Oesophagus carries food from throat to stomach.

Liver

Stomach stores and partially digests food.

Pyloric sphincter controls flow of food from stomach into duodenum.

Colon

Large intestine is made up of colon and rectum.

Appendix

Small intestine is made up of three parts – duodenum, jejunum, and ileum.

Jejunum

Anus is an opening in large intestine that faeces passes through.

Ileum

Rectum

Inferior vena cava
Liver stores and processes food and produces bile.
Ducts
Gall bladder stores bile.
Blood vessels

Liver, pancreas, and gall bladder
These three organs take part in digestion even though, since they have other body functions, they are not part of the digestive system. The liver produces bile, which is stored in the gall bladder and helps digest fats. The pancreas produces digestive enzymes that are released into the small intestine.

Absorption
Simple food molecules are absorbed into the bloodstream across the wall of the small intestine. Tiny finger-like projections called villi (singular: villus) greatly increase the surface area over which food can be absorbed.

Villus
Blood capillary network
Lacteal (part of lymphatic system)
Wall of small intestine

Imaging the intestine
A special liquid is introduced into the large intestine to show clearly its position and internal shape. This type of X-ray enables doctors to detect signs of disease inside the large intestine without having to operate.

William Beaumont
The US Army surgeon William Beaumont (1785–1853) was the first to observe how food was digested in the stomach. In 1822, Beaumont treated a patient who had shot himself in the side and was left with an opening into his stomach. Through this opening, Beaumont was able to observe the stomach's movements during digestion and to record his findings.

Food and enzymes
Enzymes are biological catalysts that speed up the conversion of one substance into another. Digestive enzymes speed up the breakdown of the complex carbohydrates, fats, and proteins that make up most of our food.

Carbohydrates
The body's main fuel, carbohydrate, comes in the form of sugars and complex carbohydrates, which include starch. Enzymes break starchy foods down into sugars such as glucose.

Glucose molecules
Starch molecule chain

Fat droplets
Fats
Fats provide the body with energy. Foods rich in fats include eggs and meat. Fats are broken down by enzymes in the small intestine to form fatty acids.

Fatty acids
Protein

Proteins
Proteins are needed for growth and maintaining the body. Protein-rich foods are meat, fish, and nuts. Proteins are broken down into amino acids.

Amino acids

FIND OUT MORE   CHEMISTRY   FOOD   HORMONES AND ENDOCRINE SYSTEM   HUMAN BODY   IMMUNE AND LYMPHATIC SYSTEM   TEETH AND JAWS

DINOSAURS

FOR 150 MILLION YEARS, from the Triassic Period until the end of the Cretaceous Period, 65 million years ago, dinosaurs lived on Earth. Their remains have been discovered in every continent including Antarctica. They formed a varied group of land-living reptiles. People who study prehistoric life, called palaeontologists, divide them into two main groups – the Ornithischia and the Saurischia. There were meat-eating and plant-eating dinosaurs. Some dinosaurs, were huge; others were only the size of chickens.

Iguanodon skull

Iguanodon skull
Gideon Mantell, an English doctor, named *Iguanodon* in 1825, noting the similarity between its teeth and those of the modern iguana. *Iguanodon*'s teeth were shaped to fit tightly together. They wore down as the dinosaur chewed its food of tough vegetation with the help of a hinged jaw.

Iguanodon tooth

Iguanodon
This was one of the first dinosaurs to be discovered. Modern reconstructions give it an outstretched tail and forelimbs that can reach the ground.

Iguanodon foot

Iguanodon

Iguanodon foot
The feet of *Iguanodon* had small hooves on the toes instead of claws, and would have made recognizable three-toed prints with rounded digits. *Iguanodon* probably walked on its toes, which, therefore, had to be strong to carry the animal's great weight.

Ornithischians

The Ornithischia, or bird-hipped dinosaurs, such as *Iguanodon*, were all herbivorous. They had a huge number of teeth – *Corythosaurus* had 2,000 – and a hinged upper jaw that allowed them to chew.

Tyrannosaurus

Saurischians

The Saurischia, or lizard-hipped dinosaurs, include the meat-eating theropods, which walked on two legs, such as *Tyrannosaurus*, and the plant-eating sauropods, which walked on four legs, such as *Diplodocus*. The sauropods were the largest ever land animals.

Tyrannosaurus tooth
Carnivorous dinosaurs had curved, pointed teeth. The sharp edges often had serrations, which helped the dinosaurs to slice through skin and meat. Palaeontologists still have to be careful when handling these teeth.

Pubis bone

Ischium bone

Tyrannosaurus skeleton
Tyrannosaurus may have hunted as well as scavenged on other dinosaurs. It had a massive skull with powerful jaws, supported by a short, flexible neck. This flexibility allowed the animal to twist its head around to wrench flesh from its prey.

Long, hollow tubular crest

Tail was used for balance.

Ischium bone

Pubis bone

Rounded, hoof-like claws

Skeleton of *Parasaurolophus*, an ornithischian

Tyrannosaurus *tore off the flesh of its prey with its teeth and claws.*

Toothless jaws

Tyrannosaurus
Although not thought to be the largest of the carnivorous dinosaurs, *Tyrannosaurus* was still an extremely fearsome predator. It walked on its hind legs with its back level and head raised. It could run very fast, its tail balancing the weight of its huge heavy body.

Fossil dung
Preserved pieces of dung are called coprolites. They contain the remains of what dinosaurs ate, such as bone fragments, fish scales, or plant remains. Scientists can study these to find out about the diet of dinosaurs.

Hips
Dinosaurs fall into one of the two main groups, according to the structure of their hip bones. The bird-hipped dinosaurs (ornithischians), such as *Parasaurolophus*, had a pubis bone in their hip girdle that sloped backward, parallel to the ischium bone. The lizard-hipped dinosaurs (saurischians), such as *Gallimimus*, had a pubis bone that sloped forward away from the ischium.

Pubis bone

Long foot bones suggests Gallimimus *could run fast.*

Skeleton of *Gallimimus*, a saurischian

Orodromeus laid up to 24 eggs.

The first dinosaurs
One of the earliest dinosaurs was *Eoraptor*, meaning "early plunderer". It was no bigger than a large dog and lived 225 million years ago (mya). As with all the early dinosaurs, it was a carnivore and walked on two legs.

Orodromeus nest

Eoraptor skull

Breeding

Dinosaurs laid hard-shelled eggs as some reptiles do today. Many dinosaurs laid a clutch of eggs in a hollowed-out nest in the ground. Several fossilized nests have been found close together, which suggests that some dinosaurs nested in colonies. The chicks developed rapidly and may have left the nest soon after hatching. Many were cared for by the parent dinosaur until they were able to look after themselves.

Richard Owen

Born in Lancaster, England, Richard Owen (1804–92) became the Hunterian Professor of the Royal College of Surgeons in 1836. As well as being an anatomist, he was a brilliant palaeontologist. He was the first to use the term "dinosaurs", which means "terrible lizards", in a report in 1842. He noted that these animals had pillar-like legs, rather than the sprawling legs of modern reptiles, and should be classified separately.

Defence

Dinosaurs protected themselves against attack from predators. Different dinosaurs developed a variety of powerful defences. For example, *Triceratops* had horns on its head, *Euoplocephalus* had a tail club, and *Tuojiangosaurus* had a spiky tail. Some of these adaptations may have had several functions, but one of them was likely to have been defence. Scientists cannot say exactly how these animals defended themselves, but it is easy to imagine.

Tuojiangosaurus
The flanks and belly of *Tuojiangosaurus* were vulnerable to attack. Near the tip of its tail were four bony spikes. These pointed up and outwards, producing a formidable defence when the dinosaur swung its tail. This animal was a type of bird-hipped dinosaur called a stegosaur. It lived in China 157-145 mya.

All stegosaurs had a double row of plates running down their back.

Small narrow head with a walnut-sized brain

Tuojiangosaurus

Defensive spikes

Short front limbs

Thumb spike

Raised nodules for protection

Euoplocephalus had thick bone plates and spikes over its back, with a large shoulder spike for added protection.

Reconstruction of Iguanodon hand

Iguanodon spike
When *Iguanodon* was first reconstructed, its large spike was placed on its beak. It is now known that the spike was on its thumb and may have been used as a defensive weapon against predators. The spike could have pierced the belly, throat, or eye of an attacker. The dinosaur may also have used it in fights for status with other *Iguanodons*, and even to help it feed.

Dinosaur skin
Occasionally, the skin, or skin impression, of dinosaurs is preserved. From these fossils we can tell that the skin of many dinosaurs was not smooth, but nodular and rough. This would have given some protection against the claws and teeth of predators. This is the skin of *Polacanthus*.

Euoplocephalus

Club was made out of several bones fused together.

Claw

Brow horn

Frill anchored the jaw muscles.

Nose horn

Euoplocephalus
This armoured ornithischian had a large bony club at the tip of its muscular tail. It could have swung this with great force, disabling a predator.

Triceratops
The ceratopsians, or horned dinosaurs, were ornithischians. Most of them had brow horns and nose horns. *Triceratops*, the largest ceratopsian, had two long horns on its brow, a short nose horn, and also a bony neck frill protecting its neck. Its head took up nearly one-third of its length. It probably used its horns to fend off predators, and males used them to deter rivals in the herd, mostly by display, but also by fighting.

Triceratops skull – side view

Triceratops skull – front view

Dinosaur discoveries
Removing dinosaur fossils from surrounding rock is tricky. Some need to be protected in a jacket made of plaster or polyurethane foam before they are taken to a laboratory. Fossils are found every year, and each discovery teaches us more about these extinct animals.

Finding dinosaur bones.

FIND OUT MORE   ANIMALS   ANIMAL BEHAVIOUR   EVOLUTION   FOSSILS   PREHISTORIC LIFE   REPTILES   SKELETON

D

Dinosaurs

Ornithischians

Heterodontosaurus was one of the first bird-hipped dinosaurs. It lived about 205 mya.

Corythosaurus had a tall crest on its head.

Six long spikes

Iguanodon could walk on two or four legs.

Styracosaurus was a short-frilled ceratopsian.

Spiky tail for defence

Scelidosaurus was the oldest-known armoured dinosaur.

Body built for speed

Hypsilophodon was once thought to have lived in trees, but its limbs were not built for climbing.

Stegoceras was a pachycephalosaur, and had a thick-domed skull.

Long thigh compared to the rest of the leg.

Stegosaurus was the largest stegosaur at 9 m (30 ft) long. It had large plates along its back.

Swinging tail club

Euoplocephalus had body armour and a tail club to protect it against attack.

Saurischians

Stiff tail helped with balance.

Deinonychus was a meat eater and may have hunted in packs.

Gallimimus was shaped like an ostrich and was one of the fastest running dinosaurs.

Toothless beak

Dilophosaurus had two high crests on top of its large head.

Flat, crocodile-like jaws

Long neck enabled Barosaurus to reach leaves at the top of trees.

Tail was used for balance at speed.

Hands could be used to grasp food.

Ankle joint

Long, clawed fingers

Baryonyx had a huge 30-cm (12-in)-long claw on each hand.

Long foot bones increased the length of the leg.

Whiplash tail used in defence.

Anchisaurus may have eaten both meat and plants.

Dagger-like teeth

Body like Archaeopteryx, the first bird

Two clawed fingers on each hand

Large hind legs were needed to bear the weight of the body.

Small arms with two-fingered hands

Compsognathus was small – only 74 cm (2.5 ft) long.

Herrerasaurus was a carnivore that lived in Argentina 228 mya.

Barosaurus resembled *Diplodocus*. It was about the same size with a shorter tail and longer neck.

Tyrannosaurus was one of the largest known land-living carnivores, weighing up to 6 tonnes.

DISEASES

JUST LIKE A MACHINE, the human body works smoothly and efficiently most of the time. However, it may occasionally stop operating normally. This may be due to an injury, such as a broken bone, but, more commonly, it is caused by a disease. Diseases occur because the body has been infected by a pathogen (germ), as in the case of influenza or food poisoning, or because of problems arising inside the body, such as heart disease or diabetes. Some diseases can be controlled and defeated by the body's immune system. More serious diseases may need drug treatment or surgery in order to cure them.

Infectious diseases

Infectious diseases are those, such as the common cold or pneumonia, that are caused by pathogens that invade the body. The most common pathogens are bacteria and viruses, although some diseases, such as thrush, are caused by fungi, and some, such as malaria, by tiny organisms called protists. They are normally destroyed by the body's immune system. Those that are not can often be dealt with by drugs.

Chickenpox causes an itchy rash that, when scratched, can leave scars.

Bacteria are in water, air, and soil, as well as many plant and animal tissues.

Bacteria
Bacteria are single-celled micro-organisms. Most bacteria are not harmful to humans. However, some multiply inside the body and produce toxins that cause disease. Bacterial diseases include typhoid and scarlet fever. Most can be treated with drugs called antibiotics.

Viruses
Viruses are tiny infective particles, not usually classed as living things. They take over a body cell's genetic material (DNA) and make copies of themselves that infect other cells. Human viral infections include colds, measles, and HIV.

HIV and AIDS

HIV

The human immunodeficiency virus, or HIV, causes AIDS (Acquired Immune Deficiency Syndrome). HIV infects and destroys the cells that form part of the body's immune system – the body's defences against diseases. HIV is transmitted by some bodily fluids, such as blood and semen. The system becomes progressively weaker, and the person becomes infected with various diseases, known collectively as AIDS.

Epidemiologist tests samples in laboratory.

Epidemiology
Epidemiology is the study of diseases as they affect groups of people. Epidemiologists are concerned with why diseases occur in a population, and their control and prevention. They have discovered links between disease and diet, environmental factors, and lifestyle. Epidemiologists first discovered the link between smoking and lung cancer.

Non-infectious diseases

If a disease is non-infectious, it is not caused by a pathogen and cannot be passed from one person to another. Non-infectious diseases include circulatory system diseases, such as heart attacks, strokes, and cancer, and respiratory diseases, such as bronchitis and emphysema.

Nutritional diseases
Nutritional diseases are caused by a lack of a balanced diet, causing a deficiency of vitamins and minerals. A child not getting enough vitamin D may suffer from rickets, where the skeleton does not form properly.

Rickets may leave sufferer with bow-legs.

Miners may develop lung problems.

Industrial diseases
Work situations may affect a person's health. Industrial processes can create harmful environments or use chemicals that cause diseases. Some miners develop a lung disease called pneumoconiosis.

Spreading infection

Most diseases are acquired from other people by skin-to-skin contact, breathing in droplets when someone sneezes or coughs, or by sexual contact without the use of condoms. Infection can also be spread through infected food, contaminated water, and insect bites. Drug users who share needles risk infections of the blood, such as hepatitis and HIV.

Sanitation
Human faeces contain bacteria and viruses that cause disease. If there is poor sanitation and human waste is discharged into rivers, people may catch diseases such as dysentery or cholera through contact with polluted water.

Some mosquitoes carry strains of malaria that are resistant to drugs.

Insects
Insects such as mosquitoes and fleas feed on human blood and can carry disease. A mosquito transmits the malaria micro-organism if it feeds on an infected person's blood.

Keeping rivers clean prevents diseases that can be caught if people drink, wash, or grow food in the water.

Preventing disease
Disease prevention is an important part of modern medicine. Diseases can be prevented by better sanitation, immunization, and improving food hygiene. Eating a balanced diet and exercising may also prevent disease.

Syringes that are not properly sterilized after use can spread disease.

Bottled water is a way of assuring water is safe in certain countries.

Pills contain measured amounts of drugs.

FIND OUT MORE   BLACK DEATH   CELLS   CURIE, MARIE   DRUGS   HUMAN BODY   IMMUNE AND LYMPHATIC SYSTEM   PASTEUR, LOUIS

DISNEY, WALT

IN 1901, A MAN WAS BORN who would change the face of entertainment. Walt Disney became interested in animation as a schoolboy; by the time he was 20 he was making short animated films. But it was his later work that changed the history of the cinema. He created a string of cartoon characters which have been favourites ever since – Donald Duck, Goofy, and, above all, Mickey Mouse. Walt Disney also made the first feature-length animated film, *Snow White and the Seven Dwarfs* (1937), which was followed by many other screen successes.

Early life

In 1906, Disney's father Elias bought a farm at Marceline, Missouri. This was where young Walt first saw animals at close quarters. He also became interested in drawing. The first he ever sold was a drawing of the local doctor's stallion, for which the doctor paid Disney a nickel.

Early animation

Disney began to make animated films in 1920. These films featured characters which were made by cutting figures out of paper. The figures could be moved while they were photographed with a hand-cranked camera.

Disney with a hand-cranked camera

Hollywood

Disney moved to Hollywood in 1923. There were no animation studios, so he set up his own. He was soon in the forefront of technical innovation, pioneering the use of synchronized sound and the three-colour Technicolor process.

Mickey Mouse

Steamboat Willie, the first cartoon to feature Mickey Mouse, appeared in 1928. This was also the first cartoon with sound. Disney himself supplied Mickey's voice, and the film was an instant success. Mickey has since appeared in many other films. He has become the instantly recognizable Disney symbol and has appeared on countless Disney merchandise products.

Walt Disney with Mickey Mouse and Donald Duck

Snow White with the seven dwarfs

Snow White

In the 1920s, cartoons were normally shown before a full-length live-action film. But in 1935, Disney had the idea of producing a full-length cartoon, *Snow White and the Seven Dwarfs* (1937). Hundreds of animators worked on the film, which was followed by many other full-length animated features.

Mary Poppins

From the 1950s onwards, Disney produced many live-action films. Some of these, such as the musical fantasy *Mary Poppins* (1964), also included animated sequences.

Julie Andrews in a scene from Mary Poppins

The Disney Club

Disney was the first US major studio to create locally produced children's programming such as The Disney Club, and is the only studio to maintain a world-wide network of production offices. This network produces more than 40 weekly Disney programmes, which reach over 300 million viewers.

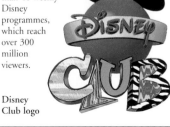

Disney Club logo

Disneyland

For many years, Walt Disney wanted to recreate the sets and characters of his films in a recreational park. The result, Disneyland, opened in 1955 in Anaheim, near Los Angeles, California. This theme park is one of the world's most popular attractions. Other parks have since opened: Walt Disney World in Florida and Disneyland ® Paris.

Disneyland

WALT DISNEY

1901	Born in Chicago, USA.
1919	Begins to make animated films.
1923	Moves to Hollywood.
1928	*Steamboat Willie,* featuring Mickey Mouse.
1937	*Snow White and the Seven Dwarfs,* the first feature-length animated film.
1940	*Pinocchio.*
1940	*Fantasia.*
1942	*Bambi.*
1955	Disneyland opens.
1964	*Mary Poppins.*
1966	Walt Disney dies.

FIND OUT MORE CARTOONS AND ANIMATION   FILMS AND FILM-MAKING   TELEVISION

DOGS

DOGS HAVE LIVED with people for more than 12,000 years. They may have started to stay near humans for food and warmth. Then people began to train dogs to work for them. They bred certain types of dog for herding and guarding other domestic animals, then for hunting and for companionship. Gradually, different types of dog developed, but it was not until the end of the 19th century that specific breeds were classified. Today, there are about 200 dog breeds throughout the world. They are more varied in their appearance and behaviour than any other domestic animal.

Siberian husky

English setter

Shetland sheepdogs

Chihuahua

Scottish terriers

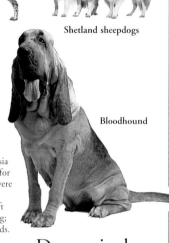

Bloodhound

Dog groups

The people of ancient Egypt and western Asia were the first to breed distinct types of dog for different purposes. By Roman times, dogs were kept for much the same reasons as they are today. There are six main groups – (from left to right) top row: working, sporting, herding; bottom row: companion, terriers, and hounds.

Domestic dogs

All breeds of domestic dog, from the Great Dane to the chihuahua, are descended from the wolf and have inherited the wolf's instincts. Like wolves, dogs are pack animals. They treat humans as part of their pack, and can be trained to accept their owner as the pack leader, and to follow his or her commands.

Borzois have sharp eyesight and hunt by sight.

Long, strong legs and a flexible body for speed

The borzoi was bred in Russia in the 13th century and used first to hunt wolves.

Dog features

The wolf is designed to chase, capture, kill, and eat its prey. It is agile, with strong legs for running long distances. Domestic dogs retain many of the features of a wolf, but through selective breeding now exist in many shapes, sizes, and colours.

Coats

There are three main types of dog coats – long, short, and wiry. Most breeds have an outer coat of guard hairs and an undercoat of shorter hairs. They moult, or shed their fur, changing their coat in spring and autumn.

Feet

Dogs walk on their toes rather than the soles of their feet. Their paw pads help with grip, as do their claws, which are non-retractable.

Short hair   Long hair   Wire hair

Senses

Dogs have highly developed senses of hearing and smell. They use these in communication and to track down their prey. The police use dogs to sniff out explosives, criminals, and drugs. The dogs can see well in the dark and are good at seeing movement in the distance.

Beagles were bred to hunt hares.

Reproduction

A female dog is pregnant for about nine weeks, then gives birth to several puppies known as a litter. At birth, puppies are blind and deaf. Their eyes open at about 10 to 12 days old and they are able to hear at 13 to 17 days old. Teeth start to grow between three and five weeks of age.

A young puppy is defenceless.

All puppies are born with short legs and a little tail.

Eyes are fully open.

1 At one week old, a puppy spends most of its time sleeping and feeding by suckling from its mother.

2 At two weeks old, the puppy takes its first wobbling steps and begins to explore. Its eyes are now open and it can hear.

3 At three weeks old, the puppy may start to eat solid food. At first, its mother will regurgitate meat for it.

4 At six weeks old, the puppy no longer feeds from its mother. It can soon be taken away from her to a new home.

FIND OUT MORE   ANIMALS   ANIMALS, BEHAVIOUR   CATS   GRASSLAND WILDLIFE   MAMMALS   POLICE   WOLVES AND WILD DOGS

Dogs

Working dogs

Great Dane makes an excellent family pet.

Mastiff existed in Britain in ancient Roman times.

Boxer is a lively and affectionate dog.

German shepherd dog is intelligent and enthusiastic.

Dalmatian, used to deter highwaymen in the 1800s.

St Bernard exists in wire- and smooth-haired forms.

Companion dogs

"Papillon" refers to the shape of the ears.

Large head

Papillon is named after the French for "butterfly".

Pekingese has a flattened face, with a broad nose.

Bulldog is a strong but affectionate dog.

Thick, harsh-textured coat

Miniature poodle, world's most popular dog in the 1950s.

Cavalier King Charles spaniel, bred in 1900s.

Pug has a soft coat and a curled tail.

Terriers

Up to 60 cm (24 in) tall

Coat comes in a variety of colours.

Airedale terrier is the largest terrier breed.

Border terrier was first bred for hunting rats.

Staffordshire bull terrier is loyal and devoted.

Tail carried upright

Boston terrier originated in Boston, USA, in the 1800s.

Smooth fox terrier is alert and tireless.

Parson Jack Russell terrier has a mostly white coat.

Long body for its height

Yorkshire terrier is a small but spirited guard dog.

Cairn terrier has a shaggy, water-resistant coat.

Australian terrier is capable of tackling a snake.

Hounds

Slightly curved tail

Long body and short legs

Strong back

Basset hound is an agile and single-minded hunter

Dachshunds can be long-, smooth-, or wire-haired.

Whippet was bred in the 1800s for racing.

Muscular neck

Rhodesian ridgeback has a ridge of hair on its back.

Afghan hound needs plenty of exercise.

Greyhound is built for speed.

Powerful hindquarters

71–90 cm (28–35 in) tall

Lurcher: individuals vary considerably within the breed.

Saluki, fast and agile, was once used to hunt gazelles.

Irish wolfhound is the tallest dog in the world.

Herding dogs

Deep muscular chest

Hair falls over the eyes

Australian cattle dog has great stamina.

Border collie is an outstanding sheepdog.

Old English sheepdog has a thick, shaggy coat.

Sporting dogs

Obvious stop on the muzzle

Water-resistant coat

Pointer is agile, athletic, and needs much exercise.

English springer spaniel is one of the largest spaniels.

Curly-coated retriever is one of the oldest breeds.

DRAMA

DRAMA HAS BEEN DELIGHTING people for at least 2,500 years. A Broadway musical, a play by Shakespeare, and a television soap opera are all different sorts of drama. What they have in common is the presence of actors, who perform a story (the play) in a theatrical setting, to entertain an audience and make them think. Dramatists (writers of drama) use their art to entertain and thrill their audience or, more seriously, to explore human character and raise questions about the nature and meaning of life.

Early drama

Western drama originated in ancient Greece, where plays were staged to honour the gods. The Greeks invented two of the most enduring dramatic forms, tragedy and comedy, which were later imitated by the Romans.

Classical Greek drama

The ancient Greeks held regular drama festivals, at which dramatists competed for prizes. Their tragedies were based on characters from Greek mythology. Their comedies ranged in style from uproarious satires to more realistic dramas.

Statuette of muse, holding a mask from Greek comedy

Renaissance and 17th century

The traditions of ancient Greek drama were revived in Renaissance Italy and spread through Europe. Many plays were written in verse. Drama thrived in the 16th and 17th centuries, the age of English playwright William Shakespeare (1564–1616) and his contemporaries.

Lope de Vega

Medieval drama

Western drama went into a decline at the end of the Roman Empire, but revived in the 10th century, with the rise of Christian religious drama. Amateur players produced plays enacting stories from the Bible, performed over a number of days. The audience watched out of doors, in market-places and other public spaces.

Religious drama, York, England, 13th century

France

The French dramatist Jean Racine (1639–99) wrote plays that were heavily influenced by Greek tragedy and often based on Greek mythology. Unusually for the time, many featured women in the title role. Another great dramatist of the era, Molière (1622–73), developed French comedy with plays that mocked the middle classes.

Phèdre (1677), by Racine

Spain

The 17th century was the Golden Age of Spanish theatre. The Spanish dramatist Lope de Vega (1562–1635) wrote some 1,500 plays; his play *Fuenteovejuna* was one of the first to deal with ordinary working people. The other great Spanish dramatist of this time was Pedro Calderón de la Barca (1600–81), who produced many tragedies and historical plays.

Realism and 20th century

From the mid-18th century onwards, drama became increasingly realistic, with playwrights portraying middle-class characters in familiar situations. Theatres were fitted with picture-frame stages and realistic sets. It was fashionable for plays to deliver a direct, moral message. During the 20th century, dramatists experimented with dialogue and plot structure, in order to challenge "realism" or give dramas a symbolic meaning.

A Doll's House (1879), by Ibsen

Realistic drama

Dramatists such as Norwegian Henrik Ibsen (1828–1906) and Swede August Strindberg (1849–1912) produced plays that attacked the narrow social attitudes of their time and sometimes shocked audiences with their frankness.

Bertolt Brecht

In his plays, the German writer Bertolt Brecht (1898–1956) put forward serious socialist messages. He constantly reminded his audience that they were watching a play, to make them think about the socialist ideas in his works, and look more closely at the world outside the theatre.

Types of drama

The many types of drama include tragedies (serious plays that deal with the downfall of a flawed but heroic individual) and light-hearted comedies (plays with happy endings). Other types include historical plays, thrillers, and musical theatre.

Waiting for Godot

(1955), by Irish writer Samuel Beckett (1906–89), is a type of modern drama known as the "Theatre of the Absurd": the plot seems to lead nowhere, suggesting life has no point.

Mother Courage (1941), by Brecht, is set during the Thirty Years' War.

The stage is empty, except for a single tree.

The heroes wait for someone who does not arrive.

Broadway

A street in New York at the heart of the city's theatre-going district, Broadway is world famous, and synonymous with the commercial theatre in North America. Broadway productions need a big budget and guaranteed audiences, so more experimental plays often appear in theatres "off-Broadway" first, and transfer to a Broadway theatre if successful.

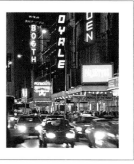

Broadcasting

Anyone with access to a television or radio can now enjoy drama every day. Sometimes these are productions of works originally written for the stage, and adapted. More common are dramas specially written for broadcasting. Many of these are run as series, so that every week, or even every day, people can watch or listen to another episode of their favourite drama. Some forms of television drama have proved especially popular, such as crime stories, adventure series, and soap operas.

O Maraja, satirical Brazilian soap opera

Soap operas
Immensely popular, these serialized television dramas usually deal with the lives and loves of "ordinary" people. Soap operas are so-called because they were at first sponsored by commercial companies such as soap manufacturers.

Actors

The skill of the actors is vital to the success of a drama. Using the right tone of voice, facial expression, or gesture, an actor creates the illusion that the audience is watching or listening to real people and events on stage or screen. Many actors study at drama school before becoming professionals, paid to appear on stage.

Drama festivals
Drama festivals are held around the world so that theatre-goers can celebrate the best in acting and writing. Plays range from traditional productions to experimental works from new writers. The Edinburgh International Festival, held annually, is world famous.

At a festival held each year in Salzburg, Austria, actors re-enact a medieval religious drama.

Chinese opera
Traditional Chinese, or Beijing, opera retells stories from historical events and Buddhist stories. The action comprises arias and recitations, mime, song, and dance, with music from an orchestra of traditional instruments, such as the lute, clappers, gongs, and drums.

Farewell My Concubine is a film about Chinese opera.

World drama

Many non-Western cultures have produced their own, distinct traditions of drama, which draw on local conditions and skills. In Asia, for example, drama draws on local mythology and tales of gods and goddesses. Such drama also uses local craft skills to produce striking costumes and masks, and may be accompanied with music played on traditional instruments.

Noh masks represent five groups: male, female, old people, the gods, and monsters.

Ritual drama
In parts of Africa, Asia, and Melanesia, traditional drama forms an important part of religious ritual. A high priest or shaman puts on a mask and costume that completely disguises him and, as he dances to music, people believe that he actually becomes the spirit he is imitating.

Papua New Guinea Trobrianders: ritual religious drama.

Noh theatre
In traditional Japanese Noh drama, actors wear elaborate costumes and masks, but perform on a bare stage. They move slowly and make special, meaningful gestures. They chant their lines, accompanied by music. Plays are performed in groups, the whole programme lasting an entire day.

Noh mask

Circuses
A circus is a form of entertainment that combines a number of different skills, such as juggling, acrobatics, clowning, and conjuring. Circuses date from the end of the 18th century. Animal acts once formed part of circus routines, but these are now less popular in the West.

Moscow State Circus

Javanese shadow puppet

In shadow plays, puppets are used to tell traditional stories.

Made from leather

The operator uses thin rods to move the puppet.

Puppetry

Puppetry is a type of drama involving puppets, figures that seem to come to life when a human operator moves them. It is one of the oldest types of drama, dating from at least the 5th century BC. One example is shadow puppetry, which is popular in Southeast Asia. A light is used to cast a shadow from the puppet onto a translucent viewing screen. The puppet then acts out a play.

Robert Lepage
The Canadian playwright and director Robert Lepage (b. 1957) has achieved world status for his experimental work. Giving everyday objects symbolic meaning, and working closely with actors, he has taken risks that, while not always a critical success, push back the boundaries of drama.

Timeline

5th century BC The Greeks pioneer tragedy and comedy.

11th to 15th centuries AD Religious drama becomes popular in Europe.

Statue of comic actor from Roman drama

1580–1642 In England, the Elizabethan and Jacobean dramatists revitalize English drama.

1600–80 The Golden Age of Spanish drama.

1782 Friedrich von Schiller (1759–1805) stages *The Robbers*, one of the plays that inspires the German Romantic movement in the 18th century.

c.1800 In Vietnam, Hat Boi theatre dramatizes tales of war and suffering.

Late 1800s "Realist" drama develops, exploring modern social issues.

1960s The "Theatre of the Absurd" subverts the conventions of the theatre.

1990s Musicals are the most popular type of play.

FIND OUT MORE — FESTIVALS · FILMS AND FILM-MAKING · GREECE, ANCIENT · LITERATURE · MEDIEVAL EUROPE · OPERA · RENAISSANCE · SHAKESPEARE · THEATRES

DRUGS

A DRUG IS ANY SUBSTANCE that, when put into the body, alters its normal workings or body chemistry. Natural body hormones, such as insulin, can act as drugs when taken in concentrated form. Medical drugs have many uses. Some, such as cough suppressants, may relieve symptoms; others, such as analgesics, deaden pain; while others, including antibiotics, treat the cause of disease. Drugs may also be taken for non-medical reasons, such as steroids to enhance sports performance and body-building. The abuse of such drugs may be illegal, and can cause physical harm.

History of drugs

Pestle
Mortar

More than 3,000 years ago, people across the world – especially in China, India, the Middle East, Europe, and North Africa – used hundreds of different substances as drugs. They included herbal and mineral extracts, and animal products, such as blood, bile, and urine. Physicians mixed these drugs using a pestle and mortar, and often combined their use with magic, superstition, and religion. Modern research has discovered that some are effective.

How drugs work

Drugs change the processes within the cells of the body. Their effectiveness depends on the dose (quantity), and method of administration (or route into the body). These routes include: absorption through the skin from a cream or a skin patch; injections into a muscle, vein, or under the skin; inhalation; eye or ear drops; or the oral route, where medication is swallowed as tablets, pills, capsules, or liquid.

Types of drugs

Drugs can be grouped by their medical uses or effects. For example, antibiotics kill bacteria, analgesics deaden pain, anti-inflammatories reduce swelling, anti-pyretics lower body temperature, and anti-coagulants help to prevent unwanted blood clots. Some drugs, such as aspirin, can be placed in more than one category.

Transdermal patches   **Syrup**

Pressurized inhaler

Chewing gum   **Suppositories**   **Pills and tablets**

Antibiotic
These drugs kill or disable germs (harmful microbes) known as bacteria. Most come from chemicals made either by fungi, or by other bacteria.

Antibiotic cream

Analgesic
Painkillers come in two types: narcotics, such as morphine, codeine, and other opiates originally from the opium poppy; and non-narcotics, such as paracetamol, which have a different origin.

Cytotoxic
The name means "cell-poisoners", but cytotoxic drugs are designed to affect only the out-of-control cells in tumours and malignancies (cancers), while leaving normal body cells unharmed. They are one type of anti-cancer drug. They are very powerful and their doses and uses must be carefully supervised.

Syringe containing cytotoxic drugs   **Tablets and capsules**

Drugs from nature
Half of modern drugs originate from plants, fungi, animals, or microbes. In ancient times, people were unable to separate the actual drug – the active ingredient – from its source. As chemistry became more sophisticated, scientists identified and purified these ingredients making the drug safer. Some drugs extracted originally from nature are now made from genetically engineered microbes.

Fresh leaves

Witch hazel   *Resin*   *Dried parts*

Paul Ehrlich
The German scientist Paul Ehrlich (1854–1915) dreamed of finding a substance that would act as a "magic bullet", by destroying invading germs, while leaving healthy body cells unaffected. He pioneered synthetic drugs (chemical agents made in the laboratory, rather than extracted from natural sources). The first of these was Salvarsan, which was a laboratory-made drug containing arsenic; it was effective against syphilis and related infections.

Drug research

In the laboratory, scientists analyse potential new drugs. They perform tests on the drug to establish its chemistry, and how it affects the body's processes. Then they test it on tissues and cells in the laboratory, on animals, and finally on human volunteers in clinical trials.

Drug research laboratory

Aspirin

Brand name – the name by which manufacturers sell a drug, e.g. Aspro.

Generic name – the name by which the active ingredient is known, e.g. aspirin.

Common chemical name – showing the chemical subgroups, e.g. acetyl-salicylic acid.

Chemical formula – lists the atoms and their numbers in the drug, e.g. $C_9H_8O_4$.

D

D

Pharmacies

The science of drugs is known as pharmacology. Pharmacy refers to both the practice of preparing and dispensing drugs, and the place where this happens. A person qualified in pharmacology is called a pharmacist (or chemist). The dispensing chemist can advise on which drugs to use for minor ailments.

Pharmacist at work

Prescription

Some drugs, known as controlled substances, are only available with a doctor's permission. A prescription is a written and signed instruction from a doctor that authorizes a pharmacist to dispense a controlled substance. Prescriptions include the name and dosage of the drug, how often the patient must take it, and any other relevant instructions.

Hospital pharmacy

Over-the-counter drugs

Over-the-counter drugs are available without a prescription. They can be bought at supermarkets and pharmacies, and are usually less powerful than prescription drugs. They have fewer side-effects or contra-indications (health problems that warn against their use), but they are still open to misuse. Pharmacists are qualified to recommend certain drug preparations, although they cannot diagnose or prescribe treatment.

Non-medical drugs

Some drugs can be taken for their non-medicinal effects on the mind and body. These effects may include the stimulation or sedation of the mind, a temporary boost to physical performance in sport, or a feeling of emotional well-being.

Wine and brandy

Caffeine is found in coffee, tea, and cola.

Coffee

Sedatives

These drugs sedate (slow down) bodily functions, including physical activity and mental agility. Sedatives can make the user feel relaxed and peaceful for a short time. They include sleeping pills, antihistamines (which suppress allergic reactions), antidepressants, and alcohol, which is probably the most widely used non-medical drug in the world.

Stimulants

These drugs temporarily stimulate (speed up) bodily functions and mental processes. However, they can cause after-effects, such as depression. Stimulants include caffeine, nicotine (in tobacco), and cocaine.

Drug abuse

This is the improper non-medical use of legal or illegal drugs for physical or psychological reasons. The feelings and mental state experienced by the taker are often very different to that person's actual behaviour, seen by onlookers. After too much alcohol, a drinker may feel bright and witty, while onlookers see a slurring bore.

Tobacco shop

Customs official arresting a drug trafficker

Illegal drugs

Some drugs are so powerful and dangerous that they are illegal almost everywhere in the world. These include LSD and mescaline (known in some countires as Schedule I drugs), amphetamines, cocaine, and narcotics (Schedule II drugs). Supplying these illegal drugs to users has become a vast international business.

Legal drugs

The legality of drugs varies greatly all over the world. As well as the drug's strength and effects, legality often depends on tradition, religion, and availability. One of the most powerful and addictive drugs is alcohol. Alcohol is fully legalized (in some countries), partly legalized (for people over 18 or 21) in others, and completely banned in others. Nicotine in the form of cigars, cigarettes, chewing tobacco, and snuff is also legal in most countries.

Group therapy session

Dependence and addiction

A person may come to depend on addictive drugs in order to function. Addiction – intense craving – is hard to control. If the user stops taking the drug, his or her body undergoes "withdrawal", which includes symptoms, such as headaches, sweating, hallucinations, and mood swings. People trying to stop using addictive drugs often find support groups are helpful.

Jonas Salk

Vaccines are substances that give the body resistance or immunity to certain infecting germs. In the 1950s, American microbiologist Jonas Salk (1914–95) developed the first effective vaccine against the crippling disease of polio (poliomyelitis). It spread into worldwide use from 1955 on. From 1960, an oral form of the vaccine, Sabin, gradually replaced the Salk injection.

Timeline

1840s Anaesthetics begin to be used during surgery.

1881 Artificial vaccine used against anthrax.

1910 Paul Ehrlich introduces chemo-therapeutic drugs.

1922 Frederick Banting and others treat diabetes using insulin, a natural body hormone.

1936 Treatment of infections improves with the advent of Prontosil, the first sulpha drug.

Fresh witch hazel

1940s Howard Florey and Ernst Chain make penicillin available as an antibiotic. It is used widely in World War II.

1956 Oral contraceptives (birth control pills) are introduced, using the natural female hormones, oestrogen and progestogen.

1967 Fertility drugs help couples conceive.

1983 Cyclosporin, an immuno-suppressant, helps prevent rejection of transplanted organs.

1990s AIDS drugs tested.

Tablets and capsules

FIND OUT MORE   FIRST AID   HOSPITALS   MEDICINE   MEDICINE, HISTORY OF   PASTEUR, LOUIS   PLANT USES

DUCKS, GEESE, AND SWANS

MOST DUCKS, GEESE, AND SWANS spend their life on or near water. They belong to a family of birds called waterfowl and are closely related to each other. They have broad beaks and short legs with webbed feet. They are good swimmers and have waterproof plumage, which keeps them dry and also helps them to float. There are about 160 species of waterfowl in the wild. Some species of duck and goose have been domesticated and are often raised on farms.

Khaki Campbell –
a domestic duck

Ducks

Ducks are the smallest and most varied waterfowl. Males are often brightly coloured and females are usually drab, which helps to camouflage them when they are sitting on their eggs. Some ducks live in coastal waters, but most live on rivers, lakes, and ponds.

Webs stretched open   *Webs closed*

Plumage
Ducks produce a waterproof oil from a gland near the base of their tail. When they preen their feathers, they spread the oil over them. This oil is so effective that a duck stays dry even when it dives beneath the surface.

Swimming
A duck's webbed feet work like paddles to push it through the water. When it pushes its feet backward, it spreads its toes to stretch out the webs between them. When it pulls its feet forward, it closes its toes to shut the webs, which then offer less water resistance.

Mute swan has a black knob at the base of its beak.

Swans

The largest waterfowl are swans, with a wingspan of up to 2.3 m (7.5 ft). Most of the eight species are white, but the Australian black swan has a black body and white flight feathers. A swan spends a lot of its time on water. It uses its long neck to reach plants below the surface.

A Mandarin duckling leaves the nest in response to its mother's call.

With its wings held wide, the duckling jumps.

Big feet and stubby wings work like parachutes to slow the duckling's fall.

A tree duckling must jump before it is a day old to find food.

Mute swan egg is an oval shape.

Swan egg

Young swans
Young swans, or cygnets, stay with their parents for a whole year, which is a long time for a bird. When they develop their adult plumage, their parents drive them away.

Nesting swans
Swans nest on the ground close to the water's edge. The female incubates the eggs for up to 38 days, and she hisses loudly at anything that comes too close. If her warnings are ignored, she attacks. Her powerful beak and wings make formidable weapons.

Tree-nesting ducks
Most ducks nest on the ground but a few lay their eggs in holes in trees. Soon after the young have hatched, their mother leaves the nest and calls to them to follow her. The ducklings are too young to fly, and instead they jump to the ground.

Geese

Unlike most waterfowl, geese usually feed on land. They eat grass, gripping it in their beaks and pulling it up with a tug. Many geese breed in the tundra of the far north. These white-fronted geese, seen here in western Scotland, fly north to Greenland after the winter.

Swan takeoff
Swans can weigh up to 13 kg (28.5 lb), which makes them among the world's heaviest flying birds. Swans cannot take off from a standing start. Instead, they have to run across the water to gain enough speed for takeoff.

The duckling walks away on landing.

MUTE SWAN

SCIENTIFIC NAME	*Cygnus olor*
ORDER	Anseriformes
FAMILY	Anatidae
DISTRIBUTION	Western Europe, parts of central Asia; also introduced into other parts of the world, including North America, Australia, and New Zealand
HABITAT	Lakes and rivers
DIET	Water plants
SIZE	Length: 152 cm (60 in)
LIFESPAN	About 20 years

FIND OUT MORE   ANIMAL BEHAVIOUR   BIRDS   EGGS   FARMING   FLIGHT, ANIMALS   PENGUINS   SEABIRDS

DYES AND PAINTS

DYES AND PAINTS are substances that are used to stain or give colour to a range of objects, from textiles and paper to buildings and machinery. The substances that give colour to dyes are called dyestuffs, which, when dissolved in water, penetrate the fibres of fabrics by means of a chemical reaction. Pigments form the colour in paints. These are held in place using a varnish-like substance called a vehicle, or binder, which also binds the pigment to the surface being painted. Throughout history, people have created colour, first by means of natural dyes and pigments, and today by using synthetic ones.

Early pigments

The first materials used as pigments were probably coloured clays, which were mixed with water or animal oils to make paint. Dyes made from plants and animals were later used to colour textiles. Common plant dyes included woad, madder, saffron, and turmeric. Animal sources included cochineal (beetle) and the Murex sea snail.

Red skin of onion gives colour

Stinging nettle

Walnuts

Turmeric leaf

Saffron powder

Root

Powder

Turmeric

Saffron crocus

Dyes

Some natural dyes still exist, but most used today are synthetic. These are organic chemicals produced by processing petroleum and coal-tar chemicals such as benzene. Most dyes are used in the textile industry, but are also used in the leather, paper, food, and cosmetics industries. The dyes can be applied to the fibre or fabric using either a direct or indirect process.

Wool can by dyed using a mordant dye, but this dye is now avoided in Western countries due to its use of potentially harmful chemicals.

Indirect dyeing

In some dyeing processes, a number of steps are needed to dye the fibre. In one process, a chemical called a mordant is first added to the fibre, which is then dyed. The mordant molecules fix the dye to the fabric.

Fabrics can be coloured using a range of dyes

Direct dyeing

In most industrial dyeing processes today, dyes can enter the fibre and colour it in one step, without the need of a mordant. The dye is dissolved in hot water, strained, and then added to the fabric. Sometimes the dye is mixed with salt to help fix the colour.

The T-shirt on the left shows how the dye has faded.

This T-shirt shows how the colour has remained fast.

Colour fastness

Two of the most important properties demanded of a dye by clothes manufacturers are its abilities to resist being washed out, and not to fade in the light. The colour fastness of a fabric also varies according to the dyeing process that is used and the type of material that is being dyed.

Paints

Paint comes in many colours and can be used as a coating on rigid structures such as houses, bridges, ships, and cars. Finer paints are used by artists to produce imaginative and colourful works of art. The pigments used to make the paints may be natural, such as rutile (titanium dioxide) or synthetic, such as phthalocyanine blue.

Industrial paints

Industrial paints are custom-made for specific jobs. Some paints contain powdered metal and metal oxides, so that the paint can protect exposed structures, such as iron bridges. Paints such as those used on cars are designed to withstand rusting and high temperatures.

Oil paints usually come in tubes so that users can squeeze out the exact amount of paint needed.

Oil paints

Artists' paints

Artists use a variety of types of paint to achieve different effects, including watercolours, oils, and acrylics. The pigments in watercolour paints are mixed with a water solution of gum arabic, in oils they are mixed in a slow-drying oil, such as linseed oil, while in acrylics the pigments are mixed with a synthetic-resin vehicle.

Paint-spraying car body

Domestic paints

Most decorating paints are made for easy application. Non-drip paints are jelly-like in the can, but flow easily when applied. Emulsion paint uses water as its vehicle, so splashes can be removed and brushes easily cleaned.

Can of non-drip paint and brush

William Henry Perkin

British chemist William Henry Perkin (1838–1907) accidentally produced the first synthetic dye, mauve, in 1856. He was attempting to make the drug quinine from coal-tar chemicals, but instead produced a purple liquid dye. This was the start of the synthetic dye industry.

FIND OUT MORE | ART, HISTORY OF | CHEMISTRY | CLOTHES AND FASHION | COAL | COLOUR | MIXTURES AND COMPOUNDS | MONET, CLAUDE | PAINTING AND DRAWING | TEXTILES AND WEAVING

EARS AND HEARING

WHEN A BEE BUZZES, a soprano sings, or a jumbo jet takes off, each generates invisible vibrations called sound waves that enter the ears, the body's organs of hearing. The sound waves travel deep inside the skull to the part of the ear that does the hearing. Here, sound waves are converted into nerve impulses that travel along nerves to the auditory, or hearing, area on each side of the brain. In the brain, the impulses are interpreted as sounds. The ears can pick up a wide range of sounds and, with the eyes, they help us to make sense of our surroundings.

Anatomy of the ear

Mostly concealed within the skull, the ear is divided into three parts. The outer ear consists of the pinna (ear flap) and the auditory canal. The middle ear is filled with air and contains three tiny bones called ossicles. The inner ear is fluid-filled and contains the cochlea and the semi-circular canals.

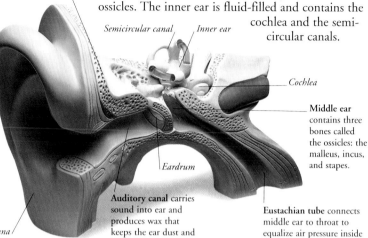

Temporal bone

Semicircular canal

Inner ear

Cochlea

Middle ear contains three bones called the ossicles: the malleus, incus, and stapes.

Eardrum

Auditory canal carries sound into ear and produces wax that keeps the ear dust and insect free.

Pinna

Eustachian tube connects middle ear to throat to equalize air pressure inside and outside the ear.

Hearing sounds

Sound waves channelled into the auditory canal cause the eardrum and the ossicles to vibrate. These vibrations travel through the fluid-filled cochlea. Inside the cochlea, sensory hair cells convert the vibrations into nerve impulses. These are carried by the cochlear nerve to the brain.

Eardrum

The eardrum, or tympanic membrane, is a taut piece of skin that separates the auditory canal from the middle ear. When sound waves hit the eardrum, it vibrates like a drum and transmits its vibrations to the ossicles of the middle ear.

Ossicles
Oval window
Semicircular canals
Malleus (hammer)
Incus (anvil)
Stapes (stirrup)
Nerves to brain
Fluid in cochlea
Eardrum
Organ of Corti
Eustachian tube

Middle and inner ear

Ossicles

The ossicles are the three smallest bones in the body. The malleus, incus, and stapes connect the eardrum to the cochlea by way of the oval window.

Air pressure

You hear most clearly when the air pressure inside the middle ear is the same as the air pressure outside your body. If the air pressure outside changes suddenly, you may not be able to hear properly. This can happen if you are a on a plane that is taking off or landing, or if you are travelling on a fast train.

Balance

Part of the inner ear helps you to balance. Sensors inside the three semicircular canals detect movements made by the head and the rest of the body. Sensors inside two adjoining chambers, the saccule and utricle, detect whether the body is upright, upside-down, or in between. Nerve impulses from the semicircular canals are analysed by the brain to assess the body's position.

Semicircular canal
Fluid
Vestibule containing saccule and utricle
Ampulla

Gymnast's outstretched arms help balance.

Semicircular canals

The three semicircular canals in each ear are filled with fluid. At the base of each canal is a bulge, called an ampulla, which contains sensory hair cells that send impulses to the brain. The three canals are set at 90° to each other, so they can detect movement in any direction.

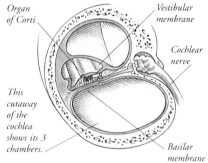

Organ of Corti
Vestibular membrane
Cochlear nerve
This cutaway of the cochlea shows its 3 chambers.
Basilar membrane

Cochlea

The cochlea is a long, coiled tube in the inner ear that is filled with fluid. It is divided by two membranes into three chambers that run lengthways. The middle of these three chambers, the cochlear chamber, contains the spiral organ of Corti, which consists of over 20,000 sensory hair cells that send nerve signals to the brain.

Bartolomeo Eustachio

Italian anatomist Bartolomeo Eustachio (1520–74) studied the detailed anatomy of the ear, as well as other body organs and systems, while he was a professor in Rome. He wrote the first full description of the ears in his book *The Examination of the Organ of Hearing*, published in 1562. Included in this was the first detailed description of the tube that links the middle ear with the throat. This was later named the Eustachian tube.

Hearing ranges

The pitch of a sound depends on the frequency of the sound waves that produced it. High-pitched sounds have a high frequency, and low-pitched sounds have a low frequency. Frequency is measured in units called Hertz (Hz). Our hearing ability decreases as we get older, from 20,000 to 12,000 Hz.

Bats' ears can hear very high-pitched sound waves called ultrasound.

20–20,000 Hz   **1,000–120,000 Hz**

FIND OUT MORE   BRAIN AND NERVOUS SYSTEM   HUMAN BODY   MUSIC   SOUND

E

EARTH

WE LIVE ON A GIANT BALL OF ROCK spinning round the Sun, which we call the Earth. The Earth is one of nine planets in the Solar System and one of the four made of rock. However, the Earth is unique, because it is the only planet in the Solar System – and perhaps even in the Universe – that can support life. The distance of the Earth from the Sun makes it neither very hot like Venus, nor icy cold like Pluto, enabling liquid water to exist on its surface. The Earth also has an oxygen-rich atmosphere. These two substances – water and oxygen – are the key factors that allow life to flourish on the Earth.

Structure of the Earth

By recording the way vibrations from earthquakes reverberate through the Earth, scientists have discovered that the Earth has an egg-like structure. At its centre is a "yolk" of metal, surrounded by an "egg-white" of soft rock called the mantle, and an outer "shell" of hard rock called the crust.

The Earth's crust consists of a number of interlocking slabs of rock called tectonic plates.

Earth's ingredients

Although more than 80 elements (basic substances) occur naturally on the Earth, the bulk of the Earth is made of iron (35%), oxygen (28%), magnesium (17%), and silicon (13%). The following elements are present in significant, but small, amounts: nickel (2.7%), sulphur (2.7%), calcium (0.6%), and aluminium (0.6%). Tiny proportions of other elements make up the remainder (0.6%).

Investigating Earth's composition
By taking rock samples from the Earth's interior, geologists have been able to understand the Earth's chemical make-up. Analysis of meteorites – solid pieces from an exploded planet – has led some geologists to believe that the Earth may have formed from the same space debris of which meteorites are made.

Solid iron

Molecule of oxygen gas

Magnesium ore (magnesite)

Locket containing crystal of silicon

Nickel ore (nickeline)

Sulphur crystals

Chondrite meteorite

Calcium-rich chalk

Aluminium ore (bauxite)

Meteorites
Meteorites are natural objects that fall to the Earth from space. They are made of iron, stone, or a mixture of both. The two main types of meteorite are called chondrites and achondrites.

Achondrite meteorite

The Earth's structure

Atmosphere is a thin surrounding layer of gases about 640 km (400 miles) deep.

Crust, Earth's outer layer of rock varies in thickness: beneath the oceans, it is 6–11 km (4–7 miles) thick, but it stretches up to 70 km (43 miles) under mountain ranges.

Mohorovicic discontinuity, or Moho, is the boundary between the crust and the mantle.

Mantle is a partially molten layer beneath the crust, extending to a depth of about 2,900 km (1,800 miles) and made largely of a rock called peridotite.

Gutenberg discontinuity is the boundary between the mantle and the core.

Outer core reaches to a depth of about 4,900 km (3,050 miles) and is made of molten iron and nickel – magnetic metals that give the Earth its magnetic field.

Inner core, like the outer core, is made of iron and nickel, but although temperatures reach 3,700°C (6,690°F), the pressure is so great that the metal remains solid.

Richard Oldham

By examining the seismographic recordings of earthquakes, the British geologist Richard Oldham (1858–1936) discovered that earthquakes produce two different kinds of vibration. He called them primary (P) waves and secondary (S) waves. Oldham's analysis revealed that P waves travel more slowly through the core of the Earth than through the mantle. He concluded that Earth's core must be liquid, which is partly true.

E

Satellite image showing Europe, Africa, India, and the Middle East

Surface details are clearly visible.

Europe

India

Middle East

Africa

Large image is assembled from hundreds of different satellite photographs.

Earth system

Planet Earth seems to operate like a vast, complex system made up of various interconnected processes that keep conditions stable and suitable for life. The atmosphere's unique make up, for example, ensures that the Earth stays at an ideal temperature for life, never heating up or cooling down by more than a few degrees. Scientists now realize that the environment must be treated with care, because a change to one part of this complex system may have unpredictable repercussions in other parts.

Earth from space
Much of what scientists know about the interrelated parts of the Earth system comes from images sent back by satellites. These images show us that the Earth is roughly spherical and reveal surface features in clear detail. Special heat-sensitive infrared photographs show the distribution of vegetation and variations in the Earth's surface temperature.

Energy regulation
The Earth system exchanges energy with its surroundings, but there is no overall gain or loss of energy. The Earth receives heat, light, and other forms of energy directly from the Sun. Some of this energy is reflected back by the clouds, oceans, land, and atmosphere; the rest is absorbed and then released back into space. The total energy the Earth gives out equals the total energy it receives from the Sun.

Infrared image of temperature variations in the Atlantic Ocean off the USA's eastern coast

Biosphere
Between the atmosphere's lowest layers and the ocean floor is a rich diversity of life, from tiny ocean organisms called plankton to the largest trees and animals. Together, these organisms form the biosphere – the living part of the planet. Satellite images can help scientists understand the complicated links between living things and the Earth.

Green: land areas where vegetation is most dense

Yellow: land areas where vegetation is least dense

Red: ocean areas where plankton is most dense

Infrared image of vegetation and plankton distribution

Blue: ocean areas where plankton is least dense

Locator map

Gaia theory

Greek statue of Gaia, 450 BC

British scientist James Lovelock (b. 1919) suggests that the Earth and all the lifeforms upon it function as if they were a single living organism. He calls this "organism" Gaia, after the Greek goddess of fertility. Like any other organism, he says, Gaia is self-regulating, meaning that it will naturally change its environment to maintain the right conditions for life – even if humans make the Earth unfit for themselves by polluting it and using up its limited resources.

Theories about the Earth
There have been many theories about the Earth that may seem strange to people today, but which were widely believed at the time. The ancient Egyptians, for example, thought that the Earth was a flat square under a pyramid-shaped sky, and people in medieval Europe believed that it was the Sun that revolved around the Earth, and not vice versa. Similarly, before technology enabled scientists to understand more about the interior of the Earth, people suggested that the Earth was hollow.

People assumed the Earth had a vast, empty core.

Hidden lands and oceans, complete with plants and animals and warmed by a subterranean Sun, were thought to lie within the centre of the Earth.

Hollow Earth theory

Search for another Earth
Astronomers have recently detected signs of the existence of planets beyond the Solar System. Wobbles in the movements of the stars 47 Ursae Majoris, 70 Virginis, and 51 Pegasi suggest that they may be orbited by planets – perhaps even ones similar to the Earth. Astronomers have found other stars with solar systems forming around them.

The yellow-and-red area may be another solar system forming around Beta Pictoris.

False-colour satellite image of the star Beta Pictoris, about 50 light years away

Timeline

c.4,600 mya The Earth and the other planets form as parts of a vast cloud of hot gas and dust circling the Sun begin to cluster together.

c.4,300 mya The Earth's crust forms.

c.4,200 mya As the Earth cools, gas bubbles and water vapour rise from the interior to form a cloudy atmosphere.

Gneiss rock

c.4,000 mya The crust and mantle separate; rain begins to fall; the atmosphere clears.

c.3,800 mya The first organisms are single-celled bacteria.

c.3,000 mya The atmosphere becomes oxygen-rich as ocean plants absorb sunlight and release oxygen into the air.

c.1,500 mya Protists, such as amoeba, are the first complex living cells; later, protists join up to form sponges – the first multi-celled organisms.

c.570 mya A huge variety of complex lifeforms develops in the Earth's seas and oceans.

Sponge

c.440–400 mya Land-based plants and animals become widespread.

c.220 mya There is a single, vast land mass, now known as Pangaea, which later breaks up into the smaller land masses we today call continents.

c.200–70 mya The era of the dinosaurs.

c.100,000 ya First modern humans appear.

FIND OUT MORE   ATMOSPHERE   CONTINENTS   EARTH SCIENCES   ELEMENTS   FOSSILS   GEOLOGY   MAGNETISM   PREHISTORIC LIFE   PLANETS   SUN

EARTHQUAKES

FROM A GENTLE RIPPLE to terrifying and violent movements in the Earth, earthquakes literally rock the world. Earthquakes are tremors in the ground, created by the sudden movement of tectonic plates – huge slabs of rock that make up the Earth's crust. The majority of earthquakes are so gentle that no one notices them, but some are so violent they destroy whole cities. An earthquake's effect and intensity are measured on different scales. In earthquake-prone countries, planning minimizes the damage earthquakes cause.

Earthquake zones

Earthquake zones
Although earthquakes can occur anywhere, they are more frequent in earthquake zones. These zones, such as Japan and California, lie near the moving margins of the tectonic plates, called fault lines.

What is an earthquake?
Tectonic plates usually slide past each other, but sometimes they get stuck together. The stress on the rocks builds up until they fault (crack). The tectonic plates then jolt past each other, sending shock waves through the ground. These vibrations, known as seismic waves, cause the earth to quake.

Epicentre
The point at which an earthquake occurs is known as the focus. Above the focus is the epicentre – the point on the Earth's surface where the effects of an earthquake are most devastating. The focus may be as much as 700 km (185 miles) below the epicentre. In 1985, an earthquake in Mexico City, with its epicentre in the Pacific Ocean, left 9,500 people dead. It measured 8.1 on the Richter scale.

Destruction diminishes as shock waves travel away from the epicentre, recording less on the Richter scale.

Earthquake that causes small object to fall rates V on the Mercalli scale.

The Mercalli scale rates an earthquake according to its effect on a scale of I–XII: a swinging light bulb measures I; extensive structural damage measures XII.

Folds form in the ground as the Earth moves.

Epicentre

Seismometer
Seismometers show seismic waves, and measure an earthquake's location and intensity on the Richter scale. The height of each line shows the wave's force.

Reading from Kobe, Japan

Tsunami
These are huge waves precipitated when an earthquake or volcanic eruption shakes the sea floor. Tsunamis roll along the ocean floor as fast as a jet plane. When they reach shallow coastal waters, they rear up into water ridges about 30 m (100 ft) high. Many tsunamis occur in the Pacific Ocean, such as the one in Hawaii, 1964 (left).

The Richter scale measures the force of an earthquake on a scale from 1–10, taken from seismograph readings of the seismic waves. Each figure represents a force 10 times greater than that of the next lowest figure.

Focus

Shock waves radiate outwards in circles from focus.

Earthquake proofing
Technology cannot prevent earthquakes but it can help limit their damage, particularly in building design. Most loss of life is caused not by the shaking ground, but by the collapse of buildings and roads, and fires started by damage to electrical equipment.

Building design
Pyramid-shaped, curved, and fire-resistant buildings and structures, such as this staircase in California, USA, bend rather than break during an earthquake. Mounting foundations on rubber also helps absorb some of the earthquake shocks.

Timeline
1556 Reports of an earthquake in the region of Shaanxi, China. Almost a million deaths.

1755 Lisbon, Portugal, is destroyed by an earthquake and the subsequent flood.

1883 Krakatoa Island destroyed by earthquake and tsunami.

1906 Quake flattens San Francisco, USA.

1964 Alaska hit by a very severe earthquake, measuring 9.2 on the Richter scale.

1964 Earthquake in Alaska generates a tsunami, which causes damage as far away as California, USA.

1976 Earthquake in China kills 255,000.

1990 In Iran 40,000 people die in quake.

1995 Kobe, central Japan, is devastated by an earthquake.

1999 Turkish quake kills 20,000 and makes 200,000 homeless.

2001 Earthquake in Gujarat, India, leaves 30,000 people dead.

FIND OUT MORE   BUILDING AND CONSTRUCTION   CONTINENTS   EARTH   GEOLOGY   OCEAN FLOOR   RADAR AND SONAR

EARTH SCIENCES

FOSSILS PROVIDE CLUES to the ages of rocks; the atmosphere provides clues to tomorrow's weather. Amongst others, these elements are studied within the discipline of Earth sciences. This is the study of the planet's physical characteristics, from volcanoes to raindrops. The different branches of Earth sciences cover all of the Earth's dynamic systems, apart from life forms, which are studied within biology. Knowledge about the Earth's history and formation also informs us about its needs, which will help ensure the future survival of the planet.

Branches of Earth sciences

The term Earth sciences has been used since the 1970s. It covers the range of subjects that were previously bracketed under the term "physical geography". Although each of the Earth sciences is a distinct study focusing on one aspect of the Earth, each is also a key element of the inter-related study of Earth sciences.

Pebbles

Granite

Anthracite, a form of coal

Palaeontology
Fossils, the remains of once living organisms preserved in sedimentary rock, are studied within the branch of Earth science called palaeontology. From fossils, scientists can work out the ages of rocks and develop a picture of the history of plant and animal life on Earth over billions of years.

Fossil of a sea creature

Earth sciences cover many different areas of study.

Geology
The oldest branch of the Earth sciences, geology is the study of the Earth's history, structure, and make-up. Although it centres on rocks and the composition of the Earth's crust, geology also relates to the other Earth sciences, except for meteorology.

Volcanology
The study of volcanoes, and the reasons why they erupt, is known as volcanology. It may involve volcanologists working close to an erupting volcano. The scientists wear special clothing to protect them from gas, heat, and flying lava bombs.

Volcanic bombs

Geomorphology
The study of landforms and the processes that shape them is known as geomorphology. It includes landforms ranging from mountains and valleys to rivers and glaciers, and the effects of different shaping processes upon them, such as the erosion caused by weathering.

Oceanography
The study of the oceans is called oceanography. It covers ocean chemistry, the ocean bed and currents (shown above by satellite), and marine life.

Geography
This is the study of the Earth's surface. Human geography looks at world patterns of human activity; physical geography studies the Earth's physical environment.

Meteorology
The atmosphere is studied within the discipline of meteorology. This focuses on the processes that make the weather, and on weather forecasting. Climatology is the study of weather patterns.

Surveying the Earth

Earth scientists can learn very little about the Earth from laboratory studies. Instead, they must make observations, collect data, and test their theories in the outside world – this may mean climbing mountains or braving earthquakes. Satellite photography has provided a vast new source of data, but most information continues to come from field work.

Survey equipment
Earth scientists sometimes need to use specific survey equipment. This laser equipment helps to monitor the movement of earthquakes.

Earth resources

The Earth provides all the materials we need for living, from the food we eat and the water we drink, to the bricks we use for building. Earth sciences help us to identify the location of these resources. They also show what damage we may be doing to them by exploiting them thoughtlessly.

Air
We need air to breathe virtually every second of our lives. However, this vital resource is becoming increasingly damaged by human pollution.

Tourmaline gemstone

Minerals
From metal for cars to concrete for buildings, nearly everything we make comes from the minerals or chemicals taken from the Earth's crust. Gems are another of its rich resources.

Water
All forms of life are dependent on water. Patterns of human activity are controlled by the need to be near a source of clean water.

Squid

Fruit

Food
Food is provided by things living on the Earth's surface. These depend on the mineral resources, water, and air provided by the Earth.

Energy
Ninety per cent of the energy we use comes from a finite supply of minerals – oil, coal, and gas – extracted from the Earth's crust.

FIND OUT MORE CLIMATE   EARTH   FOSSILS   GEOLOGY   OCEANS AND SEAS   ROCKS AND MINERALS   VOLCANOES   WEATHER

ECOLOGY AND ECOSYSTEMS

NO LIVING THING exists in isolation. It interacts with other living things and with its physical surroundings. The study of these relationships is called ecology. Ecologists consider all the organisms that live in one area as an inter-dependent community. All plants and animals rely on, and influence, vital factors in their environment, such as the supply of nutrients, food, and water. A community and its environment is called an ecosystem.

Communities

Wildlife communities exist almost everywhere you look, on land, in rivers, and in the oceans. A typical community contains a mixture of plants, various animals that feed on them or hunt one another, and organisms that burrow through the soil debris below.

Trees offer shelter for animals, and food in the form of leaves, berries, seeds, and blossom.

Insects feeding on flowers help to pollinate them.

Habitats

The habitat of a species is the surroundings in which it lives, including the rocks, soils, water, and plants. Different habitats are suitable for different species and have a certain type of community.

Mice eat seeds, and are hunted by bigger animals.

Dense undergrowth provides shelter for small animals.

Most of the tadpoles that hatch out from the frog spawn will be food for other animals.

Rotting wood is home to fungi and invertebrates.

Snails feed on the leaves of plants and are food for some birds such as thrushes.

As ferns grow, they take nutrients from the soil.

Frogs live in both land and water habitats.

Biomes

The biggest ecological units are biomes, such as deserts, rainforests, and lakes, across which similar climatic and other conditions create similar ecosystems. The plants and animals may differ across a biome, but they make up the same sort of communities with the same ecological features.

Seashores
Battered by waves and flooded by tides, seashores have few plants other than seaweeds. Animals include shellfish, rockpool fish, and wading birds.

Deserts
Cloud-free, dry climates create deserts. These are home only to plants and animals that are able to cope with extremes of aridity and temperature.

Grassland
Grassland is normal in places where there is a long dry season. It can support lots of grazing animals, some preyed on by swift-running predators. The savannah of East Africa is one of the best-known areas of grassland.

Rainforests
In hot, humid climates, dense forests develop that are home to a huge variety of animal life. Tropical rainforests cover only 10 per cent of the Earth's land surface, but contain more than half of all animal and plant species.

Ecosystems

An ecosystem contains several different wildlife communities and their habitat. Ecologists use the term to mean all the complicated interactions that take place among living and non-living things in an area. The various components of the ecosystem include sunshine, water, nutrients in the soil, bacteria, plants, and animals.

Fresh water
Lake- and river-dwelling communities include floating or submerged plants, freshwater plankton, and fish. Different species live in different parts of a river or lake, depending on the conditions that they tolerate. This is Bow Lake in the Canadian Rockies.

283

Ecological interactions

The components of an ecosystem interact with each other in lots of different ways. Rain, for example, provides water for plants. Plant growth and decay affect the form and content of soil. Soil provides a home for worms, and worms, as they move about, change the structure of the soil.

Toucans live high in the crowns of trees.

Puss moth larva cuts and chews leaves, using its sharp jaws.

Food
Perhaps the most obvious way in which living species affect one another's lives is by feeding. Most things are food for something else. For example, caterpillars eat leaves, but are themselves food for animals such as birds. The birds are food for other animals, and so on up the food chain.

Shelter
The cover and shelter that trees and vegetation provide offer much more security than bare, open ground. In a rainforest, the large trees provide toucans with shelter from the weather, a place where they can raise their young in relative safety, and protection from predators.

Transport
Animals can move around whereas plants cannot. Plants, therefore, use various methods that ensure animals carry their seeds and pollen, so that a new generation of plants can develop and grow. Bumblebees carry pollen on their legs.

Pollen sac

Bumblebees collect nectar with their tongue.

Honey fungus

Young stinkhorn fungus

Parasitism
Animals, plants, and fungi that live off other living things are called parasites. Nearly all animals and plants are host to parasites of some kind. A parasitic relationship exists between a honey fungus and a tree. The fungus steals food from the tree, usually harming it in the process.

Symbiosis

When two species have a close relationship in which both benefit, it is called symbiotic. Symbiosis often involves giving shelter in return for protection or food, and it occurs among all kinds of organisms.

Clownfish
Clownfish find shelter among the stinging tentacles of sea anemones, which do not harm them. The fish may lure in other fish for the anemones to consume.

Clownfish stay where they are protected.

Adaptation

All plants and animals are specially suited to live in their particular habitat. How they become suited, or adapted, is the key to evolution. How and where a species lives, how it gets its food, what it eats, and how it interacts with others, is known as its ecological niche.

Cacti
A cactus has adapted in many ways to desert life. For example, its leaves have adapted into spines, to prevent water from evaporating too easily. When rain does fall, a cactus stores as much water as possible in its stem.

Spines protect the swollen stem.

Cycles in nature

Nature automatically recycles the substances that are vital for life. Oxygen, nitrogen, carbon, and water are constantly being exchanged between the air, the soil, the oceans, and living things. If substances were not continuously put back into the ecosystems to be used again, the supply for organisms would soon run out and life would stop.

Carbon cycles between living and non-living things

Water cycle
Water lost by evaporation from plants, rivers, and seas, forms clouds in the atmosphere. This falls back as rain, runs into rivers and seas, and is soaked up from the soil by the roots of plants.

Carbon cycle
Organisms release carbon dioxide into the air. Carbon is also released when organisms decay, or when coal is burned. Plants absorb carbon from the air, which passes into animals that eat them.

Ecological change

Ecosystems do not always stay the same but may change over time. If an event changes the landscape, for example, high winds create a clearing in a wood, first grasses and herbs grow, then shrubs colonize the plot until trees take over once again.

The process of change from grassland to woodland is called succession.

Land erosion in Madagascar

Human impact
People's actions also change ecosystems and often the impact is so great that nature cannot repair the damage. For example, poor farming techniques sometimes cause so much soil to be eroded away from the land, that plants cannot get established and the vegetation can never recover.

| FIND OUT MORE | ANIMAL BEHAVIOUR | EVOLUTION | FOOD WEBS AND CHAINS | POLLUTION | SOIL |

ECUADOR AND PERU

TOGETHER ECUADOR AND PERU form the western side of equatorial South America, lying between Colombia to the north, Chile to the south, and Brazil and Bolivia to the east. The dominant influences in the west of the region were the Incas, who ruled until the 1500s, and the conquering Spaniards, who imposed their own culture and language. About 40 per cent of the population are *mestizos*, who are people of mixed blood resulting from intermarriage between Spaniards and Incas. Many Native Americans still live in remote Amazonian villages.

Physical features

Lying on South America's Pacific Coast, Ecuador and Peru are dominated by the jagged volcanic peaks of the Andes, whose eastern slopes descend to the hot, humid, tropical rainforest and wetlands of the Amazon Basin. To the west is the coastal strip. Peru's coast is largely arid desert, but Ecuador's coast is hot, swampy, or forested.

Mount Cotopaxi
A perfect cone capped with snow, Cotopaxi, 5,897 m (19,345 ft) is the world's highest active volcano and Ecuador's second highest peak. It lies in the Andes, which form the backbone of both Ecuador and Peru. Ecuador has 15 major volcanoes, ten of which are active. The whole region is shaken from time to time by earthquakes, which cause damage to cities.

Amazon Basin
The steamy Amazon Basin occupies the eastern regions of Ecuador and Peru. The forest is not an uninterrupted mass of trees, but contains pockets of grassland and swamps. The headwaters of the Amazon originate in this region. Much of this area is disputed territory awarded to Peru in 1942.

Regional climate
Ecuador is hot and humid along the coast, cool and fresh in the Andes, and hot with heavy rainfall in the Amazon Basin. Peru has a more mixed climate. The coastal region is dry, and kept cool by the cold waters of the Peru Current. The western part of the Peruvian Andes is fairly dry, but the eastern Andes and tropical Amazonia have heavy rainfall.

19°C (66°F) 15°C (59°F)

581 mm (23 in)

Lake Titicaca
At more than 170 km (106 miles) long, Lake Titicaca is South America's largest lake. The Uros people live here on islands that they make from the *totora* reed. They also make reed boats.

Coca
The Incas used to chew coca leaves to relieve fatigue and hunger. Today, in remote areas, coca is grown illegally to produce the powerful and dangerous drug cocaine for supply to the international drug trade. Governments are offering farmers money to destroy their coca crops and grow bananas, cocoa, or coffee instead.

Picking coca leaves, Quillabamba, Peru

Ecuador

The third smallest, most densely populated independent country in South America, Ecuador is also one of the most geographically varied and politically stable. Agriculture and oil dominate the economy. About 1,000 km (630 miles) off Ecuador's Pacific coast, the lonely Galápagos Islands, famous for their unique wildlife, are part of the country.

Quechua woman gathering gladioli for market

Oil

Since the 1970s, oil, piped from the eastern lowlands, has been the mainstay of Ecuador's economy and accounts for 40 per cent of exports. Other exports are balsa wood, shrimps, processed fish, and textiles. Most goods are exported via Guayaquil, Ecuador's main port and largest city.

Crops

Beans, maize, and potatoes are the main crops grown in the Andes. Bananas, cocoa beans, rice, coffee, oranges, and wheat are cultivated on the coast, mostly for export. Roses, carnations, gladioli, and statice (sea lavender) are grown for markets.

Bold rug designs, often with an animal theme, are woven from homespun wool fibre.

People

Native Americans make up 25 per cent and *mestizos* more than 50 per cent of the population. The rest of the people are white, black, or Asian. More than 93 per cent of the people are Roman Catholic, although some people blend Catholicism with traditional beliefs.

Otavalo market

The small town of Otavalo lies high in the Andes, north of the capital Quito. Local Indians weave brightly coloured ponchos and rugs to sell at the famous Otavalo market, which dates from pre-Inca times.

Panama hats

Originally made in the 1800s in Ecuador, to protect the heads of travellers, panama hats are constructed from the fibres of the toquilla plant. A panama can be rolled up for packing – a good one will pass through a finger ring.

ECUADOR FACTS	
CAPITAL CITY	Quito
AREA	283,560 sq km (109,483 sq miles)
POPULATION	12,500,000
MAIN LANGUAGES	Spanish, Quechua
MAJOR RELIGION	Christian
CURRENCY	US dollar

Peru

Four hundred years ago, Peru was at the heart of the Inca Empire, ruins of which still survive high in the Andes. The country has great mineral resources, yet most Peruvians are poor farmers, growing potatoes, maize, rice, and cereals for their own use, and cotton and coffee for export. Political terrorism by the Maoist Shining Path group has forced military rule in some areas.

Railways

Peru has two unconnected railway networks – the Central and Southern Railroads – both of which go from the coast to the highlands. A branch of the Central Railroad linking Lima and Huancayo in the Andes reaches 4,818 m (15,806 ft) above sea-level, making it the highest standard-gauge line in the world.

Machu Picchu

Peru's greatest tourist attraction is the ruined Inca city of Machu Picchu in the Andes. The ruins, hidden by dense forest vegetation, were discovered in 1911, when American archaeologist Hiram Bingham stumbled upon them, almost by accident. The ruins are made of stone and were built without mortar.

People

About half of Peruvians are Native American, and one-third are *mestizo*. The most populated areas are the highlands and the coastal plain. Only five per cent of people live in the remote Amazon Basin areas, including 70 Native American groups.

Jivaro man

Fishing

The cold waters of the Peru coastal current bring rich nutrients that attract large numbers of pilchards, sardines, tuna, and other fish, making fishing a major industry in Peru. However, every few years, the arrival of the El Niño current raises the temperature of the water driving away the fish and causing great hardship to the fishermen.

Sardines

Mining

Peru is a leading producer of copper, lead, tungsten, silver, and zinc and has reserves of gold, iron ore, and oil. However, low world mineral prices and industrial problems have badly affected mining.

Opencast lead mine in the Andes

PERU FACTS	
CAPITAL CITY	Lima
AREA	1,285,220 sq km (496,223 sq miles)
POPULATION	25,700,000
MAIN LANGUAGES	Spanish, Quechua, Aymara
MAJOR RELIGION	Christian
CURRENCY	Nuevo sol (new sol)

 FIND OUT MORE FARMING · FISHING INDUSTRY · INCAS · NATIVE AMERICANS · OIL · PACIFIC OCEAN · ROCKS AND MINERALS · SOUTH AMERICA, HISTORY OF · TEXTILES AND WEAVING · TRAINS AND RAILWAYS · VOLCANOES

EDISON, THOMAS

ONE OF THE GREATEST INVENTORS of all time, Thomas Alva Edison produced a number of inventions that changed the world – electric lighting, sound recording, and an early form of moving pictures, among many others. He had little formal schooling, but he was fascinated by science. He worked extremely hard, and would spend days, months, or even years experimenting in order to make something work. He often slept fully clothed on one of his worktables, so that he could start work again first thing in the morning.

Early life
Edison was born in 1847 in a small town in Ohio, USA. His teachers thought he was stupid, so his mother taught him herself, inspiring his interest in science. In 1869, after moving to New York, he improved the "ticker", a machine for relaying information about the stock market. The machine earned him $40,000.

E

Menlo Park

In 1876, using the money from his stock "ticker", Edison built an "invention factory" at Menlo Park, 39 km (24 miles) from New York City. This barn-like two-storey building was the world's first research laboratory, where a staff of scientists helped Edison to develop his ideas into devices that actually worked. In the six years that Edison worked at Menlo Park, he patented more than 400 different inventions.

Research work
At Menlo Park, Edison would come up with rough ideas and sketches. These would be refined, built, and tested by his assistants. They often had to build inventions again and again to find out why they did not work. Edison, when asked about his success, stressed the importance of these setbacks. "I failed my way to success," he said.

Organ, for experiments on sound

Edison watches to see how strongly the bulb glows.

Bench contains chemicals and other scientific equipment.

Electric light

Perhaps Edison's most important invention was the electric lightbulb. He saw that a bulb with a glowing thread or filament would work, using little electricity. It took him thousands of experiments before he discovered that the best material for the filament was carbonized cotton thread. British scientist Joseph Swan (1828–1914) invented a lightbulb at the same time as Edison, and the two men later joined forces.

Carbon filament

Patent drawing for the lightbulb

Carbon filament

Swan's electric lightbulb

Glass bulb

Edison's electric lightbulb

Lighting the city
Having developed the lightbulb, Edison went on to create a complete electric lighting system, powered by a central generator. His first power plant opened in 1882, serving 85 satisfied customers. Soon, whole cities were lit with electricity.

Other inventions

Edison patented 1,093 inventions in his lifetime. He helped make the first successful typewriter, a dictating machine, and an improved telephone mouthpiece. He came close to inventing radio, and predicted the use of atomic power.

Recording cylinder

Mouthpiece

Edison's phonograph

Handle to turn cylinder

Phonograph
The phonograph, a device for recording and playing back sounds, was Edison's favourite invention. He sketched the machine and gave it to an assistant to build. It worked, but Edison did not realize this because he had poor hearing.

Recording the voice

Kinetoscope
In 1889, Edison invented the kinetoscope, a projector with a peepshow-type viewer to go with it. Kinetoscopes were installed in special viewing parlours in the USA, and customers paid to watch short films.

THOMAS EDISON

1847	Born, Milan, Ohio, USA.
1869	Improves the "ticker", for relaying prices on the stock market.
1876	Moves to Menlo Park.
1877	Creates the phonograph.
1877	Invents the carbon microphone, for use in telephone mouthpieces.
1879	Patents the electric lightbulb.
1882	Power switched on at the Pearl Street generating station, New York.
1883	Edison and Swan form an electric company.
1889	Invents the kinetoscope.
1931	Dies, aged 84.

FIND OUT MORE

ELECTRICITY   FILM AND FILM-MAKING   INVENTIONS   PHYSICS   SCIENCE, HISTORY OF   SOUND RECORDING   TECHNOLOGY

EDUCATION

FOR A SOCIETY TO SURVIVE and progress, each generation must pass its knowledge, skills, and values on to the next. This process is called education. Passing on knowledge is so vital that most countries have established formal systems of education for teaching children, by sending them to schools and colleges. Throughout our lives we are also educated informally, by parents, friends, or the media. Education provides society with doctors, teachers, and scientists; gives industry a capable workforce; and helps maintain law and order by instructing people in social values.

Early education

In prehistoric times, elders taught children the survival skills they needed, such as how to hunt or make fire. As civilizations developed and writing was invented, formal institutions of learning – schools – were created so that some people could learn to read and write.

The ancient world

As happens today, education in the ancient world reflected the state's needs and attitudes. In warlike Sparta, for example, education was geared towards producing good soldiers. Throughout the ancient world and medieval Europe, women and the poor did not have the same acccess to education enjoyed by the male, ruling classes.

Teacher and pupil, Romano-Germanic period

Theories of education

Some theories state that people learn by practice; others, that pupils must work things out themselves in order to learn; and some suggest that pupils learn by following their emotional needs and acquiring the skills and knowledge to fulfil them. Most people probably learn in all three ways.

Beads in number units

The child learns basic arithmetic skills by creative play with special, three-dimensional equipment.

The Montessori system of education stresses that every child wants to learn. Children freely choose for themselves what and when to study.

Multiplication board

$5 \times 2 =$

Types of education

Different types of education cater for different needs. The best-known example is the general education that schools and colleges provide, in subjects such as reading, writing, and arithmetic.

Vocational

Vocational education prepares people for specific jobs; it is available through courses at school, or training at specific colleges. Skills or crafts are also passed on informally, perhaps from parent to child, when a trade is passed on from one generation to the next.

Mother teaches sewing skills to children.

Adult education

Adult education is for those who, although not full-time students, choose to continue an aspect of their education, or learn something new. The courses keep adults up-to-date, improve job prospects, and bring new interests.

Learning computer skills

Special needs

Wealthy nations can afford to provide some schools where education is tailored to the special needs of certain children, such as the physically challenged, or the highly-gifted.

Disabled boy learns sailing skills.

Socialization

The first form of education a child receives starts from birth, by his or her immediate carers. Known as socialization, it includes not only learning such basic skills as speaking, but also teaches the child how society expects that he or she should behave. The child learns from instruction, and by imitating others. Socialization also takes place at school, and through cultural influences such as television.

Table manners are a learnt form of social behaviour.

Maria Montessori

The Italian educationist Maria Montessori (1870–1952) developed teaching methods that encouraged children to work things out for themselves through practical activity, rather than simply obeying instructions. She developed her ideas while working with children with learning difficulties.

Timeline

c.3500 BC Sumerians invent writing.

3rd century BC Greek thinker Plato (427BC–347BC) proposes that education should be run by the state.

1524 German priest Martin Luther (1483–1546) advocates education be made available for all, so that everyone is able to read the Bible.

1762 French philosopher Jean Jacques Rousseau (1712–1778) argues education should prepare children to be adults.

1763 Prussians introduce compulsory schooling from the ages of 5 to 13.

1899 US educator John Dewey (1859–1952) publishes *School and Society*, an influential analysis of the social function of education.

1945 World War II ends: with the desire to build a better world, many countries reform school systems to make secondary education available to all.

1990s Education is fully recognized as vital to social and economic growth.

FIND OUT MORE

CRIME   SCHOOLS AND COLLEGES   SOCIETIES   TRADE AND INDUSTRY   WRITING

EGGS

MANY KINDS OF ANIMAL, from earthworms and insects to fish and birds, reproduce by laying eggs. An egg is a single living cell complete with a supply of food. After the egg is laid, the cell starts to divide, and gradually a young animal's body takes shape. When the animal is ready to start life in the world outside, it breaks out of the egg, or hatches. There is a great variety of eggs – large and small, with shells and without. Some animals lay just a few eggs each time and look after them carefully. Others lay thousands or millions of eggs and leave them to develop on their own.

Types of egg

Some eggs are so small that they can be seen only under a microscope; others are as big and heavy as a coconut. Animals that live in water usually lay jelly-like eggs. Animals that live on land, such as insects, reptiles, and birds, lay eggs with a hard or leathery shell. The shell helps to stop an egg drying out.

Cockroach egg package contains 16 eggs.

Packages
When cockroaches and praying mantises lay their eggs, they surround them with a special froth. The froth dries and hardens, forming a package like a tiny purse. This package protects the eggs, and the female carries it around on the end of her abdomen until the eggs are ready to hatch.

Mermaids' purses
Sharks lay some of the most unusual eggs. Instead of being round, their eggs can be flat, or even spiral. Dogfish, which are small sharks, lay eggs called "mermaids' purses". These have long tendrils with which the dogfish anchors the eggs to underwater plants.

Eggs without a shell
Frogs' eggs do not have a shell. Instead, they are surrounded by a layer of jelly. The jelly swells up when the eggs are laid, forming a floating mass that can be more than 30 cm (12 in) across.

Eggs in strings
The common toad lays eggs like those of frogs, but they are laid in strings up to 3 m (10 ft) long. As the female lays the eggs, she winds them around underwater plants. The tadpoles hatch after about two weeks.

Leopard gecko's egg

Leathery eggs
Lizards and many other reptiles have eggs with a leathery shell. Unlike amphibians, reptiles can lay their eggs in dry places, because the shell helps keep the inside of the egg moist.

American robin's egg

Chalky eggs
The shell around birds' eggs is reinforced with a substance like chalk. To hatch, most young birds peck open their shell, but some kick their way out.

Leatherhead's egg

Egg development

After an egg has been laid, a young animal starts to develop inside it. With some insects, such as the house-fly, this can take less than a day, but with birds it may take more than a month. Eggs develop more quickly if they are warm, and most birds keep their eggs warm by sitting on them. This is called incubation.

Mallee fowl
Instead of sitting on its eggs, the Australian mallee fowl buries them in a huge compost heap that it makes out of dead leaves. Heat from the giant heap keeps the eggs warm.

Development of a bird's egg
A bird's egg is divided into two main areas – the white and the yolk. The white is made of a substance called albumen. It stores water and cushions the developing chick from any sudden jolts. The yolk contains a store of food, which the chick uses up as it develops.

1 When the egg has just been laid, the part that will become the chick looks like a tiny pale spot. It lies on the upper surface of the yolk.

2 Within a day, cells in the spot start to divide to form an embryo. A network of blood vessels fans out over the yolk and supplies the embryo with food.

3 Three days after the egg was laid, the embryo is growing fast. Its eyes start to form, and tiny buds grow that will soon develop into wings and legs.

4 After seven days, the embryo has become a chick, and a special bag has formed to collect its waste. In three weeks, the chick's development will be complete.

Egg clutches

Some animals, such as queen termites, lay a steady stream of eggs, but most animals produce eggs in groups called clutches. The number of eggs in a clutch is closely linked to their size. For example, a wandering albatross has very big eggs, but it produces only one egg every two years. By contrast, a sunfish has tiny eggs, but it releases millions each time it breeds.

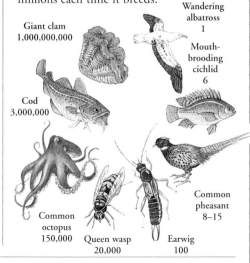

Giant clam 1,000,000,000

Wandering albatross 1

Mouth-brooding cichlid 6

Cod 3,000,000

Common octopus 150,000

Common pheasant 8–15

Queen wasp 20,000

Earwig 100

FIND OUT MORE   ANIMAL BEHAVIOUR   BIRDS   FISH   FROGS AND TOADS   INSECTS   MAMMALS   NESTS AND BURROWS   REPTILES   SHARKS AND RAYS

Eggs
Non-passerine birds

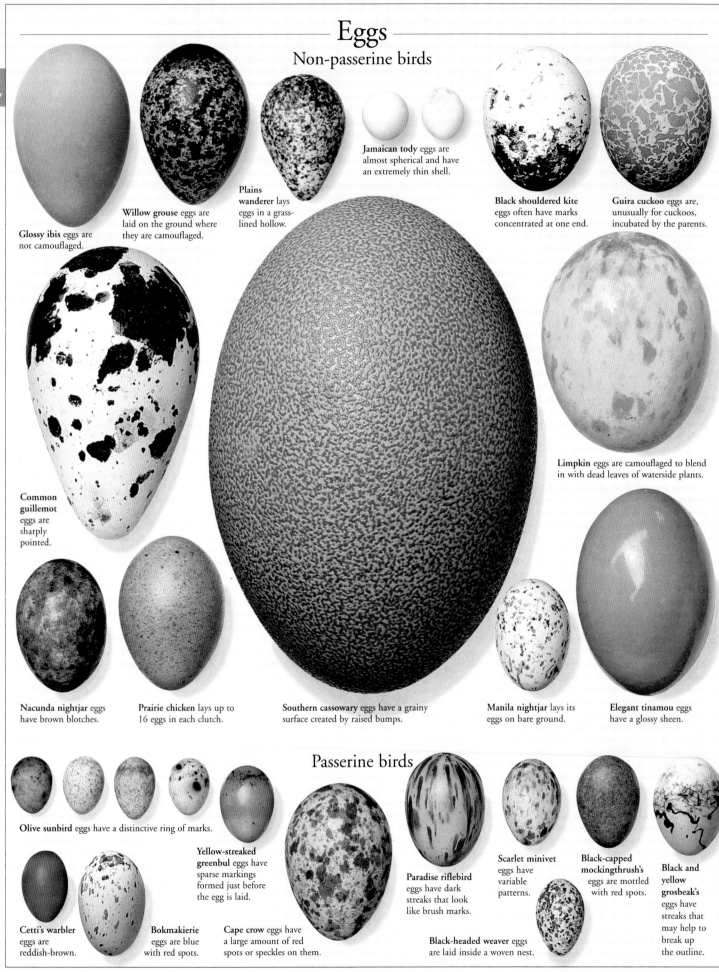

Glossy ibis eggs are not camouflaged.

Willow grouse eggs are laid on the ground where they are camouflaged.

Plains wanderer lays eggs in a grass-lined hollow.

Jamaican tody eggs are almost spherical and have an extremely thin shell.

Black shouldered kite eggs often have marks concentrated at one end.

Guira cuckoo eggs are, unusually for cuckoos, incubated by the parents.

Common guillemot eggs are sharply pointed.

Limpkin eggs are camouflaged to blend in with dead leaves of waterside plants.

Nacunda nightjar eggs have brown blotches.

Prairie chicken lays up to 16 eggs in each clutch.

Southern cassowary eggs have a grainy surface created by raised bumps.

Manila nightjar lays its eggs on bare ground.

Elegant tinamou eggs have a glossy sheen.

Passerine birds

Olive sunbird eggs have a distinctive ring of marks.

Yellow-streaked greenbul eggs have sparse markings formed just before the egg is laid.

Paradise riflebird eggs have dark streaks that look like brush marks.

Scarlet minivet eggs have variable patterns.

Black-capped mockingthrush's eggs are mottled with red spots.

Black and yellow grosbeak's eggs have streaks that may help to break up the outline.

Cetti's warbler eggs are reddish-brown.

Bokmakierie eggs are blue with red spots.

Cape crow eggs have a large amount of red spots or speckles on them.

Black-headed weaver eggs are laid inside a woven nest.

EGYPT, ANCIENT

ABOUT 5,000 YEARS ago, the great civilization of ancient Egypt grew up on the banks of the River Nile. It lasted virtually unchanged for 3,000 years. During this time the Egyptians built the first large stone buildings, invented one of the earliest forms of writing, and created a cult of the dead unlike anything known in any other culture. This cult involved preserving dead bodies, and burying them with their possessions. As a result, people today know a great deal about the ancient Egyptians.

River Nile

The River Nile was the lifeblood of the whole region. Every year the river flooded, depositing dark silt on the banks. This silt made the soil fertile and, because of this, most Egyptians lived by the river. When the Nile flooded and work in the fields was impossible, many people helped on the great royal building projects, such as the Great Pyramid at Giza.

3,000-year-old bread found in a tomb
Pomegranate
Grapes
Figs

Crops
The Egyptians cultivated wheat and barley, from which they made bread and brewed beer. The hot climate also allowed them to grow many different kinds of fruit, including figs, dates, pomegranates, and grapes.

E

Mediterranean Sea — *Nile delta*
Giza
Memphis
Saqqara
Thebes
River Nile
Extent of floodplain

Egyptian travelling boat, c.2000 BC
Steering oar
Line to test depth of water
Pole to push boat off sandbank

Sailing boats
The Nile was the main highway of Egypt. Wooden boats carried passengers and heavy cargo up and down the river. Water transport was especially useful for heavy loads, such as stones for the pyramids. Egyptian boat-builders were among the first to attach sails to their craft.

Tilling the soil
Egyptian farmers used a lightweight plough pulled by oxen. The plough had a wooden blade and a handle so that the farmer could steer it, and was effective enough to cut a furrow in the light Egyptian soil.

Egyptian farmer, c.2000 BC

Models of everyday activities, such as tilling the soil, were often found in tombs.

Pharaohs

Ancient Egypt was ruled by kings called pharaohs. The pharaohs had absolute power, and the Egyptians believed that they joined the gods in the next world when they died. For this reason, the Egyptians took special care when burying their pharaohs, mummifying them and building splendid tombs.

Pharaoh's court
A pharaoh was surrounded by officials, high priests, and ambassadors, all of whom helped him run the kingdom. The court was also the home of entertainers and the women of the royal harem. The pharaoh and courtiers lived in great luxury. They took pride in their appearance, dressing in fine linen. The women used black eye make-up, and had elaborate hairstyles.

Rameses II

Rameses II (r.1304–1237 BC) was famous for his military campaigns and great building projects. He defended Egypt against the Hittites, signing a peace treaty with them. His many buildings included the mortuary complex at Thebes on the west bank of the Nile, and the Abu Simbel temple.

Gods

The Egyptians believed in many different gods. Some were local gods, who represented each district of Egypt. Others had more general powers, such as Thoth, the god of wisdom.

Anubis, the god of death

Amun-re, king of the gods

Osiris, the god of the underworld

Bast, the cat goddess

Temples
Karnak at Thebes was the greatest of the Egyptian temples. Temples were run by priests, who maintained the building and left offerings for the gods. The most important temples had large estates and rich treasuries, so high priests were very powerful.

Bronze mirror
Comb and hair pins
Wine jar made from faience (decorated and glazed earthenware)
Containers for eye paint

Timeline

3000 BC Ancient Egyptian civilization begins; early Dynastic Period. The two kingdoms of Upper and Lower Egypt are united under Narmer.

2650 BC Step Pyramid of Zoser is built at Saqqara. It is the first pyramid and the first large-scale stone structure.

2500s BC Largest of the pyramids is built for Khufu at Giza.

2100 BC Middle Kingdom begins. Funerary (funeral) customs spread from royalty to other classes.

Giza

Saqqara

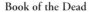

Mummification

Ancient Egyptians believed in life after death. They thought that people had a spirit as well as a body, and that for the person to live in the next world, the spirit had to be reunited with the body. They therefore preserved the body of the dead person in the form of a mummy.

Mummy cases

The Egyptians placed the mummy inside a coffin or case, and put a cover on top. By the time of the Middle Kingdom (c.2100–1550 BC), they used two coffins to give added protection from tomb robbers and animals. The coffins were decorated with writing, images of the gods, and sacred amulets, or lucky charms.

Book of the Dead

This is a series of prayers, written on papyrus, that were meant to help the dead person travel to the next world.

The Weighing of the Heart ceremony where the dead person is judged by the gods.

Thoth, the god of wisdom, writes details of the person's actions when alive.

Making a mummy

The Egyptians first removed the organs, and dried out the body with natron. They filled the body with sawdust or dry leaves, then wrapped the body in bandages.

Plate to cover the cut in the body   *Embalming tools*

Dish of natron, a natural salt used to dry out the body.

Red straps usually indicate a priest

Linen wrappings

The body's organs were placed in containers called Canopic jars.

Unwrapped mummy, showing how well preserved the body is.

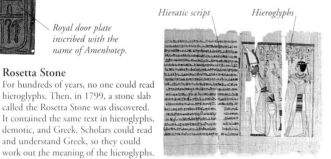

Writing

Ancient Egyptians developed a complex system of writing, called hieroglyphics, in which simple pictures represented objects. Some pictures also stood for letters. Ideas that were too complicated to be shown by one picture were written as groups of hieroglyphs.

Hieroglyphs and hieratic script

Hieroglyphs were slow to write, so the Egyptians used them mainly for sacred texts and tomb carvings. They used another, faster script, called hieratic, for business and literary texts. Later, they invented a third script, called demotic.

Royal door plate inscribed with the name of Amenhotep.

Hieratic script   *Hieroglyphs*

Rosetta Stone

For hundreds of years, no one could read hieroglyphs. Then, in 1799, a stone slab called the Rosetta Stone was discovered. It contained the same text in hieroglyphs, demotic, and Greek. Scholars could read and understand Greek, so they could work out the meaning of the hieroglyphs.

Daily life

For most Egyptians, life consisted of hard work in the fields, and on the great building projects. They ate mainly vegetables and bread, and drank beer. High officials and royal courtiers lived a much more leisurely life.

Axe head   *Axe*   *Chisel*   *Carpenter's saw*

Houses

Ancient Egyptians built houses of sun-dried mud-bricks. They covered the walls with smooth plaster. Small, high windows let in the breeze, but kept out the sun. The house pictured above belonged to a royal official, and had a garden with fruit trees.

Work

Most ancient Egyptians worked at producing their own food. Others were craft workers, making items for the home from wood, pottery, and metal. Their tools, such as saws and chisels, were very similar to the hand tools used by craftworkers today.

Ancient Egyptian amulets
Funerary amulets

Set-square amulets

Steps amulet, symbolizing the stairs on Osiris's throne.

Cartouches, containing names of the dead.

Obsidian head-rest amulets, used by ancient Egyptians instead of pillows.

Rising sun amulet, made from cornelian.

Shen amulet, symbolizing eternity

Finger amulets were placed on cuts made in the body during embalming.

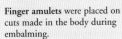
Winged-heart scarab, made from faïence.

Scarabs, sacred dung beetles that represented rebirth after death.

The Ankh, the ancient Egyptian symbol of life

Wedjat eyes, representing the eye of the god Horus, were placed on mummies to protect their health.

Girdles amulets, for protecting mummies

Papyrus columns

Sons of Horus amulets guarded the canopic jars, which held the vital organs removed from a mummy.

Soul-bird amulet

Djed pillars, amulets representing the backbone of Osiris, were thought to give the mummy strength after death.

Ushabti figures

Painted wood

Passage from the Book of the Dead

This ushabti dates from c.1500 BC.

Rensenb

Aah-mes, a clerk of the works in the Temple of Amen

Calcite (alabaster)

Egyptians believed that ushabtis came to life to work for the mummy in the afterlife.

Aah-mes

Seti I, the father of Rameses II

Cartouche containing Seti I's name.

Faïence

Pharaoh Seti I

Head cloth

Painted limestone

Heteti

Dead people were usually dressed in rich clothing.

Unnamed ushabti

Crown

Ceremonial beard

Painted limestone

Pharaoh Merenptah

Mummy with amulets

Heart scarab   *Ushabti figure*

EINSTEIN, ALBERT

$$E = mc^2$$

ALBERT EINSTEIN WAS a scientific genius who changed the way we view our universe. In 1905, he united space and time in one mathematical description. Ten years later he proposed a complete theory of gravity that explained how the universe works, relating mass and energy in the famous equation $E = mc^2$. Many people doubted his theories, but later investigation has since proved Einstein's theories to have been correct. As well as transforming the science of physics, Einstein's work paved the way for the creation of nuclear weapons.

Early life
Einstein was born in Ulm, Germany, and studied in Switzerland before graduating from Zurich's Institute of Technology in 1900. He did not fit in at school because he asked many difficult questions, and could get no work until he found a job in the Patent Office in Bern in 1902.

Special Theory of Relativity
In the early 1900s, Einstein developed the Special Theory of Relativity. This says that time is relative: it passes differently for individuals, depending on how fast or slowly they move. The faster anything travels, the slower time seems to pass. If one person travels into space close to the speed of light and another stays on Earth, time passes slower for the person in space. On their return, the person on Earth will be older.

Light beam sent by device on floor.
Light bounces off mirror on ceiling.
Train acts as "light clock" – the time taken by light, moving at constant speed, to go along train, acts as one "tick" of the clock.

Train appears stationary to man inside.
Light beam detected.
Man observes short "tick".

Light emitted from device on floor.
Woman sees long "tick".
Train has moved forward by time light beam hits mirror.
Train has moved still further by time light beam hits detector on floor.

Moving clocks
According to the special theory, time measured by a moving clock will run slower than if measured by a stationary clock. This can be demonstrated by light beams carried on a train travelling at nearly the speed of light. A person on the train sees the light travel a short distance; an observer on the platform sees it travel further because of the train's movement.

This light represents a pulsar.
This light represents a neutron star.
The twin stars make a double dent in spacetime.
These lines represent peaks and troughs in gravitational waves.

General Theory of Relativity
Einstein developed the General Theory of Relativity that explained gravity and the nature of space. He explained that as light travels the shortest path through space, when it bends space must be curved. Planets that travel round the Sun are thus following as straight a path as possible through curved space.

Making waves
Stars in a binary pulsar rotate round each other. As they move, they make waves in space. The waves carry energy from the stars, causing the stars to slow down as they lose energy. The rate that a pulsar slows in its orbit exactly matches Einstein's theory, though the first pulsar was not discovered until 1968.

Ripples in space
Einstein's theory predicted that objects jiggling around in space – such as two stars in a binary pulsar system – would make ripples in space. These ripples can be detected as gravitational waves. Subsequent experiments have proved Einstein's theory correct.

Stars rotate anti-clockwise.

Neutron star moves around pulsar.

Stars' positions change in relation to observer.

Stars continuously swap places.

Mileva Einstein
Einstein married his first wife Mileva, a mathematician and scientist in 1903. They had a daughter and two sons. Mileva worked closely with her husband and helped with her research, though to what degree she influenced his work is unknown. They were divorced in 1919.

Mileva and her son Hans Albert

Political life
In 1933, Einstein moved to America to avoid Nazi persecution as a Jew, and campaigned for a Jewish state. He realized that his theories made possible the creation of nuclear weapons, but campaigned against such weapons after World War II. In 1952, he was offered the presidency of Israel, but declined the offer.

The bomb
In the late 1930s, Einstein feared that Nazi Germany would use nuclear weapons in war, so he wrote to US president Franklin D. Roosevelt in 1939, urging the USA to begin constructing atomic weapons to counter this threat.

Explosion of atomic bomb

ALBERT EINSTEIN

1879	Born in Ulm, Germany.
1896–1900	Studies at Institute of Technology, Zurich, Switzerland.
1902–9	Works in Patent Office, Bern, Switzerland.
1905	Obtains doctorate; writes Special Theory of Relativity.
1914	Moves to Berlin.
1915	Writes General Theory of Relativity.
1921	Awarded Nobel Prize for Physics.
1933	Moves to the USA.
1952	Offered presidency of Israel.
1955	Dies in Princeton, USA.

FIND OUT MORE   NUCLEAR POWER   PHYSICS   SCIENCE, HISTORY OF   WORLD WAR II

ELECTRICITY

A FLASH OF LIGHTNING is striking evidence of the invisible energy called electricity. This energy is produced by the movement of electrons – tiny particles found in atoms of matter. Every electron carries an identical negative electric "charge". When electric charge builds up in one place, it is called static electricity. If the charge flows from place to place, it is called current electricity.

Electric circuit

The path around which current electricity flows is called a circuit. In the circuit shown here, electricity from the battery lights the bulbs. Two bulbs connected one after the other are described as being "in series". Bulbs in separate branches of the circuit are said to be "in parallel".

Ammeter measures current from battery.

Battery

Series circuit

Parallel circuit

Bulbs in series have to share the voltage, so they glow dimly.

Bulb in parallel gets the full voltage and glows brightly.

Voltmeter measures voltage across the bulb.

Electric current

Electrons pushed through the wires of a circuit form an electric current. The push on the electrons is called electromotive force (e.m.f). Voltage is a measure of e.m.f. The greater the voltage, the more current flows through the circuit.

Metal wire   *Insulation*

Electrons flow from negative charge to positive.

Battery
A battery is a source of electric current. A chemical reaction between materials in the battery separates electrons from their atoms. The battery's e.m.f makes electrons flow out of the negative terminal, around a circuit, and back to the positive terminal.

Positive terminal (+)

Ammonium chloride paste

Carbon rod

Zinc casing

Negative terminal (–)

Static electricity

Rubbing two materials together can transfer electrons from one material to the other. A material that loses electrons gains a positive charge of static electricity, and a material that gains electrons gets a negative charge.

Attracting and repelling
A positively charged balloon attracts electrons to the surface of nearby hairs, giving them a negative charge. Opposite charges attract, so the hairs are pulled towards the balloon. Charges of the same type repel (push each other away).

Lightning
A tremendous charge of static electricity builds up inside a storm cloud. A flash of lightning occurs when this charge is suddenly released as a powerful electric current.

Steel is a good conductor.   *Plastic blocks current.*

Conductors
Current can flow only through materials called conductors, whose electrons are bound loosely to their atoms and can be moved easily through the material.

Insulators
Current cannot flow through insulators. The electrons in an insulator are bound firmly to their atoms and cannot move through the material.

Generator

Most of the electricity used in homes and factories is produced by devices called generators. Inside a generator, coils of wire spin rapidly in a magnetic field. The magnetism moves electrons through the wire, creating an electric current. In this simple version, bar magnets produce the magnetic field.

Voltmeter measures voltage of current.

Electrical connections

Simple electricity generator

Coil of wire wrapped around wooden block

Bar magnet

Spinning the coil generates a current.

Circuit breakers cut off the electricity if the voltage gets dangerously high.

Meter records how much electricity is consumed.

Earth wire

Lighting circuit

Wall socket

Main circuit

Electricity supply
Electric current produced by generators in power stations reaches consumers via cables buried underground or carried by tall towers called pylons. The current alternates, which means that it changes direction many times each second. A battery produces direct current, which flows in one direction only.

Electricity in the home
Separate circuits in the home supply different voltages for different purposes. An electrical appliance takes power from the circuits through a plug that fits into a wall socket. The sockets are linked to the ground outside by an earth wire. If an electrical fault occurs, the current is diverted safely into the ground.

Michael Faraday

In 1831, the English scientist Michael Faraday (1791–1867) built the first generator after noticing that moving a magnet in and out of a wire coil made a current flow through the wire. Faraday also invented the electric motor and pioneered electrolysis (using electricity to break down substances).

Timeline

500s BC The ancient Greeks discover static electricity when they notice that amber (fossilized tree sap) attracts small objects if rubbed with wool.

Charged amber attracting feather

1752 American scientist and politician Benjamin Franklin proves that lightning is an electrical phenomenon.

1799 Italian physicist Alessandro Volta makes the first battery.

Volta's battery

1831 American physicist Joseph Henry and English Michael Faraday independently build "induction coils" – the first electricity generators.

1868 French chemist Georges Leclanché invents the Leclanché cell, the forerunner of modern zinc-carbon batteries.

1897 English physicist Joseph John Thomson discovers the electron.

FIND OUT MORE   ACIDS AND ALKALIS   ELECTROMAGNETISM   ENERGY   FRICTION   MAGNETISM   STORMS

E

ELECTROMAGNETISM

AT THE FLICK OF A SWITCH, an invisible force turns the drum of a washing machine 1,600 times every second. This force is called electromagnetism. It is a form of magnetism produced by electricity. When an electric current flows through a wire, it produces a magnetic field around the wire. Making the wire into a coil increases the strength of the magnetic effect. Winding the coil around an iron bar makes the magnetism even stronger. Any device that exerts electromagnetic forces is called an electromagnet.

Connections to battery

Compasses show magnetic field around coil.

Coil

Solenoid
A coil of current-carrying wire forms a type of electromagnet called a solenoid. The magnetic field around the coil is the same as that around an ordinary bar magnet. The field's strength depends on the number of turns in the coil and the amount of current flowing through the wire.

Electric motor

Steel casing   Coils of wire   Spindle

Permanent magnets   Iron core   Terminal

Inside an electric motor are wire coils surrounded by permanent magnets. Electricity flowing through the wire produces a magnetic field around each coil. The magnetism of the coils interacts with the magnetic fields of the permanent magnets. They push and pull on each other, making the coils rotate. This movement is used to drive machines such as electric drills.

Electric drill
An electric drill can quickly make a hole in wood, stone, and even some metals. Inside the body of the machine, gears harness the rotation of a powerful electric motor to drive the drill at high speed. A cooling fan prevents the drill from overheating.

Chuck holds drill bit tightly.

Drill bit

On/off trigger

Electric cable provides current.

Electromagnet

Most electromagnets consist of a coil of wire wrapped around an iron bar. When an electric current flows through the wire, a magnetic field forms around the electromagnet. The magnetism can be switched off by disconnecting the electricity supply.

Clamp stand   *Clamp holding iron bar*

Copper wire coiled tightly around bar

Connections to battery

Steel paper clips cling to the electromagnet.

Disconnecting the battery switches off the electromagnet's magnetic field.

Scrapyard electromagnet
Waste metal is moved around a scrapyard by a crane carrying a huge electromagnet. When the electromagnet is switched on, it picks up metal scraps containing iron. The metal is moved to a different place and then dropped by switching off the electromagnet.

Uses of electromagnetism

Some electrical appliances contain electric motors that use electromagnetism to produce movement. But electromagnetism is also used in many other ways, such as to make sound or detect hidden objects.

Loudspeaker
A loudspeaker contains a paper or plastic cone that vibrates and creates sound waves in the air around it. The cone is attached to a wire coil surrounded by a permanent magnet. The magnetic fields of the coil and the magnet interact. This causes the coil to move rapidly to and fro, making the cone vibrate.

Cone vibrates as electricity flows through coil.

Transformer   *Portable radio*

Metal detector
Inside the walk-through arch of an airport metal detector are large coils of wire carrying an electric current. Any person who walks under the arch passes through the magnetic field produced by the coils. A hidden metal object will affect the strength of the field and trigger an alarm.

Transformer
Many electrical devices use a transformer to alter the voltage of an electrical supply. Inside a transformer are two wire coils. When a varying current flows through one coil, it produces a varying magnetic field. This field causes an electric current to flow through the second coil, but at a different voltage.

Hans Christian Oersted

The Danish physicist Hans Christian Oersted (1777–1851) discovered electromagnetism in 1820. He placed a compass near a wire carrying an electric current and noticed that the compass needle was deflected and no longer pointed north. Oersted realized that the current had produced a magnetic field around the wire.

Timeline
1799 Italian physicist Alessandro Volta invents the battery, which allows scientists to experiment with electric currents.

1820 Oersted's discovery of electromagnetism opens the way for the development of the electric motor and the electromagnet.

Faraday's electric motor

1821 English scientist Michael Faraday makes an electric motor, in which a current-carrying wire rotates around the pole of a magnet. It has no practical use.

Sturgeon's electromagnet

1828 English scientist William Sturgeon builds the first electromagnet – a coil of wire around an insulated iron bar.

1883 Croatian-born physicist Nikola Tesla invents the "induction motor" – the first practical motor.

1885 American engineer William Stanley invents the transformer.

 FIND OUT MORE   ELECTRICITY   ENGINES AND MOTORS   FORCE AND MOTION   MAGNETISM   MACHINES   SOUND

ELECTRONICS

THE ELECTRONICS REVOLUTION is rapidly changing our world: whether we are at home, at work, or out shopping, we are surrounded by electronic machines and equipment. Electronics involves using devices called components to control electric currents, which are flows of tiny, electrically charged particles of matter called electrons. An electronic circuit is an arrangement of linked components – such as transistors and diodes – that manipulates current in order to carry out a specific task, such as adding numbers in a calculator.

Circuit board

The components for an electronic device, such as a radio, are attached to a circuit board, which is a flat base with metal tracks running along its underside. The components are secured to the tracks using an alloy called solder. The tracks link the components to form a circuit.

Inductors are wire coils that produce magnetic fields when current passes through them, creating a resistance that restricts the flow of current.

Variable capacitors can be adjusted to store varying levels of charge; in radios, they are used to select radio stations.

Diodes allow electric current to pass through them in one direction only.

Transistors can be used to amplify electrical signals (make them stronger) or switch circuits rapidly on and off.

Resistors allow only a fixed amount of electric current to flow through a circuit.

Light Emitting Diodes (LEDs) glow when current passes through them, and are used to indicate that a device's power supply is on.

Variable resistors allow the level of current flowing through a circuit to be adjusted.

Radio circuit board and components

Capacitors are components that store electric charge; electrolytic capacitors can store more charge than ceramic ones.

Electrolytic capacitors

Ceramic capacitors

Power cables

Integrated circuits consist of a plastic case containing a complete circuit etched on to a tiny silicon chip.

William Shockley

US physicist William Shockley (1910–89) was part of a three-man team that invented the transistor in 1947. The transistor made it possible to build tiny electronic circuits and so develop more compact electronic devices.

Remote control
Pressing a button on the remote-control of a TV – for example, to change channels – makes an LED flash pulses of infrared light to the TV set. The TV set decodes the pulses and obeys the instruction.

Semiconductors

Silicon crystal

The element silicon is a type of material called a semiconductor, because it conducts electricity only under certain conditions. The properties of a semiconductor can be altered by adding chemical impurities to it in a process called doping. Doped semiconductors are used to make diodes, transistors, and many other electronic components.

Pins connect to circuit board.

Silicon chip sealed under metal cover

Ceramic casing

Microprocessors
Many electronic devices – including computers – are controlled by circuits called microprocessors, or "silicon chips". A microprocessor is made from a single slice of doped semiconductor. The circuit, which may contain thousands of components, can carry out many complex tasks.

Uses of electronics

Electronic circuits are either analogue or digital. Analogue circuits deal with continuously varying electric currents, such as television and radio signals. Digital circuits process information in the form of thousands of on-off pulses of electric current every second.

Pocket calculator

Video-game console

CD-ROM drive

Liquid crystal display

Handset with control keys

Calculator
A calculator's digital circuits split up a calculation into a series of simple steps, each of which is performed at high speed.

Video game console
Digital circuits inside the console control the play. The console sends an analogue signal to a TV screen, which displays a picture of the game.

Television controls

Liquid crystal display

Timer and clock controls

Number keypad

Video recorder controls

TV/video remote control

FIND OUT MORE COMPUTERS ELECTRICITY ELEMENTS INFORMATION TECHNOLOGY METALS TELEPHONES TELECOMMUNICATIONS VIDEO

ELEMENTS

AN ELEMENT IS a substance composed of only one type of atom. Elements are the most basic substances in the Universe and cannot be split into anything simpler. There are 109 elements – 91 of which occur naturally, and 18 of which can be made artificially. All life on Earth is based on the element carbon, which is vital to the functioning of living cells. Oxygen is the most plentiful element on Earth. It occurs in air, water, and even rocks.

Groups of elements

Just as the members of a human family share the same characteristics, there are "families" of elements that have similar properties. An element's chemical properties are determined by the structure of its atoms. Elements in the same group have similar atomic structures.

Calcium gives bones their hardness.

Alkaline-earth metals

Calcium and magnesium belong to the group of elements called the alkaline-earth metals. They are so named because they form alkaline solutions in water, and their compounds occur widely in nature. Calcium, for example, occurs in sea shells, bones, teeth, milk, and chalk. Magnesium occurs in the substance chlorophyll, which plants use to make food by photosynthesis.

Iodine   Bromine   Chlorine

Halogens

Swimming pools smell the way they do because the halogen chlorine is put in the water to kill germs. Compounds of fluorine, another halogen, are put in water and toothpaste to prevent tooth decay. The halogens, which also include iodine, bromine, and astatine, are all strong-smelling, highly reactive non-metals.

Alkali metals

Potassium (which is used in fertilizers) and sodium (which occurs in salt) are both alkali metals. All the elements in this group are soft, extremely reactive metals. They react violently or even explosively with water to form alkaline solutions.

Reaction of potassium in water

Iron compounds are often red, black, or brown.

Iron sulphide

Iron carbide

Iron oxide

Coloured compounds of iron

Transition metals

The transition metals are a large group of hard, dense elements that conduct electricity and heat well, form coloured compounds, and some of which (iron, cobalt, and nickel) are magnetic. Other transition metals include copper, gold, chromium, titanium, platinum, and tungsten.

Noble gases

Multi-coloured street signs often contain noble gases, because each of these gases glows a different colour when electricity flows through it. Neon, for example, glows red, helium yellow, and argon blue. The noble gases are unreactive non-metals that rarely form compounds.

Elements in nature

Only a few of the naturally occurring elements can be found in their pure state. Most elements combine, or react, with other elements to form more complex substances called compounds. Pure gold can be mined directly from the ground because it is unreactive – that is, it does not readily form compounds.

Gold veins in quartz rock

Quartz rock is a compound of the elements silicon and oxygen.

Pure gold.

Allotropes

It may seem difficult to believe, but hard, sparkling diamond is made of the same types of atoms as soft, black graphite. Diamond and graphite are allotropes of carbon, meaning that they are different physical forms of the same element. Their atoms link up in different ways to make them look and behave differently.

Diamond consists of carbon atoms linked strongly to each other in a rigid framework.

Only weak bonds hold sheets together.

Graphite pencil

Graphite is made up of sheets of carbon atoms that can slide over each other easily.

Artificial elements

New elements can be created by bombarding existing elements with high-speed subatomic particles in a device called a particle accelerator. Since 1937, scientists have made 18 new elements, some of which only exist for a few millionths of a second.

Computer image of a particle accelerator collision

Hydrogen

The element hydrogen makes up 90 per cent of all the matter in the Universe. It was the first element to form when the Universe was created in the explosion known as the Big Bang. Hydrogen is a tasteless, colourless, odourless, non-toxic gas. It is the simplest of all the elements, with atoms containing just one proton orbited by a single electron. Hydrogen gives acids their acidic properties.

Electron   *Proton*

Hydrogen atom

Dmitri Mendeleyev

In 1869, the Russian chemist Dmitri Mendeleyev (1834–1907) devised a chart called the periodic table, which classified the 63 elements then known into different groups. He used the table to predict the existence of three new elements, all of which were discovered a few years later.

FIND OUT MORE   ACIDS AND ALKALIS   AIR   ATOMS AND MOLECULES   BIG BANG   MATTER   METALS   MIXTURES AND COMPOUNDS   SKELETON   TEETH AND JAWS

ELEPHANTS

THE AFRICAN AND ASIAN elephants are the only two living species of a once much larger family that was found on every continent. The African elephant is the largest land mammal, but despite its size and power it is a gentle creature. Elephants are highly intelligent, very sociable animals, that live in close family units. The African and Asian elephants are descended from different ancestors; the Asian elephant is more closely related to the mammoth than to the African elephant.

Teeth
The elephant has only four teeth, one in each quarter of the jaw. Each tooth is about 30 cm (12 in) long. As one wears down, another pushes in from behind. This can happen only six times, after which the supply of teeth is exhausted. Without teeth, the elephant can no longer eat, so dies of starvation.

Large ears

Tusks

Trunk

Diamond-shaped ridges

Pads under large feet expand when trodden on.

Tail

Features of an elephant
Everything about an elephant is oversized. Its most conspicuous feature is the long flexible trunk – an elongation of the nose. The huge tusks are overgrown incisor teeth. Besides hearing, the large ears are used as a fan to cool the elephant. They also make the animal appear larger than it really is, and spreading the ears helps intimidate a rival or a potential enemy. Soft fatty cushions on the underside of the feet spread as the elephant walks.

Elephant using tusks to dig into ground.

Tusks
A tusk is a specialized type of tooth, growing from either side of the upper jaw. Tusks are used mainly as tools and weapons. The heaviest pair of tusks ever recorded weighed 102 kg (225 lb) and 109 kg (240 lb). The longest pair measured 3.35 m (11 ft) and 3.5 m (11 ft 5 in) in length.

Skin
The skin is very wrinkled. Deep crevices increase the surface area of the skin, and allow greater heat loss. The crevices also help to trap water which then takes longer to evaporate, and helps to keep the elephant cooler for longer.

Trunk
The elephant's trunk is highly flexible and serves much the same functions as a human arm and hand. It combines great strength with delicacy, and is so versatile that it can pluck a single leaf as easily as it can lift a heavy log. Because the elephant has a trunk it does not need to lower its head while feeding, thus allowing it to remain alert. The trunk also allows the elephant to reach high above its head to browse on leaves that are out of most other animals' reach.

The elephant uses its trunk to feed.

Fingers are used to hold objects.

Nostrils
Located at the tip of the trunk, the elephant's nostrils can be raised high above its head, like a periscope, and turned in any direction to pick up traces of scent carried on the wind. The elephant relies on its sense of smell more than its other senses. While swimming, the trunk may be lifted above the surface of the water, and used as a snorkel if the elephant gets out of its depth.

Picking up scent on the wind

Fingers
As well as the nostrils, the tip of the trunk has fleshy "fingers". The African species has two opposing fingers, but the Asian elephant has only one which it uses to grip against the wide underside of the trunk. Fingers enable the elephant to perform precise movements and pick up very small objects.

Upper finger

Lower finger

Fingers of the African elephant trunk

Ivory trade
The elephant's only enemy is humans, who kill them for their tusks. In recent years, the demand for ivory has led to killing on a vast scale. From 1979 to 1989, the number of elephants in Africa was reduced from 1.3 million to 609,000.

Ivory is made into carvings and trinkets.

Types of elephant

Asian elephant
The Asian elephant, found in forests in India and south-eastern Asia, has been domesticated for at least 2,500 years. It is used for ceremonial purposes and forestry work. Of the 34,000–56,000 elephants remaining in Asia, 10,000 are working animals.

2.5–3 m (8–10 ft) tall

Small ears

Females are tuskless.

African bush elephant
The African bush elephant lives in open country and woodland in Africa south of the Sahara. It is larger, with much larger ears and a more concave back than the Asian elephant. Both males and females have tusks. Unlike the Asian elephant, it has never been domesticated.

Large ears

4 m (13 ft) tall

Elephant reaching up with its trunk.

Small rounded ears

African forest elephant
The forest elephant is a smaller subspecies of the African bush elephant, with smaller, more rounded ears. It does not need such large ears to help it keep cool, as it lives in the tropical rainforests of the Congo basin in equatorial Africa. Its tusks are slender and downward pointing.

Family group

The elephant's social organization is based upon a group of 10–12 females and their calves, led by a mature female. Harmonious relationships often develop between individual members of the group. Friendships can last for decades as elephants often live for up to 80 years. Elephants show great affection for their young, but discipline is strong, and any lapse of acceptable behaviour is dealt with firmly. Family groups often seek shade during the heat of the day, preferring to feed and drink in the cool of the evening. Elephants browse on leaves and shoots, but they also eat grass. They spend about 18 hours a day feeding, to satisfy their huge appetites.

Matriarch

Leadership of the family unit rests with the oldest and most experienced female, the matriarch, who is usually the mother or grandmother of the whole group. Each member of the group knows its position in the hierarchy and respects matriarchal authority without question.

Herd gathering

Separate family groups associate closely with each other. They often live only a few hundred metres apart, constantly coming together and drifting apart again. Occasionally, many family groups congregate in an exceptionally large herd of more than a thousand animals.

Young

Females normally conceive every four years and give birth to a single calf after 22 months' gestation. This is the longest gestation period of any animal. The newborn calf stands about 84 cm (33 in) high. Other calves from previous matings remain with their mother after the new calf is born. The older calves help to take care of their younger siblings.

Water holes

Elephants like to drink every day. They also enjoy bathing and spraying themselves with water. As the dry season advances, food and water become scarce, and they may have to walk up to 80 km (50 miles) between watering and feeding grounds. They also dig holes in some riverbeds to reach water below the surface, thereby providing water for other animals.

Bulls

Secretion shows bull is in musth.

Only immature bull calves are allowed in the family group; as soon as the bulls reach maturity they are expelled. They live alone or in small bachelor groups. Mature bulls briefly rejoin the herd when any of the cows are ready for mating.

Musth

By 25 years of age, bulls come into musth once a year. Musth is a period of aggressive behaviour where a bull picks fights with other bulls searching for a female ready to mate. A thick secretion from the temporal gland indicates he is in musth.

Fighting

Young bulls often have mock battles to test each other's strength. They are usually harmless affairs where they clash tusks and grapple with each other's trunks. Older bulls, especially those in musth, may sometimes fight in defence of territory or to establish dominance.

Young bulls sparring

Threat displays

Differences between elephants are generally resolved peacefully. Displeasure is indicated by means of a threat display. This involves head-shaking, ear-spreading, trunk-twirling, and foot-shuffling. If this fails to deter, the elephant may make a full-scale charge. This is a rare event where the elephant covers ground at rapid speed, with its trunk raised and ears outstretched, while trumpeting furiously. Threat charges are rarely carried through; the elephant usually halts or turns at the last moment.

Ears spread wide to intimidate an enemy

Communication

Touch is an important way of communicating in elephant society. When elephants meet, they greet each other by entwining trunks and touching each other's face and body. At rest, they often stand together, head to head. If a young calf misbehaves, its mother may actually use her trunk to smack it. When a calf is frightened, other elephants help to calm it by standing close, and caressing it with their trunks.

Elephants standing face to face and touching each others' heads and trunks.

Rumbling

Elephants maintain contact by means of rumbling sounds from the throat, back of the nose, and trunk. A sudden cessation of rumbling warns the herd of possible danger. Elephants are also capable of communicating over substantial distances, by low-frequency sounds which humans cannot hear.

AFRICAN ELEPHANT

SCIENTIFIC NAME *Loxodonta africana*

ORDER Proboscidea

FAMILY Elephantidae

DISTRIBUTION Africa south of the Sahara

HABITAT Open savannahs and woodlands

DIET Grasses, leaves, shoots, twigs, and other browse

SIZE Height at shoulder: 4 m (13 ft); weight: 6.1 tonnes (6 tons)

LIFESPAN 70–80 years

FIND OUT MORE   AFRICAN WILDLIFE   ANIMAL BEHAVIOUR   ASIAN WILDLIFE   CONSERVATION   ECOLOGY AND ECOSYSTEMS   GRASSLAND WILDLIFE   MAMMALS   RAINFOREST WILDLIFE

ELIZABETH I

FOR 45 YEARS from 1558–1603, a truly remarkable woman governed England. By force of personality and political skill, Queen Elizabeth I united her divided country and presided over a glorious period in the arts and culture. Yet she had to struggle all her life: her mother died when she was only three, her half-sister, Mary, put her in prison and, as an adult, she was a single woman in a world dominated by men. But Elizabeth overcame every adversity, and when she died in 1603, she left England one of the most prosperous and powerful nations in Europe.

Elizabeth I's accession to the throne, at the age of 25

Early life
Elizabeth was the daughter of Henry VIII (r.1509–47) and his second wife, Anne Boleyn. She was born in Greenwich Palace on 7 September, 1533. Elizabeth's mother was executed for treason when Elizabeth was just three years old. The future queen was imprisoned briefly while her Catholic half-sister Mary was crowned queen. Elizabeth took the throne on 17 November, 1558, after Mary's death.

Church and State
Elizabeth's father Henry VIII broke with the Roman Catholic Church in 1534, establishing the Protestant Church of England. Her half-sister Mary I (r.1553–58) tried to return England to Catholicism, but Elizabeth introduced the Anglican faith, as a compromise between Catholicism and extreme Protestantism.

William Cecil
Cecil, later Lord Burghley, served Elizabeth first as her Chief Secretary of State and, after 1572, as Lord Treasurer. He introduced many reforms and was an able adviser to the queen. He died in 1598, and his son became chief minister.

Mary, Queen of Scots
Mary was Elizabeth's heir, but also a Catholic. She became the centre of plots against Elizabeth, notably one led by Mary's page Anthony Babington. Elizabeth reluctantly had Mary tried and executed for treason in 1587.

Spanish Armada
As leader of Catholic Europe, Philip II of Spain, husband of Elizabeth's half-sister Mary, was a threat to Protestant England and encouraged plots against the queen. After the execution of Mary, Queen of Scots, Philip decided to invade England. In 1588, he sent a huge Armada of 130 ships carrying 20,000 soldiers. Harried by English ships, attacked in the English Channel, and wrecked by severe storms, the Armada was forced to return, in defeat, to Spain.

English fire ships are sent to meet the Spanish fleet.

Spanish ships escape towards the North.

Francis Drake
Between 1577 and 1580, in his ship the *Golden Hind*, Francis Drake became the first Englishman to sail around the world. He delayed preparations for the Spanish Armada by attacking the fleet while it was at anchor in Cadiz Harbour in 1587, and played an important part in its defeat the following year. He continued to attack Spanish shipping until his death off the coast of Panama in 1596.

Phoenix emblem
Elizabeth created a strong public image of herself by adopting the phoenix as her emblem. The "Phoenix Jewel", dated around 1574, shows a bust of Elizabeth, with a reverse image of the mythical phoenix rising from flames.

The famous "Phoenix Jewel"

Virgin Queen
Elizabeth spent her life surrounded by suitors, yet she never married. Powerful foreign monarchs courted Elizabeth throughout her life, eager for a stake in her flourishing kingdom, but she played her suitors off against each other for political gains. Elizabeth gloried in her role as the Virgin Queen, using it to create a national self-confidence that fuelled a flowering of the arts, distinguished by William Shakespeare, the poet Edmund Spenser, and composers such as Thomas Tallis.

Elizabeth stands on a map of her kingdom.

ELIZABETH I

1533 Born in Greenwich Palace near London, England.

1536 Elizabeth's mother, Anne Boleyn, executed for treason.

1554 Elizabeth put under house arrest by half-sister, Mary.

1558 Succeeds to the throne; appoints William Cecil as Secretary of State and Matthew Parker as Archbishop of Canterbury.

1559 Act of Supremacy makes her head of Anglican Church.

1588 Spanish Armada defeated.

1603 Dies in Richmond Palace.

FIND OUT MORE   CHRISTIANITY   DRAMA   HOUSES AND HOMES   REFORMATION   SHAKESPEARE, WILLIAM   THEATRES   SPAIN, HISTORY OF   UNITED KINGDOM, HISTORY OF

EMPIRES

Ottoman sword and scabbard

A LARGE SUPER-STATE under a single ruler is called an empire. There have been many different empires through history, from the ancient Roman Empire to the great empire of the Incas in Peru. The largest ever was the British Empire. Most empires have an army, to conquer territory and suppress revolts, and a civil service to carry out the day-to-day running of the empire and collect taxes. No empire lasts for ever – though the effect on the host country may be permanent – and empires perish for many reasons, including internal rebellion, economic decline, or the sheer difficulty of uniting many peoples under one leader.

Growth of empires

Empires grow because ruling powers want extra income from trade or taxes, or they may have territorial ambitions. Sometimes they may want to spread a religion. Would-be empires always need a strong army.

Imperial cross

Ottoman Empire
The Ottoman Turks expanded their empire by military might. At their height in the 17th century, they dominated the Mediterranean coast from present-day Greece to Tunisia.

Holy Roman Empire
Based in Germany, the leaders of this empire saw themselves as heirs to the Roman emperors. The emperors wanted to wield religious power over all western Christians, and to exert political power over the other European rulers, such as the German and Italian princes.

British Empire

The largest empire the world has ever seen had its beginnings in the 18th and early 19th centuries, when Britain acquired Australia, Canada, and a range of territories from Honduras to Hong Kong. The "jewel in the crown" of the empire was India, which Britain dominated through the East India Company. Queen Victoria (r.1837–1901) took the title Empress of India in 1876. The British Empire had a lasting influence on its territories – for both good and bad. British-style administration provided a model for local civil servants when territories gained independence. On the other hand, the British exploited local labour forces on a massive scale.

British Empire, 1918

Extent of the empire
After winning the Napoleonic Wars, and the decline of the older empires of Spain, Portugal, and the Netherlands, Britain was clearly one of the world's strongest countries. As the 19th century wore on, the already vast British Empire added parts of Africa and South-east Asia. By 1918, the empire had reached its peak.

Victoria Station, Bombay, India

Gordon of Khartoum
In 1884, two years after Egypt became part of the empire, General Charles Gordon (1833–85) came to the Sudan to aid Egyptians defending their garrisons against a local revolt. Gordon was cut off in the city of Khartoum and withstood a 10-month siege, but was finally killed. There was an outcry that a relief force had not been sent quickly enough to save Gordon, and he became a hero of the empire.

Resources of the empire
Britain had limited resources but an expanding industry, so the British used their empire as a source of raw materials, and a market for goods. The far-flung empire provided raw materials, such as cotton, gemstones, and hard wood, and raw materials included tea, rubber, tin, copper, and wool.

Timber

Cotton **Emerald**

Public works
The British made the major towns of the empire as similar to British cities as possible. They sent British engineers and architects all over the world to build government headquarters, churches, railway stations, art galleries, and public buildings. Former imperial cities, such as Bombay, still have Victorian-era administration and transport centres.

Timeline

509 BC–AD 476 Roman Empire dominates much of Europe, western Asia, and northern Africa.

221–206 BC Qin emperor unites China.

321–187 BC Mauryans rule much of India.

395–1453 Byzantine Empire established in the eastern territory of the Roman Empire.

962–1806 Holy Roman Empire dominates central Europe.

1206–1405 Mongols create an empire, including most of Asia.

1345–1521 Aztec emperors hold power in Mexico.

Conquistadore's helmet

1521–1825 Spain builds large empire in southern America.

1580–1931 British Empire increases in size.

1930s British Empire starts to decline. By the 1940s, territories are claiming independence.

Imperialism

The economic domination of Asia, North America, and Africa by Europe, the United States, and Russia from the 17th century is known as modern imperialism. Ancient imperialism peaked with the Roman Empire.

The bear, symbol of Russia, 1888

FIND OUT MORE — BYZANTINE EMPIRE · HOLY ROMAN EMPIRE · ISLAMIC EMPIRE · OTTOMAN EMPIRE · PERSIAN EMPIRES · ROMAN EMPIRE

ENERGY

WE RELY ON THE ENERGY stored in food to keep us alive and on the energy locked within fuels to drive our machines and industries. Energy is the ability to make things happen, whether it is moving something, heating it up, or changing it in some way. Energy exists in many different forms, including electricity, sound, heat, and light.

When this woman lifts the weights, she is doing work.

Her power is how long it takes her to do the work.

Weights gain potential energy.

Work

When a force moves an object, energy changes from one form to another and work is the result. This woman does work as she lifts weights. The force she applies converts the kinetic energy of her moving arms into the potential energy of the raised weights. Multiplying the force by the distance through which the object moves gives the amount of work done.

Types of energy

All energy is either kinetic or potential. Kinetic energy is the energy of moving objects, while potential energy is energy that is stored, ready for use. Energy is measured in units called joules (J).

When this frog leaps through the air, it has kinetic energy.

Kinetic energy

All objects in motion – from atoms to aircraft – possess kinetic energy. The higher the object's speed and the greater its mass, the more kinetic energy the object has.

Potential energy

An object may gain potential energy if its position or condition alters. A bungee-jumper standing on top of a bridge has potential energy – that is, the potential to fall back to Earth. When he jumps, his bungee rope gains potential energy as it stretches, because it has the potential to pull him back up again.

The jumper's potential energy changes to kinetic energy as he falls.

500 g (1.1 lb) peas
90 g (3 oz) beef
50 g (1.8 oz) sugar
500 g (1.1 lb) peeled oranges
30 g (1 oz) butter
50 g (1.8 oz) cheese

Chemical energy

Foods and fuels contain energy stored within chemical compounds. This is a type of potential energy called chemical energy. Some foods store more energy than others. All the foods above contain the same amount of energy, but you would have to eat 500 g (1.1 lb) of peas to get as much energy as you would from just 30 g (1 oz) of butter.

Power

The rate at which work is done and energy changed from one form to another is called power. Power is measured in watts (W), and is calculated by dividing the work done by the time taken to do it.

100 W fan
1,000 W iron

Electrical power

Every electrical appliance is given a power rating. If a fan has a power rating of 100 W, it shows that the fan converts 100 J of electrical energy into kinetic energy each second. Similarly, a 1,000 W iron changes electricity into heat at the rate of 1,000 J per second.

Both bulbs give out the same light.
60 W bulb (incandescent)
15 W bulb (fluorescent)
Fluorescent bulb uses less electricity.

Efficiency

Out of every 100 J of electrical energy used by a 60 W incandescent bulb, only 10 J are changed into light; the rest are lost as heat. The bulb has an efficiency of 10%. A 15 W fluorescent bulb is 40% efficient. It gives the same light using a quarter of the electricity.

Energy transfer

The Law of Conservation of Energy says that energy is always conserved – that is, it can be neither created nor destroyed. This law means that when objects gain or lose energy, the energy simply transfers from place to place, or changes into a different form.

Harvested wheat
Bread is made from wheat.
Friction occurs between brake and wheel.

1 Tremendous temperatures at the Sun's surface cause it to give out light and other forms of energy, some of which reach the Earth.

2 When sunlight falls on plants, some of the light energy transfers to the plants by a process called photosynthesis. It is stored as chemical energy.

3 Eating plant-based food, such as bread, enables you to break down the food. This releases the chemical energy and transfers it to your body.

4 Riding a bicycle changes the chemical energy into kinetic energy. If you brake, friction changes this energy into heat as you slow down.

James Joule

The unit of energy, the joule, is named after the English physicist James Joule (1818–89), who helped to develop the Law of Conservation of Energy. Joule noticed that if he rotated a set of paddles in water, the water soon became warm. He realized that the work of turning the paddles changed their kinetic energy into heat, proving that heat is a form of energy.

Timeline

1829 French physicist Gustave Coriolis introduces the term "kinetic energy".

1843 James Joule's experiments show how heat, work, and power are related.

1847 Joule and German physicists Hermann von Helmholtz and Julius Meyer independently state the Law of Conservation of Energy.

1853 Scottish scientist William Rankine devises the concept of "potential energy".

1881 The world's first electricity-generating power station opens in Surrey, UK.

1884 Irish engineer Charles Parsons invents the steam turbine.

Parsons' turbine

1905 German physicist Albert Einstein suggests that matter is a form of energy, and vice versa.

1980s Declining fossil fuel reserves and pollution bring calls for machines and industries to be more energy efficient.

E

E

Power station

Most of the energy used in homes, offices, and factories is electricity produced by power stations. Inside a coal- or oil-fired power station, chemical energy stored within fuel turns into heat energy as the fuel burns in a furnace. The heat is used to boil water into steam, which drives turbines linked to electricity generators. The electricity reaches consumers via a network of cables called a grid.

Model of a coal-fired power station

Boiler house turns water into steam.

Fumes from furnace escape via chimney.

Coal store

Connections to electricity grid

The turbine house contains the turbines and generators.

Cooling towers turn steam from the boiler back into water.

The turbine blades revolve about 3,000 times each minute.

The generator uses the motion of the turbine to produce electricity.

Turbine-generator unit in a coal-fired power station

Turbine

A turbine is a machine powered by the force of moving liquid or gas. It consists of a set of angled blades mounted on a shaft. In a power station, jets of high-pressure steam strike the turbine blades and make them revolve at high speed. The turbine shaft is connected to an electricity generator. As the shaft spins, it turns an electromagnet inside the generator, producing an electric current.

Renewable energy

Energy that is produced without permanently using up the Earth's limited resources is called renewable energy. Apart from biomass fuels, which produce smoke and other fumes when burned, renewable energy sources are pollution-free, because they harness the energy of natural phenomena such as winds and waves. As the Earth's fossil fuel reserves are gradually used up, people will have to rely much more on renewable energy sources.

Geothermal power

Below the Earth's surface, water is turned into steam by geothermal energy – that is, the energy of hot, molten rocks. By drilling a well, this steam can be harnessed to drive generators. Electricity produced in this way is called geothermal power.

Wind power

A wind turbine is a tall tower with propeller-like blades that converts the kinetic energy of the wind into electricity. As the wind blows, the turbine's blades rotate and drive a small generator. A group of wind turbines is called a wind farm.

Biomass fuels

Plant material is called biomass. Millions of people around the world burn peat, wood, animal dung, and other biomass fuels to heat and light their homes, and to cook food. Burning biomass fuels releases chemical energy stored within the plant material.

Hydroelectric power

A hydroelectric power station converts the kinetic energy of falling water into electricity. The power station sits under a dam at the end of a reservoir. Inside the power station, turbines and generators are driven by water rushing down with tremendous force from the reservoir above.

Wave power

Towers such as the one above stand in coastal waters and use the movement of the ocean's waves to produce electricity. As the waves rise and fall, they push a column of air inside the tower up and down. The to-and-fro motion of the air turns a turbine and drives a generator.

Tidal barrage

At high and low tides, huge amounts of water move up and down river estuaries. A tidal barrage is a dam across an estuary. As the tides come in and go out, some water is allowed to pass through tunnels in the dam. The tidal flow drives electricity generators built into the dam.

Solar power

Electricity produced from sunlight is called solar power. A "solar furnace" uses a vast bank of mirrors to focus sunlight on to water. The water boils into steam, which drives turbines and generators.

Fossil fuels

Coal, oil, and natural gas are called fossil fuels, because they formed underground over millions of years from the fossilized remains of plants and animals. The Earth has limited supplies of these fuels, which cannot be replenished once exhausted.

Natural gas is made up of methane and small amounts of other gases.

Petrol, diesel, and many other fuels are made from oil.

Coal consists chiefly of the element carbon.

Natural gas   Oil   Coal

Charles Parsons

The engineer Charles Parsons (1854–1931) was born in London, England, of Irish parents. He is best known for inventing the steam turbine in 1884. Power stations around the world still use steam turbines based on Parson's designs. In 1897, his boat Turbinia became the first to use a steam turbine to power its propellers.

World energy use

Around 90 per cent of all the energy used comes from fossil fuels, which give out a lot of energy when burned, but release polluting gases into the air. Nuclear power is an alternative to fossil fuels, but produces dangerous radioactive waste. Hydroelectric power is the only form of renewable energy that is used in any significant amount.

Oil 40%

Nuclear power 6%

Hydroelectric power 7%

Gas 22%

Coal 25%

FIND OUT MORE   COAL   ELECTRICITY   FOOD   HEAT AND TEMPERATURE   LIGHT   NUCLEAR POWER   OIL   SOUND   X-RAYS AND THE ELECTROMAGNETIC SPECTRUM

ENGINES AND MOTORS

EVERY MACHINE THAT MOVES OR HAS moving parts needs an engine or a motor to make it work. A motor is a machine that converts some form of energy, such as fuel or electricity, into motion. An engine is a form of motor. Engines and motors, both huge and tiny, are everywhere – in vehicles from motor cycles to airliners and railway locomotives, and in appliances around the house, in industrial machines, and in power stations.

Early engines

The first engines were developed in the middle of the 18th century, and were steam powered. During the 19th century, a new form of engine was developed: the internal combustion engine, which was lighter and had more practical uses than its predecessor.

Early four-cylinder petrol engine

E

Modern engines

Fuel efficiency, plenty of power for its low weight, and little need for maintenance are the hallmarks of the modern car engine. Many engines have electronic components that increase their fuel efficiency further.

Internal combustion engine

Most cars are fitted with internal combustion engines – so-called because they combust, or burn, fuel inside a cylinder. The power this combustion produces is harnessed by pistons and used to power the engine.

Exterior of internal combustion engine

Camshaft

Flywheel and clutch

Water pump pulley

Dipstick

Exhaust manifold

Crank-shaft

Oil filter

Camshaft controls the opening and closing of the valves. There are separate camshafts for fuel inlet and exhaust valves.

Timing belt drives the camshaft.

Spark plug

Combustion chamber is where fuel burns to force the piston down.

Sectioned view of a petrol-fuelled internal combustion engine

Distributor feeds a spark of electricity to each cylinder at the right moment, to start the fuel burning.

Valves let fresh fuel into each cylinder, and spent gases out.

Valve assembly

Exhaust manifold channels waste gases and heat to exhaust pipe.

Cylinder and piston

Oil filter

Sump reservoir for lubricating oil

The pistons slide up and down in the cylinders, providing the driving force that keeps the engine running. The number of cylinders in an engine varies; there are usually at least four, and sometimes more.

Crankshaft turns the wheels via the clutch and gearbox. Connecting rods turn the up-and-down motion of the pistons into the circular motion of the crankshaft.

Lubricating oil is pumped around the engine, continuously covering the moving parts with a thin film of oil that stops them rubbing together and wearing out.

How engines work

This sequence of diagrams shows what happens in one cylinder of a petrol engine while the engine is running. During the sequence, the piston goes down, up, down, and up again. This is called a four-stroke cycle. The cycle is repeated over and over again – up to 50 times a second when the engine is turning at high speed. In an engine with more than one cylinder, the cylinders fire one after the other to provide continuous power.

Fuel and air enter cylinder.

Inlet valve opens.

Piston moves down.

Crankshaft turns.

Valves closed

Piston moves up.

Spark plug

Valves closed

Explosion forces piston down.

Exhuast valve opens.

Piston moves up.

Induction stroke
The piston moves down, and the inlet valve opens. A mixture of fuel and air is sucked into the cylinder.

Compression stroke
The valve closes. The piston moves up again, squeezing the fuel and air into the top of the cylinder.

Power stroke
The spark plug flares and ignites the fuel which explodes, pushing the piston back down.

Exhaust stroke
The piston moves up, pushing waste gases out of the cylinder. The exhaust valve opens to let exhaust gases out.

E

Diesel engine

A diesel engine is a four-stroke engine without spark plugs. The engine's cylinder has a piston, which rises and falls, squashing the fuel-and-air mixture in the cylinder into a tiny space. The mixture gets so hot, it explodes.

Eight-cylinder diesel truck engine

Using diesels

Diesel engines are very fuel-efficient. They are used for driving electricity generators, and in vehicles that need to keep going for long periods without refuelling, such as lorries, taxis, trains, ships, and boats. Many modern cars are also fitted with diesel engines.

Steam engine

The pistons of a steam engine are moved up and down in their cylinders by steam under high pressure. The pistons are connected to rods that turn the wheels. The steam is made outside the cylinders by heating water in a coal-fired boiler, which is why steam engines are called external combustion engines.

Using steam

Until the middle of the 1900s, most railway locomotives and ships were powered by steam engines. Steam also drove many early trucks and buses. The first steam engines were used for pumping flood water out of mines, and to work industrial machines.

Steam leaves train via a funnel.

Steam engine | Firebox | Pipes heat water, which turns into steam. | Steam is fed into the cylinder. | Piston

Solar power

Petroleum and coal are fossil fuels, formed from decayed prehistoric organisms. They are expensive to produce, and create harmful gases when they burn. Solar energy is energy from the Sun. It can be used to heat houses, run air conditioning, and to generate electricity to power lightweight vehicles.

Solar panels

Sunlight can be turned into electricity by solar panels. These are made from many photovoltaic cells. The bigger the area of photovoltaic cells, and the brighter the sunlight, the larger the electric current the solar panel will produce.

Solar-powered car

The heated air turns the turbine blades at rear.

Burning fuel heats the air in the combustion chamber.

Air is sucked in the front.

Gas turbine engines

In a gas turbine, burning fuel makes a stream of hot gas that spins a set of turbine blades very fast. A shaft attached to the turbine drives a compressor that sucks air into the engine so the fuel burns.

Jet engine

High-speed aircraft have a type of turbine called a turbojet or turbofan. The stream of hot air and gases created in the engine turns the turbine, then shoots out of the back of the engine, pushing the aircraft forwards.

Turboshaft engine

Some turbine engines make ship or aircraft propellers spin. The spinning turbine turns a shaft connected to the propeller. Large hovercraft have turboshaft engines to create their air cushion and to drive their propellers. Large helicopters also have turboshaft engines to turn their rotors.

SR.N4 ferry hovercraft

Electric motors

An electric motor produces movement from electricity. Inside it are electromagnets – wire coils that become magnets when an electric current flows through them. The electromagnets are turned on and off in sequence to pull a magnetic shaft around and around. Motors are used in household appliances.

Hairdryer

Blow

The electric motor in a hairdryer turns a fan to blow air that is heated by hot wire coils. A switch adjusts the speed of the motor. The larger the current it allows through, the stronger the magnets become, and the faster the motor spins.

Suck

A vacuum cleaner has a powerful electric motor that turns an air pump. The pump sucks air through the machine, where the dust is removed from it. The motor has to generate a lot of power, so it needs electricity from the mains to drive it.

Turn

Many kitchen gadgets, such as food processors, have an electric motor that moves their working parts. Gears slow the speed of the motor, so the parts turn slowly. The electricity comes either from the mains or from batteries.

Vacuum cleaner

Food processor

James Watt

British engineer James Watt (1736–1819) improved the design of steam engines, and produced the first effective one in 1765. In 1774, he and Matthew Boulton began building steam engines for pumping water from mines. The unit of power, the watt, is named after him.

Timeline

1st century AD Hero of Alexandria, a Greek inventor, makes a novelty toy that is turned by steam.

1698 Englishman Thomas Savery (c.1650–1715) builds the first machine to provide power by using steam.

1815 British engineer George Stephenson (1781–1848) builds the first steam-powered locomotive.

Gears

1876 In Germany, Nikolaus Otto (1832–91) develops the first four-stroke petrol engine. It is a great commercial success.

1892 The diesel engine, used for driving machines, is patented by German engineer Rudolph Diesel.

1894 The *Turbinia*, the first ship with a steam-turbine engine rather than a piston engine, is demonstrated in England.

1937 The first jet engine is demonstrated by the British jet-power pioneer Frank Whittle (b. 1907).

FIND OUT MORE   AIRCRAFT   CARS AND TRUCKS   ELECTRICITY   FORCE AND MOTION   INDUSTRIAL REVOLUTION

ETRUSCANS

A PIRATE PEOPLE OF MYSTERIOUS ORIGIN, the Etruscans dominated the Mediterranean world from the 8th to the 4th centuries BC and formed a league of 12 city-states in what is now modern Tuscany, Italy. Though many of these cities – possibly the first in the area – have been lost over the centuries, superb painting and statuary remain. Etruscan fortunes, based on trade and conquest, started to decline after c.500 BC when the Romans, who had lived under Etruscan rule for a century, began to absorb their former masters into their own expanding empire.

Expansion
From their base in Etruria, the Etruscans' influence spread between the northern Alps and Naples. From 616 BC, the Tarquins, an Etruscan dynasty, ruled Rome itself.

Art

Vivid wall paintings have survived in tombs at the ancient cities of Orvieto, Veii, and Tarquinia – some dating to c.600 BC. Scenes often show dancing, religious observances, or the underworld. Etruscan art was influenced by the Greeks in subject matter and style, but as the Etruscan civilization grew it developed its own bold, colourful, and naturalistic style.

Wall painting, Tomb of the Leopard, Tarquinia

Offerings to the gods

Tomb frescoes often pictured dancing to honour the dead.

Musician

Cities of the dead
Rich Etruscans were buried in underground tombs, some of which were carved from the rock to resemble rooms. These cities of the dead contained frescoes, furniture, and lavish ornaments that tell us much about daily life.

Etruscan rock-cut tombs, Sovana

Bronze sculpture
The best sculptures were made in metal, especially bronze. Early sculptors made copies of imported Syrian or Phoenician objects, but then Greek styles became more popular.

Pan, the liveliest Greek god, in Etruscan style

Statuary
Etruscan craftworkers made statues of terracotta – a brownish-red, unglazed, fine pottery. The sculptors were particularly skilled at creating realistic human faces and figures, such as those at the precinct of Apollo in the city-state of Veii.

Etruscans adopted the letters of the Greek alphabet.

Bronze coin

Language
Though examples of Etruscan writing survive on coins and tablets, the language remains a mystery. All scholars know is that it was the last survivor of those languages spoken before Indo-European (from which all modern European languages descend) took over. The first six numbers were *mach, zal, thu, huth, ci, sa,* but no one can be certain which of them match the numbers 1, 2, 3, 4, 5, 6.

Pirates and traders

For centuries Etruscan ships dominated the area of the Mediterranean called the Tyrrhenian Sea. Feared at first as pirates, they later turned to legitimate and prosperous trade with the Phoenicians, Greeks, and Egyptians. This continued until they were eclipsed by Rome.

Fragment of marble statue

Sheep livers and cloud patterns were thought to reflect the will of the gods.

Relationship with Rome
The last Etruscan king was overthrown in 510 BC, as Rome took over the Etruscan cities one by one. Many practices, such as predicting the future by studying sheep entrails, lived on in the new Roman republic. Leading Roman families were proud of their Etruscan ancestry.

Trade
Etruscan agriculture, industry, and commerce all flourished in the period before the rise of Rome. Mineral deposits in the area were a great advantage to the Etruscans. Wealthy merchants traded metal products, such as jewellery and bronze figurines, as far away as Scandinavia and England.

Flowers

Fruit

Gold earrings

Naturalistic human features

Etruscan jewellers
were especially good goldsmiths, and surviving pieces show originality and artistry. Much gold jewellery was made for trade with Greece.

Semi-precious stones

Gold bead

Necklace

Gold medallion

Gold wreath hair ornament

City people
No one can be sure exactly which 12 walled cities formed the original Etruscan league. Ancient walls still surround modern Tuscan hill-towns, such as Orvieto. The original cities were built haphazardly, and each was dominated by temples.

FIND OUT MORE | ART, HISTORY OF | ARCHITECTURE | GREECE, ANCIENT | ITALY, HISTORY OF | METAL AND METALWORKING | RELIGIONS | ROMAN EMPIRE | SCULPTURE

EUROPE

THE SECOND SMALLEST of all the continents, Europe nevertheless has the third largest population after Asia and Africa. Rich, fertile soils, a variable but hospitable climate, and abundant natural resources have made it easy for people to live in Europe for thousands of years, establishing more than 40 nations and much wealth. Shifting land borders and inhabitants of wide ethnic diversity have caused conflict, but Europe is politically stable and is a major world power.

Physical features

Europe's landscapes range from frozen tundra and coniferous forests in the north to the balmy Mediterranean coast and arid semi-desert of central Spain. The high mountains of the Pyrenees, Alps, Carpathians, and Urals give way to the low-lying North European Plain. Rivers provide communication and transport.

Ural Mountains
The Ural Mountains in Russia separate Europe from Asia. They stretch 2,400 km (1,500 miles) from the Arctic Ocean to the Caspian Sea. The highest mountain is Narodnaya at 1,894 m (6,214 ft).

North European Plain
The vast, rolling North European Plain extends from southern England, across France and Germany, and into Russia as far as the Urals. Rich in coal, oil, natural gas, and fertile farmland, this is Europe's most densely populated area.

Alps
The high Alps dominate western Europe. Stretching 1,500 km (932 miles) from southern France, through Switzerland, Germany, Italy, Austria, and Southeast Europe, this vast arc of mountains separates northern Europe from the warmer south. The highest point is Mont Blanc in France at 4,808 m (15,774 ft).

Cross-section through Europe

Fertile farmland on France's Atlantic coast rises to the plateau of the Massif Central and the Alps at more than 4,000 m (13,125 ft) above sea-level. It then drops down to the Hungarian plain before climbing upwards again to the Carpathians and down into the Black Sea.

Bay of Biscay · Massif Central · Mont Blanc · Alps · Plain of Hungary · Carpathian Mountains · Black Sea

A — Approximately 2,400 km (1,500 miles) from A to B — B

EUROPE FACTS

AREA	10,400,000 sq km (4,000,000 sq miles)
POPULATION	704,900,000
NUMBER OF COUNTRIES	43
BIGGEST COUNTRY	Russian Federation
SMALLEST COUNTRY	Vatican City
HIGHEST POINT	Mt. El'brus 5,633 m (18,481 ft), Caucasus Mountains
LOWEST POINT	Volga Delta 28 m (92 ft) below sea-level, Caspian Sea
LONGEST RIVER	Volga
BIGGEST FRESHWATER LAKE	Lake Ladoga

Climatic zones

Europe's position and varied landscape greatly affect its climate. Apart from the far north where it is always cold, European winters are generally cool, and summers warm or hot. Europe's west coast is milder because of the Gulf Stream, which brings warm waters northwards. Mountains, such as the Alps and Pyrenees, form a natural barrier, protecting the south from the rain and cold winds that blow from the north.

Polar
Coniferous forest
Tundra
Wetland
Deciduous woodland
Scrub
Mountain
Grassland
Desert

Only shallow-rooted plants can survive the cold.

Tundra
The extreme north of Europe lies inside the Arctic Circle and has a polar climate. The vegetation there is tundra – treeless plains where much of the subsoil is permanently frozen ground called permafrost. Only in summer does the topsoil thaw and plants flourish.

Deciduous woodland
Broad-leaved woods and forests are found in many parts of Europe. The trees, which lose their leaves in winter, include the quick-growing birch and ash, and the slower-growing, longer-lived beech, chestnut, maple, plane, and oak. Today, few ancient wild forests survive, and most forest trees have been planted.

Oak leaves and acorns

Beech trees lose their dead leaves in spring when the new buds sprout.

Straight trunks provide timber for making paper, furniture, and boards.

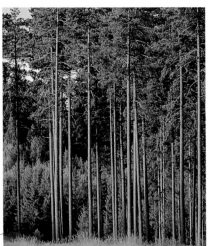

Taiga
In Russian, the word taiga means a marshy forest. The trees in the forests of northern Europe are mainly conifers, such as fir, larch, and pine. They keep their needle-like leaves even during the cold winters when they may be covered with snow for many months.

Grasslands
Large areas of Europe, such as the central *meseta* region of Spain and the steppes of southern Russia and southeastern Ukraine, are covered in vast expanses of grassland. Much of this land is used for grazing animals and growing crops. Drought can be a problem in extreme summer temperatures.

Pine-needles and cone

During the spring the grass is lush and green, but becomes scorched as summer progresses.

Many plants have small leathery leaves so they can conserve water in the summer heat.

Ice, rain, and wind make it impossible for plants to survive on the peaks.

Pyrenees
The Pyrenees form part of a vast arc of comparatively young mountains that stretch almost continuously across southern Europe and join with the Himalayas in Asia. Unlike the ancient mountains in Britain and Scandinavia, their shape is still changing because of plate movements beneath the Earth's crust. Mount Aneto is the highest peak at 3,404 m (12,962 ft).

Garrigue
The warm dry hillsides close to the Mediterranean Sea in countries such as Spain, Greece, and France are covered with thorny, often aromatic plants and low bushes. On limestone soils this vegetation is called *garrigue*, elsewhere it is *maquis*.

People
Most Europeans live in densely populated towns and cities, many of which lie on the fertile North European Plain. Living standards are generally high compared with other parts of the world, and Europeans benefit from plentiful food and good healthcare. Many countries have sizeable ethnic minorities, usually from former colonies. The majority of Europeans are Christian.

Finnish girl   **Greek boy**   **French girl**

Resources
Europe is rich in natural resources. More than half the land is used for farming a wide variety of food crops, from cereals, such as wheat, barley, and oats, to grapes, olives, citrus fruits, and salad vegetables. Europe mines 40 per cent of the world's coal and around 33 per cent of its iron ore. There are also large reserves of oil and natural gas, and lead, zinc, and other metals. Many rivers supply hydroelectric power.

Grapes

Wheat

Coal

FIND OUT MORE   CLIMATE   CONTINENTS   EUROPE, HISTORY OF   EUROPEAN WILDLIFE   FARMING   FORESTS   MOUNTAINS AND VALLEYS   ROCKS AND MINERALS   TREES   TUNDRA

EUROPE, HISTORY OF

EUROPE HAS PLAYED a much more important role in world history than its small population or size would suggest. The Greeks and Romans colonized large parts of North Africa and western Asia, and from the 15th century onwards, European nations established trading empires that spanned the globe. The Industrial Revolution of the 18th century gave Europe an economic strength which allowed it to dominate world trade, and both World Wars began in Europe. Since 1945, Europe's global influence has declined, as wealth and military power has shifted to North America and Asia.

Prehistoric Europe
The first settlers in Europe were primitive hunters who moved around in search of food. By about 5000 BC, people learned to farm and settled in villages. Bronze-working, and later iron-working, spread across the continent.

Prehistoric "Venus" figurine from Lespugue, France

Civilizations of Europe

After 900 BC, four civilizations made their successive mark on Europe. The first were the Greeks, who created powerful city states. They were followed a century later by the Etruscans in Italy. By 200 BC the Celts had settled across Europe. Finally the vast and powerful Roman Empire spanned the continent, reaching its height in AD 117.

Greek Europe
The independent city states of ancient Greece got most of their wealth from trade. Their merchants sailed around the Mediterranean, and founded colonies from Spain to the Black Sea. The most powerful Greek cities were Athens and Sparta.

Ionic-style capital from ancient Greek temple

Christian Europe

In the 4th century, Christianity became the official religion of the Roman empire, and over the next 700 years the faith spread throughout Europe. With the break-up of the Roman empire by 476 and the lack of any strong political force after then, Christianity became the single unifying force across the continent and the church gained great power.

Papal ring

Papacy
As head of the Roman Catholic Church, the popes had enormous spiritual power. Vast landholdings also gave the popes much political power, which led to many conflicts between the papacy and the leading rulers of Europe.

East and west
Attempts by the pope in Rome to establish his jurisdiction over the entire Christian Church were resisted by the Orthodox Churches of eastern Europe, centred around the ancient city of Constantinople. In 1054, this schism (split) became final, leading to a religious division in Christian Europe that survives to this day.

Orthodox icon of the Archangel Gabriel

College built around a central quadrangle

Merton College, one of Oxford's earliest colleges

Growth of education
The Church dominated education, at first through the monasteries and then the universities. The first university in Europe, specializing in medicine, was established at Salerno in southern Italy in the 9th century; others, such as Bologna, Paris, and Oxford, followed later.

Latin inscription from a Roman tomb

Roman Europe
From its foundation in c.753 BC, the city of Rome gradually expanded its power until, by the first century AD, it controlled most of Europe. The Romans gave Europe a network of roads, a common language (Latin), and a legal system, all of which survived long after the fall of the empire in the 5th century.

Nation state

By the 16th century, centralized national governments had emerged right across Europe, from Spain in the west to Russia in the east. The Holy Roman Empire had began to break up, and in countries such as England power was concentrated in the hands of the monarch who ruled with the support of a parliament, composed of members of the aristocracy and church.

The royal coat of arms of Philip II of Spain decorates the cover of one of his books.

Religious wars
The creation of new, Protestant Churches in the 16th century divided western Europe. Roman Catholic and Protestant states fought for supremacy in a series of bitter wars which lasted until the middle of the next century.

Henry IV of France was raised Protestant, but later converted to Catholicism.

Basilica in Goa, India

Overseas empires
In the 15th century, European nations built up empires. Spain and Portugal colonized Central and South America; Britain, France, and the Netherlands colonized North America and the Far East.

World imperialism

The Industrial Revolution began in Britain in the mid-1700s, and it transformed world politics and economics. Within a century, European nations were strong and rich enough to set up colonies all around the world. Only the United States of America was able to resist European influence.

Diamonds

Hemp

Cotton

Global economy

During the 19th century, European steamships took raw materials from their colonies to factories in Europe, and shipped out finished goods to markets abroad. The huge industrial cities of Europe gained vast wealth, but at the expense of poor producers in African and Asian colonies.

Nationalism

During the 19th century, many of the peoples of Europe struggled to obtain their freedom from outside rulers. In one year, 1848, Italians, Germans, Hungarians, Poles, Irish, and others fought for independence or fairer forms of government.

Fighting at Catánia, Italy, 1848

E

World wars

Austrian officer's hat

Scottish private's cap

Soldiers' hats, 1914

Twice in the 20th century, European conflicts led to war on every continent. In 1914, national rivalries resulted in a four-year war that cost 22 million lives. Germany was defeated and dissatisfied with the peace treaty. Again, war broke out in 1939. By the end of that war, in 1945, Europe was exhausted. Two superpowers, the USA and the Soviet Union, now dominated international affairs.

End of empires

World War I led to the defeat of four great European empires – Germany, Austro-Hungary, Russia, and Turkey – and weakened both Britain and France. After World War II, Europe's overseas colonies fought successfully for independence, with only France retaining sizeable overseas possessions.

The double-headed eagle symbol of Germany

Flag of Nazi Germany

Rival ideologies

Communism was established in Russia after 1917 and in Eastern Europe after 1945, while Fascism and Nazism took hold in Italy, Germany, and Spain in the years up to 1945. By 1990, parliamentary democracy, at first weak in Europe, was the dominant form of government.

Iron Curtain

After World War II, Russian troops occupied much of Eastern Europe. A clear border, known as the Iron Curtain, emerged between the Russian-dominated east and American-dominated west. The border split Germany into two countries.

Checkpoint between two sectors of the city of Berlin

Modern Europe

After World War II, French and German politicians worked together to overcome their old hostilities. Economic collaboration between the two countries developed into a formal European Union that grew to include many other western European countries. With the collapse of communism and the rise of market economies in Eastern Europe, many former communist countries lined up to join the EU.

Collapse of Communism

During the late 1980s, Russia withdrew its military and economic support from its communist allies in Eastern Europe. Popular protests then overthrew communism in every East European nation by 1990, but by the late 1990s, there was deep unrest in many East European countries.

Revolution on the streets of Romania

Willy Brandt

Willy Brandt (1913–92) was born in Lübeck, Germany, but lived in Norway during World War II, where he was active in the Resistance. As Chancellor of West Germany from 1969–74, Brandt worked to improve east-west relations and made treaties with Poland and the USSR. He was awarded the 1971 Nobel Peace Prize.

Timeline

Bronze statue of Roman legionary

C.1250 BC Mycenaean culture flourishes in Greece.

C.900 BC Greek city-states gain power.

C.753 BC Rome is founded.

C.200 BC Celts spread across Europe.

AD 117 Roman Empire is at its height.

1054 Christian Church splits into Orthodox east and Roman Catholic west.

1500s European nations use their navigation skills to explore and colonize large parts of the globe.

1914–18 World War I.

1939–45 World War II.

Mid-1700s Industrial Revolution begins to transform the European economy.

1871 The map of Europe is transformed as Germany and Italy become unified nations.

Flag of European Union

1940s–80s Europe gives up most of its colonies.

1957 EEC is set up.

1989–91 Communism falls.

1994 Outbreak of war in Southeast Europe.

2001 Euro is launched.

FIND OUT MORE
CELTS COLD WAR EMPIRES GOVERNMENTS AND POLITICS GREECE, ANCIENT HOLY ROMAN EMPIRE MEDIEVAL EUROPE ROMAN EMPIRE WORLD WAR I WORLD WAR II

EUROPE, CENTRAL

LYING AT THE HEART of Europe on the North European Plain, central Europe consists of four countries: Poland, the Czech Republic, Slovakia, and Hungary. With poor defenses because of the flat terrain, this historically troubled region has often been invaded by neighbouring powers and its country borders redrawn. At one time or another, French, Germans, and Russians have all dominated the area. After World War II (1939–45), the countries of central Europe became communist states closely tied to the former Soviet Union. Since their independence in the late 1980s, many have struggled to compete on the world market.

Roman Catholicism

In spite of repeated invasions of the area, and half a century of anti-religious communist rule, Roman Catholicism remains the dominant religion of central Europe. Throughout the region, colourful processions celebrate saints' days and other religious festivals.

Religious procession, Kraków, Poland

Physical features

Most of central Europe lies on the vast North European Plain and is largely flat, rolling farmland, broken by the low Sudeten and Carpathian Mountains in the south. In the north, rivers flow into the Baltic; in the south, they flow into the Danube on its way to the Black Sea.

Tatra Mountains
The Tatra Mountains between Poland and Slovakia are the highest part of the Carpathian Range. Their breathtaking scenery makes them popular with walkers in summer, and in winter the snow-covered peaks attract skiers.

Forests
Poland's Bialowieza National Park is the largest area of woodland in northern Europe. Some woods have survived for thousands of years, but acid rain now threatens them. One quarter of central Europe is forested.

Danube River
The Danube is 1,775 miles (2,857 km) long and links Germany and the Rhine River to the Black Sea. It is Europe's greatest waterway and is used for carrying freight and generating hydroelectric power in Slovakia.

Regional climate
Central Europe has a temperate climate with hot summers and cold winters. Winters tend to be milder in the south, except in the Carpathian Mountains and other upland areas where heavy snow falls. The summer months are often the wettest.

20°C (68°F)   -2°C (13°F)

553 mm (22 in)

Poland

This country of medieval towns and scattered farms and villages has a history of invasion and occupation by foreign powers. From 1945 to 1989, Poland was a communist state. Since the collapse of communism, however, Poland has been experiencing massive economic, social, and political change. Poland has a strong strategic position between eastern and western Europe and joined NATO in 1999.

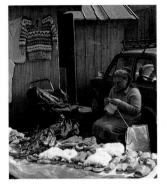

People
Like the neighbouring Czechs and Slovaks, Poles originate from the Slavic peoples of Europe. Poland has few ethnic minorities, and more than 95 per cent of the people are Polish-speaking Roman Catholics. Many Poles have a traditional way of life; local folk arts and crafts flourish. These include wood carving and colourful embroidery.

POLAND FACTS

CAPITAL CITY	Warsaw
AREA	312,680 sq km (120,720 sq miles)
POPULATION	38,800,000
DENSITY	127 per sq km (330 per sq mile)
MAIN LANGUAGE	Polish
MAJOR RELIGION	Christian
CURRENCY	Zloty
LIFE EXPECTANCY	73 years
PEOPLE PER DOCTOR	435
GOVERNMENT	Multiparty democracy
ADULT LITERACY	99%

Warsaw
Poland's capital since the 1500s, Warsaw was almost completely destroyed during World War II (1939–45). Working from original plans, paintings, and photographs, the Poles have rebuilt the city, restoring its ancient landmarks and treasured buildings. Today, the reconstructed buildings line wide streets and squares.

Old Town Square

Beet

Potato

Root crops
Poland is a major producer of rye, and also of root crops such as potatoes, sugar beets, and beets. Nearly half the land is used to grow crops or raise livestock, particularly pigs. State farms account for about 10 per cent of this land. Most privately owned farms are small, producing some crops to sell, and the rest to feed farmers' families. Farming employs a quarter of Poland's work-force.

Sugar beet

Wheat
Poland's leading grain crop is wheat, although yields are poor. Two-thirds of the wheat is fed to livestock, some, with potatoes, is used to distil vodka, and with the rest, farmers bake bread.

Industry
About one-fifth of Poland's labour force works in industry, but production in the huge old Soviet-style factories is inefficient. In order to compete on the free market, the government is slowly privatizing industry. Shipbuilding is an important industry on the Baltic Coast, and the Gdansk shipyard is one of several. Poland has a thriving iron and steel industry, and big reserves of coal, lignite (brown coal), copper, lead, silver, and zinc.

Czech Republic

The Czech Republic consists of the two ancient states of Bohemia and Moravia, which once formed part of the Holy Roman Empire. From 1918, it was part of Czechoslovakia and only emerged as an independent country in 1993, when Czechoslovakia was partitioned. The Czech Republic is central Europe's most industrialized nation, and manufacturing employs 40 per cent of its work-force.

Farming
Only five per cent of the Czech work-force is employed in farming. Much of the land is controlled by large farms owned by the state or cooperatives. Czech farms have some of the highest grain yields in central Europe, but most is fed to livestock because the Republic specializes in meat and milk production.

CZECH REPUBLIC FACTS

CAPITAL CITY	Prague
AREA	78,370 sq km (30,260 sq miles)
POPULATION	10,200,215
DENSITY	129 per sq km (335 per sq mile)
MAIN LANGUAGE	Czech
MAJOR RELIGION	Christian
CURRENCY	Czech koruna
LIFE EXPECTANCY	76 years
PEOPLE PER DOCTOR	333
GOVERNMENT	Multiparty democracy
ADULT LITERACY	99%

Prague
One of the most beautiful capital cities in Europe, Prague has remained virtually unchanged for centuries. Today, it plays host to an increasing number of visitors who come for both business and pleasure. However, air pollution caused by nearby factories poses a major problem.

St. Nicholas's Church

Bohemian glass
Since the 1300s, the Bohemians of the south have made beautifully decorated glass from the fine sands found in this region. Bohemian glass is prized for its high quality, elegance, and delicacy.

Beer
Czech beers are popular all over the world, and Budweiser, Budvar, and Pilsner are household names. Brewing traditions go back hundreds of years.

Industry
The break-up of the communist regime led to the privatization of many Czech companies. However, some of the very large factories, such as the Skoda works at Plzen, remain under state control. Czech factories are able to produce about 200,000 cars a year. As well as cars, Skoda produces locomotives, machine tools, and weapons. The Czechs also produce iron and steel, machinery, and transport equipment, although there is a trend to move away from heavy industry into consumer goods such as textiles.

Slovakia

Slovakia was the rural and poorer half of Czechoslovakia, and after its independence in 1993, the country suffered economically. Much of the land is mountainous and forested. About half is used for crops or grazing, but industry now employs a large number of workers. Most people are Slovaks, speaking their own language, but there are also some Roma and Czechs, as well as a nine per cent Hungarian minority.

Bratislava

From 1536 to 1784, Bratislava was the capital of Hungary. Now it is the capital of an independent Slovakia. The city was founded in the 10th century, and has had a university since 1467. The new parliament buildings were once the home of an archbishop. Bratislava is a Danube river port and a rail centre. Its factories make chemicals and engineering goods.

Rural life

The Slovakian countryside is a mixture of mountain villages, ancient walled towns, and castles. There are still many large state-run farms, but about 20 per cent of the land is farmed by tiny, family-run concerns. The main crops are potatoes, sugar beet, and grains. Rural life is hard, and poverty is common, driving increasing numbers of young people to towns in search of work.

SLOVAKIA FACTS

CAPITAL CITY Bratislava

AREA 49,500 sq km (19,100 sq miles)

POPULATION 5,400,000

MAIN LANGUAGE Slovak

MAJOR RELIGION Christian

CURRENCY Koruna

Folklore

Folk traditions are strong in Slovakia, where puppet shows are popular. The former Czechoslovakia is acknowledged as the original home of European puppetry. The Slovakian people enjoy folk festivals where they can dress in regional costumes and sing and dance to traditional music.

Wooden puppet

Hungary

Hungary was formed about a thousand years ago by the Magyars, an ethnic group from Russia that makes up 90 per cent of today's population. Hungary was communist from 1945 until 1990, and since then its industries have had to compete on the world market. The country's skilled scientists and engineers have succeeded in attracting foreign investment.

Thermal springs

Hungary has hundreds of hot thermal springs; their warm mineral waters are said to have medicinal properties. The country has more than 150 spring baths, which are open to the public.

HUNGARY FACTS

CAPITAL CITY Budapest

AREA 93,030 sq km (35,919 sq miles)

POPULATION 10,000,000

DENSITY 108 per sq km (280 per sq mile)

MAIN LANGUAGE Hungarian (Magyar)

MAJOR RELIGION Christian

CURRENCY Forint

LIFE EXPECTANCY 71 years

PEOPLE PER DOCTOR 286

GOVERNMENT Multiparty democracy

ADULT LITERACY 99%

Wine

Hungary is a world-class wine producer and exports a wide range of high-quality red and white wines. The best known Hungarian wine is Tokay, pronounced tok-eye. It is a sweet, rich, golden wine, widely believed to be healthful. Another well-known Hungarian wine is Bull's Blood, so-called for its dark blood-red colour.

Paprika

Hungarians grow more than 40 per cent of the world's paprika, a sweet, bright-red pepper used in cooking. One town, Kalocsa in southern Hungary, even has a museum devoted entirely to this spice. Paprika originally came from Central America. Hungarian farmers also grow rye, corn, wheat, barley, sugar beets, and potatoes, as well as grapes, olives, and figs. Sunflowers are grown for their oil.

Goulash

Hungary's most famous dish is goulash, a stew of beef with vegetables, flavoured and coloured with paprika. A pork version is called *pörkölt*. Other traditional dishes with paprika include bacon and potato casserole, and chicken paprikash.

Goulash is a traditional Hungarian stew.

Budapest

Straddling the Danube, Budapest is two cities in one – Buda on the hilly right bank, and Pest on the low-lying left bank. Buda was the old royal capital of Hungary, and has fine old buildings and the remains of a Roman town. Pest is the country's administrative and industrial centre.

The Parliament buildings in Pest, viewed from Buda

Horse breeding

Hungary has a long tradition of horse breeding, located at the great stud farms at Mezöhegyes and Bábolna. The best-known Hungarian breeds are the Nonius and Furioso, which were developed at Mezöhegyes, and the Shagya Arab at Bábolna. Today, these stud farms develop horses for taking part in shows.

Hungary's oldest stud farm at Mezöhegyes

 FIND OUT MORE   CHRISTIANITY   EMPIRES   EUROPE   EUROPE, HISTORY OF   FARMING   GOVERNMENTS AND POLITICS   HOLY ROMAN EMPIRE   HORSES   SOVIET UNION

EUROPEAN UNION

FIFTEEN COUNTRIES have joined together to form the European Union (EU). But Europe was not always at peace. Between 1870 and 1945, France and Germany were at war three times. Determined to ensure their two countries never fought each other again, the French and Germans decided to link their coal and steel industries so their nations would be forced to work together. The creation of the European Coal and Steel Community (ECSC) in 1951 led to today's European Union.

The euro
On 1 January 2002, a single currency, the euro, was fully launched in 12 countries of the European Union (EU). The notes and coins of this new currency replaced the national currencies of those nations. The only EU countries to stay out of the monetary union were Britain, Denmark, and Sweden.

E

Uniting Europe
In 1957, the ECSC evolved into the wider European Economic Community (EEC). Ten years later this became the European Community (EC). In 1991, EC leaders signed the Maastricht Treaty, which started Europe towards full economic and monetary union. When the treaty came into force in 1993, the EC became the European Union (EU).

The growing union
The European Union has 15 members. A further 13 states have applied for membership, with more considering joining. Trade and cooperation agreements are already in place between the EU and many applicants. Switzerland has close trade links with the EU, but a national referendum in 2001 rejected joining.

1 Netherlands
2 Belgium
3 Luxembourg
4 Slovenia

More countries in central and eastern Europe are intending to apply.

Date of joining
- [ ] 1957
- [ ] 1973
- [ ] 1981
- [ ] 1986
- [ ] 1995
- [ ] Membership applications

Members of the EU, 2001

Structure of the EU
The EU has three main institutions: the Commission, based in Brussels, Belgium, is the civil service which runs the EU; the Parliament, in Strasbourg, France, and Brussels, provides control over the EU; the European Court of Justice, in Luxembourg, makes sure EU laws are applied properly.

European Parliament
Every five years, adults throughout the EU go to the polls to elect 626 Members of the European Parliament (MEPs) to represent their interests. Although it does not have the same powers as a national parliament, the European Parliament advises the Commission and supervises its work and annual budget.

What the EU does
The European Union has many different roles covering economic, financial, commercial, political, industrial, agricultural, social, and cultural matters. Its two main achievements have been to establish free trade between the member states by abolishing customs duties, and to set up a common agricultural and fisheries policy.

The EU has sponsored a common European passport.

EU aid
The EU provides subsidies to the less well-off regions of Europe, for projects such as developing new industries. Much EU aid is targeted towards improving transport links in Europe, such as building roads and railways, so all regions can share in the benefits of the single market.

Jean Monnet
Jean Monnet (1888–1979) was a French economist who convinced the French foreign minister, Robert Schuman (1886–1963), that the only way to avoid another war between France and Germany was to integrate their coal and steel industries. The ECSC was set up with Monnet as its first president. His vision led directly to the development of today's EU.

Agricultural policy
In order to guarantee food supplies and increase agricultural productivity, the EU runs a very complex Common Agricultural Policy (CAP). This has established free movement of farm produce throughout the EU.

Social policy
The EU tries to improve employment for unemployed workers and young people by investing in education and training in deprived regions. It has also established a common Social Chapter of Workers' Rights.

Timeline
1951 European Coal and Steel Community (ECSC) is set up.

1957 The ECSC nations sign the Treaty of Rome, setting up the European Economic Community (EEC); a separate treaty sets up the European Atomic Energy Community (Euratom).

1967 ECSC, EEC, and Euratom merge to form the European Community (EC).

1979 European Monetary System set up to link currencies.

1991 Maastricht Treaty sets out timetable for full economic union.

1993 EC becomes the European Union (EU).

2002 The euro replaces existing currencies in 12 EU countries.

FIND OUT MORE — EUROPE, HISTORY OF · FARMING · FISHING INDUSTRY · FOOD · MONEY · TRADE AND INDUSTRY · WORLD WAR II

EUROPEAN WILDLIFE

EUROPE IS A landmass that contains many different habitats, ranging from the Arctic tundra, through broad-leaved forests, and mountainous areas, to dry, hot regions around the Mediterranean. Only deserts and tropical forests are missing from the list. European wildlife is not as rich as it once was; human intervention in the form of agriculture and forest clearance, as well as the sheer size of the human population, has diminished the number of plants and animals. Yet in undisturbed forests and wetlands, a large diversity of wildlife remains.

Broad-leaved woodland wildlife

Broad-leaved woodlands extend across Europe. The trees within them, such as oaks and sycamores, are broad-leaved, or deciduous, trees, which means they lose their leaves in winter. In spring and summer, when the leaves reappear and plants bloom, woodlands support many insects, birds, and mammals, such as squirrels and mice.

Dappled coats help to camouflage deer as they graze on grass.

Once acorns have fallen to the ground, they provide a nutritious meal for birds, squirrels, and mice.

Oak tree
Commonly found in broad-leaved woodlands, oaks provide homes and food for many animals. Insects, for example, feed on leaves and other parts of the tree, while they themselves are food for larger animals, such as birds. Acorns, the fruits of the oak, appear in late summer.

Female nut weevil drilling into acorn with her mouthparts.

Rostrum

Red fox
Red foxes live on their own or in small family groups in underground dens. They are most active at night when they hunt for rabbits, rodents, and worms. They may also eat fish and fruit.

Females flick their large, bushy tails to warn cubs of danger.

Fallow deer
Woodland provides cover and food for fallow deer. Females and young live in small herds. Males have antlers, and are solitary or live in small groups. Males and females meet during the mating season in the autumn.

Nut weevil
This beetle lives on oak trees, feeding on buds and leaves. It has a snout-like rostrum, at the end of which are its jaws. In late summer, the female makes holes in the oak's acorns. In each hole she deposits an egg. The larva that hatches from the egg feeds on the acorn.

Wetland wildlife

Europe's wetlands are rich in wildlife. Reeds, bulrushes, and marsh plants provide food and shelter for wetland animals, such as voles and otters. Insects and other invertebrates are a food source for fish and frogs, which themselves are eaten by many water birds.

Bulrushes provide nesting sites for birds.

Flower head

Bulrushes
These tall grass-like plants grow at the fringes of lakes and ponds. Their roots are often in wet soil or submerged in water, while their stems and leaves extend above the water. Bulrushes have dark, compact, cylindrical flower heads.

European kingfisher
This small bird hunts for fish and other water animals from a perch along the banks of streams and lakes. Once prey is spotted, the kingfisher plunges into the water, grabs it with its long, pointed beak, and returns to the perch to eat its meal.

European otter
Otters are strong swimmers, adapted for rapid movement in water. An otter's body is long and streamlined, its dense, glossy fur is water-repellent, and it has webbed feet. Otters hunt underwater, catching prey such as fish, water birds, and frogs. They are equally agile on land, and catch water voles and other animals that live on riverbanks.

Water vole
Water voles are good swimmers. They build tunnels in banks next to lakes and slow-moving rivers. These tunnels have chambers for food storage and nesting, and entrances that open above and below the waterline.

Edible frog
Edible frogs live in marshes and lakes, sometimes emerging at night to feed on land. They catch insects with their long, sticky tongues. Larger prey, such as newts and small fish, are caught in the jaws and pushed into the mouth with the feet.

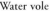
Water voles feed on plants, roots, and bulbs.

E

Alpine chough
In summer, choughs live in flocks above the tree line. They walk over rocky ground, probing under vegetation and in crevices for insects and snails. They glide on air currents, coping easily with the strong gusts of wind found at high altitude.

Mountain wildlife
The Alps and the Pyrenees are the major mountains of Europe. Vegetation changes with increasing altitude; each zone has its characteristic wildlife. Animals tend to move to lower altitudes during the cold winter months when food becomes scarce.

Mouflon
The mouflon is a wild sheep that lives in remote, mountainous regions. It feeds on grasses and other plants during the day, and rests at night. The mouflon is surefooted, moving easily over rough terrain. Males bang their heads and horns together when competing for mates.

Alpine meadow
Alpine meadows are found above the tree line and below the snow line. In summer, they are covered in a blanket of bright flowers and dwarf shrubs. These provide food for hordes of insects, which in turn are eaten by birds. Meadow vegetation is also eaten by grazing animals.

Bears eat rodents, deer, insects, salmon, carrion, tubers, and berries.

Cubs are born in dens in mid-winter.

Brown bear
These large bears live in remote forested areas of mountains and as far north as the tundra. They have no natural enemies apart from humans. In winter, brown bears usually retire to a den for a period of dormancy.

Coniferous forest wildlife
Coniferous forests of evergreen trees, such as spruce and pine, extend across northern Europe. They are dense and dark, with few ground plants. Summers are warm; winters are cold, with heavy snow falls. Many animals eat the leaves and seeds of conifers.

Norway spruce
Norway spruces have reddish trunks, dark green crowns, and grow up to 55 m (180 ft) in height. These seeds of the spruce, as well as the bark, buds, and needle-like leaves, provide food for forest animals.

Triangular outline prevents snow accumulating and snapping branches.

Pine marten
Pine martens hunt in the morning and evening, using their excellent hearing and sight to locate birds, squirrels, rabbits, and rats.

Pine martens climb trees, resting by day in tree hollows.

Common crossbill
The common or red crossbill lives in the forest canopy and is rarely seen on the ground, except when it lands to drink. Its crossed beak provides the bird with a strong "tool" for prising open the scales of pine and spruce cones. It then uses its tongue to extract the seeds.

Upper and lower parts of bill are crossed.

Arctic hare
The arctic hare lives in the coniferous forests and tundra of the far North. Its fur turns from brown in summer to white in winter, to conceal it from predators such as foxes.

Bright yellow flowers are strongly scented.

Mediterranean wildlife
The Mediterranean region of Europe has hot, dry summers, and milder and wetter winters. Aromatic plants, such as thyme, and trees such as cedar grow here. Many animals survive by sheltering in midday heat; others migrate.

Black, bristly feathers give it its other name of bearded vulture.

Lammergeier
The lammergeier lives in mountainous areas. It eats carrion, including the bones, which it drops on to rocks from a height to smash them and expose the soft marrow.

Short antenna

Spanish festoon butterfly
This brightly patterned butterfly is found on the coasts of Spain, France, and Portugal. It can be seen from late winter, when temperatures start to rise, until early summer, when mating is complete.

Zig-zag wing pattern

Ear tufts are used to signal to other lynxes.

Common lizard
A common sight in southern Europe during the summer, this lizard sunbathes in the morning to increase its body temperature, making it more active when searching for insects.

Broom
This shrub can survive the hot, dry conditions of the Mediterranean summer. The seed pods produced by the flowers dry in the sun, and split open to scatter the tiny seeds.

Spanish lynx
This cat, once found all over Spain, is now restricted to the pine forests, scrub, and sand dunes of the Coto Doñana National Park in southwest Spain. Lynx feed on rabbits and hares, deer fawns, and ducks.

FIND OUT MORE   BIRDS OF PREY   FORESTS   LAKE AND RIVER WILDLIFE   MARSH AND SWAMP WILDLIFE

EVOLUTION

THE TERM EVOLUTION refers to the theory that existing animals and plants have evolved, or developed, through a process of continual change from previous life forms. Some scientists argue that by looking at fossil evidence we can find out more about the past. Fossils have shown that primitive life forms appeared more than 3.8 billion years ago, and that vertebrates existed at least 500 million years ago. Over generations, better-adapted organisms have developed.

How a species evolves

An organism may undergo change due to a number of processes, such as natural selection and adaptation, induced by the environment in which it lives. For example, selection may have promoted larger and faster horses adapted for living on open grassy plains. In some cases, a subspecies can change so much that it becomes very different from the rest of its species.

Hyracotherium, the first in a long line of horses, appeared approximately 55 million years ago.

Four-toed hoof

Equus (modern horse) evolved around 1.64 million years ago. It originated as a plains grazer, and has a single toe forming a hoof.

One-toed hoof

Long limbs developed for speed.

The third toe became larger until the side toes eventually disappeared.

Three-toed Hipparion appeared around 15 million years ago.

Third toe

Foot of early four-toed *Hyracotherium*

Foot of three-toed *Hipparion*

Hoof of modern horse, *Equus*

Natural selection

The theory of natural selection suggests that environmental factors may favour some members of a species over others, enabling the fittest to survive. Experiments with the carnivorous plant, sundew, backed this theory. Plants that were fed meat produced more flowers and seeds than plants which were not.

Plant fed meat produces flowers.

Unfed plant has fewer flowers.

Heredity

Heredity studies how characteristics of certain individuals are passed on from one generation to the next. This process often involves the expression of a parent's dominant gene, which may mask the effect of the recessive gene.

Russian hamsters

Recessive albino gene

Dominant grey gene

Variation

Variation refers to the differences within a species. Certain variations, such as shell colour, may give certain individuals advantages over others. These individuals will have a greater chance of surviving and reproducing.

Banded snails

Shell colours allow snail to adapt to local habitat.

Mutations

Occasionally during reproduction, the process of replicating genetic material (DNA) goes wrong and produces an accidental mutation. Normally, these mutants do not live but some survive as an important source of variation on which selection operates.

Fuller's mutant teasel has curved spines, allowing easier seed dispersal.

Teasel plant

Sexual selection

Some animals choose their mates by means of sexual selection. A male, may have elaborate features, such as bright feathers, to attract a mate. Characteristics such as these, which may be beneficial to the species, are passed to the next generation.

Peacock

Adaptation

The process of adaptation occurs when an organism evolves in a certain way to make it better suited to its environment. Some people believe that this can lead to a new species, and that an animal or a plant will adapt to its surroundings so that it has a better chance of survival.

Plant-feeding finch

Insect-feeding finch

Darwin's finches

While visiting the Galápagos Islands, English naturalist Charles Darwin (1809–82) noticed the variety of finches living there. Because they resembled finches of mainland South America, he argued that each finch species had evolved a differently shaped beak to meet the needs of its particular diet.

Monarch butterfly

Viceroy butterfly

Mimicry in butterflies

Mimicry is a form of adaptation where one species has developed a resemblance to another as a means of protection. Birds find the monarch butterfly distasteful, but also avoid the similarly coloured viceroy, even though it is palatable.

Intermediates

Intermediates are thought to be the "halfway" species that should exist if one group of organism has evolved from another. In 1861, discovery of the earliest fossil bird, *Archaeopteryx*, provided important support for this theory. The fossil clearly combines the reptile characteristics of a dinosaur in its skeleton, but at the same time has the uniquely bird-like feature of feathers.

Lungfish

Living intermediates
The lungfish can breathe oxygen directly from air and has paired fleshy fins for swimming. Lungfish arose about 380 million years ago when animals first stepped on land; it is thought that the first land-going tetrapods (four-footed animals) evolved from lungfish-like intermediates.

Human impact

For centuries humans have had an impact on animal and plant habitats. For example, some animals have had to adapt to new environments created by human settlement and industry. Also, by selective breeding, scientists have altered the genetic make-up of some plants and animals to create superior crops and meat for human consumption. Fruits, such as grapes and oranges, have been bred so that they no longer have seeds and are therefore easier to digest.

Tomatoes are bred to have a longer shelf life.

Seedless orange

Seedless grape

Artificial selection
Scientists can manipulate the genetic make-up of plants and animals by artificially selecting particular strains according to need. For instance, genetically altered products, such as tomatoes with enhanced flavour, are already on sale. Dog breeders, too, can alter the temperament, shape, size, and colour of dogs. The ability to alter genetic make-up raises many ethical questions.

Shar pei dog

Impact by pollution
It was discovered that during the Industrial Revolution, light coloured peppered moths, previously camouflaged from bird predators, became vulnerable on soot blackened trees. However, darker coloured peppered moths did survive and went on to breed more dark moths.

Peppered moths

Evidence

Much of the evidence for evolution is based on fossils. These show how life originated from simple forms in the sea and then evolved to occupy land, freshwater, and air. Study of the common characteristics of organisms suggest how they could be inter-related. Also, investigations into genetics and its molecular basis have led to a greater understanding of how evolution works.

Fossil evidence
Fossils of animals and plants show that there have been significant changes throughout geological time. Fossils show how the first land living plants appeared some 440 million years ago, but were not sufficiently well established to form forests until about 320 million years ago.

Fossil of fern plant

Molecular evidence
Often, if two new species evolve from a common ancestor, their DNA begins to change. For example, both the red and grey squirrel feed on acorns. However, the red squirrel lacks the digestive enzyme which breaks down chemicals in the acorn. This has led to a decline of red squirrels in the British Isles.

Grey squirrel population outnumbers that of the red squirrel in Britain

Creation theories
Evolutionists believe that life on Earth has evolved progressively over thousands of millions of years, originally from non-living materials. However, some people argue that all life forms on the Earth were created by design, in or close to the form in which they exist today. Although creationists as a group reject the theory of evolution, many accept that life forms on Earth can change. They believe that God created various kinds of creatures that have diversified within each kind until the present day.

19th-century caricature of Charles Darwin

Armadillo forelimb

The sturdy armadillo limb is adapted for digging.

Upper arm

Chimpanzee's arm

The chimpanzee's arm is very similar to the basic vertebrate bone pattern.

Wrist bone

Finger digits

In bats, the hand and finger bones developed into supports for the membranes of the wing.

Bones of bat's wing

Comparative anatomy
French naturalist Georges Cuvier (1769–1832) demonstrated that the function of the vertebrate skeleton reflects the way in which the animal lived. Since vertebrates have a common ancestry, the structure of the skeleton has a similar plan. Armadillo limb bones may be directly compared with the arm bones of a chimpanzee, and those of a bat's wing.

Jean Baptiste de Lamarck
French naturalist Jean Baptiste de Lamarck (1744–1829) proposed a theory of evolution that broke the prevailing idea of the fixity of species. He claimed that by striving to fit into their natural surroundings, organisms changed in bodily form, and that such transformations were passed on to their offspring. According to his theory the giraffe developed a long neck by stretching to eat leaves from trees.

FIND OUT MORE · ANIMALS · BIG BANG · DARWIN, CHARLES · DINOSAURS · FOSSILS · GENETICS · HUMAN EVOLUTION · PREHISTORIC LIFE · PREHISTORIC PEOPLE

EXPLORATION

SINCE THE EARLIEST TIMES, people have been curious about the world in which they live. For more than 3,000 years, explorers have charted most of Earth's surface by land and sea. Often these brave pioneers went out into the unknown inspired by more than mere curiosity. Sometimes they went in search of riches, or to find new and less overcrowded places to live, or in a quest for scientific knowledge. In the course of mapping the world, explorers quashed many myths while bringing back true stories that could seem even stranger than fiction.

Ancient exploration

In ancient times, peoples such as the Phoenicians explored new regions in their quest for trading partners. The Greeks and Romans also discovered more about the world as their empires expanded. People began to read about far-flung places in books by classical geographers such as Strabo (c.63 BC–c.AD 21).

Xuan Zang

The Buddhist monk Xuan Zang (602–664) was one of the greatest travellers of ancient China. In 629 he set off alone on the famed Silk Road to visit India, Nepal, Sri Lanka, and Pakistan, making friends for China and studying as he went. He returned in 654 laden with the finest Asian artworks. After Xuan Zang's death, the Emperor Gaodong built the Xingjiao monastery outside Xi'an to honour him.

Exploration for trade

After the Ottomans captured Constantinople in 1453, European rulers paid sailors to find alternatives to the land route to Asia. It was soon proved quicker and cheaper to ship luxury goods such as spices and silks by sea.

Han dynasty (206 BC–220 AD) figurine

Chinese jade horse

Chinese dragon

Ivory imperial seal

Silk Road

In ancient and medieval times, there was a 6,400-km (4,000-mile) overland trade route between China and Europe, known as the Silk Road. It fell into disuse when Asian and European traders adopted new east-to-west sea routes in the 15th and 16th centuries.

Chinese silk

Bolts of silk were traded throughout the Silk Road.

Marco Polo

The Venetian pioneer trader Marco Polo (c.1254–1324) travelled overland to China, and served the Emperor Kublai Khan as a diplomat for 17 years. Back in Europe, while in prison for debt (1296–98), he dictated a hugely popular book about life in the Far East. Centuries later it helped inspire Columbus to find a new westward sea route to the East.

Kublai Khan and Marco Polo

Mongol emperor Kublai Khan

Marco Polo

Clove tree

Spice Islands

Europeans knew that valuable spices, such as cloves, grew wild in the East, and some of the greatest explorations were efforts to find the Spice Islands, which are today known as the Moluccas. Portuguese, Spanish, Dutch, and British navigators all fought to control this valuable source of trade for their countries.

Vasco da Gama

Portuguese navigator Vasco da Gama (c.1469–1524) became the first European to sail to India when he landed at Calicut (Calcutta) in 1498. Da Gama returned twice: in 1502 to avenge the deaths of some Christian traders, and for the last time, in 1524, as Viceroy of India. He died shortly after this appointment.

Aztec sacrificial knife

New World

From 1492 Europeans aimed to reach India by sailing west. When they discovered that America was in their path, they hailed this continent as a "new world". But as they explored it, they brutally plundered and destroyed the rich empires of the Aztec, Inca, and Maya.

Aztec portrait beaker

Southern Continent

For centuries Europeans believed that there was a Terra Australis Incognita – or Unknown Southern Continent. In the 17th and 18th centuries Dutch and British seamen, such as James Cook (1728–79), began to explore it, and the great continent became known as Australia.

Robert O'Hara Burke and William J Wills

Early European settlement of Australia was coastal. Burke (1820–61) and Wills (1834–61) made the first journey from Melbourne across the continent's parched interior to the northern coast. On the way back, they died of starvation in the Outback.

Death at Cooper's Creek

Exploration tools

In the days before radar, radio, and satellites were invented, navigators and explorers used a variety of hand-operated tools. Compasses, sextants, and other devices calculated their position at sea and measured distances on land. This led to more accurate charts and maps.

Angles used to determine distance

Circumferentor

Surveyor's measuring tape

Needles rubbed with a lodestone pointed north when hung on a string.

Parallel rulers were used with a chart and a compass bearing to determine a course at sea.

Lodestone, naturally magnetic iron oxide

Compasses
By the 11th century, Chinese navigators were using magnetic compasses to define their course at sea. In Europe, compasses were vital explorers' tools from the 12th century on. Early versions were magnetized needles that pointed north when hung on string. Later, encased versions enabled navigators to take more accurate readings.

Fixed points measure distances on sea charts.

Chinese compass

Set of dividers

Pundits
In the 19th century, the British in India trained Indian surveyors, known as pundits, to make maps of the Central Asian territories of Karakoram, the Hindu Kush, and the Himalaya. In 1863, one of the earliest pundits, Muhammad-i-Hameed, made the first recorded trip over the Karakoram range to Chinese Turkestan. He died after spending six months in Yarkand, but his surveying equipment and notebook containing vital topographical information were taken back to India.

Mirrors

Sextants were used to survey land.

Scale

Portable sextant, 1850

Empire building

From the 15th century, the Spanish, Portuguese, Dutch, British, and French created huge empires outside Europe. After a nation's explorers, traders, and settlers had made links with an overseas territory, it might easily come under that nation's rule as a colony. Africa, Australia, parts of Asia, and the Americas were all colonized by Europeans at one time.

Livingstone and Stanley
Dr David Livingstone (1813–73), a Scottish missionary, made three expeditions through parts of Africa previously unknown to Europeans. He disappeared when trying to find the source of the River Nile and was feared dead. A New York paper sent the journalist Henry Stanley (1841–1904), who found him on the shores of Lake Tanganyika, greeting him with the famous words "Dr Livingstone, I presume?".

Stanley's hat

Charles Sturt
Despite the presence of two great rivers, the Murray and the Darling, Australian settlers could find no river mouths on the southeast coast, so explorers searched for an inland sea. In 1828–30, Sturt (1795–1869) mapped these river systems for 1600 km (994 miles). In 1844, he explored the Australian interior, or Outback, and finally proved there was no inland sea.

Final frontiers

In 1909 and 1911 the first-ever expeditions reached the North and South Poles. Since then there have been few places on Earth left to map but, with technological advances, scientists have been able to extend exploration to include investigations of the oceans and space. In 1969, explorers landed on the Moon for the first time.

Mary Kingsley
Few women took part in the first explorations of the world. It was generally believed that only men had the courage to venture into uncharted foreign lands. However, keen English naturalist, Mary Kingsley (1862–1900), proved that this was untrue when she travelled through West Africa in 1893 and 1894, collecting fish and beetle specimens for the British Museum and making a study of African religions. In 1900 she returned to Africa to nurse soldiers in the Boer War, and died there.

Hubble Space Telescope
Astronomers can now explore time as well as space. The Hubble Space Telescope, launched in 1990, orbits Earth at a distance of 600 km (370 miles). From this distance it collects images travelling through space from millions of years ago.

Equipment box

Solar panel

Trieste submarine
The bathyscaphe, *Trieste* – a manned diving vessel designed to reach depths of up to 11 km (7 miles) in the ocean – was developed by the Swiss scientist Auguste Piccard (1884–1962). In 1960 it dived to a record 10,916 m (35,815 ft) in the Mariana Trench of the Pacific Ocean. On board were Piccard's son Jacques and Lieutenant Donald Walsh of the US Navy.

Strong hull

Steel ball in which crew travelled

Trieste, a bathyscaphe

FIND OUT MORE

AUSTRALIA, HISTORY OF   ASIA, HISTORY OF   AFRICA, HISTORY OF   CENTRAL AMERICA, HISTORY OF   COOK, JAMES   EMPIRES   POLAR EXPLORATION   SOUTH AMERICA, HISTORY OF   SPACE EXPLORATION

EYES AND SEEING

YOUR EYES ENABLE you to see by stimulating the creation of images in your brain. Each of the two eyeballs is a sphere measuring 6.25 cm (2.5 inches) in diameter. Eyeballs contain sensory cells that, when stimulated by light, send messages to the brain that are interpreted as images. Reflex mechanisms control the amount of light entering the eye, and enable the eye to focus on objects whether they are near or distant. Much of the eyeball is hidden because it is protected within the orbit, a bony socket in the skull. The delicate outer surface of the eye is also protected by the eyelids.

Eye-moving muscles

Moving the eye
Your eyes move constantly, even when you are staring. Six muscles move each eyeball and hold it in place inside its skull socket. Each muscle pulls the eye in a different direction, enabling the eyeball to move up and down, from side to side, and diagonally. Your brain controls these movements to make sure that both eyes move together.

Eyeball

Seeing

The eyes gather light from whatever you look at. The cornea and lens focus this light on the retina to produce an upside-down image. Cells inside the retina, called rods and cones, respond to light by sending nerve impulses along the optic nerve to the brain. The brain interprets these impulses so you see the image the right way up.

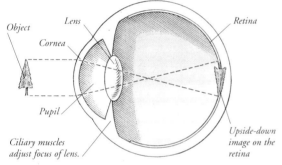

Object
Lens
Cornea
Retina
Pupil
Ciliary muscles adjust focus of lens.
Upside-down image on the retina

Iris and pupil
The iris controls the amount of light entering the eye. Muscles in the iris alter the size of the pupil, the opening that allows in light. In dim light, the pupil widens; in bright light, the pupil gets smaller.

Rods and cones
There are about 120 million rods and 7 million cones in the retina. Rods work best in dim light. Cones are responsible for colour vision and enable you to see things in detail.

Tears
Tears are released by lacrimal (tear) glands above the eye. When you blink, tears spread over the eye's surface. This keeps the cornea moist, washes away dust, and kills germs. After flowing over the eye, tears drain through two small openings at the side of the eye into the lacrimal duct, and then into the nose.

Inside the eye

The transparent cornea at the front of the eye helps to focus light as it enters. Behind the cornea are the iris, which controls the amount of light entering, and the lens, which fine focuses light on the retina. Two liquids, aqueous and vitreous humour, maintain the shape of the eyeball.

Tear gland moistens and protects eye.

Optic nerve sends messages from retina to brain.

Choroid supplies inside of eye with blood.

Eyeball lies within a protective bony socket.

Nerve

Lens alters shape to focus light.

Iris

Pupil is an opening that channels light.

Retina is a membrane at the back of the eye.

Sclera is the tough, white, outer coat of the eye.

Vision defects

The most common vision problems are long sight and short sight. In both cases the eye does not focus light properly on the retina. Some people, mainly males, have colour blindness and cannot distinguish between certain colours, most often red and green.

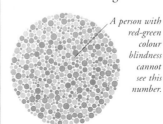

A person with red-green colour blindness cannot see this number.

Long sight
A long-sighted person sees distant objects clearly, but has a blurred view of close objects. This happens because light from near objects is focused behind the retina, rather than on it.

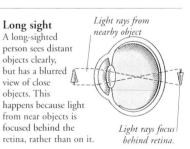

Light rays from nearby object

Light rays focus behind retina.

Short sight
A short-sighted person can see close objects clearly, but sees distant objects as a blur. Short sight is usually caused by the eyeball being longer than normal. This means that light entering the eye from distant objects is focused in front of the retina, rather than on it.

Light rays from distant object

Light rays focus in front of retina.

FIND OUT MORE   BRAIN AND NERVOUS SYSTEM   CAMERAS   CELLS   COLOUR   GENETICS   HUMAN BODY   LIGHT   MEDICINE, HISTORY OF

FARMING

BY CULTIVATING CROPS and raising animals, farms produce food and other products. Ten per cent of people in developed nations, and 60 per cent in developing countries, make their living from farming. In the West, technology makes the land highly productive, producing abundant, cheap food, and requiring fewer workers. In developing countries, farms have much lower yields because the soil or climate are often unsuitable for agriculture, and farmers, unable to afford new machines and chemicals, must rely on labour-intensive methods.

Crops

Ancient farmers bred crop plants by collecting and sowing the seed from the healthiest wild plants: the first cultivated crop was probably a kind of wheat. Today's major food crops are wheat, rice, maize (corn), and potatoes; major non-food crops include cotton and tobacco. The types and quantities of crops a farmer can grow are determined by soil and climate.

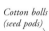
Cotton bolls (seed pods)

Cotton
The cotton crop provides fibres and oil. The main producers of the world's cotton are China and the USA.

Rice
Rice is a cereal, and the main food of half the world's people. Asia produces 90 per cent of the world's crop. Plants are grown in warm climates, usually on flooded "paddy" fields. Rice is a labour-intensive crop, which means most of the work is done by people, rather than machines.

Rice seedlings

2 days old   2–3 weeks   4–5 weeks

Harvesting rice by hand

Terraced fields

Paddy field, China

Plants are cut down, and left in bundles to dry out.

Sorting the maize harvest, Ghana

Maize
Maize is a kind of grass. There are many varieties, which can be ground into flour, eaten as a vegetable, made into oil, or used as animal feed. Maize is a major crop in the United States, Brazil, southern Africa, and parts of Asia.

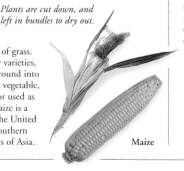

Maize

Types of farms

In the developed world, mixed farms were once common; farmers grew a few different crops and kept some livestock. Today's technology makes it advantageous for farms to specialize, raising just one kind of crop or animal with very high output. Such farming is big business. Some farmers, concerned by the possible effects on the environment, have changed to organic farming, where artificial fertilizers and pesticides are not used.

Shepherd shakes seed pods from a tree to feed sheep.

Subsistence farming
Subsistence farmers produce only enough to feed their household, with little or no surplus to sell. This is more common in developing nations where many farmers cannot afford the chemicals or machinery that would increase their yield, and rely on centuries-old farming methods.

Subsistence farming, Kenya

Commercial farming
Commercial farmers farm animals and crops intensively. They aim for a high yield and sell their produce for profit. In many countries, farmers produce too much food. When surplus crops and animals force food prices down, damaging the food industry, governments pay farmers to grow less.

Cattle fair, Argentina

Livestock

Farmers rear livestock (animals) for meat, milk, eggs, skins, and wool. In some cases, livestock is reared intensively, with many animals kept indoors in artificial conditions to encourage fast growth. By contrast "free-range" animals are reared outside; they live more like their wild counterparts, but their products are more costly.

Farmers kept goats and sheep for milk long before cattle.

Sheep's milk

Butter, from cow's milk

Cheese, from goat's milk

Dairy farming
Dairy farming is the breeding of animals for their milk and milk products. Cows are the main dairy animals, producing 10 to 15 litres (2.6 to 4 US gallons) of milk a day on average. Sheep and goats are also raised for their milk.

Sheep
The versatile sheep produces meat, wool, and milk. Sheep do not need such rich pasture as cattle: they can survive on poor quality land, and in dry or cold climates.

Sheep-shearing takes place in late spring.

Farming technology

Ever since the Agricultural Revolution in the 18th century, scientific advances in agriculture have rapidly raised farms' productivity. Artificial fertilizers, pesticides, research into selective breeding, and genetic engineering keep the increasing Western populations fed. Selective breeding programmes improve crops and livestock by combining the strengths of each parent in their offspring. By modifying genes directly in the laboratory, scientists can achieve the same results as selective breeding in a fraction of the time.

Vegetables can be bred to be regular in shape, and so more attractive to shoppers, even though there is no difference in taste.

Intensively farmed

Irregular shape

Chemicals in farming

Fertilizers enrich the soil with the minerals essential for plant growth. Animal manure is an organic fertilizer; science has also developed inorganic (artificial) fertilizers. Pesticides are chemicals that control the pests which attack crops. While these chemicals improve productivity, some chemicals get into the water supply, possibly harming human health.

Cattle raised in zero-grazing pen

Intensive rearing

Intensive farming maximizes the production of crops and livestock with chemicals and machines. Shoppers prefer cheap food: to produce this, the cost of raising livestock must be kept to a minimum. Cattle, pigs, and other animals live in controlled conditions; for example, pigs live in units, and are fed a precise mix of nutrients that make them put on the most weight in the least time.

Machinery

During the 20th century, new machinery increased farm productivity in industrialized nations, while also cutting labour requirements. Tractors, motor vehicles that pull farm machinery, quickly replaced horses as the source of pulling power on the farm. The tractor's power allowed farmers to plant and harvest crops over vast areas.

Tractors were first built in the late-19th century.

Preparing the land

To prepare the soil for sowing seed, farmers first plough the fields. The blade of a plough cuts a deep furrow in the soil and turns it over, burying weeds, which rot to enrich the soil. Harrows and cultivators are then used to break up large lumps of earth before the seed is sown.

Tractor, pulling plough

Coulter to cut into soil *Share to dig soil up* *Mouldboard to turn soil over*

Because combine harvesters work so quickly, they reap a crop at its best.

Harvesters

Machines can speed the harvest. A combine harvester both cuts a crop of wheat and separates the grain from the stalk. In less than an hour, a machine with one driver can turn two hectares of wheat into grain. Sugar, potatoes, and peas are other crops harvested by machine.

Equipment

Milking machines have changed the face of dairy farms, with farmers now able to keep much larger herds of cattle. Farmers operate machines that milk cattle twice a day, although in the Netherlands robotic machines have been introduced that milk cows whenever the cows want it. The robots place vacuum cups on the cows' teats to draw out their milk. Each cow wears a radio collar which tells the robot where to look for the udder.

Robotic milking parlour, the Netherlands

The farmer's year

The changing seasons set the pace of a farmer's work. On a livestock farm, for instance, spring is the time when lambs or calves are born. The arable (crop-growing) farm is busiest during the spring-to-autumn growing season. Apple growers must carry out different tasks through the year to produce the best crop.

Apples are the main fruit crop in cool, temperate regions. There are more than 6,000 different varieties.

Trees have been pruned so that the Sun can ripen the fruit.

To make mechanical weeding easier, the trees are grown in neat rows.

Winter: the trees take a rest from growing. The farmer prunes the branches into shapes that make the fruit easier to reach.

Bees dust pollen from blossom of one tree to that of another.

Windfalls

Farmer prunes trees.

Beehive

Modern apple trees have been bred to be small, making it easier for people to pick the fruit.

Tractor moves bins of picked apples.

Free-range pigs eat windfall apples.

Trees are sprayed and fed in spring and summer.

Late summer: the fruits ripen at the end of summer, when harvest (by hand) begins.

Autumn: harvest continues. Windfalls are used to make cider and juice.

Spring: bees from hives placed in the orchard in spring pollinate the trees.

FIND OUT MORE   FARMING, HISTORY OF   FISHING INDUSTRY   FOOD   GENETICS   INDUS VALLEY CIVILIZATION   PIGS AND PECCARIES   PLANT USES   SHEEP AND GOATS   SOIL   TRADE AND INDUSTRY

Farming
Animals farmed for produce

Chickens are bred for eggs and meat.

Peacocks are bred for their exotic plumage.

Ducks are farmed for feathers, eggs, and meat.

Sheep are bred for milk, meat, skins, and wool.

Geese are kept for meat, down, and eggs.

Red deer are bred for their meat, called venison.

Jerseys are farmed for their very rich milk.

Angora goats have a coarse undercoat and a curly wool outer coat.

Cattle are the world's most numerous farm animals.

Herefords were first bred in Britain and are now farmed in 50 countries.

Cattle are farmed for milk and meat.

Goats are farmed for milk, meat, and wool.

Goats can feed on scrubby grass and thorny branches.

Almost every part of a pig can be eaten.

Now scarce in the wild

Udders

Pigs are versatile feeders.

Ostrich chick: farmed for meat and feathers.

Saanen goats are bred in Europe for their milk.

Chinchillas, rodents bred for their soft, delicate fur.

Pigs are farmed for pork, bacon, other meat products, skins, and bristles.

Animals bred to work

Long, erect ears

Well-muscled leg

Poitou donkeys are the world's largest.

Elephants pull heavier loads than any other animal.

Camels are used as pack animals, and also farmed for wool, milk, hides, and meat.

Heavy horses, used where a farmer has no tractor.

Donkeys carry large loads on little food or water.

Mules are interbred from horses and donkeys.

Elephants are used as draught (pulling) animals in southeast Asia.

F

325

FARMING, HISTORY OF

TEN THOUSAND YEARS AGO, the first farmers began to grow crops and breed animals for food. Before that, nomadic hunter-gatherers fed on berries, plants, and wild beasts they encountered on their travels. With the emergence of farming, however, people were able to produce a reliable food supply, and to settle permanently in one place, giving rise to the world's earliest civilizations in Mesopotamia, Egypt, India, and China. Farming methods continued to evolve slowly until, in the 18th century, a so-called Agricultural Revolution led to dramatic changes. Since then, farming has become more mechanized and feeds ever greater numbers of people.

Early farmers

The first farmers tamed wild animals, kept them in herds, and used them for meat, milk, skins, and wool. By contrast, nomadic herders moved their animals constantly in search of new pastures.

Flint sickle in wooden handle

Neolithic revolution

After the New Stone Age, c.8000 BC, (Neolithic) people in western Asia began to grow crops. This type of farming supported 10 times more people than hunting and gathering.

Rice farming

Irrigation

Early farmers needed water for their crops. Rivers and artificial canal systems played a vital role in the ancient agricultural civilizations of Egypt, the Indus Valley, and China.

Agricultural revolution

From about 1750, a series of major changes ushered in the era of modern farming. Key developments included large-scale farming, the intensive breeding of livestock, and the improvement of a number of agricultural techniques – such as four-course crop rotation – all of which were first developed in Britain.

Selective breeding

Robert Bakewell (1725–95), the fifth Duke of Bedford (1765–1802), and other British stock breeders during the Agricultural Revolution, used selective breeding on their farms and estates to develop larger, healthier animals, such as cattle, goats, sheep, and turkeys, with a higher milk or meat yield. Later breeders used the same system to develop animals for a particular purpose. For example, the Camargue bull which is bred only for fighting.

Goat

Camargue bull

Crop rotation

During the Agricultural Revolution, farmers found that if they grew certain crops, such as turnips, clover, barley, and wheat in successive years, they did not need to let the land lie fallow for a year. Root crops, such as turnips, improved the soil, and therefore the quality of the next harvest.

Turnips and wheat

Black Norfolk turkey

New farm machinery

Machines, such as the thresher (formulated in 1786 by Scots inventor Andrew Meikle), eased workloads and improved productivity. Threshers, which separated the grain from the straw, became more effective after 1850 when farm workers attached steam engines to power them.

Medieval farming

Farmers in medieval Europe divided the land around their village into three fields. Each family had one 12-hectare strip of land in each field. Everyone followed the same three-year farming cycle: one field was left fallow (unused) each year to restore the soil's nutrients, and the other two grew barley, oats, rye, or wheat.

Enclosures

From the 1500s, English landowners enclosed common land with fences, ditches or hedges, to turn it into private property. As a result, the co-operative medieval system of farming gave way to a system of private ownership where land-owners made all the decisions about what to farm.

Book of Hours, 1416

Charles "Turnip" Townshend

A main forerunner of the Agricultural Revolution, Viscount Townshend (1674–1738) retired from a brilliant career in politics to concentrate on farming. He popularized a four-course rotation of crops, and pioneered "marling" (using limey clay as fertilizer). His widespread cultivation of the turnip – as a fodder crop to keep animals fed during the winter – earned him his nickname.

Green Revolution

In the 1960s, a Green Revolution took place. New "high-yield" crop varieties were developed to increase wheat and rice production, particularly in highly populated countries such as India, and China. Critics claimed this process damaged the environment through overuse of fertilizer and concentration on only a few species. Recently farmers have been rediscovering traditional farming methods and using organic fertilizers and insecticides.

Straw exits here.
Drum separates grain from straw.
Grain is fed in here.
Drive belt operates main threshing drum.
Drive wheel rotates to turn drive belt.
Coal stored here.
Steam-powered threshing machine

Seaweed, an organic fertilizer

FIND OUT MORE · BRONZE AGE · CHINA, HISTORY OF · EGYPT, ANCIENT · EUROPE, MEDIEVAL · FARMING · INDUSTRIAL REVOLUTION · INVENTIONS · KHMER EMPIRE · STONE AGE · SUMERIANS

FERNS

THE MOST ADVANCED of all the non-flowering, spore-bearing plants are the ferns and their relatives, known as the Pteridophytes. There are about 12,000 species of Pteridophyte, of which about 10,400 are ferns. The others include horsetails and club mosses. Pteridophytes are vascular plants, that is, plants whose stems contain tissues that transport water and food around the plant internally. They flourish best in warm, damp environments, but also grow where it is cool or dry.

Ferns

A typical fern plant has underground stems, or rhizomes, from which grow roots, and leaves called fronds. Upright rhizomes produce a fern with a short radiating crown of fronds, while long horizontal rhizomes produce a spreading fern. Ferns grow in a variety of places, but all have a two-stage life-cycle. The gametophyte is a small, short-lived plantlet that produces sex cells. After fertilization, a female sex cell grows into a sporophyte, which is the fern plant.

Epiphytic ferns
An epiphytic fern grows on the bough or trunk of a tree. It takes no nourishment from its host, but obtains moisture and minerals from rain and debris that become trapped among its roots.

Fronds hang clear of the branch.

Radiating fronds

Tree ferns
Tree ferns have woody, fibrous trunks topped with a crown of fronds. They are found in all climates, most frequently in the tropics and sub-tropics. The tallest species reaches 20 m (65 ft).

Base of dead fronds

Water ferns
Some ferns are aquatic. They either root into mud in fresh water, or float free. This *Azolla* species floats. Its tiny roots dangle in the water below a mat of fronds.

Male fern
Ferns similar to this male fern, so-called because of its vigorous growth, are found in woods all around the world. This species has stiff, bright green fronds. Each blade is divided into "leaves" called pinnae (singular: pinna), each of which is further divided into pinnules.

Pinna and pinnules

A full-grown frond may reach as much as 150 cm (5 ft) long.

Young frond

The frond continues to lengthen as the lower parts unfurl.

A developing male fern plant

Stipe is the "stalk" of the fern.

Rhizome

Root

1 Frond buds develop on the rhizome. Each bud produces just one frond. It takes up to three years for a bud to develop and a frond to start growing.

2 A frond can grow rapidly because all the cells of the stalk and leaflets are fully formed, though very small. They just have to expand.

3 A male fern produces tall fronds, each on a scaly stipe. Fertile fronds are the last to unfurl, so that the spores are released in the summer.

Club mosses

These small plants grow on damp ground or on rainforest trees. Their creeping stems are covered with tiny leaves arranged in a spiral. Spores are carried in modified leaves on fertile stems.

Horsetails

The stiff upright stems of horsetails grow in dense patches from underground stems. Branches are arranged in whorls, although fertile stems often have no branches. Tiny brown leaves grow in rings around the stems and branches. Spores are borne in cone-like structures on the tip of fertile stems.

Sterile stem

Fertile stem

The life-cycle of a fern

Sori

Pinna

Sorus

Sporangia

Dry weather causes the sporangium to burst at a weak spot.

Sex organs are carried on the underside of the gametophyte.

Archegonium containing female sex cells

Antheridium containing male sex cells

New fern plant – the sporophyte

Spores

Gametophyte is a thin green plantlet.

Fertile fronds have sori (singular: sorus), usually on the lower surface of each pinna.

Within each sorus are clusters of sporangia, which contain the spores.

Sixty-four spores develop inside each sporangium. The sporangium then bursts, releasing all the spores.

A spore landing on damp soil germinates into a gametophyte. This bears male and female sex organs.

Male sex cells swim in a film of soil moisture to the female sex cells and then fertilize them.

The first female sex cell to be fertilized grows into a fern plant.

FIND OUT MORE   MOSSES AND LIVERWORTS   PLANTS   PLANTS, ANATOMY   PLANTS, REPRODUCTION   RAINFOREST WILDLIFE   TREES

F

FESTIVALS

ALL OVER THE WORLD, people set aside special days each year to enjoy themselves at festivals. These public celebrations are held for many reasons: they may be linked to a community's religious beliefs, mark the changing seasons, or honour important events in a country's history.

Streamers are hung from a pole.

Day of the Dead
On 1 November, Mexicans celebrate the Day of the Dead, to honour people who have died. Families have picnics by the graves of their relatives, decorate the streets with flowers and carved skeletons, and eat sweets shaped like skulls and coffins.

Papier-mâché skeleton

Calendar festivals

The majority of festivals are held at the same time each year. Many religions have adapted the celebrations of early peoples to their own ends: the Christian Christmas and the Hindu Diwali are held around the same time as ancient feasts marking the onset of winter.

Children's Day
To mark Children's Day (5 May) in Japan, streamers in the shape of carp are hung out. The strong, energetic fish is seen as a good role model for young children.

Harvest festivals

Ancient peoples thought that thanking the gods would ensure a good crop the next year, and people still celebrate festivals based on this idea. There are many festivals in Africa and Papua New Guinea that celebrate the yam crop, and the Oktoberfest beer festival in Germany began as thanks for the crop of hops.

Radishes
On Christmas Eve, townspeople in Oaxaca, Mexico, celebrate their radish crop by carving large, recently harvested radishes into elaborate shapes, which they use to decorate market stalls and restaurants. Food is served on chipped plates, which are saved for the occasion and smashed at the end of the night.

Corn
In England, people often used the last of the year's corn to make a figure called a corn dolly. The dolly kept the corn spirit alive through the winter, ensuring another good harvest the next year.

Traditional English corn dolly

Carnivals

Originally, carnivals were pagan festivals to celebrate the rebirth of nature in spring. Later, they became associated with the Roman Catholic festival of Lent. The start and duration of the carnival season varies from country to country.

Carnival in Venice
This famous Italian carnival first began in the 11th century. Traditionally, many revellers wear masks. They originally did this to hide their faces while they behaved outrageously.

Float pulled by tractor

Mardi Gras float

Caribbean carnival
Carnival in the Caribbean combines African and European traditions; dance, costume, and music are important parts of African religious beliefs.

Mardi Gras
In many Roman Catholic countries, carnival is by tradition a last chance for merry-making before the start of Lent, the weeks of fasting that come before Easter. Thousands of people enjoy the week-long Mardi Gras carnival in New Orleans, USA, which is named after the French for "Fat Tuesday". This refers to Shrove Tuesday, the day before Lent begins, when all the fats in the home must be used up. Another spectacular Mardi Gras carnival is held in Rio de Janeiro, Brazil.

Modern festivals

Most festivals set up today mark non-religious events. The Olympics celebrate excellence in sports; the Edinburgh festival in the UK promotes the performing arts.

Mime artist, Edinburgh Festival

Roskilde
Thousands of fans attend this summer rock music festival in Denmark.

Political festivals

Significant political dates are often the cause for regular celebration. Festivals mark the anniversary of a nation's independence or a great leader's birthday: in the USA, there is a holiday on George Washington's birthday.

May Day
Once a springtime fertility festival, May 1 is a now a public holiday to honour workers. In Russia, May Day is marked with trades union parades.

FIND OUT MORE CHRISTIANITY   FILM AND FILM-MAKING   FOOD   HINDUISM   SPORT   UNIONS, TRADE

FEUDALISM

IN PARTS OF MEDIEVAL ASIA and Europe, a system arose for organizing society known as feudalism. In the feudal system, the king gave land to powerful barons, who then gave land and protection to lesser lords, and so on through to the peasants. Each level was then expected to fight to protect its overlords whenever needed. European feudalism started in the late 9th century, and spread all over the continent. Outside Europe, the feudal system operated in Palestine during the Crusades, and also in Japan, where samurai gave military service to their overlords in return for land.

Lords and vassals

In the European feudal system, the only person who actually owned land was the king. When the king granted land to a baron, the baron knelt and pledged to be the king's vassal (servant). Lesser lords swore a similar oath to the barons and became their vassals, and peasants swore allegiance to the lords. Bishops were also the king's vassals, and held nearly as much power as the barons.

Feudal counsel
Kings and barons often asked for advice, or counsel, from their vassals when making any important decisions. This 14th-century French manuscript shows Philip VI of France judging Robert of Valois, helped by the bishops on his right hand and the barons on his left.

Feudal contract
The people owed their loyalty to the monarch. This "contract" meant that Philip VI could – and did – tax his subjects heavily to finance the Hundred Years War.

Derisive image of king with cat, not crown, on his head

King
Although the king owned the land, he could rarely afford to keep an army. He was often in conflict with the barons, on whom he relied for his warriors.

Barons
The most powerful of all the nobles, the barons got their lands directly from the king. Because they provided the royal army, they had great power and prestige.

Local lords
Local knights got their land (or manor) from the barons. In return, they fought for the barons when needed. As time went on, local lords often paid a tax called scutage (shield money) instead of fighting, and the king used this money to hire professional soldiers. In peacetime, they farmed and kept order.

Peasants
The peasants, at the bottom of feudal society, got their plots of land from the local lord of the manor. He allowed them to farm this land; in return, they paid rent in produce and money. The peasants also contributed several days' labour on "public" projects such as road- and bridge-building.

How feudalism began

The great emperor Charlemagne insisted that all his nobles swear loyalty to him. This bond beween lord and warrior began the feudal system. Over the next two centuries, feudalism spread through France, Germany, northern Italy, the Slav countries, and finally the British Isles and Sicily.

Mounted warriors
Warriors riding horses to war became more common after 950. These warriors were the first knights. They had great prestige, and became an important part of the feudal system.

The manor

Farmland and its ownership was the most important part of feudalism, and the manor was the administration centre of the system. The lands surrounding the manor house were divided into the demesne (for the lord's own use), the arable (granted in parcels to the peasants), and the meadow lands (used by everyone for livestock).

Ightham Mote, England

The manor house
Every manor house had a hall. This acted as the dining and living room for the family, and also a general reception room where the peasants paid their rent. The kitchen was at one end of the hall, beside a pantry and buttery (store room for drinks). Buildings in the courtyard outside included workshops and cattle-sheds. The whole complex was often surrounded by a moat for protection.

The Hall, Ightham Mote

Domesday Book

For the feudal system to work well, the ruler needed detailed information about the land and who lived on it. William of Normandy, who introduced feudalism to Britain, had a complete record made of all land ownership in England in 1085–86. This became known as the Domesday Book.

The book is the most complete record of land-holding in medieval Europe.

William I

The illegitimate son of Duke Robert I of Normandy, William (c.1028–1087) conquered England in 1066. He introduced the feudal system to the island, and replaced Saxon nobles with Norman lords.

FIND OUT MORE   CHARLEMAGNE   HUNDRED YEARS WAR   KNGHTS AND HERALDRY   MEDIEVAL EUROPE   NORMANS   SAMURAI AND SHOGUNS

FILMS AND FILM-MAKING

IN 1895, THE Lumière brothers held the first public film screening, in a room below a Parisian café. The black and white images flickered on a silent screen, yet the audience was enthralled. The magic of the movies has continued ever since. Technology developed rapidly: sound arrived in 1927, colour in the 1930s, and today's complex films often involve stunning special effects. Film production is now an international industry, generating great wealth and employing thousands worldwide.

Pre-production

Film-making begins long before the cameras start to turn. After a studio (a film-making company) agrees to make a movie, a script is prepared, the budget drawn up, actors and skilled crew hired, and the entire production planned to the last detail.

Pictures represent each shot.

The producer

A producer decides which film to make, finds the money to finance it (often millions of pounds), and brings together the stars, script, and director.

Storyboard

With one small picture for each shot, a storyboard is important in planning a film and gives an idea of what it will look like. Notes outline the action and dialogue.

Casting

It is vital to the success of a movie to cast (place) actors who suit their parts artistically. Audiences have their favourites, so the choice of a popular star can turn a promising film into a huge box-office success.

Focus puller has a seat at top of crane to adjust the focus on the camera lens.

The set designer uses sketches and models to design the set.

The set

The film scenery, or set, is often purpose-built, to simulate the right atmosphere without the film crew leaving the studio. An actor who, on screen, seems to swagger into a saloon in the rough Wild West, may, in fact, be in a studio in Bombay, Hollywood, or Paris.

The set decorator finds props and decorates set.

Powerful light

Boom holds microphone near actor but out of shot.

RAMIREZ SALOO

Boom operator sits here to position the microphone.

Crane raises the camera above the actors' heads.

The camera and camera equipment on set are moved by the grip.

The camera operator sits here to work the camera during shooting.

Director's folding chair next to camera

When the actors move, grips push the stand to move the microphone.

Production

When filming begins, a movie set is crowded with equipment, and each piece is the responsibility of a specific member of the crew. Between takes (sequences of filming), everyone works frantically to ensure that everything is adjusted exactly as the director wants. Off the set, props, wardrobe, and make-up have their own staff on hand.

The director

Responsible for the artistic side of the film-making process, the director is the most important person on set. Directors control the action and judge how well each take brings the script to life. They consult with experts in each department, such as the director of photography, who is responsible for the way the film looks.

Motion pictures

The continuous action on a movie screen is, in fact, an illusion. What we are watching are thousands of still photographs, taken rapidly one after the other. A film camera shoots 24 photographs (frames) every second, and when the images are projected at the same rate, our eyes merge the pictures together. Over 27 m (90 ft) of film is shot for just one minute of cinema.

Post-production

Separate scenes in a film are shot in whatever order suits the crew. Then the director chooses the best sections, and the film editor links them in the right sequence to tell the story. While working closely with the director and other technicians, the editor carefully aligns the sound track and pictures, and adds the special effects.

Screen to view the film

Loudspeaker plays back sound track

Editing table

Editing

The editor cuts up the disjointed sequences of film, cutting between frames, and splices them together. Cuts are viewed at an editing table.

Sound track

Music, the actors' speech, and any background sound effects are each recorded separately and then combined to make the sound track.

Types of films

From the simplest short cartoon film to a full-length feature with an all-star cast, films cover every subject. There have been notable films on many topics, but some of the most successful movies have been in areas where film can add an extra dimension, such as the vivid settings of fantasy and space adventures or western movies, the special effects of science-fiction and horror films, or the singing and dancing of American musicals.

Babe is a piglet who believes he is a sheepdog.

Babe, 1995

Comedy

The first films were silent, yet the comic antics of the actors made audiences roar with laughter. Today, comedies range from biting social commentaries to the gentle humour of an animal film such as *Babe*.

Charlie Chaplin

One of the best-loved comedians of the silent screen, Chaplin (1889–1977) moved to the USA from London as a young man. He appeared in over 60 short films and 11 full-length comedies, including *City Lights* and *Modern Times*. His characterization of a tramp, who keeps a sense of humour despite great hardship, was based on observation of poor people on the London streets.

Jean-Louis Barrault Arletty

Les Enfants du Paradis, 1944

Romance

Love stories are always popular. The romantic *Les Enfants du Paradis* was made in German-occupied France during World War II; in 1979, French critics voted it the best French film ever made.

Horror

German film makers were the first to realise that audiences like being frightened: directors were making horror movies in Germany by 1913. By the 1930s, horror had caught on in Hollywood, where it has been popular ever since. *Frankenstein* appeared in 1931. More than 100 films have been based on the same theme since.

Boris Karloff as Frankenstein's monster

Going to the movies

By the 1930s, going to the cinema was popular entertainment, but in the 1950s television took over and the film industry declined. Recently, movie-going has grown popular again. Today, multiplex cinemas screen many films at the same time, offering audiences a wide choice of pictures.

Special effects

Anything can happen on film, thanks largely to the special effects department, a complex and skilled area of film-making. Effects may range from animals that seem to talk, to horrific dripping wounds, or people appearing to fly through the air.

Eyes, nose, and mouth operated by motors.

— *Dog, from* The Storyteller

Motor

Le Grand Rex cinema, Paris, France

Picture palaces

Following the arrival of sound in 1927, cinemas were built in most towns in North America, Europe and Australia. With their impressive architecture, the cinemas of the 1920s and 1930s were often called picture palaces.

Dramatic lighting

Neon sign

Make-up

Actors wear make-up to look natural under the bright film lights. Make-up also helps when an actor must look unnatural. A make-up artist can make an actor look much older, or use latex rubber and lining colours to add dreadful wounds. In horror and science-fiction films, make-up is used to turn people into aliens.

Make-up in Terminator 2

Movie models

Where it is too costly, dangerous, or impossible to use the real thing, filmmakers may turn to models. Tiny models stand in for massive spacecraft in science-fiction films. A talking animal may be a puppet, or an actor in costume whose remote-controlled mask is operated by a puppeteer. This kind of puppetry is called animatronics.

Blue screen

To create the illusion that a character is flying, an actor is filmed in front of a blue screen. Wind machines make his clothes flutter, as if air is moving past. An optical printer then combines the sequence with footage shot from a plane, or of a simulated space environment. The printer re-photographs images from each film onto a single frame, to blend the two films seamlessly.

Actor held by wires

Computers

Computers can manipulate images to create extraordinary special effects. Programs also allow operators to draw and animate characters on screen. Changes are much easier to make here than in animation which has been hand-drawn frame by frame.

Disney's Toy Story *is a computer-generated film.*

© Disney

Hype and merchandise

The cost of film production means it is vital to make the public eager to see a movie, so that the producers can earn back their investment and make a good profit. Publicists work hard to sell a film before it opens. They inform journalists, and arrange for the actors to appear on television talk shows. This process is known as hype. Selling items related to a movie, such as socks or a mug, is another way of making more money.

Batman logo

Batman merchandise
™ & © 1996 DC Comics

Timeline

1895 The Lumière brothers open the first public cinema in Paris, France.

1913 By this date, Hollywood, Calif., is the centre of the US film industry.

Academy Award (Oscar)
© A.M.P.A.S. ®

1920s Russian director Sergei Eisenstein (1898–1948) introduces cross-cutting, showing bursts of action one after the other so they seem to happen simultaneously.

1927 The Academy of Motion Picture Arts and Sciences is set up; in 1929, it honours filmmakers for the first time.

1927 *The Jazz Singer*, made in the US, is the first full-length film with sound.

1932 The "three-strip" process is introduced by the Technicolor company, and colour films, originally developed much earlier, begin to take off.

Technicolor three-strip camera

1941 US actor-director Orson Welles (1915–85) releases *Citizen Kane;* it explores new techniques in lighting, dialogue, and the use of camera lenses.

1952 The CinemaScope process introduces widescreen cinema.

1960s *Nouvelle Vague* ("New Wave") film-makers in France introduce influential new techniques.

1980s The VCR allows people to see films at home.

1990s Special effects techniques are advanced.

FIND OUT MORE

CAMERAS   CARTOONS AND ANIMATION   EDISON, THOMAS   VIDEO

F

Film posters

United States

The Gold Rush (USA, 1925), a classic silent film, is touching yet very funny.

Raging Bull (USA, 1980) is one of the most influential films of the 1980s.

Blade Runner (USA, 1982) portrays a bleak Los Angeles in 2019.

Do the Right Thing (USA, 1989) develops from comedy to social comment.

Europe

The Battleship Potemkin (USSR, 1925), commissioned by Soviet leaders to put across a powerful political message, is still referred to as a masterpiece of cinema.

Metropolis (Ger. 1926) is a disturbing vision of an "ideal" city in the year 2000.

Pelle the Conqueror (Den/Swe. 1987) won top international awards.

Oceania

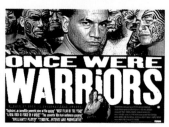

Once Were Warriors (NZ, 1994): a great success critically and at the box-office.

Four Weddings and a Funeral (UK, 1994) is a light-hearted, appealing romance.

Women... (Spain, 1988) is a manic farce from talented director Pedro Almodóvar.

The Piano (Aust. 1993), directed and written by Jane Campion, won three Oscars.

Africa

Yeelen (Mali, 1987) tells the story of the struggle between a father and son.

The Sixth Day (Egypt, 1986), directed by Youssef Chahine, starred actress Daleeda.

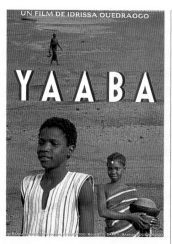

In **Yaaba** (Burkina, 1989), a friendship develops between a boy and an old woman cast out by other villagers.

Asia

Ran (Japan, 1985) is based on *King Lear* by Shakespeare; the battle scenes are superbly staged and shot.

Pather Panchali (India, 1956) brought its director, Satyajit Ray, world recognition.

Raise the Red Lantern (HK, 1991) looks at a woman's life in 1920s' China.

FINLAND

A LAND OF LAKES AND FORESTS, Finland is bordered by Russia to the east, the Baltic Sea to the south, and Sweden and Norway to the west and north. Finland shares government of Lapland, in the Arctic Circle, with Sweden and Norway. Finland was ruled by Russia until 1917, and, as a result, Finns have more in common culturally with the east than with their Scandinavian neighbours. A wealthy, liberal nation, Finland was the first European country to give women the vote.

FINLAND FACTS

CAPITAL CITY	Helsinki
AREA	338,130 sq km (130,552 sq miles)
POPULATION	5,200,000
MAIN LANGUAGES	Finnish, Swedish
MAJOR RELIGION	Christian
CURRENCY	Euro
LIFE EXPECTANCY	77 years
PEOPLE PER DOCTOR	333
GOVERNMENT	Multi-party democracy
ADULT LITERACY	99%

Physical features

From the air, Finland is a patchwork of lakes, peat bogs, and trees. Forests dominate the land, and water covers about ten per cent of the country. There are some 98,000 islands within the lakes, and 30,000 off the coast. The Arctic north, including part of Lapland, is a bleak area of rocky tundra.

Forests
Pine, spruce, and birch trees cover 80 per cent of Finland, making it the ninth most forested country in the world. The forest is most dense just south of the Arctic Circle and is often covered in snow.

33°C (91°F) 17°C (62°F)   -41°C (-42°F) -6°C (21°F)

618 mm (24 in)

Lakes and islands
Finland has more than 60,000 lakes, mainly in the southeast, carved out by glaciers in the last Ice Age. Many islands are scattered in the lakes and off the warm southwest coast, including 6,000 of the Åland Islands.

Climate
Finland has short, bright summers and long, cold winters when lakes often freeze up to 1 m (3 ft 3 in) deep. The Arctic north sees midnight sun in its 73-day summer.

Barren 7.5%   Forest 80%
Built-up 0.25%   Wetland 0.5%
Tundra 1.5%   Farmland 10.25%

Land use
Dense forests and a maze of lakes, rivers, and peat bogs mean only 11 per cent of Finland's land can be used for crops or grazing animals. Despite this, farmers produce all of the country's dairy foods. The forests support a valuable timber industry, and the waters are used for fishing and hydroelectric power.

People
Almost half of the population lives around Helsinki. Families are close-knit, and most homes have a sauna, or hot, steamy relaxation room. Women enjoy equal rights and about 50 per cent pursue a career.

Kirkniemi paper mill

Cooling off after the sauna

Farming and industry
Finland produces all of its own food. Most crops are grown in the southwest and on the sunny Åland Islands. The country is a world leader in the production of plywood, wood pulp, and paper, and these alone make up 30 per cent of the total exports. Furniture and high-tech manufacturing compete in world markets and, with the service sector, employ the majority of the work-force.

Helsinki

Standing on a peninsula and several islands in the Gulf of Finland, the vibrant capital of Helsinki has about 770,000 inhabitants. Tree-lined avenues and a colourful market back onto a busy harbour. Only half of the city's area has been developed, leaving parkland for the residents to enjoy.

The bustling Helsinki harbour

17 per sq km (44 per sq mile)   67% Urban   33% Rural

FIND OUT MORE   ARCTIC OCEAN   ENERGY   EUROPE, HISTORY OF   FISHING INDUSTRY   FORESTS   GLACIATION   LAKES   PAPER   SCANDINAVIA, HISTORY OF   TRADE AND INDUSTRY   WINTER SPORTS

FIRE

BURNING OUT OF CONTROL in forests or cities, a fire leaves a trail of destruction. Yet life without the benefits of fire is unimaginable. We use fire in power stations, car engines, and kitchens, to provide electricity and transport, or to cook food. Early humans realized the value of fire about half a million years ago – perhaps when lightning set a tree on fire. Learning to control and use the flames helped them hunt, clear land for farming, survive in colder climates, and eat foods that were inedible when raw. No wonder some religions still worship fire as a hungry god.

Flame is a glowing gas, produced in burning.

Combustion or burning
Fire is the heat and light produced when fuel burns. This process is known as combustion. The fuel can be any flammable material (one that can catch fire). The material must first be heated to a temperature called the ignition temperature; above this, it will burst into flame. As a fire gets hotter, more fuel catches alight, and the flames spread. Gases and vapours burn quickly; liquids and solids take longer to burn.

Using fire

To make fire do useful work, the supply of air or fuel must be controlled to keep the flames burning evenly. Furnaces, cooking stoves, and power plants use fire for the heat energy it produces. Heat is not always the main purpose of creating fire. In a car engine fuel burns explosively. Expanding gases drive the vehicle; the heat produced is wasted.

Welder at work

Welding
Many industrial processes rely on combustion. In the welder's torch, oxygen and acetylene gas mix and produce a flame hot enough to melt steel.

Fire-engine with hydraulic platform, used to reach awkward spaces.

Cooking
Many foods must be cooked before they can be eaten. When food is heated, chemical changes take place that improve its taste and make it easier to digest. Early people ate raw food until they discovered cooking, probably by accident.

Some booms are up to 62 m (203 ft) long.

Rescue platform

Arm, or boom

Built-in hose

Leg for support

Making a fire

In the past, there were two main methods of starting a fire: raising the temperature until flames appeared, or striking sparks to set light to tinder. Cigarette lighters still start fires by using the spark of flint on steel.

Mouthpiece steadies drill   *Wooden drill*

String

Modern model of bow drill

Hearth

Bow drills
Rapidly turning the string of a bow drill causes friction at the tip, which starts flames.

Piston handle is pumped to compress air.

A fire piston works like a bicycle pump: compressing air in the tube raises the temperature until the tinder (flammable material) inside catches alight.

Tinder stored in box

Lid with candle holder

Steel

Flint

A tinder box contains flint, which makes sparks when struck against metal (the steel).

Matches
Invented in 1827, these wooden splinters were tipped with chemicals. The chemicals were ignited by heat, generated by rubbing the tip against sandpaper. Safety matches burn only when rubbed against a specially coated strip on the matchbox.

Cooking with fire

Fighting fire

Fires feed on fuel, air, and heat; removing any one of these puts out the flames. Firefighters spray a blaze with water to remove heat and to create a blanket of steam that chokes off the air supply.

Myths about fire

The power and danger of fire made ancient peoples wonder about its origin. Myths that explain how people learned to tame flames occur in many separate cultures. Most fire myths involve a hero who brings fire to the world.

Prometheus
In Greek mythology, the chief god, Zeus, hid the secret of fire from mortals (humans) to punish them for a trick that a lesser god, Prometheus, had played on him. But Prometheus snatched a glowing ember from the Sun, and brought fire to the Earth.

Prometheus

FIND OUT MORE   FOOD   HEAT AND TEMPERATURE   INVENTIONS   LIGHT   PREHISTORIC PEOPLE

FIRST AID

FIRST AID RANGES from cleaning a small wound and covering it with sticking plaster, to dealing with serious injuries at a major disaster. But its main aims are the same: to save life, prevent the casualty's condition from worsening, promote healing and recovery, and arrange for expert help at the earliest opportunity. Recently, first aid has advanced greatly due to a better understanding of the body's needs in serious injury or disease, improved medical equipment, and mobile communications. It now plays an even more vital role in saving lives, and speeding a casualty's recovery.

At the scene

Effective first aid – the temporary treatment of injury or illness while waiting for medical aid – relies on correctly assigning priorities. At an accident, one of the first priorities is to summon the emergency services.

Scene of a motorcycle accident

Assessing conditions

Experienced first aiders know that noisy casualties are not necessarily the most hurt. At a multiple accident, they assess quickly the condition of all casualties, then concentrate available first aid on the most seriously injured. In hospitals, this assessment is known as triage.

Raising the alarm

A telephone call is usually the best way to get help. Special telephones are located in areas such as motorways, but calls to the emergency services are free on all telephones. Shouting, waving flags, or firing flares are all alternative methods.

Spanish public telephone

Further danger

First aiders should never place themselves or others in danger. Before treating the casualty, they should try to make the area safe. Fire, traffic, electricity, and unsafe structures are some of the hazards that may delay treatment.

Fire extinguisher

ABC of first aid

ABC stands for the body's three vital needs. "A" stands for airway: the airway needs to be open so that oxygen-containing air can enter the lungs. "B" stands for breathing, by which the body inhales fresh air and expels stale air. "C" stands for the circulation of the blood, which distributes oxygen around the body. When dealing with an unconscious casualty, the first aider must check that the casualty has a clear airway, is breathing, and has a pulse that indicates blood circulation.

Two fingers pressing lightly on a pulse point

Checking for a pulse

The heart pumps blood around the body, causing a pulse. A first aider can check the heart is still beating by feeling for this pulse in arteries located in the neck or wrist.

Airway
Inhaled foreign bodies or fluid can block the airway. By tipping the head back and straightening the airway, a first aider can look for blockages.

Breathing
If breathing stops, the first aider may blow air at regular intervals through the casualty's mouth into their lungs. This is called artificial ventilation.

Circulation
If a pulse is absent, the first aider may carry out heart massage (external chest compression) to try to stimulate the heart into action.

First-aid kit

In many countries, the law requires workplaces and schools to keep first-aid kits. The contents should be kept in a clean, marked container and be re-stocked regularly. Because there is a danger of misusing drugs, the contents of some kits are restricted to sterile wound dressings.

Safety scissors
Forceps (tweezers)
Painkillers
Bandages and sterile dressings
Eyebath
Cottonwool or similar absorbents
Elasticated bandage for treating sprains

First-aid kit for use in the home

Bent leg and arm in front of body prevent casualty rolling onto front.

An extended head and neck keeps the airway open and prevents the tongue blocking throat.

Recovery position

Recovery position
If the casualty is breathing but unconscious, the first aider may gently place him or her in the recovery position until expert help arrives. However, it is important to remember that a person involved in a bad accident may have damage to bones and nerves. First aiders should avoid moving the casualty, unless it is vital to save life.

FIND OUT MORE

DRUGS · HOSPITALS · MEDICINE · MEDICINE, HISTORY OF · NIGHTINGALE, FLORENCE · PLANTS, USES OF

FISH

THE FIRST FISH appeared in the seas 470 million years ago. Today, more than 20,000 species have been described, ranging from the great whale shark to the pygmy goby. Fish live in freshwater streams, rivers, and lakes, and in saltwater seas and oceans. A few, including eels and salmon, migrate from salt to fresh water. Some fish are fierce predators, and because of this many others have evolved a range of methods of defence. Although most fish leave their eggs and young to look after themselves, some species protect their young.

Fins
Most fish have a dorsal fin, paired pectoral and pelvic fins, and a tail for movement. In some fish, fins have become specialized as lifting foils, walking legs, suckers for holding on, or poisoned spines for protection.

Scales
Most fish have a covering of backward-facing scales that help to streamline them. Bony fish have either flat, oval, or square overlapping scales, while sharks have tooth-like structures buried in the skin.

Dorsal fin

Caudal, or tail, fin

Operculum (gill cover)

Pectoral fin **European carp**

Anal fin

Pelvic fin

Gills
Almost all fish have gills for breathing. The sharks and rays have paired gills in the throat, with openings to the outside known as gill slits. Bony fish have paired gills at the back of the head, with one opening covered by a flap of skin known as the operculum.

Fish features

Fish have a number of features in common. They breathe through gills, and are generally streamlined in shape with paired body muscles along each side. They have a tail for propulsion, fins for steering, and scales for protection. Their heads contain paired eyes and an obvious mouth with teeth.

Swim bladder
Bony fish have a swim bladder containing air, and they are able to fill and empty it at will. In many bony fish the swim bladder controls buoyancy, allowing the fish to move up and down in the water.

Swim bladder   *Stomach*

Gills

Inside a fish   *Heart*

Flatfish

Flatfish spend most of their lives lying on their sides, half buried and camouflaged in the sand on the seabed. Like most fish, the young develop in eggs. They hatch into normal larval fish that swim "the right way up" in the plankton.

10 days old

1 The larval fish has an eye on either side of its head.

17 days old

2 One eye gradually "migrates" to the other side of the head.

35 days old

3 An adult flatfish lies on one side. Its eyes are on top.

Fish groups

The fish are divided into three groups: jawless and primitive fish (cyclostomes), which include the lampreys and hagfish; cartilaginous fish (elasmobranchs), which include the sharks, rays, and ratfish; bony fish (teleosts), which include the more familiar fish, such as herring, cod, plaice, trout, eels, goldfish, sticklebacks, and guppies.

Caudal fin   *Dorsal fin*

Great white shark

Gill slits

Pectoral fin

Sharp teeth

Pike

Jawless fish
Hagfish and lampreys have funnel-shaped mouths. Lampreys attach themselves to other fish with their mouths and rasp away flesh with their teeth. Hagfish are scavengers.

Sea lamprey

Bony fish
These fish are divided into two groups – those with jointed bony fin rays, such as most fresh- and saltwater fish, and those with fleshy fin lobes, such as lungfish.

Cartilaginous fish
Sharks and rays have large mouths with many teeth in rows that are continually being replaced. Their skeletons are made of cartilage (gristle), instead of bones.

Where fish live

There are fish living wherever there is water. Some fish live in oceans, the largest numbers living in the shallow seas of the continental shelf. The most brightly coloured fish live on coral reefs. Other fish live on muddy, sandy, or rocky seashores, in estuaries, in rivers and streams, and even in temporary puddles.

On land
Inhabitants of Indo-Pacific mudflats and mangrove swamps, mudskippers are able to leave the water. They can stay on land for hours, absorbing oxygen through the mouth and pharynx. They have eyes on top of their heads for all-round vision.

Mudskipper

Red mullet

Rainbow trout

Oceans
The oceans provide a range of habitats for fish. Light-producing fish live in the deepest ocean trenches, while other fish live near hot volcanic vents. Some, such as sharks, roam the open oceans searching for smaller fish to eat.

Fresh water
Fish live in fast-flowing streams, slow-moving rivers, ponds, and lakes, and are suited to their habitat. Some have to be powerful swimmers or have suckers for holding on to stones. Others live in shoals or are camouflaged to avoid predators.

Protection

As well as scales, fish use colour, camouflage, or poisonous spines to protect themselves. The spiny puffer fish can take in water or air and swells up to more than twice its size. Some eels use an electric discharge, while other fish live in shoals, making it difficult for a predator to pick out any one individual.

Clown fish

Colour
Fish use colour to warn other fish that they are poisonous. Colour also helps some fish hide from predators. The fish's colour depends on its lifestyle. Cave fish have no colour; deep-sea fish are black; open-sea fish are a silvery colour.

Cutting blade
The surgeon fish has a formidable cutting blade that lies in a groove. This defensive structure is a developed scale and is as sharp as a surgeon's scalpel. If attacked, the fish erects the blade and slices its opponent with a blow from its tail.

Plaice

Camouflage
Some fish look like the plants among which they live. The triple tail looks like a mangrove leaf, and the leafy sea-dragon and sargassum fish look like seaweed. The plaice can change colour to match the surrounding seabed.

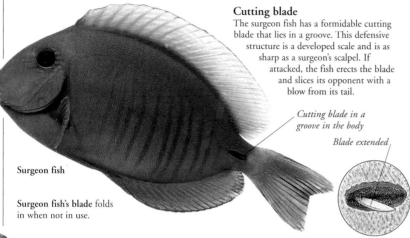

Cutting blade in a groove in the body

Blade extended

Surgeon fish

Surgeon fish's blade folds in when not in use.

Weever fish

Poison
Several fish are poisonous. The weever fishes are extremely dangerous. They lie partly buried and camouflaged in sand, waiting for food. The spines on their gill covers and dorsal fin can inject poison into anyone who steps on one.

Food

Many larger fish, including sharks, groupers, pikes, and barracudas, are predators and catch and eat their prey. Most smaller shoal fish feed on plankton, which floats around in the water. Some fish are bottom feeders, such as plaice, while others are grazers, such as the parrot fish, which rasps organisms from rocks.

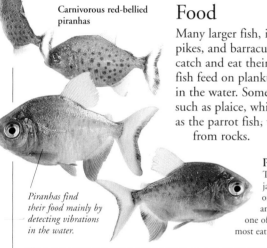

Carnivorous red-bellied piranhas

Piranhas find their food mainly by detecting vibrations in the water.

Cleaner fish
Fish called cleaners, such as some wrasses, have "cleaning" stations where they wait for customers. The customers allow the cleaners to remove bits of food and parasites from their skin, gills, fins, and even right inside their mouths.

Cleaner wrasse at work

Piranhas
These South American fish have strong jaws and sharp triangular teeth. A shoal of carnivorous piranhas can strip an animal to the bone in minutes. They are one of the most feared types of fish, but most eat mainly fruit and nuts.

Angler fish with lure

Angler fish
Angler fish usually live in deep water. They have a dorsal fin ray modified into a fishing line, with a lure on the end to attract their prey. They can swallow fish much larger than themselves.

Reproduction

Most bony fish lay eggs in the water, and these are then fertilized by a male's sperm. The parents usually leave the eggs to their fate, but some species protect their young in their mouths, in pouches, or in nests. Some sharks, such as the dogfish, lay eggs in an egg case, while others bear live young.

Sticklebacks
Male sticklebacks make a nest and attract females by doing a zigzag dance. The female lays her eggs in the nest, and the male fertilizes them. He then protects the nest from any intruder until the young hatch and are ready to fend for themselves.

Male three-spined stickleback

Seahorses
Within 10 seconds of mating, the female seahorse transfers 200 fertilized eggs into the brood-pouch of the male. The male carries them around with him for four weeks until they are ready to hatch. The male then "gives birth", and the young seahorses swim away.

Male stickleback's underside turns red in the breeding season.

Stickleback eggs

Salmon
The Atlantic salmon lays its eggs in upland streams. The young, called parr, live there for three years; then they are called smolt. The smolt swim down-river to the sea and travel across the Atlantic. At maturity, the salmon return to spawn in the same stream where they hatched.

Adult salmon will leap up waterfalls on their journey upstream to spawn.

FIND OUT MORE   CAMOUFLAGE AND COLOUR   LAKE AND RIVER WILDLIFE   MARSH AND SWAMP WILDLIFE   MIGRATION   OCEAN WILDLIFE   POISONOUS ANIMALS   SHARKS AND RAYS

Fish
Marine

Blenny lives in shallow water and often rests on the bottom.

Royal gramma fish identifies itself to a mate with dazzling colours.

Zebra pipe fish hides in eel-grass.

Large black spots look like spots on a panther.

Cuckoo wrasse is a colourful fish that lives in British waters.

Red mullet is probably the most important commercial marine fish in the world.

Panther grouper is a lethal predator like its namesake.

Extremely poisonous fin ray spines

Both eyes are on the upper surface.

Plaice is a flat fish and can change colour to merge with the seabed.

Juvenile lumpsucker

Clown triggerfish has a spiny dorsal fin that it can lock erect like a trigger.

Lumpsucker has sucker-like fins for clinging safely to stones and rocks in rough seas.

Lionfish is brightly coloured, which warns its enemies that it is deadly poisonous.

Large free dorsal fin rays

Spiny boxfish has a rigid body from which it gets its name.

Port Jackson shark produces an egg case, or "mermaid's purse", in which the young develop.

John Dory sucks up its food in a tube formed by extendable jaws.

Hatchetfish lives in the deep sea and has luminescent lights along its sides.

Butterfish is well camouflaged among the browny-green seaweed-covered rocks where it lives.

Blue-ringed angelfish is flattened from side to side, making it difficult to see from the front.

Angelfish are often brightly coloured.

Large sensitive eyes for seeing in the dark

Freshwater

Bitterling lays its eggs in a freshwater mussel.

Large eyes for accurate shooting

Minnows live in shoals for protection.

Minnows are small silvery fish that live in clean, fast-flowing, freshwater streams.

Archerfish shoots a jet of water above the surface to capture its insect prey.

Uncoloured guppy, or toothcarp, bears its young alive, unlike most fish, which lay eggs.

Blue-ribbon eel is long and thin, allowing it to hide in narrow crevices.

Neon tetra is a very small, brightly coloured, tropical fish, often kept in aquaria.

F

FISHING INDUSTRY

LONG BEFORE FARMING BEGAN, people fed themselves by hunting fish and land animals. Today, the fishing industry continues this hunting tradition. Fishing vessels go to sea from every country with a coastline. Small boats, such as the stern trawler, have few crew members, and fish within a day's sailing of their home port. The biggest fishing ships can stay at sea for months, and freeze their catch on board.

Fishing with lines
To catch valuable tuna, fishing boats trail a line as long as 180 km (112 miles, 97 nautical miles). Branching off this line are 200 smaller lines, each ending in a baited hook. This arrangement is known as a drifting longline.

Sea fishing

Most sea fish live within 50 m (165 ft) of the surface. They are concentrated in the shallow waters around the coasts of continents. In the past, the supply of sea fish appeared limitless. However, intensive fishing in areas that were once rich in fish, such as the Grand Banks of North America, has driven cod and other popular species to the edge of extinction.

Deep-water fishing
To catch demersal fish (those that live near the ocean floor), fishing boats sink bag-shaped nets in the water. The fish are trapped by towing the net along the bottom (trawling) or drawing the neck of the net closed (seine fishing). The boat then hauls in the net to land the catch.

Stern trawler

Fish-finding equipment in wheelhouse shows the crew where to find the biggest catch.

Deck winch drags the full net towards the boat.

Hoist lifts the net on to the boat.

P40

Crew launch the trawl net over the boat's stern.

Lobster pot

Traps
Bait lures lobsters into this basket-like "pot", which rests on the seabed in shallow water. Its funnel-shaped entrance makes escape impossible. Fish traps take many different forms: the Mediterranean tuna trap, for example, is like a maze of net corridors anchored to the seabed. There are even special aerial traps for catching flying fish.

Seine fishing

Net closes like a purse, entrapping fish.

Weighted net hangs down from floats.

Surface fishing
Many species of pelagic fish (those that live near the surface) swim together in large groups called shoals, and it is these shoals that fishing boats seek. They catch them by enclosing the shoal in a purse seine net, which is like a circular curtain. Pulling a line closes the bottom of the net, preventing the fish from escaping.

Freshwater fishing

Only 5 per cent of the world's fish catch comes from freshwater sources, such as rivers and lakes. However, in non-industrialized nations freshwater fishing with lines and nets is a vital industry, especially on great lakes such as those in East Africa's Rift Valley. In industrialized nations, anglers have to pay to fish on the few remaining stretches of unpolluted water.

Fur and feather make hook resemble an insect.

Freshwater rods

Barb

Point

Double hook   Treble hook   Fly-fishing bait   Weight

Ocean mammals
The oceans are also home to mammals. Fishing for whales, the world's largest mammals, has now almost ceased because their numbers fell so low. The fur of the seal makes it a target for hunters, and although few fishing vessels catch dolphins deliberately, many dolphins die because they become entangled in abandoned nets.

In the past, whaling crews made beautiful carvings out of the bones and teeth of sea mammals.

Fish farming
Just as farming produces meat more efficiently than hunting, farming fish is more efficient than catching them. Fish farms breed fish carefully to give good-quality stock, and protect the young fish in ponds or enclosures from predators. Carp and trout are the main freshwater farm fish.

Angling
Fishing for sport is known as angling, and is as ancient as fishing for food. Anglers fix a hook to a thin line and then cast it into the water using a long, flexible rod. To lure fish, anglers bait the hook with worms or insects. They may also use a "fly", which is a hook disguised as an insect.

FIND OUT MORE	FARMING	FISH	FOOD	SHIPS AND BOATS	SPORT	WHALES AND DOLPHINS

FLAGS

FOR HUNDREDS of years, people have used flags as emblems, signals, or rallying points. Among the earliest flags were those flown in battle, so that soldiers could identify their leader and tell each side apart. The flag has since developed as a means of communication, used to send rapid signals, or as a symbol representing a nation or group. Every country has its own flag, as do many states and most political organizations.

Cap Becket Toggle Upper hoist canton Upper fly canton

Sleeve

Flag pole

Lower hoist canton Lower fly canton

Halyard – long rope that runs the length of the pole.

Finial Looped clip

Parts of a flag

A flag is usually made from brightly coloured fabric and is square or rectangular in shape – although more varied shapes, such as streamers, banners, and long, narrow pennons, were once popular. It is divided into four quarters (cantons): those near the pole are the hoist, and the others the fly. A special emblem often appears in the upper hoist canton.

Flying the flag

In Europe, flags are attached to the pole by passing the toggle through a loop (becket) in another rope (halyard). In the USA, flags have eyelets to which clips are attached. Inglefield clips have a quick-release mechanism, and are popular at sea. Parade flagstaffs are topped with decorative finials.

Toggle and becket

First flags

Many ancient armies carried standards, carved symbols on the end of a pole. The Roman standard first introduced cloth flags. These hung from horizontal poles, to make them easy to carry on horseback.

Homemade flag

The first flag was probably a piece of brightly coloured cloth tied to a stick. A plain red flag spelt danger to early peoples, just as it does today.

Finial on top of pole could show legion badge

Cloth dyed with natural earth pigment

Badge of legion

Pride of a legion

The Roman standard was awarded to a military unit only as a reward for special endeavour.

LEG II AVG

Name of legion

Uses of flags

Flags communicate across language barriers. At sea, the International Code of Signals is a system of signalling with flags: the meanings are the same in every language. In both sports and politics, flags also send messages that are understood universally.

Red Cross flag

Flag of the United Nations

The dove on the Greenpeace flag, a symbol of hope

Rallying cries

Modern flags may be developed to identify political movements, or for international medical or environmental groups. The emblems and colours represent the organization's ideals: for instance, a white background stands for peace, while olive branches symbolize reconciliation.

Soccer flags are raised to signal when the ball has gone out of play.

Golf flags are attached to slender pins to mark the holes on a course.

Sports flags

Flags are used in many sports for marking out the area of play or signalling to participants.

Plastic marker flags

Political symbols

A symbol on a national flag can sum up political ideals that would otherwise take many words. The former Soviet red flag with its hammer and sickle symbol represented the workers and farmers who took part in the Russian Revolution.

Semaphore

This method of signalling with just two flags is still used at sea. Signallers can spell out a message quickly, simply by changing the position of their arms. Red and yellow flags are chosen because they can be seen over long distances.

A B C D E F G H I J K L M N

O P Q R S T U V W X Y Z

FIND OUT MORE   FOOTBALL   PEACE MOVEMENTS   ROMAN EMPIRE   SHIPS AND BOATS   SIGNS AND SYMBOLS   SOVIET UNION   UNITED NATIONS

International Code of Signals
Alphabet and single flag messages

A I have a diver down; keep well clear at slow speed.

B I am taking in, or discharging, or carrying dangerous goods.

C Yes.

D Keep clear of me; I am manoeuvring with difficulty.

E I am altering my course to starboard.

F I am disabled; communicate with me.

G I require a pilot (or, I am hauling nets).

H I have a pilot on board.

I I am altering my course to port.

J I am on fire and have dangerous cargo on board; keep well clear of me.

K I wish to communicate with you.

Two-flag messages

DX I am sinking.

L You should stop your vessel instantly.

M My vessel is stopped and making no way through the water.

N No.

O Man overboard.

P All persons should report on board as vessel is about to proceed to sea.

NG You are in a dangerous position.

Q My vessel is healthy and I require free pratique [permission to trade].

R [No single letter meaning]

S My engines are going astern.

T Keep clear of me; I am engaged in pair trawling.

U You are running into danger.

AC I am abandoning my vessel.

V I require assistance.

W I require medical assistance.

X Stop carrying out your intentions and watch my signals.

Y I am dragging my anchor.

Z I require a tug.

NH You are clear of all dangers.

Numerals

ONE   TWO   THREE   FOUR   FIVE

SIX   SEVEN   EIGHT   NINE   ZERO

FLIES

THEY MAY BE PESTS AT TIMES, but flies are remarkable insects. As their name suggests, they have mastered the power of flight. Fast and agile in the air, flies dart about, hover, and make lightning turns. There are about 90,000 different insects that we call flies. About 75,000 of these are true flies, which have only one pair of wings and belong to the insect group Diptera. The remainder form many other groups of insects with two pairs of wings. Unlike most other types of fly, the larvae of true flies are completely different from the adults. Often called maggots, they have simple bodies with no legs and are little more than eating machines.

Feeding

Fly larvae feed on foods such as microscopic organisms, living flesh, plants, and dung. The mouthparts of adult flies are adapted for a liquid diet. They have extendible tubes to draw fluids into their bodies. The feeding habits of flies cause many health problems worldwide, from stomach upsets to more serious illnesses such as cholera.

Abdomen swollen with blood

Tsetse fly

Bloodsuckers and predators
Bloodsuckers and flies that catch prey have piercing mouthparts that cut holes in their victims. They inject anti-clotting agents to keep blood flowing, or poison to kill the prey. Enzymes are also released to help break down the body contents.

Hoverfly

Nectar and waste feeders
Flies that feed on nectar or decaying matter have soft pads on the ends of their sucking mouthparts, that help soak up liquid food. On solid food, flies deposit saliva, then suck up the partly digested juice that results.

Features of a true fly

The body of an adult fly is clearly divided into three main parts: the head, thorax, and abdomen. The head bears the sucking mouthparts and a bulging pair of compound eyes, between which sprouts a pair of antennae. Attached to the thorax are the fly's six legs and its membranous wings. The abdomen contains most of the body organs.

Long hairs on thorax

Head

Antenna

Sponge-like mouthparts

Close-up of mouthparts

Compound eye

Sense hairs

Single pair of wings

Haltres of a crane fly

Blue iridescence on abdomen

The soles of the feet have taste buds on them.

Mouthparts
The mouthparts of a blowfly end in soft spongy pads that enable them to suck up liquids.

Bluebottle feeding

Flight stabilizers
True flies have a single pair of wings; the hindwings have developed into club-ended stubs called halteres. Halteres act as balancing organs that improve the fly's flight control and make it easier to change direction.

Breeding

After mating, female flies lay hundreds of eggs on a suitable feeding site for the larvae, that develop from the eggs. These sites may be in dung, soil, or water, or on leaves, dead bodies, or living animals. The larvae eat voraciously, and grow into pupae within which they change into their adult shape and form.

Robber flies mating

Bluebottle larvae

Mating
Before mating, flies may go through elaborate courtship rituals. Fruit flies dance on leaves, and gnats dance in the air. After mating, female robber flies commonly eat their mates.

Larvae
Fly eggs often hatch out into larvae on dead animals, which they begin to eat. The larvae, also called maggots, may live longer than the adult flies into which they develop.

Aquatic larvae

Mosquitos and many other bloodsucking flies lay their eggs in water. The larvae that develop float upside-down on the surface. They breathe through a tube attached to the abdomen, that pokes above the water. After pupation, the adult emerges to fly away.

Tube takes in air.

Mosquito larva

Types of fly

In addition to true flies, many other kinds of fly exist that all have two pairs of wings, such as dragonflies and mayflies. The young that emerge from their eggs have a more complicated body structure than the larvae of true flies – some even look like wingless versions of the adults.

Giant compound eyes

Dragonflies
Dragonflies are large predators. They dart around in seach of other insects that they catch in flight with their long legs. They lay their eggs in water.

Long antenna

Caddis flies
Adult caddis flies always live near water. Their larvae live underwater, and carry with them a protective case made of plant debris or sand.

Mayflies
Young mayflies live below water. After growing wings, they leave the water and form swarms in the air. The adults mate, lay their eggs, then die a few hours later.

Long, thin legs

Lacewings
Lacewings often hibernate in houses over winter. The adults and larvae prey on other insects such as aphids. They are weak fliers.

Delicate wings

BLUEBOTTLE

SCIENTIFIC NAME	*Calliphora erythrocephala*
ORDER	Diptera
FAMILY	Calliphoridae
DISTRIBUTION	Europe
HABITAT	Fields, meadows, houses, and buildings
DIET	Rotting flesh, faeces, and other decomposing organic matter; adults also eat nectar
SIZE	Length 10 mm (0.4 in)
LIFESPAN	Larvae: 7 days; pupae: 8–10 days; adults: unknown

FIND OUT MORE ARTHROPODS • DISEASES • EGGS • FLIGHT, ANIMAL • INSECTS • MARSH AND SWAMP WILDLIFE

FLIGHT, ANIMAL

THE ONLY ANIMALS CAPABLE of powered flight are birds, bats, and insects. Some other animals can glide for short distances. Flight is very useful. It helps the animals to find food, escape from predators, and migrate long distances. Flying animals need wings, powerful wing muscles, a streamlined shape, and a lightweight body. They also need to eat lots of food to give them the energy to flap their wings.

Minla in flight

Birds

A bird's wings are an aerofoil shape – curved on top and slightly hollow underneath. As the wings move through the air, a difference in air pressure is created above and below, which lifts the bird up into the air. A bird steers by changing the angle of one or both wings, twisting its wings, and spreading and twisting its tail.

Hovering
Hummingbirds are among the birds that hover. They beat their wings in a figure-of-eight pattern, producing lift on both the upstroke and downstroke. They can also fly sideways, straight up and down, backwards, and even upside-down.

Between flaps, the bird folds its wings and rests.

Tail used to steer and change direction

Red-tailed minlas have an up-and-down flight.

Forward flight
Most small birds, such as this minla of eastern Asia, fly by flapping their wings up and down. As the wings go down, they push air backwards, moving the bird forwards. As the wings go up, the feathers at the wingtips move apart to allow air to slip through.

Feathers closed for the downstroke

Swan taking off

Gliding albatross

Gliding
Some large birds rarely flap their wings. Albatrosses and other large seabirds glide on strong winds rising off the waves. Albatrosses can travel for hundreds of kilometres a day. Large land birds, such as vultures and eagles, float on columns of rising hot air called thermals.

Taking off
Small birds take off by jumping into the air and flapping their wings. They may take off straight from the ground or from a perch. A large, heavy bird, such as a swan, cannot do this. It needs to run along while flapping its wings to create enough lift for take-off.

Insects

A small insect, such as a mosquito, flaps its wings 1,000 times a second. Most insects flap about 520 times a second. Dragonflies are the fastest insect fliers, reaching nearly 300 km/h (190 mph). Some insects, such as flies, have one pair of wings. Others, such as bees, have two pairs.

Vertical muscle contracts, moving the wings up.

Horizontal muscle contracts, moving the wings down.

Wing muscles
Insect wings developed from their hard body covering. They are not modified legs, like the wings of birds or bats. Insects do not have any muscles on the wings. Instead, their wing muscles are inside the thorax, the middle part of the body.

Cockchafer take-off
The cockchafer is a beetle with two pairs of wings. The front wings are hard wing cases, which are held out of the way during flight. They give the beetle some lift when it flies fast. The flexible back wings flap up and down to provide the power for flight.

Bats

The only mammals able to fly, bats are more acrobatic than birds. They have four large pairs of flight muscles and several smaller pairs, while birds have only two pairs. Each wing consists of skin stretched between four long fingers.

Wing is made of an elastic membrane covered with skin.

The bat flexes its arm bones up and down to flap its wings.

Long narrow wings are for fast flight in open areas.

Horseshoe bats find prey by echolocation.

Thumbs are used for clinging to surfaces.

Gliding animals

Some animals can glide slowly downwards. They have developed large fins, or webs or flaps of skin, which they spread out to slow their fall. They have to be able to judge speeds and distances accurately.

Flying squirrel
Flaps of skin allow a flying squirrel to glide up to 100 m (330 ft) between trees. The squirrel uses its tail as a rudder, and has sharp claws to grasp the surface on landing.

Flying squirrel

Flying fish
To escape predators, flying fish swim fast along the surface, then take off and glide for up to 50 m (160 ft), with their huge fins held out.

Flying gecko
The gecko (above) has flaps of skin along the sides of its body and tail. It spreads out the flaps to glide between trees. It has webbed feet to help with steering.

Flying fish

FIND OUT MORE AIRCRAFT ANIMALS BATS BIRDS FLIGHT, HISTORY OF INSECTS MIGRATION

FLIGHT, HISTORY OF

EVERY DAY, MILLIONS OF PEOPLE fly to destinations all over the world. Planes are a common sight in the skies, but, despite their widespread use, they were first developed only about 90 years ago. The urge to fly is ancient, but by the start of the 20th century, the only flying machines were hot-air balloons, airships, and gliders. World War I stimulated the development of aeroplanes and, by the end of World War II, advances had resulted in jets and rockets. Since then, flight technology has produced supersonic planes and space travel.

Flying machine designed by Leonardo da Vinci in the 15th century

Copying the birds
Wings are the part of an aircraft that provide the upwards lift needed to keep it in the air. Successful aeroplanes were impossible to build before people understood how wings worked. Early attempts at flight concentrated on copying the flapping action of birds, which proved to be impractical because a human's muscles are far too weak. Many "bird men" were killed trying to fly.

First controlled flight
The first controlled flight of a powered aeroplane took place on 17 December 1903 in Kitty Hawk, North Carolina, USA. The plane, *Flyer I*, flew 36 m (119 ft) in a flight that lasted under 12 seconds: it is nonetheless perhaps the most famous flight of all time. *Flyer I* was designed and built by the Wright brothers, Orville and Wilbur, after years of experiments with kites and gliders. It was powered by a petrol engine they built themselves.

Flyer I climbed to a height of 3 m (10 feet).

Wilbur Wright watches his brother Orville take off.

Warplanes
The military's interest in the potential of aeroplanes as weaponry was central to the advancement of flight technology. During World War I (1914–18), warplanes were transformed from being slow and vulnerable to being fast, easily manoeuvrable fighting machines. Huge bomber and fighter planes were made in this period.

Protective clothing worn by World War I pilots included flying helmet, goggles and gauntlets.

Biplane of 1917

Biplane
World War I pilots flew biplane (twin-winged) fighters. Built from wood and fabric, biplanes were sturdier than monoplanes, but flying them was little fun. The cockpit was open to the cold and wet, and to spits of oil from the engine. Larger fighters had a second cockpit for a navigator and gunner. Single-seaters had a machine gun that fired through the spinning propeller.

Airships
Airships are held aloft by a vast gas-filled envelope and driven forward by engines with propellers. Airships were an important form of passenger and military transport until long-distance aircraft were developed in the 1940s.

Modern age
The basis for the modern aeroplane first appeared in the 1920s. It was a monoplane (single-winged) aircraft. The wing was made of metal, as was the fuselage. All aircraft had piston engines and propellers until the late 1930s, when a new type of engine, the jet, was invented.

Amelia Earhart
American aviation pioneer Amelia Earhart (1898–1937) set several long-distance flight records. She was the first woman to fly solo across the Atlantic. In 1937, in a bid to fly round the world, she disappeared near New Guinea.

Harrier GR5 jet fighter

Jets
A turbojet engine allows aircraft to fly much faster and more quietly than a propeller engine. Jet aircraft were increasingly used after World War II and became standard for fighter aircraft and for long-distance passenger planes.

Boarding pass
Airline ticket

Passenger flight
Fast, comfortable, and affordable air travel had become accessible by the 1960s. Today, millions of passengers fly around the world in the Boeing 747, a so-called "jumbo jet" which has quiet, turbofan engines.

Ariane launch vehicle

Space flight
The first rockets powerful enough to reach space were built in the late 1950s. Today, modern launch vehicles and re-usable spacecraft, such as the Shuttle, make going into orbit almost an everyday event.

FIND OUT MORE   AIRCRAFT   AIRPORTS   AIRSHIPS AND BALLOONS   LEONARDO DA VINCI   SPACE EXPLORATION   TRANSPORT, HISTORY OF   TRAVEL   WARPLANES   WEAPONS

FLIGHTLESS BIRDS

FLYING IS A VERY USEFUL WAY of moving, but it does have drawbacks. It uses a lot of energy, and it is possible only for animals with a light body. During the course of evolution, some birds have given up flight and the problems it brings. Instead, they run, or, as is the case with penguins, they swim; some can move extremely fast. There are about 40 species of flightless birds alive today, including kiwis, emus, and the world's biggest bird, the ostrich. Many more flightless species, including some record-breaking giants, existed in the past, and some of today's species are also in danger of extinction.

Long neck with sparse feathers

Weak, fanlike wings used in courtship rituals.

Females are slightly smaller than males, with brown plumage instead of black.

Two large clawed toes on each foot

Ostrich crèche
Young ostriches are guarded by an adult male. Several families of chicks gather together, forming a group called a crèche.

Kiwis

These medium-sized birds are found only in the forests of New Zealand. Their wings are only about 5 cm (2 in) long, and their body is covered with a unique plumage that looks like hair. Kiwis are nocturnal and because they have poor eyesight, they find food mainly by smelling it.

Ostrich

The ostrich is the world's largest bird. It can run at up to 65 kmh (40 mph), and uses its speed and stamina to outdistance most of its enemies. An ostrich's feet have two toes, and each toe ends in a large claw. If an ostrich is cornered, it uses these claws as deadly weapons to defend itself.

Hatching
The shell of an ostrich egg is thicker than a china mug, but not as hard. The young ostrich breaks out by kicking and pecking at the shell.

Sensory, whisker-like feathers at the base of the beak

1 The chick turns its body as it pecks and pushes at the shell.

2 Half the shell is in pieces, and the chick is almost free of the egg.

3 The chick tumbles out and will soon start to look for food.

Small wings are hidden under the body plumage.

Hard "helmet," or casque

Rheas escape from danger by running away.

Cassowaries
These large, flightless birds live in dense forests in northern Australia and New Guinea. They use their claws as weapons and have been known to kill people.

Rheas
There are two species of rheas, both of which live on the open plains in South America. Young rheas have bright stripes, but the adults are grayish-brown.

Strong legs with large feet

This egg is shown in proportion to the kiwi above.

Probing beak
The kiwi has nostrils at the tip of its long, curved beak, instead of near its head. It uses its beak to find food on the forest floor.

Kiwi egg
The kiwi's egg is 13 cm (5 in) long, and is a quarter of the female's weight. Relative to her body, the female kiwi lays the largest eggs of all birds.

Emus
Found only in Australia, emus are the second largest birds in the world, after the ostrich. Emus live in large flocks and wander long distances in search of food. They can cause problems on farms by raiding crops.

OSTRICH

SCIENTIFIC NAME	*Struthio camelus*
ORDER	Struthioniformes
FAMILY	Struthionidae
DISTRIBUTION	Tropical western and eastern Africa, and southern Africa
HABITAT	Savannah and semi-desert
DIET	Fruit, seeds, leaves, small animals
SIZE	Height up to 2.4 m (8 ft); weight up to 154 kg (340 lb)
LIFESPAN	About 30 years

FIND OUT MORE AUSTRALIAN WILDLIFE BIRDS EGGS FLIGHT GRASSLAND WILDLIFE PENGUINS SOUTH AMERCIAN WILDLIFE

FLOWERS

THE FIRST flowering plants appeared about 120 million years ago. They are now the largest group of plants, and are widespread. Flowers are the advanced reproductive structures of plants. The majority of them are pollinated by the wind or by animals. Over millions of years, flowers and insects have co-evolved to produce some very complex and interesting relationships.

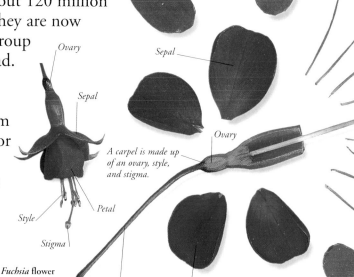

Petal

Anther

Filament

A stamen is made up of an anther and a filament.

Ovary

Sepal

Stigma

Sepal

Style

Ovary

A carpel is made up of an ovary, style, and stigma.

Style

Petal

Stigma

Fuchsia flower

Flower stalk

Sepals enclose the flower when in bud.

Anthers produce pollen grains.

When the anthers are ripe, they split to release masses of pollen.

Petal

Petals are brightly coloured to attract insects.

The **flower** is the structure that brings about sexual reproduction in the plant.

Parts of a flower

A plant's reproduction organs are inside the flowers. Stamens are male and produce pollen. The female organs are called carpels. These contain ovules, which develop into seeds. A ring of petals attracts pollinators, and sepals protect the flower when in bud.

Pollination

In order for seeds to develop, a flower has to be pollinated. Pollen from the stamens of a flower of the same species must stick to the plant's stigma. Cross-pollination occurs when pollen from one plant lands on the flowers of another. If a flower is pollinated by its own pollen, it is called self-pollination.

Bee at a *Narcissus* flower

Insect pollination
Flowers are mostly pollinated by insects. These are attracted to the flowers by their petals, a scent, and a supply of nectar or pollen to eat. The pollen sticks to a visiting insect and is carried to another flower.

Freesia

Tobacco plant

Wattle

Scent and colour
The colour and scent of a flower attract insects or other animals. Drops of sugary nectar secreted at the base of the petals provide food for the insects, which are dusted with pollen while they drink. Flowers are often sweetly scented, but some smell unpleasant, especially those pollinated by flies.

Water pollination
Aquatic plants may have aerial, submerged, or floating flowers. A few use the surface film of water to carry pollen. The flowers float in shallow dips. The pollen slides into these and pollinates the flowers.

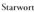

Starwort

Wind pollination
Some plants rely on wind to waft their pollen from one flower to another. Their flowers may have no petals, or just tiny ones. They are often arranged in catkins with conspicuous stamens and stigmas.

Hazel catkins and pollen

Bird pollination
Many flowers that rely on birds to pollinate them are red or orange – colours that attract birds. The flowers tend to be tubular so that birds can dip their beaks in. Stamens dust the birds' heads with sticky pollen.

Hummingbird at a thistle flower

Mammal pollination
Important mammal pollinators include some species of tropical bat and many types of tiny Australian possum. They pollinate flowers as they feed on nectar and pollen.

Pygmy possum feeding on a *Banksia* flower

Insect mimics

Many orchids have such specialized partnerships that only one type of insect serves as a pollinator. Some orchids look and smell so like a female insect, that males of that species try to mate with them, picking up pollen as they do so.

Bee orchid

An orchid's pollen is produced in small clumps called pollinia.

The bee orchid can be pollinated by a bee, but is often self-pollinated by the wind.

Part of the flower looks and smells just like a bee.

FIND OUT MORE | CARNIVOROUS PLANTS | FRUITS AND SEEDS | INSECTS | PLANTS | PLANT ANATOMY | PLANT REPRODUCTION | PLANT USES | TREES | WINDS

Flowers

Insect-pollinated

Urn-shaped flowers

Bramble pollinators include beetles and bees.

Bell heather is pollinated by short-tongued bees.

Primrose flowers appear in the spring.

Brown lines on the petals guides insects to the nectar.

Hollow-stemmed asphodel has hollow stems and leaves.

Each flower contains a drop of nectar.

Red clover has a head of tubular flowers.

Greater periwinkle is pollinated by bees.

Domed hood

Mirror orchid has pollen in clumps called pollinia.

Anemone pavonina is pollinated by insects.

Magnolia flowers have thick, waxy petals.

Corn marigold flowerhead has many tiny flowers.

Fox and cubs has strap-shaped ray florets.

Bastard balm attracts bees with its large petal.

Dwarf elder has small flowers clustered together.

Early dog violet has dark veins, which guide insects.

Wild pansy is pollinated by long-tongued bees.

Insects crawl into the bell-shaped flowers.

Foxglove is pollinated by bumblebees.

Umbels of tiny yellow flowers

Thorow-wax has clusters of flowers called umbels.

Marsh cinquefoil has much larger sepals than petals.

Red valerian has tiny tubular flowers pollinated by moths and butterflies.

Carline thistle has yellow flowers surrounded by stiff, spiny bracts.

Honeysuckle has scented flowers which attract honeybees and hawk moths.

Cornflower has scented flowers and is pollinated by flies and bees.

Common rockrose is pollinated by insects, but can be self-pollinating.

Red campion is pollinated by long-tongued bees and also by hoverflies.

Bird- and mammal-pollinated

Petals bend back so that birds are dusted with pollen.

Fuchsia is pollinated mostly by birds.

Passionflower is pollinated by nectar-drinking birds.

Silver wattle flowers attract birds and possums.

Nasturtium flowers are pollinated by birds.

Stamens and stigmas on a long column

Hibiscus dusts hawk moths and birds with pollen.

Urn plant flowers are surrounded by spiny bracts.

Wind-pollinated

Spike of petal-less flowers

Broad-leaved pondweed has a dense spike of flowers.

Greater plantain has purple anthers.

Anthers protrude from the tiny green flowers.

Armenian oak has male flowers in yellow catkins.

Long slender catkins

Sand couch has flowers in stalkless spikelets.

Female flowers

Alder has male flowers in long, dangling catkins.

Stinging nettle has catkins of male or female flowers.

FOOD

WE ARE WHAT WE EAT: our bodies get the energy and nourishment they need from our daily diet. Not having enough of the right food, or eating too much of the wrong food, causes ill-health. Food and eating are important in other ways too. Many countries have a distinctive cuisine (cooking style), which reflects the eating habits of its people and the ingredients available locally. In many industrialized nations, cooking is a hobby as well as a necessary task. Today there is concern about levels of chemicals in food, and many people choose an organic diet.

Fast food is food that is mass-prepared and served quickly in takeaway outlets. The hamburger is a popular fast food in many western countries.

A delicacy in France

Popular in Japan

Made with pig's blood

Jews and Muslims do not eat pork

Frog's legs   Seaweed   Black pudding   Snails   Pork sausages

Processing and preserving

Even before they are cooked, most foods must be processed to make them ready for cooking: for example, wheat must be ground into flour before it can be baked as bread. Preserving food allows it to be stored for use later; this reduces the risk of shortages, and prolongs availability. A food industry has grown up to provide the food we eat, and process, preserve, and package it.

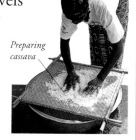

Preparing cassava

Cassava
Many foods are indigestible without processing but bitter cassava, the main food in many tropical areas, is actually poisonous. Grating, pressing, and heating the root removes the deadly cyanide it contains.

What is food?

Anything humans can digest counts as food. Worldwide, diets vary widely: food habits are influenced by availability, climate, and religious, moral, or social factors. Ideally, a daily diet should include staple, energy-giving carbohydrates, such as rice or pasta, plus proteins, fats, vitamins, and minerals. In reality, poverty or warfare make this impossible in many places.

Preparing food

Although some foods, such as salad vegetables and fruit, are delicious when raw, many foods need to be cooked first. Cooking makes food tastier and easier to digest. Cooking root vegetables, for instance, makes their starch grains absorb water, swell, and burst, releasing essential nutrients.

Salad

Fennel

Orange

Steaming fish is a healthy way to cook it.

Cooking methods
There are many cooking methods, such as simmering food in water, which heats it to just under 100°C (212°F). Only a few foods, such as eggs, cook at temperatures lower than this. Grilling or frying in oil heats food to a much higher temperature, cooking it faster.

Food preservation:
freezing peas

Viner

Frozen peas

1 Until frozen peas were invented, the only peas most people could eat were dried or tinned. A machine called a viner harvests the peas when they are sweet enough to be frozen. It tumbles them in a drum to remove the pods. These are ploughed back into the field as fertilizer.

2 Once at the factory, the peas are washed and blanched. They are then carried on a conveyor to the freezing chamber. On the way, jets of cold air prevent them sticking together. In the chamber, the peas are blast-frozen at a temperature of -18°C (-2°F).

3 Before packaging, the peas are assessed for quality and taste. Fresh vegetables begin to lose their nutrients as soon as they are picked. Because these peas have been frozen within two and a half hours, they are fresher than fresh peas in a shop.

Cocoa beans

Chocolate
Chocolate is a food product derived from the cocoa bean. The Aztecs of Mexico enjoyed a chocolate drink, flavoured with chilli. When the Spanish conquered Mexico in the 16th century, they introduced the drink to Europe. People began to eat solid chocolate from about 1630, but chocolate bars were a luxury until the 20th century.

Frozen food
Freezing food to preserve it dates from prehistoric times in cold regions. Following the appearance of home electric refrigerators in 1913, frozen vegetables first went on sale in the USA in 1930.

Peas in the pod

Frozen vegetables

Hunger and famine

Each year, 800 million people cannot get enough food to lead healthy lives, despite food surpluses in other parts of the world. Children suffer most. Malnutrition in children severely damages their physical and mental development. Every year in the developing world, famine (widespread starvation) occurs when insects, plant diseases, drought, or warfare destroy crops, and a harvest fails.

FIND OUT MORE   DIGESTION   FARMING   HEALTH AND FITNESS   TRADE AND INDUSTRY

Food

Types of food

Uncooked rice

Puffed rice cakes

Grains of wheat

Bread made with wheat flour

Maize

Tortilla chips

Rice is a staple food for Southern Asia and parts of Africa.

Wheat is a staple in North America, Europe, Australia, and parts of Asia.

Maize (corn) is a staple food in some African, Asian, and American countries.

Potatoes

Lettuce

Soybeans

Coconut

Watermelon

Honeycomb

Starchy roots are a good source of carbohydrate.

Vegetables are an important source of vitamins.

Pulses (beans and peas) are rich in protein.

Nuts and seeds can be pressed to make oils.

Fruits are an important source of vitamins.

Sugars and honey sweeten food.

Duck

Lobster

Cheese

Olive oil

Chillis

Vanilla

Meat is a major protein source.

Fish and shellfish are a low-fat protein source.

Eggs are a valuable source of protein.

Milk and milk products provide protein and important minerals.

Fats and oils store energy.

Spices and herbs add flavour to a meal.

World cookery

Chicken

Mussels

Prawns

Salad

Australia: meats grilled out-of-doors on a barbecue

India: vegetable curry and *roti* (wheat bread)

France: *bouillabaisse,* fish soup, served with bread

Mexico: *buritto,* a pancake with chilli, meat, beans

Spain: *paella,* rice simmered with chicken, seafood, and spices

Raw salmon

Vietnam: spring rolls filled with pork, prawns, noodles

Morocco: chicken baked with spices

United States: pork ribs with black-eyed peas

China: roast duck with an aromatic seasoning

Parmesan cheese

Yorkshire pudding

Italy: *fettucini,* a kind of pasta, in a tomato sauce

Thailand: *pad thai,* Thai fried noodles

Japan: *sushi,* extremely fresh, raw fish, with rice and seaweed

United Kingdom: roast beef, gravy, and roast potatoes

Russia: *borscht* (beetroot soup) with *blinis* (pancakes)

FOOD WEBS AND CHAINS

THE LIVES OF DIFFERENT species in a wildlife community are linked together through the process of feeding. As plants and animals grow and are eaten by others, energy and food substances locked up in their body tissues pass on along a chain. These food chains interlink with one another, and the resulting network is called a food web. The number of different animals and plants in a community is naturally balanced. If the balance is upset it can affect the whole web.

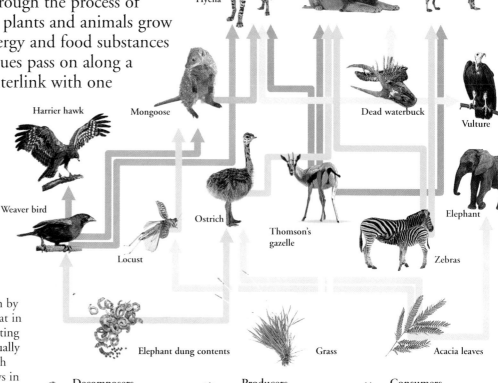

Hyena · Lion · African hunting dog · Harrier hawk · Mongoose · Dead waterbuck · Vulture · Weaver bird · Ostrich · Thomson's gazelle · Elephant · Locust · Zebras · Elephant dung contents · Grass · Acacia leaves

Food webs

In a simple food chain, a plant is eaten by a herbivore (a plant-eating animal), that in turn is eaten by a carnivore (a meat-eating animal). In nature, food chains are usually longer than this, and they connect with other chains to form a web. The arrows in this diagram show how different plant foods on a typical African savannah are eaten by a range of animals, that, in turn, provide food for various other animals.

Decomposers
Some animals, fungi, and bacteria feed on dead or waste plant and animal tissue. They turn it back into simple substances, which plants use to grow.

Producers
In ecology, plants are called producers. They start the food chain by using the sun's energy to produce food from simple substances.

Consumers
Animals are known as consumers because they get the biological material they need for life from the plants or other animals that they eat or consume.

Top predator

The tawny owl at the top of this food chain is known as the top predator. An owl needs to eat many weasels and rodents to meet its energy needs.

The number of animals or plants represents the amount of energy available to the next level.

Trophic pyramids

Ecologists call each stage in a food chain a trophic level. These levels can be represented as a pyramid. Animals use much of the energy they gain from their food to grow. They also use energy to live, to move about, breed, feed, and avoid their enemies. This means that at each trophic level there is less energy available to the next level.

Secondary consumers

Weasels are secondary consumers because they get energy from the plants through other consumers. There are more weasels in a community than the owls that hunt them.

Primary consumers

Mice and voles get energy directly from plants. They use a lot of energy; many are needed to support the weasels.

Primary producers

Energy is stored in plants. It takes a large quantity to support the rodents.

Population cycles

A change in the population of one species affects the population of other species in the food chain. The lemming population in the tundra and Arctic rises and falls on roughly a four-year cycle. When there are lots of lemmings, Arctic foxes, which hunt them, breed more successfully, so their numbers increase too.

Arctic fox

Giant African land snail

Partula snail

Upsetting the balance

When the giant African land snail was taken to Pacific islands, the snails destroyed vegetation because there was nothing to prey on them. Another type of snail was released to eat their eggs, but these began to wipe out the native *Partula* snail instead.

FIND OUT MORE   ANIMALS   AFRICAN WILDLIFE   ECOLOGY AND ECOSYSTEMS   ENERGY   FOOD   GRASSLAND WILDLIFE   PHOTOSYNTHESIS   RAINFOREST WILDLIFE

FOOTBALL

THE VARIOUS FORMS OF FOOTBALL are among the most popular sports to play and watch. Association football, or soccer, is played in almost every country by men and women. Rugby games are less widespread, but the new professional rugby union is becoming increasingly international. American football, although watched worldwide on television, is played little outside the United States. Other "national" games include Australian football, played chiefly in the state of Victoria, and Gaelic football, an Irish game.

Soccer ball

Soccer

Soccer is a kicking game played 11-a-side. The goalkeeper is the only person allowed to handle the ball. The object is to propel the ball into the opposition's goal with a foot or the head. A game lasts 90 minutes, with a 15-minute interval plus, in some knock-out competitions, an extra 15 minutes each way.

Soccer pitch

Helmet

Face mask made from unbreakable plastic coated in rubber

Shoulder pads

Upper arm pad

Rib pads tie to shoulder pads.

Hip pad

Breeches

Thigh pad

American football

A handling game, American football is played 11-a-side with limitless substitution from 40 players or more. It is divided into short bursts of action as the attacking team advances in a series of "downs". Points are awarded chiefly for touchdowns and field goals.

American football

American football field

Equipment
To withstand the crunching tackles and blocks, players wear extensive protective padding under their uniform, the amount and type depending on their role. Players wear a number from 1 to 99 to identify them.

World Cup
The soccer World Cup is as popular as the Olympics. About 170 countries enter competitions to qualify for the 32 places in the finals, which take place every four years.

Pelé
Brazilian soccer star Pelé (b. 1940) won universal acclaim when he inspired Brazil to win the World Cup for the first time in 1958. His performances in Brazil's 1970 triumph have gone down in soccer folklore. In a first-class career he scored 1,281 goals.

Women's soccer
In 1991, the first women's soccer World Cup was held, and women's soccer was accepted as an Olympic sport in 1996. In many countries, girls now begin playing soccer at school.

Australian football
Australian football is played 18-a-side on a huge oval field. Players kick, catch, and run with the ball which must be grounded every 10 m (33 ft). A goal, kicked between the inner posts, is worth six points; a behind, kicked inside the outer posts, scores one point.

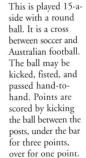

Rugby

The rugby codes are rugby union and rugby league. They are handling games featuring running, hand-to-hand passing, tackling, and kicking. Points are scored for a try – touching the ball down over the opposition goal line, or a goal – kicking the ball over the cross bar and between the posts. The two codes have a slightly different ball and pitch.

Rugby union ball

Rugby union pitch

Rugby union
This is played 15-a-side with eight forwards, two halfbacks, four three-quarters, and one full-back. It features scrums (shown here), line-outs to restart play, and tactical kicking. Tries score five points and conversions two points.

Rugby league
Rugby league is played 13-a-side. A tackled player may rise and play the ball with his foot. After six successive tackles, a team must give up the ball to the other team. Tries score four points, goals one or two.

Gaelic football
This is played 15-a-side with a round ball. It is a cross between soccer and Australian football. The ball may be kicked, fisted, and passed hand-to-hand. Points are scored by kicking the ball between the posts, under the bar for three points, over for one point.

FIND OUT MORE   BALL GAMES   OLYMPIC GAMES   TENNIS AND OTHER RACKET SPORTS   SPORT

FORCE AND MOTION

THE WORLD IS NEVER STILL – traffic and pedestrians rush along busy streets, clouds race across the sky, and the Earth turns on its axis and whirls around the Sun. Forces make all this motion, or movement, possible. A force is a push or a pull that causes an object to start or stop moving, or to change its speed or direction. When forces combine, they can hold things still or make things balance. The study of the way objects move when forces act upon them is called dynamics.

Speed and acceleration

An object's speed is how far it moves in a period of time. Speed in a particular direction is called velocity. Acceleration is the rate at which an object's velocity changes.

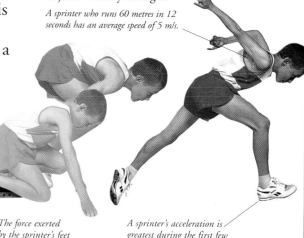

A sprinter who runs 60 metres in 12 seconds has an average speed of 5 m/s.

The sprinter's feet push against the starting blocks.

The force exerted by the sprinter's feet propels him forward.

A sprinter's acceleration is greatest during the first few seconds of a race.

Combining forces

Equal forces acting on an object in opposite directions will have no effect. If the forces are not equal, or if they do not act in opposite directions, they will combine to give an overall force called the resultant.

Pulling force

Resultant

Pulling force

Resultant
Two tugboats helping an ocean liner into port do not pull in the direction the ship needs to travel. They pull at an angle to each other so that the resultant force moves the ship straight ahead.

Terminal velocity
Gravity pulls a parachute downwards, but air resistance pushes upwards with an equal force. There is no resultant, because the forces cancel each other out. The parachute cannot accelerate, so it falls to the ground at a constant speed, known as terminal velocity.

"Flying buttresses" support the walls.

Equal masses

Equilibrium
An object is in equilibrium when the forces acting upon it balance. This set of scales is in equilibrium when two equal masses are placed on the pans, because gravity pulls on each pan with the same force.

Statics
Statics is the study of forces acting on stationary objects in equilibrium. It is important in building design, because a building will collapse if the forces acting upon it do not balance.

Inertia

An object's mass makes it resist a force that tries to change its state of motion, whether it is moving or at rest. This resistance is called inertia. The greater an object's mass, the more inertia it has. For example, the same force will accelerate a small car more than a loaded truck, because the car has a smaller mass and less inertia.

Momentum
When a moving object collides with a stationary one, the result depends upon a quantity called momentum. An object's momentum is calculated by multiplying its mass by its velocity. For example, a heavy bowling ball has more momentum than a light plastic ball moving at the same velocity, because it has a greater mass.

The mass of the bowling ball gives it enough momentum to scatter the pins.

The lighter plastic ball has a smaller mass and simply bounces off the pins.

Archimedes

Archimedes (c.287–212 BC) was a Greek mathematician and inventor who studied forces and how they could be used by simple machines. He founded statics, discovered why objects float and sink, and worked out the principles behind levers and pulleys.

Newton's laws of motion

In 1687, English physicist Sir Isaac Newton devised three laws to summarize the principles of force and motion.

Force ➡   Motion ➡

First law
An object continues in a state of rest or constant motion unless a force acts upon it. The inline skater in the picture will keep on rolling at the same speed until a force, such as friction, acts to stop him.

Second law
An object's acceleration is equal to the size of the force acting upon it divided by the object's mass. This inline skater's acceleration depends on how heavy he is and how hard he is pushed.

Third law
For every force there is an equal force acting in the opposite direction. Forces act in pairs, so when A pushes B, an equal and opposite force acts on A, making both inline skaters move apart.

Circular motion

A free-moving object will naturally move in a straight line. Centripetal force is needed for the object to move in a circle. This is a force that pulls an object towards the centre of a circle, constantly changing its direction and stopping it from moving off in a straight line. A motorcycle uses centripetal force to travel around a bend.

Friction between the tyres and the road provides centripetal force.

FIND OUT MORE   FRICTION   GRAVITY   MACHINES   MAGNETISM   PRESSURE

F

FORESTS

A THIRD OF THE WORLD'S land surface consists of forest – areas of land covered by dense tree cover. Each forest is an ecosystem – a group of animals and plants interacting with the physical environment and one another. More plants and animals live in forests than in any other environment. Forests differ according to the climate – boreal, temperate, or tropical. They help maintain the Earth's natural balance; trees absorb and release gases which regulate the climate.

Tropical forest

Tropical forests, or rainforests, tend to thrive in warm and wet climates. The porous soil is generally rich in aluminium and iron. In one hectare there may be more than 200 species of trees, hundreds of birds, mammals, and reptiles, and thousands of insects.

Emergent trees rise up to 60 m (197 ft).

Canopy of trees 15 m (50 ft) above the ground

Plants twine around branches.

Understorey contains shrubs and young growth.

Tropical forest

Each forest has layers of vegetation. In a tropical forest emergent trees poke through the top. Below are the canopy, the understorey, and the forest floor.

Broad leaves of deciduous trees grow rapidly in summer, and are shed in winter.

Temperate forest

Tropical forest
Temperate forest
Boreal coniferous forest

Down-angled branches allow the trees to shed the weight of the snow in cold climates without breaking them.

Forest floor is dark with little plant growth, but vegetation decay enriches the soil.

Temperate forest

These forests are found in mild or temperate climates, where winters are cool and summers are warm. The majority of trees are deciduous, such as oak and beech. Many temperate forests have been cleared for farmland because the soil beneath is very fertile.

Boreal coniferous forest

In cool, northern, or boreal regions, such as North Asia, there are vast areas of boreal forests, sometimes known as taiga. These dense forests contain hardy coniferous or evergreen trees, such as spruce, pine, fir, and larch trees.

Soil beneath these trees is acid and infertile.

Boreal coniferous forest

Afforestation

More people are becoming aware of the value of forests. In Southeast Asia, new forest land is created with tree-planting programmes. Some forests are now conservation areas.

Deforestation

Each year, forest land the size of Washington State, USA is destroyed. Trees are cut down for farmland or timber. Deforestation can cause huge environmental problems, disturbing the soil and forest life. Fewer trees to absorb carbon dioxide may also disrupt the climate.

Cattle ranching
Huge areas of rainforest in Brazil are cut down for cattle-ranching, which exhausts the soil within a few years.

Slash and burn
Nomadic farmers slash and burn forests for farmland. After a few years, they move on to allow the soil to regenerate.

Overgrazing
A shortage of land forces nomadic farmers to stay in one place. The land is over-grazed, and the soil dries up.

FIND OUT MORE   CLIMATE   ECOLOGY AND ECOSYSTEMS   PLANT USES   POLLUTION   RAINFOREST WILDLIFE   SOIL   TREES   WOODLAND WILDLIFE

F

FOSSILS

THE REMAINS AND TRACES of past life forms are called fossils. All living organisms are potential fossils, but only a few are preserved. The most common fossils are those of hard parts of animals and plants. Only rarely is soft tissue fossilized. Sometimes, trace fossils, such as footprints, are found. The study of fossils, called palaeontology, is crucial to our understanding of life.

Graptolite

Conodont

Fossil dating
Some fossils, such as graptolites and conodonts, evolved and became extinct over geologically short periods of time. This makes them useful for dating the rocks in which they are found.

How a fossil is formed

In order for something to fossilize, it must be buried quickly by sediment, such as sand or mud, before it decomposes. Fossils form in a variety of ways, depending on the environment in which the animal or plant lived, and the conditions after it was buried.

The skeleton may be broken up.
Water deposits sediment.
Erosion of the rock brings the fossils nearer the surface.

1 After death, the soft parts of a *Triceratops* decompose quickly, leaving just the hard skeleton and horns.

2 Through time, the bones are buried under thick layers of sediment and harden to form fossils.

3 The layers of sediment turn to rock. They may be pushed up or folded to form mountains.

4 Erosion exposes the bones. Palaeontologists can then collect and study the dinosaur remains.

Studying fossils

The study of the evolution of environments and natural communities is an important part of palaeontology. This limestone contains fossils of different animals, such as trilobites and corals. It shows a community that existed on the seafloor more than 400 million years ago.

Limestone from Much Wenlock, England

Coral
Fossil corals are common because they have a hard skeleton. Soft-bodied animals, such as sea anemones and jellyfish, would have lived in the same community, but are unlikely to have fossilized.

Trilobite
Trilobites were arthropods that lived in the sea. They shed their shells regularly, as modern arthropods do, and these shells are often found as fossils. They are divided into three distinct parts, or lobes, hence the name "trilobite". A few fossils of soft parts have been found.

Types of fossil

Fossils range from microscopic plants and animals to the huge bones of dinosaurs. They can be almost unchanged from the original or replaced by minerals.

Amber
The fossilized resin of trees, called amber, often contains trapped insects and other small animals and plants. The trapped fossils are often preserved with much detail.

Volcanic ash
This child's body was buried by volcanic ash at Pompeii, Italy, in AD 79. Ash turns to rock quickly. A buried animal or plant may rot away to leave a hollow, which, if filled with plaster, forms a cast.

Trees
Fossilized trees, such as these *Lepidodendron* trunks and roots, can be preserved as internal moulds of the bark. The inside rots away and is replaced by sand.

Bones
Vertebrate fossils are made of many parts and are usually found as single pieces. If conditions are right, a skeleton can be preserved whole, as in this *Diplomystus*, an ancestor of the modern herring.

Females were larger than males.

Ammonite shells replaced with iron pyrites, or "fools' gold".

Jurassic ammonite

Petrification
These monkey-puzzle cones have been turned to stone, or petrified. This happened when silica-rich waters crystallized within the cells of the cones.

Concretions
Hard lumps, or concretions, are often formed around fossils in sediments. This concretion reveals the fossil shell and mould of a clam.

Ammonites
These molluscs were abundant in the seas of the Mesozoic Era. Their shells were made of the mineral aragonite and were often replaced by other minerals during fossilization.

Georges Cuvier

A French zoologist, Georges Cuvier (1769–1832) realized that the parts of the body were interrelated. For example, an animal that has hooves is a herbivore, and must have herbivore's teeth. He identified a fossil as a marsupial from a jaw.

FIND OUT MORE   ARTHROPODS   DINOSAURS   EVOLUTION   GEOLOGY   PREHISTORIC LIFE

F

Fossils

Invertebrates

Raphidonema is a sponge from the warm waters of the Cretaceous Period.

Didymograptus are Ordovician graptolites. They floated in oceans.

Trachyphyllia is a Miocene solitary coral.

Lonsdaleia lived as a colony during the Carboniferous Period.

Lovenia is a heart urchin with a flattened shell.

Archaeogeryon is a deep-water Miocene mud crab.

Mesolimulus is a horseshoe crab of the Jurassic and Cretaceous Periods. It has a horseshoe-shaped shell.

Viviparus is a freshwater snail.

A stalk attached the brachiopod to the sea floor.

Terebratula is a brachiopod, also known as a lamp shell.

Lingula is a brachiopod with a thin shell.

Stem made up of disc-like plates.

Dimerocrinites is a sea lily, or crinoid, from the Silurian and Devonian Periods.

Vertebrates

Eighth lower left tooth

Carcharocles is an extinct shark.

Rectangular body scales

Dapedium is a fish from the shallow seas of the late Triassic and Jurassic Periods.

Macrocranion from the Eocene Period resembles a living hedgehog without the spikes.

Pointed skull   *Long hind leg*

Rana is a true frog that first appeared in the Eocene Period.

Raphus is a huge, extinct, flightless pigeon, commonly known as the dodo.

Nostril

Ichthyosaurus is a sea reptile of the Jurassic Period.

Ring of bones around the eye

Nostril

Dagger-like teeth

Dimetrodon is a mammal-like carnivorous reptile of the Permian Period.

Eye socket

Plants

Collenia is an alga of the Precambrian and Cambrian Periods.

Ficus is a fig which first appeared in the Eocene Period.

Porana is a Miocene flower.

Trapped spider

Stigmaria are the root-bearing branches of a Carboniferous club-moss.

Amber is fossilized tree resin or gum.

Populus is a poplar, almost identical to poplars today.

Carved jet

Jet is a type of fossilized wood.

Growth rings

Quercus is oak. It first appeared in the Eocene Period.

Polished, petrified wood

Ribbed seed

Trigonocarpus is the seed of a Carboniferous seed fern.

FRANCE

THE LARGEST COUNTRY in western Europe, France stretches from the Pyrenees in the south to the English Channel in the north. A founder member of the European Economic Community (now European Union), France plays a key role in world affairs. It is a leading industrial nation, although some five per cent of the population works in farming. The first of the modern republics, France includes Corsica, Guyana, and various islands in the Caribbean and Pacific Ocean.

FRANCE FACTS

CAPITAL CITY	Paris
AREA	551,500 sq km (212,930 sq miles)
POPULATION	57,800,000
MAIN LANGUAGE	French
MAJOR RELIGION	Christian
CURRENCY	Euro
LIFE EXPECTANCY	78 years
PEOPLE PER DOCTOR	333
GOVERNMENT	Multi-party democracy
ADULT LITERACY	99%

River Seine
From its source in the east, the River Seine crosses Paris, before winding its way north to the Atlantic Ocean. France's river network, which also includes the Loire and the Rhône, is used for transport and for irrigating farmland.

The Seine in Normandy

Corsican *maquis*

Physical features
France's landscape varies from undulating fields in the north to sparse hills in the Massif Central, and mountains in the Alps and Pyrenees in the south.

Corsica
With an area of 8,630 sq km (3,350 sq miles), Corsica is the third largest Mediterranean island. Fragrant, thorny scrub called *maquis* covers the slopes of towering granite peaks, and rich fertile valleys are used to graze sheep and grow vines. The capital is Ajaccio.

Climate
Northwest France, particularly Brittany, is mild but damp. The east has hot summers and stormy winters. Summers in the south are dry and hot, and forest fires are common. In the Pyrenees and Alps, winter snowfalls are heavy, making these ideal areas for skiing.

39°C (102°F)   -17°C (1°F)
18°C (64°F)   3°C (37°F)
584 mm (23 in)

Barren 1%
Farmland 60%
Forest 36%
Built-up 3%

Land use
France's fertile farmland includes gently rolling pastures and fields of wheat and sugar beet in the north, and vineyards and lavender fields in the south. Much of the Massif Central is pasture land for grazing sheep.

Paris
The Louvre Museum lies on the fashionable Right Bank of the River Seine, which divides the city. The Left Bank is traditionally home to students, artists, and the famous Eiffel Tower. One of the world's most beautiful and most visited capitals, Paris is the cultural and political centre of France.

The Louvre Museum

People

People of French descent make up about 94 per cent of the population. Among these are several groups who speak their own languages and have strong independence movements. These include the Bretons of Brittany in the north, about 500,000 Basques in the Pyrenees, and the Corsicans.

107 per sq km
(278 per sq mile)

75% Urban   25% Rural

Ethnic groups
France's five million immigrants include mainly North African Muslims and economic migrants from South and Central Europe. Most live and work in the cities.

Leisure

Football, rugby, cycling, and tennis are all popular sports in France, as are horseracing and Formula 1. The French Open is a major international tennis championship.

Tour de France
Each year, more than a hundred of the world's leading professional cyclists compete in this famous cycle race over a 3,400-km (2,113-mile) route in 24 one-day stages.

Boules
Throughout France, groups of people playing *boules* are a common sight in the town or village square. *Boules* is France's national game and involves rolling heavy balls at a smaller target ball.

Farming

The French grow a variety of crops, such as wheat, barley, sugar beet, and grapes for making wine. About a third of all the farmland is pasture for grazing cows and sheep, which are reared for milk to make dairy products, and for meat.

Cantal

Livarot

St.-Nectaire

Cheese
France produces more than 365 kinds of cheese, from cow, sheep, and goats' milk. These include St.-Nectaire, Cantal, and Livarot, and the famous Brie, Camembert, and Roquefort. Milk and butter are also important exports.

Cereals
France's main cereal crop is wheat, which grows on large farms in the north of France where the soil is good.

Wine
The wines of Bordeaux, Burgundy, Champagne, and the Rhône valley are sold worldwide. France is the leading producer and controls quality strictly.

Food

French cuisine is world famous, and words such as café, restaurant, paté, and quiche are common in many languages. Special French dishes include *bouillabaisse* (fish soup), *escargots* (snails), and *grenouilles* (frogs' legs).

Prawn

Slice of lemon

Whelk

Lobster / *Mussel*

Industry

France has strong chemical, steel, electronics, and manufacturing industries, and an active aerospace programme. Nuclear power provides three-quarters of the country's electricity. Perfume and fashion are also a major source of income.

Perfume
French perfumes, such as Chanel, are world famous. Many are made from the fragrant oils extracted from roses, jasmine, and lavender that grow in the southeast of the country.

Tourism
The fashionable resorts of the Côte d'Azur in southeast France attract thousands of tourists every summer. France is now the world's leading tourist destination, attracting 75 million visitors each year.

Car production
Most French drivers buy French cars, such as this Renault Espace. Other makes include Peugeot and Citroën. The French car industry ranks fourth in the world.

Transport

France boasts the world's fastest train, the TGV, which can travel at speeds of up to 300 kmh (186 mph). A direct service now runs to England via the Channel Tunnel.

Monaco

This tiny independent principality on the Côte d'Azur derives its income from tourism, banking, sales tax, and gambling. It has close ties with France.

Grand Casino
The people of Monaco pay very little tax and earn more per head than any other country in the world. The gaming rooms and roulette wheels of the Grand Casino in Monte Carlo are open to anyone with money to spend.

MONACO FACTS

CAPITAL CITY	Monaco
AREA	1.95 sq km (0.75 sq miles)
POPULATION	32,000
MAIN LANGUAGE	French
MAJOR RELIGION	Christian
CURRENCY	Euro

FIND OUT MORE   CARS AND TRUCKS   CLOTHES AND FASHION   CYCLING   EMPIRES   EUROPE, HISTORY OF   EUROPEAN UNION   FARMING   FRANCE, HISTORY OF   TRADE AND INDUSTRY   TRAINS AND RAILWAYS

FRANCE, HISTORY OF

THE LARGEST COUNTRY in western Europe, France has dominated European history ever since the Franks conquered the country in the 5th century. Its vast natural wealth and large population have enabled a succession of rulers, such as Charlemagne in the 9th century, Louis XIV in the 17th, and Napoleon in the 19th, to create powerful empires that spanned Europe. Despite three bitter wars with Germany between 1870 and 1945, France emerged as one of the world's superpowers. Today, France is a leading member of the European Union, and one of the wealthiest countries in the world.

Horses heads, carved c.10,000 BC

Prehistoric France
The first inhabitants of France were prolific artists. More than 20,000 years ago, they adorned caves at Lascaux and elsewhere with lifelike pictures of animals. They also carved likenesses of animal heads from bone, antler, and rock.

Samian ware bowl

French potters made this type of ware in the Roman period.

Roman France
Between 58 and 51 BC, a Roman army led by Julius Caesar conquered France. The new province of Gaul was one of the richest in the empire. Trade flourished, and the Romans built many roads and bridges. They also introduced growing grapes for wine.

Franks
In 486, the Franks from Germany routed the last Roman governor of Gaul and took control, giving France its name. At first the Franks continued with Roman customs, but their empire broke up in civil wars. The 8th-century kings Charles Martel, Pepin the Short, and Charlemagne restored order.

Charlemagne

Medieval France
In common with other European rulers, the power of the French kings was always limited by the strength of local nobles. Despite this weakness, France became one of the richest countries in Europe during the 11th century. Major trade fairs in the Champagne region attracted merchants from all over Europe, and trade and commerce flourished.

Angevin Empire
As a result of marriage and war, Henry II of England (r.1154–89) ruled much of western and northern France. His vast realm was called the Angevin Empire, after the county of Anjou. For years it was a threat to French unification.

Château Gaillard, an Angevin castle

Religious wars
The Reformation split France, with many Catholics becoming Huguenots (Protestants). In 1562, civil war broke out between the two sides; religious toleration was agreed by the Edict of Nantes in 1598, but tension remained high. In 1685, Louis XIV revoked the Edict, and many Huguenots fled to England and Holland.

Renaissance France
Joan of Arc, who fought the English for independence, was burnt at the stake in 1431. During the 15th century, the French kings drove out the English, and united their country. They also crushed the power of the nobles. During the next century, the ideas of the Italian Renaissance entered France. New châteaux were built, and the arts flourished.

Golden age
The 17th and 18th centuries were a golden age of the arts. Royal support led to the founding of the Gobelins tapestry works in 1602 and the royal pottery at Sèvres in 1756. The nobility supported artists such as Watteau and Fragonard, dramatists such as Racine, Molière and Corneille, the writer Montaigne, creator of the essay, and the fable-writer La Fontaine.

Bourbons
Under the Bourbon kings, France emerged as the major power in Europe during the 17th century. Habsburg-ruled Spain and Austria – enemies of France – were defeated, and all power was centralized under the king. Industry and commerce were supported, and France established colonies in North America and India.

Palace of Versailles
In order to increase his own power, and reduce that of the nobility, Louis XIV built this vast new palace outside Paris. Some 36,000 people worked on the building, decorating it with the best examples of French art and design. At the centre was the king's bed chamber, where Louis received guests.

Hand-painted figures

Gilded decoration

Sèvres porcelain vase

Louis XIV
During the long reign of Louis XIV (r.1643–1715), the power of the French kings reached its height. Louis believed in the divine right of kings to rule, and governed without parliament. He reorganized the army and expanded French territory. But his lavish lifestyle left France almost bankrupt.

Monarchy and empire

After the defeat of Napoleon in 1815, France had a series of short-lived, weak governments. The restored Bourbon monarchy was overthrown in 1830 and King Louis Philippe lost his throne in 1848. The resulting Second Republic collapsed when its president, Louis-Napoleon (r.1852–70), became emperor. In spite of these problems, France grew prosperous.

French Revolution

Revolution broke out in 1789, sweeping away the king and nobility. A new National Assembly was set up, and swore the famous tennis court oath, that they would not disband until France had a proper constitution. Napoleon Bonaparte became Emperor in 1804, marking the end of the revolutionary period.

Revolution of 1848

In February 1848, Parisians rose up against their ineffectual king, Louis Philippe. A republic was set up, with Louis-Napoleon, a nephew of Bonaparte, as president. Radical reforms were promised, but in 1852 Napoleon became emperor.

Revolutionaries in Paris, 1848

Infantryman's pack, Franco-Prussian War

Franco-Prussian War

Although successful at home, Napoleon III was no match for Bismarck, chancellor of Prussia. In 1870, rivalry between France and Prussia led to war, but the French armies were unprepared and were soon defeated. France lost the provinces of Alsace and Lorraine to Germany.

Third Republic

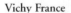

The Third Republic (1870–1940) was riven with internal disputes and conflicts between moderates, radicals, socialists, and royalists. Between 1918 and its collapse in 1940, there were 44 governments and 20 different prime ministers. Yet France stayed one of the leading states in Europe, with a worldwide empire and a strong economy.

J'Accuse, writer Emile Zola's pamphlet supporting Dreyfus

Dreyfus case

In October 1894, French army captain Alfred Dreyfus was court-martialled for treason, for passing military secrets to Germany. But a mistake had been made, and a campaign to free Dreyfus began. He was cleared in 1906, but the case split the nation between his supporters and those who refused to change the verdict.

Vichy France

In 1940, German forces invaded France. French general and right-wing politician Marshal Pétain set up a government in Vichy, central France. This government collaborated with the occupying forces; opposition was led from London by Charles de Gaulle, leader of the Free French. Vichy France was occupied by the Germans in 1942.

Cross of Lorraine

Flag of the Free French

Modern France

After the liberation of France from German occupation in 1944, a Fourth Republic was set up to govern the country. Like its predecessor, it was weak and was brought down by the unrest caused by the Algerian war in 1958. Charles de Gaulle then set up the Fifth Republic, aiming to restore French prestige and prosperity.

May 1968

In May 1968, students demanding more money for education demonstrated against high defence spending. Riots broke out in Paris and elsewhere, with fighting between police and students. A general strike ensued, and de Gaulle's government was weakened.

After the riots, Paris, May 1968

Charles de Gaulle

Charles de Gaulle (1890–1970) trained as a soldier, rising to command an armoured division. On the fall of France in 1940, he fled to Britain and called on French people to resist German occupation. As leader of the Free French, he did much to boost French morale during the war. In 1958 he became president, leading his country until he resigned in 1969.

Algerian war

In 1954, Algeria, one of several African countries colonized by France, demanded that it be granted its independence. This led to conflict with the many European settlers in the country. The French army supported the settlers in their wish to remain French and waged a vicious war against the Algerian rebels. Algeria finally won its independence in 1962.

Timeline

58–51 BC Gaul (present-day France) becomes part of the Roman Empire.

AD 486 The Franks take control of the country.

1337–1453 France and Britain fight the Hundred Years' War.

Encyclopedie, 1751

1589 Henry IV becomes first Bourbon king.

1643–1715 France reaches height of its power under Louis XIV.

1789 Revolution breaks out in Paris.

1848 After a revolution, the short-lived Second Republic is established.

1870–71 Third Republic set up.

1870s Impressionist movement founded by Claude Monet and other French painters.

Claude Monet, Waterlilies

1914–18 France fights Germany in World War I.

1946 Fourth Republic established after World War II.

1958 De Gaulle takes power and introduces Fifth Republic.

1950s–90s France is a leading member of European Union,

FIND OUT MORE   EUROPE, HISTORY OF   FRENCH REVOLUTION   GERMANY, HISTORY OF   MEDIEVAL EUROPE   NAPOLEON BONAPARTE   NAPOLEONIC WARS   ROMAN EMPIRE   WORLD WAR I   WORLD WAR II

FRANKLIN, BENJAMIN

INVENTOR, PRINTER, PUBLISHER, writer, scientist, politician, diplomat, and an author of both the US Declaration of Independence and the US Constitution – there was nothing Benjamin Franklin did not turn his hand to. He was born into a poor family, but had a fertile mind very receptive to new ideas. He invented items such as the lightning conductor and bifocal spectacles, but he is most respected for his contribution to the founding of the USA. He is sometimes known as the "wisest American".

Early life
Benjamin Franklin was born in 1706 in the American port of Boston. He was the son of a candle and soap maker, and left school at 10 to help in his father's business. Later he worked for his half-brother James, printer and publisher of a newspaper to which Benjamin contributed. After disagreements with James, he left Boston in 1723 to work as a printer in Philadelphia.

Printer
Franklin prospered as a printer. As publisher of the popular *Poor Richard's Almanac* between 1732–57, he introduced numerous common-sense sayings that have since become part of the American language. He also set up an academy that later became the University of Pennsylvania.

Poor Richard, 1733.
AN
Almanack
For the Year of Chrift
1733,
Being the Firft after LEAP YEAR:

Scientist
In 1748, Franklin handed over his printing business to his foreman so that he could devote his life to science. He researched the nature of electricity, and this work led to him inventing the lightning rod, to protect tall buildings from lightning. He also worked out a theory of heat absorption and tracked the paths of storms across the sky.

Bend caused by lightning.
Lightning rod

Lightning
In 1752, Franklin flew a kite in a thunderstorm to prove that lightning is electrical. Electricity from the thunderclouds flowed down the string to a metal key tied on it near the ground. Sparks flew from the key, showing the presence of the electrical charge in the sky.

Franklin experimenting with a kite and lightning

Inventor
Franklin was a tireless inventor, using his scientific knowledge to devise a number of inventions that were designed to make human life safer and more comfortable. These ranged from bifocal spectacles – combining two lenses of different strength in one frame to correct both close and distant vision – to a musical glass "armonica". Among his useful inventions were the lightning rod and an energy-saving stove still made today.

The armonica was played by rubbing the fingers gently on the edges of the glasses.

Stove
Among Franklin's many inventions was a practical stove that made use of the heat that would otherwise have escaped up the chimney. Stoves like this were installed in many American houses.

Armonica
In the early 1760s, Franklin built a musical instrument made up of a series of glass bowls, graduated in size and fitted one inside another. By rotating a spindle, the edges of the bowls passed through a trough of water. Contact with the musician's fingertips produced a penetrating sound. Composers such as Mozart and Beethoven wrote music for this strange device.

Statesman
During the American Revolution, Franklin was a member of the committee that wrote the Declaration of Independence, which he signed in 1776. Later that year, he sailed to France to win diplomatic recognition for the new nation. When the war ended, he was one of the main US negotiators in the peace talks.

Constitution
In 1787, Franklin helped to write the new American constitution. Although his proposal for a single-chamber congress was rejected, he negotiated a compromise between the different authors which resulted in the constitution that survives today.

Franklin (left) talks to the French king and queen (seated, right) and members of their court

BENJAMIN FRANKLIN

1706	Born in Boston, USA
1723	Begins work as a printer
1732–57	Publishes *Poor Richard's Almanac*
1752	Conducts famous experiment with lightning
1776	Helps to draft Declaration of Independence
1781	Chosen as one of the US negotiators with Britain
1787	Member of group which draws up US constitution
1790	Dies in Philadelphia

 FIND OUT MORE

AMERICAN REVOLUTION · ELECTRICITY · EYES AND SEEING · GOVERNMENTS AND POLITICS · INVENTIONS · MUSICAL INSTRUMENTS · UNITED STATES, HISTORY OF

FRENCH REVOLUTION

IN 1789, REVOLUTION BROKE OUT in France when people rose up against poverty and injustice. The French Revolution swept away the power of the monarchy and ended the traditional social order. When the revolution began, poverty was widespread, the king was unpopular, and people resented the clergy and nobility. Following the formation of the National Assembly, France was declared a republic, the king was executed, and, for a while, terror reigned. In 1799, Napoleon came to power, and the revolution ended.

Revolutionary Paris

The key events of the revolution occurred on the streets of Paris. Various political groups sprang up, such as the Jacobin Club, which relied on the Parisian *sans culottes* for support.

National Assembly

In 1788, France ran out of money, and King Louis XVI called the Estates General, representing clergy, nobility, and middle classes. The Third Estate formed a National Assembly, seized lands, and drew up a new constitution.

Rights of Man

The National Assembly issued the *Declaration of the Rights of Man and the Citizen,* stating that "Men are born and remain equal". Women's rights were not included, but the ideals of "liberty, equality, and fraternity" inspired everyone.

Storming of the Bastille

In 1789, angry demonstrators seized the Bastille, a prison that had been a symbol of oppression for many years. This act sparked a wave of rebellion. Outside Paris, peasants attacked the country houses of the nobility they hated.

Coarse working blouse

The bonnet rouge, or red bonnet, symbolized freedom. It looked like the cap worn by freed Roman slaves.

Reign of Terror

By 1792, the revolution was under threat. There were food shortages, royalist uprisings in the countryside, and a threat by Prussia to invade and restore the monarchy. Extremists, known as Jacobins, grew in power, declaring a republic and executing the king in 1793. They set up the Committee of Public Safety, and a reign of terror began. Anyone suspected of being an enemy of the revolution was arrested and guillotined. Thousands died. By 1794, the leaders of the Committee were themselves executed, and the terror was over.

Guillotine

Named after a French doctor, the guillotine consisted of a wooden frame, with a sharp blade mounted on it, which sliced off the victims' heads. This killing machine was quicker than previous methods of execution, and was, therefore, thought to be more humane.

Sharpened blade fell on victims' necks.

Robespierre

A lawyer by profession, Maximilien Robespierre (1758–94) was one of the leaders of the revolution. He headed the Jacobin Club, and, by 1793, was leader of the Committee of Public Safety that conducted the Reign of Terror. In 1794, he, too, went to the guillotine.

Revolutionaries

The revolutionaries were men and women from all social classes: lawyers, peasants, workers. Street revolutionaries were known as *sans culottes* (without breeches) because they wore striped trousers. Two rival revolutionary groups emerged: the Girondins and the more radical Jacobins.

Marseillaise

From 1792, revolution spread outside French borders. A soldier composed the *Marseillaise* as a revolutionary marching song. Today, it is France's national anthem.

White was the colour of the royal family.

Red and blue were the colours of Paris.

Striped trousers

Strong leather shoes

1788 France bankrupt. Louis XVI summons Estates General.

May 1789 Third Estate forms National Assembly,

Louis XVI

14 July, 1789 Paris mob storms the Bastille; French Revolution begins.

27 August, 1789 National Assembly issues *Rights of Man.*

October 1789 Women march to Versailles from Paris to demand bread.

1791 The French revolution inspires a slave rebellion in Haiti.

1792 National Assembly abolishes monarchy. France becomes a republic and goes to war with Austria and Prussia.

1793 Louis XVI executed. Counter-revolution breaks out. Revolutionary war spreads across Europe.

1793–4 Reign of Terror.

1795 The Directory, a more moderate board of governors, is formed and takes power.

1799 Napoleon overthrows Directory and takes power.

1798–99 Revolution inspires uprisings in Ireland.

FIND OUT MORE — AMERICAN REVOLUTION — EUROPE, HISTORY OF — FRANCE, HISTORY OF — GOVERNMENT AND POLITICS — NAPOLEONIC WARS

FREUD, SIGMUND

ONE HUNDRED YEARS AGO, people viewed the workings of the human mind as a great mystery. Sigmund Freud helped to make sense of that mystery. Because of his innovative ideas, he is often known as the father of psychiatry. Freud was an Austrian doctor who worked in Vienna almost all his life. He researched the meaning of dreams, how the unconscious mind works, and how events in our past influence the actions we take. In developing the science of psychoanalysis, he provided insights that have affected every aspect of modern life.

Early life
Freud was born into a Jewish family in 1856 in Freiburg (Pribor), in what is now the Czech Republic. In 1859 his family moved to Vienna. Freud was a brilliant student, coming top of his class in school for six years. In 1873 he began to study medicine at Vienna, and in 1881 he qualified as a doctor.

Psychoanalysis

In 1886, Freud began to specialise in neuroses, or nervous diseases. To find out what was causing his patients' illnesses, he used first hypnotism and then free association – instructing his patients to say whatever came into their head in the belief that they would reveal the cause of their illness. Freud published his ideas in 1895 in *Studies on Hysteria*, the first-ever account of psychoanalysis – the interpretation and treatment of mental disorders.

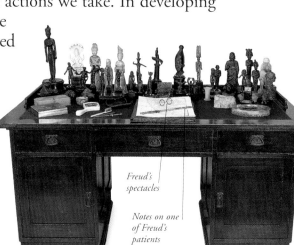

Freud's spectacles

Notes on one of Freud's patients

Freud's couch

Analyst's couch
Much of Freud's work consisted of listening to his patients as they talked about themselves. The patient lay on a couch in Freud's study, and Freud sat at his desk, surrounded by his collection of ancient Egyptian statues, listening and taking notes. This technique, devised by Freud, is still used widely today. Many of Freud's books are made up largely of case studies – reports of the psychoanalytic sessions and the conclusions Freud drew from them.

The Psychopathology of Everyday Life (1904)

The Interpretation of Dreams (1900)

Interpretation of dreams
Freud believed that beneath our conscious mind is a submerged unconscious that governs much of our behaviour. Dreams are the way in which the unconscious comes to the surface. He published this theory in *The Interpretation of Dreams* in 1900.

Chair is made in the shape of a person.

Freud's chair

Freudian slips
In his book *The Psychopathology of Everyday Life* (1904), Freud explained how slips of the tongue can reveal hidden, unconscious wishes. Freud made many connections between what we say and do and what we actually mean.

International Psychoanalytical Association

Early in his career, Freud attracted intense hostility to his work, but gradually his ideas were accepted. In 1902, he established a psychoanalytical society in Vienna, and in 1910 he set up the International Psychoanalytical Association (IPA) to promote his ideas. Regular IPA meetings and discussions helped Freud confirm his theories about the mind and spread them to a wider audience.

Carl Gustav Jung
The Swiss psychiatrist CG Jung (1875–1961) and Freud lectured together in the USA in 1909. Jung was the first president of the IPA, but resigned in 1914 because he disagreed with Freud about the origins of neurosis. He later created his own school of thought about the mind's workings.

Later life

In the 1920s, Freud developed a new theory that the mind is made up of three parts – the id, which contains impulses, the ego, which represents reasoning, and the superego, the self-critical area. He was developing this theory when he left Austria in 1938 because it was occupied by Nazi Germany.

Anna Freud
In 1938, Freud moved to London, where he died in exile the following year. His work was carried on by his youngest daughter, Anna (1895–1982). A qualified teacher, she specialized in child psychiatry. She founded and directed a world-famous clinic for child therapy in London and wrote several books.

SIGMUND FREUD

1856 Born in Freiburg, Moravia.

1859 Family moves to Vienna.

1886 Begins work as a specialist in nervous disease.

1900 *The Interpretation of Dreams.*

1910 Sets up International Psychoanalytical Association.

1923 Has his first operation for cancer of the jaw; publishes *The Ego and the Id.*

1938 Leaves Vienna for London; publishes *An Outline of Psychoanalysis.*

1939 Dies in London.

FIND OUT MORE: BRAIN AND NERVOUS SYSTEM | GERMANY, HISTORY OF | HOSPITALS | MEDICINE | MEDICINE, HISTORY OF

FRICTION

DRAGGING A HEAVY OBJECT across the floor is difficult because of friction, a force that opposes motion. Friction occurs between any two surfaces that are in contact, because even seemingly smooth surfaces have microscopic ridges and troughs that make them grip one another. Friction is greater between rough surfaces than smooth ones. Static friction stops surfaces at rest from moving. Dynamic friction slows down surfaces in motion.

Static friction

Friction acts between these two masses and the wooden slope. Static friction on the stationary block is great enough to prevent it from moving. The moving block has overcome static friction, but it then produces dynamic friction, which limits its speed.

Gravity makes the mass on the smooth surface overcome static friction and slide down the slope.

Smooth surface

Rough surface

The rougher surface increases the force of static friction and prevents the mass from sliding.

Using friction

Friction can be useful. Without friction, no one would be able to walk or run. Friction helps people's shoes grip the ground and stops their feet from sliding out from under them. In the same way, friction enables a vehicle's tyres to grip the road. Most brakes use friction to slow a vehicle down. Friction between surfaces always produces heat, and sometimes electricity.

The pattern on the soles of these shoes is designed to create friction to give maximum grip.

Balloon charged by friction

Disc brakes
When the rider of this motorcycle applies the brakes, a pad presses against the metal disc fixed to the wheel. The rubbing action of the pad against the moving disc produces friction and slows the wheel enough to stop the motorcycle.

Brake pad unit

Disc

The brakes glow as the racing car slows down.

Friction and electricity
Rubbing two objects together can produce a charge of static electricity. Friction between a T-shirt and a balloon will dislodge negatively charged electrons from the atoms of the shirt. The electrons transfer to atoms in the balloon and give it a negative charge, while the shirt becomes positively charged. Opposite charges attract, so the negatively charged balloon clings to the positively charged shirt.

Friction and heat
In cold weather people often rub their hands together to warm them. Friction between two surfaces always produces heat. When a racing car brakes at high speed, the brakes glow red as the energy of the car's movement is changed into heat.

Reducing friction

If two moving machine parts rub together, friction will eventually damage them. Friction in machines generates heat and wastes a great deal of energy. Most methods of reducing friction involve keeping the surfaces apart in some way.

1-kg (2-lb) mass

Mass moves smoothly over flat surface.

Steel roller

Rollers
The rollers under this 1-kg (2-lb) mass allow it to move smoothly over a flat surface. The mass and the surface are not in contact, so there is no friction between them. If the mass is pushed or pulled, the rollers will roll instead of dragging over the surface.

Axle passes through centre.

Outer ring attaches to wheel.

Ball bearing
A ball bearing is a device used to reduce friction between a wheel and its axle. As the wheel turns, the steel balls in the bearing roll around and prevent the wheel and axle from rubbing together.

Lubrication
Using a fluid such as oil to make machine parts move more smoothly and reduce wear is called lubrication. The oil coats the surfaces of the moving parts, preventing them from rubbing together.

Air resistance
Dynamic friction between the air and a moving object is called air resistance. Streamlining gives an object a smooth shape so that air flows more easily around it. Here, smoke trails blown over a streamlined car show how the air moves over its surface.

Hovercraft
A hovercraft overcomes the problem of friction by using high-pressure air as a lubricant. Fans pump air from the atmosphere into a flexible skirt around the craft's hull. This powerful downward jet of air allows the craft to hover over the water, reducing friction with the water's surface to a minimum. Large propellers on top of the craft move it quickly across the water.

Christopher Cockerell
In 1953, English engineer Christopher Cockerell (1910–99) began working on ways to reduce the friction between a ship's hull and the water. His solution was to lift the vessel above the water on a cushion of compressed air. In 1959, after making successful models, he produced the world's first practical hovercraft, called the SR-N1.

FROGS AND TOADS

THE CROAKING SOUNDS of frogs and toads are often heard in spring as they try to attract a mate. Frogs and toads are amphibians – cold-blooded animals that live both on land and in water. In Europe, they are easy to distinguish – frogs have slimy skins and live mainly in the water; toads have dry, warty skins and live mainly on land. In the tropics, they are more diverse and harder to tell apart. There are more than 2,600 species of frog and toad, living in most parts of the world where there is fresh water. Their habitats range from lakes and marshes, to rainforests, mountains, and deserts.

Features of frogs and toads

Frogs and toads have porous skin – water and air can pass through it – enabling them to breathe through their skin as well as their lungs. Most have sharp teeth, and can see and hear well. They have four legs, varying in length between species. Frogs range in size from a few centimetres long to the West African Goliath frog, which is 40 cm (16 in) in length. Some unusual species are the hairy frog – the male grows hair in the breeding season – and the Borneo flying frog that glides between trees.

Feeding

Most tadpoles are herbivorous, while adult frogs and toads are insectivorous or carnivorous. Prey includes insects, worms, spiders, fish, other frogs, or small reptiles, depending on species. Most species catch insects with their long sticky tongues. Larger frogs and toads rely on ambush. Giant horned toads and bullfrogs have powerful jaws and wide mouths and can even eat mice.

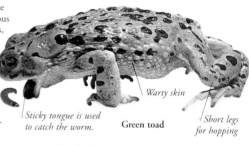

Sticky tongue is used to catch the worm.
Warty skin
Green toad
Short legs for hopping

Hind legs in full stretch
Feet push off from the ground.
Frog in a streamlined position in mid-flight
Eyes closed for protection
Webbed feet
Frogs swim by pulling their hind legs towards their bodies, then kicking them backwards, so pushing themselves forwards through the water.

Leaping and swimming

Long-legged frogs, such as this Northern leopard frog, can jump more than 30 times their own length in a single leap. When swimming, its long webbed toes help propel it through the water. Short-legged frogs walk, crawl, or do short hops. Some species, such as spade-foot frogs, have feet that can burrow into loose earth. Toads usually have short legs and can only hop weakly or walk. Some species, such as the natterjack toad, can run.

Back legs are long and very powerful.
Front legs are held back.
Northern leopard frog
Frogs use their front legs like brakes when they enter the water.

Reproduction

Most frogs and toads mate in water. The male fertilizes the eggs externally as the female lays them; a few species fertilize eggs internally. Some bear live young; others form "mating-balls" of a female and several males. The eggs develop into tadpoles that live in water and breathe through gills. The tadpoles change into air-breathing adults with lungs.

The dark dots develop into tadpoles.
The eggs stick together.
Tadpole uses its tail to swim.
Tiny buds from which front legs will grow.
Back legs
Tail eventually disappears.

Life-cycle of a common frog

1 Eggs stick together to form frogspawn. Each egg contains a dark centre that will become a tadpole. Many eggs are infertile and die, or are attacked by fungus or predators.

2 The newly hatched tadpole lives in the water and breathes through external gills. Most species at this stage are herbivorous and feed on plants.

3 By 6–9 weeks, the tadpole has grown considerably in size. The hind legs have developed. The tadpole now prepares to metamorphose, or change, into a froglet.

4 At 12 weeks, the tail has almost receded. The tadpole has become a froglet. It is now ready to leave the water to begin its adult life – partly on land.

Croaking

Frogs and toads croak to attract mates. Normally, it is the males that croak, using inflatable vocal sacs in the throat. Each species has its own distinctive croak so that the calls of the male only attract females of the same species. This avoids mating between different species in regions where there are many similar frogs and toads.

Painted reed frog
Vocal sac

Defence

Some frogs have poisonous skin that they advertise with bright colours. Others such as tree frogs may secrete bad-tasting sticky substances. Many toads, including cane toads, have poison-secreting glands. Large species, such as horned toads, give painful bites.

Poison dart frog

This South American frog is the most poisonous frog in the world. Its bright skin warns predators that it is poisonous to eat.

Skin is highly toxic.
Golden poison dart frog

Red belly

Fire-bellied toad

Fire-bellied toads in Europe have drab backs but bright red bellies. If threatened, the toad exposes its belly. This flash of colour frightens away predators.

Tree frogs

Tree frogs move with ease within trees. They have sticky discs on their toes and an opposing thumb enabling them to grip most objects, even smooth surfaces. Flying frogs are tree frogs with very large webbed feet that enable them to glide downwards from branch to branch.

Sticky pads on their toes enable them to grip branches.
Red-eyed tree frog

NORTHERN LEOPARD FROG

SCIENTIFIC NAME *Rana pipiens*

ORDER Anura

FAMILY Ranidae

DISTRIBUTION Northern and western USA and Canada, as far south as New Mexico

HABITAT Found in most habitats, even those far from water, which explains its other name of "meadow frog"

DIET Insects

SIZE Length 9–11 cm (3.5–4.5 in)

LIFESPAN Up to 6 years (in captivity)

FIND OUT MORE   AMPHIBIANS   CONSERVATION   EGGS   LAKE AND RIVER WILDLIFE   MARSH AND SWAMP WILDLIFE   POISONOUS ANIMALS   RAINFOREST WILDLIFE   URBAN WILDLIFE   WOODLAND WILDLIFE

Frogs

Colours help camouflage frog in earth and leaf litter.

Asian painted frogs are burrowers that emerge onto the surface at night and inflate themselves if touched.

Foam-nesting frogs lay eggs in self-made foam in trees above water, into which the tadpoles drop.

Colour varies from deep red to pale orange.

Tomato frogs from Madagascar live on land, but breed in slow-moving or stagnant water.

Eyespots look like eyes to confuse predators.

Chilean four-eyed frogs have eyespots on their backs that deter predators.

Large digital discs help it land after gliding.

Malayan flying frogs cannot fly, but glide downwards.

Bright colours indicate it is poisonous to eat.

Yellow and black poison dart frogs live in cracks in riverside rocks.

Long fingers and toes

Paradoxical frogs develop from tadpoles twice their length and shrink as they "grow".

A diet of tiny invertebrates makes skin poisonous.

Green and black poison dart frogs have toxic skin.

Golden mantellas are poisonous frogs from Madagascar. They feed on small invertebrates.

Very wide mouth

These toads can reach 20 cm (8 in) in length.

African bullfrogs are large, carnivorous frogs that feed on other frogs, reptiles, and even mice and rats.

Smooth, slimy skin

Common frogs are becoming rarer, partly due to the loss of wetland areas.

White's tree frogs are large Australian frogs.

Sticky pads below fingers

Toads

Smooth skin is unusual for a toad.

Asian tree toads have flat digital discs, enabling them to climb riverside trees.

These toads run rather than hop.

Natterjack toads, also called running toads, are the rarest toads in Britain.

Developing eggs

Male midwife toads carry their eggs on their backs until they hatch into the water.

Fleshy horns project over eyes to enhance leaf-like appearance.

Asian horned toads resemble dried leaves, to escape discovery on the forest floor.

Narrow fingers used for feeding.

Webbed feet

African clawed toads are totally aquatic.

Warty skin

Ornate horned toads may even eat others of the same species.

Ornate horned toads from Argentina are large, aggressive toads with huge appetites.

Cane toads were originally from South America.

Cane toads were introduced to Australia to control sugar cane pests, but have become pests themselves.

Mexican burrowing toads live in dry areas, rarely emerging onto the surface.

FRUITS AND SEEDS

CHERRIES, TOMATOES, and pea pods are all fruits. A fruit is the part of a plant that contains and protects the seeds. A fruit forms after a flower has been pollinated. First the petals wither and fall, then the part of the flower called the ovary swells. This becomes the fruit, containing one or several seeds, which are the plant's way of reproducing itself. Inside the fruit, the seeds are supplied with nutrients through tiny stalks connecting them to the fruit wall. As the seeds grow, the fruit ripens. Some fruits are sweet and juicy and may be edible; others are inedible, or even poisonous.

Parts of a fruit

In some fruits, the fruit wall, or pericarp, has three distinct layers – an outer epicarp, a middle mesocarp, and a hard, inner endocarp. These layers are easy to see in fleshy fruits, such as plums, but in other fruits the layers are not so clear. The fleshy part of an apple, for example, is actually formed from the receptacle – the swollen tip of the flower stem.

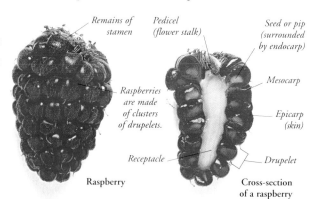

Remains of stamen

Pedicel (flower stalk)

Seed or pip (surrounded by endocarp)

Raspberries are made of clusters of drupelets.

Mesocarp

Epicarp (skin)

Receptacle

Drupelet

Raspberry

Cross-section of a raspberry

How a fruit develops

Once a flower has been pollinated and fertilization has taken place, its ovary becomes known as a fruit. This fruit and the tiny seeds within begin to develop and grow. Gradually the fruit enlarges, and as it matures, its shape, colour, and texture also change. When a juicy, edible fruit such as this melon ripens, its flesh becomes very sweet and succulent.

The flower is brightly coloured and attracts insects that will pollinate it.

After pollination, the ovary starts to swell.

The flower is no longer needed, so it shrivels up and dies.

The fruit begins to form.

The fruit grows larger as it ripens.

The fruit has ripened and contains hundreds of seeds deep inside.

A melon is a kind of berry.

Parts of a seed

All seeds contain a tiny embryo and seed leaves called cotyledons, which are full of stored food. These are all enclosed in an outer seed coat, called a testa. The embryo has a minute root called a radicle and a tiny stem called a plumule. When the seed germinates, the food store provides nourishment for the tiny seedling.

Testa (seed coat)

Embryo

Cotyledon (seed leaf)

Testa

Apple seed

Cross-section of an apple seed

Seed dispersal

Plants need to spread their seeds to increase their chance of survival. Seeds are dispersed by wind, water, and animals. In some plants, parts of the fruit wall or flowerhead also help to spread the seeds. As the fruit dries, the fruit wall splits open and the seeds are scattered.

Dispersal by burial

Seeds are a valuable source of food for mammals and birds. Squirrels and other rodents bury acorns and other nuts, then forget to dig them up. These grow into plants where they were left.

Squirrel burying nuts

Bird dispersal

Brightly coloured orange and red berries attract birds, which like to feed on them. The birds swallow the berries whole but digest only the fleshy part. The seeds pass out, unharmed, in the bird's droppings.

Redwing

Water dispersal

Some fruits and seeds float. Their fruit wall contains oil droplets or air to make them buoyant. Coconut palm fruits float in the sea until they are washed up on a beach.

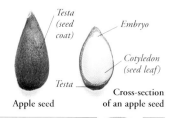

Coconut growing on a beach

Wind dispersal

Light fruits and seeds are spread by the wind. The seeds of a columbine are scattered when the breeze shakes the seed head. Maple tree seeds have papery wings to carry them on the wind.

Columbine seed head

Animal dispersal

Some seeds are encased inside hooked fruits that can easily become trapped in the fur of mammals. They are carried along by the animals and drop off later in another place.

Bison with seeds trapped in fur

Types of fruit

Simple fruits have a single ovary; compound fruits have more than one. When ripe, some fruits remain succulent; others become woody and hard, or dry and papery, such as larkspur. False fruits develop from other flower parts in addition to the ovary.

Berries

Berries have a combined mesocarp and endocarp layer. They often have many seeds that each have a tough seed coat, or testa.

Grapes

False fruits

In most false fruits, the receptacle swells to enclose the true fruit. Tiny true fruits may also be fixed to the surface of the receptacle.

Pear

Drupes

Drupes, or stone fruits, have a thick, fleshy mesocarp and a woody endocarp – the stone. Fruits such as raspberries are made up of many tiny drupelets.

Plum

Dry fruits

Dry fruits often have lids or seams that open to release the ripe seeds. This capsule has round openings called pores.

Love-in-a-mist capsule

FIND OUT MORE BIRDS FLOWERS FOOD MAMMALS PLANTS PLANTS, ANATOMY PLANTS, REPRODUCTION PLANT USES RATS AND OTHER RODENTS

Succulent fruits

Berries

Kiwanos have a spiky rind to prevent animals from eating them until the seeds are ripe.

Avocados have a single large seed and oily flesh.

Redcurrant seeds are spread by birds.

Persimmons are juicy berries with many seeds.

Grapes each have a tiny stalk and grow in large clusters.

Tomato seeds are covered in a jelly layer that protects them while inside an animal's gut.

Melons are a firm-walled kind of berry called a pepo.

Gooseberry seeds are embedded in juicy flesh.

Lemons are citrus fruits with flesh made of juice-filled hairs.

Lychees have a fleshy layer that grows from the seed stalk.

Rambutans have very hairy skin.

Kiwis have black seeds embedded in firm green flesh.

Drupes and drupelets

Peaches have juicy flesh and a single seed protected inside a woody stone.

Cherries have a single seed inside a hard stone.

Apricots are cultivated fruits that have a single seed inside a woody stone.

Blackberry fruits each consist of many single-seeded drupelets.

Nectarines are a cultivated variety of peach with a smoother skin.

Damsons are small plums. Their seeds are spread when animals eat the flesh.

Mangoes have a large, single seed and sweet flesh.

Greengages are a kind of plum with green or yellow flesh.

Loganberries are made up of many single-seeded drupelets.

Plums have juicy flesh and a single seed inside a stone.

Sago palm fruits have a corky layer that allows them to float.

Coconuts are the fruit of a palm tree.

False fruits

Rowan berries are the swollen tips of the flower stem. They enclose the real fruit.

Apple flesh is the swollen tip of the flower stem, and the pips are the seeds.

Fig fruits are tiny woody pips contained in a fleshy swollen flower stem.

Strawberries consist of a red fleshy receptacle covered in tiny fruits.

Quinces have hard flesh and a seed-filled core.

Breadfruits have many fruits in a large, fleshy flowerhead.

Dry fruits

Honesty has a papery fruit and flat seeds.

Dandelion fruits have hairs that help them float in a breeze.

Goosegrass fruits have hooks that cling to animals' fur.

Sycamore fruits have wings that carry them on the wind.

Larkspur fruits split open to release the seeds.

Hogweed fruits are papery and contain two seeds.

Laburnum pods split to release the hard seeds.

Poppy capsules contain masses of tiny seeds.

Burdock has a head of hooked fruits.

Acorns are nuts with a tough, woody fruit wall.

Sweet chestnuts are enclosed in a spiny case.

Beech nuts are arranged in threes inside a rough case.

FURNITURE

EVERY DAY, PEOPLE SIT on chairs, sleep in beds, and eat from tables. All these are items of furniture, the movable equipment of a home. At one time, furniture was handmade, so most homes contained only basic, functional pieces. A wide range of more affordable furniture became available when production was mechanized in the 19th century. Today, furniture design is largely determined by function, cost, size, and fashion.

The chairs in this Roman sculpture are similar to modern chairs.

Early furniture
Different cultures have produced very similar furniture. The ancient Egyptians had folding beds, and the Romans had armchairs. The earliest furniture to survive was sealed in Egyptian tombs.

Antique furniture
Antiques are objects made more than 100 years ago. Antique furniture was usually handcrafted, using fine materials, in many different styles. Antiques are frequently considered valuable and are highly prized by collectors today.

An 18th-century cabinet

Types of furniture

Furniture made for use in a home is designed to be as comfortable as possible. Choices of shape and fabric let the buyer express personal taste. Office furniture is usually plainer and more functional. Furniture is found outdoors in the form of litter bins, street lamps, and bus stops.

Domestic furniture
Most homes have a bed or a futon. Originally created in Japan for modern, urban life, the futon saves space by serving as a bed at night and a sofa during the day.

Office furniture
Modern office furniture, such as this Anglepoise lamp, is designed to be practical, sturdy, and long-lasting.

The lamp head is easily adjusted.

The heavy base provides balance.

Street furniture
Despite having similar functions, street furniture looks very different all over the world. This elaborate public drinking fountain is in Paris, France.

How an armchair is made

Most modern furniture is mass-produced by machine rather than handcrafted. Furniture such as sofas and armchairs have machine-made parts that are fitted together by hand and then upholstered. This armchair is made from materials that have been built up around a wooden frame.

Steel springs attached to the frame help spread a person's weight evenly.

Arms are cushioned with foam padding and a fleece layer.

Upholsterer fits the fabric covering securely into position.

Castors are small wheels beneath the chair that allow it to be moved easily.

Metal springs make the chair comfortable to sit on.

Layers of metal mesh and hessian hold the springs in place.

Cushions are filled with foam or feathers.

Fabric covering is durable.

Upholstery
A layer of padding called upholstery covers the basic wooden frame of a chair. Upholstery also refers to the way in which fabric is fitted to the frame. The top layer of fabric is chosen from a range of colours, patterns, and textures.

Interior design
In furnishing a room, people try to choose colours, pictures, fabrics, and furniture that go well together. This process is known as interior design. It began in Europe in the 16th century, when furniture makers were first given charge of entire rooms to decorate as a unified whole.

Soft furnishings
Soft furnishings are materials such as rugs, cushions, and curtains. These materials are chosen to make a room comfortable and to help create its overall look.

Cushions and wallpaper borders are coordinated.

William Morris
The British designer, artist, and socialist William Morris (1834–96) was active in many areas. He was influential in the design of furniture and fabrics, argued for a return to handcrafted furniture, and founded the Arts and Crafts Movement for design.

FIND OUT MORE   ARCHITECTURE   ART, HISTORY OF   CRAFTS   DESIGN   EGYPT, ANCIENT   HOUSES AND HOMES   MUSEUMS

English furniture

Lights

Iron candlestand,
late 17th century

Brass candlesticks,
early 18th century

Bronze storm lamp,
early 19th century

Gilt gaslight pendant,
mid 19th century

Glass electric pendant
with brass edgings, c.1900

Standard lamp,
1930–40

Chairs

Carved oak armchair,
c.1620

Walnut chair,
c.1680

Beech armchair with
caned seat, c.1815

Upholstered chair with beech
and walnut frame, c.1860

Ebonized beech
side-chair, c.1890

Birch veneered
plywood chair, 1989

Tables and cabinets

Pine and oak side-table gilded
in Chinese style, c.1690

Mahogany and walnut table
on a tripod stand, c.1760

Rosewood side-
table, c.1800

Combined games and
needlework table, c.1830

Mahogany table in
Moorish style, c.1895

Maple veneer side-
table, late 1930s

Queen Anne cabinet on chest,
walnut veneer on a pine frame, c.1700

Shelves projecting
from back panel

Painted panels
showing signs
of the zodiac

Open shelf

Moorish
style
decoration

Cupboard
with painted
panel set
into door

Double
glazed doors

Mahogany cabinet with inset painted panels and
decoration, designed by Lewis F Day in 1880

Oak bookcase with fluted columns,
handcrafted in a traditional style, 1993

GALAXIES

A HUNDRED billion galaxies exist in the Universe. Each consists of a vast collection of stars, gas, and dust. They started life thousands of million of years ago, slowly forming into distinctive shapes. Each galaxy can contain billions of stars. Gravity keeps the stars together and keeps the galaxies in clusters.

Milky Way

About 500 billion stars make up the spiral-shaped Milky Way. The arms contain young, hot, bright stars; older, dimmer stars make up the nucleus. A thin halo of old stars surrounds our Galaxy. The Sun is in one of the arms, about two-thirds of the way from the centre. It orbits the centre of the Galaxy once every 220 million years.

The Milky Way is about 100,000 light years wide and 13,000 light years across at the central hub.

Spiral arm in profile — *Central hub*

Types of galaxies

Most galaxies have a central ball of stars, the nucleus, and many have a flattened disc coming out of this. Astronomers have classified galaxies into three main types based on these features. No one knows why galaxies become a particular shape. It may be to do with how fast a galaxy spins and how quickly stars form inside.

Elliptical

About 60 per cent of galaxies are ball-shaped collections of old stars. They range in shape from round to flattened ovals. Astronomers describe their shape with the letter *E* followed by a number between *0* and *7* – the higher the number, the flatter the galaxy.

Spiral

A hub of older stars is surrounded by a flattened disc with spiral arms containing younger stars. The shape of a spiral is described by the letter *S,* followed by a letter between *a* and *d* to indicate how tightly wound the arms are and the size of the hub.

Classification of galaxies by shape

E0 E3 E5 E7 Sa Sb Sc SBa SBb SBc

Irregular

About 10 per cent of galaxies are irregular. They are collections of stars with no distinctive shape or structure, and do not fit into any of the classifications. They are smaller than the average galaxy and contain large amounts of gas and dust.

Barred spiral

These galaxies consist of a central bar of older stars with arms containing younger stars coming from the ends of the bar. Barred spirals are described as *SB* followed by a letter from *a* to *d* to indicate how tightly wound the arms are and the size of the hub.

Active galaxies

Unusually large amounts of energy are emitted from some galaxies. This energy may come from an object that is visible, such as a quasar, or from an invisible object, such as the lobes of a radio galaxy. How the energy is created is uncertain, but evidence suggests it could be from a supermassive black hole at the centre of the galaxy.

Quasars

Quasars are the brightest, most distant, fastest moving, and youngest objects visible outside the Milky Way. Thousands are known, each emitting huge amounts of energy. They are found at the heart of large galaxies.

Radio galaxies

Powerful radio energy is emitted by radio galaxies. The energy comes from lobes at either side of the visible core, and is detectable with radio telescopes. Centaurus A is the nearest active galaxy: it is 16 million light years away.

Core — *Lobes*

Centaurus A

Colliding galaxies

Galaxies can collide as they move through space, as is happening (left) with two galaxies in the constellation of Boötes. Such collisions will change the shape of a galaxy or result in a merger.

Edwin Hubble

In 1923, the American astronomer Edwin Hubble (1889–1953) proved that there are galaxies other than the Milky Way. The next year he classified galaxies according to their shape. He went on to show that galaxies are moving away from each other, and so provided proof that the Universe is expanding.

Galaxy clusters

Galaxies are grouped together in clusters. The Milky Way belongs to a cluster of about 30 galaxies called the Local Group. The Virgo Cluster (right) contains about 2,500 galaxies, mostly spirals.

Superclusters

Clusters of galaxies group together into superclusters that spread across many millions of light years. In turn, hundreds of superclusters group together to form huge walls and filaments, such as the Stick Man, which stretch for hundreds of millions of light years.

The Stick Man contains millions of galaxies.

FIND OUT MORE   ASTRONOMY   BIG BANG   BLACK HOLES   GRAVITY   STARS   UNIVERSE

GALILEO GALILEI

THE ITALIAN SCIENTIST Galileo Galilei was one of the greatest astronomers and physicists of all time. He was the first person to use a telescope to look at the heavens. He started a branch of physics called mechanics, showing that nature obeyed mathematical rules. His belief that science should be based on observation made him one of the first modern scientists. It also led him into trouble, because his views about the Solar System went against those held by the Roman Catholic Church.

Early life
Galileo was born in Pisa, Italy, in 1564. After school he went to the University of Pisa to study medicine. But Galileo was more interested in mathematics and physics, and left without a degree. By the time he was 25, he was back at the university – as professor of mathematics.

Telescope

In 1609, Galileo heard of the invention of the telescope and made one of his own. He used it to look at the heavens and made many astronomical discoveries. He noticed that the planet Venus has phases like the Moon. This gave support to the theory of Nicolaus Copernicus that the planets went round the Sun.

Moving bodies

In the 16th century, people believed that the Sun moved around Earth. Galileo did not agree with this, and developed Copernicus's theory of Earth moving around the Sun.

Falling feather

Coin falls at same speed

Gravity
Galileo showed that all objects fall at the same speed, no matter what their weight. Previously, people had believed that heavier objects fell faster. There is a story that Galileo proved his theory by dropping objects from the leaning tower of Pisa, but this is probably not true. He certainly did an experiment like this, in which objects of different weights were dropped in identical jars from which the air was pumped out.

Replica of Galileo's telescope, 1609

Artist's impression of the Milky Way

Planet with two moons

Planet with ringlike formations

Galileo's drawings of Saturn

Milky Way
In 1610, Galileo built a telescope that could magnify 1,000 times. It enabled him to see thousands of stars that no human being had ever seen before. He trained his new telescope on the Milky Way and found that it was a vast collection of stars, clustered together in groups of various sizes.

Planets and moons
Through his telescope, Galileo saw what he at first thought were two small moons orbiting the planet Saturn. He drew these "moons" in his notebooks, but later worked out that they were Saturn's now-famous rings. He also discovered the four moons that orbit the planet Jupiter, and was able to examine the craters on our own Moon.

The Starry Messenger
In March 1610, Galileo published many of his discoveries in his book, *The Starry Messenger*. The book also showed that Copernicus was right to say that the Earth moved around the Sun, and that the Roman Catholic Church's idea of an unmoving Earth at the centre of the Universe was wrong. *The Starry Messenger* infuriated many churchmen.

Crater on Moon

Illustrated pages from *The Starry Messenger*, 1610

Inquisition

Galileo's support for Copernicus's ideas outraged the Catholic Church because the priests thought that the Earth should be at the centre of the Universe. In 1633, the Church called Galileo to appear before its court, or inquisition, in Rome. The court ordered him to deny his beliefs under threat of torture. Galileo was forced to agree that Earth was the centre of the Universe, but was heard to mutter, "Yet it *does* move".

Trial of Galileo

GALILEO GALILEI

1564 Born, Pisa, Italy.

1589 Becomes Professor of Mathematics at Pisa University.

1609 Makes his first telescope.

1610 Publishes *The Starry Messenger*.

1632 Publishes *Dialogue*, explaining the two theories of the universe.

1633 Sentenced by the Inquisition.

1642 Dies under house arrest at Arcetri, Italy.

FIND OUT MORE   FORCE AND MOTION   PLANETS   SCIENCE, HISTORY OF   STARS   SUN AND SOLAR SYSTEM   TELESCOPES

GANDHI, MOHANDAS

WHEN THE VAST AND HEAVILY populated nation of India gained independence from Britain in August 1947, one man more than any other was responsible for that achievement. Mohandas Gandhi united the different communities of India and led them to independence. He believed in non-violent protest and despised the racial violence of his homeland. He became known as Mahatma, or "great soul". Although he did not live long enough to see the results of his work, Gandhi is remembered today as the instigator of three movements crucial in the 20th century: the campaigns against racism, colonialism, and violence.

Early life
Mohandas Kamarchand Gandhi was born in Porbandar, India, in 1869. Educated in India and Britain, he trained in law and became a barrister in 1889. In 1893 he moved to work in South Africa. While there, he edited a newspaper called *Indian Opinion* and campaigned against racial injustice, forcing the South African government to grant Indians rights of permanent citizenship in 1914.

Indian nationalism

The British had controlled India since the 18th century, but many Indians wanted to govern themselves. In 1915, Gandhi returned from South Africa and became one of the leaders of the independence movement. He led many peaceful campaigns against British rule, using the tactic of non-violent civil disobedience. He called this method Satyagraha ("holding to the truth"). It was copied by many civil-rights campaigners around the world.

Gandhi with Jawaharlal Nehru, leader of the socialist wing of Congress

Congress
The Indian National Congress Party was founded in 1885. Its members wanted to increase Indian participation in government and represent all religions and cultures. During the 1920s, under the leadership of Gandhi and Jawaharlal Nehru, Congress took the lead in campaigning for Indian independence.

Imprisonment
During his many campaigns, Gandhi was often imprisoned by the British for civil disobedience. But after each spell in prison, Gandhi emerged more powerful and more respected than before. His personal prestige was so high that people began to call him Mahatma, the "great soul". He alone seemed able to unite the diverse elements of the independence movement that represented the many different religions and cultures in the huge subcontinent of India.

Gandhi's spectacles

Gandhi's sandals

Gandhi lived a simple life, wearing plain clothes and keeping only a few possessions.

Gandhi's watch

Salt march
The British controlled the production of salt in India. This monopoly forced up prices and was very unpopular. In 1930, Gandhi led a 320-km (200-mile) march to the sea to get his own salt and thousands joined him on the way. Gandhi was imprisoned for civil disobedience, but the march showed the power of Satyagraha.

Social reforms

In 1937, the Indian provinces received a large measure of home rule. The Congress Party took control of seven of the 11 provinces and began to reform the country. Gandhi pushed for social, economic, and educational improvements designed to rebuild India. He encouraged crafts such as spinning cotton, because he believed that small cottage industries could help India's villages.

Gandhi spinning cotton

Independence

In 1947, India gained its independence. Hindus in the Congress Party wanted a united India, but Muslims wanted a country of their own. The country was, therefore, divided into India and Pakistan, a division Gandhi bitterly opposed.

Assassination
Gandhi took little part in the independence talks, but threatened to fast to death to protest against the violence between Hindus and Muslims. In January 1948, he was assassinated by a Hindu fanatic who resented his concern for the Muslims.

Monument at the place where Gandhi died

MOHANDAS GANDHI

1869	Born in Porbandar, India.
1889	Becomes a barrister in England.
1891–93	Works as a lawyer in India.
1893–1915	Works in South Africa.
1920s	Takes control of Congress Party with Nehru.
1930	Leads salt march to the sea.
1942	Launches Quit India campaign during World War II, and is interned until 1944.
1945	New British government promises independence by 1947.
1947	India gains its independence.
1948	Gandhi is assassinated.

FIND OUT MORE

EMPIRES HINDUISM HUMAN RIGHTS INDIA, HISTORY OF SOUTH AFRICA, HISTORY OF

GARBO, GRETA

SOPHISTICATED, SUPERIOR, scornful, and beautiful, Greta Garbo was everyone's idea of the perfect film star. The daughter of a poor labourer in Stockholm, Sweden, she conquered Hollywood in the 1920s and 1930s. Her audiences adored her, but at the height of her career she retired, becoming a recluse and never showing her face in public again. Yet this most celebrated actor received no Oscars, only a belated special award for her unforgettable films.

Early life

Greta Gustafson was born in the Swedish capital of Stockholm in 1905. Her family was poor, and she worked from an early age in a barber's shop and a department store. Her first film part was in *How Not to Dress*, a publicity film for the store.

Training

Early in her career, Garbo appeared as the female lead in a slapstick comedy, *Peter the Tramp*. She then applied for and won a scholarship to Sweden's Royal Dramatic Theatre training school, where she was soon playing small parts on stage.

Mauritz Stiller

While at training school, Garbo was spotted by the Swedish film director Mauritz Stiller. Stiller was best known for such films as the comedy *Love and Journalism,* and the sexually charged movie *Erotikon*. Stiller took a special interest in Garbo's career, gave her the surname Garbo, and made her into a star.

Garbo and Mauritz Stiller

First success

Garbo's first major film role was as the star of *The Atonement of Gösta Berling*. The film was a romantic tale of a priest set in the Swedish countryside. The premiere in Stockholm in 1924 attracted a huge audience and launched Garbo on her film career.

Still from *Gösta Berling*

Hollywood

In 1925, after the success of *Gösta Berling,* Garbo moved to Hollywood, the centre of the US film industry. She signed a contract with Metro-Goldwyn-Mayer (MGM) and began filming *The Torrent*. Her first major success was *Flesh and the Devil,* made in 1926 and directed by Clarence Brown. By 1927, she was earning $5,000 a week from MGM. In all, Garbo made 24 films in Hollywood, and became one of the most famous, and best-paid, film stars in the world.

Studio system

Film-making in Hollywood was dominated by a few large companies, such as MGM, Paramount, and Warner Bros. These and other studios kept actors and directors on tight contracts, so that they could not work for a rival company. As a result, Garbo was forced to star in films she did not like.

"Garbo talks!"

In 1930, the first sound film starring Garbo appeared. The publicity slogan was "Garbo talks!". The film, *Anna Christie,* had a heroine with a Swedish accent. The producers thought this would be an ideal role for Garbo. They believed that audiences might not otherwise accept her heavily accented voice.

Anna Karenina

Garbo's reputation as a tragic heroine was established by *Anna Karenina* (1935), based on the novel by the great Russian writer Leo Tolstoy. The film won numerous awards and confirmed Garbo's reputation as the leading actress of her day.

Garbo laughs

Garbo's reputation was as a serious, intense actress. In 1939, she astounded audiences with her relaxed performance in the romantic comedy *Ninotchka.* Publicity for the film made much of her laughter in this role.

A life apart

In 1941, Garbo announced her retirement from making films, having no wish to disappoint her admirers by growing old on screen. Despite her success in Europe, her popularity was declining in the USA. She became an American citizen in 1951 and led the life of a recluse, although she remained friends with many famous people.

"I want to be alone" was Garbo's famous wish after her retirement in 1941.

GRETA GARBO

1905 Born in Stockholm, Sweden.

1924 Stars in *The Atonement of Gösta Berling,* her first major film.

1925 Moves to the USA and signs contract with MGM.

1930 Has her first talking role, in *Anna Christie.*

1935 *Anna Karenina.*

1938 Nominated for an Oscar for *Camille.*

1939 *Ninotchka.*

1941 Retires from film-making.

1954 Honoured at Academy Awards.

1990 Dies in New York.

FIND OUT MORE   CAMERAS   FILMS AND FILM-MAKING   LITERATURE

GARDENS

LIKE LANDSCAPES in miniature, gardens are set-aside areas of land where plants are grown to provide beauty and relaxation. Gardens have a practical purpose too. From ancient times, they have helped people nurture plants for food and medicine. They reduce noise and air pollution in cities, and create a refreshing environment in a hot climate. Glorious landscaped gardens can enhance the finest modern buildings, and botanic gardens are places of scientific study.

Shears, for cutting hedges

Thick blades

Used for digging soil

Spade and fork

Watering can

Trowel

Hand fork

Tools

Gardeners use a variety of tools. Some have hardly changed in hundreds of years, such as forks. Mechanical aids such as the lawnmower, invented in 1832, are relatively new developments.

Development of gardens

Gardens have an ancient history. They were planted in Mesopotamia, China, Egypt, Persia, and Greece. The Romans spread knowledge of gardening to northern Europe during their rule of the Mediterranean lands. From the 4th century AD, when Roman power declined, monks continued the tradition of cultivating plants in monastery gardens. European gardens were enclosed by abbey or castle walls until the Renaissance.

China and Japan

Gardens in China and Japan often have a religious significance, where nature itself is honoured. This tradition is centuries old. For Zen Buddhists, landscaped gardens of raked gravel, where a rock may represent a mountain, are places of silent meditation.

Temple garden, Kyoto, Japan

Clipped shrubs

Islamic gardens

North African Moors created shady courtyard gardens, with pools and fountains to reflect the sky and cool the air. When they conquered Spain in the 8th century, the Moors took the style to Europe, as seen in the Court of the Myrtles, the Alhambra, Spain.

Renaissance formality

During the Renaissance in the 14th century, architects planned gardens as settings for the grand houses they designed. Fashionable gardens were formal, open, and regular, reviving a style established by the Romans.

Villa Lante, Bagnaia, Lazio, Italy

Botanic gardens

In botanic gardens, specimen plants are collected and cultivated for scientific study. They developed from the herb or physic gardens tended by medieval monks, where plants were grown for medicinal purposes.

18th-century naturalism

The Jardin Anglais (English garden) style spread through Europe during the 18th century. The trend was first set by the English architect William Kent (c.1685–1748), who planned less formal gardens than had been common previously. He used an open style, which he believed to look more natural, to set off the formality of his buildings.

This small Classical temple, in a wooded glade, is typical of the Jardin Anglais style.

Chiswick House, London, England

Plant collectors

From the late 1600s, European explorers returned from their world expeditions with many new and exotic varieties of plant. Serious plant-collecting expeditions began in the 18th century, bringing back specimens for scientific study and to decorate gardens.

The peony, a native of China, was taken to Europe by plant collectors.

Roberto Burle Marx

Brazilian garden designer Roberto Burle Marx (1909–1994) created stunning gardens for modern buildings in Brazil, using only plants native to his country. He made Brazilians more aware of the amazing plants found in their countryside.

Wildlife gardens

In the 20th century, gardeners became more interested in the wild creatures that inhabited their plants, trees, and ponds. Instead of treating them as pests, they welcomed wildlife. Careful planting of a wildlife garden creates many different habitats, encouraging the widest possible range of animal visitors.

Gardeners plant flowers that attract insects.

FIND OUT MORE   ARCHITECTURE   BUDDHISM   ISLAMIC EMPIRE   MEDICINE, HISTORY OF   MONASTERIES   PLANT USES   RENAISSANCE

GASES

WHEN YOU CATCH an unpleasant smell given off by a chemistry experiment, your nose is detecting the presence of a gas released by a chemical reaction. A gas is a type of matter with no fixed shape or volume. Not all gases have a smell, and many are invisible, but all are made up of tiny, fast-moving particles that move rapidly and randomly.

Condensation

Tiny droplets form on the inside of a cold window when water vapour in the air is cooled by the glass and turns into liquid water. The change of a gas to a liquid is called condensation. As a gas cools, its particles lose energy and slow down. The forces between the particles grow stronger and pull them together to form a liquid.

Vapour
A gas normally forms when a liquid boils. However, a type of gas called a vapour sometimes forms when a liquid is below its boiling point. Paint, for example, dries when liquid particles at its surface gain enough energy to escape into the air as a vapour.

Brownian motion

Dust particles can often be seen dancing in shafts of sunlight. Their random, jittery path is caused by tiny, unseen air molecules that bombard the dust particles. This motion – called Brownian Motion after Robert Brown (1773–1858), a Scottish biologist – shows that gas particles are constantly moving.

Gas jar of air

Partition is removed.

Gases diffuse.

Glass partition

Gas jar of bromine

Diffusion
When a jar of bromine gas and a jar of air are placed together, the gases quickly intermingle as their moving particles spread out to fill all the available space. This process is called diffusion. Food cooking in the kitchen is soon smelt throughout the house as gas particles released by the food rapidly diffuse in the air. Diffusion also occurs when solids and liquids dissolve to form solutions.

Gas particles
The forces between the speeding particles of a gas are too weak to hold them in one place, so the gas spreads out.

Nitrogen dioxide gas soon escapes from the beaker and mingles with the air.

Copper and nitric acid react, releasing brown nitrogen dioxide gas.

Gas laws

The gas laws are a set of proven theories that allow scientists to predict how a gas will behave when there is a change in its volume, pressure, or temperature. The laws apply only when a gas is held in a sealed container.

Charles's Law
This law, formulated by French physicist Jacques Charles (1746–1823), states that the volume of a gas at a constant pressure is proportional to its temperature. Thus, when the temperature of the gas halves, so does its volume.

1 When a gas-filled balloon is cooled in liquid nitrogen at -196°C (-321°F), the gas particles slow down.

2 The particles strike the balloon walls less often, so the gas volume shrinks, and the balloon collapses.

3 As the gas warms again in the air, the gas particles speed up, the volume expands, and the balloon reflates.

Properties of gases

A gas quickly spreads out to fill any available space because its free-moving particles travel in all directions. The higher the temperature of a gas, the more energy its particles have and the faster they move. The pressure of a gas is linked to the number of collisions between the gas particles and the walls of its container: the more frequent the collisions are, the greater the pressure the gas exerts.

Amedeo Avogadro

In 1806, an Italian lawyer named Amedeo Avogadro (1776–1856) gave up his legal career to devote himself to the study of physics. In 1811, Avogadro proposed that equal volumes of all gases at the same temperature and pressure will contain the same number of particles. This is now called Avogadro's Law.

The air molecules collide more often with the syringe walls, so the air pressure rises.

Pushing in the plunger reduces the volume.

Boyle's Law
Put your finger over the end of a syringe, push in the plunger, and you will feel the air pressure in the syringe rising. The air obeys Boyle's Law, formulated by the Irish physicist Robert Boyle (1627–91). The law states that when a gas is at a constant temperature, its pressure is inversely proportional to its volume. In other words, if the volume halves, the pressure doubles.

Pressure inside the can blows off the lid.

Pressure Law
Heating a sealed can raises the air pressure inside the can until it is so great that the lid blows off. The air obeys the Pressure Law, which states that when a gas's volume is constant, its pressure is proportional to its temperature. This means that if the gas's temperature doubles, so will its pressure.

| FIND OUT MORE | AIR | ATOMS AND MOLECULES | HEAT | LIQUIDS | MATTER | PRESSURE | SOLIDS |

GENETICS

EACH PERSON IS UNIQUE, but he or she also inherits some characteristics and even appearance from his or her parents. The study of how characteristics are passed on from parents to offspring is known as genetics, and it affects all forms of life. At the centre of the process is the deoxyribonucleic acid (DNA) molecule, which exists inside every living cell and contains a complex chemical "code" that controls the way in which life forms are put together and operate. DNA is composed of genes, and DNA, in turn, makes up chromosomes. All of these microscopic structures live in the nuclei of cells.

DNA

A DNA molecule contains all the information required to make and operate a specific organism. DNA is found in the nucleus of a cell and is a long structure which consists of two strands twisted together to form a double helix. The strands are linked by four chemicals called bases: thymine, adenine, cytosine, and guanine.

"Backbone" of strand is made from sugar and phosphate molecules.

Thymine   Adenine

Cytosine   Guanine

Replicating DNA

DNA is unique in its ability to replicate, or copy, itself. When a cell divides (reproduces), DNA information is passed on unchanged. During replication, the DNA strands separate, and DNA building blocks, nucleotides, line up, matching the original sequence of bases to form two new and identical DNA molecules.

New strand

Original strand

Cytosine-guanine base pair

Adenine-thymine base pair

Two strands coil round each other to form a double helix.

Nucleotide

Replication fork

DNA replication

Original double helix, or parent DNA molecule

An albino squirrel is a mutation.

Chromosomes

A chromosome is a thread-like structure found in the nucleus of a cell. Chromosomes store DNA and carry DNA molecules when a cell reproduces by dividing. Most human cells contain 46 chromosomes, divided into 23 pairs; 23 chromosomes are derived from each of the parents.

Chromosomes, stained and paired

Chromosome defects

A chromosome defect can result from the wrong number of chromosomes, a missing piece of chromosome, or an unnecessary extra piece. Alternatively, there may be a "mistake" in part of the DNA. Any of these can cause a genetic disorder before or after birth, or later in life.

Genetic defect causes malformed feet.

Mutations

A mutation is an accidental change in the structure of part of a DNA molecule, or sometimes in the number or shape of chromosomes. Mutations may result in new or unusual characteristics.

Variations

While members of a species look similar, they are not identical, as we can see from people around us. Variation happens because each individual receives a unique combination of DNA from its parents during reproduction.

Variations in types of flowers

Genes

A gene is the basic unit of inheritance, a small segment of a DNA molecule. There are about 100,000 genes in the 46 human chromosomes. Genes contain the instructions to construct proteins, which control cell activities. Therefore, genes help to determine the characteristics of an organism.

Genotype and phenotype

The genotype is the overall genetic blueprint for an organism. The phenotype is what an organism actually looks like, based on genotype and environment.

Alleles

Each gene has two or more forms called alleles. They control the same characteristic (for example, eye colour) but different versions of it (for instance, blue or brown).

Grey-blue eye, round-shaped, with long eyelashes, and large eyelid

Dark brown eye, almond-shaped, with short eyelashes

Medium-brown eye with fine eyelashes, and small eyelid

A length of DNA molecule

Franklin, Watson, and Crick

The discovery of the DNA molecule was a collaborative effort. Rosalind Franklin (1920–58) completed groundbreaking work, which was consolidated in 1953 by Francis Crick (b.1916), James Watson (b.1928), and Maurice Wilkins (b.1916). Watson, Crick, and Wilkins shared the 1962 Nobel Prize.

James Watson, American biologist

Rosalind Franklin, British biochemist

Francis Crick, British scientist

G

Heredity

Heredity is the transmission of characteristics from one generation to the next. These inherited characteristics, such as size, shape, and colour, are determined by genes passed on by parents. When different forms of the same genetic characteristic meet (for example, blue and brown eye colour), some genes are dominant (effective) and some are recessive (ineffective).

Family inheritance

Children inherit genetic traits and characteristics from parents.

Each child is unique because it inherits a different mix of genes from its parents.

Each child resembles, but is not identical to, its parents.

Sex chromosomes

Whether an animal is male or female is determined by one pair of chromosomes called the sex chromosomes. In humans and other mammals, a female's sex chromosomes are identical and are called XX. In males, one chromosome is smaller, and the pair is called XY.

Human X chromosome

Mutation in gene in this area causes a form of muscular dystrophy.

Mutation in gene here causes an eye disease.

Mutation in gene here causes cleft palate.

Mutation in gene here causes haemophilia, a disease that affects blood clotting.

Sex determination
Sperm and eggs each carry one sex chromosome. Eggs carry an X chromosome, and sperm carry an X or a Y. When a sperm and an egg meet during fertilization, there is a 50:50 chance of producing a male (XY) or a female (XX), depending on which chromosome the sperm is carrying.

Most ginger cats are male.

Tortoiseshell cats are always female.

Sex-linked inheritance
Sex chromosomes also carry genes that determine other characteristics apart from an animal's sex. More of these sex-linked genes are found on X chromosomes than Y. So some characteristics are specific only to males or to females.

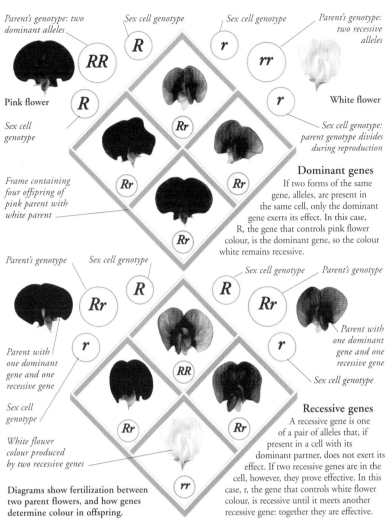

Parent's genotype: two dominant alleles

Pink flower

Sex cell genotype

RR

Sex cell genotype

R

Sex cell genotype

r

rr

Parent's genotype: two recessive alleles

White flower

Sex cell genotype: parent genotype divides during reproduction

Frame containing four offspring of pink parent with white parent

R

Rr

Rr

Rr

Rr

Rr

Dominant genes
If two forms of the same gene, alleles, are present in the same cell, only the dominant gene exerts its effect. In this case, R, the gene that controls pink flower colour, is the dominant gene, so the colour white remains recessive.

Parent's genotype

Rr

Sex cell genotype

R

Sex cell genotype

R

Parent's genotype

Rr

Sex cell genotype

r

Parent with one dominant gene and one recessive gene

Sex cell genotype

Parent with one dominant gene and one recessive gene

Sex cell genotype

r

RR

Rr

Rr

White flower colour produced by two recessive genes

rr

Recessive genes
A recessive gene is one of a pair of alleles that, if present in a cell with its dominant partner, does not exert its effect. If two recessive genes are in the cell, however, they prove effective. In this case, r, the gene that controls white flower colour, is recessive until it meets another recessive gene: together they are effective.

Diagrams show fertilization between two parent flowers, and how genes determine colour in offspring.

Genetic code

DNA contains the instructions to make the proteins that construct the cell and control its functions. Four chemical bases – adenine (A), cytosine (C), guanine (G), and thymine (T) – combine in pairs to form a sequence, or code. The cell then translates this code and produces a protein.

Human Genome Project
The genome is the complete set of genes found in the nucleus of every body cell. In the 1980s the Human Genome Project set out to identify all of those genes by working out the sequence of bases. In 2001 they announced the existence of some 30,000 genes.

Genetic codes are made up of bases (A, C, G, T).

Genetic engineering

Genetic engineering involves taking genes from one cell and inserting them into another cell. This gives the cell new characteristics, which are determined by the transferred gene. In the future, genetic engineering may be used on human cells, so that genetic disorders can be eliminated.

Genetically modified (GM) food
Food products can also be altered by genetic modification or engineering. For example, scientists can genetically engineer certain fruits and vegetables, so that they do not rot so quickly. There is much debate about the safety of GM foods.

Genetically modified tomatoes

FIND OUT MORE   BIOLOGY   CELLS   DISEASES   FOOD   HUMAN BODY   PLANTS, REPRODUCTION   REPRODUCTION

GEOLOGY

PEOPLE ONCE THOUGHT that the Earth was just a simple ball of rock. Recently geologists have shown that it is much more complex. Geology is the study of the Earth's history, structure, and composition. Originally only the study of rocks and rock structures, the scope of geological study broadened after the discovery in the 1960s that the Earth's crust is made up of giant, continually moving plates. These plates affect everything from the creation of continents to the eruption of volcanoes. The science of geology also helps us to locate mineral reserves, and to understand our environment.

Inner core of solid metal
Outer core of molten metal
Mantle of hot fluid rock
Crust of solid rock

Structure of the Earth
Geophysicists and geochemists study the structure of the Earth. Geophysicists focus on its physical processes, such as the circulation of heat deep inside; geochemists study the Earth's chemical composition.

Seismographs
The seismic waves, earthquake vibrations, are picked up by seismographs. These can reveal to geologists the structure of the rock they have passed through.

Seismographs

Rock and field geology

Petrology is the study of rocks and minerals. Surveys and rock samples indicate the occurrence of different rocks beneath the landscape, their structure, and their history.

The rock strata
Many rocks were formed in strata (layers) of sediment deposited on the seabed. Stratigraphy is the study of these layers. A break in a sequence of rock layers is called an unconformity, shown as a red line on the models below.

James Hutton
Scottish–born James Hutton (1726–97) was the founder of modern geology. With his collection and analysis of rock formations, he proved that the Earth was more than just a few thousand years old, and that all its rocks and land-forms had been formed over millions of years.

Angular unconformity – the older rock strata below the unconformity are at a different angle to the new layers.

Parallel conformity – strata either side of unconformity dip at the same angle.

Limestone pavement

Evidence of old landscape shaped long before the rocks above were formed.

Disconformity – an irregular eroded surface between parallel strata.

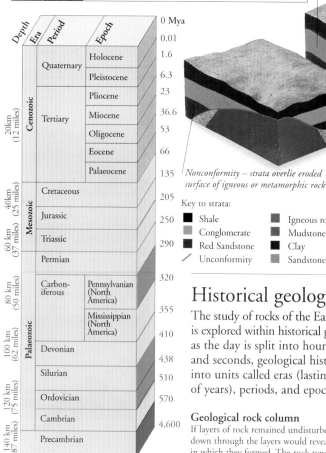

Depth	Era	Period	Epoch	Mya
				0
				0.01
		Quaternary	Holocene	1.6
			Pleistocene	6.3
			Pliocene	23
20km (12 miles)	Cenozoic	Tertiary	Miocene	36.6
			Oligocene	53
			Eocene	66
			Palaeocene	135
40km (25 miles)		Cretaceous		205
	Mesozoic	Jurassic		250
60 km (37 miles)		Triassic		290
		Permian		320
80 km (50 miles)		Carbon-iferous	Pennsylvanian (North America)	355
			Mississippian (North America)	410
100 km (62 miles)	Palaeozoic	Devonian		438
		Silurian		510
120 km (75 miles)		Ordovician		570
		Cambrian		4,600
140 km (87 miles)		Precambrian		

Nonconformity – strata overlie eroded surface of igneous or metamorphic rock

Key to strata:
- ▪ Shale
- ▪ Conglomerate
- ▪ Red Sandstone
- / Unconformity
- ▪ Igneous rock
- ▪ Mudstone
- ▪ Clay
- ▪ Sandstone

Rock strata models

Geologist's hammers

Chisels

Goggles

Tools
In order to examine the Earth's structure, geologists need some basic tools. These are goggles to protect their eyes from fly-ing rock chips, and a hammer and chisel for collecting rock samples.

Club hammer for use with chisels.

Historical geology
The study of rocks of the Earth's crust is explored within historical geology. Just as the day is split into hours, minutes, and seconds, geological history is split into units called eras (lasting millions of years), periods, and epochs.

Geological rock column
If layers of rock remained undisturbed, a column cut down through the layers would reveal the sequence in which they formed. The rock types shown along the side of this visual representation of geological time, are the predominant rocks of each period.

Key:
- / Sandstone
- / Mud
- / Shale
- / Limestone
- / Metamorphic

Geologists locate rock structures likely to contain oil; drilling can confirm this.

Exploration and survey
Each mineral in the Earth's crust is linked to a different type of geological structure. After using satellite and aerial surveys to target a particular area, the geologist then uses specific instruments to pinpoint the mineral.

FIND OUT MORE EARTH EARTHQUAKES EARTH SCIENCES FOSSILS ROCKS AND MINERALS VOLCANOES

GERMANY

THE FEDERAL REPUBLIC of Germany lies at the heart of Europe, bounded by nine other nations and the Baltic and North Seas. Since the country was reunified in 1990, it is, more than ever, a link between east and west for both trade and culture. Germany is one of the world's wealthiest nations and Europe's leading industrial power. It was a founder member of the European Union and plays a key role in international affairs. Germany has the second largest population in Europe after Russia.

Physical features

Germany has a varied landscape. It includes lakes, heaths, and islands in the north, fertile pastures and great forests in the centre and southwest, and great mountains, such as the Bavarian Alps, in the south.

GERMANY FACTS	
CAPITAL CITY Berlin	
AREA 356,910 sq km (137,800 sq miles)	
POPULATION 82,200,000	
MAIN LANGUAGE German	
MAJOR RELIGION Christian	
CURRENCY Euro	
LIFE EXPECTANCY 78 years	
PEOPLE PER DOCTOR 286	
GOVERNMENT Multi-party democracy	
ADULT LITERACY 99%	

River Rhine

The Rhine is one of Europe's most important rivers. It rises in the Swiss Alps and flows into the North Sea at Rotterdam in the Netherlands. The total length is about 1,320 km (820 miles), nearly half of which is in Germany. Long barges regularly carry freight such as coal, grain, and timber. Many tourists visit the southern part of the Rhine to see the scenery, vineyards, and castles that flank its sides.

Black Forest

Germany's Black Forest lies in the southwest of the country. The name comes from the dark conifers that clothe its mountain slopes and provide timber for the traditional wooden houses. Tourists flock to the region, attracted by the beauty of the scenery, spa resorts, such as Baden-Baden, and Lake Constance, which lies nearby.

Climate

Northern and central Germany have mild summers, and cool, damp winters. The southern and mountainous areas, such as the Harz Mountains, the Black Forest, and Bavaria, have much hotter summers and cold winters with heavy snow.

39°C (101°F)   -30°C (-21°F)
19°C (66°F)   -1°C (30°F)
563 mm (22 in)

Land use

Germany has relatively few natural resources, and forest covers almost half the country. Most of the land is fertile and is used for growing crops or raising animals.

Barren 0.5%   Farmland 45.5%
Forest 48.5%   Built-up 5.5%

Berlin

The Brandenburg Gate in Berlin symbolizes the reunification of Germany in 1990 when the Berlin Wall, built after World War II (1939–45) to separate East and West, was demolished. Always a thriving centre of art and culture, there are plans to rebuild this grand capital, Germany's largest city.

Brandenburg Gate

379

People

About 92 per cent of the people are Germans. Turks make up the largest minority group of more than 2,000,000, having gone to Germany in the 1960s to boost the labour force. Since 1990, many immigrants have arrived from eastern Europe. Some racial discrimination has caused social tension.

235 per sq km
(609 per sq mile)

87% Urban 13% Rural

Society
German society prides itself on equal opportunities and a comprehensive social welfare system, with free education and healthcare. Germans are environmentally aware, and the influence of the Green Party has led to strict anti-pollution policies.

Leisure

The Germans love sports and outdoor activities. Many enjoy hiking and cycling in the countryside, or canoeing and sailing on the lakes and rivers. In winter, skiing and skating are popular. Germans also excel at football, tennis, and motor-racing.

Skiing
Snow-covered slopes in the Bavarian Alps provide Germans with plenty of opportunities to practise their skiing. Children begin the sport early. Many people also travel to nearby French and Swiss ski resorts.

Football
The German national team has won the World Cup three times, as well as the Euro '96 cup against the Czech Republic. Association football, or soccer, is the most popular sport in Germany both for players and spectators, and there are many clubs.

Farming

Only three per cent of Germany's labour force work on the land, yet the country grows about two-thirds of all the food it needs. Crops include cereals, potatoes, and other vegetables. Pigs and cattle are reared.

Grapes

Crops
Germany's chief cereal crops are barley, oats, rye, and wheat. Sugar beet for refining to produce sugar is also widely grown. Grapes grow best in the areas bordering the Rhine and Moselle rivers, and are used for producing Germany's world-famous white wines.

Wheat

Sugar beet

Dairy
The lush green pastures of Germany's Allgäu valley, in the Alps, are ideal for grazing dairy cattle for milk, butter, and cheese.

Food

German people enjoy traditional smoked sausages, smoked meats and cheese, *sauerkraut* (pickled cabbage), and smoked and pickled fish, usually eaten with good, sourdough bread and a glass of cold beer. They also make tasty soups, sweet and savoury dumplings, and enjoy afternoon *Kaffee und Kuchen*, coffee with cakes.

Lid keeps flies out of beer.

Gherkin Salami

Wurst

Smoked sausage

Beer stein Selection of meats *Bread*

Industry

Over the last 50 years, Germany has become one of the world's leading industrial nations, and is an important manufacturer of cars, trucks, electrical goods, ships, and chemicals. The heart of German industry lies in the Ruhr, once a major coal-producing region.

Cars
Germany is one of the world's largest car manufacturers. Volkswagen is an internationally renowned make. Other famous brands are BMW, Mercedes-Benz, and Porsche.

Transport

Germany has an excellent transport system with 14 international airports, major sea ports in Hamburg and Bremen, and a highly efficient rail and road network. Canals and rivers, such as the Rhine and Ruhr, carry as much freight as the roads.

Inland waterways
Many of Germany's rivers are linked by canals, like the Danube-Main canal, creating an extensive network that makes long-distance freight transport practical.

Shipbuilding
Hamburg, Germany's largest port on the mouth of the Elbe river, has a long tradition of shipbuilding, as has Bremen on the mouth of the River Weser. Germany leads the rest of Europe in shipbuilding, and ranks highly in the world.

Precision work
Electronic devices such as calculators, computers, and electrical equipment such as this drill, form a large part of Germany's industrial output. The country also produces precision optical equipment.

Autobahns
Germany has Europe's most elaborate motorway network stretching almost 11,400 km (7,084 miles), with no speed limit. The first *Autobahn* was built in the 1930s for military use.

FIND OUT MORE CARS AND TRUCKS EUROPE EUROPE, HISTORY OF EUROPEAN UNION FARMING FOOTBALL GERMANY, HISTORY OF PORTS AND WATERWAYS SHIPS AND BOATS

GERMANY, HISTORY OF

ALTHOUGH THERE HAVE ALWAYS been German speakers living in Europe, a single German country did not exist until 1871. For much of its history, Germany consisted of many small kingdoms, duchies, and other states, kept apart by rivalries. Unification was eventually achieved under the diplomatic and military leadership of the north German state of Prussia. German industrial strength allowed the new nation to dominate Europe, but defeat in two world wars left the country divided again. In 1990, Germany reunited, and once more became the major economic power of Europe.

German tribes
In about 370, Huns from Asia swept into Germany, forcing native German tribes to pour into the neighbouring Roman Empire. Within a century, Rome had collapsed, and Germanic tribes such as the Visigoths and Franks controlled much of western Europe.

Brooch made by Germanic Lombard tribe

Medieval Germany
In 962, Otto I of Saxony united the German kingdoms in the Holy Roman Empire. This empire was long-lasting but weak, as local rulers fought to protect and increase their own power. Despite this disunity, the country became increasingly rich. By the late 15th century, German cities such as Augsburg controlled European banking and finance.

Ulm cathedral

Coming of Christianity
From the 5th century onwards, individual Germans became Christian. Some churches, such as Ulm Cathedral, were founded in the early 7th century, but it was not until the mission of St Boniface in the early 8th century that most of the people converted to Christianity.

Seal of Hamburg

Hanseatic League
The cities of northern Germany worked together to support their trading interests. In 1241, Lübeck and Hamburg concluded a treaty that led to the growth of the Hanseatic League, a trading alliance that dominated commerce in northern Europe. At its height there were 160 cities in the League.

Isenheim Altarpiece, by Mathias Grünewald

German Renaissance
In the 15th century, the Renaissance spread to Germany. Artists such as Albrecht Dürer (1471–1528) perfected the technique of the woodcut, Hans Holbein (1498–1543), working mostly in Switzerland and England, produced superb portraits, and Mathias Grünewald (1480–1528) painted religious masterpieces.

Peasants' War
In the 16th century, there was much tension between Catholics and Protestants in Germany. In 1524, peasants in southern Germany exploited the confusion to rise up and demand social reforms. The revolt was crushed in 1526.

Peasant rebellion in southern Germany

Inscription says that the owner "Fights for God".

Treaties of Westphalia
When the treaties ended the Thirty Years' War in 1648, German agriculture and commerce were in ruins, and the population had been reduced by half. The Habsburgs were seriously weakened by the years of conflict and Germany was more disunited than ever before, split into no fewer than 234 states and 51 independent cities.

German rapier of the 1630s

Thirty Years' War
In 1618, a revolt broke out in the Protestant province of Bohemia against the rule of the Catholic Habsburgs. War spread through Germany as Protestant princes rebelled against the Habsburgs. Other nations, notably France and Sweden, entered the war on the Protestant side to end Habsburg domination of Europe.

Prussian by 1648

Prussian by 1772

•Hamburg
•Berlin
•Cologne
•Frankfurt
Augsburg •
•Prague
• Munich

Prussian lands in Europe

Rise of Prussia
Prussia was one of the few German states to emerge from the Thirty Years' War with increased power. Under successive rulers, Prussian territory expanded across most of northern Germany and, by 1795, also included western Poland.

Frederick the Great

Frederick, King of Prussia from 1740–86, laid the foundations of later Prussian greatness. An inspired military leader, his diplomacy enabled Prussia to expand by outwitting Austria and Russia. At his death, Prussia was Europe's foremost power.

G

German unification

After Napoleon's defeat in 1815, many Germans wanted to unite as one nation. A confederation of states was set up, but it was too weak to last. In 1861, Wilhelm I became king of Prussia. Prussia's strength grew, and the other German states agreed to unite with Prussia. At last, in 1871, Wilhelm was made emperor of a united Germany.

Prussian power

A strong army gave Prussia the power to defeat France in the Franco-Prussian War of 1870–71. Prussian strength also enabled the newly-united Germany to negotiate a powerful and advantageous alliance with Austria-Hungary and Russia in 1881. This gave Germany great influence throughout the Continent.

Prussian army officer's helmet

Otto von Bismarck

Otto von Bismarck (1815–98) became chief minister of Prussia in 1862. In a brilliant series of diplomatic and military campaigns he removed all foreign influence from Germany, making Prussia the leading German state. He was chancellor of Germany for 19 years.

Imperial Germany

Under Wilhelm I and Wilhelm II, Germany became the leading power in Europe. Germany sought its "place in the sun" by acquiring colonies in Africa, China, and the Pacific, but its aggressive foreign policy led to world war in 1914 and the collapse of its empire in 1918.

Industrialization

Between 1870 and 1914, Germany's population rose from 33 to 65 million, and its industrial output quadrupled. The Ruhr Valley became the centre of large iron, coal, steel, and armaments industries. This industrial power helped Germany to become the most powerful state in Europe by 1914, and helped provide resources and finances for World War I.

Factories, Ruhr Valley

Chair by Bauhaus designer Marcel Breuer

Breuer's chair, angular in appearance, is typical of Bauhaus design.

The Bauhaus School of Art was founded in Wiemar 1919. It revolutionized the teaching of art by combining it with the skills of craft.

Nazi swastika and eagle badge

Badge of the SS, the Nazi security force

Weimar Germany

In 1918, following its defeat in World War I, Germany became a republic. A new constitution was agreed in 1919 in the town of Weimar, where the National Assembly met until it moved back to Berlin in 1920. However, Germany was badly affected by economic problems in the 1920s. and by 1932, over 5 million people were unemployed.

The rise of the Nazis

The unfavourable terms of the peace settlement after World War I, together with the economic failures of the 1930s, saw Germany crippled by high unemployment and hyper-inflation, and led to a desire for change among the people. Support grew for the Nazis, an extreme nationalist party led by Adolf Hitler that took power in 1933. The Nazis promised to rebuild Germany's strength and power. It was Hitler's imperialist ambitions that were one of the causes of World War II.

Statuette of soldier

Modern Germany

After World War II, the country was occupied by French, British, US, and Russian troops. In 1949, Germany was divided in two, with a communist, Russian-backed state in the east and US-backed capitalist state in the west.

Living conditions in West Germany were much better than in the east.

Housing complex, East Germany

Reunification

In the late 1980s, Russian control over East Germany weakened. The Berlin Wall, which divided the former capital, was taken down in 1989, and free access between the two countries was guaranteed for the first time. By October 1990, the two halves of Germany were politically united once more.

People flocked to Berlin to see The Wall come down.

Demolition of the Berlin Wall

Timeline

The medieval castle of Pfalz

962 Otto I of Saxony establishes Holy Roman Empire.

1241 Hamburg and Lübeck combine to form Hanseatic League; German trade prospers.

1517 German monk Martin Luther begins Protestant Reformation.

1618–48 Thirty Years' War devastates Germany.

1740–86 Frederick the Great rules Prussia.

1815–66 German Confederation tries to unite Germany.

1871 Wilhelm I is made German emperor.

1871–90 Bismarck governs as chancellor.

1914–18 Germany fights in World War I, is defeated, and empire collapses.

1919 Weimar Republic is established.

Banknote, 1931

1931 German economy crashes; prices rise, the currency becomes worthless, and many suffer unemployment.

1939–45 Germany fights in World War II.

1949 Germany divided into East and West.

1990 East and West Germany reunited as a single state.

FIND OUT MORE ARMIES   BARBARIANS   COLD WAR   EUROPE, CENTRAL   EUROPE, HISTORY OF   FRANCE, HISTORY OF   HOLOCAUST   HOLY ROMAN EMPIRE   WORLD WAR I   WORLD WAR II

GERONIMO

A CENTURY AFTER the native people of North America fought the white settlers to stay on their land, one name is remembered above all others. As a fearless warrior, Geronimo had no equals. In his early 20s, he lost his entire family to Mexican raiders, and he determined to fight to the death to safeguard his Apache way of life. Only in old age, defeated by the superior arms of the US government, did he surrender, ending his days as a wealthy farmer, revered by people across the USA.

Massacre
In 1858, a band of Mexican raiders killed Geronimo's mother, wife, and children. Geronimo was filled with a deep hatred of white people, and decided to spend the rest of his life fighting them.

Early life
Geronimo was born in about 1829 in Arizona, southwest USA. He was a member of the Mimbreño Apache tribe, and his Apache name was Goyanthlay. Spaniards called him Geronimo.

Native American encampment

Apaches
The Apaches lived among the arid mountains and deserts of southwest USA. Because their land was unsuitable for farming, they earned a living hunting and raiding for food. This brought them into conflict with the many settlers who were moving into the area from Mexico and the eastern USA.

The young warrior
As a young warrior, Geronimo was trained to shoot, track enemies or wild animals across the land, map out a new and unfamiliar terrain, and survive for days away from camp. He also learned the skill of travelling through the countryside over vast distances without being observed. For recreation, he took part in Apache games such as the loop-and-pole game (left), arrow shooting, and wrestling.

Sharp metal blade

Bowl of pipe

Ornately carved wooden shaft

Warfare
Geronimo was a skilled warrior who many times had to fight for his life. With only a small group of followers, he managed to pose a threat to large numbers of US law enforcers. His ability to move quickly and quietly across the land, thus avoiding detection, created great fear among local settlers. If he was followed, he and his men would split up. Their understanding of the country enabled them to vanish into the bush.

Apache tomahawk pipe

Reservations
As European settlers pushed west, Native Americans were forced into special areas called reservations. The Native Americans were, therefore, excluded from their traditional lands and prevented from roaming over vast areas as they had done before. In response, many tribes broke out and raided neighbouring areas.

Raiding
US officials tried to reform the San Carlos reservation, but Geronimo and his followers continued their raiding. Overwhelmed by the superior force of the US Army, Geronimo was forced to surrender in 1886.

Geronimo (far right) before his surrender

San Carlos reservation
In 1877 Geronimo and 16 of his warriors were captured by US forces and marched 400 miles to the San Carlos reservation in Arizona. The new reservation was brutal and corrupt, with suppliers making vast fortunes at the expense of the native inhabitants. Many resentful and half-starved Apaches left the reservation to go on raids.

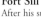

Fort Sill
After his surrender, Geronimo was sent first to Florida, then Alabama, and finally, in 1894, to Fort Sill, Oklahoma. He sold native American handicrafts, became a farmer, adopted Christianity, and appeared at the 1904 St Louis World's Fair and in President Theodore Roosevelt's inaugural parade in 1905. To the end of his life, he hoped to return to his native southwestern mountains.

GERONIMO

c.1829 Born in Arizona, USA.

early 1850s Raiders kill his family.

late 1850s Accepts Cochise, head of the Chiricahuas, as his leader, and marries a Chiricahua wife.

1876 Retreats into the Sierra Madre mountains and raids both sides of the US–Mexican border.

1877 Confined to the San Carlos reservation, but continues to raid the surrounding lands.

1886 Surrenders; exiled to Florida.

1894 Confined to Fort Sill.

1909 Dies at Fort Sill.

FIND OUT MORE

HUMAN RIGHTS   NATIVE AMERICANS   UNITED STATES, HISTORY OF

GIRAFFES

WITH ITS MASSIVE neck and long legs, the giraffe is the world's tallest animal. Despite its ungainly appearance, it is very graceful. Giraffes live in the savannahs of Africa – grasslands with a few trees and bushes. Their distribution closely follows that of the acacia trees on which they feed. They avoid open grassland because of their feeding habits, but also because their size makes them conspicuous in the open. There is only one species of giraffe, but eight subspecies, which differ mainly in the colour and pattern of their coats.

Thick rubbery lips and saliva protect a giraffe's tongue and mouth from thorns.

An adult male giraffe can stand 5.3 m (17.5 ft) high.

Short mane

The giraffe's long neck has the same number of vertebrae as other mammals, but they are larger.

Hoof

Reticulated giraffe

Reticulated giraffes have regular russet-coloured markings.

Browsing
The giraffe's great height is a specialized adaptation for browsing the upper branches of trees. Leaves and small twigs form the greater part of the giraffe's diet. It also eats shoots, flowers, fruit, seed pods, even bark, but never grass. Many acacias and other trees have vicious thorns to discourage browsing, but the giraffe's tongue is well equipped to get past such strong defences.

Drinking
For an animal as tall as the giraffe, drinking presents special problems. To lower its head the giraffe has either to bend its knees forward or to extend its forelegs out to either side. This awkward posture greatly reduces the animal's field of vision, leaving it vulnerable to attack.

Features of a giraffe
Massive shoulder blades carry the huge muscles that support the giraffe's head and long neck. Its hind legs are shorter than its forelegs, but the angle of the back makes them appear shorter than they really are. By breaking up its outline against its surroundings, a giraffe's coat markings help to camouflage it.

Herds
Giraffes usually live in small groups of up to about 12 females and their calves. Adult males live apart and visit the herd only for mating. Occasionally, giraffes gather together in large groups of up to 70 animals that stay together for a few days, or sometimes just a few hours.

Coat markings
Giraffe markings range from regular geometric patterns to irregular fuzzy-edged patterns. Old males darken with age and may become almost jet black.

Reticulated giraffe

Rothschild's giraffe

Masai giraffe

Giraffes have exceptionally good eyesight.

Standing still and staring towards a potential threat acts as a warning sign of danger.

Median horn

The horns are covered with hairy skin.

Horns grow on the crown of the head above the eyes.

Large nostrils

Horns
Giraffes of both sexes have a pair of short stubby horns, about 30 cm (12 in) in length in an adult male. Some giraffes, such as the reticulated giraffe, have a third (median) horn in the middle. Rothschild's giraffe also has a small pair of horns behind the ears, for which reason it is often known as the "five-horned giraffe".

Necking
Necking is a form of ritualized sparring that determines dominance within a group. It begins with one bull challenging another by advancing towards it with its head held high, legs rigid, and neck erect. After much preliminary jostling, one bull swings its head in a huge arc, in an attempt to strike its opponent's neck with its head.

Giraffe's neck is very flexible.

Okapi
The giraffe's only living relative, the okapi, is a much smaller animal, with shorter limbs and neck. While the giraffe lives in herds for mutual protection and is active by day, the forest-dwelling okapi is a solitary animal, active by night. It lives in the tropical rainforests of Zaire. The okapi's vision is poor, but its hearing and sense of smell are acute and more useful in the forests where visibility is limited.

Males have horns

Large ears

Deep chestnut-coloured coat

Creamy-white, or light grey, markings help camouflage the okapi.

Striped legs

RETICULATED GIRAFFE

SCIENTIFIC NAME	*Giraffa camelopardalis reticulata*
ORDER	Artiodactyla
FAMILY	Giraffidae
DISTRIBUTION	Africa south of the Sahara
HABITAT	Savannahs
DIET	Leaves, shoots, small twigs, flowers, and fruit
SIZE	Height: males 5.3 m (17.5 ft); females 4.5 m (15 ft)
LIFESPAN	25 years

FIND OUT MORE   AFRICAN WILDLIFE   CAMOUFLAGE AND COLOUR   GRASSLAND WILDLIFE   MAMMALS   PLANT DEFENCE   RAINFOREST WILDLIFE

GLACIATION

THE SHAPING OF THE LANDSCAPE by ice is called glaciation. All over the world there are landscape features that were formed during past ice ages by glaciers, huge moving rivers of ice, and even bigger mounds of ice called ice sheets. In cold places, such as the polar regions, glaciers and ice sheets are still present, and glaciation still continues. The landscape created by ice is dramatic. Glaciers carve out deep, trough-like valleys, ice sheets pile up huge quantities of debris, and the icy conditions around can shatter rock into jagged peaks and knife-edge ridges.

How a glacier forms

Glaciers are created when layers of snow are compacted in icy mountain regions to form rivers of ice, which slowly creep downhill until they melt. The ice on the surface of the glacier cracks, forming deep crevasses, and both the surface and the underside of the glacier are covered with debris plucked away from the valley sides by the sheer weight of the passing ice.

Valley glaciers
In high mountain ranges, such as the Alps and the Himalayas, glaciers form in valleys as snow slides from the peaks of the mountains. These are called alpine glaciers. Where these emerge from the mountains, they may cause piedmont glaciers, so called because they spread out in the shape of a foot.

Cirque, the deep hollow where the glacier begins.

Frost shatters rocky summits into jagged "horn peaks".

Valley glacier, Norway

This glacially carved edge is called an arête.

Bergschrund, the deep crack at the head of a glacier

Frost-shattered ridges form knife-edges, or arêtes.

Glacial erosion
Glaciers have immense erosive power. In some places this works through abrasion; the moving ice acts like sandpaper, scraping away the rock with the huge amount of rock debris trapped in its base. Sometimes, it simply sweeps away loose rock shattered by the cold. Occasionally, it can freeze round rocks and literally picks them up.

Frost-shattered rock falls on to the ice as lateral moraine along the side of the glacier.

Ice fills the valley.

Crevasses fill with debris and water.

U-shaped valley
It takes many thousands of years, but over time a glacier can carve out a very distinctive, deep, U-shaped trough of a valley. If this reaches the coast and fills with seawater, it is called a fjord.

Huge quantities of subglacial moraine are swept along underneath the glacier.

Ice fall, where the ice flows over a step in the valley floor.

Medial moraine – a band of moraine formed as two glaciers flow together.

Debris is swept along beneath the glacier.

Lateral moraine forms terraces along the valley side.

Holes in the ice fill with debris, which is left behind when the ice melts.

Subglacial streams often leave winding ridges of debris called eskers.

Meltwater lakes fill up behind debris in front of the glacier.

Terminal moraine is the band of debris across the snout of a glacier

Fjords
Fjords are steep-sided, narrow coastal inlets, formed where glaciers have ground out deep valleys along existing riverbeds. When the ice melted, the valleys were flooded as the sea-level rose. The coast of Norway has many fjords.

Traces of glaciation
Glaciers carry huge quantities of debris, called moraine, which either fall on to the glacier from the mountains above or are swept away from the rock beneath. The moving ice pushes this debris into giant piles, or leaves it scattered over the landscape as the ice melts.

Lower end of the glacier

Melt-water chamber

Drumlins are half-egg shaped piles of subglacial moraine.

G

Mount Kilimanjaro, Tanzania

Snow-line

Above a certain height, called the snow-line, the air is so cold that the snow never melts. In the tropics the snow-line is well over 5,000 m (16,000 ft), but comes down to 600 m (1,900 ft) in Greenland and is at sea-level at the North and South Poles.

Avalanches

The snow cover on steep slopes is often far from stable. If the layers are not well compacted, even a slight disturbance – a falling rock, a skier, or even a shout – can make an entire snowfield collapse in an avalanche.

A powder snow avalanche such as this can produce shock waves powerful enough to explode buildings.

Ice sheets and caps

Ice sheets are huge layers of ice, thousands of metres thick, that may cover not just a single valley but an entire continent. Ice caps are smaller dome-shaped sheets of ice that cover a mountain. The sheets of ice over Antarctica and Greenland are also called ice caps. The ice deep within the polar ice caps first fell as snow many millions of years ago.

Formation of an ice cap

Ice caps form gradually by accumulation as snow falls, stays frozen, and is compacted by the addition of new snow. Some ice is lost by "ablation" (melting and evaporation), but if the ice is formed faster than it is lost, then the ice cap grows.

1 An ice cap forms when the snow covering a peak remains frozen all year.

2 Fresh snowfalls compact the snow beneath, turning it into dense crystals.

3 Eventually, the lower layers are compacted into solid opaque ice.

Icebergs

Icebergs are huge chunks of ice that have broken off from the edge of an ice sheet or glacier to float in the sea. They are generally rounded or block-like in shape. Icebergs float because ice is less dense than water, but it is only a little less dense, so about one-eighth of the iceberg is visible above the surface

Ice sheets are thousands of metres thick, but vary in extent and depth between summer and winter, which effects the Earth's climate.

Isolated mountaintops jutting through the surface of an ice cap are called nunataks.

Glacier moves by sliding over melted ice.

Rocks under glacier are slowly eroded.

Ice fall – crevasses form where glacier flows over steep rock.

Around 10,000 icebergs a year break away from the glaciers in Greenland.

When Arctic glaciers reach the sea, the tides and waves heave the ice up and down, cracking bits off to float away as icebergs, a process known as calving.

Only about 12 per cent of an iceberg is visible above the surface of the ocean.

Icebergs may be broad and tabular (flat). They are often hundreds of kilometres long and may last for years before melting.

It is estimated that the average age of the ice in an iceberg is 5,000 years.

Titanic disaster

Because most of an iceberg is hidden below the surface, it can pose a real hazard to shipping if one drifts across sea lanes. In 1912, the luxury liner *Titanic* sank after a collision with an iceberg, resulting in the loss of about 1,500 lives.

Louis Agassiz

Swiss-American geologist Louis Agassiz (1807–73) realized that past ice ages had shaped the landscape. In 1836, he noted that glaciers are not static, but move, and found rocks that had been scoured by glaciers. He concluded much of northern Europe had at one time been covered by ice.

Shaded areas show the extent of the ice cover during the last ice age.

Ice Age

There is no doubt that ice ages have occurred several times in the Earth's past. Some geologists believe they are linked to the variations in the energy reaching Earth from the Sun as the Earth wobbles and tilts in its orbit. Others think there may be some other trigger for an ice age.

FIND OUT MORE   ARCTIC   ANTARCTICA   GEOLOGY   POLAR EXPLORATION   POLAR WILDLIFE   RAIN   RIVERS   TUNDRA

GLASS

FEW MATERIALS have the same remarkable properties as glass. It is transparent, easy to shape and clean, does not rot, and resists attack by most chemicals. Glass is also cheap to produce because it is made from sand, one of the most common materials on Earth. When sand is heated with other materials, it turns into a liquid, which, when cooled, solidifies into glass. Although the glass looks crystalline, it still has the structure of a liquid, and is termed a "supercooled" liquid.

Ancient glass

Decorative glass objects have been found in ancient Egyptian tombs dating back to 2500 BC. After the invention of the blowpipe in about 100 BC, glass was made across the ancient world, particularly in Rome.

Roman glassware, dating from 1st century AD

Types of glass

Three main ingredients are used to make glass: pure silica sand, soda ash, and lime. These are heated in a furnace to about 1,400 °C (2,500 °F), to produce soda-lime glass. This is the ordinary glass we use to make bottles and windows. Different kinds of glass can be made by adding other ingredients.

Lead glass

Also called crystal glass, lead glass contains lead oxide, which makes it easy to cut. The cut glass exhibits a diamond-like sparkle.

Lead crystal

Optical glass

Optical lenses are made from pure glass. A variety of substances, such as lead and titanium, are added to give glass its optical properties.

Spectacles

Magnifying glass

Heat-resistant glass

Boron oxide is sometimes added in the glassmaking process to produce heat-resistant borosilicate glass.

Heat-resistant glass jug

Fibreglass

Glass may sometimes take the form of fibres, which are used for loft insulation, reinforcement for plastics, and fibre-optic cables.

Fibreglass

Stained glass

Stained glass is normally used to create decorative windows, using pieces of coloured glass set in a lead framework. Medieval stained glass may seem richer to the eye because it is full of impurities.

Stained-glass window

Working glass

Glass is easy to work, but only when it is in a molten state. The most common method of shaping glass is blowing by craftworkers or machines. Other methods include pressing molten glass into a mould, a traditional technique still used today, and casting it into a mould to make lenses.

Sheet glass

Sheet glass was originally made by drawing a ribbon of molten glass vertically upwards. However, this caused distortion. Today, it is made by floating molten glass on a bath of molten tin. This float glass is of even thickness throughout and shows no distortion.

Glass building

Glassblowing

Most glassblowing is done mechanically, but traditional methods, shown in the following sequence, are still used for making special objects.

Molten glass

Iron rod

Strong shears

Measuring mould

1 An iron rod is dipped into the furnace to pick up a gob (lump) of molten glass. The glassblower cuts off the correct quantity of glass needed using special glass shears, and drops it into a measuring mould.

Shaping mould into which the shaped parison is fitted.

Blowing glass

The semi-finished glass shape is called a parison.

2 The glassblower picks up the molten glass from the measuring mould on a blowing-iron, then blows air through the iron, to shape the glass and form a parison.

Layers of steam protect and cushion the glass.

3 With further blowing, the glass expands and takes its final shape inside the mould. At the same time, the rod is spun to stop the object showing signs of joints from the mould.

The bottle shows no signs of the joint between the two halves of the mould.

4 The glassblower removes the final object from the mould, and smooths the mouth of the bottle by reheating it in the furnace and shaping it.

Bottles ready to be recycled

Recycling glass

Glass is an easy material to recycle because it melts readily. It is recycled, not for the purpose of conservation, but to save energy because the original glassmaking process requires such high temperatures. In Europe alone, about four million tonnes of glass are recycled each year.

 FIND OUT MORE ARCHITECTURE CHURCHES CRYSTALS AND GEMS EYES AND SEEING PLASTICS AND RUBBER POLLUTION ROCKS AND MINERALS ROMAN EMPIRE

G

GODS AND GODDESSES

SINCE PREHISTORIC TIMES, humans have worshipped gods and goddesses – spirits that are believed to control nature and human destinies. The mythology that surrounds them attempts to explain the how and why of life, and account for forces that are beyond human control. The rituals associated with these supernatural beings, or deities, are a powerful force in binding societies together. The variety of gods and goddesses worshipped around the world reflects the diversity and power of human imagination.

Mother goddess

Every culture had a mother goddess, one of the earliest deities, who represented nature and fertility. In ancient Egypt, she was called Isis and may have been a model for the Christian Madonna.

Hades and Persephone

Venus figure, c.4000 BC

Persephone
In Greek mythology, Hades, god of the underworld, abducts Persephone. She returns to the world for six months every year, bringing spring and summer.

Durga
In Hinduism, Durga is the powerful warrior-goddess. She is often represented with a beautiful face and 10 arms, each one holding a weapon.

Gods

Much of what we know of gods and goddesses was passed down by men rather than women, so male gods – often gods of war – predominate in mythology. Many myths portray the struggle between good and evil. Some deities are kind and just, while others, such as the Norse god Loki, commit acts of evil and treachery on other gods or humans. Gods may be depicted either in human form, or as part-human and part-animal.

Thor

In Norse mythology, Thor was the god of the sky, rain, thunder, and farming. Thor's hammer, known as Mjollnir, made thunderbolts when the god threw it. Norse gods such as Thor and Odin were worshipped in parts of Scandinavia up until the 12th century.

Thor fighting frost giants

Mars was popular in Rome.

Mars

Mars, god of war, was said to be the father of Rome's founder. Many Roman gods were equivalent to earlier Greek versions: Mars was called Ares in Greek mythology, and Demeter, goddess of spring, was Persephone.

Sacrifices

A sacrifice is an offering of an animal, plant, possession, or even a human life, to please or pacify a deity. In ancient cultures, sacrifices were made to gods and goddesses on special days or at important ceremonies. Ancient Romans marked such occasions with a *suovetaurilia,* a special sacrifice involving a bull, a ram, and a pig – the most valuable items of Roman livestock.

Wicker man
Roman historians recorded that Celtic tribes in Gaul (France) placed human sacrifices inside wickerwork figures, then burnt them alive. Wicker figures are still burnt at festivals in Spain.

Mountain-top sacrifice

The Aztecs offered human sacrifices to the god of the Sun, Tezcatlipoca. This deity was the most feared of the Aztec gods and thousands, usually prisoners of war, were sacrificed in his name. The Aztecs carefully chose their victim, who was accorded great honours for one year. Then, on the day of the sacrifice, a priest cut open the victim's chest and offered his heart up to Tezcatlipoca.

Aztec warrior and his prisoner of war

Priests

In many societies, priests are the human links between the natural world and the supernatural world of the gods. They are thought to have special, often magical power, and may carry out sacred rites.

Priest in traditional costume

Priest's costume
Costumes convey authority and represent tradition. The priest's costume of the Nkimba people of the Congo, West Africa, includes an ornate carved wooden mask and a grass net decorated with feathers.

Shaman's mask
The shamans of Native American tribes wore masks representing a guardian spirit. This showed the connection between the human and spirit worlds.

Oracles

The term "oracle" describes a direct communication with a deity though the mouth of a priest. The most famous oracle was at Delphi in ancient Greece, at a temple to the god Apollo. In Greek mythology, the heroes Oedipus and Heracules consulted the oracle, whose replies to questions were always ambiguous.

Delphi Oracle, Greece

FIND OUT MORE   AZTECS   CELTS   EGYPT, ANCIENT   GREECE, ANCIENT   MAYA   RELIGIONS   ROMAN EMPIRE   WITCHES AND WITCHCRAFT

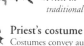

Mask "transforms" into eagle head.

Gods and Goddesses

Nature

Mayan rain god

Men is an Anatolian Moon god.

Luna drives a chariot across the night sky.

Luna is the Roman Moon goddess.

Syrian river god

Aztec agricultural god

Ceres is the Roman corn goddess.

Poseidon is the Greek god of the sea.

Silvanus is the god of uncultivated land.

Celtic god of rivers

Apollo is the Roman Sun god.

Hephaistos is the Greek god of fire.

Balls of thunder

Japanese god of thunder and lightning.

Love and Fertility

Artemis is the Greek goddess of fertility.

Cupid is the Roman god of love.

Aphrodite is the mother of Eros.

Eros is a god of love.

Attis is the Egyptian goddess of fertility.

Priapus is the Roman god of fertility.

Venus is the Roman goddess of love and beauty.

Aphrodite is the Greek goddess of love and beauty.

Juno is the Roman goddess of marriage and maternity.

War and Death

Cerberus is a dog that guards the underworld.

Hades is the Roman god of the underworld.

Proserpina is the Roman queen of the underworld.

Ares is the father of Eros.

Athena is the Roman goddess of war.

Ares is the Greek god of war.

Serapis is an Egyptian god of the dead.

Osiris is the Egyptian god of the underworld.

Antlered Celtic goddess

GOODALL, JANE

FROM 1960 TO 1995, Jane Goodall spent 35 remarkable years devoted to studying chimpanzees in the wild, and became one of the world's most respected and influential zoologists. She began her painstaking research alone in the middle of the tropical forest in Tanzania, East Africa, and steadily built up one of the foremost centres for field research on primates. Her observations and those of her colleagues revolutionized our knowledge of chimpanzee behaviour and shed light on our own human ancestry.

Early life
Jane Goodall was born in London, England, in 1934. As a teenager she dreamed of studying wildlife in Africa, and the ambition never faded. In 1957, with savings from a summer job as a waitress, she embarked on a trip to Kenya. There she approached the famous anthropologist Louis Leakey, and told him she wanted to work in Africa. Leakey gave her a job as a secretary.

Research

In spite of Jane Goodall's lack of formal training, Louis Leakey decided to help her realize her dream. In 1960, he raised funds for her to begin a research programme at Gombe, Tanzania. She has been based there ever since. In the 1960s, most primatologists studied captive animals in zoos. Goodall's task was different – to gain the confidence of the chimps and study them at close quarters in their natural environment.

Goodall with one of the chimps at Gombe

Tool used to open bees' nests

Fishing stick

Wooden chisel

Communication

Goodall was fascinated by the way the chimps used sounds, gestures, and expressions to communicate with each other. Every noise conveyed a different message, and gestures and body movements were also forms of communication.

Displays
Goodall saw how body movements act as visual displays of emotion and intent. Males issue threats to rivals by charging forward with their fur raised, often dragging branches or throwing stones. Early on, Goodall noted that groups of chimps would react to coming rainfall with an agitated "rain dance".

Charging display

Touch
Goodall observed that chimps would often pat, embrace, or kiss as a way of calming distressed individuals. She also saw them grooming each other's fur. This has a calming effect and strengthens social bonds.

In her lonely observation posts in the jungle, Goodall made careful drawings of the chimps' use of tools and other behaviour.

Two of Goodall's notebooks

Working methods
Goodall worked by spending day after day alone in the forest with the chimpanzees. Gradually, she won their confidence and they accepted her. She filled her notebooks with descriptions of the chimpanzees, and wrote freely of the emotions, personalities, and intelligence of the chimps.

Toolmaking
One of Goodall's most startling discoveries was that wild chimps are good toolmakers. They use objects as tools, modifying them to suit their purpose. She saw chimps stripping twigs to make probes for "fishing" termites from their nests, and chewing clumps of leaves to make sponges for getting water from shallow pools.

Conservation

Goodall championed the cause of chimpanzee conservation and campaigned for better conditions for captive chimps. In 1977, she launched the Jane Goodall Institute for Wildlife Research, Education, and Conservation in the USA. By the late 1990s, it had branches in the UK, Canada, and Tanzania.

Goodall campaigning for chimpanzees

JANE GOODALL

1934	Born in London, England.
1957	Travels to Kenya and meets Louis Leakey.
1960	Establishes research station at Gombe, Tanzania.
1965	Gains doctorate from Cambridge University.
1971	Publishes *In the Shadow of Man*, first of several influential books.
1977	Founds Jane Goodall Institute.
1991	Launches international youth environmental programme, "Roots and Shoots".
1995	Receives Hubbard Medal.

FIND OUT MORE   AFRICAN WILDLIFE   CONSERVATION   LEAKEY FAMILY   MONKEYS, AND OTHER PRIMATES

GOVERNMENTS AND POLITICS

A GOVERNMENT IS an institution which makes the political decisions about running a country. Governments and politics are individual to each country because they result from that country's unique history and culture. Yet despite those differences, the systems of government and the issues of political debate are similar everywhere, for they concern how to govern the country best for the benefit of the people.

The orb symbolizes a monarch's spiritual authority over his or her subjects.

The crown symbolizes sovereignty.

German orb

Russian Imperial crown

Prussian sceptre

The crown jewels (crown, orb, and sceptre symbolize the monarch's authority.

Types of government

There are almost as many types of government as there are countries in the world. The three main types of government are republican, monarchical, and dictatorial, although these have many variations. Anarchists believe that governments are not necessary.

Republic
Most countries in the world are republics, that is, where electors vote for their head of state as well as for their government. The power of the president ranges from holding real political power, as in the USA, to being a symbolic figurehead, as in India.

Monarchy
In a monarchy, the head of the royal family is head of state and is succeeded by his or her closest relative in hereditary succession. In most monarchies, such as Britain or Japan, the monarch has little real power, but in countries such as Morocco, Saudi Arabia, or Jordan, the king holds considerable political power.

Dictatorship
Many countries in the world have at one time or another been ruled by dictators, that is, single rulers with absolute power. Most dictators gain power either through a military take-over or by seizing leadership from an existing ruler, as Saddam Hussein did in Iraq in 1979. Dictators eliminate any opposition to their rule.

Democracy

In a democracy, electors vote for a government from a range of political parties. There are two main types of democracy: presidential, where voters elect the president who then runs the government and may choose the prime minister; and parliamentary, where voters directly elect the government of their choice.

Presidential
As the President of Ireland, Mary McAleese (b.1951), is the symbolic head of the nation. In France and Russia, the president chooses the prime minister.

Old Parliament House, Canberra, Australia

Parliamentary
Parliamentary systems exist in both republics and monarchies. Parliament is made up of politicians from different political parties. Electors vote for the party or individual of their choice, and the government is drawn from the largest political party in parliament. The leader of this party becomes head of government. Most nations in the world are parliamentary democracies.

How government works

Each country has its own system of government, usually consisting of four separate parts. The executive governs the country, the legislature makes the laws, the civil service carries out those laws, and the judiciary ensures the laws are applied fairly.

Legislature
The legislature is the place where laws are made and the executive is held to account for its actions in governing. The legislature is made up of elected representatives, and often consists of a lower house of parliament, where laws are made, and an upper house, which keeps a check on the lower house. The British upper house (the House of Lords) is unique in mainly consisting of hereditary, not elected, members.

Parliament House, New Delhi, India

Civil service
The role of the civil, or public, service is to administer the country. Once the executive has proposed a law, and the legislature has passed it, the civil service implements it. Civil servants are non-political and work for whichever government is in power. Their work ranges from local issues, such as street lighting, to national issues, such as defence.

Pentagon, USA

Judge calls court to order with a gavel.

Judiciary
The judiciary makes sure laws are carried out fairly. Judges sit in judgment in individual cases, and also review the operation of the law or suggest changes to improve it. The judiciary is independent from the executive and legislature to maintain its neutrality.

Executive
The executive's role is to govern the country. In parliamentary democracies, the executive consists of senior ministers and the prime minister, who sit in the Houses of Parliament. In the USA, the executive, such as the Secretary of State, Colin Powell (b. 1937), is chosen by the president and is separate from the Houses of Congress.

Elections

In a multi-party democracy, every three to five years voters go to the polls to elect their government, choosing the politicians who will represent them from a list of candidates. Elections are an opportunity for politicians to present their ideas for the government of the country, and for the electorate to debate and consider matters of interest and concern to them. In the past, elections were local, personal affairs, in which candidates for office tried to meet each elector in person. Today, most electioneering is carried out by advertising and television.

Voting

The electors vote in secret for the candidate of their choice by marking a ballot paper. The ballots are then counted and the winning candidate is elected. In many countries, electors rank candidates in order of preference. A system of proportional representation (PR) then ensures that the candidates with the most preferences are elected.

Political parties

Political parties are formed to represent particular political beliefs, such as the Socialist Party in France or the Christian Democratic Party in Germany, or to represent particular areas of a country, such as the Scottish Nationalists, who wish to see Scotland become independent from Britain. Political parties are active at local and national levels in getting their supporters out to vote and in attracting new voters to their cause.

Swedish Christian Democratic Party

French Socialist Party

Politicians

People become politicians for different reasons. Some people stand for election because they believe in serving the public, or have a particular skill that would be useful in government. Others stand to represent a particular political viewpoint. In the USA, the cost of a campaign restricts candidates to those with money.

US Democratic Convention, 1996

Politics

Politics is the organization of political debate and discussion in a country. That debate can take place in a formal setting as in parliament, or informally. Any subject can be discussed, from major issues such as the economy or international relations, to local issues such as the siting of a new road.

Chamber of the House of Commons, London, UK

Political beliefs

Different political beliefs play a large part in determining how a country is governed. Left-wing ideologies, such as communism and socialism, favour a large role for the state acting on behalf of its citizens, while right-wing ideologies, such as capitalism, favour individual action and responsibility by citizens.

Capitalism

Capitalism is the system in which wealth and profit in the hands of a few people drive the country's economy. Capitalism can lead to great differences in income between rich and poor.

Socialism

Socialism is the system in which the economy is controlled by the state for the benefit of the whole community. Countries such as the Netherlands and Sweden aim for a more equal distribution of wealth.

Fascism

Fascism is the system of government under which total authority resides in the leader of the country, who pursues nationalist and militarist policies. Like other far-right ideologies, fascism glorifies the state for providing strong national leadership.

Communism

Communism is the system in which land and property are owned by the whole community and each person is paid according to their needs and abilities. China and North Korea are examples of communist countries.

Public pressure

Everyone can play a part in politics, from full-time politicians to individuals who are concerned about a particular issue or event. Apart from elections, individuals can bring pressure to bear on governments, both by participating in public protest, such as strikes and demonstrations, and by joining pressure groups that are set up to campaign for particular issues, such as protecting the environment or civil liberties.

Protest groups

In order to force an issue into the public view, it is sometimes necessary to take direct action. Recently, protest groups have achieved success against the siting of nuclear weapons and the proposed building of new roads.

Pressure groups

Pressure groups play an important part in focusing attention on issues of public concern. Environmental pressure groups, such as Greenpeace, raise public awareness on issues of pollution or environmental damage that cross national borders.

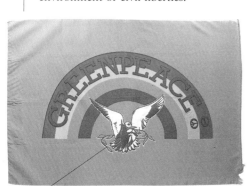

Dove bearing olive branch symbolizes hope.

Machiavelli

Niccolò Machiavelli (1469–1527) was a civil servant in the Florentine Republic in Italy. He was a realist who observed the political chaos of his times and urged governments to pursue practical, realistic politics rather than lofty political ideals. In his book *The Prince* (1532), he described politics as the art of the possible and pointed out what a government can do rather than what it ought to do.

FIND OUT MORE COLD WAR EUROPE, HISTORY OF EUROPEAN UNION HUMAN RIGHTS LAW PEACE MOVEMENTS UNIONS, TRADE UNITED NATIONS WARFARE WOMEN'S MOVEMENT

GRASSES, RUSHES, AND SEDGES

THESE THREE GROUPS of plants are all monocotyledons – flowering plants whose seedlings possess a single cotyledon, or seed leaf. In common with many other monocotyledons, grasses, rushes, and sedges have long, narrow leaves with parallel veins. They are all wind-pollinated and, therefore, do not have showy blossoms to attract animals. Instead, they have tiny flowers grouped in spikes or clusters. These produce large amounts of dry pollen.

Flowerheads at the top of tall, leafy stems

Flower stem, or culm

Yorkshire fog

Grasses

There are about 9,000 species of grass, including cereal crops such as wheat and barley. They are the most widespread flowering plants. Grass plants often grow close together to make a turf. Each plant has a mass of fibrous roots, leafy shoots, and flowerheads borne on long stems.

Cross-section of sedge flower stem

Sedges

The sedge family includes true sedges, cottongrasses, club-rushes, and galingales, totalling about 4,000 species. Unlike grasses, sedges have leaves in tufts around the base of the stem. The flower stem is usually leafless and three-angled.

Male flowers at the top of the spike have withered and fallen.

Fruits explode out of the ripe flower spike.

Cross-section of rush stem

Rushes

The 400 or so species of rush are small to medium-size plants. They are found mostly in the damper habitats of temperate and mountain regions. Rushes have green, white, or brown flowers that turn into dry fruits called capsules. Leaves may be flat like grass leaves, or cylindrical. The stems of all rushes are circular in cross-section.

Ripe flower spike

Tightly packed female flowers

Reed mace
Often wrongly called bulrushes, these tall plants grow in shallow, slow-moving or still water. There are about 15 species in their own family. Each plant has a flower spike made up of densely packed flowers. This splits open when ripe, releasing a mass of single-seeded fruits.

When these leaves are cut off, new shoots grow from the base of the plant.

Tillers
The reason grasses can tolerate the pressures of constant grazing or mowing is that new leafy shoots arise from buds at ground level. This kind of branching is called tillering.

Woody bamboo canes have many uses, from kitchen utensils to scaffold poles.

Soil particles are trapped and held by a network of rootlets.

Bamboo
About 830 tropical and sub-tropical species of grass have tough, woody stems. These are called bamboos. The tallest species reaches 35 m (115 ft) tall.

Soil binding
The roots of grass plants growing close together make a densely interwoven mat. This stabilizes loose, dry soils and prevents erosion of all kinds of soil.

FIND OUT MORE ECOLOGY   FARMING   FLOWERS   PLANTS   PLANTS, ANATOMY   PLANTS, REPRODUCTION

Grasses

Timothy grass is a nutritious pasture grass.

Soft brome grass is common on verges and wasteground.

Smooth meadow grass has graceful flowerheads.

Couch grass is a weed in gardens and farmland.

Anthers hang outside flowers.

Sweet vernal grass is a pleasant-smelling grass.

Stiff, compact flowerhead

Crested dogstail is a widespread grass.

Cocksfoot grass has short, stiff flower spikes.

Flowerheads resemble cocks' feet.

Branched flowerhead

Spreading flowerhead

Delicate feathery awns

Closely packed flowerheads

Needle grass has rigid stems and narrow, in-rolled leaves.

Bermuda grass is common in warm parts of the world.

Large quaking grass has thin-stemmed flowerheads that tremble in the breeze.

Great brome grass has been introduced to many countries from the Mediterranean.

Tufted hair grass grows into large tussocks 2 m (6.5 ft) tall.

Rushes and sedges

Soft rush is a very common rush of bogs and marshes.

Common sedge spreads on creeping underground stems.

Clusters of flowers borne up the stem

Hairy sedge has hairy leaves and fruits.

Woodrush has fine hairs on the margins of its leaves.

Greater tussock sedge has stiff leaves with finely toothed edges.

False fox sedge has sharp-angled triangular stems.

Pendulous sedge has long drooping flower spikes.

Greater pond sedge grows beside rivers and ponds.

GRASSHOPPERS AND CRICKETS

FAMOUS FOR THEIR ATHLETIC LEAPS and chirping calls, grasshoppers and crickets are among the largest and most distinctive of insects. Most are weak fliers and prefer to move by walking or jumping. They live mainly in grasslands and rainforests, but some live in deserts and caves, and a few wingless species burrow underground. Grasshoppers tend to be active by day, but crickets are out and about after dark; in many parts of the world their constant chirps fill the night air.

Features of a grasshopper

Grasshoppers have long bodies, big heads, large eyes, and downward-pointing mouthparts. Their long, thickened forewings protect delicate hind wings, which they use mainly for flying. Grasshoppers use their powerful, long hind legs for leaping. Bumps on the hind legs rub against the forewings to make sounds.

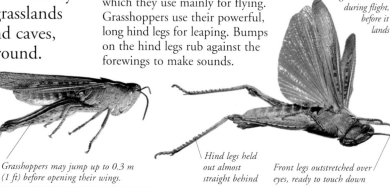

Wings outstretched during flight, before it lands

Grasshopper gains height by holding its wings back.

Grasshoppers may jump up to 0.3 m (1 ft) before opening their wings.

Hind legs held out almost straight behind

Front legs outstretched over eyes, ready to touch down

Leaping
Propelled forward by snapping their hind legs straight, grasshoppers can out-jump all other insects. If danger threatens or if the grasshopper wants to move to another clump of vegetation, it springs into the air, opens and flutters its wings to prolong the leap, and drops down as much as 1 m (3.3 ft) ahead.

Long, strong back legs

Compound eye

Front legs

Grasshopper poised, ready to leap

Common field grasshopper

Crickets
Crickets are similar to grasshoppers but differ in some key features: their hearing organs are on their legs rather than abdomen; they have longer antennae, sometimes longer than their bodies; and they make sounds by rubbing their wings together.

Long antenna

Bush cricket

Eardrum on legs
Crickets have a swelling below the knee that consists of a drum-like membrane, called a tympanum, on either side of the leg. This is the cricket's ear and is sensitive to sound vibrations.

Cricket's leg showing eardrum

Locust swarms
Locusts are grasshoppers. After heavy rains, lush plant life grows, creating the right conditions for locusts to breed in large numbers. Swarms of up to 50 billion set out across the land. They devastate crops and plants, causing famine.

Swarm of locusts in Ethiopia

Reproduction
During mating a male grasshopper or cricket transfers tiny packets of sperm to the female to fertilize her eggs. She then uses a spike-like ovipositor to place batches of up to 100 eggs at a time into the soil or into plant stems and leaves. Tiny nymphs – miniature versions of the parents – hatch from the eggs. They moult and grow many times until they reach adult size.

Grasshopper rubs its legs rapidly against its wings to generate sounds.

Male has laid a sperm sac that is being taken up by the female.

Ovipositor

Bush cricket transferring sperm sac

Stridulation
The rapid rubbing sounds made by grasshoppers and crickets are known as stridulation. To amplify the sounds, crickets rub veins and ridges on both wings together; grasshoppers rub ridges on their legs against a tough vein on their wings. Breeding males produce stridulations to attract mates. Sounds are characteristic of each species and uttered at specific times of the day.

Feeding
Most grasshoppers feed on leaves, buds, and other parts of plants that they chew with their mouthparts. Crickets have a more varied diet. Many eat plants but also catch and devour other insects – in fact, some bush crickets are dedicated hunters. Crickets that live in houses and caves scavenge on dead and waste matter.

Bush cricket eating a grasshopper

Great green bush cricket

Defence
Many grasshoppers and crickets are brown or green so they are less visible to predators. Others have brightly coloured hind wings that they flash to warn off enemies. Some have elaborate camouflage, with body parts resembling leaves and plant stems.

Weta

Legs raised in warning posture

Foaming grasshopper

Bright colours confuse predators

Posture
Large crickets, called wetas, have spines on their hind legs. If disturbed, they raise their hind legs into a threatening posture to frighten predators.

Flash coloration
At rest, only the outer wings of this grasshopper are exposed. If disturbed, it flashes its lilac inner wings to confuse enemies, as the colour disappears when it settles.

Warning coloration
This grasshopper eats poisonous plants and stores the poisons in its body. Its bright stripes warn predators that it is unpleasant to eat.

COMMON FIELD GRASSHOPPER

SCIENTIFIC NAME	*Chorthippus brunneus*
ORDER	Orthoptera
FAMILY	Acrididae
DISTRIBUTION	Europe
HABITAT	Dry open areas with short grass
DIET	Grass and other low-lying plants
SIZE	Length: males up to 18 mm (0.7 in); females up to 23 mm (0.9 in)
LIFESPAN	6–7 months

FIND OUT MORE ARTHROPODS CAVE WILDLIFE CAMOUFLAGE AND COLOUR GRASSLAND WILDLIFE INSECTS NORTH AMERICAN WILDLIFE

GRASSLAND WILDLIFE

GRASSLANDS SUSTAIN MORE ANIMALS than any other type of land habitat. This is because each species eats a different type, or part, of the grass. In this way, the various species of herbivore can share the same habitat without competing for food. On the African plains, for example, zebras eat the tops of grasses, wildebeest prefer the middle layers, while Thomson's gazelles graze close to the ground. Tall grasses also provide shelter for myriad insects, and a refuge for small animals, such as birds and rodents, many of which live in burrows due to the lack of shelter from trees.

Prairies of North America

Eurasian steppe

Savannahs of Africa

Pampas of South America

Australian grasslands

Giraffes browse on trees.
Zebras and springboks graze on grass.

Giraffes, springboks, and zebras grazing on the African savannah

Grasslands

Grasslands cover 25 per cent of the Earth's land surface. The world's principal grasslands are the Eurasian steppe, the savannahs of Africa, the pampas of South America, the prairies of North America, and the Australian grasslands. Grasslands are areas where it is too dry for many trees to grow, but tough grasses grow in abundance. Grasses can withstand constant grazing by animals, and recover quickly from damage by fire, flood, or drought.

Mammals

Grasslands sustain a wide variety of mammals, mainly herbivores, often in large numbers. The herbivores support a population of carnivores, while scavengers, such as hyenas, jackals, and vultures, dispose of their remains. Typical grassland mammals include zebras in Africa; prairie dogs and coyotes in North America; maned wolves in South America; marmots in Eurasia; and kangaroos in Australia.

Blackbuck
Blackbucks are a type of antelope that once roamed the Indian grasslands in herds of up to 10,000. More recently, hunting has reduced their numbers, and there are now more blackbucks in Argentina and Texas, where they have been introduced, than in their original homeland.

Males have slender, spiralled horns.

Pairs of African wild dogs run down animals larger than themselves.

Huge ears and good sense of smell help to locate prey.

Patagonian hare
The Patagonian hare, or mara, looks like a hare but is closely related to the guinea pig. It lives in burrows in groups of 30–40, in the Argentinian pampas and the stony Patagonian desert.

Long, thin legs help hare run fast.

American bison
The most characteristic animal of the Great Plains of North America, the bison once numbered 50–60 million. By the 1880s, the huge herds had been almost destroyed by hunting. Only 500 remained, but given protection, numbers rose to 25,000. The bison now live in herds of up to 50 animals.

African wild dog
The wild dog lives in packs of up to 12 on the open savannahs of Africa. It employs a very effective method of communal hunting; having singled out an animal, such as a zebra or gazelle, from the herd, a pair of dogs chases it until they are tired, when a fresh pair takes over. Relays of dogs continue in this way until the prey is exhausted, and the pack closes in for the kill.

Invertebrates

Invertebrates are of great importance in tropical grasslands. They feed on dead vegetation, helping decompose it, and make nutrients available to plants. They also bring subsoil to the surface, helping to keep the soil healthy.

Ant lion
Ant lion larvae build pits in sandy soil and wait at the bottom for an ant or spider to dislodge grains of sand. Once alerted, the larva squirts sand at its victim, making it slide into the pit where the ant lion seizes it in its powerful jaws.

Termites
Tropical grasslands are dotted with termite nests, each containing several million of these insects. Termites are an important food source for many animals, especially echidnas, numbats, aardvarks, and pangolins.

Dung beetle
Dung beetles roll dung into balls, which they lay eggs in, and push into holes. The larvae hatch and feed on the dung.

Queen termites have huge, swollen bodies and can lay up to 30,000 eggs a day.

Termite nest may be 6 m (20 ft) high.

Reptiles

Many reptiles live in grasslands where they can tolerate the harsh conditions during the dry season. However, when the grass is short it provides little cover in which to hide, so reptiles need to be camouflaged. Many grassland snakes and lizards are dull coloured, with brown or grey mottled markings that blend into the surroundings.

Large claws help it to catch prey.

Strong jaws and sharp, curved teeth help it catch snakes, rabbits, and birds.

Perentie

Reaching a length of 2 m (7 ft), the perentie is the largest of the Australian monitor lizards. It lives in grasslands and among rocky outcrops in deserts. Like other monitors, the perentie is a carnivore with a voracious appetite. It also eats carrion. If threatened, it inflates its body, hisses, and lashes out with its tail.

The perentie can lash its huge tail from side-to-side in self-defence.

Grass snake

This small, non-venomous reptile lives in grasslands close to water. It is a strong swimmer, and catches much of its prey, such as fish, frogs, and newts, in water. If attacked, it releases a bad smell, or feigns death by lying on its back, with its tongue hanging out. Grass snakes hibernate in winter, usually in holes in the ground.

Grass snakes usually lay a clutch of up to 30–40 eggs in decaying vegetation.

Puff adder

Hidden within the grass stems of the African savannah lurks the slow-moving, dangerous puff adder. Camouflaged in the grass, it lies in wait for prey. It produces a powerful venom for immobilizing prey, such as rodents and frogs, and as a means of defence, against mongooses, secretary birds, and eagles.

Mottled markings break up outline against the grass.

Birds

Grasslands support many birds, among them bustards, guineafowl, francolins, long-legged seriemas, and the secretary bird. Many birds nest on the ground as there are few trees. The burrowing owl even goes underground and nests in burrows on the American prairies. Other birds, such as weaver birds, flock in droves to the same isolated tree to weave their basket-shaped nests.

Emu

The emu is the second largest bird in the world, after the ostrich. It is flightless and lives on the Australian grasslands, where it feeds on grasses, berries, fruit, and insects. Emus live in small, nomadic flocks, moving long distances in search of food and water. They are powerful runners, covering the ground in 2.7 m (9 ft) strides, reaching speeds of up to 50 kmh (30 mph) over short distances. Males incubate the eggs and look after the chicks.

Long, shaggy feathers

Bare skin on neck

Long legs for running

Greater bustard

A turkey-sized, ground-dwelling bird with a wing span of up to 2.4 m (8 ft), the greater bustard lives in the open grasslands of Asia and southern Europe. It is famous for the male's spectacular courtship display. He inflates the air sac on his throat, and twists his back and tail feathers forwards, transforming himself from a drab grey colour into a shimmering white mass.

Long neck gives bustard a clear view over the grass.

Indian white-backed vulture

Vultures are a group of carrion-eating birds of prey. They perform a vital role of scavenging and keeping the environment clean by disposing of waste. Indian white-backed vultures hunt, by soaring on thermal currents from where they can spot a kill; once sighted, the vultures land to feed on the remains. The sight of vultures spiralling down draws other scavengers to the kill.

Vulture feeding on a goat

Plants

Grasslands sustain numerous types of grass, among the best known are red oat grass in Africa and buffalo grass in America. Which species grow depends on altitude, temperature, soil type, and rainfall. Grassland trees often have deep roots to reach water supplies far below the ground, allowing them to survive during the dry season. Some trees can store water. The baobab tree can store about 9,000 l (2,400 gal) of water in its huge swollen trunk.

Acacia tree

The characteristic tree of Africa's arid and semi-arid grasslands is the flat-topped umbrella tree, *Acacia tortilis*. This tree is protected from grazing animals by sharp thorns, but these do not deter giraffes, which manage to pluck the leaves and blossoms. Acacias produce a mass of pods that fall to the ground providing food for many animals. Acacias also provide welcome shade for the animals of the savannah.

Fluffy, white seed heads

Pampas grass

The Argentine pampas extends from the foothills of the Andes to the Atlantic coast. Many of the grasses that grow there can be up to 2.5 m (8 ft) high.

Petals and bracts are covered with small hairs.

Anemones

When the snow retreats on the Asian steppes, many wild flowers, including anemones and peonies, grow amidst the sea of grass.

FIND OUT MORE ANTS AND TERMITES BIRDS OF PREY BUFFALO AND OTHER WILD CATTLE DEER AND ANTELOPES GRASSES, RUSHES, AND SEDGES PLANTS, DEFENCE WOLVES AND WILD DOGS

G

GRAVITY

WITHOUT GRAVITY, we would fly off the spinning Earth and into space. Gravity is a force of attraction that acts between any two objects. The objects can be as large as galaxies or as small as subatomic particles. The strength of the gravity between two objects depends on their masses and the distance between them. Objects with large masses exert a strong force of gravity. Objects far apart attract each other weakly.

Centre of gravity

Every object consists of tiny particles of matter. Each of these particles has a small force of gravity acting upon it. Together, the forces act like a single force pulling downwards at just one point, called the centre of gravity. An object will balance when it is supported in line with its centre of gravity. Balancing is easiest if the object has a low centre of gravity.

Centre of gravity is directly below the string, making the object very stable.

Gravity in space

Gravity is a universal force, because it acts between any two objects, wherever they are in the Universe. The force that keeps our feet firmly on the ground is the same one that holds huge clusters of stars together as galaxies.

Galaxies
A typical galaxy is about 100,000 light-years across. The stars are so massive that gravity can still act over this huge distance, preventing the stars from drifting off into space.

Path of orbit

Gravitational force on the Earth

Planetary orbits
Gravity holds the planets of the Solar System in orbit around the Sun. Venus and the Earth have similar masses, but because Venus is closer to the Sun than the Earth, the force of gravity keeping it in orbit is greater.

Gravitational force on Venus

Orbital path of Mercury over 4 years

Orbit shifts over time.

General Relativity
In 1915, German-born physicist Albert Einstein published his Theory of General Relativity. This theory sees gravity not as a force, but as a curvature of space caused by bodies of matter. In 1919, the theory was used successfully to explain why Mercury's orbit gradually varies over time.

Weight

The force of gravity acting on an object is called weight. Like all forces, weight is expressed in units called newtons (N). An object's weight is directly related to its mass. On Earth, 1 kg (2.2 lb) of matter weighs about 10 N.

The force of gravity acting on the ball is constant.

Balls slow down as they are thrown upwards.

Balls speed up as they fall.

Gravity tries to pull the balls downwards.

Apple weighs about 1 N.

Newton meter measures weight and other forces.

Apple has a mass of 100 g (3.5 oz).

Earth's gravity

Gravity always acts towards the centre of the Earth, defining the "downwards" direction at every point on the planet's surface. Gravity pulls a juggling ball towards the ground, slowing it as it rises, and speeding it up as it falls. The ball also pulls on the Earth, but the Earth is so massive that the ball's gravity has no noticeable effect.

Moon's gravity
The Moon is smaller and has less mass than the Earth, so the force of gravity is weaker on the Moon. A hammer on the Moon weighs one-sixth of its weight on the Earth. It takes 1.1 seconds for a hammer to fall 1 m (3.3 ft) on the Moon, but only 0.44 seconds on the Earth.

Earth   Moon

Aristotle

The Greek philosopher Aristotle (c.384–322 BC) believed that heavy objects fall faster than lighter ones. Aristotle's ideas were accepted until the Italian scientist Galileo Galilei (1564–1642) showed that gravity pulls all objects to Earth at the same speed.

Tides
Twice each day, the waters of the ocean rise a little and then fall back. This movement is called a tide, and it is caused by the pull of the Moon's gravity. The Sun also influences tides. When the Earth, Sun, and Moon are in line, their combined gravity produces tides that are higher than normal, called spring tides.

Harbour at low tide

Timeline

4th century BC Aristotle proposes that stones fall to the ground simply because they are heavy, and that smoke rises because it is light.

1604 Italian scientist Galileo Galilei investigates how objects fall to Earth.

17th century English physicist Isaac Newton publishes his Law of Gravitation, perhaps inspired by seeing an apple fall from a tree.

Model showing how space curves around a planet.

1915 Einstein's Theory of General Relativity describes gravity as a curvature of space.

1919 English astronomer Arthur Eddington (1882–1944) obtains proof of Einstein's theory by observing light, reaching Earth from a distant star, being bent by the Sun's gravity.

FIND OUT MORE   EINSTEIN, ALBERT   FORCE AND MOTION   MATTER   MOON   NEWTON, SIR ISAAC   OCEANS AND SEAS

GREAT DEPRESSION

ON 24 OCTOBER, 1929, the world's financial heart – the New York Stock Exchange – stopped beating. Share prices crashed, consumers stopped investing, banks failed, and millions of people lost their jobs. Within a year, a severe economic depression gripped the world, and governments struggled to cope with the crisis. Ill-thought-out economic policies led to social unrest and the rise of right-wing authoritarian governments in Europe. The Great Depression lasted for a decade; it ended when the threat of war resulted in the need for workers to produce armaments.

Roaring Twenties
Once western economies had recovered from World War I, they entered a period of rapid growth. High public confidence, low interest rates, and optimistic investments created a boom in the 1920s. Women enjoyed greater freedom, and most people spent more on leisure and entertainment than ever before.

A fashionable 1920s' "flapper"

US magazine front cover, 1926

Wall Street Crash

In 1929, after years of rising share prices, the Stock Exchange on New York's Wall Street saw a dramatic crash (fall) in prices. The crash bankrupted many companies and private citizens.

Bread line, New York, 1932

Jarrow marchers on their way to London

Soup kitchens
Many people lost their life savings after the Wall Street Crash, and bankrupt companies had to lay off their workers. With no work and no social security system, millions of American families faced poverty and hunger. Every town opened soup kitchens to provide at least one good meal a day.

Jarrow March
By the early 1930s, the effects of the Depression had spread to Britain, Germany, and the rest of the world. Poverty was rife. In 1936, 200 unemployed workers marched 444 km (276 miles) from Jarrow, northeast England, to the capital, London, demanding jobs. Almost 70 per cent of Jarrow's workers were out of work.

A family in the Texas Dust Bowl, 1938

Dust Bowl

In the United States, years of over-farming and drought caused dust storms throughout the mid-western states during the 1930s. Thousands of farmers, already hit hard by the Depression and suffering desperate poverty, were forced to abandon their land to seek work in the fruit farms of California. Few found it. Their plight was immortalized in John Steinbeck's classic novel, *The Grapes of Wrath* (1939).

Rearmament

From the 1930s, world leaders took action to combat unemployment: the USA's President Roosevelt started the New Deal to get people back to work. However, it was renewed war in Europe that ended the Depression. Armament factories producing aeroplanes and tanks created new jobs and revitalized the world economy.

New Deal
In 1932, FD Roosevelt won the US presidential election against President Hoover. He pledged "a new deal for the American people", establishing agencies to regulate business, start public works programmes, and build a series of huge hydroelectric power plants, such as the Hoover Dam, in order to provide employment.

Italy's Fascist leader Benito Mussolini taking the salute at a rally

Rise of Fascism
The Depression caused much tension. Socialists agitated for reform, but some countries looked to right-wing solutions. Italy had had a Fascist government since 1922; Germany got one in 1933, and Spain in 1936. Authoritarian governments across Europe quashed dissent from workers and left-wingers.

Hoover Dam, Nevada, USA

Franklin D Roosevelt
Roosevelt (1882–1945) became Democratic senator for New York in 1910, and Assistant Secretary to the Navy from 1913–1920. In 1921 he developed polio and was paralysed, which confined him to a wheelchair for the rest of his life. He returned to public life in 1928 as governor of New York, and won the 1932 presidential election. He promised "direct, vigorous action" against the Depression, and won re-election three times. He led the USA to victory in World War II.

Timeline
1929 Wall Street Crash.

1930 World unemployment doubles.

1931 Britain forms national government to deal with crisis.

1932 More than 1 in 4 workers unemployed in USA; unemployment in Germany triples to 5.6 million.

1933 Hitler comes to power in Germany, with promises to get the country back to work through rearmament and national expansion.

1933 Slow recovery begins in USA and Europe.

1939 Outbreak of war in Europe ends Depression as workers are employed in armament factories.

 FIND OUT MORE — GERMANY, HISTORY OF · UNITED STATES, HISTORY OF · WORLD WAR II

GREAT ZIMBABWE

Southern Africa • Kilwa

Madagascar

Sofala

Great
Zimbabwe •

ONE OF AFRICA'S GREATEST archaeological mysteries is the walled city of Great Zimbabwe. This massive granite zimbabwe – a word literally meaning chief's court – was begun in the 13th century. By the 14th century, it had become the capital of a vast kingdom that stretched between the Zambezi and Limpopo rivers. The people of Great Zimbabwe were mainly farmers, but the city was also the main centre for trade and religion. However, by 1450, Great Zimbabwe had been abandoned for reasons that remain a mystery. Today its ruins stand in modern Zimbabwe, the southern African country named after this remarkable walled structure.

Rise of Great Zimbabwe
Great Zimbabwe's first city started as a farming settlement, possibly as early as the 2nd century. As well as rearing and selling cattle, its people mined for gold and copper on the Zimbabwe plateau. By the 12th century, long-distance trade based on gold and copper was passing through the city from the east coast of Africa. As Great Zimbabwe rose in importance and wealth, it was rebuilt in stone and increased in size.

Great Enclosure
Built of massive granite blocks, the Great Enclosure is a huge dry stone wall that surrounded the city, providing protection for Great Zimbabwe's people. Inside the enclosure, people lived in circular houses made from daga (a gravel-like clay) and roofed with thatch. There were also small oval enclosures – but, like the stone conical tower, their purpose remains a mystery. Near to the enclosure was a hill complex, which was used for religious rituals.

The conical tower was 9 m (27 ft) high, and made of solid stone.

Roofless oval enclosures

Masonry incorporates massive boulders

Round thatched huts

Outside wall was 5 m (16 ft) thick at the base and 9.75 m (32 ft) high.

Chevron pattern decorated parts of wall.

Great Enclosure, Great Zimbabwe

Farming
Great Zimbabwe at its height had 10,000 people living in and around it. Most people were farmers in the surrounding areas. They herded cattle and grew millet, sorghum, and vegetables, which they sold to the many traders visiting the walled city.

Zimbabwean cattle

Hill complex

Hill complex
The religious centre, where the ancestors' spirits were worshipped, was built on a hill near the Great Enclosure. At the front of the complex, there was a public space where the mambo (ruler) conducted sacred rites.

Conical tower
A massive and mysterious cone-shaped tower stands inside the Great Enclosure. Some archaeologists think it may be a monument celebrating the power and wealth of the rulers of Great Zimbabwe.

Ancestor worship
The people of Great Zimbabwe worshipped the spirits of their dead rulers, known as ancestors. In sacrificial rites, they killed calves, and offered the meat to ancestor spirits on beautifully carved soapstone dishes. They placed the dishes in sacred places outside the hill complex.

Birds
Eight carved soapstone birds have been found at Great Zimbabwe. They stood in sacred places on 1-m (3-ft) high soapstone columns. Each of the birds may represent a royal ancestor, and one of them is now used as the symbol of the modern state of Zimbabwe.

Soapstone bird on column

Trade
The prosperous trading centre of Great Zimbabwe was situated on one of the trade routes that linked southern Africa to the east coast. Traders from Sofala and Kilwa (in modern Mozambique) obtained gold and copper from Great Zimbabwe to export to Arabia and Asia.

Metal exports
The people of Great Zimbabwe mined gold, copper, iron, and tin on the Zimbabwe plateau. Cross-shaped ingots were exchanged for trade goods from Asia, such as beads, glassware, and ceramics.

Copper ingot

Karl Mauch
A German self-taught geologist, Mauch (1837–75), travelled southern Africa from 1865 to 1872. During his nine months in Great Zimbabwe (1871) he drew diagrams of the ruins and sketched the carved stone and metal objects found there. Much of today's knowledge of the area is based on Mauch's diaries.

Timeline
c.900 Iron Age (Shona) people settle between the Zambezi and the Limpopo rivers in southern Africa.

1100s Trade passing through Great Zimbabwe to Africa's East Coast increases.

1200s Zimbabwean gold being exported to Asia.

1250 Building in stone begins at Great Zimbabwe.

Early 1400s Great Enclosure is completed; and Great Zimbabwe reaches its greatest extent.

1450 Great Zimbabwe is abandoned, probably because its people leave to look for new and better farmland.

FIND OUT MORE   AFRICA, HISTORY OF   METALS   MALI EMPIRE

GREECE, ANCIENT

MORE THAN 2,500 YEARS AGO one of the world's most influential civilizations flowered in mainland Greece. From the 8th until the 2nd centuries BC, Greek writers, thinkers, and artists made a huge contribution to western culture – especially in politics, drama, mythology, architecture, and literature. Greek civilization declined when, after defeating the Persians and peacefully colonizing much of Europe, they were absorbed into the Roman Empire.

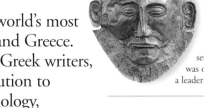

Mycenaean civilization
The Mycenaeans formed the first great mainland Greek civilization (c.2700–1120 BC), and were the forerunners of classical Greece. These Bronze Age traders and warriors ranged all over the Mediterranean area from their settlement at Mycenae. The gold mask was once thought to be of Agamemnon, a leader in the legendary Trojan War.

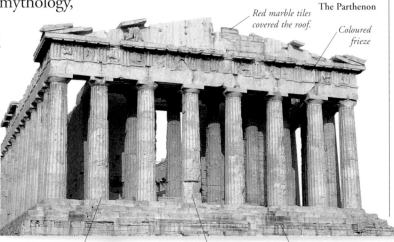

Red marble tiles covered the roof.

The Parthenon

Coloured frieze

Reliefs decorated the exterior.

Temples were built on stepped platforms.

White marble columns

Polis

Ancient Greece was made up of hundreds of separate city-states. Some were hardly bigger than villages, while others were based around great cities, such as Sparta or Athens. Each of these city-states was known as a polis (plural: poleis). Laws, festivals, and government systems varied, and there was often war between rival poleis, despite their common Greek background. The need for land led some poleis to colonize other parts of the Mediterranean between the 8th and 6th centuries BC, and in this way ancient Greece expanded.

Ancient Greece, c.4th century BC

Sparta
Life in Sparta was disciplined and harsh. Spartans trained both girls and boys to excel at sports and feats of endurance. To strengthen military power, all the boys went on to become soldiers. After helping Athens defeat the Persians in 480 BC, Sparta conquered Athens in the Peloponnesian War (431–404 BC), and became master of Greece.

Spartan warrior

Athens
From the 6th century BC, Athens was governed by a form of democracy (rule by the people), in which all male citizens voted. In the 5th century BC, thanks to its powerful navy, Athens had a maritime empire in the Aegean Sea, and its 250,000-strong population enjoyed a golden age of art and culture. After their triumph against the Persians, the Athenians celebrated by building a massive "fortified citadel" – the Acropolis. The Parthenon (447 and 432 BC) was the most important temple in the Acropolis, and was dedicated to Athena.

Clash of the Titans
The Greeks believed that the world was originally inhabited by giants called Titans. Their ruler, Cronos, swallowed his children alive, so that they could not overthrow him. One son, Zeus, escaped this fate when his mother gave Cronos a clothed stone to swallow instead. Zeus grew up in secret, made Cronos vomit up his siblings, defeated the other Titans in battle, and made himself king of the gods.

Cronos eating his children

The Legend of Troy
Little of the ancient city of Troy (in modern Turkey) remains. Homer's *Iliad* says that a Greek army besieged Troy for 10 years in the late Mycenaean Age (c.1250 BC). This became known as the Trojan War. According to legend, Athena advised the Greeks to smuggle their soldiers into the city inside a huge wooden horse, and in this way they gained victory.

Model of Trojan Horse

Mount Olympus

Ancient Greeks believed that various deities (gods and goddesses) watched over ordinary mortals from a cloud-palace above the highest mountain in Greece – the snow-capped Mount Olympus. The deities who lived there were also known as Olympians. Each Olympian had specific responsibilities: Poseidon was in charge of the sea, Athena of wisdom and the arts, Apollo of music and poetry, and Demeter of crops. The supreme god was Zeus, lord of sky and earth. Greek cities regarded different deities as their special protectors. For example, Athens was devoted to the cult of Athena.

Oracle at Delphi
Ancient Greeks consulted the gods for advice or prophecies at holy places called oracles. The most famous oracle in Greece was at Delphi. People went there to ask questions at Apollo's shrine about religious or political matters. A high priestess went into a trance to give Apollo's answers. Most gods had their special shrine, but they competed with each other for the best ones. Legend has it that Athena won a competition against Poseidon over the Parthenon in Athens, the largest city in Greece, and he had to move his shrine to Attica.

Poseidon was Zeus's brother and god of the sea.

Part of a trident

Poseidon is usually shown holding a fish.

Poseidon, god of the sea

Homer
The Greek poet Homer probably lived in the 7th or 8th century BC. He is believed to be the author of two of the world's greatest epic poems: the *Iliad*, which is about the siege of Troy, and the *Odyssey*, which describes the wanderings of the hero Odysseus after the Trojan War. According to to later writers, Homer was blind.

Ceres, goddess of the harvest

Cloak

Chiton, or full tunic

Culture

Ancient Greek art and science was of the highest standard, and set the standard for European culture for centuries. "Greece, though conquered," wrote the Roman poet Horace, "brought the arts to the uncivilized Latin peoples" (Romans) – and through them to modern Europe.

Sculpture

Ancient Greek sculpture was famous for its naturalness, beauty, and perfect proportions. Statues related to all aspects of life, including religious worship and sport. Those of deities, such as Ceres, were popular among farmers, and were left at shrines to ensure a good harvest.

Drama and architecture

The ancient Greeks learned much from the Egyptians about using stone in their architecture – but their theatres were original. In the golden age of Athens (400s BC), dramatists, such as Aeschylus, Sophocles, and Euripedes wrote tragedies that are still performed.

Epidaurus theatre

Amphora

Human figures at a banquet

Art

Red-figure painting replaced black-figure in c.530 BC. Most red-figure vases (amphorae) were made from Athenian clay. Subjects were usually male, and were often shown banqueting or engaged in athletics.

Pericles

From 443 BC, Pericles (c.495–429 BC) was the most important politician and general in Athens. A great public speaker and champion of democracy, he strengthened and expanded the Athenian empire after defeating the Persians. He also made Athens the most splendid city in Greece by arranging for the Parthenon and other buildings to be built on the Acropolis, a rocky hill overlooking the city.

Language and literature

Ancient Greek, like Latin, is known as a "classical" language. Many great works of Greek literature have survived by authors such as Hesiod and Appolonius (poets), Thucydides (a historian), and Plato (a philosopher).

Greek inscription of thanks to Asclepius, the god of medicine

Alphabet

The word "alphabet" (used in many modern languages, including English) was formed by joining the first two letters of ancient Greek: alpha and beta. The Cyrillic alphabet of eastern Europe also grew out of the Greek alphabet.

Greek-Persian wars

After 545 BC, the mighty Persian Empire took over Greek cities in Ionia, the easternmost part of Greek territory. When Athens tried to lend support to the cities (499–494 BC), the Persians invaded mainland Greece, but were driven back at Marathon. Ten years later, an alliance between Athens, Sparta, and other Greek cities defeated another massive Persian expedition on land and sea at Salamis.

The Treasury, Delphi

Battle of Marathon

In 490 BC, a Persian force sailed across the Aegean Sea, and landed in Attica. On the plain of Marathon, against all odds, it was heavily defeated by an army of Athenians and their allies. The Athenians built a treasury at Delphi to mark this victory, filled it with Persian spoils, and dedicated it to Apollo, the god of war.

Jason and the Argonauts *Poseidon* *The Clashing Rocks*

Battle of Salamis

In 480 BC, the Persian emperor Xerxes the Great led a huge force along the shores of the Aegean Sea. As central Greece fell, the Athenians evacuated their city. A smaller Greek fleet then lured the Persians into battle in the straits between the mainland and the island of Salamis – and defeated them decisively.

Philip of Macedon

Warrior-king Philip II ruled Macedon, a northern state in Greece, from 359 to 336 BC. A strong king and a great diplomat, Philip made Macedon the dominant power in the Greek world. He was murdered on the point of invading Persia, but by then had laid the foundations for his son, Alexander, to continue his military feats.

Jason and the Argonauts

Even today, Greek myths are rewritten, and made into plays and films. Few tales are as dramatic as the quest by Jason and his ship, the *Argo*, to steal the Golden Fleece of the Sun from a watchful dragon. On their journey, Jason and his crew (including the hero Herakles) were helped and hindered by many gods, monsters, witches, and giants.

Timeline

Detail from amphora

c.2700–1120 BC Myceneaen civilization flourishes.

c.750–550 BC Greeks colonize areas in Italy and Africa.

560–510 BC Athenian influence spreads.

510 BC Cleisthenes, an Athenian statesman, introduces democracy to Athens.

c.510–366 BC Peloponnesian League forms, led by Sparta.

499–494 BC Revolt against Persia by Ionian Greeks.

490 BC Battle of Marathon.

480–479 BC Greeks repel Persian invaders at Salamis and Plataea.

477 BC Athens and Ionian Greeks form Delian League against Persia.

459 BC Sparta defeats Athens in first Peloponnesian War.

443–429 BC Pericles dominant in Athens.

431–404 BC Sparta wins second, or Great, Peloponnesian War.

378–371 BC Thebes overthrows Sparta as leading Greek power.

359–323 BC Reigns of Philip II and his son Alexander the Great of Macedon.

Hephaistos, god of fire

FIND OUT MORE ART, HISTORY OF ALEXANDER THE GREAT CITIES ETRUSCANS EUROPE, HISTORY OF GODS AND GODDESSES MINOANS PERSIAN EMPIRES ROMAN EMPIRE SOCRATES

GREECE AND BULGARIA

ALTHOUGH Greece and Bulgaria share a border, high mountains separate the two countries, making communication difficult. Greece and Bulgaria are quite different. Three-fifths of the Greek mainland is mountainous, and only one-third of the land is cultivated. By contrast, Bulgaria is much more fertile with a strong agricultural tradition. Greece has a strong history of democratic government, while Bulgaria is only just emerging from almost half a century of communist rule.

Physical features

Surrounded by sea on three sides, the country of Greece is made up of the mainland, the Peloponnese peninsula, and more than 2,000 islands. It is a mixture of high mountains, dry, dusty plains, and dramatic coastlines. Land-locked on three sides, Bulgaria has broad fertile valleys, separated by the Balkan and Rhodope mountains.

Regional climate
Greece has very hot, dry summers and cooler winters. The northern mountains have cold winters. Annual rainfall is low, and the country suffers from water shortages. Bulgaria, by contrast, has warm summers and cold, snowy winters, with a high rainfall – especially in the mountains.

44°C (111°F)   -25°C (-13°F)
24°C (75°F)   6°C (43°F)
525 mm (20.5 in)

Danubian Plain
The mighty River Danube forms most of Bulgaria's northern border with Romania, flowing through the vast and fertile Danubian Plain that extends across the width of the country. This rolling farmland is used for grazing sheep, goats, and cattle, and for cultivating a variety of crops including sunflowers, which are grown for their oil.

Crete
The largest of the Greek islands at 8,380 sq km (3,235 sq miles), Crete lies 100 km (62 miles) southeast of the Greek mainland. More than 600,000 people live on the island, and one third of Cretans are farmers. Many people work in tourism.

Mount Olympus
Much of central and western Greece is made up of steep, rugged mountains, many of which are capped with snow for several months of the year. Mount Olympus is Greece's highest peak at 2,917 m (9,570 ft). Once thought to be the home of the gods, it is now a national park with busy ski resorts.

Orthodox Church

Greece is the only official Christian Orthodox country in the world. Priests are responsible community figures and play an important part in national events. Most Greeks and Bulgars belong to the Eastern Orthodox Church, which split from the Roman Catholic Church in 1054. Each country has its own branch of the Church, which also flourishes in other parts of eastern Europe, and Russia. Around one tenth of the world's Christians belong to the Orthodox Church.

Greek Orthodox priest

Greece

One of Europe's oldest nations, Greece gained independence from almost 500 years of Turkish rule in 1830. Although it is the poorest member of the European Union, the country has a thriving tourist industry and a large shipping fleet. The Greek people have a strong national unity, based on their deep-rooted Orthodox religion, and a language that has remained in use for 2,700 years.

Parsley · Tomato · Cucumber · Aubergine · Olives

Farming
High mountains and poor soils make farming difficult in Greece. However, agriculture employs about 23 per cent of the work-force, mainly on small, traditional farms. The main crops are olives, citrus fruits, salad vegetables, tomatoes, and grapes. Small herds of sheep and goats produce meat, and milk for cheese and yoghurt. Greece is the world's third largest producer of olive oil.

GREECE FACTS

CAPITAL CITY Athens

AREA 131,990 sq km (50,961 sq miles)

POPULATION 10,600,000

DENSITY 81 per sq km (210 per sq mile)

MAIN LANGUAGE Greek

MAJOR RELIGION Christian

CURRENCY Euro

LIFE EXPECTANCY 78 years

PEOPLE PER DOCTOR 250

GOVERNMENT Multi-party democracy

ADULT LITERACY 97%

Food
The Greeks love to eat outdoors in the warm summer months. Meals are simple and tasty and consist mainly of tomatoes, salad, olives, feta cheese, lamb, some fish, and yoghurt made from sheep's milk. Retsina, a wine flavoured with pine resin, is often served with food.

Athens
Home to almost one-third of the Greek population, Athens is famous for its ancient buildings, such as the Acropolis and the 2,400-year-old ruins of the Parthenon temple. On certain days, cars are banned from the capital to protect the ruins. Nearby, pinewoods and mountains provide a retreat from the busy city.

Ruins of the Parthenon temple

Tourism
Each year, more than 12,000,000 tourists visit Greece, attracted by its warm climate, ancient monuments, and beautiful islands. Tourism is the mainstay of the economy and employs thousands of Greeks each summer.

Greek islander selling sponges to tourists

Shipping
Greece has the world's largest merchant fleet, and relies on ships to move goods between the many islands. The narrow Corinth Canal, built in 1893, links the Ionian and Aegean seas, providing important access to Athens.

Bulgaria

From 1944 to 1989, Bulgaria was part of the Russian communist bloc. Since gaining independence, Bulgaria is slowly adapting to a democratic government and a western-style economy. About 85 per cent of Bulgaria's population are Bulgars, with minorities of Turks, Macedonians, and Roma. The small groups have suffered discrimination, but are gaining power in parliament.

Tourism
Bulgaria's Black Sea coast is becoming increasingly popular as a holiday destination, in particular the towns of Varna and Burgas. New airports serve western tourists, whilst Russians cross the Black Sea by ferry. Many new resorts have been built, and the natural beauty of the coastline, with its sandy beaches, pine forests, and old fishing villages, is often spoiled by high-rise hotel developments.

Resort near Varna

BULGARIA FACTS

CAPITAL CITY Sofia

AREA 110,910 sq km (42,822 sq miles)

POPULATION 8,200,000

DENSITY 74 per sq km (192 per sq mile)

MAIN LANGUAGE Bulgarian

MAJOR RELIGIONS Christian, Muslim

CURRENCY Lev

LIFE EXPECTANCY 72 years

PEOPLE PER DOCTOR 286

GOVERNMENT Multi-party democracy

ADULT LITERACY 98%

Sofia
Bulgaria's capital is also its largest city, with more than one million inhabitants. Founded by the Romans, it is now the cultural and economic centre, with one-fifth of the country's industry. The Alexander Nevsky Cathedral was built in the 1870s to celebrate liberation from Turkish rule.

Alexander Nevsky Cathedral

Energy
Twenty-five per cent of Bulgaria's electricity comes from the Kozloduy nuclear power station built by the former Soviet Union in an earthquake zone. Increased safety measures have been introduced since 1990. Bulgaria imports 70 per cent of its energy due to poor coal and oil resources, and has built a hydroelectric generator.

Farming
Near the town of Kazanlúk in the Balkan Mountains, vast fields of roses are grown. The petals, picked at dawn in midsummer, are used to produce attar, the essential oil of roses, which is used in perfume manufacture. Farther south, in the Maritsa valley, tobacco plants are grown and dried for cigarettes. Black grapes grown on the Danubian Plain are used for making high-quality red wine.

FIND OUT MORE   CHRISTIANITY   EUROPE, HISTORY OF   EUROPEAN UNION   FARMING   GREECE, ANCIENT   POLLUTION   PORTS AND WATERWAYS   SHIPS AND BOATS   SOVIET UNION

GROWTH AND DEVELOPMENT

AS THE HUMAN BODY grows and develops, it follows a regular sequence of changes. After birth, a human being passes through infancy, childhood, puberty and adolescence, and into adulthood. The body grows at different rates at different times. Rapid growth, called a growth spurt, occurs during infancy and again at puberty, while growth is steady throughout childhood, but ceases in adulthood. In later life, the body ages as it becomes less efficient. Eventually, one or more of the body's systems stop working, and a person dies.

Changing proportions

Different parts of the body grow at different rates. Changing body proportions can be compared by fitting photographs of children and young adults into a panel that makes them appear the same height. The panel divides each body into eight equal parts. The head, for example, makes up one quarter of the height of a newborn baby, but only one eighth of the height of a 20-year-old.

2 months	2 years	4 years	7 years	12 years	20 years
55 cm (1 ft 10 in)	86 cm (2 ft 10 in)	110 cm (3 ft 8 in)	120 cm (4 ft)	145 cm (4 ft 10 in)	175 cm (5 ft 10 in)

From baby to child

During the first two years of life, a young human being grows and develops rapidly. A six-week-old baby is helpless and must have everything done for it, but by the age of two years, the baby can walk, talk, and feed itself. Growth and development is marked by a series of age milestones at which children have learned certain skills.

8 months
The baby can sit up by herself, will try to crawl, and can stand if supported. She turns towards the sound of a familiar voice, and can imitate simple sounds.

6 weeks
The baby sleeps when not being held or fed, and cries when distressed. She can follow objects with her eyes and listen to a person talking.

6 months
The baby can sit supported with her head up and back straight. She holds objects, squeals, and babbles.

10 months
The baby can crawl rapidly, pull herself up to a standing position, point to and pick up objects. She says her first words, usually "mama" and "dada".

Toddler can walk a few steps on her own.

Child needs help getting dressed but can put on own shoes and socks.

Child can dress and undress herself.

14 months
The child can stand alone and may walk without help. She speaks a few words, and tries to indicate what she wants.

2 years
She can run and jump, turn the pages of a book, identify pictures of familiar objects, and form a few short phrases.

4 years
The young girl now has good balance and can hop on one foot. She can draw simple pictures and copy some letters.

Developing bones

The skeleton is formed before birth from flexible cartilage. During childhood, this is replaced by bone, as revealed by X-rays. The skeleton continues to get larger and harder during the teenage years.

A newborn baby's skeleton is made of both bone and cartilage. Unlike bone, cartilage cannot be seen on an X-ray.

By the age of 6, the wrist bones are forming so that there are now more bones. Other bones have got harder and bigger.

By the age of 16, the 27 bones that make up the fingers, palm, and wrist, are now mature, hard, and adult in size and form.

Adolescence and puberty

Adolescence is the whole process of growing up from a child to an adult. During adolescence, changes occur to a person's body and in the way they think and feel. Puberty is part of adolescence during which the body grows rapidly and changes shape, and boys and girls become sexually mature and able to reproduce.

Puberty in boys   Puberty in girls

Changes during puberty

In girls, puberty begins between the ages of 10–14. The body becomes rounder, breasts grow, and periods begin. In boys, puberty begins between the ages of 12–16. The body becomes more muscular, the testes produce sperm, and the voice deepens.

Ageing

Growing old is a normal part of life. Humans age because the body's cells gradually become less efficient. Signs of ageing usually appear after 40 years of age. The body becomes less mobile, hair thins and turns grey, and the skin wrinkles. Bones become brittle and can break more easily. Exercise and a healthy diet can help to slow down the ageing process.

FIND OUT MORE BRAIN AND NERVOUS SYSTEM   HORMONES AND ENDOCRINE SYSTEM   HUMAN BODY   MUSCLES AND MOVEMENT   REPRODUCTION   SKELETON

GULF STATES

SAUDI ARABIA, Yemen, Oman, Kuwait, United Arab Emirates, Qatar, and Bahrain – make up the Arabian Peninsula. Six of these countries – all except Yemen – have coastlines on the Gulf and are often called the Gulf States. As a result of the rich oil deposits in the region – about half the world's total – many of these countries are wealthy, and the region is politically very important. In the past 50 years, there has been great industrial and social change in what was an underdeveloped region. Even so, most of the land is uninhabited.

Physical features

Nearly all of the Arabian Peninsula is dry desert, sandy or rocky, with some rugged, bare mountains near the coast. There are small fertile areas along the coasts, in some mountain regions, and at oases. Most of the fresh water for cities and industry comes from large desalination plants that remove salt from and purify sea water from the Gulf.

Red Sea
The warm, salty waters of the narrow Red Sea, 2,000 km (1,243 miles) long, separate Africa from Asia. The Red Sea is connected to the Mediterranean Sea by the Suez Canal, which was built in 1869 to provide a route for ships between Europe and eastern Asia.

Yemeni Mountains
These rugged mountains in the west of Yemen reach a height of 3,760 m (12,336 ft). The western slopes are well watered by rain blowing in from the Red Sea and are extensively cultivated by terracing. The climate is ideal for growing coffee, grapes, and cotton.

Najd Desert
The Najd is a vast area of stony desert plateau at the heart of Saudi Arabia. Some Najdi people still live here, leading a semi-nomadic existence tending camels and sheep, although many are moving into towns. Saudi Arabia's largest desert is the uninhabited Rub' al Khali, in the south, known as the "Empty Quarter".

96°C
(36°F)
63°C
(17°F)

118 mm (4.5 in)

Regional climate
Most of the region is very dry and hot all year, although winter temperatures in northern Saudi Arabia and Kuwait may drop below freezing. Only southwest Saudi Arabia and north Yemen receive rain. Some desert areas have no rain for years at a time.

Islam

For almost 1,500 years, Islam has been the dominant religion in the Gulf States. Muslims, the followers of Islam, believe in one god, Allah, and the prophet Muhammad, who was born in the Saudi Arabian town of Mecca. In many countries, life is interrupted five times a day while people pray.

Worshippers outside the mosque, Dubai

Saudi Arabia

The largest and most important country in the Arabian Peninsula, Saudi Arabia is 95 per cent hot, dry, and inhospitable desert. The most populated areas lie along the Gulf and Red Sea coasts. Founded in 1922 by Ibn Saud, Saudi Arabia has grown wealthy as a result of its vast oil reserves, discovered in 1938. It has major refining and petrochemical industries and spends freely on farming, education, and agriculture.

Riyadh

Saudi Arabia's capital since 1932, Riyadh is a modern city of around two million people. Lying among oases of orchards and palm groves, it is the centre of Saudi Arabia's commerce and government. Buildings range from smart, modern skyscrapers, erected since 1950, to poor shacks.

Saudi-Cairo Bank

People

Most Saudi people are Muslim Arabs. They take their religion seriously and interpret the Qur'an, the Islamic holy book, strictly. Women must wear veils and may not drive cars. However, about 33 per cent of schoolchildren are girls, and women may take certain jobs, such as nursing and teaching.

Mecca (Makkah)

Every year, two million Muslims visit the Ka'ba shrine in the Great Mosque at Mecca, birthplace of Muhammad and Islamic holy city. All Muslims should make a pilgrimage, or *hajj*, to Mecca at least once in their lives.

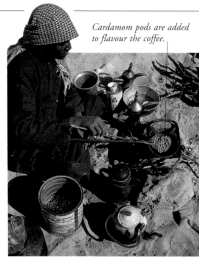

Cardamom pods are added to flavour the coffee.

Bedouin

Nomadic Bedouin roam the vast desert, grazing their camels, sheep, and goats in oases. They live in portable tents, but the government is trying to persuade them to give up their wandering life to settle in cities.

Lentils   Dates

Farming

Massive irrigation projects using desalinated sea water to irrigate vast, circular fields now make it possible for Saudi farmers to cultivate wheat, fruit, and vegetables. Farming employs one-eighth of the work-force.

Tomato

SAUDI ARABIA FACTS

CAPITAL CITY	Riyadh
AREA	2,149,690 sq km (829,995 sq miles)
POPULATION	21,600,000
DENSITY	10 per sq km (26 per sq mile)
MAIN LANGUAGE	Arabic
MAJOR RELIGION	Muslim
CURRENCY	Saudi riyal
LIFE EXPECTANCY	71 years
PEOPLE PER DOCTOR	588
GOVERNMENT	Absolute monarchy
ADULT LITERACY	77%

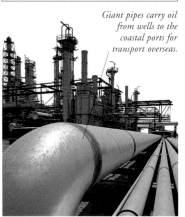

Giant pipes carry oil from wells to the coastal ports for transport overseas.

Oilfields

Saudi Arabia has the world's biggest oil and gas reserves – a quarter of the world's total – and is the world's leading oil exporter. Income from oil has improved living standards.

Yemen

Formerly two separate countries, Yemen was united in 1990. The north is mountainous, with a narrow, fertile coastal strip on the Red Sea coast, where cotton and grapes are grown. The arid Rub' al Khali desert, or "Empty Quarter" covers the northeast. Yemen's main source of income is oil, some of which is refined in the port of Aden.

Traditional coffee pot

Coffee

Yemen produces fine coffee beans, and coffee drinking is thought to have originated here. Mocha coffee is named after the port of Al-Makha from where it was exported. Yemenis chew *qat*, shoots of a narcotic shrub, with coffee.

YEMEN FACTS

CAPITAL CITY	Sana
AREA	527,970 sq km (203,849 sq miles)
POPULATION	18,100,000
MAIN LANGUAGE	Arabic
MAJOR RELIGION	Muslim
CURRENCY	Yemeni riyal

Sana

Yemen's modern capital, Sana, sits in the centre of the country, 2,380 m (7,808 ft) above sea-level. With a population of about half a million, it is a modern commercial and industrial centre with historic buildings, markets (*souks*), and ornately decorated mosques.

Oman

Ruled by a sultan, the Sultanate of Oman is mostly desert, with a narrow fertile strip along the Gulf of Oman in the north, where most of the people live. Oil has brought the country great prosperity. About 75 per cent of the people belong to the Islamic Ibadi sect, which adopts a liberal attitude towards women. Pakistani Baluchis make up one-quarter of Omanis.

OMAN FACTS

CAPITAL CITY	Muscat
AREA	212,460 sq km (82,030 sq miles)
POPULATION	2,500,000
MAIN LANGUAGES	Arabic, Baluchi
MAJOR RELIGIONS	Muslim, Hindu
CURRENCY	Omani rial

Sardines

Anchovy

Fishing

Omani fishermen catch 118,000 tonnes of fish a year in the rich waters of the Arabian Sea and Gulf of Oman. The main catches are anchovies, cod, cuttlefish, sardines, and tuna. The country exports dried fish and fish meal.

City of the sands

Archaeologists have discovered the remains of a city, believed to have been built in about 3000 BC, buried beneath the sands of southern Oman. They think it may be the remains of the legendary lost Arabian city of Ubar.

Kuwait

Oil has transformed Kuwait, a tiny desert country at the northern end of the Gulf, into one of the world's most prosperous nations. Iraq's invasion of Kuwait, in 1990, was quelled by a United Nations force after a brief war. Since its liberation, Kuwait has built a wall to separate its territory from Iraq.

Oil
Kuwait has about ten per cent of the world's total oil reserves. The oil industry, which attracts large overseas investment, accounts for more than 80 per cent of the country's export earnings. Kuwait also has reserves of natural gas.

Kuwait City
The country of Kuwait is named after its capital city, which was founded in the 18th century. Situated on the shores of a natural harbour, Kuwait City is modern, built on a grid pattern with many attractive houses. The country's affluence is reflected in its glittering skyscrapers.

KUWAIT FACTS

CAPITAL CITY	Kuwait City
AREA	17,820 sq km (6,880 sq miles)
POPULATION	2,000,000
MAIN LANGUAGES	Arabic, English
MAJOR RELIGION	Muslim
CURRENCY	Kuwaiti dinar

Free education
The revenue from the oil industry enables the Kuwaiti government to provide its children, both male and female, with free education, from nursery level to university. The Kuwaiti people have some of the world's highest salaries, pay no income tax, and receive free health care and social services.

United Arab Emirates

The United Arab Emirates (UAE) is a federation of seven small states: Abu Dhabi, Ajman, Dubai, Fujairah, Ras al Khaimah, Sharjah, and Umm al Quaiwan. Each ruled by its own independent emir, or sheik, they unite for international matters and to sell the oil that has made them rich.

Fishing
All the states bordering the Gulf have busy fishing fleets. In high summer they also send divers down to collect pearls from the pearl oysters. This industry has flourished for many hundreds of years.

Pearl develops from a grain of sand inside the shell.

UNITED ARAB EMIRATES FACTS

CAPITAL CITY	Abu Dhabi
AREA	83,600 sq km (32,278 sq miles)
POPULATION	2,400,000
MAIN LANGUAGES	Arabic, Farsi
MAJOR RELIGION	Muslim
CURRENCY	UAE dirham

Mina' Jabal 'Ali port
The UAE is one of the world's leading exporters of natural gas and oil, both of which leave the country via Mina' Jabal 'Ali port, the world's largest artificial harbour. Since less than three per cent of the UAE land can be cultivated, the port is also used to import food products.

Tourism
Hot sun, sandy beaches, and duty-free shopping make the UAE an attractive winter holiday resort for visitors from Europe and Japan (summer is too hot for tourism). The federation is gradually building up its tourism. Other attractions include trips into the desert, luxury hotels, and traditional markets.

Qatar

A small peninsula in the Persian Gulf, Qatar, like other Gulf States, depends on natural gas and oil for its wealth. Although most of the country is desert, Qatar grows most of its own food by tapping reserves of underground water. Qatari women are free to drive cars and not to wear veils.

QATAR FACTS

CAPITAL CITY	Doha
AREA	11,000 sq km (4,415 sq miles)
POPULATION	699,000
MAIN LANGUAGES	Arabic, Farsi
MAJOR RELIGION	Muslim
CURRENCY	Qatar riyal

Foreign workers
Only 20 per cent of the people are native-born Bedouin Qataris. The country has had to import workers from India, Asia, Iran, and other Arab countries to cope with the work produced by the oil industry. Almost 90 per cent of the population live in the capital, Doha.

Bahrain

Three inhabited islands and 30 smaller ones make up the small country of Bahrain. The oil reserves that made it rich are now running low, but the country has plenty of natural gas. Bahrain has a long history, and 4,000 years ago was a transit port for trade with India.

BAHRAIN FACTS

CAPITAL CITY	Manama
AREA	680 sq km (263 sq miles)
POPULATION	617,000
MAIN LANGUAGES	Arabic, English
MAJOR RELIGIONS	Muslim, Christian
CURRENCY	Bahrain dinar

Women's role
Bahrain is the most liberal of the Gulf States. Although the people are Muslim, women are not obliged to wear the veil. They have equal access to education and many follow careers.

FIND OUT MORE | ASIA, HISTORY OF | DESERTS | ENERGY | FARMING | FISHING INDUSTRY | ISLAM | ISLAMIC EMPIRE | MOSQUES | OIL | PORTS AND WATERWAYS

GUNS

FROM A BOOMING cannon to a pocket pistol, all firearms (guns) work on the same principle: a controlled explosion in one part of the gun propels a shell or bullet out of a tube or barrel. Firearms appeared in Europe in the early 14th century; although they were feeble at first, in time they changed warfare forever. Armour could not stop bullets, nor castle walls withstand cannon balls. Without guns, no nation could resist invasion for long; armed with them, European peoples colonized most of the world.

15th-century illustration of a battlefield shows cannons in action.

Origins of guns
The first guns were cannons, known to have been in use before 1326, when drawings of them appeared in a book. At first smiths built the barrels from strips of iron. Safer, cast cannons came into use a century later, when bell-founders began to make them by filling a mould with liquid metal.

G

Small arms
Soldiers carry small arms for individual use. These compact, lightweight weapons may have a stock for bracing the gun against the shoulder, or they may be fired from the hand. Most fire bullets rapidly from preloaded magazines. Some are very powerful: a modern rifle can fire a bullet more than 1,800 m (2,000 yards).

.45-calibre bullet

Automatic Colt 1911 A1 pistol

Artillery
A gun is described in terms of calibre, which is the width of the hole through its barrel, or the weight of the shell it fires. The shells of artillery (heavy firearms) are big enough to destroy buildings. Artillery includes mortars, with a fairly short range, or longer-barrelled, long-range guns.

Howitzer in use

Muzzle — *Barrel*

Pistols
A pistol is easy to hide under clothing, and quick to fire. It has a short barrel and so cannot be aimed accurately at distant targets. It is most useful in close fighting or for self-defence.

Trigger

Magazine rounds

Spring pushes bullets up.

Muzzle (front)

Shield protects gun crews

Breech (back), where ammunition is loaded.

Mountain howitzer

Plastic hand guard

Submachine gun

30-round magazine stored here.

Pistol grip

Automatic weapons
Set to automatic, many small arms will continue to fire as long as the soldier holds back the trigger.

Hiram Maxim
American-born inventor Hiram Maxim (1840–1916) developed the first practical automatic machine gun in 1884. Maxim guns fired so quickly that by World War I (1914–1918) soldiers no longer fought on horseback, but tried to hide from the bullets in trenches.

Howitzers
A howitzer is a field gun, which may be towed or self-propelled to the battlefield. Its barrel and aim is midway between that of a mortar and a gun. Shells can be fired at a high angle, so that they fly above hills or other defences before reaching enemy targets.

Sniper's rifle *Barrel* *Stock*

Rifles
Rifling (spiral grooves) inside the barrel of a gun makes the bullet spin in flight, improving accuracy. Self-loading rifles use the energy from firing a bullet to expel the cartridge case, and load the next shot.

10-round magazine *Rifles are fired from the shoulder.*

Ammunition
The missile that a gun fires, the propellant (explosive charge), and the means of firing it, are known together as ammunition. The first guns fired round stones, propelling them from the barrel with loose gunpowder, lit with a hot wire. From the mid-19th century on, following the introduction of rifled gun barrels, shells were long and pointed in shape. Today, in all but the biggest guns, a metal cartridge holds the missile, propellent, and means of firing together.

Machine gun belt, World War I

250 rounds on the belt

Armour-piercing shell, fired by anti-tank gun.

Bullet, for .44 revolver

Gun control
A few civilians need to own guns for security, target shooting, pest control, and other uses. However, guns are dangerous, and most countries control ownership. Many people believe these controls should be stricter to stop criminals getting hold of and using guns, and to reduce the number of shooting accidents.

Gun safety poster, USA

Used by 5.56-mm (.22-in) calibre gun

Rifle cartridge

Machine gun bullet

FIND OUT MORE ARMS AND ARMOUR WARFARE WEAPONS WORLD WAR I

GUPTA EMPIRE

AT THE BEGINNING of the fourth century, India was made up of a number of separate kingdoms. In 320, Chandragupta I, ruler of Magadha, who was named after the warlike Mauryan ruler, took over neighbouring kingdoms to found the Gupta Empire. Under his successors, the empire expanded to include much of India, and became the greatest Asian country of the time, lasting about 150 years. It was a golden age of Indian painting, architecture, sculpture, and literature.

Magadha

Gupta Empire

How the empire was run

The Guptas ran their empire as a group of small regions, or sub-kingdoms. Each sub-kingdom had its own ruler, but all were under the control of the emperor in Magadha. The first two Gupta emperors expanded the empire, while the later emperors had the task of holding the territory together.

Gupta coins had symbols, such as horses, on them instead of portraits.

Chandragupta I
In his short reign, the fierce Chandragupta I (320–330) expanded his territories by conquest, and by his marriage to Princess Kumara Devi of the Lichchavi tribe.

Samudragupta
Chandragupta I's son (r.330–376) extended the empire into Bengal, central India, and the valleys of the upper Yamuna and Ganges rivers.

Chandragupta II
Named after his grand-father, the third Gupta had a long and peaceful reign (376–415), during which Indian art and literature began to flourish.

Art and literature

During the Gupta period, Indian artists created some of their finest works. Magnificent palaces and temples contained the highest quality sculpture and paintings. Classical forms of music and dance, created under the Guptas, are still practised today all over Asia.

Exteriors of the Buddhist cave-shrines at Ajanta, western India

Padmapani, the "lotus-bearer"

Bodhisattva

Musician with lyre

Sculpture

Lifelike sculptures adorned Gupta shrines and palaces. The most popular subjects were people who had made donations to the shrine, the Buddha and scenes from his life, and people known as Bodhisattvas (those who have reached the Buddhist goal of enlightenment and help others to do likewise). Many sculptures, such as the seated musician, were made of terracotta.

The golden age of learning

Under the Guptas, universities expanded and became famous for philosophy, medicine, and logic. The Sanskrit language was also developed, and was used for major epic stories. One of the finest writers of the period was Kalidasa, who lived during the reigns of Chandragupta II and Kumaragupta. His works include comedies, poems, and heroic plays which are still performed.

Sanskrit inscription

Wall paintings

There are more than 30 Buddhist shrines and monasteries in the Ajanta hills. The walls of many of these were decorated with colourful frescoes, or wall paintings. This was a fashion that continued for hundreds of years. The paintings show scenes from the life of the Buddha, and other devotional subjects.

The figures are dressed in Gupta-period costumes.

A procession of elephants

Wall paintings are a good source of information about life in the empire.

Painting from the Jataka stories, Cave 17, Ajanta

Fa-Hsien

In 399, Fa-Hsien, a Chinese Buddhist, went to India to study the sacred writings of Buddhism. In the 10 years he was there, he wrote about life under the Gupta emperors. His writings form one of the most important sources for the history of this period.

Cave-shrines

Many of the Buddhist cave-shrines in western India were cut out of the cliffs – a task which must have taken years of labour with the simple tools the Guptas used. The cave-shrines are dark but beautifully decorated with sculptures and paintings. The Buddha in this example is making the gesture known as *abhaya mudra*, or "have no fear".

Timeline

320 Chandragupta I founds the Gupta Empire.

330–376 Samudragupta expands the empire from the Indus River to the Bay of Bengal, and up into the northern mountains.

Bodhisattva

376–415 Chandragupta II makes the empire secure, and encourages trade.

415–450 Kalidasa composes most of his poetry in the reign of Kumaragupta (415–455).

c.450 Empire begins to collapse under pressure from invading Huns.

554 The Gupta dynasty ends when the last emperor dies.

Silver Gupta horseman

 FIND OUT MORE   BUDDHISM   HINDUISM   INDIA, HISTORY OF   MAURYAN EMPIRE   SHRINES

GYMNASTICS

THERE ARE TWO MAIN BRANCHES of gymnastics – artistic and rhythmic. In artistic gymnastics, the gymnasts perform on fixed apparatus, such as bars and beams. In rhythmic gymnastics, they perform routines with apparatus such as hoops and balls. Other gymnastic sports include sports acrobatics and trampolining. In major artistic gymnastic competitions, the apparatus is set out on a large platform, or podium, and several events take place together. The competitors are awarded marks out of 10 by a panel of judges.

Men

There are six events in men's competitions. They are the floor, pommel horse, vault, rings, parallel bars, and high bar. Boys and men usually wear a singlet with shorts or white trousers. Men's gymnastics calls for strength as well as balance and dynamic movement.

Pommel horse
The pommel horse needs arm and shoulder strength. The gymnast moves back and forth along the horse, swinging his legs up and over, supporting himself on his hands only.

Parallel bars
The bars are a good all-round test for men. There is a wide choice of movements that a gymnast can perform, including swings and balances, and support and strength moves.

The ribbon is attached to a wand.

Ribon

Ball

Clubs

Rope

Hoops

The ribbon is made of silk.

Rhythmic gymnastics
Performed only by women and girls, rhythmic gymnastics consists of five individual exercises – ribbon, clubs, ball, hoop, and rope. There are also group exercises performed by a team, usually with two different pieces of apparatus.

Holding a position to show strength

Floor
Men's floor exercises last 50 to 70 seconds and feature balances as well as somersaults and handsprings. Gymnasts must not step off the square mat.

Rings
More strength is needed on the rings than on any other apparatus. Gymnasts must hold some positions for two seconds and must not swing on the ropes.

Vault
This is the shortest event. Boys and men perform only one vault. Until they are about 13, boys vault across the horse, but after that they vault along its length.

High bar
High bar routines contain continuous swinging moves. The gymnast circles around and around, with turns, twists, and changes of direction and grip.

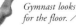
Springing into a flic flac

Women vault across the width of the horse.

Women vault across the width of the horse.

Vault
Women and girls have two vaults in a competition, the better of the two marks counting. Different turns and somersaults are used, especially as the gymnast thrusts off the horse before landing neatly.

Women

There are four women's events – the floor, beam, asymmetric (uneven) bars, and vault. In competitions there is also an overall championship. Women and girls usually wear one-piece leotards with short or long sleeves. Women's exercises call for balance and agility, and floor exercises include elements of dance.

Beam
The beam is 5 m (16.4 ft) long and only 10 cm (4 in) wide. Gymnasts must perform deliberate movements and graceful balances. The leading gymnasts can perform somersaults and backflips.

One leg is brought over first.

Gymnast looks for the floor.

Floor
The women's floor routine is performed to music. Women and girls have from 60 to 90 seconds. Gymnasts are expected to include dance steps in their routine, as well as spectacular running somersaults.

Asymmetric bars
This is possibly the most difficult of the women's appparatus. The gymnast must make full use of two bars 2.3 m (7.5 ft) and 1.5 m (5 ft) high, swinging and changing grip. The routine must have a flowing rhythm with no stops or hesitations.

Nadia Comaneci
Romanian gymnast Nadia Comaneci (b.1962) became the first person to score a maximum 10 points in Olympic competition, at the age of 14. She scored seven 10s in the 1976 Montreal Olympics, winning the overall gold medal as well as separate golds for the bars and beam.

Trampolining
This is an excellent exercise routine for practising moves such as twists and somersaults, and it is also a sport in itself. There are solo competitions and synchronized pairs. Judges award marks for difficulty and how well a routine is performed.

Sports acrobatics
This type of gymnastics comprises tumbling, pairs, and group events. Tumbling is like the floor exercises, but performed on a straight, sprung track. The routines in pairs (men, women, or mixed), the trio (women), and fours (men) are like those of circus acrobats.

A mixed pair balance

FIND OUT MORE   OLYMPIC GAMES   ROMANIA, UKRAINE, AND MOLDAVIA   SPORT

Gymnastics
Sports acrobatics

Clasps hands firmly

Leans back

Keeps her body tensed

The base rests much of his body on the floor.

Leg positions can be varied.

The top holds her body in a straight line.

The top keeps her body still.

The top lifts and straddles her legs.

The base carries his partner's weight on his legs.

Counterbalance: gymnasts use their weight against each other.

Shoulder balance: a simple, stable position.

Simple balance: the base supports the top.

Stag balance: elegance contrasts with strength.

Straddle lever balance: an advanced position.

Rhythmic sequences

Gymnast performs to music.

Moves elegantly throughout the sequence.

Full side bend

The gymnast keeps her arm straight.

Graceful arm position

1 Swings hoop around the waist.

2 Lets a side of the hoop drop.

3 Jumps through the hoop.

4 Carries hoop to the side.

1 Carries the ball to one side.

2 Circles the ball out behind.

3 Spirals to the other side.

4 Rises into an arabesque.

Artistic, floor

This move is known as a Y-balance.

Legs held together and straight

Stretching his arms upwards helps the gymnast stand.

Keeps toes pointed

Gymnast presses legs together.

Gymnast tucks his body down into a roll.

Moves round in quarter turns

Gymnasts generally prefer to work barefoot.

The gymnast moves smoothly into each stage of the exercise.

Head tucked in

Spread fingers

1 Gymnast holds balance for two seconds.

2 Springs into a dive.

3 Upwards and forwards into a dive roll.

4 Lands on hands and rolls.

5 Rolls onto feet and comes up to stand.

6 Kicks up to a handstand, then turns round by moving his hands.

Artistic, beam

The beam, used only in women's gymnastics, is very difficult. For safety's sake, a gymnast must progress from floor skills, to a low beam, then a practise beam.

The gymnast learns to walk, turn, and sit on a beam first.

Head up, back straight

Looking ahead

In competition, judges deduct points for wobbly or faulty landings.

The gymnast tries to jump as high as possible.

Toes pointed

She bends her knees as she lands.

1 Gymnast mounts the side or end of the beam.

2 Performs low move, known as a V-sit.

3 The gymnast begins a W-jump.

4 With one step, takes off from both feet.

5 She points one leg forward and tucks the other behind.

6 Prepares to land.

7 She keeps a steady balance.

HEALTH AND FITNESS

IF A MACHINE is treated with care and given proper maintenance, it is more likely to function efficiently. Similarly, the human body is most likely to function to the best of its ability if it is kept fit and healthy. Health may be defined as the state of being well in body and mind. Fitness is an indication of how efficiently the body's muscles, heart, and lungs are working. If people are fit, they can deal with the requirements put upon their bodies by everyday activities, such as walking and lifting, but also with sudden demands, such as sprinting for a bus. Mental health – the mind's fitness – is also important for well-being.

What is health?

When someone is in good health it means their body is working to its full potential and is not impeded by physical or mental diseases. People's health may suffer as they become older, if they eat a poor diet, if they are poor, if they are exposed to pollution, or work in a harmful environment.

Outdoor play contributes to the healthy development of children.

Maintaining health

Many people in developed countries are overweight, take little exercise, and eat too much fatty food. This makes them unfit, and often unhealthy. Following a balanced diet with plenty of fresh fruit and vegetables and not too much fat, combined with regular exercise, aid better health.

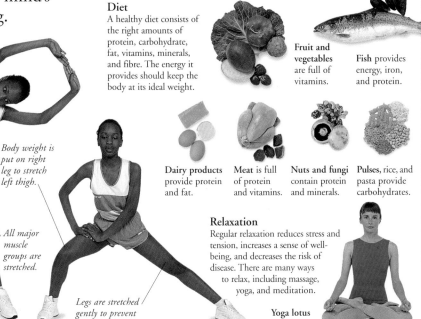

Diet
A healthy diet consists of the right amounts of protein, carbohydrate, fat, vitamins, minerals, and fibre. The energy it provides should keep the body at its ideal weight.

Fruit and vegetables are full of vitamins.

Fish provides energy, iron, and protein.

Dairy products provide protein and fat.

Meat is full of protein and vitamins.

Nuts and fungi contain protein and minerals.

Pulses, rice, and pasta provide carbohydrates.

Exercise
The human body requires exercise to improve fitness. Exercise makes the heart and lungs work more efficiently, and strengthens muscles and bones. This helps keep the body flexible.

Stretching side lateral muscles and abdomen

Clothing is loose and comfortable.

Body weight is put on right leg to stretch left thigh.

All major muscle groups are stretched.

Gentle stretching is a good way to start an exercise programme

Training shoes should be used.

Legs are stretched gently to prevent any strain.

Relaxation
Regular relaxation reduces stress and tension, increases a sense of well-being, and decreases the risk of disease. There are many ways to relax, including massage, yoga, and meditation.

Yoga lotus position

Mental health

Mental health is the fitness of the mind. Problems may be caused by heredity or emotional problems caused by relationships or lifestyle. Keeping fit, discussing problems, and seeking professional help can all improve a person's mental health. Some people are affected by mental illnesses that have been caused by brain disorders.

Doctors who look after mental health are called psychiatrists.

Public health

Public health is concerned with the effect environment has upon a population's health, and how the health of the community can be improved. Workers in this field are interested in, for example, good housing, effective sanitation, reducing air pollution, and the immunization of children and adults against infectious diseases.

Sanitation
Sanitation is the provision of clean drinking water, enclosed sewers, and drains. It stops food and water being contaminated by potentially fatal pathogens (germs) from human waste and helps stop the spread of disease.

Poor sanitation in slums in 19th-century England

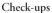
Syringe

Immunization
Immunization protects people from disease. It involves injecting them with small amounts of pathogens of a certain disease. This stimulates the body to produce antibodies that fight the disease, producing protection.

Check-ups

A doctor carries out a check-up, or physical examination, to make sure that a person is healthy, and to look out for anything that may be wrong. During a check-up, the doctor will ask the patient how he or she feels, look at and feel the patient's body, use a stethoscope to listen to breathing and the heart, and measure blood pressure.

Doctor examines girl's throat

| FIND OUT MORE | DISEASES | DRUGS | FOOD | HUMAN BODY | MEDICINE | SOCIETIES, HUMAN | SPORT |

HEART AND CIRCULATORY SYSTEM

THE HEART IS A FIST-SIZED muscular pump that beats non-stop, 24 hours a day, sending blood around the body along a massive network of tubes called blood vessels. Together, they make up the circulatory system. The larger blood vessels divide repeatedly to form smaller vessels, which travel to every cell in the body, supplying them with oxygen from the lungs and nutrients from digested food, and carrying away waste. Blood helps defend the body against infection and also distributes heat around the body, helping to maintain its temperature.

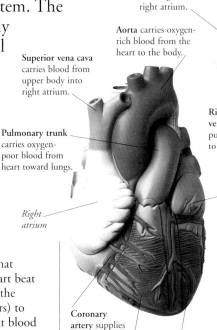

Right atrium receives oxygen-poor blood from body.

Tricuspid valve prevents blood flowing backward from right ventricle into right atrium.

Aorta carries oxygen-rich blood from the heart to the body.

Superior vena cava carries blood from upper body into right atrium.

Pulmonary trunk carries oxygen-poor blood from heart toward lungs.

Right atrium

Left atrium receives oxygen-rich blood from lungs.

Semilunar valve stops blood flowing back into right ventricle.

Left ventricle pumps blood to body.

Right ventricle pumps blood to lungs.

Left atrium

Septum is wall that separates ventricles.

Coronary artery supplies heart with blood.

Right ventricle

Left ventricle

How the heart beats

The wall of the heart is made of cardiac muscle that contracts automatically. The two halves of the heart beat together to pump blood around the body. Inside the heart, blood passes from the atria (upper chambers) to the ventricles (lower chambers). Valves ensure that blood cannot flow backwards through the heart. Each heartbeat is not a single contraction, but consists of three stages.

Heart

The heart consists of two muscular pumps, left and right, which lie side by side. Each pump is divided into a smaller upper chamber, or atrium, and a lower chamber, or ventricle. The left ventricle has a thicker wall because it has to pump blood around the body; the thinner-walled right ventricle pumps blood to the lungs.

Right atrium

Left atrium

Tricuspid valve

Bicuspid valve

Aorta

Pulmonary artery

Right ventricle

Left ventricle

1 During the first stage (diastole) both the atria and the ventricles are relaxed. Blood flows into and fills both atria. The semilunar valves at the exit points of the ventricles are closed.

2 During the second stage (atrial systole) the tricuspid and bicuspid valves between the atria and the ventricles open. Both atria contract and squeeze blood into the ventricles below them.

3 During the third stage (ventricular systole) the ventricles contract to push blood out of the heart. The tricuspid and bicuspid valves close, while the semilunar valves open.

Monitoring heart rate during exercise.

Heart rate
The heart normally beats about 70 times per minute. This is your heart rate. It changes according to the oxygen demands of the body. If you exercise, heart rate increases to pump more oxygen-carrying blood to your muscles.

William Harvey
English doctor William Harvey (1578–1657) was the first person to show that blood circulated around the body. Before Harvey, it was thought that blood ebbed and flowed along blood vessels rather like the tide coming in and going out. Harvey concluded that blood travelled in one direction only, and that it was pumped by the heart.

Blood

Blood is a liquid transport system that travels to every cell in the body. It supplies body cells with oxygen and nutrients, and carries away waste products. Blood consists of billions of blood cells floating in a yellowish liquid called plasma. There are three types of blood cells: red blood cells, white blood cells, and platelets. Red blood cells make up 99 per cent of all blood cells. A soft tissue inside bones called red marrow produces blood cells.

Platelets
Platelets are cell fragments that help stop blood leaking from injured blood vessels. If a blood vessel is damaged, platelets gather at the wound and stick to each other to form a plug.

White blood cells
White blood cells defend the body against infection. There are three main types. Granulocytes and monocytes engulf invading germs; lymphocytes release chemicals that destroy germs.

Red blood cells
Red blood cells are packed with a red substance called haemoglobin. Haemoglobin picks up oxygen in the lungs and releases it as blood passes through other parts of the body.

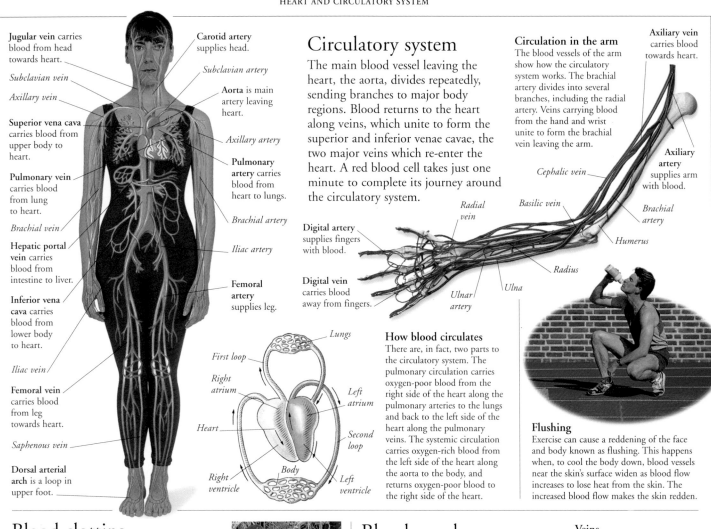

Jugular vein carries blood from head towards heart.

Subclavian vein

Axillary vein

Superior vena cava carries blood from upper body to heart.

Pulmonary vein carries blood from lung to heart.

Brachial vein

Hepatic portal vein carries blood from intestine to liver.

Inferior vena cava carries blood from lower body to heart.

Iliac vein

Femoral vein carries blood from leg towards heart.

Saphenous vein

Dorsal arterial arch is a loop in upper foot.

Carotid artery supplies head.

Subclavian artery

Aorta is main artery leaving heart.

Axillary artery

Pulmonary artery carries blood from heart to lungs.

Brachial artery

Iliac artery

Femoral artery supplies leg.

Circulatory system

The main blood vessel leaving the heart, the aorta, divides repeatedly, sending branches to major body regions. Blood returns to the heart along veins, which unite to form the superior and inferior venae cavae, the two major veins which re-enter the heart. A red blood cell takes just one minute to complete its journey around the circulatory system.

Digital artery supplies fingers with blood.

Digital vein carries blood away from fingers.

Radial vein

Ulnar artery

Ulna

Radius

Circulation in the arm

The blood vessels of the arm show how the circulatory system works. The brachial artery divides into several branches, including the radial artery. Veins carrying blood from the hand and wrist unite to form the brachial vein leaving the arm.

Axiliary vein carries blood towards heart.

Cephalic vein

Basilic vein

Axiliary artery supplies arm with blood.

Brachial artery

Humerus

Lungs

First loop

Right atrium

Heart

Right ventricle

Body

Left atrium

Second loop

Left ventricle

How blood circulates

There are, in fact, two parts to the circulatory system. The pulmonary circulation carries oxygen-poor blood from the right side of the heart along the pulmonary arteries to the lungs and back to the left side of the heart along the pulmonary veins. The systemic circulation carries oxygen-rich blood from the left side of the heart along the aorta to the body, and returns oxygen-poor blood to the right side of the heart.

Flushing

Exercise can cause a reddening of the face and body known as flushing. This happens when, to cool the body down, blood vessels near the skin's surface widen as blood flow increases to lose heat from the skin. The increased blood flow makes the skin redden.

Blood clotting

When a blood vessel is damaged, clotting reduces the loss of blood. Platelets accumulate at the wound and stick together to form a plug. Red blood cells are trapped in threads of fibrin to form a clot. White blood cells prevent infection beneath a hard outer scab.

Skin

Fibrin thread

White blood cells

Red blood cells

Blood vessel

Platelet

Scab

Platelet

Fibrin

Chemicals in the blood and damaged cells trigger the production of the protein fibrin. This forms strands which trap red blood cells into a clot. A hard crust, called a scab, forms over the clot to protect the wound.

Blood vessels

There are three types of blood vessels: arteries, veins, and capillaries. Arteries divide into smaller vessels called arterioles, which themselves divide into a network of capillaries. Blood then passes to venules and veins.

Arteries

Arteries carry blood away from the heart. They have thick, muscular walls that can withstand the high pressure produced when the heart beats. Arteries usually carry blood that is rich in oxygen.

Veins

Veins carry blood towards the heart. They have thin walls because pressure inside them is low. They contain valves to prevent blood flowing backwards.

Arteriole

Artery

Capillary network

Venule

Valve

Vein

Thin wall of vein

Thick wall of artery

Capillaries

Capillaries are the tiny blood vessels that carry blood between arterioles and venules. They supply individual cells with food and oxygen and remove wastes.

Karl Landsteiner

Austrian/American Karl Landsteiner (1868–1943) discovered the existence of blood groups, and made safe blood transfusion a reality. In 1900, Landsteiner showed that red blood cells may clump together when blood from different people is mixed. He worked out the ABO blood group system, and was awarded a Nobel Prize.

Blood groups

People belong to different blood groups, depending on the antigens (chemicals) in their red blood cells. The ABO blood group system has two antigens, A and B. It has four blood groups: A (carries A antigen); B (carries B antigen); AB (carries both antigens); and O (carries neither).

Regular blood donors are given a donor badge.

Blood compatibility

Blood transfusion is the donation of blood by one person to another. People who share the same blood groups can give or receive blood safely because their blood is compatible. In an emergency, however, people with type O blood can give blood to any other group.

FIND OUT MORE   CELLS   FIRST AID   HEALTH AND FITNESS   HORMONES AND ENDOCRINE SYSTEM   HUMAN BODY   IMMUNE AND LYMPHATIC SYSTEM   LUNGS AND BREATHING   MEDICINE   MUSCLES AND MOVEMENT

HEAT AND TEMPERATURE

H

IN GREEK MYTHOLOGY, Icarus flew too close to the Sun and plummeted to his death as the Sun's heat melted his waxen wings. Heat is a type of energy that can indeed melt wax, and many other substances. The temperature of a substance – how hot or cold it is – can be thought of as how much heat energy that substance contains. More precisely, temperature is a measure of the average energy possessed by the moving particles of matter inside the substance.

Column of mercury or alcohol

Metal indicator

Column moves along scale.

Digital readout

Mercury or alcohol well

Heat-sensitive probe

Liquid   Maximum-minimum   Digital

Thermometers

A device that measures temperature is called a thermometer. A liquid thermometer contains a column of mercury or alcohol that expands and contracts as the temperature changes, moving up and down a scale. A maximum and minimum thermometer records the highest and lowest temperatures over a certain period, using metal indicators that are moved by a liquid column. A digital thermometer contains a heat-sensitive electronic probe. The probe produces an electric current that varies with changes in temperature.

Thermal expansion

Heating a substance gives its particles more energy so that they move faster and farther. The particles take up more room and increase the volume of the substance. This is known as thermal expansion.

Ball passes through ring.

Flame heats ball.

Bunsen burner

Ring is moved away.

Hot ball is now too wide to pass through ring.

1 This cold metal ball passes easily through the hoop. The ball is a solid object, composed of millions of tightly packed, vibrating particles.

2 A hot flame heats the ball, giving its particles more heat energy.

3 The extra energy increases the size of the particles' vibrations, making them take up more space. The ball expands and will no longer pass through the ring.

Temperature scale

Just as the scale on a ruler shows length in centimetres or inches, a temperature scale shows temperature in units called degrees Celsius (C), degrees Fahrenheit (F), or kelvin (K). Most temperature scales are defined by two "fixed points". The Celsius scale uses the melting and boiling points of water as its fixed points.

Absolute zero

There is no upper limit to temperature, but there is a lower limit, called absolute zero (-273°C, -459°F, 0K), at which atoms and molecules are stationary. Scientists have managed to achieve temperatures within a millionth of a degree of absolute zero. The study of how matter behaves at very low temperatures is known as cryogenics.

Cryogenics scientist at work

100°C (212°F, 373K): water boils

58°C (136°F, 331K): highest recorded temperature on Earth

43.3°C (110.3°F, 316.3K): normal body temperature of a sparrow

37°C (98.4°F, 310K): normal human body temperature

28.1°C (82.6°F, 301.1K): normal body temperature of echidna (spiny anteater)

18°C (64°F, 291K): normal room temperature (water is in its liquid state)

0°C (32°F, 273K): freezing point of water

Celsius scale

Producing heat

Heat can be produced in a number of ways, including by friction, through chemical reactions, and using an electric current.

Drilling machine

Heat from friction

The American scientist Benjamin Thompson (1753–1814) discovered that friction produces heat. At his weapons factory in Germany, he noticed that when a drilling machine bored into a gun barrel, friction between the two objects made the gun barrel extremely hot.

Heat and chemical reactions

Athletes often use a device called a hot pack to treat a sprained limb. The pack contains powdered iron that reacts with oxygen from the air when the pack is shaken. The heat from the chemical reaction warms the joint and eases the pain.

Heat and electricity

An electric current always produces heat. When current flows through an electric toaster, for example, the heat produced raises the temperature of the wire element so that it glows red-hot and toasts bread.

Element

Refrigerator

A refrigerator is a machine that is used to chill food, drinks, and other items. A liquid called a refrigerant flows through pipes inside the refrigerator. The liquid absorbs heat from the refrigerator's contents and evaporates. The vapour is compressed and pumped into a tube on the outside of the refrigerator. As the vapour passes through the tube, it loses heat to the surrounding air and condenses back to a liquid.

Tube is called a condenser.

Refrigerant absorbs heat from inside refrigerator and loses it to air outside.

Insulated walls

Pump circulates refrigerant.

Rear view of refrigerator

Water molecules gain heat from the hot pan and vibrate faster.

Bubbles appear as the water molecules use heat from the flame to break free from each other and form steam.

Latent heat

When a liquid is at its boiling point, an input of heat energy will not raise the liquid's temperature any further. Instead, the extra energy enables particles in the liquid to break free from each other and form a gas. This energy is called latent heat. The energy is released again if the gas condenses into a liquid. Latent heat is also absorbed when a solid melts, and released when a liquid freezes.

Thermal motion

All matter is made up of moving particles. This movement is called thermal motion. The temperature of an object is a measure of its thermal motion. Heating the object makes its particles vibrate faster and raises its temperature.

Radiation

All objects give out energy in the form of infrared rays, which are similar to X-rays. A hot object, such as a light bulb, gives out a lot of infrared rays. These rays will heat up any object that absorbs them. Dull surfaces absorb infrared rays well, but shiny surfaces reflect them. Infrared rays are invisible, but you can feel their effect. The closer you put your hand to a light bulb, the warmer it feels, because the radiation is more intense.

The bulb emits visible light rays and invisible infrared rays.

30.2°C (86.36°F) 25.5°C (77.9°F) 22.5°C (72.5°F)

Thermometers measure heat radiated by lamp.

Propagator

Seeds sprout and grow more rapidly in warm conditions, so they are often planted in a tiny greenhouse called a propagator. Sunlight passes through the propagator's plastic cover and warms the seeds and soil, which radiate the heat back out again as infrared rays. The rays cannot pass through plastic, so the heat is trapped inside and the temperature rises.

Convection

The way heat travels as moving currents through a gas or a liquid is called convection. If a tank of water is heated from below, the warm water at the bottom will rise as it expands and becomes less dense. The cooler, denser water above sinks to take its place. Soon, this cooler water also warms and starts to rise, creating a circulation of water called a convection current.

Warmer, less dense water rises.

Cooler, more dense water sinks.

Tank is heated from below.

Dissolving potassium permanganate crystals show the movement of the water.

Heat conduction

When a substance is heated, its vibrating particles knock against neighbouring particles and pass on some of their thermal motion, spreading heat throughout the substance. This is called conduction. Heat always conducts from a warm substance to a cooler one. The warm air in a room can lose heat through a window. Heat conducts from the warm air to the window, and then to the cooler air outside.

Temperature outside is 18.3°C (65°F).

Temperature inside is 21.7°C (71°F).

Thermometer records temperature difference across window.

Heat conductors

Some materials – called conductors – conduct heat better than others. If you press wax on to the ends of metal and plastic spoons in hot water, the wax on the metal spoon melts first. This is because metal is a better conductor.

Heat conducts up the spoons.

Wax melts and slides down the handle.

Metal conducts faster than plastic.

Hot or cold?

A marble tile feels colder than a carpet at room temperature. Marble is a better conductor than carpet. Marble takes heat rapidly away from the body, making the marble tile feel much colder to the touch than the carpet.

Marble tile   Carpet

Heat insulators

Poor conductors of heat, such as plastics, wood, cork, and air, are known as insulators. Using such materials to reduce heat loss from an object is called insulation. When these two jars are filled with water at 80°C (176°F) and left for 15 minutes, the jar covered in bubble wrap retains the most heat. Bubble wrap (plastic filled with pockets of air) is a good

27°C (80.6°F)   42.4°C (108°F)

Bubble wrap

Uninsulated jar   Insulated jar

Airtight stopper

Hot or cold liquid

Vacuum between double walls of flask

Shiny walls reflect heat radiation.

Vacuum flask

A vacuum flask keeps drinks hot or cold by stopping the transfer of heat to or from the liquid. Conduction can only occur through matter, so the flask has two walls with a vacuum between them to prevent conduction. Shiny walls reflect heat radiation, while the flask is sealed with an airtight stopper made of a good insulator.

FIND OUT MORE   ELECTRICITY   ENERGY   FRICTION   GASES   LIQUIDS   MATTER   METALS   SOLIDS   X-RAYS AND THE ELECTROMAGNETIC SPECTRUM

HEDGEHOGS AND OTHER INSECTIVORES

THE ORDER INSECTIVORA, which means insect-eating, contains more than 370 species, including hedgehogs, moles, shrews, and tenrecs. Most of these mammals, especially the shrews, are highly active and have to eat almost constantly to sustain themselves. They have poor eyesight, but a good sense of smell. They rely on smell to find their prey of worms and snails as well as insects. Insectivores have sharp teeth for preying on invertebrates. The hedgehogs and some tenrecs are protected from predators by spines.

Hedgehogs

Like most insectivores, hedgehogs are nocturnal, solitary animals that associate only to mate. Each adult animal needs its own territory in order to find enough to eat. Not all hedgehogs are spiny, but the European and desert hedgehogs have a thick covering of spines on the top of the head and body to protect them against predators such as foxes.

Hedgehog spines

A European hedgehog has about 5,000 spines. These are hairs modified into sharp, stiff tubes. Hedgehogs are born with their first coat of pale spines flat under the skin, but these come through within a few hours. At two days old, the hedgehog's dark spines start to grow.

When threatened, a hedgehog raises its spines.

Each spine is controlled by muscles in the hedgehog's skin.

Spines normally lie flat over the hedgehog's body.

For extra protection, a hedgehog can roll into a prickly ball.

European hedgehogs build up a layer of fat during the summer to sustain them during the winter when they hibernate.

Young hedgehogs accompany their mother to find food.

The long snout bears many highly sensitive whiskers which the hedgehog uses to find its way around and also to locate food.

A female hedgehog usually has two litters of young each year.

Young hedgehogs stay with their mother until they are about seven weeks old.

Ordinary fur grows on the chest and belly.

Moles

Moles live underground in a system of tunnels that they dig through the soil. They are well adapted for this existence, having a compact body, short legs, tiny eyes, and no protruding ears. They are active day and night, looking for food such as worms, insect larvae, and beetles.

Fur lies in no particular direction, so that the mole can push backward or forward through its tunnels.

Molehills

Mounds of soil, often called molehills, are the result of a mole's tunnelling activities. The mole pushes loose soil to the surface up short vertical tunnels.

Strong claws for loosening the soil.

A nest under the mound

Mole feet

The front paws are broad with large claws, and do the digging. The hind feet are narrower with sharp claws, and are used to push soil to the surface.

Shrews

These small mammals have a long snout and short legs. They are highly active and need a constant supply of food to keep them alive. Shrews are extremely aggressive and will attack one another if they meet. Many predators avoid shrews because of a foul-smelling secretion that they can produce from scent glands.

Tenrecs

The 30 species of tenrec live only on the island of Madagascar. Some swim, some climb, and others live underground. Some have spines, others look more like shrews. They have many young. The common tenrec may have 34 in one litter.

Shrews eat up to 130 per cent of their body weight every day.

EUROPEAN HEDGEHOG

SCIENTIFIC NAME *Erinaceus europaeus*

ORDER Insectivora

FAMILY Erinaceidae

DISTRIBUTION Europe, east into Russia. Introduced to New Zealand

HABITAT Farmland, suburbs, woodland, and mountains

DIET Beetles, worms, caterpillars, other invertebrates, small mammals, and carrion

SIZE Length: 25 cm (10 in)

LIFESPAN 4–7 years

FIND OUT MORE   ANIMALS   ANIMAL BEHAVIOUR   HIBERNATION

HERONS, STORKS AND FLAMINGOS

HERONS AND THEIR relatives are distinctive birds, with long, slender legs and a large beak. Most of them eat fish and other water animals, and can wade out into the water to look for food without getting their feathers wet. Herons hunt by stealth, and several species have developed remarkable fishing techniques. Flamingos catch their food by straining it through fibrous plates in their beak. Although storks have long legs, most of them do not wade, but catch their food on land. Many of these birds are sociable animals, living and nesting in large flocks or colonies. This gives them some protection from predators.

Neck is hunched at rest and in flight.

Herons often rest with one leg raised.

Cattle egret
This small heron lives near cattle and other grazers, and snaps up the small animals that they disturb. In recent years, cattle egret have become one of the world's most widespread birds.

Bittern
Bitterns live in dense reedbeds where they are perfectly camouflaged. When threatened, they point their beak skyward and sway gently. This makes them look like the reeds moving in the wind.

Juvenile goliath heron

Adult goliath heron

Long, straight legs

Herons

There are about 60 species of heron. They live all over the world, except Antarctica and the far north. Most live close to water, and they often nest in groups. They usually build their nests out of sticks and reeds in a tree or bush.

Black heron fishing
The African black heron strides into the water and raises its wings like an umbrella. This casts a shadow on the surface, which probably helps the heron to see any fish swimming below.

Fishing

Many herons, including the goliath heron, catch fish by wading into the water and then keeping absolutely still with their necks hunched. When a fish swims near, the heron crouches down toward the surface, then suddenly stretches out its neck and stabs the fish with its beak. Other herons have developed different fishing techniques.

Green heron
This heron usually hunts at night when many small animals are active. It often perches, legs bent, on a low branch, ready to pounce on its prey.

Marabou stork

This stork has one of the largest wingspans of all birds.

Long legs and toes

Flamingo skull

Flamingos

Many of the five species of flamingo live in shallow, salty lakes where little else survives. They feed with their head upside down, using their uniquely shaped beak to filter tiny animals and plants from the water.

Storks

There are 19 species of stork. Some feed by wading into water, but others live in quite dry places. The giant African marabou stork is a scavenger. It feeds on already dead animals, in the same way as vultures, but it will also eat live prey, such as insects, fish, rats, and small birds.

Fishing with bait
The North American green heron throws small twigs or pellets into the water. It waits for fish to be attracted by this bait and catches them when they come within range.

Colonies
Flocks of flamingos can contain more than 2 million birds. They build mound-like nests with mud that they scrape up with their beaks.

Nests
White storks migrate long distances and return to the same place in Europe every year to breed. They are traditionally encouraged to nest on houses because they are supposed to bring luck.

GOLIATH HERON

SCIENTIFIC NAME	*Ardea goliath*
ORDER	Ciconiiformes
FAMILY	Ardeidae
DISTRIBUTION	Africa, Arabian peninsula, India
HABITAT	Coasts, lakes, rivers, marshy ground
DIET	Mainly fish
SIZE	Length: 150 cm (59 in)
LIFESPAN	About 25 years

FIND OUT MORE
BIRDS   BIRDS OF PREY   LAKE AND RIVER WILDLIFE   SHOREBIRDS

HIBERNATION

DURING WINTER, as temperatures drop and food becomes scarce, some animals hibernate to survive the harsh conditions. Hibernation is a resting state in which the animal's body temperature falls to just above that of its surroundings, and its metabolic rate (the rate at which it consumes energy) drops dramatically. The animal resumes its active lifestyle in the spring. Hibernation is triggered by shortening day length, a fall in temperature, or by the animal's internal biological clock. Some other animals rest, or remain dormant, to withstand adverse conditions.

Rodents
Rodents, such as dormice and woodchucks, form the largest group of hibernating mammals. Many smaller rodents living in the northern hemisphere hibernate in the winter months when the plant material and small animals they feed on are in short supply. Some construct nests in tree hollows or underground in which they curl up, to minimize heat loss, and go into a deep sleep. Many species wake periodically either to eat, drink, or urinate, to get rid of accumulated waste.

Hibernation
Rodents, bats, and insectivores are all mammals that hibernate. Their small size allows them to cool down and warm up quickly. Some animals eat more in early winter to build up fat stores to use while hibernating; others wake every few weeks to feed on food in their nest. A squirrel shows changes typical of a hibernating mammal; its metabolic rate drops to 1 per cent of normal, and its body temperature falls from 37°C (99°F) to 4°C (39°F). When it emerges its body weight will have fallen by 40 per cent.

Nest of straw and grass

Hibernating dormouse

Dormouse curled up in its nest

Natterer's bat

Bats
Many temperate species of bat hibernate when their insect food disappears. They often hibernate in large numbers and cluster together to conserve warmth. The site where bats hibernate is called a hibernaculum; it may be a cave, mine, tree hollow, or a deserted building.

Hummingbird in nest

Birds
Most birds migrate to avoid cold winters; a few such as the North American poorwill enter a state of torpor and hibernate. Many hummingbirds show a form of daily hibernation. At night, their body temperature falls, enabling them to survive cooler conditions without consuming much energy.

European badger
Badgers live in forests where they dig extensive burrows called setts. In winter, badgers rarely leave their sett. They curl up in nesting material and go into a dormant state, living off fat reserves accumulated in summer and autumn. Dormancy can last for seven months in Siberia.

Dormancy
Some large mammals, such as bears and badgers, that live in northern parts of North America and Europe, go into a resting state, called dormancy, during winter. Dormancy differs from hibernation; the animal's body temperature does not drop significantly, and it can wake up quickly if danger threatens. However, this small fall in body temperature, combined with a lack of activity, produces significant energy savings for the animal.

Bear feeds on berries to build up fat reserves.

Brown bear
The brown bear lives in Asia, North America, and Europe. In summer it builds up fat on which it lives in winter. In autumn, the bear excavates a den, lines it with vegetation, and goes into its winter "sleep". Its body temperature falls by 5°C (9°F), and its metabolic rate drops by 50 per cent. The bear emerges in spring weighing half what it did in the autumn.

Cabbage white butterfly pupa

Diapause
Diapause is the insects' equivalent of hibernation. Some insects enter diapause to survive adverse conditions, such as cold or lack of food. During diapause, growth and development are suspended, usually at the egg or pupa stage of the life cycle. For example, if the cabbage white butterfly lays her eggs in late summer, the pupal stage goes into diapause over winter, resuming development in spring.

Aestivation
Aestivation is a state of dormancy, shown by animals such as African lungfish, during hot, dry summers. Lungfish live in places that flood in the wet season and bake in the dry season. As river levels fall, the lungfish digs a burrow in the mud, ending in a chamber. The fish curls up in the chamber, secretes a protective mucus bag around itself, and remains there for up to six months until the rains come.

Lungfish emerging

African lungfish

FIND OUT MORE   ANIMAL BEHAVIOUR   BATS   BEARS   HEDGEHOGS AND OTHER INSECTIVORES   MAMMALS   MIGRATION   RATS AND OTHER RODENTS

HINDUISM

THE OLDEST OF THE GREAT world religions, Hinduism began in India at least 5,000 years ago. Hindus believe in one great power, or supreme god, called Brahman, that exists in everything. They believe in a cycle of death and rebirth – when we die, our souls live on in another person, animal, or plant. The goal of the Hindu is to live such a good life that the soul breaks this cycle and itself becomes part of Brahman. There are some 733 million Hindus, mostly living in Asia.

Vishnu

Hindus know Vishnu as the preserver. They believe that when there is danger to the Earth, Vishnu protects it. His main task is to keep the balance between good and evil powers. To do this, he has visited the Earth in nine different human and animal forms, including the lord Rama and the god Krishna.

Vishnu

Gods

Hindus worship many gods, each of which represents part of Brahman. Some of the gods can take different forms. Hindus can choose a favourite god; two of the most popular are Hanuman, the intelligent monkey-god, and Lakshmi, the goddess of beauty and wealth. But the most important of all is the holy trinity of Vishnu, Shiva, and Brahma. This group of three makes up Brahman, the supreme god.

Shiva

Hindus know this god as the destroyer. Shiva destroys things which are no longer needed, but also allows new things to be created, so he is said to control life and death. He is shown in many forms. As Lord of the Dance, he brings the dance of life to an end so the new cycle of life can begin.

Shiva beats a drum to summon up a new creation.

His left foot is a symbol of liberation.

Brahma

As the creator of the Universe, Brahma has four arms to symbolize the four points of the compass. He has four faces so he can look in all directions at the same time. These features also suggest that Brahma can be in all places at all times.

These figures represent holy scriptures.

Shiva bears a flame as a symbol of destruction.

The ring of flames represents the energy of the Universe.

Shiva dances on the defeated figure of the demon of ignorance.

Ganesha

Ganesha, the elephant-headed god of wisdom and strength, is the son of Shiva and Parvati. Hindus worship him at the beginning of journeys because he is thought to remove obstacles.

Sacred texts

Hinduism has many sacred books that explain the religion and instruct people how to lead their lives. The oldest texts are four books known as the *Vedas*. These contain hymns to the gods and texts telling priests how to carry out their duties. At the end of the *Vedas* are the *Upanishads*, which are philosophical discussions about religious belief. The *Puranas* are a series of books discussing and explaining the Vedas. The *Laws of Manu* provide teachings about everyday life.

Rig-Veda

The oldest and most sacred of the *Vedas* is the *Rig-Veda*. It contains some 1,000 hymns of praise to 33 of the most important of the gods. Like the other *Vedas*, it was originally composed in around 1200 BC, and passed on by word of mouth. The texts were written down in Sanskrit in around AD 1400.

Indra is the Vedic god of conquest. He is a warrior and a destroyer of demons.

In the Bhagavad-Gita, Krishna drives the warrior Arjuna's chariot.

The epics

Two great epic poems tell stories in which the gods come to Earth. The *Mahabharata* is probably the longest poem ever written. Its 100,000 verses tell of Vishnu visiting Earth as Krishna. It contains the text known as the *Bhagavad-Gita*, the Song of the Lord. The *Ramayana* tells a story in which Vishnu comes to Earth as lord Rama.

Blue houses in Jodhpur were for Brahmins.

Caste system

Hinduism divides people up into four separate groups, or varnas. The four groups are Brahmins (generally priests), Kshatriyas (soldiers and rulers), Vaishyas (traders and farmers), and Shudras (servants). These broad divisions are split into smaller groups called jatis, or castes. Traditionally, people would not have anything to do with castes lower than their own, but nowadays there is much more social flexibility.

H

Festivals

Throughout the Hindu year, festivals celebrate the gods in a variety of ways. At Janmashtami, Hindus commemorate Krishna's birthday with readings of the *Bhagavad-Gita* and gifts of sweets. Divali, the festival of lights, remembers the story of lord Rama's victory over his enemies and his lamp-lit procession home.

Pilgrims come to bathe in the River Ganges.

The sacred water is said to wash away one's sins.

Holi
The festival of Holi is held for two days in spring to celebrate the rescue of Krishna from the clutches of the demoness Holika, who was burnt to death by Vishnu. After worship a bonfire is lit to symbolise good overcoming evil. Dancing and processions take place.

Pilgrimages
Going on a pilgrimage to a holy place is important for many Hindus. They may go to a shrine or to a place where one of the gods is said to have appeared on Earth, believing that their prayers are more likely to be answered if said at such a place. A favourite goal for pilgrimage is a holy river, particularly the River Ganges, in north-western India. Varanasi on the Ganges is India's most sacred city.

On the second day of Holi, people of all castes cover each other with coloured powders.

Sacred cows
The white cow is a Hindu symbol of the soul, and cows are sacred in Hinduism. They are allowed to rove freely, and there are penalties for killing a cow. Hindus may drink milk and use cow dung as fuel, but must not kill cows for food. The cow's status is part of a wider respect for life and many Hindus are vegetarians.

Daily traffic in the city of Delhi skirts around seated cows.

Worship

Since Hindus believe that god is in everything, any human activity, done well, can become an act of worship. But Hindus also perform special acts of worship at least once a day. They may worship in a temple, but the most common place for worship is in the home, in front of a shrine to a favourite god. Rituals include meditation and reciting sacred texts and prayers. Hindus light candles, make offerings to the gods, and waft incense around the shrine.

Vishnu is the main image.

Krishna and his half-brother Balarama are shown with Vishnu.

Shesha the serpent protects Vishnu.

Shrines
The household shrine is the focus of daily worship. It may contain an image of one of the principal gods, plus pictures of other deities. It may also have a container full of water from the sacred River Ganges. Although some shrines are elaborately decorated, others may be as simple as a shelf or holy picture in the corner of a room.

Puja
Before puja (worship) takes place, the image of the god is washed, dried, and anointed with turmeric or sandalwood powder. Offerings such as flowers, fruit, and cooked food are made to the god. The worshipper stands or sits in front of the shrine, reciting holy texts.

Incense burner

Burning incense welcomes the god to his shrine.

Kamal

This scent-shaker is shaped like the lotus flower, the symbol of creation.

Yoga
All Hindus strive to break the cycle of rebirth (samsara) and merge with Brahman. They believe that one way of achieving this state is through following the physical and mental disciplines of yoga. There are different types of yoga, but all aim to attain ultimate spiritual enlightenment.

A Hindu carrying out yoga exercises.

The temple's tall towers symbolize mountains that are sacred dwelling places of the gods.

The shrine room is in the inner sanctum.

The very fabric of the temple is sacred.

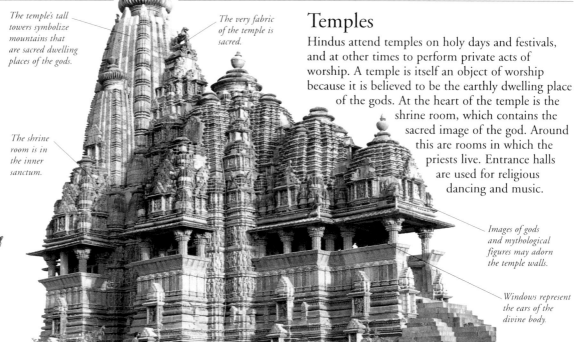

Temples

Hindus attend temples on holy days and festivals, and at other times to perform private acts of worship. A temple is itself an object of worship because it is believed to be the earthly dwelling place of the gods. At the heart of the temple is the shrine room, which contains the sacred image of the god. Around this are rooms in which the priests live. Entrance halls are used for religious dancing and music.

Images of gods and mythological figures may adorn the temple walls.

Windows represent the ears of the divine body.

FIND OUT MORE
FESTIVALS   GODS AND GODDESSES   INDIA, HISTORY OF   INDUS VALLEY CIVILIZATION   LITERATURE   RELIGIONS   SHRINES   SIGNS AND SYMBOLS   WRITING

HIPPOPOTAMUSES

SPENDING THE DAY submerged in water, hippopotamuses emerge at dusk to feed on nearby grasslands. Well-used pathways lead to their feeding grounds. There are two species of hippo – the common hippo and the pygmy hippo – both of which live in the equatorial regions of Africa. The common hippo is the third largest land animal after the elephant and the white rhino. Common hippos have a huge appetite and can consume vast quantities of grass. In places where they are numerous, they may destroy the vegetation for a considerable distance from the river or lake in which they live, sometimes causing serious soil erosion.

Common hippopotamus

The common hippo is a very large and aggressive animal. It is the second heaviest land animal after the elephant. Despite its huge size and legs that seem too short for its enormous barrel-like body, it can move at surprising speed. Anything coming between it and the water is liable to be attacked. Hippos make a variety of noises from bellowing to snorting.

Skin

Hippo skin is smooth and almost hairless except for a few bristles on the nose, in the ears, and on the tail. Underneath the skin is a thick layer of fat. Pores on the skin exude drops of a thick pink fluid that acts as a sunscreen and a lubricant. The fluid is also thought to disinfect wounds sustained by males during fights.

Scars are usually the result of sparring between adult males.

Small ears

Hippos feed on grass.

School of hippos

The common hippo lives in groups of 20–100 animals called schools. A school spends the day partly submerged in water or wallowing in mud pools. Hippos establish a territory with males around the edge, and females and young in the centre. Males are excluded from the female area except in the breeding season. Any male approaching too close will be attacked by the females.

Young

Thirty-four weeks after mating, the female gives birth to a single young. Birth normally takes place on land, but occasionally in water. The newborn hippo can swim, walk, and run within a few minutes of being born. If a female temporarily leaves the territory, she puts her calf in the care of another female.

Bristles on nose

Males open their huge mouths to display their large teeth and tusks.

Teeth

Prominant tusks project more than 60 cm (24 in) from the gums.

Threat displays

Males challenge each other by opening their mouths to maximum gape. If this fails to deter a rival, they may rise up out of the water and try to slash each other with their tusks. Ferocious fights often develop between rival males and may lead to serious injury.

Eyes, ears, and nostrils appear above the water surface.

Hippos spend up to 18 hours a day submerged in water.

Hippo underwater

The common hippo, whose name means "river horse", is more at home in water than on land. When submerged it can hold its breath and seal its nostrils and ears. Normally, it stays underwater for 3–5 minutes before having to surface to breathe, but, if necessary, it can remain submerged for considerably longer. It swims easily and may walk along the bottom of the riverbed.

Hippo walking on the bottom of a riverbed.

Pygmy hippopotamus

The pygmy hippo is about one-fifth the size of the common hippo. It swims well, but is less aquatic than the common hippo. It lives in marshland and swamp forest where it makes tunnel-like tracks through the undergrowth. If alarmed it seeks refuge in dense undergrowth. The pygmy hippo is a shy, nocturnal animal living alone or in pairs. It spends most of the day resting and feeds during darkness on swamp plants, fruit, and leaves.

Round head and body

Thick skin

COMMON HIPPOPOTAMUS

SCIENTIFIC NAME	*Hippopotamus amphibius*
ORDER	Artiodactyla
FAMILY	Hippopotamidae
DISTRIBUTION	Tropical Africa
HABITAT	Rivers, lakes, and estuaries
DIET	Grass and aquatic vegetation – up to 45 kg (100 lb) per day
SIZE	Height: 1.52 m (5 ft); weight: 4.06 tonnes (4 tons)
LIFESPAN	50 years

FIND OUT MORE   AFRICAN WILDLIFE   CONSERVATION   LAKE AND RIVER WILDLIFE   MAMMALS   MARSH AND SWAMP WILDLIFE

HISTORY

THE STUDY OF HISTORY is an attempt by people today to understand the lives of people in the past. Historians – the people who study history – look at primary sources – those writings and artefacts that have survived – and try to piece together a realistic picture of life in previous years. But not every piece of historical evidence survives to the present day, and that which does survive can sometimes be interpreted in many different ways. As a result, history is a complex and sometimes controversial subject that excites considerable debate among historians and non-historians alike.

Parasaurolophus skull, a type of duckbill dinosaur

Prehistory
Writing has existed for around 5,500 years. The period before written records is called prehistory. Archaeologists study material evidence, such as bones, fossils, and artefacts, to help them understand prehistoric periods, such as the Stone Age.

Records of history
All primary sources, whether photographic or written, need careful study, because they may be biased, that is, illustrate a subjective (personal) viewpoint.

Lenin

Propaganda
Historical evidence may be altered to serve political needs. The Soviet Union saw a power struggle between Josef Stalin (1879–1953) and Leon Trotsky (1879–1940) after the death of Lenin. When Stalin became leader, he had Trotsky removed from all official photographs.

Trotsky appeared in the original of this photograph.

Meroë pyramid, Sudan

Sources of history
What we know of history is based on material evidence, such as buildings, roads, tools, artworks, and clothes; written evidence, such as books; and oral evidence handed down through generations. All these sources provide valuable information about past societies and the people who created them.

Material evidence
By piecing together material evidence, historians can discover much about the people of the time. The Bayeux Tapestry is the record of a known historical event – the Norman invasion of England (1066). But when historians study it more closely, they discover a wealth of information, not just about the event the tapestry is relating, but about life of the time generally – and even about the women who made the tapestry.

English soldiers

Norman knights

Normans attack the English, Bayeux Tapestry

Dark Ages
Historians often label historical periods, though people of the time may not have agreed with the label. The chaotic period in Europe after the Roman Empire fell (c.500) is often called the Dark Ages, yet in places it was a time of culture and learning.

The Book of Durrow, c.800

Chinese letter, written on a scroll

The larger the document, the more useful it is to a historian.

Written evidence
Books, diaries, poems, letters, account books, receipts, state documents, and newspapers are all written evidence and help historians in their work. But written evidence needs careful study, because it is often personal, and has to be balanced against other accounts or other types of evidence to gain a more rounded picture of past events.

EP Thompson
Edward Thompson (1924–93) was an important English social historian. His best-known work, *The Making of the English Working Class* (1965) studied the politics and protests of ordinary people as opposed to the history of political leaders.

Oral history
Many societies know their own history, even though they have not written it down. In West Africa, storytellers known as *griots* record the history of their tribes through lengthy narrative stories set to music. In the 1960s and 1970s, there was a move towards sociological history, whereby historians recorded the stories of people previously left out of historical record-making, such as women and the working classes.

Warrior's mother, Kenya

Timeline
c.400s BC Herodotus writes history of the Greek–Persian wars.

c.800 Monks begin the Anglo-Saxon Chronicle.

1380s Arab historian Ibn Khaldun writes *Kitab al-Ibar,* to explain why civilizations rise and fall.

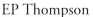

Ammonite, prehistoric material evidence

1800s History established as an academic subject, with the emphasis on primary sources, rather than interpretation.

1860s Karl Marx (1818–83) argues a view of history in which economic factors determine events.

1930s French historians of the Annales school concentrate on social history.

1960s Historians focus on people previously ignored in accounts of history, such as women.

1992 US historian Frances Fukuyama argues that the fall of communism "ended" history.

FIND OUT MORE   ARCHAEOLOGY   MARX, KARL   RUSSIAN REVOLUTION   SEVEN WONDERS OF THE ANCIENT WORLD

HITTITES

A WARLIKE PEOPLE, known as the Hittites, flourished from 1600 to 1200 BC, when they had one of the most powerful armies of the ancient world. They settled in Anatolia (central Turkey) around 2000 BC, then established control over the area from their great fortified capital at Hattusas. Gradually, the Hittite kingdom expanded into Syria, where they clashed with Egypt, and the growing might of Assyria. Despite their fearsome reputation, the Hittites were astute politicians, and preferred diplomacy to armed conflict where possible. Eventually, attacks from outside forces, combined with famine, put an end to their empire.

The Hittite Empire covered most of Turkey and Anatolia at its height, c.1300 BC.

Teshub was often portrayed holding a weapon.

A three-pronged lightning fork

Chariot warfare

From 2000 BC the introduction of horses, the development of the bit, and strong, spoked wheels transformed the chariot from a humble cart pulled by asses, into a dangerous weapon which changed warfare in the Near East. The Hittites were masters of this weapon.

Battle of Kadesh

The world's earliest battle that can be reconstructed was between the chariots of the Hittite king, Muwatallis, and the Egyptian Rameses II at Kadesh in 1286 BC. Chariots continued to be important to ancient armies for over 2000 years.

Rameses II

Diplomacy

The Hittites favoured diplomatic marriages to secure peace, especially with Egypt. For instance, after the Battle of Kadesh, a Hittite princess was married to a pharaoh. On another occasion, an Egyptian queen, possibly Tutankhamun's widow, wrote to the Hittite king asking to marry one of his sons.

Politics

Hittite rulers were supreme commanders of the army (and chief judges and high priests). The greatest king was Suppiluliumas I (r.1380–1346 BC), who conquered all Syria, between the Euphrates and the sea. Though he took this territory through military might, he kept it by bribing his Egyptian rivals with gold. Many Syrian gods were accepted by the Hittites as leading deities, including Teshub, who symbolized storms and the destruction of war.

Ugarit

A wealthy trading city on the Mediterranean coast, Ugarit was a main area of conflict between the Hittites and the Egyptians because of its location. It was abandoned in the turmoil that destroyed the Hittite Empire. Archaeologists have unearthed one of the world's earliest cuneiform alphabets here.

Teshub, the Hittite storm god

Head-dress, indicating high status

Art and literature

Hittite myths emphasize divine warfare, and many feature Teshub defeating evil outside forces. In the remains of their hilltop capital at Hattusas (modern Boghazkoy, Turkey), stone reliefs in the city wall show helmeted warriors, and some of the many Hittite gods. Tiny figures, crafted in gold, have been found. These depict kings and gods, and wear the distinctive upturned boots of a mountain people.

Hittite wall relief

Neo-Hittites

The Syrian city-states belonging to the empire adopted Hittite hieroglyphics and art. After the collapse of the empire, this influence continued, and the cities became known as the Neo-Hittite states.

Food and drink

The main crops were barley and wheat, which were used for making bread and brewing beer. The Hittites also grew fruits, such as apples, figs, and apricots, and they made wine from grapes. Bees produced honey, and farmers raised sheep, oxen, and cattle.

Apple

Figs

Apricots

Short-sleeved tunic

Upturned boots

Gold figurine, possibly of a Hittite king

Timeline

Hittite warhorse

1600–1400 BC
The first Hittite kingdom is established in Anatolia.

1595 BC King Mursili I sacks Babylon, but does not remain.

1550 BC The fortified Hittite capital is established at Hattusas.

c.1460 BC Tudhaliyas II begins conquests that establish last phase of empire.

1380–1346 BC Suppiluliumas commands a vast empire stretching from present-day western Turkey to north Syria. Hattusas (modern Boghazkoy) is the main cultural influence in the area.

1299 BC One of the earliest known battles takes place, between Hittite and Egyptian forces, at Kadesh.

1283 BC Peace treaties are signed between Hittites and Egyptians.

1200 BC The growth of the Assyrian Empire, forces invading from the north and west, and famine combine to destroy the Hittite Empire.

FIND OUT MORE | **ASIA, HISTORY OF** | **ASSYRIAN EMPIRE** | **BABYLONIAN EMPIRE** | **EGYPT, ANCIENT** | **PERSIAN EMPIRES** | **SUMERIANS**

HOLOCAUST

BETWEEN 1939 AND 1945, six million European Jews were systematically murdered by the German Nazi regime. Some were killed in their own towns, but most died in concentration camps. This mass murder of Jews is known as the Holocaust, after a Biblical term meaning "slaughter by fire". It was a deliberate national policy established by Adolf Hitler and his Nazi followers to wipe out all traces of Jewish life and culture. Jews have been persecuted throughout history, but the Holocaust, which slaughtered nearly 70% of Europe's Jews, is history's worst example of anti-Semitism. Today, people still ask how such an atrocity was allowed to happen.

Star of David
From 1933, the Nazis began to segregate (separate) German Jews from the rest of the population. Jews had to wear the yellow Star of David to identify them, and they were banned from public places. Nazi propaganda encouraged hatred, and people attacked Jewish shops and homes.

Warsaw Ghetto

Warsaw Ghetto
In 1939, Germany invaded Poland. The capital, Warsaw, was home to half a million Jews, who were rounded up, forced to live in a ghetto (part of the city cut off from the rest), and given starvation rations. In 1943, the Jews made a brave and desperate attempt to fight back, but this uprising was mercilessly crushed. By the time Soviet troops liberated Warsaw in 1945, only 200 Jews remained alive.

Concentration camps
Special concentration camps were built by the Nazis to detain people considered "undesirable", particularly Jews. From 1941, many camps were set up throughout eastern Europe, including Chelmno, Treblinka, and Auschwitz. These were literally death camps, built to achieve Hitler's "final solution" of exterminating all European Jews. Thousands of men, women, and children were led into chambers where they were killed with a cyanide compound, Zyklon B, introduced through vents in the walls. Non-Jews were also killed, including gypsies and the disabled.

Entrance to Auschwitz

Auschwitz
One of the most feared death camps was Auschwitz (Oswiecim) in Poland, where some 12,000 victims a day were gassed and their bodies cremated. It was this burning in the death camps that gave the Holocaust its name.

Death camps were in eastern Europe

Deportation
European Jews from France to Greece were rounded up, loaded onto trains, in cattle cars, and deported to death camps. local people hostile to Jews often helped the Nazis to do this. Up to a thousand people were forced into each train, and deprived of food and water. On arrival, survivors were sent to the gas chambers.

Jewish resistance
Despite the power of the Nazis, the Jews did resist oppression. During the war, there were revolts by Jews in ghettoes, such as Warsaw, and even in the concentration camps, such as Sobibor. Elsewhere, small bands of Jews formed partisan groups that fought heroically in enemy territory, attacking Germans, and destroying military stores and railway tracks.

Liberation
From 1942, news of the death camps began to reach the West. It was only in 1945, however, that the full story emerged. When the Allied forces liberated the camps, they found, to their horror, huge mounds of skeletal people either dead or dying.

Timeline
1925 Adolf Hitler publishes *Mein Kampf* (My Struggle). In it, he states his anti-Semitism (hatred of Jews).

1933 Hitler becomes Chancellor and begins the persecution of German Jews. First camp is built at Dachau.

1935 Nuremberg Laws declare Jews to be second-class German citizens.

9–10 Nov 1938 "Kristallnacht" (Night of Broken Glass), Germany. People attack more than 7000 Jewish shops and homes, and 30,000 Jews are sent to concentration camps.

1941 Hitler, Eichmann, and other leading Nazis announce their "final solution". Death camps are set up throughout Europe for mass slaughter.

1943 Warsaw Ghetto Uprising. Nazis kill or deport more than 56,000 Jews in four weeks.

1945 Allied forces liberate concentration camp in Eastern Europe.

1962 First tree is planted in Israel's Avenue of the Righteous, which commemorates non-Jews who saved Jewish life during World War II.

Anne Frank
Born in Frankfurt, Anne Frank (1929–45) was a German Jew. In 1933, she and her family fled to Amsterdam, Holland, to escape persecution. In 1941, the Nazis invaded Holland, and from July 1942, Anne and her family were hidden by friends. While in hiding, she wrote a diary that is now world famous. In August 1944, the family was betrayed and sent to the concentration camps. Anne died in Bergen Belsen camp at the age of 16.

FIND OUT MORE   COLD WAR   EUROPE, HISTORY OF   GERMANY, HISTORY OF   JUDAISM   WORLD WAR II

HOLY LAND, HISTORY OF

OVER THE CENTURIES, THIS VARIED region of mountains, deserts, and marshes has had shifting borders, various conquerors, and many names, including Canaan, Zion, Israel, Judah, and Palestine. The area is holy to three world religions: Judaism, Christianity, and Islam. Jews believe it is the Promised Land God gave them, and that Abraham, father of the Jews, settled there in about 1900 BC. The land is holy for Christians because Jesus Christ lived there; and for Muslims, Jerusalem is sacred as the site of many of Muhammad's activities. The Bible records mainly Jewish history in this region.

The Holy Land

This crossroads between Europe, Africa, and Asia has been conquered by Babylonians, Persians, Greeks, Romans, Arabs, Byzantines, Ottomans, and British in turn. Today it includes Israel, and parts of Jordan and Syria.

Jericho

Excavations show that the walled city of Jericho may be the oldest settlement in the world. According to the Bible, it was destroyed many times in its history – once by Joshua, who led the Israelites after the death of Moses.

Jerusalem

Over the centuries Jews, Christians, and Muslims have all fought for access to holy shrines, such as Solomon's Temple. This has caused many wars in one of the world's holiest cities.

Solomon's Temple

This temple, completed by Phoenician craftsmen in 957 BC, housed the Ark of the Covenant, and was the first permanent Jewish religious centre. In 587 BC, the Babylonians destroyed the first temple. It was rebuilt in 37 BC but destroyed by the Romans in AD 70. All that remains today is the so-called Wailing Wall on the west side.

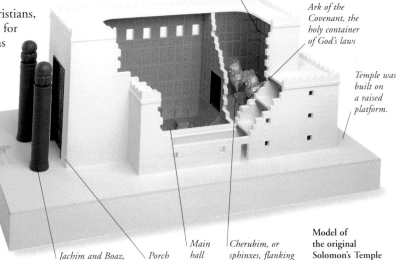

Holy of holies, inlaid with gold

Ark of the Covenant, the holy container of God's laws

Temple was built on a raised platform.

Jachim and Boaz, the bronze columns

Porch

Main hall

Cherubim, or sphinxes, flanking the Ark

Model of the original Solomon's Temple

Church entrance

Holy Sepulchre Church

In the 12th century, Crusaders rebuilt a Christian church on Mount Calvary, Jerusalem, where Jesus Christ was crucified. The church contains Greek Orthodox, Roman Catholic, and Armenian chapels. In a grotto underneath is the empty tomb of Jesus.

Dome of the Rock

This massive rock is sacred to Muslims because Muhammad is said to have risen to heaven from this spot. It is sacred to Jews because Abraham is said to have prepared his son Isaac for sacrifice here.

Philistines

The Philistines were part of a group of warriors also known as the Sea Peoples. In about 1100 BC, the Philistines threatened the Israelites, who had settled the southern coast of Palestine (in modern Israel). The Israelites lived subject to the Philistines for 200 years until the Israelite King David (r.1013–973 BC) managed to subdue them.

Slingshots.

David and Goliath

Goliath, a huge Philistine champion, challenged the Israelites to present a man for single combat. No one dared respond until David, a young shepherd, volunteered. Against all the odds, he knocked Goliath out with one slingshot, and cut off his head. David went on to become Israel's greatest king, and made Jerusalem a great political and religious centre.

Timeline

c.8000 BC Evidence of human settlement, Jericho.

c.1900 BC The patriarch Abraham settles in Canaan.

c.1200s BC The Exodus: Moses leads the Israelites out of slavery in Egypt.

Holy Sepulchre Church

1033–1013 BC Reign of Saul, first king of Israel.

1013–933 BC Reigns of David and Solomon.

587 BC Babylonians destroy first Jewish temple, Jerusalem.

AD 33 Romans crucify Jesus Christ in Jerusalem.

AD 70 Romans destroy the second Jewish temple at Jerusalem.

636 Muslim rule begins.

1096–1291 European Crusaders fight to control the territory.

1948 Declaration of the state of Israel.

King Solomon

The son of King David and his wife Bathsheba, Solomon (r.973–930 BC) built the first temple at Jerusalem, and a number of cities. He was famous in ancient Israel for making profitable foreign alliances, and, during his reign, Israel reached its greatest extent of territory. Myths present Solomon as very wise, but he was actually a rather harsh and despotic ruler.

FIND OUT MORE ARCHITECTURE   CHRISTIANITY   CRUSADES   ISLAM   ISRAEL   MYTHS AND LEGENDS

HOLY ROMAN EMPIRE

FOR MORE THAN 800 years, most of central Europe was loosely tied together in the Holy Roman Empire, an attempt to revive the old Roman empire, with backing from the Christian Church. It was founded in 962. After 1273, the Habsburg family of Austria won the throne and dominated the empire from then on. The emperors were elected by seven German princes and crowned by the Pope in Rome. The emperor had little power, but the title made him political leader of Europe.

Jewelled cross

Crown is set with enamel plaques.

10th-century imperial crown

Otto's German lands

The empire in 987

Emperors were also kings of Italy.

The empire
From its foundation in 962 until the mid-13th century, the Holy Roman Empire included much of Germany, the Low Countries, Switzerland, Austria, and northern Italy. Over the next centuries, it shrank, but it remained dominant in Germany.

Otto I: the birth of empire
In 936, Otto, a descendant of Charlemagne, became king of Germany. He defeated the Magyar invaders at the battle of Lech in 955 and went on to conquer northern Italy. In 962, the Pope crowned him Holy Roman Emperor.

Habsburgs

The Habsburgs took their name from a castle in Switzerland and held vast estates in Switzerland, Austria, and southern Germany. In 1273, a member of the Habsburg family became Rudolf I of Germany and then the Holy Roman Emperor. With a few short breaks, the Habsburgs ran the empire until its end in 1806. Under their rule, the interests of the empire were secondary to those of increasing Habsburg family power.

Maximilian I married Mary of Burgundy in 1477 and acquired Burgundy.

Philip I, son of Maximilian, married Juana of Castile and Aragon in 1496.

Mary of Burgundy

Struggle for power
The emperor was the supreme secular (worldly) ruler of Christian Europe; the Pope was its supreme spiritual ruler. The two often clashed. In 1076, Pope Gregory VII deposed Emperor Henry IV. The conflict led to a decline in the power of the emperors over the next few centuries.

Charles V

Habsburg power in Europe reached its peak in 1519, when Charles V (1500–58) became emperor. He acquired vast lands from each of his grandparents, including Spain and its empire in America. Charles kept this empire together until 1556, when he gave up the throne and divided his empire between his brother Ferdinand, who became emperor on Charles's death in 1558, and his son Philip, who ruled Spain, Italy, and the Low Countries.

Ornate Renaissance decoration

The Schweizertor, a gate to the Hofburg

Imperial Vienna

The Habsburg capital was the Austrian city of Vienna. It was one of the leading cities in Europe, with fine churches, palaces, and other civic buildings. The centre of Habsburg power was the Hofburg Palace, a vast complex including imperial apartments and government offices.

Charles's brother, Ferdinand I, married Anna and inherited Bohemia and Hungary.

Charles V, son of Philip, inherited Spain through his mother, Juana and the Habsburg lands from his grandfather Maximilian.

Maria Theresa
In 1740, Emperor Charles VI died, leaving his daughter Maria Theresa on the throne. Prussia and France disputed her right to inherit the throne and declared war. Maria was an inspired leader and managed to keep her empire together, making Austria into a powerful, centralized state.

Timeline

800 Charlemagne crowned.

962 Otto, king of Germany, becomes first Holy Roman Emperor.

1076 Pope overthrows emperor Henry IV and establishes papal power over emperor.

1273 Rudolf I becomes first emperor from the Habsburg family.

Imperial knight

1517 Reformation under Martin Luther results in a divide between German Protestant princes and the Catholic emperor.

1519 Charles V is crowned emperor and becomes most powerful man in Europe.

1556 Charles splits his empire between brother Ferdinand and son Philip; Habsburg Austria dominates the Holy Roman empire.

1806 Francis II abolishes the Holy Roman empire.

FIND OUT MORE CHARLEMAGNE · CHRISTIANITY · GERMANY, HISTORY OF · REFORMATION · ROMAN EMPIRE

HORMONES AND THE ENDOCRINE SYSTEM

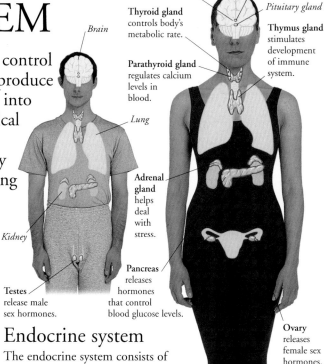

Hypothalamus is part of the brain that controls the pituitary gland.

Pineal gland regulates body's internal clock.

Pituitary gland

Thyroid gland controls body's metabolic rate.

Thymus gland stimulates development of immune system.

Parathyroid gland regulates calcium levels in blood.

Brain

Lung

Kidney

Adrenal gland helps deal with stress.

Pancreas releases hormones that control blood glucose levels.

Testes release male sex hormones.

Ovary releases female sex hormones.

THE ENDOCRINE SYSTEM is one of the body's control systems. It consists of endocrine glands that produce chemicals called hormones, and release them into the bloodstream. The hormones act as chemical messengers and instruct specific areas of the body to carry out certain actions. Hormones usually work slowly and have a long-lasting action, regulating processes such as growth and reproduction.

How a hormone works

The blood carries hormones throughout the body, but they only affect certain target cells within target tissues. The hormone attaches itself to a site on the surface of a target cell. This locking-on causes changes inside the target cells, which produce the required action. For example, the pancreas releases the hormone insulin in order to reduce levels of glucose molecules in the blood. Insulin does this by stimulating the body cells to take in glucose.

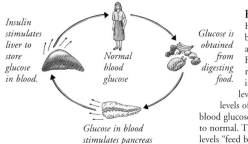

Insulin stimulates liver to store glucose in blood.

Normal blood glucose

Glucose is obtained from digesting food.

Glucose in blood stimulates pancreas to release insulin.

Hormone levels
Hormone levels in the blood are controlled by a feedback mechanism. For example, insulin is released from the pancreas in response to increased levels of glucose. Higher levels of insulin will then cause blood glucose levels to return back to normal. The lowered glucose levels "feed back" to the pancreas, which produces less insulin.

Endocrine system

The endocrine system consists of many glands scattered throughout the body. Glands are the same in men and women, except for the reproductive glands. The pea-sized pituitary controls many other glands. Some organs are linked to the endocrine system because, as well as having other functions, they also release hormones. The pancreas, for example, produces digestive enzymes and releases hormones.

H

Urine test

Urine sample

Colour chart

Diabetes
Diabetes is a condition that occurs when blood glucose levels become very high because the pancreas cannot produce enough insulin. Doctors can monitor blood glucose levels by measuring the amount of glucose in a urine sample.

Pituitary gland

The pituitary gland releases at least eight hormones. Some affect body functions directly, while the remainder stimulate other endocrine glands to produce hormones of their own. The pituitary gland has two parts, or lobes. The anterior lobe produces and sends hormones around the body; the posterior lobe releases hormones produced in the hypothalamus.

Hypothalamus

Nerves carry hormones from hypothalamus to posterior lobe.

Blood vessels carry hormones around body.

Tissues release hormones received from hypothalamus.

Posterior lobe

Anterior lobe

Jokichi Takamine

Japanese chemist Jokichi Takamine (1854–1922) was the first person to isolate a pure sample of a hormone. Using extracts of adrenal glands, he prepared crystals of a substance that increased blood pressure in animals. This substance was later called adrenaline.

Prolactin

Prolactin is a hormone that is produced by the anterior lobe. It stimulates the production of milk when a woman breastfeeds her baby. When the baby sucks on the nipple, prolactin is immediately released from the mother's pituitary gland.

Growth hormone

The anterior lobe produces growth hormone, which encourages the body to grow. It works by stimulating the body's cells to divide. Although growth hormone affects all tissues, its main targets are bones and skeletal muscles. Growth hormone is most active in childhood and adolescence.

Adrenaline

If you have ever been frightened and felt your heart pounding, you have experienced the effects of adrenaline. It is a hormone that helps the body react to danger. When the adrenal glands release adrenaline, your breathing and heart rate speed up, and blood flows to your muscles so you can run from danger.

FIND OUT MORE   BRAIN AND NERVOUS SYSTEM   DIGESTION   GROWTH AND DEVELOPMENT   HUMAN BODY   REPRODUCTION

HORSE RIDING

PEOPLE RIDE HORSES for leisure and in competitions, which are often described as equestrian (from *equus*, meaning horse). These include show jumping, eventing, and dressage, all of which test the horse's ability to jump or perform special movements, and each of which appears in the Olympic programme. Equestrian events also include racing events – flat racing, steeplechasing, and hurdling – where jockeys ride specially bred horses called thoroughbreds. Other riding sports include polo, in which teams of riders compete to score goals.

Hard hat is essential.

Riding
Riders learn how to start, stop, steer and control the speed of a horse using their hands, legs, and body-weight. The natural gaits of a horse are the walk, trot, canter, and gallop.

Bridle

Reins

Stirrup

Saddle

Horse breaks into a canter from a trot.

Show jumping

This involves riders taking their horses around a set course of jumps which may include artificial gates, a wall, and a water jump. Competitors receive faults if their horse refuses or knocks down a jump, or exceeds the specified time. The competitor with the fewest faults wins.

Rider keeps looking ahead.

Rider's hands move up the reins to allow the horse to use his head and neck.

Rider leans forward from the hips.

Landing

Jumping a single pole

Horse draws up his hind legs and stretches to clear the jump.

Horse tucks up his forelegs.

Taking off

Puissance
This show jumping competition tests the ability of a horse to jump high fences. From four to six fences are jumped, the number being reduced and the height raised for each round.

Racing

Racing can be flat or over jumps. Some events such as the English Grand National – a steeplechase – are world famous and attract thousands of spectators and involve heavy betting on different runners. Horses may have to carry extra weights under the saddle, as well as the jockey (rider).

Polo
This game is played four-a-side on a large field. Players mounted on polo ponies use mallets to strike a ball into their opponents' goal. A game consists of up to eight seven-minute periods called chukkers. Riders usually change ponies after every chukker.

Dressage

In dressage, each competitor guides his or her horse through paces, figures, manoeuvres, and halts (stops). Judges award points for the quality of the performance. Dressage is a formal sport and riders wear top hat and tails or military uniform; it needs a high degree of discipline and schooling.

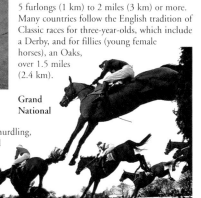

Flat racing
Horses are raced over distances from 5 furlongs (1 km) to 2 miles (3 km) or more. Many countries follow the English tradition of Classic races for three-year-olds, which include a Derby, and for fillies (young female horses), an Oaks, over 1.5 miles (2.4 km).

English Derby

Grand National

Jumping
The main types of jumping races are hurdling, for three-year-old horses upwards, and steeplechasing for four-year-olds upwards. Hurdles are low and may be knocked over; steeplechase fences are larger and include ditches and water jumps.

Eventing

In three-day eventing, riders take their horses through a different discipline each day to test all aspects of the horse's abilities. Dressage tests a horse's obedience and show jumping its powers of recovery. There is also a four-phase endurance test which includes a steeplechase.

Cross-country
The cross-country phase may cover 7 km (4.3 miles) with about 30 fixed obstacles of all kinds. The course has to be completed in a set time to avoid time penalties. The jumps are often spectacular and include water, slippery grass banks, steps, solid walls, and drops.

Mark Todd
A New Zealand eventer, Mark Todd (b. 1956) won the individual three-day event gold medal at the 1984 and 1988 Olympics on the horse Charisma. He was deprived of a third successive gold when his mount broke down on the second day after scoring well in the dressage.

FIND OUT MORE   EVOLUTION   HORSES   MAMMALS   MONGOL EMPIRE   OLYMPIC GAMES   SPORT

HORSES

ALL MEMBERS OF THE HORSE family, which includes zebras and asses, are social animals. In the wild, they live in family groups which join to form a herd. People first tamed horses about 6,000 years ago, and today there are more than 300 breeds of domestic horse. They can be divided into three groups: heavy horses, light horses, and ponies, which are less than 14.2 hands high (1.47 m or 4.8 ft).

The horse
Naturally grazing animals, horses in the wild eat grasses and shrubs. In each jaw, they have six incisor teeth for cutting and 12 molars for chewing. They rely on their sharp senses to survive, using taste and smell to check their food, and hearing and sight to detect danger. If they face possible danger, their first defence is to run away.

Dapple grey

Dun

Skewbald

Light bay

A foal will drink its mother's milk until it is about one year old.

Five-week-old foal

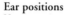

Ear positions
Horses can move their ears separately to pick up sounds, and the position of their ears is a good indication of their mood. Ears forward show interest; one ear forward and one back means the horse is not sure; ears back show aggression or fear.

Leg of modern horse

Leg of early horse

Side toe

Reproduction
A female horse carries her young in her womb for about 11 months. Within an hour of its birth, a young horse, called a foal, will get up and is soon able to run. In the wild, it has to keep up with the herd.

Hooves and feet
Modern horses have one toe on each foot, protected by a hoof. It has taken 50 million years for them to evolve. The first horses, which were the size of small dogs, had a pad with four toes on the forefeet and three on the hind.

Colours
Originally, the colour of a horse's coat may have provided camouflage. Today, horses are bred in several colours. In some, the legs, mane, and tail are a different colour from the rest of the body. Some horses have white markings on the face and legs.

Movement
Horses can travel using four main patterns of leg movements, called gaits. These are the walk, trot, canter, and gallop. The gallop is the fastest, but a horse can gallop only short distances. Humans have bred horses to perform other artificial gaits, such as the paso done by the Peruvian paso, and the tölt done by the Icelandic pony.

The walk is a four-beat gait. The horse moves its legs in turn.

The trot is two-beat. Opposite fore and hind legs move together.

The canter has three beats.

In the canter, one leg moves, then a diagonal pair, then the last leg.

All feet are off the ground together.

The gallop is like the canter, but paired feet go down separately.

Horse family
The horse belongs to the family of mammals called the *Equidae*. Also in this family are donkeys, zebras, the wild asses of Africa and Asia, Przewalski's wild horse of Mongolia, and the recently discovered Riwoche wild horse of Tibet.

Zebras
There are three species of zebra, each with a different pattern of stripes. Herds of all species live wild in tropical Africa.

Wild asses
The three species of wild ass are the African wild ass, and the onager and kiang of Asia. This kulan is a type of onager.

Donkey
Descended from the African wild ass, donkeys have great strength and stamina.

Przewalski's
An ancient breed of horse, it has been reintroduced into the wild.

Herds
Members of a herd are close friends. They communicate using a variety of sounds, smells, and body language. For example, if a horse is startled, it will raise its head and tail, arch its neck, and flare its nostrils. This alerts the others, which prepare to run.

Zebra

Feral herds
These wild horses in Australia, called brumbies, are described as feral. They are domesticated horses now running wild.

FIND OUT MORE — EVOLUTION — FARMING — GRASSLAND WILDLIFE — HORSE RIDING — TRANSPORT, HISTORY OF

Horses

Light horses

Strong build

Irish draught was originally used for work on small Irish farms.

Saddlebred is an American horse with a high action. It is a brilliant show horse.

Australian stock horse is an all-rounder, with great endurance and stamina.

Pinto is also called the paint horse. It comes in a variety of types and sizes.

Camargue horses live in semi-wild herds in the Rhône delta, France.

Strong arched neck

Welsh cob is a bold horse. It is extremely hardy and easy to keep.

Compact body

Hackney horse is often used in showring harness competitions.

Lipizzaner is used in the Spanish Riding School of Vienna, Austria.

Long tail and mane

Morgan descends from one stallion. named Justin Morgan after his owner.

Andalucian is a Spanish breed from which the Lipizzaners derive.

Tennessee walking horse is good-tempered. It has three smooth gaits.

Big joints

Hanoverian is popular in Germany for show-jumping and dressage.

Appaloosa as a breed was first bred by the Nez Percé Indians of North America.

Quarter horse is claimed to be the most popular horse in the world.

Arab is the oldest breed and is accepted as the original source of all breeds.

Orlov trotter is a tall lightly built horse. It was first bred in Russia.

Thoroughbred is the fastest horse breed, with almost perfect proportions.

Barb comes from Morocco in North Africa. It is one of the oldest horse breeds.

Ponies

Dartmoor is noted for its long, low action.

Good sloping shoulders

Connemara is fast and a brilliant jumper.

Exmoor lives on Exmoor in southwest England.

American Shetland is used mostly as a harness pony.

Australian pony has an excellent temperament.

Compact body with depth through the girth

Welsh mountain pony is hardy as well as beautiful.

Shetland is up to 102 cm (40 in) high, but is strong enough to carry a man.

Highland is sure-footed, strong, and docile. It is known to be long-lived.

Icelandic horse can carry heavy weights, at speed, over long distances.

New Forest pony is a friendly, comfortable riding pony.

Fjord comes from Norway and is descended from Przewalski's horse.

Tail set low

Falabella is a miniature horse. standing up to only 7 hh (70 cm/28 in).

Heavy horses

Deep, strong neck

Suffolk punch is very powerful. It was used as an all-round farm horse.

High withers

Clydesdale originated in the Clyde Valley, Scotland, in the 18th century.

Shire is the heaviest of the draught breeds. It is gentle and easy to handle.

Percheron is a French breed containing a great deal of Arab blood.

Short back

Ardennais falls into two types – a lively, light draught, and a heavy type.

Large, rounded quarters

Belgian draught is also known as the Brabant. It is a very old breed.

HOSPITALS

ANCIENT ROME HAD special places where sick people could receive medical treatment – the world's earliest hospitals. Today, hospitals have more responsibilities: patient care, health education, and medical research. Whether general or specialist, most hospitals have wards for in-patients, clinics for out-patients, operating theatres for surgery, and pharmacies for dispensing drugs. Trained staff, such as doctors and nurses, care for patients using complex equipment, while non-medical staff, such as cooks, porters, cleaners, and engineers, are crucial in making the hospital function. In some poorer countries, there may be only one hospital for every million people.

Specialist hospitals

Some specialist hospitals focus on groups of patients, such as women or children. Others concentrate on groups of diseases, such as eye problems, psychiatric disorders, or neurological (nerve-and-brain) diseases. Teaching hospitals train nurses, doctors, and other medical staff.

Children's hospital

Hospitals specializing in the care of sick children use scaled-down equipment, such as surgical instruments, bandages, beds, and chairs. Wards are bright and cheerful for the small patients, and there are toys and games. Parents are able to stay in nearby hospital rooms.

Child's teddy

Flying eye clinic, China

Eye clinics

Ophthalmology – the branch of medicine concerned with eye and sight problems – requires exceptionally detailed and precise equipment, and specialist facilities for patients who may be temporarily unable to see. Some large countries with remote regions, such as China or Australia, can provide these facilities in a mobile form – usually a small plane.

Staff

Doctors usually work in different hospital departments for several years, to gain general training, before choosing a speciality. Nursing staff may also specialize, for example, in paediatrics (children), psychiatry, or intensive care. A hospital's staff usually includes radio-graphers, laboratory technicians, physio-therapists, and anaesthetists.

Nurses

Nurses attend to patients' comfort and daily needs, such as feeding and washing. They also carry out medical tasks, such as taking and recording pulse rate and body temperature, and giving edications.

General nurse

Equipment

Modern equipment – especially that modified to be mobile – is crucial in hospitals. In an emergency, some of the most useful pieces include breathing apparatus (face masks or tubing), long syringes to administer fast-acting drugs, such as heart stimulants, and fluid products for intravenous infusions (drips).

Forceps and syringes   *Face mask*   *Balloon pump*

Oxygen cylinder and trolley

Drug boxes

Drawers

Emergency trolley

Stethoscope

General hospital

A general hospital provides medical facilities for a large area. Its wards cater for patients with common health problems. More complex cases are referred to a specialist hospital. General hospitals also arrange community services, such as visits by nurses.

Chart   Hospital beds in a ward

Wards

In-patients usually stay in dormitory-type wards. They are separated into medical and surgical groups of children, men, women, and the elderly. Patients with infectious diseases usually stay in isolation rooms.

Ambulance, New York, USA

Accident and emergency

The A&E department receives medical emergencies, such as accident or heart-attack victims. The patient's problem is identified and stabilized, after which he or she may be sent home, or transferred to a suitable general ward.

Premature baby in incubator   Neo-natal intensive care unit

Intensive care unit

In intensive care, expert staff attend gravely ill patients round the clock. Electronic equipment continually monitors their vital processes, such as heartbeat and breathing.

Waiting room

Out-patients

Out-patients attend the hospital to undergo screening tests or have minor surgery. They do not stay overnight.

FIND OUT MORE   DRUGS   FIRST AID   MEDICINE

HOUSES AND HOMES

EVERYONE NEEDS A HOME, to provide comfort and shelter from the weather. It usually takes the form of a permanent house, although some people live in temporary structures, such as tents. Houses differ greatly around the world. They vary in what they are made of, because builders usually use local materials; in their structure, because their features must cope with local weather; and their plan. But they all provide a place for the inhabitants to sleep, eat, and cook.

Brick from local mud

Straw woven into matting

Overhanging thatched roof keeps off rain and provides shade.

Wooden poles support roof.

Early houses
From the earliest times, people built their houses out of materials that were available locally. Houses such as this African example have been made for thousands of years and are still built today. A wall of mud bricks is covered by a thatched roof supported on wooden pillars.

Inside a house

A modern house includes many parts that are normally hidden from view. Many of these are to do with the services – such as running water, drainage, heating, and electricity – that are provided for the occupants. Water tanks are concealed in the roof space, pipes and wiring are hidden behind plaster, and drains are dug below ground level.

Water tanks in the attic store cold water piped in from the water mains.

Wooden roof truss

Wooden floor

Inner leaf of concrete blocks

Outer leaf of bricks

Window, framed with wood or PVC

Wooden front door with porch

Box containing electricity meter

Concrete foundations

Central-heating radiator

Insulation cavity between wall leaves

Pipe carries all waste to mains drain.

Rainwater cylinder

Central-heating boiler

Wooden joists support floor.

Drainpipes take rainwater from gutter.

Roof covered with concrete tiles

Solar panel

Construction
Modern houses in Europe and North America are most commonly made of brick, timber, and concrete. A popular building method is to construct an inner wall or "leaf" of concrete blocks, which are faced with an outer leaf of more attractive bricks. Wood is used for floors, doors, and roofing supports.

Japanese house
Traditional Japanese houses have a timber framework. The gaps between the timber uprights are filled with wooden panels or sheets of paper to let through some sunlight. The rooms are designed to be covered by a set number of standard-sized straw mats called tatami mats.

Flats and apartments

In towns and cities, where space is limited and many people want to live near the centre, the answer is often to build upward, creating blocks of flats. This type of home became common in the 19th century, when cities began to expand quickly, and new devices such as steam cranes made it easier to lift building materials high up.

Roman apartments
The ancient Romans were the first to build blocks of apartments. In cities such as Rome and Ostia, rising ground rents and growing populations encouraged the trend, and many brick-and-concrete five- or six-storey apartment blocks were built.

In Ostia, the ancient Romans built flats above street-level shops.

Modern flats made of concrete and steel, in France

Modern apartments
From Paris to New York, apartment blocks are common in cities. Each apartment is linked to the ground by metal fire escapes to prevent residents from being trapped if there is a fire.

| FIND OUT MORE | AFRICA, HISTORY OF | ARCHITECTURE | BUILDING AND CONSTRUCTION | CITIES | CRAFTS | FURNITURE | INDUSTRIAL REVOLUTION | JAPAN | ROMAN EMPIRE |

Houses and homes

Permanent homes

Troglodyte houses hollowed out of rock, eastern Turkey

Stilts protect occupants from vermin and floods.

Wooden stilt-house with thatched roof, Malaysia

Adobe house built from sun-dried clay bricks, New Mexico, USA

Thick walls and few windows keep house cool.

Decorated mud house, Saudi Arabia

Turf provides insulation.

Stone-built palace

Small windows help to conserve heat.

Sloping roof to shed snow.

Farmhouse covered with turf and built into hillside, Iceland

Wooden house on stilts, Canada

Wooden log house, Switzerland

Wooden log cabin with overhanging roof, Wyoming, USA

Stone cottage with thatched roof, Donegal, Ireland

Large roof space for storage.

Wooden cross-braces add strength.

Dormer windows provide extra space on upper floor.

Wood-framed house with brick panels, Germany

Tall outcrop of sandstone

Summer Palace, Wadi Dahr, Yemen

Wooden panels give extra protection against weather.

Wooden house with clapboard panels, USA

Temporary and movable homes

Gypsy horse-drawn caravan, UK

Dome of compressed snow

Tunnel entrance

Inuit igloo built from blocks of snow and ice, Canada

Thick layer of felt covers the entrance.

Shepherd's cabin woven from bundles of straw, Spain

Wooden poles bound at top into a cone shape.

Circular entrance

Yurt made from layers of felt lashed to a circular frame, Mongolia

Tepee made of buffalo hides over poles, Arizona, USA

H

HUMAN BODY

ALTHOUGH WE ALL LOOK different, we are identical in the way our bodies are constructed and function. Each human body is built up from 12 major systems, including the digestive system, skeletal system, and muscular system. These systems interact to produce co-ordinated, active, intelligent humans. The study of the body's structure is called anatomy. Externally, the only consistent anatomical differences between humans are between males and females.

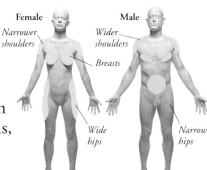

Female
Narrower shoulders

Male
Wider shoulders

Breasts

Wide hips

Narrow hips

Anatomy

The human body is divided into the head and neck, the trunk (consisting of the chest, abdomen, and pelvic region), and the arms and the legs. Men and women differ in their external genitals and in the places where fat accumulates (shown in green).

From cells to systems

The body's billions of cells are organized into tissues. Each tissue consists of similar types of cell. One or more types of tissue work together inside an organ, such as a bone or a lung. Organs are linked together to form a system that has one or more major roles. Together the systems are collected together to form the body.

The skeleton is a framework of bones that supports the body.

The end of a bone is normally covered by cartilage.

Compact bone

Thigh bone

Spongy bone

Skeleton
The adult skeletal system is made up of 206 bones. The skeleton provides a framework that supports the body, protects internal organs, and provides attachment points for muscles.

The body is made up from hundreds of billions of cells.

Ligaments are strips of tissue that hold bones together at joints.

Movable joints between bones make the skeleton flexible.

Bone cell

Nucleus

Cytoplasm

Cell membrane

Compact bone

Lacuna

Haversian canal

Circular layers of compact bone

Body
The skeleton and the other major body systems form the living human body. The body's systems do not work in isolation, however. For example, the skeleton is supplied with blood vessels, lymph vessels, and nerves, and requires muscles to move it.

Cell
Osteocytes, or bone cells, are spider-shaped cells that make up the tissues that form a bone. Osteocytes are found in spaces called lacunae that are scattered about the hard matrix (material) found in bone tissue. Their job is to maintain the hard matrix.

Tissue
Compact bone is one of the tissues that makes up a bone. It consists of layers of hard bone around a central tube called the Haversian canal. This carries blood vessels which supply the osteocytes with food and oxygen.

Organ
Each bone consists of different tissues. Compact bone is a bone's hard outer covering. Spongy bone and bone marrow are tissues found inside bones. Cartilage is the slippery tissue found in joints.

Body systems

Each body system contributes to the body's normal functioning. Together, the body's systems are controlled by the nervous and endocrine systems. They enable us to move, talk, and perceive the world, while our internal processes run automatically.

Muscular
The muscular system moves and supports the body. It consists of over 620 skeletal muscles attached to bones.

Nervous
The nervous system controls the body's activities. It consists of the brain and spinal cord, and a network of nerves.

Circulatory
The circulatory system transports material around the body. It consists of the heart, a network of blood vessels, and the blood.

Digestive
The digestive system supplies the body with food. It consists of the mouth, oesophagus, stomach, and intestines.

Integumentary
The integumentary system is the body's outer, protective covering and consists of skin, hair, and nails.

Respiratory
The respiratory system supplies the body with oxygen. It consists of the nose, throat, trachea, and lungs.

Urinary
The urinary system removes waste. It consists of the two kidneys, the ureters, the bladder, and the urethra.

Endocrine
The endocrine system regulates many body processes. It consists of glands that make hormones.

Lymphatic
The lymphatic system protects the body against disease. It consists of a network of lymph vessels.

Reproductive
The reproductive system enables us to produce children. Male and female systems are different.

FIND OUT MORE

BRAIN AND NERVOUS SYSTEM   CELLS   GROWTH AND DEVELOPMENT   HEART AND CIRCULATORY SYSTEM   HUMAN EVOLUTION   MUSCLES AND MOVEMENT   REPRODUCTION   SKELETON   SKIN, HAIR, AND NAILS

HUMAN EVOLUTION

MUCH DEBATE HAS SURROUNDED the evolution of humans. However, most scientists are now agreed that modern humans, *Homo sapiens*, are the sole survivors of a number of human species that evolved from the common ancestor of humans and apes some six million years ago. Climatic changes forced our earliest ancestors out of the tropical forests and into open woodlands and grasslands. The challenge of these new habitats resulted in important changes, such as the ability to walk upright and an increase in brain size.

Evolutionary tree

The evolutionary sequence from the earliest human ancestors is not a straight line, but is instead a "tree" with many dead ends. Because the fossil evidence is limited, scientists disagree about how many human species have existed and which were ancestors of others. This evolutionary tree provides a simple guide to relationships but does not necessarily indicate ancestry.

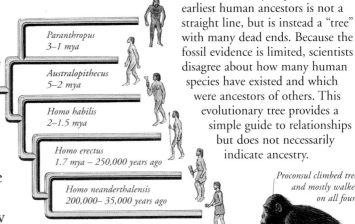

Common ancestors

Paranthropus
3–1 mya

Australopithecus
5–2 mya

Homo habilis
2–1.5 mya

Homo erectus
1.7 mya – 250,000 years ago

Homo neanderthalensis
200,000– 35,000 years ago

Homo sapiens
100,000 years ago

Proconsul climbed trees and mostly walked on all fours.

Proconsul

Proconsul is the earliest known member of the hominoids, the group to which apes and humans belong. It lived in the tropical rainforests of East Africa between 24 and 18 million years ago. Compared to its ancestors, *Proconsul* had a large brain.

Australopithecines

The Australopithecines are thought to be the earliest hominids (human-like people). Although ape-like, with a small brain and projecting jaws, *Australopithecus* stood upright and walked on two feet. This is known from its leg bones and backbone, and from 3.7 million–year–old footprints found at Laetoli in Tanzania.

Lucy

"Lucy" is the name given to the most complete Australopithecine skeleton yet discovered, found in Ethiopia in 1974. It was an adult female, 3.18 million years old. Lucy was about 1.1 m (3 ft 6 in) tall.

Projecting jaw and low forehead

Long arms and short legs

Chimpanzees

The chimpanzee is our closest living relative. Chimpanzees and humans share over 98 per cent of their DNA (genetic material). Chimpanzees and gorillas are known collectively as the African apes. About six million years ago, humans and African apes split from their common ancestor to evolve separately.

Paranthropines had small brains and flattened faces.

Paranthropines

The Paranthropines were strongly built "man-apes" that lived in southern and eastern Africa between three and one million years ago. They were probably descended from the Australopithecines, but were not part of the evolutionary pathway that led to modern humans.

A male Paranthropus was about 1.35 m (4 ft 4 in) in height.

Homo

Homo is the genus, or group of species, to which modern humans belong. It probably evolved from the Australopithecines between three and two million years ago, although there is no direct evidence for this. Early members of the genus showed increasing brain size and the ability to make tools.

Homo habilis

"Handy man" is the earliest known species of *Homo*. It lived in the woodlands and savannahs of Africa. *Homo habilis* had a brain size of 650 to 800 ml. It made and used simple stone tools, and was a successful forager and scavenger.

Flat face and slender jaw

Reconstruction of *Homo habilis*

Homo erectus

Homo erectus was the first human to leave Africa and move to Europe and Asia. It had a sloping forehead, flattish face, and a brain size between 850 and 1100 ml. These humans exploited more habitats than their ancestors, and were the first to use fire.

Neanderthals

Neanderthals were the first humans to have adapted to life in the cold climates of Europe and Asia. They had strong physiques and large brains. They wore clothes, made a range of tools, and used fire to keep warm. They were the first humans to bury their dead.

***Homo erectus* skull**

Homo sapiens

Modern humans first evolved in Africa. *Homo sapiens* has a large brain, considerable intelligence, and the ability to use language. Humans increasingly took control of their surroundings as they developed agriculture, societies, and technology.

A modern human has an average brain size of 1400 ml.

Prominent brow

***Neanderthal* reconstruction**

Face is straight rather than forward-jutting.

FIND OUT MORE   ARCHAEOLOGY   BRONZE AGE   DARWIN, CHARLES   EVOLUTION   FOSSILS   GENETICS   HUMAN BODY   LEAKEY FAMILY   PREHISTORIC PEOPLE   SKELETON   STONE AGE

HUMAN RIGHTS

MOST OF US BELIEVE that as human beings we have certain rights – to say what we want, to be treated fairly, and not be discriminated against because of our gender, colour, age, religion, sexual orientation, or ethnic group. These and other rights are human rights we carry with us wherever we live. In many countries, these rights are written into national law, but in others they are denied. Recently, world attention has focused on countries that deny their citizens basic human rights. Despite this, abuses of human rights are still common.

Justice is often symbolized as a blindfolded figure, holding a pair of scales.

A fair trial is a basic human right.

What are human rights?
Human rights are those rights and privileges which people possess, regardless of the country they live in. Basic human rights include the right to freedom of speech, political liberty, and religious freedom. Some people believe that the right to the necessities of life, such as food and clean water, should also be viewed as basic human rights. These are often lacking in areas of severe poverty.

Clean water

Bills of Rights

Many countries have incorporated a declaration of human rights into their constitutions. In France, for example, the Declaration of the Rights of Man and of the Citizen, written in 1789, today forms part of the constitution of the French Republic.

The US Bill of Rights
The first ten amendments to the US Constitution constitute the US Bill of Rights. It includes the right to freedom of worship, the right to bear arms, and the Fifth Amendment (the right to remain silent to avoid self-incrimination); witnesses took this in the 1950s to protect themselves against investigations into "un-American activities".

Taking the Fifth Amendment, 1950s

Modern human rights

The horrors of world war and countless atrocities in the 20th century have led people to believe that the only way to protect human rights is by setting an international standard to which all countries agree. Since 1945, many international agreements have been signed to protect the rights of oppressed people around the world.

Universal Declaration
In 1948, the United Nations passed a Universal Declaration of Human Rights to serve as "a common standard of achievement for all peoples and all nations". American Eleanor Roosevelt (1884–1962), chair of the UN Commission on Human Rights and widow of a former US president, was the person most responsible for getting the Declaration approved.

Eleanor Roosevelt

Civil rights

Civil rights are those rights that people enjoy in individual countries and that are protected by law. Civil rights include basic human rights, as well as political rights such as the freedom to join a trade union. Where civil rights are denied, popular movements may be formed, committed to repair the injustice.

© Amnesty International

Amnesty International
Set up in 1961, Amnesty International is a global pressure group, which campaigns for the release of people "detained anywhere for their beliefs, colour, sex, ethnic origin, language, or religion".

The European Court ruled against corporal punishment in schools.

Amnesty symbol

European Court of Human Rights
The European Court, which meets in Strasbourg, France, exists to hear human rights cases from the whole of Europe. Individuals can bring cases against their government if they believe their human rights are threatened.

Freedom of expression
The right to express your views without fear of censorship or persecution, for example, in speaking against a government, is a fundamental human right. But it is denied in some countries, where newspapers and television are heavily censored, and people are not allowed to demonstrate or express their views in public.

Amnesty leaflet against censorship

Minority rights
The law is often used unfairly against certain groups of people whose culture has minority status within their society. Ethnic, religious, and other minorities have all had to protest in order to receive the rights already enjoyed by the majority of the population.

As a minority, homosexuals have had to campaign for equal civil rights in many countries.

Rigoberta Menchu

Guatemalan human rights activist Rigoberta Menchu (b.1959) has campaigned since she was a teenager to secure and protect the rights of the native people in her country, who have been oppressed by Guatemala's military rulers. Menchu's own parents and brother were killed by the security forces. She was awarded the Nobel Peace Prize in 1992 for her work.

FIND OUT MORE — FRENCH REVOLUTION — PEACE MOVEMENTS — SLAVERY — SOCIETIES, HUMAN — UNITED NATIONS — UNITED STATES, HISTORY OF — WOMEN'S MOVEMENT

HUNDRED YEARS' WAR

IN 1337, EDWARD III of England (r.1327–77) began a bitter war with France that was to last for over 100 years. Edward and his successors felt they had a claim to the French throne, but they also wanted to protect their inherited lands in south-western France. In the beginning, under Edward III and his great-grandson Henry V, England seemed to be winning. Then, as the independent duchy of Burgundy abandoned the English and joined forces with the French army, fortunes changed, and France began to win. In the end, the French drove the English from their country, leaving Calais as the only English possession on the European mainland.

Cord pulled back
Bolt
French crossbowman

Yew wood stave *Hemp string* **English longbowman**
Ash wood arrow shaft

Opponents

In battles such as Crécy (1346) and Agincourt (1415), the French used cavalry charges, which were easily broken by the English using their new, powerful weapon, the longbow. From the 1420s on, the French rebuilt their army and began to use rapid assaults, which broke the English army and gave victory to the French.

French crossbows
The crossbow was a slow but powerful weapon. After each shot, a lever or winder mechanism pulled back the string for the next shot. This took 30 seconds, during which time the bowman was open to attack.

English longbows
The longbow was quicker to reload than the crossbow. An archer could shoot up to 12 arrows per minute. One arrow could pierce armour from as far away as 180 m (600 ft) – but they were not as accurate as the crossbow bolts.

Early phases of the war

Helped by their Burgundian allies, the English had many successes until 1429, when the French, under the brilliant leadership of Joan of Arc, defeated them at Orléans. The French-Burgundian alliance of 1435 proved too strong for England, which steadily lost its French lands.

England • Calais · France · Aquitaine

1340–1360
The English inherited Aquitaine, and, in 1347, captured Calais. In 1359, they attempted to invade French territory. The French held them off, and the Treaty of Brétigny followed in 1360.

Burgundy · *English allegiance* · France

1360–1429
Although the English had lost Aquitaine by 1429, they had gained territory in northern France, including Normandy. Within 30 years they lost everything until, by 1453, their only possession in France was Calais.

Leaders of the war

The personalities and military skills of Joan of Arc and Henry V of England inspired their followers with courage and trust. The dukes of Burgundy were crucial for a different reason: they held the balance of power between England and France.

The Black Prince
Named because he wore black armour, Edward (1330–76) was the eldest son of Edward III. He fought at Crécy and Poitiers, and ruled Aquitaine in the 1360s.

Charles VII of France
Charles VII (r.1422–61) was not crowned King of France until 1429, after the victory at Orléans. He was then able to organize an army against the English.

Philip the Good
Philip (1396–1467), duke of Burgundy, was an English ally at first, but then changed sides and helped France to victory. He built his dukedom into one of the most powerful in Europe.

Henry V

Henry V (r.1413–1422) of England captured major cities, such as Rouen, and led his men to many victories. Through his marriage to Catherine of Valois, he would have inherited the French throne from his father-in-law, King Charles VI of France, but he died before Charles. Shakespeare's play *Henry V* describes Henry's achievements.

Joan of Arc

Joan of Arc (1412–31) heard voices telling her to free France. At 17, she led the French to victory against the English. Later, she was captured and sold to the English, who burnt her at the stake as a heretic. In 1920, she was declared a saint.

Timeline

1346 Battle of Crécy: England builds up strength in France.

1360 Peace of Brétigny: Edward III acquires Aquitaine and gives up other French claims.

1415 English victory at Agincourt; Henry V controls Normandy.

1420 Henry V named heir to French throne.

1422 Charles VI and Henry V die.

1429 Joan of Arc liberates Orléans and escorts Charles VII to Reims to be anointed as king of France.

1431 Joan of Arc is burnt at the stake as a heretic.

1435 Council of Arras: Burgundy joins forces with the French army.

1453 French victory at Castillon: England loses all her French lands, except Calais.

FIND OUT MORE | ARMS AND ARMOUR | EUROPE, HISTORY OF | FEUDALISM | FRANCE, HISTORY OF | MEDIEVAL EUROPE

HYENAS

THE EERIE CACKLING LAUGH of the spotted hyena is one of the characteristic sounds of the open grasslands of Africa. There are three main types of hyena – spotted, striped, and brown. The spotted hyena is the largest; all three have large, broad heads and powerful jaws. Their front legs and shoulders are larger and more powerful than their weaker hindquarters. Although hyenas look rather like dogs, they are in fact more closely related to the cat family.

Spotted hyena

The spotted hyena is the most aggressive and most numerous member of its family. It is usually found in open country, but sometimes also on the forest fringes. Spotted hyenas' furtive movements and liking for carrion have given them a reputation for cowardice and dependence on the kills of other animals, but they are in fact predators in their own right. They have an important ecological role in keeping herds of hoofed animals moving. By forcing these animals to move to fresh grazing grounds, hyenas help to conserve the habitat.

Large, broad head with very powerful jaws

Sloping shoulders

Red-brown coat with dark spots

Forelegs are longer than hind legs.

Large sharp canine teeth

Powerful heavy jaws

Clan

Spotted hyenas live in clans of between 10–100 animals. They scavenge by day and hunt by night. Members of the clan work together and are capable of driving lions off their kill, and may even kill an old solitary lion. Females are larger than males and the most dominant female presides over the clan.

Jaws

Bones and marrow form an important part of the spotted hyena's diet. Unlike any other carnivores, it will even eat hard tusks and horns. To cope with this diet, the spotted hyena's jaws and teeth are immensely powerful, and capable of crushing the heaviest of bones.

Feeding

Spotted hyenas scavenge the remains of other animals' kills, but also kill their own prey, frequently taking young gazelles, wildebeest calves, and zebras. They may hunt singly but are more effective in packs. The pack size varies according to the availability of prey in their territory.

A pack of hyenas feeding on a carcass.

Young

Normally, two to three cubs are born in an underground burrow. They can see immediately. Several females often establish a nursery where they and their young live together communally. One female remains in the burrow to guard the cubs while the others go in search of food. The cubs are not fully weaned until they are 18 months old.

Cubs play together but may also fight fiercely, to establish who will become the most dominant.

Female hyenas nurse the young cubs.

Types of hyena

The hyena family consists of four species: the spotted, striped, and brown hyenas, and the aardwolf, which is sometimes placed in a separate family. The spotted and striped hyenas live in Africa and Asia; the brown hyena and the aardwolf are confined to southern Africa.

Brown hyena

Essentially a desert species, the brown hyena is unaggressive, shy, and so secretive that it is seldom seen. At night it searches for the remains of other animals' kills. It lives in southern Africa, mainly in Namibia and Botswana.

Wispy brown coat

Striped hyena

A much smaller animal than its spotted cousin, the striped hyena inhabits an area from India to the Middle East and southwards to Tanzania. It is less predatory and less aggressive than the spotted hyena and tends to be more solitary by nature. It lives in rock clefts, caves, or burrows.

Long wispy mane

Striped body and legs

Aardwolf

A timid animal, the aardwolf spends the day underground, often in another animal's abandoned den. It has weak jaws, small, widely spaced teeth, and a long flexible tongue – adaptations to the termites and other insects on which it feeds. To deter predators it emits an evil smell from an anal gland.

Small head

Striped coat

SPOTTED HYENA

SCIENTIFIC NAME *Crocuta crocuta*

ORDER Carnivora

FAMILY Hyaenidae

DISTRIBUTION Northern and eastern Africa and southern Asia

HABITAT Open grassland

DIET Mainly carrion, but is also an opportunist predator and will kill large animals, such as zebras, antelopes, and gazelles

SIZE Height at shoulder: 79 cm (31 in); weight: 80 kg (175 lb)

LIFESPAN 20 years

FIND OUT MORE | AFRICAN WILDLIFE | ASIAN WILDLIFE | CATS | DESERT WILDLIFE | GRASSLAND WILDLIFE | MAMMALS

IMMUNE AND LYMPHATIC SYSTEMS

EVERY DAY THE BODY IS INVADED by disease-causing micro-organisms called pathogens, or germs. The immune and lymphatic systems are the body's defence against these pathogens. The immune system is a collection of cells that keep detailed records of invading pathogens so, if they reappear, they can be destroyed, making you immune to that disease. The lymphatic system drains fluid called lymph from tissues, filters out any pathogens, and returns the lymph to the bloodstream.

Tonsils guard throat against infections.

Neck lymph nodes

Thoracic duct empties lymph into a main vein.

Groin lymph nodes

Knee lymph node

Lymphatic system

The lymphatic system consists of a network of tubes called lymph vessels that reach all parts of the body, and several lymphatic organs. Lymph is carried by the vessels to the main lymph ducts which empty into the bloodstream.

Heart

Spleen is a lymph organ that also stores blood.

Lymph node removes pathogens from lymph.

Network of lymph vessels

Lymph nodes

Lymph constantly leaves the bloodstream and flows through the spaces surrounding cells. It passes through lymph nodes, which are small swellings of the lymph vessels that clean and filter the lymph. Inside each lymph node is a network of fibres which supports large numbers of two types of immune system cells, lymphocytes and macrophages.

Cutaway of a lymph node

Outer capsule

Lymph vessel carries lymph into lymph node.

Network of fibres and white blood cells

Valve ensures lymph flows in one direction.

Lymph vessel carries lymph away from node.

Blood capillary

Tissue fluid passes into lymph vessel.

Lymph capillary   Tissue cell

Lymph vessels

The smallest lymph vessels are capillaries. Excess fluid drains through the walls of lymph capillaries from the surrounding tissue. Lymph capillaries join to form larger lymph trunks.

Lymphocytes
Lymphocytes, found in the lymph nodes recognize and destroy specific pathogens using chemicals that are called antibodies. Lymphocytes are also to be found circulating within the bloodstream.

Macrophages
Macrophages are cells with voracious appetites that detect, engulf, and destroy viruses, bacteria, cancer cells, and any other foreign material in the lymph that passes through the lymph node.

Immunization

Immunization gives a person protection against a specific disease. There are two types of immunization. In active immunization, a vaccine containing some dead pathogens is injected into the body to stimulate the immune system to make antibodies. Passive immunization involves injecting antibodies and gives short-term protection.

Hypodermic syringe   Vaccine   Dead pathogen   Antibody locked onto pathogen.   Real pathogen   Antibody

1 A vaccine containing dead or weakened pathogens is injected into the body.

2 The immune system produces antibodies and keeps a "memory" of the pathogen.

3 If the real pathogens enter the body, large numbers of antibodies are released.

Quilt for AIDS charity

AIDS
Acquired Immune Deficiency Syndrome (AIDS) is caused by the Human Immunodeficiency Virus (HIV). A person with AIDS becomes infected with diseases that the body would normally fight off. This is because HIV attacks and destroys immune system cells. In time, the immune system weakens and the person becomes unable to fight infections and eventually dies.

Lady Mary Wortley Montagu

Lady Mary Wortley Montagu (1689–1762) was an English author who introduced an early form of immunization against smallpox to England. In Turkey, she had seen people scratching pus from small-pox blisters into the skin of healthy people to protect them from catching smallpox. She had her children "vaccinated" and publicized the method.

Allergies

If you have an allergy, it means that your immune system has wrongly identified a harmless substance, called an allergen, as being harmful. The body's reaction to these allergens produces symptoms such as sneezes and rashes. Common allergens include pollen, fur, dust, shellfish, and strawberries.

Strawberry

A skin patch test is used to identify possible allergens.

FIND OUT MORE   CELLS   HEALTH AND FITNESS   HEART AND CIRCULATORY SYSTEM   HUMAN BODY   MEDICINE   MEDICINE, HISTORY OF   PASTEUR, LOUIS

INCAS

IN THE 15TH CENTURY, the Incas created a great empire in Peru. They were a group of Native American peoples who used military might and skilled organization to build what was then one of the world's biggest nations. Their empire took in most of the great mountain range of the Andes and huge areas of desert and rainforest. In 1532, Spanish adventurers conquered the Incas.

Inca Empire

Machu Picchu

Cuzco

Peru

Farming terraces

Central plaza (square)

Palace

Temple of the Sun

Machu Picchu

Cuzco

The Inca capital was called Cuzco, from the Inca word meaning "centre". It is 3,400 m (11,000 ft) up in the mountains. Cuzco was an awe-inspiring city, made great by the emperor Pachacuti Inca. At the centre of the city was the Temple of the Sun. Many Inca remains survive in the modern city.

Machu Picchu
The Incas built their cities using great blocks of rock so finely cut that they fitted together without cement. Machu Picchu, high in the Andes Mountains, is the most spectacular remaining example of Inca architecture. Its stone buildings clinging to the mountain could accommodate thousands of people.

Inca industry

The state collected manufactured goods, such as food, wool, and clothing, which were kept in storehouses. Every town had at least two storehouses: one for the ruler, one for the rest of the people. Goods were transported by llamas along a large network of paved roads.

Quipus
The Incas had no system of writing, but they kept records by knotting different coloured strings on to a stick or cord known as a quipu. They could record figures such as the numbers of wool bales or the amount of births in a year using this method.

Agriculture
The Incas introduced terraced farming, which enabled crops to be grown on steep slopes. Bird droppings and fish heads were used as fertilizer. Most of the work was done collectively, and most of the land was owned in common by the local community.

Inca society

At the top of society were the Inca ruler and his relatives. They could be identified because they were allowed to enlarge their ears with huge ornaments. Some of the nobles left their palaces in Cuzco to rule outposts of the empire. Ordinary people were organized into groups of villages called ayllus. Each ayllu was governed by an elected council of elders. Sometimes the emperors moved groups of people around the empire, so that they could place loyal people in areas that were otherwise difficult to govern.

Cup with emperor's portrait

Workers
Inca workers produced some goods for themselves, and some for the emperor and nobles. These provided the state with the resources for public works and other royal projects.

Emperors
The Incas believed their rulers were descended from the Sun god, so they were worshipped as holy beings. This portrait of an Inca emperor decorates a cup used in religious rituals.

Religion

Chief of the gods was the creator Viracocha, who was worshipped by the Inca priesthood and nobility. Next in importance was the Sun god, Inti, claimed by royal Incas as their

Sun god

ancestor. Other Inca deities included gods of the Moon and stars. The earth god was also central, because the Incas relied on farming for wealth and food.

Pachacuti
Pachacuti Inca was crowned in 1438. With his son, Topa Inca, Pachacuti enlarged the territory of the Inca state. He came to dominate many provinces, was a great organizer, and an effective administrator.

Spanish conquest
Shortly before the Spanish ships reached Peru's coast, civil war broke out among the Incas. The Spaniards, led by Francisco Pizarro (c.1475–1541), took advantage of this division and captured the Inca Empire for the King of Spain.

Spanish coins

| FIND OUT MORE | FARMING, HISTORY OF | GODS AND GODDESSES | SOUTH AMERICA | SOUTH AMERICA, HISTORY OF | SPAIN, HISTORY OF |

Inca arts and crafts
Gold items

Gold figurines of gods were often left as offerings in the tombs of prominent Incas.

Small tomb figure was made of cast gold.

Belt ornaments were made of gold cut and hammered into shape.

Head attached to neck with soldered joint

Statuette of llama is made of cast gold.

Everyday items

Mouthpiece

Cat-like head with bared fangs

Clay trumpet has twin cat-like heads, which may have represented a god.

Pipes are made from quills.

Panpipes have different-length tubes for each note of the scale.

Alpaca-head handle

Stone container is made in shape of alpaca.

Drawstring bag is decorated with tapestry bearing design showing Peruvian llamas.

Pottery vessel has elaborate base; its exact use is unknown.

Flat-sided vessel could be hung on the back of a llama.

Stone bowl is decorated with a religious procession.

Jug is painted with simple geometric design.

Wooden beaker was made for Spanish conqueror Pizarro.

Tall, narrow neck

Carrying ring

Copper chisels may have been used for woodcarving.

Inca pots were often made in standard shapes; a common design had a conical base, long, flaring neck, and twin carrying handles; this type of pot was used for carrying water and beer.

Beaker decorated with Inca royal figures

INDIA AND SRI LANKA

SEPARATED FROM other Asian countries by the Himalayas in the north, India forms part of a subcontinent that also includes Pakistan, Bhutan, Bangladesh, Nepal, and the island of Sri Lanka, which lies 32 km (20 miles) to the south. India is the world's seventh largest and second most populated country. Poverty is a serious problem, but India is self-sufficient in food production and increasingly industrialized, counting among the world's largest economies.

Physical features

The Himalayan peaks form a natural border in northeastern India. The Indo-Gangetic Plain is drained by the Ganges and Indus rivers and stretches from Pakistan to Bangladesh. The Thar Desert is on the Pakistan border. The peninsula land slopes west from the Western Ghats across the Deccan Plateau to the Bay of Bengal.

Western Ghats
The Western Ghats mountains stretch along India's west coast, rising to a height of 2,695 m (8,842 ft). Forests of tropical palms cover the lowlands west of the mountains, and lush, evergreen rainforest, home to tigers and elephants, cloaks the slopes. To the east is dry, deciduous forest.

Ganges
At 2,700 km (1,678 miles) the Ganges is the biggest river in India, flowing through a vast, highly populated plain. Its source is 4,200 m (13,779 ft) above sea-level in an ice cave in the Himalayas. It ends in a huge delta that is mostly in Bangladesh. For Hindus, the Ganges is a sacred river.

Sri Lanka
Just off the southeastern tip of India lies the island of Sri Lanka, which is a country in its own right. At the centre of the island are high mountains surrounded by a low coastal plain. Like southern India, Sri Lanka has a tropical climate with two monsoon seasons each year. However, the southwest has no dry season and is humid all year, while the northeast is drier, with open forest and grassland.

Religions
For most Indians, religion is a way of life, governing thoughts and actions, and giving a sense of identity. About 80 per cent of Indians are Hindus. Muslims make up 11 per cent, and Christians and Sikhs about five per cent. Sri Lanka is mainly Buddhist.

Hindu priest

46°C (115°F)   -14°C (7°F)
31°C (88°F)   14°C (57°F)
640 mm (25 in)

Climate
Heavy and persistent monsoon rains soak India and Sri Lanka between June and September. The coolest season is from November to March. Winter temperatures rarely fall below 20°C (68°F) except in the high Himalayas, and may top 50°C (122°F) on northern plains in summer.

India

With more than 450 million voters, India is the world's largest democracy. In 1947, the country became independent of Britain, and was left with a vast rail network, international ports, and working farms and factories, all of which have contributed to its industrial success. Today, India has many industries and large modern cities, although millions of people still live in extreme poverty. India has rich mineral resources, including oil, iron, bauxite, coal, and manganese.

Forest 42%
Built-up 1.5%
Wetland 1%
Farmland 40%
Grassland 11.5%
Desert 4%

Land use
Most of India's farmland is used for growing fruit and cereals, and the country is largely self-sufficient in food. With such a large population to feed, demand for farmland is high, and many Indian forests have been felled to make way for crops. Some of the land is used for mining.

INDIA FACTS

CAPITAL CITY	New Delhi
AREA	3,973,190 sq km (1,147,949 sq miles)
POPULATION	1,000,000,000
MAIN LANGUAGES	Hindi, English
MAJOR RELIGIONS	Hindu, Muslim
CURRENCY	Rupee
LIFE EXPECTANCY	63 years
PEOPLE PER DOCTOR	2,500
GOVERNMENT	Multi-party democracy
ADULT LITERACY	57%

People
Most Indians live according to the caste system, which indicates their role in society, who they can marry, and the work they can do. However, the caste system is now more flexible than in the past. Women have equal rights by law, but rarely in practice. Several measures to reduce India's rising population have been initiated by the state, but have remained largely unsuccessful.

341 per sq km (883 per sq mile)

28% Urban   72% Rural

Indian family

Films are often packed with stars, dancing, action, and romance.

Film-making
India has a highly successful film industry and makes more films than any other country including the USA. The centre of the film industry is "Bollywood" – India's Hollywood – in Bombay.

Music
India has a long and varied musical tradition. There are two classical forms of music: *Hindustani* and *Carnatic*. Both are based on the *raga*, a mixture of melody and scales. Typical classical instruments include the *sitar* and the *sarod* (which are both lutes), flutes, drums, and the European violin. Folk music varies from region to region and is played on at least 500 different kinds of instruments.

Sitar

Food
The traditional Indian food is curry, a sauce flavoured with a subtle blend of spices, such as turmeric, cardamom, ginger, coriander, nutmeg, and poppy seed, eaten with meat or vegetables. Meat dishes, mainly lamb and chicken, are savoured in the north. In southern India, vegetables and pulses such as *dhal* (lentils), coconut, and fresh sea food are enjoyed with curry. Rice and unleavened breads, such as *chapatis*, *parathas*, and *poori*, are eaten with meals.

Boiled rice
Vegetables in a spicy curry sauce

New Delhi
Purpose-built by the British as India's capital, New Delhi has a population of 301,000 and lies 5 km (3 miles) from the old city of Delhi, with 16,000,000 people. Compared with Delhi's winding streets, temples, mosques, and bazaars, New Delhi has tree-lined boulevards and spacious parks.

Jama Masjid, Delhi

Farming
About two-thirds of Indians are involved in agriculture. Many are poor farmers who grow just enough food to feed their families. Others work on plantations producing cash crops, such as tea, rubber, coffee, sugar, bananas, mangoes, cotton, and tobacco. India exports timber, including teak, sandalwood, and rosewood. Cattle are reared for butter and ghee, but not for beef, forbidden by the Hindu religion.

Bananas
Sesame seeds
Mango

Industry
The country's economy is still based on small, cottage industries. But, aided by a large, cheap work-force, India's industry is growing rapidly. In the south, Bangalore is now a centre for electronics, and many international companies have factories there. India also exports machinery, cut diamonds, textiles, clothing, and chemicals.

Electronics worker

Transport
Railways in India total 62,810 km (39,030 miles). Every year they carry two-thirds of all freight and three billion passengers. India has 2,160,000 km (1,342,000 miles) of roads, only half of which are paved. Only one person in 300 owns a car, but buses are widely used and very crowded. In rural areas, ox carts are common, and in cities, people ride bicycles, scooters, or travel by taxi and rickshaws.

Kashmir
In 1947, Pakistan and India separated. Since then, they have disputed ownership of the former princely state of Kashmir. Part of Kashmir lies in the Indian state of Jammu and Kashmir. The rest is ruled by Pakistan, which claims it all because most of the people who live there are Muslims. Fighting breaks out from time to time.

Kashmiri winters are cold.

Sri Lanka

 Known as Ceylon since 1796, Sri Lanka adopted a new name and constitution in 1972. It is separated from India by the Palk Strait, and is made up of one large island and the several coral islets of Adam's Bridge. In 1960, Sri Lanka became the world's first nation to choose a woman as prime minister, Sirimavo Bandaranaike. Since 1983, civil war has raged between the Sinhalese, who rule the government, and the Tamils, who are fighting for independence.

Tamils

The Tamils, a mainly Hindu minority ethnic group, have been campaigning for an independent state in the northern peninsula of Jaffna since the 1980s. They object to the control of the government by the majority Sinhalese, most of whom are Buddhist. The Tamil Tigers, a ruthless guerrilla group, have fought many fierce battles in which up to 50,000 people have been killed.

Tamil man

SRI LANKA FACTS

CAPITAL CITY Colombo

AREA 65,610 sq km (25,332 sq miles)

POPULATION 18,800,000

MAIN LANGUAGES Sinhala, Tamil

MAJOR RELIGIONS Buddhist, Hindu

CURRENCY Sri Lankan rupee

Procession of decorated elephants in Kandy's Perahera Festival

Colombo

Sri Lanka's capital and chief port, Colombo, was developed by the Portuguese after 1507. The commercial capital is at Fort, so-called as it was a military garrison during Portuguese and Dutch occupation from the 16th to the 18th centuries. Today's city has a population of 2,241,000. It is a blend of old and modern buildings, with a busy bazaar area known as the Pettah. There are also Buddhist and Hindu temples and mosques.

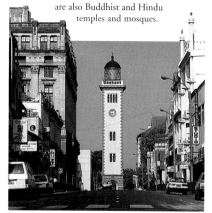

The Fort

The Sacred Tooth

At the heart of Sri Lanka is the Buddhist holy city of Kandy, with a population of more than 100,000. There, in a gold casket inside the Dalada Maligawa (Temple of the Tooth), is a tooth that is said to have come from Buddha's funeral pyre (fire) in 486 BC. Every August, in the grand Perahera procession, the tooth casket is paraded on the back of a sumptuously decorated elephant.

Education

At 92 per cent, Sri Lanka has one of the highest Asian literacy rates. It has nearly 19,000 schools and 12 universities, including an Open University. Begun in 1980, it was modelled on the British Open University, a self-instructional learning scheme, aided by television, recordings, and mailed course materials.

Cloves – pungent

Chicory – bitter

Lemon – sour

Rock salts – salty

Sage leaves – astringent

Sweet potato – sweet

Ayurvedic medicine

The traditional Hindu form of medicine called Ayurvedic medicine is practised throughout Sri Lanka. Its name comes from the Ayurveda, an ancient treatise on healing that divides foods into six tastes. A healthy diet combines all of these. Ill-health can be cured by adjusting their intake. Sri Lanka also has an extensive national health service.

Farming

Most Sri Lankans live in the humid southeast of the island. About 38 per cent are poor farmers growing rice, sugar-cane, cassava, and sweet potatoes for their own consumption, or working on plantations producing tea, rubber, and coconuts for export. Nearly 30 per cent of the land is used for crops, and almost seven per cent for grazing cattle, buffaloes, and goats.

Rice

Coconut

Buddha figure carved from sapphire.

Tea

Sri Lanka is the world's largest tea exporter. The tea is still marketed abroad as Ceylon tea. There are more than 2,000 tea estates. Their teas are described as high-grown, medium-grown, or low-grown, according to their height above sea-level. The best quality comes from the cooler climate of the central highlands. The tea is hand picked, mostly by women, to preserve the delicate leaves. The pickers are paid by the basketful.

Dried tea leaves

Tea leaves

Gemstones

Sri Lanka produces brilliant gemstones, which are found near Ratnapura, the "City of Gems", which lies southeast of Colombo. It is especially noted for its sapphires. Other gems include deep yellow topazes, large rubies, and amethysts. Many are made into jewellery.

Tourism

Despite the civil war, Sri Lanka's tourist industry is beginning to flourish. Increasing numbers of Europeans in search of winter sun visit the island's beautiful palm-shaded sandy beaches and coral reefs. Buddhists from all over the world make pilgrimages to the sacred Buddhist city of Kandy.

 FIND OUT MORE   ASIA, HISTORY OF   BUDDHA   BUDDHISM   CRYSTALS AND GEMS   FARMING   FILMS AND FILM-MAKING   HINDUISM   INDIA, HISTORY OF   MEDICINE   MUSIC

INDIA, HISTORY OF

THE SUBCONTINENT OF INDIA has been home to some of the world's great civilizations. Dynasties such as the Buddhist Mauryans, the Hindu Guptas, and the Muslim Mughals spread their cultures and religions across India. As a result, India has remained dominated by a host of different cultures, a fact that has made it difficult to unify under one ruler. The Mughal Empire declined in the 18th century, and Britain added India to its empire, imposing strong rule from outside. India became independent in 1947, when the Muslim state of Pakistan was also created.

Buddhist and Hindu empires

In 324 BC, Chandragupta Maurya, king of Magadha, eastern India, began to conquer northern India. He founded the Buddhist Mauryan Empire, the first to unite the subcontinent. His dynasty was followed by the Guptas, a family of Hindu rulers who controlled India from c. AD 320 to c.700.

Nalanda University, founded during the Gupta period

Chola statue of a goddess

Elaborate head-dress shows high status.

Chola metalworkers cast bronze statues decorated with fine details.

Gupta Empire
India flourished under the Guptas. They promoted education, founding some of the earliest universities, and encouraged the arts of architecture, painting, sculpture, dancing, and music. The writers of the period produced books in the Sanskrit language that are still read today.

Imperial Cholas
The Cholas, from southeastern India, were a Hindu people. In the late 9th century, they took over much of southern India and what is now Sri Lanka, ruling the area from the city of Tanjore. A seafaring people, their merchants sailed west to Arabia and east to China, organizing their trade efficiently and introducing India's first money.

Statues such as this were often commissioned from the artists of southern India by Chola merchants, many of whom were very wealthy.

Ancient India

People have lived on the Indian subcontinent for about 400,000 years. Some came to India from western Asia; others probably sailed on primitive boats from eastern Africa. By 2500 BC, the subcontinent's first civilization was developing on the banks of the Indus River.

Indus civilization
This culture flourished from c.2500–1600 BC. It was based in large, well-planned cities near the Indus River (in what is now Pakistan). The people grew corn, wove cotton, and wrote a script we are unable to read.

Steatite seal from Indus Valley, 2500–2000 BC

Aryan culture
Around 1600 BC, hordes of nomads moved out of the area between the Black and Caspian Seas. Some of them moved into the area around the Indus. Ancient religious texts called the Vedas describe their life, their gods, and their system of social castes or classes, which later spread to the rest of India.

Statue of Surya, a god of the Aryans

Coming of Islam

Between the 8th and 12th centuries, many Muslim invaders from Arabia and western Asia attacked India. By 1206, a Muslim sultan, based in Delhi, ruled the whole of the northern Indian plain. Under the Delhi sultans and the later Mughal emperors, large areas of India were under Islamic rule. India's Muslim rulers built fine cities, but some were intolerant of other religious faiths.

Mughal dagger

Complex engraved decoration

Sharp steel blade

Tomb of the Muslim emperor, Tughluq Shah, near Delhi.

Delhi Sultanate
In the 13th and 14th centuries, the sultans of Delhi ruled much of northern India, from the Punjab in the west to Bihar in the east. But this empire was unstable. The sultans always had to fight opposition from Hindu states in southern India, and from the Mongols, who conquered Delhi in 1398.

Mughal Empire
The Mughals ruled India from 1526. Under their greatest emperor, Akbar, they brought prosperity to India, but after 1700, their power was weakened by opposition from Hindu southern India. Mughal emperors remained on the throne until 1858, but they had little power.

Aurangzeb
The last great Mughal ruler, Aurangzeb (1618–1707), became emperor in 1658. In 1678, there was a Hindu revolt against his rule and Aurangzeb began a series of costly wars against the Hindus. He expanded the empire, but bankrupted it with his wars, and it began to break up on his death.

I

East India companies

In 1600, European countries founded East India companies to trade in India. England's company set up forts at Madras, Bombay, and Calcutta and began to trade in textiles. The English used the company to rule India, making alliances with local princes and driving out French colonists. Portugal also set up an Indian colony at Goa.

Figure is finely carved and painted.

Gilt

Statue of Portuguese East India Officer

British India

In the late 1700s, the British East India Company defeated rival European colonists and established an empire based on the three "presidencies" of Bombay, Madras, and Bengal. By 1850, the company ruled some three-fifths of India, with the rest run by local princes who were subject to the British.

Indian soldier's belt

Bullet pouch

Chain mail extension to protect hand

Powder flask

Fastens to arms with straps

Tubular arm guard

Double-edged blade

Handle made of steel

Recurved dagger

Indian mutiny

In 1857–58, there was a mutiny of Indian troops in the British army, arising from British insensitivity to Indian customs and religions. The rebels took large areas of India, but the British soon regained the territory, restoring order by July 1858, after much bloodshed.

The British parliament took a greater part in Indian government after the mutiny.

British rule

After the Indian mutiny, the British disbanded the East India Company. The British adopted a more positive attitude towards the Indian people. A new government department was formed and an official called a Viceroy ruled on behalf of the crown. However, the Indian people remained far poorer than the British.

Building the railway system in India

Rise of industry

During the 19th century, India became an industrialized country. The British built Asia's largest rail network in India, and developed steamship and telegraph services. India exported raw materials to British factories, but also built its own steel and textile mills.

Independence

In 1885, the Indian National Congress was founded to campaign for Indian rights. By the 1920s, under the leadership of Mohandas Gandhi, it was demanding Indian independence. A long campaign of resistance to British rule followed, but it was not until the end of World War II, in 1945, that Britain agreed to make India an independent state.

India
Pakistan

Lahore

Delhi

Dhaka

Modern Bangladesh

Indian Ocean

Indian Ocean

Sri Lanka

Pakistan

During World War II, the Muslim League, led by Muhammad Jinnah, demanded a separate independent Muslim state in the Indian subcontinent. In 1947, the Muslim country of Pakistan was created, originally in two parts. In 1971, after a war between the two parts, East Pakistan became the independent state of Bangladesh.

Nehru

Jawaharlal Nehru (1889–1964) was one of the leaders of the Indian National Congress and was imprisoned nine times for his political activities. In 1947, after India's independence, he became India's first prime minister. He funded industry and developed India's role as a superpower. Nehru's daughter, Indira Gandhi, became prime minister in 1966.

Regional superpower

Under Nehru, India avoided alliances with major states. This policy of non-alignment gave India great power in its own right, power which increased when India supported East Pakistan in its civil war with West Pakistan in 1971.

Chemical works, India

First Indian National Congress

Congress Party

The Indian National Congress had led India's independence movement. After 1947, it became the Congress Party. It controlled India for much of the period after independence, under the leadership largely of members of Nehru's family: Nehru himself (prime minister 1947–64), his daughter Indira Gandhi (1966–77; 1980–84), and her son Rajiv (1984–89).

Timeline

c.2500 BC Rise of the Indus Valley civilization.

c.1600 BC Aryan nomads invade western India.

326 BC Alexander the Great invades the Punjab.

324–320 BC Mauryan dynasty.

Terracotta Mother Goddess figure from Mohenjo-Daro, Indus Valley civilization.

320–c.700 Gupta Empire.

711 First Muslim invasions of India.

1206–1526 Sultans of Delhi rule northern India.

1526–1707 The Mughal Empire is established and reaches its peak.

1600 British East India Company is founded.

1746 War between British and French colonists in India.

1858 Indian mutiny defeated; British impose direct rule.

Mohandas Gandhi, campaigner for independence

1917–44 Mohandas Gandhi leads campaign of resistance to British rule.

1947 India and Pakistan become independent.

1971 New state of Bangladesh formed.

1990s Efficient agricultural methods provide India with a healthier economy.

FIND OUT MORE

ALEXANDER THE GREAT | EMPIRES | GANDHI, MOHANDAS | GUPTA EMPIRE | INDUS VALLEY CIVILIZATION | MAURYAN EMPIRE | MUGHAL EMPIRE | UNITED KINGDOM, HISTORY OF